The
Proficient
Reader

Proficient Reader

THIRD EDITION

Ira D. Epstein
Ernest B. Nieratka
LaGuardia Community College, CUNY

Houghton Mifflin Company   Boston   New York

To our mothers, Molly Epstein and Helen Rose Nieratka.
Without their labor our labor would have been for naught!

and

With love and gratitude to our families,
Fredda, Sheri, and Ronit
Edy, Steavan, and Kevan

Senior Sponsoring Editor: Mary Jo Southern
Senior Associate Editor: Ellen Darion
Senior Project Editor: Cathy L. Brooks
Production/Design Coordinator: Jodi O'Rourke
Senior Manufacturing Coordinator: Priscilla Abreu
Senior Marketing Manager: Nancy Lyman

Cover designer: Linda Wade
Cover image: Keith Thompson/Tony Stone Images

Acknowledgments appear on page 515.

Printed in the U.S.A.

Library of Congress Catalog Card Number: 98-72021

ISBN: 0-395-87794-6

123456789-CS-03 02 01 00 99

CONTENTS

Preface   xi
To the Student   xv

UNIT ONE
Reading and Literacy   1

Introduction   2
READING STRATEGY: ANSWERING QUESTIONS USING CUE WORDS   5

1. FREDERICK DOUGLASS, from *The Life of an American Slave*   9
   READING STRATEGY: READING NARRATIVES   10
   READING STRATEGY CHECK: CUE WORDS   11
   ◆ **The Reading**   12
   MARKED COPY   14
   PROCESS GUIDE   15
   READING STRATEGY: PREDICTING VOCABULARY   18

2. HELEN KELLER, from *The Story of My Life*   29
   READING STRATEGY: COLLECTING IDEAS   29
   READING STRATEGY CHECK: PREDICTING VOCABULARY   31
   ◆ **The Reading**   32
   MARKED COPY   35
   PROCESS GUIDE   37
   READING STRATEGY: FRAMING AN ANSWER I   40

3. SAM LEVENSON, from *Everything But Money*   41
   READING STRATEGY CHECK: COLLECTING IDEAS   42
   ◆ **The Reading**   42
   PROCESS GUIDE   45
   READING STRATEGY: MARKING TEXT   48

4. MALCOLM X, from *The Autobiography of Malcolm X*   51
   READING STRATEGY: CONNECTING IDEAS   51
   READING STRATEGY CHECK: MARKING TEXT   53
   ◆ **The Reading**   53
   MARKED COPY   57
   PROCESS GUIDE   59
   READING STRATEGY: WRITING A SUMMARY   62
   Reading Journal   67

5. Vince Nowell, "Why We Should Read"   67
   Reading Strategy: Reading Argument and Persuasion   68
   Reading Strategy Check: Writing a Summary   70
   ◆ The Reading   70
   Process Guide   73
   Reading Journal   74

6. Ira D. Epstein and Ernest B. Nieratka, "The Proficient Reader"   75
   Reading Strategy: Reading Exposition—Part I   75
   Reading Strategy Check: Previewing   79
   ◆ The Reading   79
   Marked Copy   89
   Process Guide   92

7. Geoffrey Rubinstein, "History of Printing"   93
   Reading Strategy: Reading Exposition—Part II   94
   Reading Strategy Check: Making All the Strategies Work for You   98
   ◆ The Reading   99
   Process Guide   107
   Reading Journal   114

8. Bernard Malamud, "A Summer's Reading"   114
   ◆ The Reading   115

THE TECHNOLOGY CONNECTION   121

9. Mary Purpura and Paolo Pontoniere, "In His Book, The Printed Word Will Live On"   121
   ◆ The Reading   122

MAKING CONNECTIONS: Reading and Literacy   124
LIBRARY ASSIGNMENT: The Week I Was Born   125

UNIT TWO
Work and Careers
129

Introduction   130

1. Barbara Garson, "McDonald's—We Do It All For You"   134
   Reading Strategy: Framing An Answer II   134
   Reading Strategy Check: Previewing   137
   ◆ The Reading   138

2. "So You Want to Be a Physician/Ophthalmalogist" 153
   READING STRATEGY: READING INTERVIEWS 153
   READING STRATEGY CHECK: COLLECTING IDEAS 155
   ◆ **The Reading** 157
   Reading Journal 164

3. ANNE W. CLYMER AND ELIZABETH McGREGOR, "Solving the Job Puzzle" 165
   READING STRATEGY: SUMMARIZING EXPOSITION 165
   READING STRATEGY CHECK: CONNECTING IDEAS 168
   ◆ **The Reading** 170

4. "Tomorrow's Jobs" 178
   READING STRATEGY: READING AND INTERPRETING GRAPHS 178
   READING STRATEGY CHECK: SUMMARIZING TEXT 186
   ◆ **The Reading** 186
   PROCESS GUIDE 201
   Reading Journal 204

5. ROBERT LEWIS, "Looking for Work in All the Right Places" 205
   READING STRATEGY: EVALUATING INFORMATION ON THE INTERNET 205
   READING STRATEGY CHECK: FRAMING AN ANSWER 211
   ◆ **The Reading** 212
   PROCESS GUIDE 217

6. JAMES MICHENER, "Work to Make the World Work Better" 223
   READING STRATEGY: EVALUATING QUALIFICATIONS AND SOURCES 224
   READING STRATEGY CHECK: READING ARGUMENTATION AND PERSUASION 228
   ◆ **The Reading** 229

7. JAN HALVORSEN, "How It Feels to Be Out of Work" 234
   READING STRATEGY: DETERMINING THE AUTHOR'S PURPOSE 234
   READING STRATEGY CHECK: EVALUATING SOURCES 236
   ◆ **The Reading** 237
   PROCESS GUIDE 239
   Reading Journal 241

8. ANITA SHREVE, "The Day the Mommies Went Home" 241
   READING STRATEGY: READING SATIRE 242
   READING STRATEGY CHECK: MARKING TEXT 243
   ◆ **The Reading** 244
   PROCESS GUIDE 248
   Reading Journal 249

9. RICKY GRIFFIN, "Managing Workforce Diversity in Organizations" 250
   READING STRATEGY: STUDYING A TEXTBOOK CHAPTER AND PREPARING FOR AN EXAM 251
   READING STRATEGY CHECK: APPLYING THE STRATEGIES 273
   ◆ The Reading 275
   MARKED COPY 298
   Reading Journal 309

10. BARBARA HOLLAND, "The Day's Work" 309
    ◆ The Reading 310

THE TECHNOLOGY CONNECTION 319

11. WILLIAM BRIDGES, "Change and the Transformation of Work" 319
    ◆ The Reading 320

MAKING CONNECTIONS: Work and Careers 325
LIBRARY ASSIGNMENT: Career Exploration 326

UNIT THREE
Mass Media

329

Introduction 330
READING STRATEGY: READING TABLES 336

1. LINDA ELLERBEE, "Television Changed My Family Forever" 339
   READING STRATEGY CHECK: READING NARRATIVES 340
   ◆ The Reading 341

2. TOM BROKAW, "Only Good If You Can Trust It" 344
   READING STRATEGY CHECK: DETERMINING THE AUTHOR'S PURPOSE 345
   ◆ The Reading 345
   PROCESS GUIDE 347

3. SHIRLEY BIAGI, "Introduction to the Mass Media" 348
   READING STRATEGY: MAPPING INFORMATION 348
   READING STRATEGY CHECK: READING TEXTBOOK CHAPTERS 351
   ◆ The Reading 352
   PROCESS GUIDE 370
   Reading Journal 374

4. JIM TRELEASE, "Television" 375
READING STRATEGY: DETECTING AND EVALUATING BIAS 376
READING STRATEGY CHECK: MARKING TEXT 377
◆ The Reading 377
PROCESS GUIDE 392

5. JEFF GREENFIELD, "Don't Blame TV" 394
READING STRATEGY: READING COMPARATIVELY 394
READING STRATEGY CHECK: SUMMARIZING 397
◆ The Reading 398
PROCESS GUIDE 402
Reading Journal 404

6. KATHLEEN TYNER, "Can Your Students Read TV?" 404
READING STRATEGY: ALLUSIONS 405
READING STRATEGY CHECK: USING CUE WORDS 407
◆ The Reading 408
PROCESS GUIDE 411

7. JEFFREY SCHRANK, "The Language of Advertising Claims" 413
READING STRATEGY: CONNOTATION AND DENOTATION 413
READING STRATEGY CHECK: ALLUSIONS 416
◆ The Reading 418
PROCESS GUIDE 425
Reading Journal 426

8. CHRISTINE LAPHAM, "The Evolution of the Newspaper of the Future" 427
READING STRATEGY: READING JOURNAL ARTICLES 428
USING THE STRATEGIES: PUTTING IT ALL TOGETHER 430
◆ The Reading 432

9. JOHN CHEEVER, from *Bullet Park* 440
◆ The Reading 440

THE TECHNOLOGY CONNECTION 444

10. JOE SALTZMAN, "Too Much Information, Too Little Time" 445
◆ The Reading 445

MAKING CONNECTIONS: Mass Media 447
LIBRARY ASSIGNMENT: Exploring an Issue in Television 448

UNIT FOUR
The Family

Introduction 452

1. JACQUELYN MITCHARD, "The New Traditional Family" 455
   ◆ **The Reading** 455

2. IAN ROBERTSON, "Family" 458
   ◆ **The Reading** 458

3. STEPHANIE COONTZ, "The Way We Weren't—The Myth and Reality of the 'Traditional' Family" 475
   ◆ **The Reading** 476

4. ARLIE HOCHSCHILD with ANNE MACHUNG, "The Second Shift: Working Parents and the Revolution at Home" 482
   ◆ **The Reading** 482

5. DR. BENJAMIN SPOCK, "Put Family First" 490
   ◆ **The Reading** 491

6. MAYA ANGELOU, from *Keeping Families Together: The Case for Family Preservation* 492
   ◆ **The Reading** 493

7. BARBARA KINGSOLVER, "Quality Time" 496
   ◆ **The Reading** 497

THE TECHNOLOGY CONNECTION 505

8. ERMA BOMBECK, "Technology's Coming . . . Technology's Coming" 505
   ◆ **The Reading** 506

MAKING CONNECTIONS: The Family 509
LIBRARY ASSIGNMENT: The Family, Past and Present 510

Acknowledgments 515
Index 519

PREFACE

WHAT WE BELIEVE ABOUT TEACHING AND READING

In the course of teaching reading at the college level for many years, we have given much thought to two related questions: (1) How do students master the reading process? And (2) What is the most meaningful, effective way to prepare our students for the demands of college reading and studying? *The Proficient Reader* grew out of our desire to share the very positive results we have had with our approach to these questions. Using the text, we continue to learn from our students, colleagues, and other users. In the third edition we attempt to incorporate new features and rework tested ideas based on this collective experience.

The Proficient Reader starts from the premise that students learn best about the process of reading if they are, at the same time, acquiring new and relevant knowledge. In other words, students who are given the opportunity to explore topics central to their lives—literacy, work, media, and family— will more readily master vital reading and thinking strategies.

We found that when assigned readings are grouped thematically (as they would be in college "content" courses), students engage more actively in learning the reading process. Because readings within each unit resonate and relate integrally to each other, students find them both more interesting and more realistic, that is, closer to what they actually encounter in later courses. And, as in college, readings in *The Proficient Reader* encompass many styles, viewpoints, lengths, rhetorical modes, and levels of difficulty.

Although selections at a variety of levels are included, *The Proficient Reader* is geared to the needs of inexperienced readers. It is designed to allow students to practice and improve their reading strategies in a supportive yet realistic context. Early units contain a wealth of instruction on reading strategies, all linked to specific readings. This "applied" method of presentation allows students to grasp the strategies and thus gain that pleasure that comes from comprehending and connecting with ideas in written material. Later units contain less support material and are structured to help students achieve independent proficiency.

Through thematically arranged content and integrated support features, *The Proficient Reader* expresses our basic belief: to succeed in college and afterwards, students need to be urged beyond surface-level comprehension and encouraged to confront issues, make judgments, and connect ideas.

SPECIAL FEATURES OF THIS TEXT

The following features, which were popular in the first two editions, are retained in the third edition:

Thematic Organization

The text is divided into four thematic units: Reading and Literacy, Work and Careers, Mass Media, and The Family. Each unit is self-contained. Exercises and strategies that support learning accompany the material.

Varied Readings

Within each unit, selections are culled from a range of different sources, such as newspapers, magazines, books, textbooks, government studies, interviews, the Internet, and works of fiction. Each unit contains examples of narrative, expository, and argumentative and persuasive writing.

Integrated Reading Strategies

A variety of reading strategies is provided. Rather than combine all of these into one section, the strategies are provided either before or after an appropriate reading so that students can see their immediate, relevant application. Unit Four does not include strategies in order to encourage students to apply the strategies that they have already learned.

Critical Thinking Strategies

Crititical thinking strategies reinforce the reading-writing connection by asking students to examine interrelationships among the readings. Included in the critical reading strategies are determining the author's purpose, reading comparatively, detecting and evaluating bias, and determining tone and attitude and connotation and denotation.

Support Features

Gearing Up   These prereading questions and activities are designed to activate students' prior knowledge and prepare them for the topic in the reading.

Marked Copy   These annotated versions of articles contain notes and symbols that signal ideas, raise questions, draw attention to certain ideas and phrases, and teach annotation techniques. Complete marked copies accompany some articles. In other instances, we mark the first page or a portion of the text and encourage the student to continue the process.

Process Guides   These extended study aids walk students through some of the more challenging material (about one-half of the readings) and provide additional support through extended questioning, explanation, and strategy reinforcement. Some sample answers are provided for the first two readings.

Library Assignment   At the end of each unit, the instructor can assign a project that takes the student to the library for additional exploration of the unit's theme. Topics include "The Week I Was Born" and "Career Exploration." When appropriate, strategies for incorporating the Internet are included.

NEW TO THIS EDITION

Internet Connection

As the Internet becomes a tool for publishing and accessing a wide variety of information, *The Proficient Reader* makes use of this resource in a number of ways. The first three units contain at least one article that appears on the Internet at the time of our writing. Thus Unit One has an article on the history of printing, and Unit Three has a selection about the evolution of newspapers. We feel strongly that even if students do not have access to the Internet, they need to begin to understand its rich potential for accessing information. Whenever applicable, end-of-unit library assignments incorporate use of the Internet. For example, the second unit's library assignment focuses on career exploration and uses numerous resources available to the potential job candidate. There is also a strategy on evaluating Internet sources.

Many New Readings

A number of new readings ensure up-to-date coverage of themes. Of the thirty-eight readings in the textbook, twenty-five are new to this edition.

Increased Emphasis on Critical Reading and Thinking

Coverage of critical reading and thinking strategies has been expanded, and exercises have been added. The link between these strategies and the selections has been strengthened.

Study Skills Receive New Emphasis

Such features as mapping ideas and preparing for exams have been added to this edition.

New Strategies

A number of new strategies are introduced and applied to readings. They include Connotation/Denotation, Reading Visuals, Reading Allusions, and Mapping Ideas.

Framing Answers

New attention is devoted to writing, particularly to responding appropriately to textbook comprehension questions. The Framing Answers strategy appears in the first two units.

Collecting Ideas and Connecting Ideas

The strategy of Making Connections, found in the first two editions, has been further expanded and divided into two parts, Collecting Ideas and Connecting Ideas. Each unit gives students an opportunity to gather and organize ideas and concludes with questions and activities that require them to review and synthesize the material of the unit.

The Technology Connection

We close each unit of the textbook with a section titled The Technology Connection that contains readings about technology. We feel strongly that technology relates to the four units of the textbook and that it will continue to affect us in many ways. This concluding section relates technology to one or more of the unit's issues. No vocabulary exercises are provided.

Expanded Instructor's Resource Manual

This manual includes model answers for all of the questions and representative exercises in the text. Instructors are provided with guidelines and suggestions on how to approach various articles and exercises. Related materials are included that can be duplicated for classroom use or made into transparencies.

Reading Strategy Check

Almost every article in the first three units is accompanied by a strategy section that introduces a new strategy. The strategy check feature then draws attention to relevant strategies introduced previously.

Reading Journal

Students are introduced to the idea of keeping a reading journal. Through this activity they are further encouraged to think about the text and make various connections.

Reading Survey

In the section To the Student, students are given the opportunity to review their reading habits and attitudes through a survey instrument. There is a section focusing on goal setting.

ACKNOWLEDGMENTS

We wish to thank our distinguished panel of reviewers and our colleagues at LaGuardia Community College for their many helpful suggestions. We would like to thank our sponsoring editor, Mary Jo Southern, for her strong support for this project; our development editor, Ellen Darion, for her insight, patience, and sense of humor; and our project editor, Cathy Brooks, for her exceptional attention to details and schedules. Finally, we wish to express our sincere appreciation to our families for their encouragement and forbearance.

TO THE STUDENT

This section is devoted to you, the user of this text. This introductory material is intended to acquaint you with the features of the book. Because the book has an approach that you probably have not seen before, reading about what is coming will make your study more productive.

USING THE TEXT

The purpose of this book is to help you improve your reading ability. The key word here is *you*. With a strong effort on your part and help from your instructor, you will see improvement.

The book contains three major elements:

1. The content of the readings

2. The instructions for the reading strategies

3. The support features

The reading content is the subject matter about which you will read and learn. The reading strategies are steps and procedures you will apply to become actively engaged in the reading process and in thinking about the content. The support features are a series of learning aids and supplementary materials in the form of questions, guides, and models. They are provided to give you a fuller understanding of the content and to increase your ability to read effectively.

Readings

The Proficient Reader is organized into four units: Reading and Literacy, Work and Careers, Mass Media, and The Family. A theme is a set of facts, ideas, and opinions related to a common topic. Each theme is a self-contained unit consisting of readings of varying difficulty. The selections are taken from different sources, including textbooks, journals, novels, newspapers, and the Internet. The four themes were selected because of their interest, importance, and interrelatedness.

Here's What You Can Expect in Each Unit:

1. An introduction designed to prepare you for the ideas that follow.

2. Readings that are a mixture of narrative, argumentation and persuasion, and exposition.

3. Exercises and strategies designed to aid your understanding and reading efficiency.

4. Comprehension questions designed to measure your understanding.

5. Various other exercises that guide you in making connections among ideas within a theme and, ultimately, in connecting ideas across all four themes. At the end of each unit, a library assignment lets you explore the theme further by using the resources of a media center or library.

Reading Strategies

Even the best reading materials do not by themselves communicate thought. You, the reader, must actively sort out ideas and take in, organize, and use the information you have gained. We want you to learn productive strategies to apply throughout your reading. *The Proficient Reader* provides an in-depth study and application of a core of reading strategies: previewing, predicting vocabulary, comprehending text, collecting and connecting ideas, and a number of critical reading strategies.

Each of the strategies will be introduced one at a time and applied to material. At regular intervals the strategy will be referred to in a strategy check to assist you in continuing to apply it to the readings.

Support Features

In addition to the readings and strategies, we have found that most students benefit from extra assistance and guidance. *The Proficient Reader* provides three major support features designed to give you a broader understanding of the subject matter and make you a more effective reader: Gearing Up, Marked Copy, and Process Guide.

Gearing Up   As mentioned earlier, each article is preceded by a set of Gearing Up questions and activities designed to activate your prior knowledge and prepare you for the material you will read. For example, before reading the article "Solving the Job Puzzle," you are asked to explain why people work, other than to make money. Before reading about what it was like to spend part of childhood without television, you are directed to interview a family member or friend who grew up without TV.

Marked Copy   The first three units present a Marked Copy—an annotated version of an article—for your study. A Marked Copy contains the original text together with notes and markings that signal ideas, raise questions, and help extend the meaning of the text by drawing attention to certain features, structures, and phrases. The Marked Copies can also serve as models if your instructor asks you to develop your own marked version of the unmarked textbook selections and other material.

Process Guide   Process Guides are provided for the most challenging articles. These study aids direct you through a careful reexamination of an article. The guides provide additional background information and raise questions that you respond to on the lines provided. For the first two articles, we supply some model answers. Later Process Guides are more open-ended and challenging. The Process Guides serve two purposes. First, they clarify and elaborate on the content of the articles. Second, they reinforce reading strategies and explain how they apply to an article.

PREREADING STRATEGY: AN EXERCISE IN USING THE TEXT

Throughout the book, strategies are introduced in relation to specific articles. We have done this for two reasons. First, we believe it is unproductive to merely read about a strategy without seeing it applied in context. Second, we believe strategies should be introduced one at a time. A series of unapplied strategies could be overwhelming and more difficult to learn.

The first strategy introduced, Previewing, is not attached to a specific article but rather to the text as a whole. The Previewing strategy will be reintroduced later in the book, and previewing exercises are included throughout. The previewing exercise that follows will give you an overview of the book and prepare you for your reading and studying.

Previewing Material

The term *previewing* consists of two parts: *pre* means "before," and *view* means "to see." In previewing written material, you attempt to get an idea of what you are about to read. Your goal is to obtain a general sense of the purpose, organization, and features of the material before you engage in a careful reading. By getting a "feel" for an article early on, you gain a general overview of the major points it considers.

Previewing is part of an exploration process. It is intended to help you achieve purposeful reading. After completing the previewing process, you should be able to pose some meaningful general questions about the material you will read. By asking questions of yourself, you set up some goals to meet in your reading. Previewing should also help you think about the structure and content by focusing your attention on certain features of the material.

Previewing can be done with all kinds of written material. You can preview a newspaper article by studying its headline, subheadings, and any accompanying graphics. You can preview a complete textbook by looking at the table of contents, index, preface, and chapter headings.

Previewing Exercise

1. What is the title of this textbook?

2. What does the title suggest that the text will discuss?

3. Who are the authors, and when was the textbook published?

4. Skim the first two paragraphs under the heading "Using the Text" (page xv). What is the message?

5. Look at the table of contents.
   a. How is the textbook organized?
   b. What are the titles of the four units?

    c. List some strategies and support features in Unit One.
    d. How is each unit concluded?

6. Study the index. What terms and words appear frequently? What does the frequent appearance of some words suggest about the content?

    Throughout the textbook, you will be encouraged to preview. With practice, you will be able to frame your own questions and select appropriate key features for examination when you preview other material.

Reading Survey and Reading Journal

The Reading Survey, which immediately follows, and the Reading Journal are new to the third edition. The Reading Survey is our effort to give you and your instructor a sense of you as a reader. We think that it is very important for you to be aware of your reading habits and have the opportunity to set reading goals.

    The Reading Journal is the written form of what might be considered the ultimate strategy—your awareness of what is happening while you are reading a text. Since we consider your awareness of your current reading habits (survey) and your ongoing awareness and record of your progress (journal) as vital, we include both of these features in the introductory section before you begin work with the themes of the book.

READING SURVEY

Before beginning your work in this textbook it would be helpful for you to provide answers to the following reading survey. There are no set answers. Each person will have a different response based on his or her background, experiences, and feelings. Don't rush your answers—take time and reflect on your responses.

Reading: general perceptions

1. Some people feel that reading is valued in our society, whereas others do not. Discuss your position.

2. Describe what makes a proficient (skilled, competent, accomplished, expert) reader.

3. Estimate the time you think a proficient reader spends reading each week:

    for school

    for work

    for pleasure

Reading: self-perceptions (or self-assessment)

4. Explain how reading is important to you and your success in school and life.

5. Consider your current schedule and estimate the number of hours you will spend reading each week for the following:

   school

   work

   pleasure

6. Rate yourself as a reader by selecting one of the following terms:

   (a) excellent (b) very good (c) good (d) fair (e) poor

7. Describe your reading strengths and weaknesses.

   Strengths:

   Weaknesses:

8. Describe any difficulties you experience when reading.

9. Describe the types of reading you enjoy most and least.

   Most enjoyed:

   Least enjoyed:

10. List the types of reading material you find easiest and hardest to read.

    Easiest:

    Hardest:

11. Do you read for pleasure (books, magazines, hobby-related materials)? List some examples of materials you read for pleasure.

12. Do you read a newspaper?

   If so, list the paper's name.

   How often do you read the paper?

   List the section or part that you enjoy reading most.

13. Do you read magazines?

   If so, list their names.

   Describe what you find most interesting in the magazines that you read.

14. Describe the most difficult reading assignment you ever faced.

15. List the steps you take when you come upon reading material that is difficult to understand.

16. Describe the steps you take when you come upon unfamiliar vocabulary.

17. Describe steps you could take to improve your reading proficiency.

Reading Goals

18. Discuss the improvement you would like to see in your reading and studying.

19. Discuss the improvement you would like to see in your vocabulary development.

20. Describe what you would like to accomplish by the time you finish this reading course.

READING JOURNAL

As you read your assignments in *The Proficient Reader*, we are suggesting that you maintain a Reading Journal in which you make regular entries. The Reading Journal is the written record of your reading effort and a reaction to what you read. Writing about your reading helps you to organize your thinking and requires that you reflect upon your understanding. The Gearing Up and comprehension exercises that appear before and after the readings require a written response to very specific questions. Unlike this type of writing, your journal will be more informal. Here you can explore and develop your thoughts, feelings, and reactions.

In most cases *you* will select the aspects that you wish to comment on. Your Reading Journal allows *you* to become more actively involved in your reading and to control which aspects of your reading you might wish to share, examine, and explore. For example, you might wish to express your personal thoughts and feelings about certain individuals, pose questions to an author, note memorable language and images, or examine your reading process. To illustrate just some possibilities, consider the following hypothetical reactions to an imaginary text.

Wow, That was inspirational—especially the words...I never realized that...

How can he say that?! That's ridiculous!

Lorem ipsum dolor sit amet, consectetuer adipiscing elit, sed diem nonummy nibh euismod tincidunt ut lacreeet dolore magna aliguam erat volutpat. Ut wisis enim ad minim veniam, quis nostrud exerci tution ullamcorper suscipit lobortis nisl ut aliquip ex ea commodo consequat, vel illum dolore eu feugiat nulla facilisis at vero eros et accumsan et iusto odio dignissim qui blandit praesent luptatum zzril delenit au gue duis dolore te feugat nulla facilisi. Ut wisi enim ad minim veniam, quis nostrud exerci taion ullamcorper suscipit lobortis nisl ut aliquip ex en commodo consequat. Duis te feugifacilisi per suscipit lobortis nisl ut aliquip ex en commodo consequat. Duis te feugifacilisi. Lorem ipsum dolor sit amet, consectetuer adipiscing elit, sed diem nonummy nibh euismod tincidunt ut lacreeet dolore magna aliguam erat volutpat.

This reminds me of something I read about last week...

I'm lost...I can't figure out what's going on and the vocabulary is...

Why do I find this so boring? Maybe because...

This was really long but I was able to stick with it because...

By reflecting on and responding to your reading, you should see your progression and growth in the learning process. You will also see that your journal does not have to be associated only with the reading course you are now taking. If you wish, you can carry over your journal efforts to other college classes as well as to your personal daily reading.

Getting Started

You should use a separate notebook for your journal. Note the current day and the title of your current reading, the type of reading, and your purpose in reading the material. What follows is up to you unless your instructor asks you to focus on some particular aspect of your reading. To help you in your efforts, we have provided a broad outline of three general categories that you may wish to consider.

A. *The content.* In exploring the content you could consider the following:

- Capture in a sentence the author's thesis
- Write a brief summary of the reading
- Describe something new that you learned
- Discuss any connection between the article and other readings and/or experiences

B. *The process.* The following might be applicable when examining your reading process:

- Note how much time you spent on the reading
- Discuss your reading techniques for handling the material
- Describe any difficulties you may have had and state how you handled them or your plan to resolve them

C. *The response (affect).* It is important to note your feelings, opinions, and reactions when you read. Here are some points to consider:

- Describe your initial and final reaction to the material
- Discuss what you liked or disliked about the reading
- Explore and analyze your reactions—why do you feel this way?

We have found that a useful way to "break the ice" and help you begin the journal writing process is to provide a series of sentence starters:

This reading was important because . . .

I disagree with . . .

The strongest image, event, idea to me was . . .

I wonder why . . .

I'm puzzled or bothered by . . .

I'm upset by . . .

I realized that . . .

I discovered . . .

I'm curious to learn . . .

I feel strongly that . . .

I was amazed that . . .

I see a problem with . . . because . . .

I see a relationship between this reading and . . .

At various points in the text you will see the following icon: 📄 This will alert you that a journal entry will be suggested. Of course you can choose to create your own topic, or your instructor may suggest an issue for exploration.

You may be wondering what students choose to include in their journals. The following examples may give you some ideas.

Sample Journal Entries

Consider a student's reaction to the preface as a sample journal entry.

Date: September 20, 2000

Reading: Preface to The Proficient Reader

Type: Introductory message

Purpose: To find out what the authors are doing in the book.

Content: The authors are telling me things about their textbook. One thing they say is different from other reading books is that the readings in a unit will all be related to the same subject.

Process: I tried to survey the material in the Preface by using the headings. I learned this in another class. I discovered that there were things I didn't understand, like the part called Gearing Up. How can I answer questions when I haven't read the story?

Response: I found out that there are a lot of different parts to the book. At this point it seems like a lot of work. I also looked over the whole book. I didn't find any multiple choice questions. It looks like I'll be doing a lot of writing.

The previous example followed the model setup exactly. You may be asked to submit entries in a more casual manner. Here are three additional samples of that type of entry.

Sample 1—Student response to the Preface and To the Student

I'm not sure why I'm taking this course. I may not be the greatest reader in the world but I don't think I need much help. Then again, it is early and I guess I should keep an open mind.

Sample 2—Student writing about the content of the Frederick Douglass reading

I was amazed to see how determined the author was to learn to read. With very little instruction, he was able to learn the basics and continue to learn even though his mistress was turned against him.

Sample 3—Student writing about the process of reading "History of Printing"

This article was very difficult for me. First of all, there were many words that were new. I couldn't even guess at their meaning. Using the dictionary didn't help much with these words because the definitions were confusing. What seemed to help the most was a classmate who was familiar with the topic because she had written a term paper on this subject.

After you have kept your journal for a few weeks, you will have an opportunity to examine your reading growth and explore how your reading behavior may have changed.

HOW TO USE THIS TEXTBOOK: A GUIDE

Reading and studying require time, effort, strategy, and thought. You are advised to prepare yourself for what you are about to read, maintain an open mind, and, when you are finished, reflect on what you have read.

This textbook has many features designed to help you gain the most from your reading and studying. As a guideline, we suggest an overall approach for using the text:

1. Answer the Gearing Up questions that precede each reading.

2. Work through any reading strategy that is provided.

3. Read an article through once without stopping to get a general idea of the content. Then return for a more careful, critical reading.

4. Answer the questions that follow the reading, noting any that pose problems for you. Even if questions haven't been assigned, it is recommended that you read them. Questions help direct your thought and give you clues about an article's focus.

5. Apply the vocabulary procedure.

6. Study the Marked Copy when one is provided.

7. Complete the Process Guide when one is provided. Afterward, reexamine your answers to the questions, paying particular attention to those that were perplexing at first.

Throughout the text you will be guided through additional activities, such as making connections among readings, writing summaries, and library assignments. The various exercises and assignments in *The Proficient Reader* will help you learn the strategies you need for successful, enjoyable reading in college and beyond.

Additional Suggestions

We are quite aware that you may have trouble with one of the articles or you may have some difficulty in understanding the directions or strategy instruction. You can expect that some of these problems will be handled in class. However, like most of us, you won't discover that you really don't understand something until you sit down to do your homework away from school and the instructor's help. We hope that before you give up on a particular piece you will follow our general advice given above on reading the book. Also, we offer the following suggestions as a way to see you through problem areas.

1. Focus on the title.   Pay particular attention to the title of the article or strategy section. In most cases, titles are the authors' means of signaling the topic—the subject that the reading matter will discuss. Being aware of the topic helps you to focus your attention on a specific area. In fact, one way to determine if you are comprehending at least something from the text is to be able to explain the title in a few sentences in your own words. If you understand little else, concentrate on the title and build on this.

2. Activate related knowledge.   Bring to mind what you know about the topic. This conscious effort to connect what you may already know about the area is an excellent way to prepare yourself for ideas and information. Also, by thinking about what you already know, you may anticipate what the author is going to tell you. Sometimes you may know about the author's subject but you do not recognize the words chosen to express the ideas.

3. Locate the thesis or topic sentence.   This sentence is the major statement the author will make about the subject. If you're able to identify the thesis, you are well on the way to understanding the article. What if you are uncertain or lost? Focusing on the first few sentences or the first paragraph is a good next step, because often the author's thesis is in this location. You can probably understand why. The author is trying to communicate and needs to tell the reader what to look for in the article. Locating the thesis up front is the author's effort to tell the reader early on where the text is headed.

4. Look for textual and graphic clues.   Beyond the title, an article, particularly a textbook chapter, may contain a series of headings and subheads or notes in the margin. These are efforts by the author and editor to signal the direction of the text. Even though the introductory material may be unclear, the body of the text, particularly when it contains examples, may help fill in your uncertainty about the first section. Newspapers, magazines, and many of the current textbooks use a feature called an "inset" to highlight an idea. An inset is a large-print restatement of an idea found within the body of the text that is usually boxed off or boldfaced to draw your attention to the point. Such an inset is a strong clue about what the author and editors think is important. Graphs, charts, tables, and pictures may also help you understand the text.

5. Focus on knowns.   Concentrate on what you do know about the material. Often in a science or technical passage you will be thrown by the new vocabulary. It is not necessary to understand every word or idea in a text to be able to make basic sense of it. If you are conscious of your reading behavior, categorize ideas as follows:

Clear and understood   **(+)**

Fuzzy, not completely clear   **(?)**

Not understood   **(??)**

A major step forward in improving comprehension is becoming aware of what you know and what you don't know or are uncertain of. When you discover something that you cannot work through because of the complexity of the idea, your unfamiliarity with the vocabulary, or your lack of background knowledge and experience in the area, mark the margin with a single **(?)** or double question mark **(??)** and draw a wavy line under the area. This then becomes a quick reference when the instructor asks for questions.

6. Consult alternative sources.   We all have difficulty reading certain texts. Rather than dismiss the task as overwhelming or ignoring it, there are other ways to work through the problem. One of those ways is to consult other sources. For example, the basic principles usually taught in a beginning accounting course have been stated somewhat differently by dozens of authors in as many books. Some books may be very clear on certain ideas and less clear on others. Proficient readers consult other works and do not feel that they must be able to crack every concept in the assigned text to be successful with the ideas contained in it. In an alternative text you may find the key sentence you need or the perfect example to aid your understanding.

7. The running start.   We humans are pretty amazing creatures. Our brains continue to work even when we are not focused or are sound asleep. For this reason, we believe it is good advice to take a jump into an assignment even when you don't have sufficient time to work through it properly. It may be worth your while to acquaint yourself with an upcoming text (even when it is not due the next day) as a way of focusing your thinking on the upcoming material. Examining the title and the other impressions you may gain from a preview may simplify your careful reading at a later date. Beginning to establish preliminary expectations may help you to begin to make connections in the hours you are not devoting to the task.

The
Proficient
Reader

Reading and Literacy

READINGS IN UNIT ONE

1. From *The Life of an American Slave* by Frederick Douglass

   Frederick Douglass describes the difficulties he encountered in his attempts at learning to read as a slave.

2. From *The Story of My Life* by Helen Keller

   Helen Keller recounts how she learned to read despite being blind and deaf.

3. From *Everything But Money* by Sam Levenson

   Sam Levenson reveals how his family helped foster a love and respect for books.

4. From *The Autobiography of Malcolm X* by Malcolm X with Alex Haley

   Malcolm X explains how he improved his reading in prison and how reading opened up a new world to him.

5. "Why We Should Read" by Vince Nowell

   Vincent Nowell replies to an inquiry he received from schoolchildren who questioned the value of reading.

6. "The Proficient Reader" by Ira D. Epstein and Ernest B. Nieratka

   The authors of this textbook examine the reading process and suggest strategies for reading improvement.

7. "History of Printing" by Geoffrey Rubinstein

   Geoffrey Rubinstein traces the development of printing and examines its effects on society.

8. "A Summer's Reading" by Bernard Malamud

   Bernard Malamud explores how a young man trying to find direction in his life turns to reading in an effort to gain respect.

9. "In His Book, The Printed Word Will Live On": An interview with Professor Geoffrey Nunberg by Mary Purpura and Paolo Pontoniere

   Geoffrey Nunberg discusses the future of the book in an era of electronic documents and digital technologies.

INTRODUCTION

Reading is making sense of written language. Learning to read and write leads to **literacy:** the ability to process, understand, and create written works. In the larger sense, we use the word *literate* to mean well informed or educated. Understandably, society is concerned about the literacy of its members, because reading is important for society as well as the individual. The world community benefits from literate individuals exercising their literacy. Being able to read makes it more possible for a person to function effectively within our modern society. In their textbook, *The Teaching of Reading,* Dallmann, Rouch, Chang, and Deboer describe the uniqueness of reading.

> Reading is essential to the existence of our complex system of social arrangements. But it is more than that. It is the means by which every age is linked to every other. It makes possible man's capacity for "time binding," the ability to perceive himself and the fluid universe around him in the historic process. If all the inventions of a hundred years were destroyed and only books were left, man could still be man, in the sense intended by the idealists, the poets, the great creators. Reading is a humanizing process.

Being literate lets us sample many experiences not possible in daily living. In books we find advice, information, satisfaction, comfort, inspiration, guidance, strength, escape, and challenge. We can enter another world or become deeply involved in our own. According to Daniel Boorstin, former librarian of Congress, "the book is the reservoir of all ideas that we have forgotten and will be the depository of ideas still unborn." Poets and thinkers have cherished books, whereas tyrants and the close-minded have tried to keep books from people or control their contents because they feared the ideas they contained. Book burnings were common in Puritan America and in Nazi Germany. In contrast, when people have struggled for freedom and fulfillment for themselves and others, they have placed great value on freedom of the press. Franklin Delano Roosevelt, the thirty-second U.S. president, remarked, "We all know that books burn, yet we have the greater knowledge that books cannot be killed by fire. People die, but books never die. . . . Books are weapons . . . make them weapons for man's freedom."

Reasons for Reading

We live in the age of information. Each day we are besieged by vast amounts of information coming from books, newspapers, and magazines as well as from newer forms of communication such as the Internet. As people have learned more and more about the world, the written word has recorded the flood of new ideas and information. Libraries cannot hold all the books, journals, and newspapers published each year. Without technology such as microfilm and compact disc systems, the storage capacity of libraries would be overwhelmed. But even these newer technologies assume the ability to read in order to gain information and acquire knowledge. Bill Gates, head of the Microsoft Corporation, commented on the value of reading in our information age and what it means to him personally:

> It is pretty unlikely that people will become knowledgeable without being excellent readers. Multimedia systems are beginning to use video and sound to deliver information in compelling ways, but text is one of the best ways to convey details. I try to make sure I get an hour or more of reading each week night and a few hours each weekend. I read at least one newspaper every day and several magazines each week. I make it a point to read at least one news weekly from cover to cover because it broadens my interests. If I read only what intrigues me, such as the science section and a subset of the business section, then I finish the magazine the same person I was before I started. So I read it all.

But reading involves more than access to the spread of new information. As anyone who has ever curled up with a good book knows, reading is a source of boundless pleasure. Other leisure activities may be limited by one's age, one's finances, or other circumstances—but not reading. Holbrook Jackson, the English writer, observed: "The time to read is any time: no apparatus, no appointment of time and place, is necessary. It is the only art which can be practiced at any hour of the day and night, whenever the time and inclination comes, that is your time for reading; in joy or sorrow, health or illness." As long as books and libraries exist, the reader is free to explore an ever-expanding universe of dreams and ideas, plots and theories, mysteries and musings.

Expanded Literacy in the Workplace

Reading also has a very practical application: economic survival. Today it is difficult to get and hold a decent job without adequate reading skills. As our society becomes more technologically oriented and more complex, the level of literacy expected of workers continues to increase and reading proficiency assumes greater significance. Many jobs go unfilled because of the lack of qualified applicants. Having a literate work force is essential to the future of our country.

Competition and the continuing information explosion will make inservice training for employees more common than ever before. Remaining competent in a job will depend on the ability to master new knowledge. Furthermore, advances in computer technology will not make reading obsolete. Sophisticated equipment such as computers and word processors is only another means of handling, storing, and printing written language. To use these devices, people will need to read—and to read well.

Millions of people in the work force are, or will be, changing careers. Many will make this change against their wishes as job market conditions force them to retrain and relearn. Those who are able to adopt and assimilate new information will be in the best position to secure the new jobs. Furthermore, as the job market continues to change, those in training now and in the future will find that work requires much more background knowledge and greater technical understanding—and thus broadened reading skill.

What You Can Expect in This Unit

In this unit, you will study a number of articles on the subject of literacy and reading and learn reading strategies that you can apply to textual materials.
After completing this unit, you should be able to do the following:

Content

- Describe the route to literacy taken by different individuals
- Discuss literacy's impact on individuals
- Explain technology's role in promoting literacy

Process

- Analyze the writing pattern of an author
- Distinguish between expository and narrative text
- Provide examples of the following writing patterns: (a) Comparison and contrast; (b) Simple listing; (c) Cause and effect

Strategies

- Preview texts
- Predict and confirm unfamiliar terms
- Mark texts

As you read about reading in this unit, you will be asked to focus on your own process of reading. This textbook aims to help you become a proficient, self-monitoring reader. The Reading Survey (page xviii) and Reading Journal (page xx) components will help in this process. You will discover that there are different ways to read. The way you approach a reading task depends on your purpose for reading, your background, and the type of material. There are no "ten easy steps." Reading requires time and effort, but it will generously reward all the time and effort you invest.

An Introduction to Reading Strategy: A Definition

The term *strategy* refers to a plan of action toward reaching a goal. People use strategy all the time to help them move toward an objective more efficiently. Professional athletes spend as much time in strategy sessions as they do on the field or court. Teams view videotapes of their opponents to look for weaknesses and opportunities to use their own strengths. Big league sports is more than a matter of ability and desire. Game strategy is a crucial element in performance excellence.

Strategy should also help you become a proficient reader and a good student. Successful study is more than a matter of ability and desire. Proficient students have a plan to succeed in their studies, and the plan incorporates a strategy for reading and studying that will help them read more effectively.

 # READING STRATEGY

Most of the readings in the first three units have a section marked Strategy. The strategy section is divided into two areas:

1. *Strategy introduction and instruction.* In this section a strategy is introduced for the first time. Here you will find a rationale for the strategy: a set of reasons why we feel the strategy will work for you. After the introduction, the strategy will be explained with examples.

2. *Strategy application.* The next section will apply the strategy to a reading. Usually the strategy will come before the article and will make suggestions about reading it. For example, the strategy that precedes the Douglass article is Reading Narratives. Suggestions will be made on reading stories like the one by Frederick Douglass. However, sometimes strategies are introduced after the reading, such as Writing a Summary that follows the Malcolm X reading. So that you fully understand the article to make the most of the strategy discussion, we have held the summarizing strategy until after you have worked through all the additional study assistance found in the Marked Copy and Process Guide. In the application part, you will find more instruction and examples from the reading.

 # READING STRATEGY CHECK

The Reading Strategy Check will occur in the Strategy section. It is a short reference to strategies that have been introduced before but will not receive the extensive treatment received when a strategy is introduced for the first time. It reminds you that to change your reading behavior, you need to continue to apply your strategies. The check will direct you to apply a particular strategy at some point in the upcoming reading and may provide hints and support for your effort.

 # READING STRATEGY
ANSWERING QUESTIONS USING CUE WORDS

You may have noticed that the introduction section titled What You Can Expect in This Unit (p. 4) contained a series of action verbs such as *explain,* *describe,* and *analyze.* We refer to these terms as "cue" words because they signal or suggest a specific course of action. Becoming familiar with cue words is an important feature of this textbook.

The purpose of reading is to understand the author's message. The word *understand* can have various meanings. It can mean being able to describe an author's position on an issue, to evaluate that position, or to synthesize various points within the reading and connect them to other readings. In the first case, you understand by relating or representing the author's statements. In the second, you understand by making judgments about the author's statements. In the third, you understand by bringing together several points you have gained from your reading and making new observations of your own. In testing your understanding of an assigned reading, your instructor may develop questions that will ask you to describe, evaluate, or synthesize what you have read. Learning to recognize the cue words in such questions will help you respond.

APPLICATION

The comprehension questions that follow the selections in this text usually begin with a very important cue word. These cue words ask you to answer in specific ways, for example, *describe, explain, illustrate,* or *analyze.* Such terms, once learned, provide you with an effective strategy for answering questions. The following chart shows some cue words, their definitions, and examples of their use in test questions. Study the chart, and then complete the exercises that follow.

Cue Word	Definition	Example
1. *List, identify, name, state, cite*	Give a series or number of.	Q. List three (3) American League baseball teams. A. The New York Yankees, the Detroit Tigers, and the Cleveland Indians are American League teams.
2. *Illustrate*	Give an example.	Q. Illustrate the use of figurative language in the story. A. "It rained cats and dogs" is an example of figurative language used in the story.
3. *Describe*	Give an account that presents a picture or story to the person who reads or hears it.	Q. Describe your route to school. A. I walk to the corner of Reader's Lane and make a right turn. I walk one block to Book Street and take the M-15 bus three miles to school.

Cue Word	Definition	Example
4. *Define*	Give the meaning of a word or expression to clarify its meaning.	Q. Define the term *preview.* A. To *preview* means to look ahead at material to know what's coming.
5. *Paraphrase*	Put in your own words.	Q. Paraphrase: "Four score and seven years ago, our forefathers brought forth on this continent a new nation." A. Eighty-seven years ago, our leaders established the United States.
6. *Explain*	Give reasons for, make understandable, make clear.	Q. Explain the reason for previewing. A. Readers who preview remember more information and understand it better.
7. *Agree or disagree*	Accept or reject the idea expressed.	Q. Agree or disagree with the following statement: "Women are naturally superior to men." Cite the reasons for your position. A. I agree that women are naturally superior to men because they are healthier and live longer.
8. *Compare and contrast*	Give similarities and differences.	Q. Compare and contrast New York City and Bloomington, Indiana. A. *Comparisons:* Both places have opera most Saturday nights, and both have residents from many different countries. *Contrasts:* New York has 8,000,000 people and traffic congestion. Bloomington has 50,000 people and very little traffic congestion.
9. *Analyze*	Examine the parts of what follows; break it down into smaller units for examination.	Q. Analyze the formula SQ3R (a procedure for improving reading developed by Francis P. Robinson). A. SQ3R means Survey, Question, Read, Recite, Review: *Survey*—Look over the upcoming material. *Question*—Formulate questions based on the survey. *Read*—Read closely. *Recite*—State the material's meaning in your own words. *Review*—Look over all material, focusing on key spots.

Cue Word	Definition	Example
10. *Summarize*	Report the main points briefly to give the highlights.	Q. Summarize the introductory lecture to the course. A. The instructor described the content of the course, outlined student responsibilities, and explained the grading standards.
11. *Interpret*	Give your personal perception; give your own understanding.	Q. Interpret the poem "The Box." A. To me, "The Box" represents the pressure of life from which there is no escape.
12. *Critique*	Give a personal perception; give your own understanding.	Q. Critique Hemingway's *The Old Man and the Sea.* A. I found the book stimulating. Hemingway poses some important questions, and the way in which they are handled guarantees the book's lasting value.
13. *Support*	Provide evidence or proof for.	Q. Support your choice among the candidates. A. I support candidate X because she had the most experience.
14. *Refute*	Provide proof or evidence against.	Q. Refute the donut diet's claims. A. I refute the donut diet because the nutritional breakdown does not meet the minimum standards set by the government agency.

CUE WORD EXERCISE

Use your knowledge of cue words to answer the following questions. If necessary, refer to the chart.

1. Identify three colleges other than your own.

2. Illustrate what the following statement means: "You can lead a horse to water, but you can't make him drink."

3. Describe your route to school.

4. Define the term *reading.*

5. Paraphrase the following statement: "Genius is 99 percent perspiration and 1 percent inspiration."

6. Explain the author's rationale for using the themes of Reading and Literacy, Work and Careers, Mass Media, and The Family in this textbook.

7. Agree or disagree with the following statement: "Lincoln can be considered a great president." State the reasons for your position.

8. Compare and contrast watching television with reading a book.

9. Analyze the homework assignments in your courses this term. Which assignments will take the most time, and which the least?

10. Summarize the major ideas contained in the preceding section: Introduction to Unit One.

11. Intepret the symbols found on a United States dollar bill.

12. Critique a movie or television show that you have recently seen.

13. Support the ideas of free higher education for all citizens.

14. Refute the ideas of year-round schooling for elementary and secondary students.

from

The Life of an American Slave

FREDERICK DOUGLASS

Frederick Douglass (1818–1895) was born into slavery and was sold several times in southern slave markets. He secretly taught himself to read and write and through his autobiography provided an eyewitness account of the slavery system in pre–Civil War America. Douglass eventually gained his freedom and became a famous lecturer, writer, and orator. He also served as a U.S. minister to Haiti. As a leader of black people, he was an eloquent spokesperson for freedom and the abolition of slavery. The Life of an American Slave, *Douglass's autobiography, was published in 1845 and later revised.*

GEARING UP

1. Recall what you know about the slavery system in America before the Civil War. Think of the history you have studied, the books you have read, and the television programs and movies you have watched. What was it like to be a slave? List three things that illustrate what life was like for a slave.

2. Imagine being forbidden to learn to read. If you got caught, you would be beaten or maybe even killed. Nevertheless, you had a strong reason to learn. Discuss the steps you would take to learn reading, and describe how you would try to avoid getting caught.

 # READING STRATEGY

READING NARRATIVES

To narrate means to tell a story. Like the fairy tales and bedtime stories read to you as a child, these narratives tell what occurred. You are presented with a sequence of happenings and asked to follow along and participate as events unfold.

In reading narratives it will help you to focus your thinking on several questions.

1. What is the author's purpose?   Determining the author's purpose will help you understand the article's intent. For example, if the article is humorous, the author's basic purpose was probably to entertain you. On the other hand, if the article seriously examines a critical decision point in a person's life, you might decide that the author wants to convey a certain attitude about an important issue.

2. What incident has the author selected to tell about?   An author has many possible events to choose from in telling a story. Examining the nature of the chosen event may help you learn what the author considers important.

3. Who is involved, and what is the setting?   Considering the identity of the character(s) will help you understand the author's intent. For example, a U.S. Civil War battle might have a different message if seen from the perspective of a Southern (Confederate) soldier as opposed to a Northern (Union) fighter.

4. What happens in the story?   You are looking for a plot or set of actions in a story. What happens and how it happens reflect the author's decision to tell something and also how she decides to talk about it. Sometimes an author clearly lets you know what she thinks about what happened.

5. Does any special mood (tone) emerge?   Discovering the tone is often a matter of inference. If the author uses words that typically convey happiness, such as *smile, sunny,* and *laughter,* he might intend to describe a joyous event. On the other hand, words that typically represent sadness, such as *sorrow, downcast,* and *depressed,* might indicate a sad occurrence.

6. What does the author want us to remember? What point is being made?
Authors write for a variety of reasons. Certainly among them is the belief that they have something important to say. Discovering this idea is a key to understanding the thrust of the article. Sometimes a point is made very clear. For

example, imagine a story that reports a frantic student's effort to study all night for an important exam after a semester of little effort only to fall asleep during the examination. The writer may end by clearly saying, "The moral of the story is that daily preparation is the key to success."

APPLICATION

The Douglass article and the three that follow it are narratives in which the authors reveal something about their lives. Because the readings are excerpts, they tell only a portion of a larger story. The four individuals you will meet explain what learning to read was like for them and describe the role that reading played in their lives. They give eloquent testimony to the meaning of literacy. To help you gain the most from these narratives, consider the questions in the narrative strategy after you have worked through each reading. Here are some key points to keep in mind:

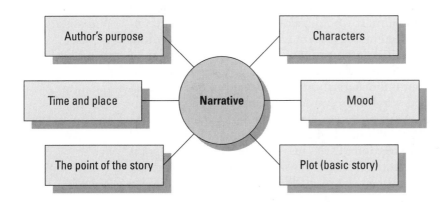

 # READING STRATEGY CHECK
CUE WORDS

You were introduced to the strategy of answering questions using cue words in the introduction to this unit (see pages 5–8). You were advised that it is important to know the meaning of a set of cue words—action words (such as *explain, define, list,* and *compare*) that require you to respond to a statement in specific ways. Knowing the exact meaning of these words will help you write an appropriate response to questions. The questions after Douglass use these cue words. You may wish to review the cue words—particularly the terms used in the Douglass questions (*cite, describe,* and *explain*)—before framing your response.

The Reading

from The Life of an American Slave

by FREDERICK DOUGLASS

1   Very soon after I went to live with Mr. and Mrs. Auld, she very kindly
commenced to teach me the A, B, C. After I had learned this, she as-   *commenced*
sisted me in learning to spell words of three or four letters. Just at this point
of my progress, Mr. Auld found out what was going on, and at once forbade   *forbade*
5   Mrs. Auld to instruct me further, telling her, among other things, that it was
unlawful, as well as unsafe, to teach a slave to read. To use his own words,
further, he said, "If you give a nigger an inch, he will take an ell. A nigger
should know nothing but to obey his master—to do as he is told to do.
Learning would *spoil* the best nigger in the world. Now," said he, "if you
10   teach that nigger (speaking of myself) how to read, there would be no keeping him. It would forever unfit him to be a slave. He would at once become
unmanageable, and of no value to his master. As to himself, it could do him
no good, but a great deal of harm. It would make him discontented and un-   *discontented*
happy." These words sank deep into my heart, stirred up sentiments within
15   that lay slumbering, and called into existence an entirely new train of   *slumbering*
thought. It was a new and special revelation, explaining dark and mysterious
things, with which my youthful understanding had struggled, but struggled
in vain. I now understood what had been to me a most perplexing diffi-   *perplexing*
culty—to wit, the white man's power to enslave the black man. It was a
20   grand achievement, and I prized it highly. From that moment, I understood
the pathway from slavery to freedom. It was just what I wanted, and I got it
at a time when I least expected it. Whilst I was saddened by the thought of
losing the aid of my kind mistress, I was gladdened by the invaluable in-   *invaluable*
struction which, by the merest accident, I had gained from my master.
25   Though conscious of the difficulty of learning without a teacher, I set out
with high hope, and a fixed purpose, at whatever cost of trouble, to learn
how to read. The very decided manner with which he spoke, and strove to
impress his wife with the evil consequences of giving me instruction, served
to convince me that he was deeply sensible of the truths he was uttering. It
30   gave me the best assurance that I might rely with the utmost confidence on
the results which, he said, would flow from teaching me to read. What he
most dreaded, that I most desired. What he most loved, that I most hated.
That which to him was a great evil, to be carefully shunned, was to me a great   *shunned*
good, to be diligently sought; and the argument which he so warmly urged,   *diligently*
35   against my learning to read, only served to inspire me with a desire and determination to learn. In learning to read, I owe almost as much to the bitter
opposition of my master, as to the kindly aid of my mistress. I acknowledge
the benefit of both.

QUESTIONS

1. Cite the event that convinced Frederick Douglass of his need to read.

2. Why was Douglass's master, Mr. Auld, so furious when he found out that Douglass was learning to read?

3. Discuss how the ability to read would be a form of power that Douglass could use.

4. Determination and effort are important parts of learning. Describe how Douglass showed these qualities.

5. Explain how Douglass might have continued learning to read despite his master's prohibition. (There is no information in the excerpt that answers this question. You are being asked to speculate on the basis of what you know.)

EXTENDING YOUR VOCABULARY

Directions

Below you will find incomplete sentences using what we call "target words" from the reading. These words are in the right-hand margin. (More on target words is on pages 18-20.) Read each sentence, consider the target word's meaning, and compose an ending that would make sense. Many sentence endings are possible.

Example

acknowledge: After receiving the science award, Maria turned to her

teacher and said: "I want to acknowledge _____

_____ "

possible answer   After receiving the science award, Maria turned to her

teacher and said: "I want to acknowledge all the time and

support you gave me."

commenced: Because the audience was noisy, the speaker commenced

his remarks _____

forbade: She forbade her child to _____

discontented: The newlyweds became discontented after _____

_____

slumbering: After discovering two students slumbering in class, the

instructor _____

perplexing: "What I find perplexing," the detective remarked, "is how _____ "

invaluable: Her invaluable suggestions _____

shunned: The new neighbors felt they were being shunned by the fact that _____

diligently: The farmer worked diligently because _____

 MARKED COPY

The Reading

from The Life of an American Slave

by FREDERICK DOUGLASS

1   Very soon after I went to live with Mr. and Mrs. Auld, she very kindly
     commenced to teach me the A, B, C. After I had learned this, she as-
     sisted me in learning to spell words of three or four letters. Just at this point
     of my progress, Mr. Auld found out what was going on, and at once forbade
5   Mrs. Auld to instruct me further, telling her, among other things, that it was
     unlawful, as well as unsafe, to teach a slave to read. To use his own words,
     further, he said, "If you give a nigger an inch, he will take an ell. A nigger
     should know nothing but to obey his master—to do as he is told to do.
     Learning would *spoil* the best nigger in the world. Now," said he, "if you
10   teach that nigger (speaking of myself) how to read, there would be no keep-
     ing him. It would forever unfit him to be a slave. He would at once become
     unmanageable, and of no value to his master. As to himself, it could do him
     no good, but a great deal of harm. It would make him discontented and un-
     happy." These words sank deep into my heart, stirred up sentiments within
15   that lay slumbering, and called into existence an entirely new train of
     thought. It was a new and special revelation, explaining dark and mysterious
     things, with which my youthful understanding had struggled, but struggled
     in vain. I now understood what had been to me a most perplexing diffi-
     culty—to wit, the white man's power to enslave the black man. It was a
20   grand achievement, and I prized it highly. From that moment, I understood
     the pathway from slavery to freedom. It was just what I wanted, and I got it
     at a time when I least expected it. Whilst I was saddened by the thought of
     losing the aid of my kind mistress, I was gladdened by the invaluable in-
     struction which, by the merest accident, I had gained from my master.
25   Though conscious of the difficulty of learning without a teacher, I set out
     with high hope, and a fixed purpose, at whatever cost of trouble, to learn
     how to read. The very decided manner with which he spoke, and strove to
     impress his wife with the evil consequences of giving me instruction, served
     to convince me that he was deeply sensible of the truths he was uttering. It
30   gave me the best assurance that I might rely with the utmost confidence on
     the results which, he said, would flow from teaching me to read. What he
     most dreaded, that I most desired. What he most loved, that I most hated.
     That which to him was a great evil, to be carefully shunned, was to me a great

Mrs. Auld helps

Why does Mr. Auld object?

Frederick's reactions to Auld's objections

*The main point—FD understands the power of literacy

Frederick's mixed feelings

Frederick's determination

The results from learning to read

35 good, to be diligently sought; and the argument which he so warmly urged, against my learning to read, only served to inspire me with a desire and determination to learn. In learning to read, I owe almost as much to the bitter opposition of my master, as to the kindly aid of my mistress. I acknowledge the benefit of both.

Frederick "thanks" his owners
?

PROCESS GUIDE

This reading excerpt is taken from the autobiography of Frederick Douglass, a former slave. An excerpt is part of a larger whole. In this case key events occur before and after the events that are narrated. The author assumes that the reader is aware of what has already occurred, which can make excerpted material difficult to read. Usually, however, you will understand the excerpt by itself or with the help of some minimal background information. Douglass wrote his narrative before the Civil War, over 150 years ago.

1. Read the first sentence of the article. What is unusual about it? (Try to frame your own answer before you look at the model.)

Model Answer*   The kind of English that was used 150 years ago is different from today's English. Douglass says that Mrs. Auld "very kindly commenced to teach me the A, B, C." A modern version might read, "She was nice enough to start teaching me the alphabet."

There are other examples of old-style language in the article. With careful reading and with the help of the Process Guide, you can understand Douglass's meaning and get a "feel" for nineteenth-century language.

2. Read through the first eight lines of the article. Is Douglass writing in a narrative mode (telling a story) or an expository mode (explaining information)?

Model Answer   This article is written in the narrative mode, or story form. A narrative can be recognized because it has characters, a setting or location, and a plot. In contrast, exposition can be recognized because it deals with fact and ideas.

3. In the Frederick Douglass article, identify the following:

Characters _____

Setting (time and place) _____

Events (List the major events briefly.)_____

———————————

*Some sample answers are provided for you in the first two process guides of the unit. They represent one possible answer. There is no one correct answer.

_____

_____

_____

4. Paraphrase (put in your own words), in one or two sentences, the plot given in the first eight lines.

_____

_____

Model Answer   Douglass is instructed by Mrs. Auld in some basic reading, but it stops when her husband finds out. Mr. Auld said that it was illegal and dangerous.

5. In the next section of the story, Douglass reports the words of his master, Mr. Auld, urgently explaining why there was such great fear about a slave learning to read. From Auld's reasons for keeping slaves illiterate, what can you infer (what conclusions can you draw) about Auld's values, priorities, and motivations?

_____

_____

Model Answer   Auld's own words suggest he is motivated by fear, racism, insecurity, selfishness, and greed. He has a good deal in slavery and doesn't want to lose it. He knows the tremendous power that comes with the ability to read, and he wants to keep that power for himself.

✦ **NOTE**   As we stated at the beginning of the Process Guide, this reading is an excerpt from a book. If you read all of Douglass's autobiography, *The Life of an American Slave*, you would be able to answer the above question more completely. You would have a fuller understanding of the greed, selfishness, fear, ignorance, and insensitivity that motivated Auld and other slave owners. You would also better understand why Auld's remarks to Douglass intensified, rather than discouraged, Douglass's desire for learning. Even without reading the entire book, however, you can *infer*, or draw a conclusion about, the answer to the question by using (1) relevant information in the excerpt, (2) your general knowledge of human nature, and (3) your background knowledge about slavery.

Using the relevant information in the excerpt, you can infer that Auld is fearful, because he says it is "unsafe" to teach a slave to read and that reading would make the slave "unmanageable." You can infer that Auld is greedy and selfish by his demand for total obedience, without which the slave has "no value to his master."

Using your knowledge of human nature, you can infer that Auld is fearful by imagining him as an ordinary man who sees his authority being threatened. When a person—particularly an insecure person—has power over someone else, the idea of surrendering that power may be hard to bear. Auld knows that if slaves received an education, his own power over them would vanish. He could no longer maintain the fiction that they were somehow less than human beings.

Using your background knowledge of slavery, you can infer that Auld was part of a racist system that perpetuated slavery for its own advantage for hundreds of years. Other information you have about institutionalized slavery in the United States, gained from your reading, school studies, conversations, movies, and television, can help you infer what motivates Auld. ✦

6. Now try to infer why Auld believes that a slave who was taught to read would become unmanageable and unfit to serve his master.

_____

_____

Model Answer   Slave owners tried hard to prevent communication among slaves on different plantations in part by forbidding literacy. The fear of slave revolts was always great, and in fact many did occur. Masters did not want slaves to be able to plan rebellions with written messages or read any documents connected with plantation business. In addition, slave owners feared that if slaves learned to read, they might come across material that questioned the slavery system. For example, the Bible tells us that if a slave runs away from his master, that slave is free. Many slave owners believed strongly in the Bible, but only in those sections that did not question slavery.

7. In lines 14–18, Douglass describes the effect his owner's words had on him. Read these lines again and paraphrase the impression they made on Douglass.

_____

_____

Model Answer   Auld's words had a very great effect on Douglass, but not the effect Auld wanted. By stressing the power of literacy to destroy the master-slave relationship, Auld made Douglass realize that literacy was the way to freedom.

8. In lines 20–22, Douglass claims that he now understands the slavery system. Once again, you must infer what Douglass understands; it is not directly stated. Read these lines again. Can you determine what Douglass now understands?

_____

_____

Model Answer   *Douglass understood that a key factor in keeping people slaves was to keep them ignorant. Gaining literacy was a key to unlocking the chains of slavery.*

9. Douglass states that he had mixed feelings about what happened. What were the causes of these feelings?

Cause of sad feelings

_____

Cause of happy feelings

_____

10. In the last two sentences, Douglass thanks two people for helping him learn to read. Who are the people, and why does he thank them?

Model Answer   *He thanks Mrs. Auld for her initial lessons and Mr. Auld for his strong opposition to those lessons. His master's opposition encouraged and motivated Douglass to learn to read despite the risks.*

✦ **NOTE**   You might expect Douglass to be grateful to his master's wife because she taught him the alphabet. You probably would not expect him to thank the master who had opposed his reading. Douglass explains that his master's opposition to his learning prompted him to work even harder. It is an ironic turn of events.

At this point, you may be wondering how Douglass actually managed to learn to read. After all, this excerpt shows only how he began the learning process; it does not supply the details. An additional excerpt is included on pages 25–28 to fill some of the missing details. The complete picture is provided in Douglass's autobiography, which is available in libraries and on the Internet. ✦

READING STRATEGY

PREDICTING VOCABULARY

Predicting Vocabulary is a technique to help you learn new words. Unlike the usual approach that centers your attention on an unknown word, this strategy focuses on the larger meaning of the text that surrounds the unknown word. The idea is that you are using the rest of the text to help you figure out what you don't know. Two powerful forces will allow you to predict the meaning of unknown terms: your general knowledge and your built-in sense of English grammar. Consider the following:

"The child found that pulling the little red _____ was difficult."

Try to predict a word that fits in the blank using the context that surrounds the blank.

Perhaps you were able to predict that a good choice for the blank was *wagon.* Several factors allowed you to make this choice, among them:

1. The grammar of the sentence requires a thing (a noun) to fit the blank.

2. The missing word must be something little (unlike a school bus), that can be colored red, and pulled by a child even with some difficulty.

3. The phrase "little red wagon" is a common one in the language and is almost a cliché, an expression that is overworked and used too frequently.

However, the first context may not have provided you with enough clues to make a good guess or prediction. Notice how added information might help you predict the missing term. "The child found pulling the little red _____ was difficult because the wheels were bent." Of course, this is a simple example, and the words you will encounter will be more difficult than *wagon.* However, you will have the advantage of a full story context that surrounds the unknown words.

When you read the Frederick Douglass narrative, you noticed that certain words are printed in the right margin. These terms we called *target words.* It is useful to learn their meanings, if you don't already know them, so that you can better understand the Douglass narrative and other readings in which the words occur. Predicting Vocabulary is a good strategy for studying these terms because you will learn the meaning of the target words, but, more importantly, you will learn a process that can be used in all your reading. After a general explanation of the strategy, you will see the method applied to the Douglass excerpt as a model for study.

Before You Get Started

The Predicting Vocabulary strategy will work best if you do the following:

1. First, preview the article.

2. Second, read the material through at least once, without stopping, to get a general impression of the article.

Steps in the Predicting Vocabulary Strategy

The following five-step procedure is to be used with the target words identified in the right margin of the text and with other words you may not know. The steps are given here in abbreviated form accompanied by a flow chart that illustrates the procedure. Each step is then explained in detail followed by an application to the Douglass article.

1. List the target word (the words in the margin or other unknown terms).

2. Study the context—the material surrounding the target word.

3. Write a synonym or definition if you're sure of the word's meaning in the context given. If you're not sure or have no idea, predict the meaning based on the context.

4. Check predictions in the dictionary. If correct, mark a (√); if not, mark an (X).

5. Write a sentence using the target word.

Begin

List target word

Do you know the meaning of the word?

No → Make a prediction

Yes ↓

Write a synonym/ definition

Use a dictionary to confirm whether the prediction was correct

No → Mark an X over your prediction

Yes ↓

Mark a check (√) in the check box

Write the correct dictionary definition

Create a sentence with the target word

End

Terminal — Indicates the start or end of a process

Data — Represents the information that goes into or comes out of a process

Decision — Indicates a point at which a decision must be made

Let's apply the procedure to a sample paragraph whose target words appear italicized in the right margin.

SAMPLE TEXT

At present, my knowledge of computers is superficial, but I expect to gain extensive knowledge when I finish my degree. I am confident that I have chosen the right field of study.

present / superficial
extensive
field

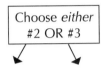

Choose *either*
#2 OR #3

1 Target Word	2 Synonym/ Definition	3 Prediction	4 Dictionary Confirmation	5 Sentence
present	right now			At the present time I'm single.
superficial		~~important~~	Surface or limited understanding	I don't want a lawyer with superficial training.
extensive		wide, vast	√	She has extensive knowledge about art.
field	area of knowledge			The field of medicine interests me.

STEP #1

List the target word: Most readings have target words that appear *italicized* in the right-hand margin. Record these words in the designated space of your chart. In the above example the target words *present, superficial, extensive,* and *field* have been listed in the first column.

    Your next step will be to *either* (a) write a synonym or definition for each word *or* (b) predict its meaning. But, before doing so, you will need to *carefully examine the target word's context.* A word can have multiple meanings depending on how it is used. Be sure to consider the ideas presented immediately before and after the target word. In the example above, the words *present* and *field* can have several meanings depending on how they are used in a sentence. For example, one can receive a birthday *present;* one can be *present* for a class; or one can *present* an award. In the example above, the word *present* has yet another meaning.

STEP #2

Write a synonym or definition: If you know or think you know the meaning of the target word, write a synonym or definition of the term in the appropriate column. A *synonym* is a one-word substitute for the target word; a *definition* expresses the meaning of the target word in a short phrase. Note that in the sample chart the student completed the "Synonym/Definition" for the target words *present* and *field* because the student was sure of the meanings of these words. If you have completed step 2 because you knew the meaning of the target word, skip to step 5. If the target word is new or unfamiliar to you, proceed to step 3.

STEP #3

Make a prediction: If you are unsure or have no idea of what the target word means, make an educated guess, or predict what it could mean given its use in the sentence. Write your prediction in the column labeled "Prediction." In the sample chart the student was not sure of the meanings of *superficial* and *extensive,* and entered good guesses, or predictions, in the appropriate column. Not all your predictions will come close to the mark, but many will if you pay close attention to the context. You will find that whether your prediction is right or wrong, you will absorb and remember the correct definition more thoroughly if you have tried to puzzle it out first. Now move on to step 4.

STEP #4

Confirm predictions in the dictionary: When you are uncertain of a target word's meaning, look it up in the dictionary. Check all your predictions against the dictionary definitions. If your prediction was off the mark, write the correct definition in the fourth column, and cross out your prediction. In the sample chart, the prediction for *superficial* was inaccurate, so the student crossed out the prediction and entered the correct definition in column 4. If you predicted correctly, make a check mark in the same column. In the sample chart the prediction for *extensive* was correct, so the student put a check mark next to it in the "Dictionary Confirmation" column.

When you look up a term, you may find that the dictionary lists a number of meanings for it. Look for the meaning that fits the context of the story. If more than one meaning seems to fit, make a note of all of them and consult your instructor.

STEP #5

Write a sentence: In the fifth column of the chart, write a sentence using the target word, keeping the same meaning the word has in the article. Thus in the first target word of the example, *present,* you should not write a sentence in which *present* is used to mean "a gift" or "not absent." The student has written the sentence "At the present time I'm single," which keeps the same meaning as that in the sample paragraph: "right now." Creating your own sentence will help you remember the word and make it part of your growing vocabulary. Show your sentences to your instructor to confirm that you have used your new words correctly. You will have an additional opportunity to test and use your target words in the vocabulary exercise that will follow most readings.

Applying the Vocabulary Strategy to the Frederick Douglass Reading

The first target word in the Frederick Douglass excerpt is *commenced,* in the sentence "She very kindly commenced to teach me the A, B, C." The first step is to list the target word on your chart as it is done here:

Choose *either*
#2 OR #3

1 Target Word	2 Synonym/ Definition	3 Prediction	4 Dictionary Confirmation	5 Sentence
commenced				

If you know the meaning of the word, enter a synonym or a short definition in column 2. If you don't know the meaning of the word, go to column 3 and make a prediction, or "an educated guess," and enter your response. For example, a prediction for *commenced* could be the word *decided.*

Choose *either*
#2 OR #3

1 Target Word	2 Synonym/ Definition	3 Prediction	4 Dictionary Confirmation	5 Sentence
commenced	----------	decided		

In context, the prediction would read, "She very kindly decided to teach me the A, B, C." *Decided* is a reasonable prediction, because it makes sense and sounds right (that is, it is grammatical) in context.

After predicting all your target words, confirm or check your work in the dictionary. Looking up *commenced* in the *American Heritage Dictionary,* you would discover that it means "to start or begin." You would also note the word is marked (*v.*) for "verb," so your original prediction of *decided* is the correct part of speech. But *decided* indicates merely that someone made up his or her mind to do something, whereas *commenced* means that something was actually begun. So write the correct meaning of *commenced* in the "Dictionary Confirmation" column and mark an "X" through the inaccurate prediction, *decided.* Finally, write your own sentence in column 5.

Choose *either*
#2 OR #3

1 Target Word	2 Synonym/ Definition	3 Prediction	4 Dictionary Confirmation	5 Sentence
commenced	----------	~~decided~~	began, started	The wedding ceremony commenced on time.

You may find that on first learning new terms, it is difficult to work them into sentences. The words can seem foreign and unfamiliar. With effort and imagination, however, you can invent a sentence that uses the new word correctly. This process will help you to make the new word your own. Your instructor can check your sentence to make sure you are on the right track.

The Douglass Story Continues

The next excerpt from the autobiography continues the story of Douglass's early quest for literacy. It is not supported with a marked copy or process guide. You are on your own. You do have the advantage of reading the first supported excerpt and you should have a good sense of the story line. The strategy of reading narratives continues to apply. If you study this excerpt, reconsider your answer to question 5 that appears after the first excerpt (see page 13). The information given in the second excerpt will allow you to amend your speculative answer with one based on facts from the text.

from The Life of an American Slave

by FREDERICK DOUGLASS

Chapter 7

1   I lived in Master Hugh's family about seven years. During this time, I succeeded in learning to read and write. In accomplishing this, I was compelled to resort to various stratagems. I had no regular teacher. My mistress, who had kindly commenced to instruct me, had, in compliance with the advice and direction of her husband, not only ceased to instruct, but had set her face against my being instructed by any one else. It is due, however, to my mistress to say of her, that she did not adopt this course of treatment immediately. She at first lacked the depravity indispensable to shutting me up in mental darkness. It was at least necessary for her to have some training in the exercise of irresponsible power, to make her equal to the task of treating me as though I were a brute.

2   My mistress was, as I have said, a kind and tender-hearted woman; and in the simplicity of her soul she commenced, when I first went to live with her, to treat me as she supposed one human being ought to treat another. In entering upon the duties of a slave-holder, she did not seem to perceive that I sustained to her the relation of a mere chattel, and that for her to treat me as a human being was not only wrong, but dangerously so. Slavery proved as injurious to her as it did to me. When I went there, she was a pious, warm, and tender-hearted woman. There was no sorrow or suffering for which she had not a tear. She had bread for the hungry, clothes for the naked, and comfort for every mourner that came within her reach. Slavery soon proved its ability to divest her of these heavenly qualities. Under its influence, the tender heart became stone, and the lamblike disposition gave way to one of tiger-like fierceness. The first step in her downward course was in her ceasing to instruct me. She now commenced to practise her husband's precepts. She finally became even more violent in her opposition than her husband himself. She was not satisfied with simply doing as well as he had commanded; she seemed anxious to do better. Nothing seemed to make her more angry than to see me with a newspaper. She seemed to think that here lay the danger. I have had her rush at me with a face made all up of fury, and snatch from me a newspaper, in a manner that fully revealed her apprehension. She was an apt woman; and a little experience soon demonstrated, to her satisfaction, that education and slavery were incompatible with each other.

3   From this time I was most narrowly watched. If I was in a separate room any considerable length of time, I was sure to be suspected of having a book, and was at once called to give an account of myself. All this, however, was too late. The first step had been taken. Mistress, in teaching me the alphabet, had given me the *inch*, and no precaution could prevent me from taking the *ell*.

4   The plan which I adopted, and the one by which I was most successful,

was that of making friends of all the little white boys whom I met in the street. As many of these as I could, I converted into teachers. With their kindly aid, obtained at different times and in different places, I finally succeeded in learning to read. When I was sent of errands, I always took my book with me, and by going one part of my errand quickly, I found time to get a lesson before my return. I used also to carry bread with me, enough of which was always in the house, and to which I was always welcome; for I was much better off in this regard than many of the poor white children in our neighborhood. This bread I used to bestow upon the hungry little urchins, who, in return, would give me that more valuable bread of knowledge. I am strongly tempted to give the names of two or three of those little boys, as a testimonial of the gratitude and affection I bear them; but prudence forbids;—not that it would injure me, but it might embarrass them; for it is almost an unpardonable offence to teach slaves to read in this Christian country. It is enough to say of the dear little fellows, that they lived on Philpot Street, very near Durgin and Bailey's ship-yard. I used to talk this matter of slavery over with them. I would sometimes say to them, I wished I could be as free as they would be when they got to be men. "You will be free as soon as you are twenty-one, *but I am a slave for life!* Have not I as good a right to be free as you have?" These words used to trouble them; they would express for me the liveliest sympathy, and console me with the hope that something would occur by which I might be free.

5   I was now about twelve years old, and the thought of being *a slave for life* began to bear heavily upon my heart. Just about this time, I got hold of a book entitled *The Columbian Orator.* Every opportunity I got, I used to read this book. Among much of other interesting matter, I found in it a dialogue between a master and his slave. The slave was represented as having run away from his master three times. The dialogue represented the conversation which took place between them, when the slave was retaken the third time. In this dialogue, the whole argument in behalf of slavery was brought forward by the master, all of which was disposed of by the slave. The slave was made to say some very smart as well as impressive things in reply to his master—things which had the desired though unexpected effect; for the conversation resulted in the voluntary emancipation of the slave on the part of the master.

6   In the same book, I met with one of Sheridan's mighty speeches on and in behalf of Catholic emancipation. These were choice documents to me. I read them over and over again with unabated interest. They gave tongue to interesting thoughts of my own soul, which had frequently flashed through my mind, and died away for want of utterance. The moral which I gained from the dialogue was the power of truth over the conscience of even a slaveholder. What I got from Sheridan was a bold denunciation of slavery, and a powerful vindication of human rights. The reading of these documents enabled me to utter my thoughts, and to meet the arguments brought forward to sustain slavery; but while they relieved me of one difficulty, they brought on another even more painful than the one of which I was relieved. The more

I read, the more I was led to abhor and detest my enslavers. I could regard them in no other light than a band of successful robbers, who had left their homes, and gone to Africa, and stolen us from our homes, and in a strange land reduced us to slavery. I loathed them as being the meanest as well as the most wicked of men. As I read and contemplated the subject, behold! that very discontentment which Master Hugh had predicted would follow my learning to read had already come, to torment and sting my soul to unutterable anguish. As I writhed under it, I would at times feel that learning to read had been a curse rather than a blessing. It had given me a view of my wretched condition, without the remedy. It opened my eyes to the horrible pit, but to no ladder upon which to get out. In moments of agony, I envied my fellow-slaves for their stupidity. I have often wished myself a beast. I preferred the condition of the meanest reptile to my own. Any thing, no matter what, to get rid of thinking! It was this everlasting thinking of my condition that tormented me. There was no getting rid of it. It was pressed upon me by every object within sight or hearing, animate or inanimate. The silver trump of freedom had roused my soul to eternal wakefulness. Freedom now appeared, to disappear no more forever. It was heard in every sound, and seen in every thing. It was ever present to torment me with a sense of my wretched condition. I saw nothing without seeing it, I heard nothing without hearing it, and felt nothing without feeling it. It looked from every star, it smiled in every calm, breathed in every wind, and moved in every storm.

7   I often found myself regretting my own existence, and wishing myself dead; and but for the hope of being free, I have no doubt but that I should have killed myself, or done something for which I should have been killed. While in this state of mind, I was eager to hear any one speak of slavery. I was a ready listener. Every little while, I could hear something about the abolitionists. It was some time before I found what the word meant. It was always used in such connections as to make it an interesting word to me. If a slave ran away and succeeded in getting clear, or if a slave killed his master, set fire to a barn, or did any thing very wrong in the mind of a slaveholder, it was spoken of as the fruit of *abolition.* Hearing the word in this connection very often, I set about learning what it meant. The dictionary afforded me little or no help. I found it was "the act of abolishing;" but then I did not know what was to be abolished. Here I was perplexed. I did not dare to ask any one about its meaning, for I was satisfied that it was something they wanted me to know very little about. After a patient waiting, I got one of our city papers, containing an account of the number of petitions from the north, praying for the abolition of slavery in the District of Columbia, and of the slave trade between the States. From this time I understood the words *abolition* and *abolitionist,* and always drew near when that word was spoken, expecting to hear something of importance to myself and fellow-slaves. The light broke in upon me by degrees. I went one day down on the wharf of Mr. Waters; and seeing two Irishmen unloading a scow of stone, I went, unasked, and helped them. When we had finished, one of them came to me and asked

me if I were a slave. I told him I was. He asked, "Are ye a slave for life?" I told him that I was. The good Irishman seemed to be deeply affected by the statement. He said to the other that it was a pity so fine a little fellow as myself should be a slave for life. He said it was a shame to hold me. They both advised me to run away to the north; that I should find friends there, and that I should be free. I pretended not to be interested in what they said, and treated them as if I did not understand them; for I feared they might be treacherous. White men have been known to encourage slaves to escape, and then, to get the reward, catch them and return them to their masters. I was afraid that these seemingly good men might use me so; but I nevertheless remembered their advice, and from that time I resolved to run away. I looked forward to a time at which it would be safe for me to escape. I was too young to think of doing so immediately; besides, I wished to learn how to write, as I might have occasion to write my own pass. I consoled myself with the hope that I should one day find a good chance. Meanwhile, I would learn to write.

8   The idea as to how I might learn to write was suggested to me by being in Durgin and Bailey's ship-yard, and frequently seeing the ship carpenters, after hewing, and getting a piece of timber ready for use, write on the timber the name of that part of the ship for which it was intended. When a piece of timber was intended for the larboard side, it would be marked thus—"L." When a piece was for the starboard side, it would be marked thus—"S." A piece for the larboard side forward, would be marked thus—"L. F." When a piece was for starboard side forward, it would be marked thus—"S. F." For larboard aft, it would be marked thus—"L. A." For starboard aft, it would be marked thus—"S. A." I soon learned the names of these letters, and for what they were intended when placed upon a piece of timber in the shipyard. I immediately commenced copying them, and in a short time was able to make the four letters named. After that, when I met with any boy who I knew could write, I would tell him I could write as well as he. The next word would be, "I don't believe you. Let me see you try it." I would then make the letters which I had been so fortunate as to learn, and ask him to beat that. In this way I got a good many lessons in writing, which it is quite possible I should never have gotten in any other way. During this time, my copy-book was the board fence, brick wall, and pavement; my pen and ink was a lump of chalk. With these, I learned mainly how to write. I then commenced and continued copying the Italics in Webster's Spelling Book, until I could make them all without looking on the book. By this time, my little Master Thomas had gone to school, and learned how to write, and had written over a number of copy-books. These had been brought home, and shown to some of our near neighbors, and then laid aside. My mistress used to go to class meeting at the Wilk Street meetinghouse every Monday afternoon, and leave me to take care of the house. When left thus, I used to spend the time in writing in the spaces left in Master Thomas's copy-book, copying what he had written. I continued to do this until I could write a hand very similar to that of Master Thomas. Thus, after a long, tedious effort for years, I finally succeeded in learning how to write.

from

The Story of My Life

HELEN KELLER

Helen Keller (1880–1968) lost her sight and hearing shortly before her second birthday. Throughout her early life, she was completely without spoken or written language. However, with determination and the help of Anne Sullivan, a patient and understanding teacher, Keller gradually learned to use sign language and to read. She went on to graduate from college, write books, and inspire millions of people, both blind and sighted.

In the following excerpts, Keller describes her early attempts at learning to read and reveals the wonderful world that books opened up to her.

GEARING UP

1. Our senses—hearing, seeing, smelling, touching, and tasting—play a crucial part in our learning. Which senses do we generally use in learning to read? Explain how we use these senses.

2. How is it possible for someone who can neither hear nor see to learn to read? How can instructions be given when the learner can neither see nor hear the instructor?

 ## READING STRATEGY

COLLECTING IDEAS

College life would be easier if all you had to do was read a single article, answer a few questions, and then go on to the next reading without having to relate the information to what you had learned previously. But in college you will be expected to grasp relationships among ideas and information found in articles, books, and lectures. You must add new ideas and information to what you had previously known to deepen your knowledge of those ideas.

Because all four narrative selections in this unit present information about the role that reading, books, and literacy played in each author's life, it is possible for you to connect information from one article to another. However, before you can make connections, you must collect the information in some way.

For these selections, it is particularly useful to focus on three areas as you collect information. Try to relate the information and ideas to your own experiences with reading and literacy. The first area concerns the way these individuals learned to read. As you read the narratives, think about how you learned to read and how your learning is a continuous process. The second area is the role that effort and determination play in reading. Consider how these authors exerted effort. What actions did they take? What efforts do you make in your reading? The third area is the notion of power, that is, the usefulness of literacy. As you will see, these writers understood the power of the printed word.

Application: How to Collect Ideas

It is easy to say, "Collect ideas and relate them." But how do you do this? This discussion will focus on the first part of the statement, collection. Later in the unit another strategy will be presented, Connecting Ideas, which focuses on how information from different sources can be unified. One way to collect information from your reading is to map out ideas on a chart. You can use a chart such as the one that follows to write down your past ideas on the subject and your present reactions to the readings.

Issues	Myself	Douglass	Keller	Levenson	Malcolm X
The process: how reading is learned					
The role of effort: how effort is shown					
The power of reading: the potential impact					

The chart allows you to organize information from the readings and your reactions to them. You should compose a similar chart in your notebook or on a large sheet of paper. Begin by completing the part of the chart that deals with yourself. Your answers will come from your personal experiences. In the first block labeled, "The process: how reading is learned," you should enter the steps that you encountered on the way to learning to read, perhaps through experiences like attending preschool and watching *Sesame Street*.

After completing the column labeled "Myself," you should begin to focus on the four narratives. You will not find each category addressed by
every article. It may be necessary to infer about a category based on what the
article gives you and what you may know beyond that. In addition, you may
have to revise your initial entries based on new information. For example,
you may have read the first Frederick Douglass excerpt and completed the
appropriate part of the chart. However, if you continued to read the second
excerpt from his narrative, you may have had to revise your initial response.
You can make changes to the chart at any time. Collecting your ideas on a
chart will help you retain and organize ideas. Moreover, the chart will serve
as a data bank for your later effort at connecting the ideas you have gathered.
You will find this method of collecting information even more valuable
when you study for tests, particularly essay exams. The chart is constructed
to accommodate the first four articles and your responses to the issues. We
think you will discover that the other articles in the unit can also be studied
in this manner.

READING STRATEGY CHECK
PREDICTING VOCABULARY

You were introduced to the strategy Predicting Vocabulary after the Frederick Douglass reading. It was stated that proficient readers often predict unknown words using the story line and the sentence. For example, a target
word in Douglass (line 23) is *invaluable.* If you were uncertain of the term's
meaning you might have predicted *unlikely,* since it would be unlikely that
a master would provide instruction to a slave. Even though this is not the
correct meaning, a prediction of this sort would not change the basic meaning of the story. Later, by using the dictionary, you could confirm that the
term meant "very helpful." Your incorrect prediction would be crossed out
and the correct definition would be inserted. The process might appear as
follows:

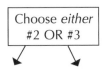

Choose *either*
#2 OR #3

1 Target Word	2 Synonym/ Definition	3 Prediction	4 Dictionary Confirmation	5 Sentence
invaluable		~~unlikely~~	Very helpful	The dictionary is invaluable.

We encourage you to continue using the Predicting Vocabulary strategy in the other readings. The Helen Keller reading contains target words in the margin. The first is *devoured* in paragraph 5. List *devoured* under the target word category and then decide, based on your study of the context, whether you know the word or not. Enter your word in either the synonym/definition column (if you know the term) or in the prediction column (if you are not sure). Confirm your prediction after you have made choices for all the target words. Finally, make sure that you compose a sentence using the target word. Pay particular attention to the target word *consequence*. It is not used in its most familiar form (as in "truth or consequences").

The Reading

from The Story of My Life

by HELEN KELLER

Chapter 7

1   The next important step in my education was learning to read. As soon as I could spell a few words my teacher gave me slips of cardboard on which were printed words in raised letters. I quickly learned that each printed word stood for an object, an act, or a quality. I had a frame in which I could arrange the words in little sentences; but before I ever put sentences in the frame I used to make them in objects. I found the slips of paper which represented, for example, "doll," "is," "on," "bed" and placed each name on its object; then I put my doll on the bed with the words is, on, bed arranged beside the doll, thus making a sentence of the words, and at the same time carrying out the idea of the sentence with the things themselves.

2   One day, Miss Sullivan tells me, I pinned the word girl on my pinafore and stood in the wardrobe. On the shelf I arranged the words, is, in, wardrobe. Nothing delighted me so much as this game. My teacher and I played it for hours at a time. Often everything in the room was arranged in object sentences.

3   From the printed slip it was but a step to the printed book. I took my "Reader for Beginners" and hunted for the words I knew; when I found them my joy was like that of a game of hide-and-seek. Thus I began to read. Of the time when I began to read connected stories I shall speak later . . .

Chapter 21

4   I have thus far sketched the events of my life, but I have not shown how much I have depended on books not only for pleasure and for the wisdom they bring to all who read, but also for that knowledge which comes to others through their eyes and their ears. Indeed, books have meant so much more in my education than in that of others, that I shall go back to the time when I began to read.

5   I read my first connected story in May, 1887, when I was seven years old, and from that day to this I have devoured everything in the shape of a printed page that has come within the reach of my hungry finger tips. As I have said, I did not study regularly during the early years of my education; nor did I read according to rule.

devoured

6   At first I had only a few books in raised print—"readers" for beginners, a collection of stories for children, and a book about the earth called "Our World." I think that was all; but I read them over and over, until the words were so worn and pressed I could scarcely make them out. Sometimes Miss Sullivan read to me, spelling into my hand little stories and poems that she knew I should understand; but I preferred reading myself to being read to, because I liked to read again and again the things that pleased me.

7   It was during my first visit to Boston that I really began to read in good earnest. I was permitted to spend a part of each day in the Institution library, and to wander from bookcase to bookcase, and take down whatever book my fingers lighted upon. And read I did, whether I understood one word in ten or two words on a page. The words themselves fascinated me; but I took no conscious account of what I read. My mind must, however, have been very impressionable at that period, for it retained many words and whole sentences, to the meaning of which I had not the faintest clue; and afterward, when I began to talk and write, these words and sentences would flash out quite naturally, so that my friends wondered at the richness of my vocabulary. I must have read parts of many books (in those early days I think I never read any one book through) and a great deal of poetry in this uncomprehending way, until I discovered "Little Lord Fauntleroy," which was the first book of any consequence I read understandingly.

earnest

retained

consequence

8   One day my teacher found me in a corner of the library poring over the pages of "The Scarlet Letter." I was then about eight years old. I remember she asked me if I liked little Pearl, and explained some of the words that had puzzled me. Then she told me that she had a beautiful story about a little boy which she was sure I would like better than "The Scarlet Letter." The name of the story was "Little Lord Fauntleroy," and she promised to read it to me the following summer. But we did not begin the story until August; the first few weeks of my stay at the seashore were so full of discoveries and excitement that I forgot the very existence of books. Then my teacher went to visit some friends in Boston, leaving me for a short time.

9   When she returned almost the first thing we did was to begin the story of "Little Lord Fauntleroy." I recall distinctly the time and place when we distinctly read the first chapters of the fascinating child's story. It was a warm afternoon in August. We were sitting together in a hammock which swung from two solemn pines at a short distance from the house. We had hurried through the dish-washing after luncheon, in order that we might have as long an afternoon as possible for the story. As we hastened through the long grass toward the hammock, the grasshoppers swarmed about us and fastened themselves on our clothes, and I remember that my teacher insisted upon picking them all off before we sat down, which seemed to me an unnecessary waste of time. The hammock was covered with pine needles, for it

distinctly

had not been used while my teacher was away. The warm sun shone on the pine trees and drew out all their fragrance. The air was balmy, with a tang of *balmy* the sea in it. Before we began the story Miss Sullivan explained to me the things that she knew I should not understand, and as we read on she explained the unfamiliar words. At first there were many words I did not know, and the reading was constantly interrupted; but as soon as I thoroughly comprehended the situation, I became too eagerly absorbed in the story to notice mere words, and I am afraid I listened impatiently to the explanations that Miss Sullivan felt to be necessary. When her fingers were too tired to spell another word, I had for the first time a keen sense of my depri- *deprivations* vations. I took the book in my hands and tried to feel the letters with an intensity of longing that I can never forget.

10   Afterward, at my eager request, Mr. Anagnos had this story embossed, and I read it again and again, until I almost knew it by heart; and all through my childhood "Little Lord Fauntleroy" was my sweet and gentle companion. I have given these details at the risk of being tedious, because they are in *tedious* such vivid contrast with my vague, mutable and confused memories of ear- *vivid / mutable* lier reading.

11   From "Little Lord Fauntleroy" I date the beginning of my true interest in books. During the next two years I read many books at my home and on my visits to Boston. I cannot remember what they all were, or in what order I read them; but I know that among them were "Greek Heroes," LaFontaine's "Fables," Hawthorne's "Wonder Book," "Bible Stories," Lamb's "Tales from Shakespeare," "A History of England" by Dickens, "The Arabian Nights," "The Swiss Family Robinson," "The Pilgrim's Progress," "Robinson Crusoe," "Little Women," and "Heidi," a beautiful little story which I afterward read in German. I read them in the intervals between study and play with an ever-deepening sense of pleasure. I did not study nor analyze them—I did not know whether they were well written or not; I never thought about style or authorship. They laid their treasures at my feet, and I accepted them as we accept the sunshine and the love of our friends. I loved "Little Women" because it gave me a sense of kinship with girls and boys who could see and hear. Circumscribed as my life was in so many ways, I had to look between *circumscribed* the covers of books for news of the world that lay outside my own.

QUESTIONS

1. Describe Keller's process in learning to read.

2. Discuss Keller's attitude toward learning to read.

3. What value did books have for Keller? Explain your answer.

4. In what ways did Keller depend on Anne Sullivan, her teacher?

5. The article presents two different times in Keller's reading life. Compare and contrast the information Keller provides about her reading process in Chapter 7 with the information she gives in Chapter 21.

EXTENDING YOUR VOCABULARY

devoured: The lion devoured _____

earnest: Her earnest goodwill gesture was not _____

retained: During the heavy rains the sandbag wall retained
                  _____

consequence: Their loss of the first race was of no consequence be-
                  cause _____

distinctly: The witness remarked: "I distinctly _____ "

balmy: I enjoy balmy weather because _____

deprivations: Despite my many childhood deprivations, I still
                  _____

tedious: When I watch a tedious movie, I _____

vivid: Vivid memories can _____

mutable: I could see that his feelings were mutable by the fact that
                  _____

circumscribed: The child's activities became very circumscribed because
                  _____

 MARKED COPY

The Reading

from The Story of My Life

by HELEN KELLER

Chapter 7

1   The (next important step) in my education was learning to (read.) As soon as
    I could spell a few words my teacher gave me slips of cardboard on
    which were printed words in <u>raised letters</u>. I quickly learned that each
    printed word stood for an object, an act, or a quality. I had a frame in which
    I could arrange the words in little sentences; but before I ever put sentences
    in the frame I used to make them in objects. I found the slips of paper which
    represented, for example, "doll," "is," "on," "bed" and placed each name on
    its object; then I put my doll on the bed with the words is, on, bed arranged
    beside the doll, thus making a sentence of the words, and at the same time
    carrying out the idea of the sentence with the things themselves.

2   One day, Miss Sullivan tells me, I pinned the word girl on my pinafore
    and stood in the wardrobe. On the shelf I arranged the words, is, in,
    wardrobe. Nothing delighted me so much as this game. My teacher and I

Margin notes:
things already happened

raised letters?

Helen learns that words and sentences have meaning

played it for hours at a time. Often everything in the room was arranged in object sentences.

3   From the printed slip it was but a step to the printed book. I took my "Reader for Beginners" and hunted for the words I knew; when I found them my joy was like that of a game of hide-and-seek. Thus I began to read. Of the time when I began to read connected stories I shall speak later . . .

connected stories?

Chapter 21

4   I have thus far sketched the events of my life, but I have not shown how much I have depended on books not only for pleasure and for the wisdom they bring to all who read, but also for that knowledge which comes to others through their eyes and their ears. Indeed, books have meant so much more in my education than in that of others, that I shall go back to the time when I began to read.

continuation of events

Importance of books

5   I read my first connected story in May, 1887, when I was seven years old, and from that day to this I have devoured everything in the shape of a printed page that has come within the reach of my hungry finger tips. As I have said, I did not study regularly during the early years of my education; nor did I read according to rule.

note time reference

"hungry finger tips"

6   At first I had only a few books in raised print—"readers" for beginners, a collection of stories for children, and a book about the earth called "Our World." I think that was all; but I read them over and over, until the words were so worn and pressed I could scarcely make them out. Sometimes Miss Sullivan read to me, spelling into my hand little stories and poems that she knew I should understand; but I preferred reading myself to being read to, because I like to read again and again the things that pleased me.

raised print?

7   It was during my first visit to Boston that I really began to read in good earnest. I was permitted to spend a part of each day in the institution library, and to wander from bookcase to bookcase, and take down whatever book my fingers lighted upon. And read I did, whether I understood one word in ten or two words on a page. The words themselves fascinated me; but I took no conscious account of what I read. My mind must, however, have been very impressionable at that period, for it retained many words and whole sentences, to the meaning of which I had not the faintest clue; and afterward, when I began to talk and write, these words and sentences would flash out quite naturally, so that my friends wondered at the richness of my vocabulary. I must have read parts of many books (in those early days I think I never read any one book through) and a great deal of poetry in this uncomprehending way, until I discovered "Little Lord Fauntleroy," which was the first book of any consequence I read understandingly.

Helen begins to read

books made an impression

8   One day my teacher found me in a corner of the library poring over the pages of "The Scarlet Letter." I was then about eight years old. I remember she asked me if I liked little Pearl, and explained some of the words that had puzzled me. Then she told me that she had a beautiful story about a little boy which she was sure I would like better than "The Scarlet Letter." The name of the story was "Little Lord Fauntleroy," and she promised to read it to me the following summer. But we did not begin the story until August; the first few weeks of my stay at the seashore were so full of discoveries and excitement that I forgot the very existence of books. Then my teacher went to visit some friends in Boston, leaving me for a short time.

The role Anne Sullivan plays

9   When she returned almost the first thing we did was to begin the story of "Little Lord Fauntleroy." I recall distinctly the time and place when we distinctly read the first chapters of the fascinating child's story. It was a warm after noon in August. We were sitting together in a hammock which swung

from two solemn pines at a short distance from the house. We had hurried through the dish-washing after luncheon, in order that we might have as long an afternoon as possible for the story. As we hastened through the long grass toward the hammock, the grasshoppers swarmed about us and fastened themselves on our clothes, and I remember that my teacher insisted upon picking them all off before we sat down, which seemed to me an unnecessary waste of time. The hammock was covered with pine needles, for it had not been used while my teacher was away. The warm sun shone on the pine trees and drew out all their fragrance. The air was balmy, with a tang of the sea in it. Before we began the story Miss Sullivan explained to me the things that she knew I should not understand, and as we read on she explained the unfamiliar words. At first there were many words I did not know, and the reading was constantly interrupted; but as soon as I thoroughly comprehended the situation, I became too eagerly absorbed in the story to notice mere words, and I am afraid I listened impatiently to the explanations that Miss Sullivan felt to be necessary. When her fingers were too tired to spell another word, I had for the first time a keen sense of my deprivations. I took the book in my hands and tried to feel the letters with an intensity of longing that I can never forget.

10   Afterward, at my eager request, Mr. Anagnos had this story embossed, and I read it again and again, until I almost knew it by heart; and all through my childhood "Little Lord Fauntleroy" was my sweet and gentle companion. I have given these details at the risk of being tedious, because they are in such vivid contrast with my vague, mutable and confused memories of earlier reading.

11   From "Little Lord Fauntleroy" I date the beginning of my true interest in books. During the next two years I read many books at my home and on my visits to Boston. I cannot remember what they all were, or in what order I read them; but I know that among them were "Greek Heroes," LaFontaine's "Fables," Hawthorne's "Wonder Book," "Bible Stories," Lamb's "Tales from Shakespeare," "A History of England" by Dickens, "The Arabian Nights," "The Swiss Family Robinson," "The Pilgrim's Progress," "Robinson Crusoe," "Little Women," and "Heidi," a beautiful little story which I afterward read in German. I read them in the intervals between study and play with an ever-deepening sense of pleasure. I did not study nor analyze them—I did not know whether they were well written or not; I never thought about style or authorship. They laid their treasures at my feet, and I accepted them as we accept the sunshine and the love of our friends. I loved "Little Women" because it gave me a sense of kinship with girls and boys who could see and hear. Circumscribed as my life was in so many ways, I had to look between the covers of books for news of the world that lay outside my own.

Margin notes:
- Ms. Sullivan introduces Helen to Little Lord Fauntleroy
- Note details
- Helen reacts—feelings of frustration
- Helen asks for the book to be embossed
- Helen reads many books
- *The power of literacy in Helen's life

 # PROCESS GUIDE

1. The account you just read is part of Helen Keller's autobiography. How can you tell that this is an excerpt?

_____

Model Answer   The heading "Chapter 7" indicates that six chapters precede it. In addition, the reading opens with the words "The next important step in my education . . ." This suggests that events have already taken place.

✦ **NOTE** At first, Keller learned the alphabet manually—by feeling and touching. Miss Sullivan spelled words using her hands, and Keller, her hand upon Sullivan's, would follow along to feel the letters. After she learned some words, Keller used raised print to learn to read. She had special books in which each printed letter was raised on the page to a height about the thickness of a thumbnail. Keller moved her fingers over the page and felt the letters. ✦

2. Keller says she learned that each printed word represented something. How did she bring life to these printed words?

_____

_____

_____

3. In paragraph 3, the author signals that she is moving to a new idea. How is this indicated? _____

Model Answer   *She tells us, "From the printed slip it was but a step to the*

printed book."

✦ **NOTE** Like most beginning readers, Keller started out with simple books. She does not say whether one of her early books, *Reader for Beginners,* was printed in a special way, but we can probably assume that it used raised letters. This is not to be confused with Braille, which is a special alphabet that Keller learned at the Perkins Institute in Boston. A printed page of Braille consists of a system of raised dots embossed in paper by hand or machine and read by touch. Each letter, number, and punctuation mark is indicated by the number and arrangement of one to six dots in a cell, or letter space, two dots wide and three dots high. The characters are embossed from the back of the paper, working in reverse direction, and are read from the face of the paper in the normal reading direction. This excerpt tells us little more about her early reading except that Keller enjoyed finding words she knew. In the next excerpt, we learn about her efforts to move beyond simple material to longer, more complex stories printed in Braille. ✦

4. The next excerpt is from Chapter 21 of Keller's autobiography. How does the author indicate that events have already taken place?

_____

Model Answer   *The phrase "thus far" (up to this point) shows that things have*

already happened. Now Keller tells her readers that she will focus on the important

role that books played in her life.

5. What does Keller mean by "knowledge that comes to others through their eyes and their ears"?

_____

_____

_____

6. The author talks about her reading experiences at age seven and mentions reading her first "connected" story. What does she mean?

_____

_____

_____

Model Answer   At first, Keller learns to spell and read a few words. She realizes

that printed words have meaning, and she practices reading using a beginner's

reader. Then she advances to a story consisting of several chapters—a "connected

story," as she refers to it.

7. In paragraph 5, why does Keller use the expression "my hungry finger tips" as she describes her pursuit of reading?

_____

_____

_____

◆ **NOTE**   Keller's expression *my hungry finger tips* has special significance. To understand the meaning, recall how Keller learned to read by using books with raised print. To do so, she used her fingertips to feel the letters.

This type of expression is an example of figurative language. Writers use figurative language when they wish to extend the meaning of what they are saying. They don't expect readers to understand their expressions in a literal (word-by-word) sense. Figurative language occurs in our everyday language. If someone is upset, we may ask, "What's eating you?" We are not suggesting that the person is really being eaten. In fact, we cannot understand the intended meaning of the expression if we take it literally.   ◆

8. What does Keller mean when she says, "I read them over and over, until the words were so worn and pressed I could scarcely make them out." How did the words become "worn and pressed"?

_____

_____

READING STRATEGY

FRAMING AN ANSWER I

Producing appropriate answers on examinations and homework assignments is obviously a valuable ability for students. Perhaps you have been frustrated when you felt that you knew certain material but were told that you answered incorrectly. Producing good answers requires more than just knowing the material. For example, consider the first question you were asked to answer after the Douglass article, "Cite the event that convinced Frederick Douglass of his need to read."

Most of our students claim that they understand the reading upon which this question is based. In fact, their discussion in class suggests that they do. However, when they approach this question, some produce an incorrect answer, such as "Frederick Douglass was convinced that literacy would be a way out of slavery for him." Incorrect responses like this one result from a lack of experience with analyzing questions and also from a lack of strategy. The process of approaching questions and constructing good answers can be broken down into steps:

1. Understanding the question (cue words and other key terms)

2. Reading the text and/or searching your mind for related ideas

3. Selecting the relevant information

4. Constructing the answer (organizing, paraphrasing, and using transitions)

5. Editing the response

(The discussion here will focus on the first step, understanding the question. The other steps will be covered later in the book.)

Usually wrong answers come from not truly understanding the question and transforming it into something known to be true but not asked for. Let us look at the question again: "Cite the event that convinced Frederick Douglass of his need to read." Breaking up the question in the following way may help you see the parts.

> 1 {Cite the event} 2 {event that convinced Douglass} 3 {convinced of need to read}

Part 1 is the opening direction headed by the cue word *cite*. As you may recall, *cite* means to list or state. The question is asking you to cite or name the *event*. Usually when students respond inappropriately with Douglass's feelings about the slave system, they miss the meaning of the word *event* and its key role in the sentence. An *event* is an activity that takes place in time and space and can be witnessed. Thus whatever is cited or named must be something that has been seen or heard by Douglass and not something that takes place in his mind. In this case the event is hearing his master's words about the slave situation. The event then convinced (persuaded to believe) Douglass that he needed to read.

Application

The selection by Helen Keller is followed by a number of questions as are the other readings. A first step in answering the questions appropriately is to make certain that you know the meanings of the cue words and other key terms that often begin a question. Cue words specify the kind of information that you are to provide in your answer and the form it is to take. After consulting the questions, you may wish to review the cue word chart on pages 6–8. For example, the fifth question reads as follows:

5. The article presents two different periods in Keller's reading life. Compare and contrast the information Keller provides about her reading process in Chapter 7 with the information she gives in Chapter 21.

The question can be mapped out for clarity:

Chapter 7,   Chapter 21,
Reading Process Information   Reading Process Information
(one time in Helen's life)   (another time in Helen's life)

"*Compare and contrast.*" The cue word list tells you that "compare and contrast" means to look for similarities and differences. In the case of Keller, you are to look for events or activities in Keller's reading process that are the same and not the same in the two excerpts. *Hint:* Remember that the question is asking about Helen Keller's reading process and not what might be common for many hearing and sighted people.

from
Everything But Money

Sam Levenson

Sam Levenson began his career as a teacher and became nationally known as a humorist through his appearances on radio and television. Levenson was noted for his amusing autobiographical accounts of family life and school. His numerous books include In One Era and Out the Other, You Don't Have to Be in *Who's Who* to Know What's What, *and* Everything But Money.

GEARING UP

1. Cite some language and cultural problems immigrants might face as they try to adjust to life in a new country.

2. Discuss the role family members can play in encouraging a child to learn to read.

 # READING STRATEGY CHECK

COLLECTING IDEAS

You were introduced to the strategy of "collecting ideas" in the *Helen Keller* reading. It was suggested that one way of following an issue or idea over a number of articles was to construct a chart such as the model on page 30. If you have studied the narrative selections, you may have entries for both Douglass and Keller. When you finish your work with Sam Levenson, return to the chart and enter the appropriate information for Levenson. Remember, not every article addresses every issue. If information is inferred rather than directly stated, you might note this with some type of marking [* inference]. If there is no information given or no inference possible, leave the box blank or write in [NI] for *no information.*

The Reading

from Everything But Money

by SAM LEVENSON

1   Plants could not flourish in our flat, but books did. They grew and multi-   *flourish*
plied in the dark. They were displayed, dusted, protected, and referred to
with reverence. I respected them long before I could read them. In this sense,
again, I was a privileged child. I was heir to an ancient tradition of love of   *heir*
learning. Our household heroes were almost exclusively men of learning,
spiritual leaders, poets, musicians, philosophers. We hung their pictures on
our walls, along with our diplomas.

2   My parents told us how in the old country when a child began his religious education his first book was strewn with raisins and almonds as a symbol of the sweetness of knowledge. The first song I remember my mother
singing to me was a sort of hymn in praise of education. It is perhaps the only
folk song of its kind and it had to come from the "People of the Book." It
was sung, naturally, in Yiddish. I have put it down freely rendered as I re-   *rendered*
member it:

Around the Fireplace

There's a fire on the hearth
And the house is warm
And the little ones, all of them,
Learn their A, B, C.
Say it, little ones, say it, precious ones,
What you're learning here.
Say it once again, and even once again,
Say your A, B, C.

When you will older be
You will understand
How many tears have fallen on these pages,
How much heartbreak felt here, too.

Say it, little ones, say it, precious ones,
What you're learning here.
Say it once again, and even once again,
Say your A, B, C.

3   In my elementary-school-graduation autograph book Papa wrote in Hebrew the words "My son, make thy books thy companions. Let thy cases and shelves be thy pleasure grounds and gardens. . . ."

4   I recently found the entire quotation. It was written by Judah Ibn Tibbon in twelfth-century Spain. It continues from where Papa left off with ". . . pluck their roses, take their spices and their myrrh. If thy soul be satiated and weary change from garden to garden, from furrow to furrow, from prospect to prospect, then will desire renew itself and thy soul be filled with delight."   *satiated*

5   Compulsory education was not regarded by my people as a legal imposition but as a golden opportunity—part of the dream that had brought millions of immigrants to America. The word "culture" brought tears even to Papa's eyes, but he could not make sense out of the stuff they were teaching us in school, like "The cow says, 'Moo, moo,' the pig says 'Oink,' the dog says, 'Bow wow.'"   *compulsory imposition*

6   "What's the matter with these animals?" Papa used to say. "Can't they talk English?"

7   My childish fingers riffled through the pages of books my older brothers were reading. I was awestricken by the big words, and I looked forward to the day when I might understand them. Children's books didn't come into my life until I had children of my own. I never read *Alice in Wonderland* until my children did. My "Wonderland" as a child was the mysterious books all about me as yet unread. I imagined what was in them. When I got to read them later in life I found them even more exciting than I had dreamed. I still open an unread book with delicious anticipation.   *riffled*   *awestricken*

8   My older brothers used books as a ladder to elevate themselves to the point where they could see beyond our block. They stole a glimpse of the great, free world of ideas. Our bookshelves reflected the expanding intellectual horizons of the family. Papa's traditional prayer books were joined by

Plato, Shakespeare, Voltaire, Tom Paine, Ingersoll, Tolstoy, Dostoevsky, Shaw, Dreiser, Whitman. . . . Papa must have suspected that some of the boys were going off in directions alien to his traditions, but he was tolerant.   *alien*

9   We spent much of our time in the public library for two reasons: they had the books we could not afford to buy, and they had steam heat. I admired my brothers' library cards, which were heavily stamped with dates of withdrawals. This to my mind was status—a dog-eared, smudgy library card. I tired to match their record. I withdrew and returned books at the rate of two or three a day. I had to have a dirty library card.

10   And the humiliations I had suffered to get the card in the first place! I had to get references from my school principal and "two responsible citizens." I got the OK of the principal, but where was I to find a responsible citizen, one who, according to the librarian, had his name in the telephone book? I gave the candy-store phone number. That got me into trouble. I had to produce a birth certificate. Mine had been lost. They began to question my legitimacy.

11   When I took out my first book I caused quite a stir at the signing-out desk. At the secret request of my cousin Sophie, who was too embarrassed to do it for herself, I withdrew *What Every Girl Should Know.* The librarian put a question mark in red beside the name Samuel on my card.

QUESTIONS

1. Describe how education was regarded in the Levenson household.

2. What was Levenson's inspiration for learning to read?

3. Levenson states, "My older brothers used books as a ladder to elevate themselves to the point where they could see beyond our block." Explain what he means by this statement.

4. Paraphrase the statement "Papa must have suspected that some of the boys were going off in directions alien to his tradition, but he was tolerant."

5. Explain why Levenson caused a stir when he checked out his first library book.

6. What object bore high status for Levenson? Do you think this item is typical of a status symbol? Why or why not?

7. Levenson is noted for the humor in his writing. Cite two examples from the story that show this humor.

8. Is Levenson's experience with reading typical of immigrant families? Explain.

EXTENDING YOUR VOCABULARY

flourish: The university's music program began to flourish when

_____

heir: He became heir to the throne after _____

rendered: As she rendered a Spanish folk song into English, she real-
                 ized that _____

satiated: After being satiated with praise, the young violinist started
                 to _____

compulsory: The seat belt law became compulsory because _____
                 _____

imposition: Driving the neighbor's children began to be an imposition
                 when _____

riffled: As she riffled through the book she realized _____
                 _____

awestricken: Standing at the foot of Niagara Falls, the children were
                 awestricken by _____

alien: While studying the alien customs of the remote tribe, I dis-
                 covered that _____

 PROCESS GUIDE

1. Levenson is writing through the eyes and experiences of an immigrant
   family. In the first four paragraphs of the article, he describes the high es-
   teem books received in his household. Using the following table, cite information from each paragraph that demonstrates this viewpoint. In the
   "Book Statement" column, paraphrase the message about books. In the
   "View Holder" column, identify the person who holds this viewpoint.

Paragraph	Book Statement	View Holder
1		
2		
3		
4		

2. What can you conclude from Levenson's statements about books?

_____

_____

3. Levenson begins paragraph 5 with a complicated sentence. You need to understand this statement to fully appreciate the rest of his message. If you had some difficulty with this sentence, you could have proceeded in two ways. First, you could have looked up the terms *compulsory* and *imposition* and attempted to integrate their marriage into the context of the sentence. Second, you could have made a prediction about their meanings and continued reading. The latter process may have helped you understand this sentence as it connects to the rest of the article. Try paraphrasing this sentence.

_____

_____

4. Levenson stresses his father's regard for "culture" (the arts) by saying that even the word "brought tears even to Papa's eyes." Why would the mention of an idea move someone to tears?

_____

_____

5. Paragraph 7 signals a particular time in Levenson's life with the words *childish fingers.* This suggests that the remarks that immediately follow will relate to his childhood. What does Levenson say in the next sentence that indicates his early feelings about reading?

_____

6. In the third sentence, Levenson shifts to a later period when he had children of his own. Why does he do this?

_____

7. The time shifts in paragraph 7 may make it difficult to determine whether the events are taking place in Levenson's childhood or adulthood. It will help you to separate the events into two categories as follows:

Childhood	Adulthood

8. In paragraph 8, Levenson continues the theme of the value of literacy. He uses the literary form called *simile.* A *simile* is a comparison using *like* or *as.* In this case, to what object does Levenson compare books?

_____

✦ **NOTE**   Levenson's brothers used books to discover worldly ideas, views, and thoughts beyond those found in their immediate neighborhood. He says, my older brothers use books "as a ladder to elevate themselves to the point where they could see beyond our block." This is an example of figurative language. If you took this expression literally, you would visualize Levenson's brothers piling book upon book to create a ladder-like heap and them climbing to the top to look out beyond their neighborhood. To be understood, this expression must be read figuratively—that is, by reading books Levenson's brothers gained many worldly experiences and broadened their horizons beyond the immediate neighborhood. ✦

9. Levenson gives some evidence of the influence of books on his family. Try paraphrasing the sentence "Our bookshelves reflected the expanding intellectual horizons of the family."

_____

_____

✦ **NOTE**   Another difficult sentence concludes paragraph 8: "Papa must have suspected that some of the boys were going off in directions alien to his traditions, but he was tolerant." Here an informed frame of reference can make the meaning of the statement come alive. In the play and later movie *Fiddler on the Roof*, Tevye, when faced with new ideas (ideas foreign to his background and upbringing), quickly responds, "What about tradition?" Tevye believes certain things must continue to be done according to practices established long ago. Tradition offers us a map of what must be done. Like Tevye's beliefs and practices, the prayerbooks, prayers, and blessings of Levenson's father were traditional. When Tevye's daughter announces her wish to marry someone outside the faith, Tevye responds with great anguish—how could his own child abandon tradition by marrying a non-Jew? Similarly, Levenson's father faced a situation where his children were being introduced to "newer" ideas. No doubt the authors on the bookshelf next to Papa's traditional prayerbooks had some nontraditional ideas. ✦

10. How did Levenson's father respond to these "alien" ideas?

_____

_____

11. In paragraphs 9 through 11, Levenson demonstrates what he is best known for: humor. Briefly paraphrase the humorous example for each paragraph listed:

Paragraph 9 _____

_____

Paragraph 10 _____

_____

Paragraph 11 _____

_____

 # READING STRATEGY
MARKING TEXT

Proficient reading is an active process. Marking text as you read is one way to stay active and involved. By **marking** we mean using symbols to indicate ideas and features and writing brief marginal notes to capture the author's message. To some extent, marking text is like holding a conversation with an author: You can signal your agreement with a point, register your doubts or reservations, and list your questions for discussion in class and later study. Marking text has these advantages:

1. It provides a record of your understanding.

2. It gives you reference points for questions.

3. It serves as a source for examination review.

4. It keeps you actively engaged in your reading.

The marked copies accompanying the Douglass and Keller articles are two examples of applying the marking-text strategy. We highlighted significant ideas, noted transitional points in the author's thoughts, and identified key words and phrases. Study these and other examples of the marking-text technique in this book. With practice and attention to some basic principles, you will become proficient in this technique.

How and What to Mark

There are two important steps in marking text. First, you need to learn *how* to mark text. Second, you need to learn how to decide *what* to mark.

One marking strategy students often use is underlining. Perhaps you have seen a student-marked textbook in which just about everything is underlined or highlighted. This may seem like a useful exercise to students at the time they are doing it. However, often the student must reread almost all the material just to determine why something was marked.

When text is underlined or highlighted with no discrimination between the markings, the value of using that form of marking is lost. It is quite inefficient, for example, to use underlining to signal both those things that are most significant and those that you don't understand. Marking everything the same way means that when you go back to the material, you must repeat all the reading and thinking steps that led you to conclude that something was important and something else was hard to understand. Significant ideas and points not understood are two different categories, and they should be marked differently. As you will see, a range of marking techniques is available to you, and each should be used selectively.

MARGINAL NOTES

One helpful marking technique is to write brief notes in the margin of your book, responding to or questioning the material you are reading. (See samples of marginal notes on pages 14 and 35.) Marginal notes obviously take more time than underlining or other kinds of shorthand notation, but they are extremely useful. Writing them keeps you involved with what you are reading, almost as if you are having a conversation with the author. Later, these notes bring to mind your thoughts as you were reading a certain section of text.

OTHER TYPES OF MARKING

To be useful, your text markings should follow a consistent pattern. Some suggested notations follow; you can also devise your own.

1. **Underline.** Underline only what seems important. Sometimes it is difficult to determine what is important until you get through the whole article. Therefore, your best approach is to read through an article once without stopping to mark it. Underlined material will be more meaningful if it is accompanied by a marginal note that briefly explains your reasons for the underlining.

2. **Double underline.** Use a double underline to distinguish the most important items you have already underlined. If you have underlined, say, five times on a page, another reading of the article will reveal that not all of the underlined material is of equal importance. If double underlining is not practical due to the text spacing, use a pound sign (#) in the margins as an alternative.

3. (Circle.) Circle key words and phrases in the text. Suppose you read the following: "The purpose of this article is to argue the case (against) capital punishment." It is important to note the position the author is taking on an issue. In this example it would be useful to circle *against*, because that word clearly shows the author's opinion of the issue.

4. **Asterisk (*).** Use an asterisk to mark the one or two major points in an article. Often even a long article has essentially one main idea. If you use the asterisk selectively, you will be able to skim the article, note your placement of the asterisks, and quickly recapture the main points. For textbook chapters, use one asterisk per section that is set off by headings.

   When the author's central thesis is implied rather than directly stated, use the asterisk to mark a marginal note you have written that briefly captures the point of the article.

5. **Arrow (→).** Use the arrow to mark transitional points in the text, that is, points where the author is moving on to a new topic and is relating the material to come to what has already been discussed. Sometimes the author signals transitional points with subheadings, which clearly announce that a new topic is about to be discussed. At other times, the author signals a new topic by means of transitional words: "Let us examine another issue that supports the Geneva accords." "A historical perspective seems to argue against the current trend. For example, ..."

6. **Question mark (?).** The question mark may be the most valuable marking symbol. It is your signal to yourself that things are unclear or confusing and thus need further study or explanation. Marking your texts with question marks gives you a convenient listing of the difficulties that can be asked of your instructor. To further refine the question mark symbol, we suggest the following: Use one question mark (?) for things that are somewhat unclear or fuzzy. Use two question marks (??) to indicate that a particular section of the text makes no sense at all and is totally confusing.

Application

As a first exercise in marking text, we have chosen the excerpt from *Everything but Money* by Sam Levenson. Because we want you to mark this article, a marked copy is not provided in the textbook.

If you have been following the guidelines set at the beginning of this unit, you began the reading by responding to the Gearing Up questions before the article. You then read the article through without stopping and returned for a second, more careful reading in which you focused on new vocabulary words and ideas that may have escaped you on the first pass. Normally, at this point you would be ready to mark the text. However, we have purposely put the marking exercise after the Process Guide to let you become as familiar with the material as possible.

In the Levenson article, notice the frequency of the word *book* and related words like *reading, library,* and *education.* You may choose to mark these terms with symbols or a brief note, since key words and phrases are an important feature to consider. Study the text carefully to determine the author's main point. Then mark it with an asterisk (*) and write a brief note in the margin paraphrasing that statement.

For the remainder of the article, mark the statements you believe are significant. You may wish to review the marking scheme suggested earlier. Also, make brief marginal notes to interpret your markings.

Further Practice

Like any newly acquired skill, becoming proficient at "marking text" will require time, practice, and the study of additional models. With this in mind, we have provided a partially marked copy for *The Autobiography of Malcolm*

X (pages 57–59) and a partially marked copy for "The Proficient Reader" (pages 88–91). Try a markup before you consult these examples, and try to continue with the marking strategy in this text and others you are using.

✦ **NOTE**   Perhaps you have already been using some effective way to mark text that you have devised on your own. If so, stick with your good habit and only adopt those suggestions that will work for you. ✦

from
The Autobiography of Malcolm X

MALCOLM X

Malcolm X, a noted black civil rights leader, reformer, author, and speaker, was born Malcolm Little in Omaha, Nebraska, in 1925. At a fairly young age he served time in prison, where he became familiar with the religious teachings of the Black Muslims. After being paroled from prison, he became active in the Black Muslims movement and later went on to establish a new black organization. He was assassinated in 1965 at a rally in New York City. In this narrative, Malcolm X reveals how reading opened up a whole new world for him both while in prison and after gaining his freedom.

GEARING UP

1. Describe how prison life is portrayed on television, in movies, and in the press.

2. Must a person attend school to be educated? List at least three other ways a person can gain knowledge.

READING STRATEGY
CONNECTING IDEAS

To connect means to join together or relate in some way. A true benchmark of the college learning experience is synthesis. The expectation is that you will be synthesizing (putting together) information from a variety of sources. Your compilations will focus on the relationships among various ideas. A group of random facts will probably not have much significance, but take these pieces of isolated data, organize them into a meaningful pattern, and you have useful information.

In the strategy section before the Helen Keller article, you were shown the strategy of *collecting ideas.* You were told that one way of doing this was to prepare a chart (see page 30). You may find it useful to consult the chart at this point.

What can you do with collected facts? Make connections by relating ideas. If you have studied two or more articles in the first unit, you can use your data to make connections regarding reading and literacy issues. For example, consider the following question:

> Compare and contrast the *initial* reading steps (how reading was first learned) by Frederick Douglass and Helen Keller.

You may recognize that this question is trying to get at the process first used by these individuals. We are assuming that you in fact studied these two articles and collected information on the chart. If so, examine the section labeled *process.* (Note: You can still follow this discussion even if you didn't complete this portion of the chart.)

First, examine the information you have collected. As a sample, consider the following information:

Collected Information

Frederick Douglass	learned the alphabet and a few short words from his master's wife. After that he used his creativity to learn new words. (This subsequent learning is found in the continuation of the text found after the process guide.)
Helen Keller	was taught the manual alphabet used by the deaf. Her teacher instructed her in using raised letters on cardboard.

Application

Now, how do you respond to the question? If you recognize the cue words *compare and contrast,* you are aware that the question is asking for similarities and differences in the reading process for the two individuals. This means connecting information from the two narratives. Begin by restating the question somewhat differently in answer form and then relate it to the two.

Answer: There are similarities and differences between the reading process for Frederick Douglass and Helen Keller. First, Frederick Douglass was

Note the use of the term similarities and differences— compare & contrast

taught the alphabet. (Similarly,) Helen Keller was also taught the alphabet. → *the comparison*
(But for) Helen the process was different because she was blind and deaf. Her → *the contrast*
instructor formed the manual alphabet so that Helen could feel the shapes of
her hands. Miss Sullivan also connected the raised cardboard letters that Helen
could feel to common objects that were part of her everyday life.

 # READING STRATEGY CHECK

MARKING TEXT

The strategy of "marking text" was introduced after the selection by Sam
Levenson. We hope you made the effort to mark this article. You will mark
an article somewhat differently than your fellow classmates depending on
your background, the purpose you have in reading the article, and the experience you have with this strategy. You may want to consider building up to
the strategy in stages. When people begin to train for the marathon, they do
not begin the first day by running twenty-six miles. They start off with
shorter distances and build gradually. Similarly, you might begin by focusing on what you are uncertain of and noting this uncertainty with a question
mark (?). A next step might be to mark the main point with an asterisk (*).
As we noted in the strategy discussion, use this device sparingly. If used
sparingly with an accompanying marginal note, the asterisk will quickly
help you locate the author's main message and your own thoughts about it.

The Malcolm X selection is accompanied by a marked copy. We encourage you to try your own before you study the marked copy provided. Additional marked copies are provided in the first three units.

The Reading

from The Autobiography of Malcolm X

by MALCOLM X with ALEX HALEY

1   I became increasingly frustrated at not being able to express what I wanted
to convey in letters that I wrote, especially those to Mr. Elijah Muhammad. In the street, I had been the most articulate hustler out there—I had   *articulate*
commanded attention when I said something. But now, trying to write simple English, I not only wasn't articulate, I wasn't even functional. How
would I sound writing in slang, the way I would *say* it, something such as,
"Look, daddy, let me pull your coat about a cat, Elijah Muhammad—"

2   Many who today hear me somewhere in person, or on television, or
those who read something I've said, will think I went to school far beyond
the eighth grade. This impression is due entirely to my prison studies.

3   It had really begun back in the Charlestown Prison, when Bimbi first
made me feel envy of his stock of knowledge. Bimbi had always taken charge
of any conversation he was in, and I had tried to emulate him. But every   *emulate*

book I picked up had few sentences which didn't contain anywhere from one to nearly all of the words that might as well have been in Chinese. When I just skipped those words, of course, I really ended up with little idea of what the book said. So I had come to the Norfolk Prison Colony still going through only book-reading motions. Pretty soon, I would have quit even these motions, unless I had received the motivation that I did.

4   I saw that the best thing I could do was get hold of a dictionary—to study, to learn some words. I was lucky enough to reason also that I should try to improve my penmanship. It was sad. I couldn't even write in a straight line. It was both ideas together that moved me to request a dictionary along with some tablets and pencils from the Norfolk Prison Colony school.

5   I spent two days just riffling uncertainly through the dictionary's pages. I'd never realized so many words existed! I didn't know *which* words I needed to learn. Finally, just to start some kind of action, I began copying.

6   In my slow, painstaking, ragged handwriting, I copied into my tablet everything printed on that first page, down to the punctuation marks.

7   I believe it took me a day. Then, aloud, I read back, to myself, everything I'd written on the tablet. Over and over, aloud, to myself, I read my own handwriting.

8   I woke up the next morning, thinking about those words—immensely proud to realize that not only had I written so much at one time, but I'd written words that I never knew were in the world. Moreover, with a little effort, I also could remember what many of these words meant. I reviewed the words whose meanings I didn't remember. Funny thing, from the dictionary first page right now, that "aardvark" springs to my mind. The dictionary had a picture of it, a long-tailed, long-eared, burrowing African mammal, which lives off termites caught by sticking out its tongue as an anteater does for ants.

9   I was so fascinated that I went on—I copied the dictionary's next page. And the same experience came when I studied that. With every succeeding *succeeding* page, I also learned of people and places and events from history. Actually the dictionary is like a miniature encyclopedia. Finally the dictionary's A section had filled a whole tablet—and I went on into the B's. That was the way I started copying what eventually became the entire dictionary. It went a lot faster after so much practice helped me to pick up handwriting speed. Between what I wrote in my tablet, and writing letters, during the rest of my time in prison I would guess I wrote a million words.

10   I suppose it was inevitable that as my word-base broadened, I could for *inevitable* the first time pick up a book and read and now begin to understand what the book was saying. Anyone who has read a great deal can imagine the new world that opened. Let me tell you something: from then until I left that prison, in every free moment I had, if I was not reading in the library, I was reading on my bunk. You couldn't have gotten me out of books with a wedge. Between Mr. Muhammad's teachings, my correspondence, my visitors—usually Ella and Reginald—and my reading of books, months passed without my even thinking about being imprisoned. In fact, up to then, I never had been so truly free in my life.

11   The Norfolk Prison Colony's library was in the school building. A variety of classes was taught there by instructors who came from such places as Harvard and Boston universities. The weekly debates between inmate teams were also held in the school building. You would be astonished to know how worked up convict debaters and audiences would get over subjects like "Should Babies Be Fed Milk?"

12   Available on the prison library's shelves were books on just about every general subject. Much of the big private collection that Parkhurst had willed to the prison was still in crates and boxes in the back of the library—thousands of old books. Some of them looked ancient: covers faded, old-time parchment-looking binding. Parkhurst, I've mentioned, seemed to have been principally interested in history and religion. He had the money and the special interest to have a lot of books that you wouldn't have in general circulation. Any college library would have been lucky to get that collection.

13   As you can imagine, especially in a prison where there was heavy emphasis on rehabilitation, an inmate was smiled upon if he demonstrated an unusually intense interest in books. There was a sizable number of well-read inmates, especially the popular debaters. Some were said by many to be practically walking encyclopedias. They were almost celebrities. No university would ask any student to devour literature as I did when this new world opened to me, of being able to read and *understand*.   *rehabilitation*

14   I read more in my room than in the library itself. An inmate who was known to read a lot could check out more than the permitted maximum number of books. I preferred reading in the total isolation of my own room.

15   When I had progressed to really serious reading, every night at about ten P.M. I would be outraged with the "lights out." It always seemed to catch me right in the middle of something engrossing.   *engrossing*

16   Fortunately, right outside my door was a corridor light that cast a glow into my room. The glow was enough to read by, once my eyes adjusted to it. So when "lights out" came, I would sit on the floor where I would continue reading in that glow.

17   At one-hour intervals the night guards paced past every room. Each time I heard the approaching footsteps, I jumped into bed and feigned sleep. And as soon as the guard passed, I got back out of bed onto the floor area of that light-glow, where I would read for another fifty-eight minutes—until the guard approached again. That went on until three or four every morning. Three or four hours of sleep a night was enough for me. Often in the years in the streets I had slept less than that. . . .   *feigned*

18   I have often reflected upon the new vistas that reading opened to me. I knew right there in prison that reading had changed forever the course of my life. As I see it today, the ability to read awoke inside me some long dormant craving to be mentally alive. I certainly wasn't seeking any degree, the way a college confers a status symbol upon its students. My homemade education gave me, with every additional book that I read, a little bit more sensitivity to the deafness, dumbness, and blindness that was afflicting the black race in America. Not long ago, an English writer telephoned me from London, asking questions. One was, "What's your alma mater?" I told him, "Books."   *dormant*

confers

afflicting

alma mater

You will never catch me with a free fifteen minutes in which I'm not studying something I feel might be able to help the black man.

QUESTIONS

1. Describe Malcolm X's feelings when he tried to compose a letter.

2. Identify the course of action that Malcolm X followed to solve his literacy problem.

3. Analyze Malcolm X's effort to improve his reading. Do you think this is a commonly used strategy? Explain.

4. Malcolm X says, "The ability to read awoke inside of me some long dormant craving to be mentally alive." Explain.

5. What was Malcolm X's alma mater? How is his answer different from what is usually expected?

6. Malcolm X learned to improve his reading and writing in prison. What lesson(s) can we learn from his achievement?

EXTENDING YOUR VOCABULARY

articulate: In order to become more articulate, I decided to
                  _____

emulate: The people I choose to emulate are _____

succeeding: At first the guests arrived slowly, but with each succeeding hour, _____

inevitable: After not sleeping for two nights it was inevitable that
                  _____

rehabilitation: I went to a rehabilitation center in order to _____

engrossing: When I read something that is engrossing, I _____

feigned: I feigned illness so that I could _____

dormant: Today the volcano is dormant, but perhaps next week it
                  _____

confer: At the ceremony honoring the governor, the university chose to confer _____

afflicting: This disease should be taken seriously because it is afflicting _____

alma mater: Colin Powell's alma mater is _____

MARKED COPY

The Reading

from The Autobiography of Malcolm X

by MALCOLM X with ALEX HALEY

1   I became (increasingly frustrated) at not being able to express what I wanted to convey in letters that I wrote, especially those to Mr. Elijah Muhammad. In the street, I had been the most articulate hustler out there—I had commanded attention when I said something. But now, trying to write simple English, I not only wasn't articulate, I wasn't even functional. How would I sound writing in slang, the way I would *say* it, something such as, "Look, daddy, let me pull your coat about a cat, Elijah Muhammad—"

Why was Malcolm X frustrated?

2   Many who today hear me somewhere in person, or on television, or those who read something I've said, will think I went to school far beyond the eighth grade. This impression is due entirely to my prison studies.

Impact of prison

3   It had really begun back in the Charlestown Prison, when Bimbi first made me feel envy of his stock of knowledge. Bimbi had always taken charge of any conversation he was in, and I had tried to emulate him. But every book I picked up had few sentences which didn't contain anywhere from one to nearly all of the words that might as well have been in Chinese. When I just skipped those words, of course, I really ended up with little idea of what the book said. So I had come to the Norfolk Prison Colony still going through only book-reading motions. Pretty soon, I would have quit even these motions, unless I had received the motivation that I did.

Malcolm X is impressed by fellow inmate's knowledge, but he has difficulty reading

4   I saw that the best thing I could do was get hold of a dictionary—to study, to learn some words. I was lucky enough to reason also that I should try to improve my penmanship. It was sad. I couldn't even write in a straight line. It was both ideas together that moved me to request a dictionary along with some tablets and pencils from the Norfolk Prison Colony school.

Dictionary use

5   I spent two days just riffling uncertainly through the dictionary's pages. I'd never realized so many words existed! I didn't know *which* words I needed to learn. Finally, just to start some kind of action, I began copying.

6   In my slow, painstaking, ragged handwriting, I copied into my tablet everything printed on that first page, down to the punctuation marks.

Plan of action: copying a dictionary

7   I believe it took me a day. Then, aloud, I read back, to myself, everything I'd written on the tablet. Over and over, aloud, to myself, I read my own handwriting.

8   I woke up the next morning, thinking about those words—immensely proud to realize that not only had I written so much at one time, but I'd written words that I never knew were in the world. Moreover, with a little effort, I also could remember what many of these words meant. I reviewed the words whose meanings I didn't remember. Funny thing, from the dictionary first page right now, that "aardvark" springs to my mind. The dictionary had a picture of it, a long-tailed, long-eared, burrowing African mammal, which lives off termites caught by sticking out its tongue as an anteater does for ants.

A sense of accomplishment

9   I was so fascinated that I went on—I copied the dictionary's next page. And the same experience came when I studied that. With every succeeding

continuation of effort

page, I also learned of people and places and events from history. Actually the dictionary is like a miniature encyclopedia. Finally the dictionary's A section had filled a whole tablet—and I went on into the B's. That was the way I started copying what eventually became the entire dictionary. It went a lot faster after so much practice helped me to pick up handwriting speed. Between what I wrote in my tablet, and writing letters, during the rest of my time in prison I would guess I wrote a million words.

10   I suppose it was inevitable that as my word-base broadened, I could for the first time pick up a book and read and now begin to understand what the book was saying. Anyone who has read a great deal can imagine the new world that opened. Let me tell you something: from then until I left that prison, in every free moment I had, if I was not reading in the library, I was reading on my bunk. You couldn't have gotten me out of books with a wedge. Between Mr. Muhammad's teachings, my correspondence, my visitors—usually Ella and Reginald—and my reading of books, months passed without my even thinking about being imprisoned. In fact, up to then, I never had been so truly free in my life.

Results of his efforts

11   The Norfolk Prison Colony's library was in the school building. A variety of classes was taught there by instructors who came from such places as Harvard and Boston universities. The weekly debates between inmate teams were also held in the school building. You would be astonished to know how worked up convict debaters and audiences would get over subjects like "Should Babies Be Fed Milk?"

Role of library

12   Available on the prison library's shelves were books on just about every general subject. Much of the big private collection that Parkhurst had willed to the prison was still in crates and boxes in the back of the library—thousands of old books. Some of them looked ancient: covers faded, old-time parchment-looking binding. Parkhurst, I've mentioned, seemed to have been principally interested in history and religion. He had the money and the special interest to have a lot of books that you wouldn't have in general circulation. Any college library would have been lucky to get that collection.

13   As you can imagine, especially in a prison where there was heavy emphasis on rehabilitation, an inmate was smiled upon if he demonstrated an unusually intense interest in books. There was a sizable number of well-read inmates, especially the popular debaters. Some were said by many to be practically walking encyclopedias. They were almost celebrities. No university would ask any student to devour literature as I did when this new world opened to me, of being able to read and *understand*.

14   I read more in my room than in the library itself. An inmate who was known to read a lot could check out more than the permitted maximum number of books. I preferred reading in the total isolation of my own room.

Malcolm X becomes a serious reader

15   When I had progressed to really serious reading, every night at about ten P.M. I would be outraged with the "lights out." It always seemed to catch me right in the middle of something engrossing.

16   Fortunately, right outside my door was a corridor light that cast a glow into my room. The glow was enough to read by, once my eyes adjusted to it. So when "lights out" came, I would sit on the floor where I would continue reading in that glow.

17   At one-hour intervals the night guards paced past every room. Each time I heard the approaching footsteps, I jumped into bed and feigned sleep. And as soon as the guard passed, I got back out of bed onto the floor area of that light-glow, where I would read for another fifty-eight minutes—until the guard approached again. That went on until three or four every morning. Three or four hours of sleep a night was enough for me. Often in the years in the streets I had slept less than that. . . .

18   I have often reflected upon the new vistas that reading opened to me. I knew right there in prison that reading had changed forever the course of my life. As I see it today, the ability to read awoke inside me some long dormant craving to be mentally alive. I certainly wasn't seeking any degree, the way a college confers a status symbol upon its students. My homemade education gave me, with every additional book that I read, a little bit more sensitivity to the deafness, dumbness, and blindness that was afflicting the black race in America. Not long ago, an English writer telephoned me from London, asking questions. One was, "What's your alma mater?" I told him, "Books." You will never catch me with a free fifteen minutes in which I'm not studying something I feel might be able to help the black man.

*What reading does for Malcolm X

 # PROCESS GUIDE

1. In paragraph 1 Malcolm X claims that writing a letter caused him frustration. By contrast, what does Malcolm X say that he could do well?

   _____

   _____

2. The first three paragraphs of the text shift back and forth in time—the events are not listed in the order in which they occurred. One way to avoid confusion about time sequence is to rearrange events in chronological order, that is, the order in which they actually occurred. In the article, events are reported in the following sequence:

   1. I became increasingly frustrated. . . .

   2. In the street, I had been the most articulate hustler. . . .

   3. But now, . . . I wasn't even functional.

   4. Many who today hear me. . . .

   5. It had really begun back in the Charlestown Prison, . . .

   6. So I had come to the Norfolk Prison Colony still going through only book-reading motions.

      Now rearrange these events on the basis of when they actually occurred. The first event is listed for you.

   1. In the street, I had been the most articulate hustler. . . .

   2. _____

   3. _____

   4. _____

   5. _____

6. _____

3. Malcolm X says he encountered a problem when he tried to read. What was the problem, and what did he do to solve it?

   _____

   _____

   _____

4. So far, you have focused on specifics. Now consider the overall ideas. Malcolm X's excerpt is storylike, that is, narrative material. It is part of a larger work: Malcolm X's autobiography. As such, it has a character, a setting (location), and a plot (the action that takes place), all of which are evident in the first four paragraphs. Reread these paragraphs and fill in the following blanks according to the information given thus far.

   Character(s) _____

   Setting _____

   Plot _____

5. In paragraphs 5 through 8, Malcolm X reports his reading and writing efforts. What did he do and how does he regard his accomplishments?

   _____

   _____

   _____

6. Read paragraphs 6 and 7 again. Put in your own words (paraphrase) what Malcolm X did.

   _____

   _____

   _____

7. Paragraph 8 relates Malcolm X's feelings about what he had done. Read the paragraph again and describe his thoughts.

   _____

   _____

   _____

8. What did Malcolm X do as a result of his accomplishments and his success with the dictionary?

   _____

   _____

   _____

✦ **NOTE**   Note that in paragraph 9 Malcolm X is describing a process. He is sharing with the reader the actions he took. For example, in the third sentence of paragraph 9 he says, "With every succeeding page, I also learned of people and places and events from history." This sentence shows the cause-and-effect pattern:

Cause		**Effect**
Malcolm X read	→	Malcolm X learned
(This happened)	→	(This resulted) ✦

9. Another example of the cause-and-effect pattern occurs in the first sentence of paragraph 10: "As my word-base broadened, I could for the first time pick up a book and read and now begin to understand what the book was saying." Which part of this statement is the cause and which is the effect?

   Cause (action that occurred) ————————————————

   Effect (results) ————————————————————

10. In paragraph 10, Malcolm X describes how reading became a very important part of his life. He was so involved with reading that "months passed without my even thinking about being imprisoned." He concludes the thought by saying, "Up to then, I never had been so truly free in my life." Does this thought make sense to you? (How could someone in prison say that he had never been so truly free?)

   ————————————————————————————

   ————————————————————————————

11. Malcolm X explains that the well-read inmates were considered "almost celebrities" by the other prisoners. Does this seem likely given what you know about prison? Explain.

   ————————————————————————————

   ————————————————————————————

12. Reread the last sentence in paragraph 13. How did Malcolm X respond to books once he could read well?

   ————————————————————————————

   ————————————————————————————

13. In paragraphs 14 through 17, Malcolm X describes how he became deeply involved in reading. What evidence does he present to show his intense interest in reading?

   ————————————————————————————

   ————————————————————————————

14. In paragraph 18, how does Malcolm X say that reading changed him?

_____

_____

✦ **NOTE**   Malcolm X learned that many black people were not getting the kind of information about black history and racism that he was getting from his reading. He came to realize that there is power in reading. Recall that the power of literacy is also a theme in the Frederick Douglass excerpt. After hearing his master's harsh words to his wife about teaching a slave to read, Douglass began to see the power of literacy as a step to his freedom.   ✦

15. The last four sentences of paragraph 18 conclude the article with an anecdote (a brief, amusing story). What happened?

_____

_____

16. Do you think the English writer expected Malcolm X's answer? Explain.

_____

_____

17. Now that you have finished the Process Guide, summarize the article in your own words.

_____

_____

_____

_____

_____

READING STRATEGY

WRITING A SUMMARY

Have you ever seen a movie and afterward told a friend what the film was about? If you related the essential points of the movie accurately, you gave your friend a good summary. People often summarize events in their lives. When asked about our day at work, we usually give a condensed account of the most important things that happened. Television and movie critics typically include a summary of the program or film in their reviews. Children provide brief yet remarkably comprehensive and accurate summaries of their favorite bedtime stories. Instructors ask students for summaries of assigned material in class and on exams. Thus, a summary can be defined as a condensation or short version of a text that retains the ideas of the author and captures the spirit of the author's attitude toward the material.

Why Write Summaries?

Why should you develop the ability to summarize written material? How can summary writing help you in your reading?

- Summarizing allows you to be an active reader. To write a summary, you must sort out relationships among ideas and incorporate what you read into your own base of knowledge.

- Summarizing allows you to check your understanding of written material. To summarize well, you must read closely, locate the main ideas, select and condense the most significant of those main ideas, and *express them in your own words.*

- Summarizing allows you to show your understanding of written material. On multiple-choice tests, you are provided with possible answers and simply have to choose the correct one. On an essay exam, however, you must provide the essential information, often in the form of a summary. Even when an exam question does not specifically call for a summary, you can effectively use brief summaries of your reading to back up your points. You will also use summaries in research papers. In a research paper, you must consider many ideas, sort through them, and, using proper documentation of your sources, recount the relevant information you have gathered.

- Summarizing allows you to remember what you have read. Once you have written a summary, you can recall the material's central ideas much more easily. Your retention will improve because you took the time to express the central ideas in your own words.

- Finally, summarizing reinforces your writing and thinking skills. It demands clarity, coherence, and accuracy on your part.

Steps in Writing a Summary

Writing a summary takes time. You should not expect to produce a good summary without exerting some effort. Sometimes you will read a selection and understand and remember it so well that you can sit down and write a summary easily. In other cases, you will have to struggle with the material to produce a good summary.

The following suggestions will help you create effective summaries:

1. *Preview the material.* Look at the title and subheadings. Look at the first sentence in each paragraph. Note any boldface or italicized print, lists, or charts. Try to get a general sense of what you are about to read.

2. *Read the material once without stopping.* You are trying to get your first impression of the author's message. Don't worry if not everything is clear on this first reading.

3. *Reread the material.* This second reading requires more care and concentration than your first effort. You must become more actively involved. We suggest the following:

   a. *Ask questions.* Question as you read. Interact with the text. Ask yourself questions beginning with key words such as *who, what, where, when, why,* and *how.* (Who is speaking? What is being said? Why is this important? How is the writer presenting the information?)

   b. *Mark the text.* Underline key words, phrases, and sentences. Make marginal notes next to key elements in the text. Paraphrase (put in your own words) the material you mark. You will use these notes in writing your summary.

   c. *Organize your notes.* Try to arrange the notes you have made in a logical way. Group related items or ideas. As you do this, ask yourself, "What is the subject of this information? What idea covers most of this information?"

4. *State the main idea.* If the author provides a statement that clearly expresses the central focus of the article, try to paraphrase it. If no such sentence is provided, you will have to create your own. Such a sentence is important because you will use it near the beginning of your summary to present the main idea of the reading. This sentence will depend largely on the type of material you are reading. (For example, is the author trying to explain, persuade, or describe?)

After you have completed these steps, write your first draft. In most cases, expect to create at least two drafts. First, identify the reading you are about to summarize and state the author's central idea. Next, include whatever supporting information is needed to give your reader a clear picture of what the writer says. Remember, you cannot include everything—if you did, it wouldn't be a summary. Writing a summary means you choose what to delete and what to combine. Your summary should not include your personal opinions; "editorializing" is appropriate only in reaction papers or critiques. Accurately report only the author's ideas.

Use your own words. Merely copying sentences from the source does not reflect your understanding of the material. Furthermore, if you use another person's words, you must remember to use quotation marks and to give proper credit. If you don't, you run the risk of committing plagiarism—using the thoughts or words of another.

Finally, be concerned with how you connect your sentences. Do your ideas flow smoothly, or are you merely stringing together separate, unconnected ideas? To avoid this pitfall, use transitional words such as *first, next, also, although, however,* and *finally.*

One test of an effective summary is whether it would give someone who has not read the original text a good idea of what that text contained. Another way to evaluate your summary is to pretend the author told you all about the article and then asked you to briefly convey his or her message to someone else in your own words.

Major Points to Keep in Mind When Writing a Summary

1. Write an opening statement that identifies the reading and accurately states the central idea.

2. Include the essential points the author makes to support the central idea.

3. Condense ideas, keeping the essential and eliminating the unnecessary.

4. Use your own words.

5. Write complete sentences, and use smooth transitions between ideas.

6. Avoid giving your own opinion.

Application

Now we will examine the Malcolm X article and consider how to write a summary of it. First, this is narrative material, so you can expect a story or a sequence of events to be presented. Although this is an excerpt, it gives enough information to establish what the author is trying to communicate. After you have previewed the article and given it a first reading, certain impressions are probably clear to you. The setting is prison, and Malcolm X is relating a particular episode that occurred there. A second, closer reading will reveal much more information. Questions you can ask include: Who is speaking? What is being said? What is the central focus? As you answer these questions, note that Malcolm X repeats certain ideas. For example, words such as *dictionary, copying, writing, words, books, reading,* and *library* appear repeatedly. The recurrence of these key terms confirms the author's subject.

Because this is narrative material, you can expect a sequence of events to unfold. Note how the author takes us through the following chain of events:

I became increasingly frustrated at not being able to express what I wanted to convey in letters that I wrote . . .

But every book I picked up . . . I really ended up with little idea of what the book said.

I saw that the best thing I could do was get hold of a dictionary . . .

I spent two days just riffling uncertainly through the dictionary's pages.

Finally, . . . I began copying.

I read back, to myself, everything I'd written . . .

I woke up the next morning, thinking about those words . . .

I was so fascinated that I went on . . .

I suppose it was inevitable that as my word-based broadened, I could for the first time pick up a book and read and now begin to understand . . .

These sentences express the basic idea the author is trying to communicate: how he taught himself to improve his reading and writing while in prison. The remainder of the article discusses the effects of Malcolm X's newfound ability to read. Consider the following excerpts:

> imagine the new world that opened.
>
> in every free moment I had, . . . I was reading . . .
>
> I never had been so truly free in my life.
>
> I read more in my room than in the library itself.
>
> the new vistas that reading opened to me
>
> reading had changed forever the course of my life.
>
> the ability to read awoke inside me some . . . craving to be mentally alive.
>
> My homemade education gave me . . . a little bit more sensitivity to the deafness, dumbness, and blindness that was afflicting the black race in America.

A Model Summary

Now you can organize this information into a summary. Begin by identifying and stating the article's main idea:

In this excerpt from his autobiography, Malcolm X reveals that he learned to improve his reading ability in Norfolk Prison Colony. He explains how reading changed his life.

After stating the main idea, you must tell the reader why this event occurred and what happened afterward:

At first, Malcolm X wanted to improve his writing. He used a dictionary and copied words. After a time, his vocabulary improved and he was able to read and understand more. Malcolm X turned more and more to reading, and he read at every available opportunity. He explained that his ability to read opened up a new world of ideas, made him aware of his people's history, and made him feel free even though he was still in prison.

Here is another summary of the same article:

The excerpt from The Autobiography of Malcolm X reports on how reading changed Malcolm X's life. While in prison, Malcolm X is frustrated when trying to compose a letter and read a book. He decides to do something about this problem and begins copying a dictionary. He becomes excited about his progress and what he is learning. He claims that once he could understand what he was reading, a whole new world opened up for him. Malcolm X concludes that the source of his education, his "alma mater," was books.

READING JOURNAL

In the To the Student section you were introduced to the Reading Journal. As was noted, the Reading Journal is intended to be introspective; that is, it represents a kind a diary. You are encouraged to log your responses to the ideas in the readings and also reflect on the process of reading them. The four autobiographical accounts presented different aspects of learning to read in a variety of settings. Perhaps your instructor has given you a specific assignment in regard to the narratives. If not, here are suggestions to help you get started with your journal entries.

- **Content**

  Explain how the ability to read made a difference in the authors' lives.

- **Process**

  Which of the narratives was hardest and which was easiest for you to read? Explain your response.
  Cite an instance where you had trouble reading one of the narratives. How did you try to remedy the situation?

- **Response**

  How might you feel if you were facing the circumstances of the narrative authors? According to your view, which author faced the greatest challenge in learning to read? If you could express your feelings in a letter to any author, what would you say?

Why We Should Read

VINCE NOWELL

Vince Nowell is a writer and also works as a curriculum consultant and substitute teacher in California. Nowell's article is in the form of a letter he wrote to students in response to a question posed by their English teacher. Their instructor was frustrated when her students asked her, "Why read?" To solicit help, the teacher wrote to the local newspaper and invited members of the community to write to her students about the impact of books on their lives.

GEARING UP

1. Imagine being asked the following question by a first grader who was learning to read: "What value is there in learning to read?" How would you respond?

2. How would have Frederick Douglass, Helen Keller, Sam Levenson, and Malcolm X responded to the above question?

3. What advantages (if any) do books have over electronic devices such as VCRs and televisions in presenting information?

READING STRATEGY
READING ARGUMENT AND PERSUASION

In the previous readings, we examined the mode of *narrative* writing. In the article that follows, we will consider a second form of writing: argument and persuasion. **Argument and persuasion** are intended to appeal to logic (reasoning) and emotions (feelings). The writer's aim is to convince the reader to think, feel, and/or react in a certain way. In constructing an argument, the writer establishes a particular viewpoint and usually presents evidence or uses reasoning to support it. In trying to persuade, the writer usually makes an emotional as well as rational appeal to get the reader to accept the desired point of view.

The news sections of a newspaper aim to present a factual recounting of events. By contrast, the editorial page expresses opinions about particular issues, and editorial writers commonly use argument to make their points. For example, editors may argue that increasing the speed limit from 55 to 65 miles per hour on certain interstate highways will result in more traffic fatalities and therefore is not worth the tradeoff in time saved for motorists. To support their position, they present data from traffic studies in ten states.

A common use of persuasive writing is advertising. The advertiser constructs a message to convince you that you need a particular product or service. Similarly, candidates for political office attempt to convince you that, based on their stands on various issues, they are best qualified to represent you.

In reading an argumentative or persuasive essay, consider the following questions:

1. What is the writer's major idea? How is this idea supported? (Does the writer use facts and figures, historical evidence, analysis, or comparison and contrast? Is the writer's opinion the sole basis for the argument?)

2. What is the writer's attitude toward the subject? What words does the writer use to express the message? (Is the writer calm, upset, ironic, serious, bitter?)

3. What is the writer's purpose? (To argue a point? To convince the reader to adopt a particular view?)

4. What is the writer's agenda? (For example, politicians want to be elected; car dealers want to sell cars; clergy members want to boost their congregations.)

As you read, be aware of the writer's argument and consider alternative points of view. Keep an open mind, and be tolerant of other ideas. There is always at least one other way of looking at an issue. In his essay *On Liberty*, John Stuart Mill, the nineteenth-century English philosopher and political theorist, stated:

> The only way in which a human being can make some approach to knowing the whole of a subject, is by hearing what can be said about it by persons of every variety of opinion, and studying all modes in which it can be looked at by every character of mind. No wise man ever acquired his wisdom in any mode but this.

Each unit in this textbook contains articles whose purpose is to argue a point or persuade readers to adopt a particular view. Following are examples of contradictory opinions about the four themes addressed in this book:

Unit One: Reading and Literacy

Computers will eventually eliminate the need to read.

Computers will make reading more important than ever.

Unit Two: Work and Careers

Women belong in the home, not in the workplace.

Women, like men, deserve an equal opportunity to work.

Unit Three: Mass Media

Children's advertising is often misleading and teaches wrong values.

Children's advertising helps children learn to be consumers and make choices.

Unit Four: Family

The family will soon become an extinct institution.

Families evolve. They are here to stay and will survive.

Application

The title of the article that follows, "Why We Should Read," clearly states the issue that the author will discuss. As you read this essay, pay particular attention to Mr. Nowell's statements about the value of reading. How does he try to convince you? What evidence does he provide to support his statements? You may find it useful to reexamine the questions given earlier in the strategy. The author's tone—his attitude toward literacy—is clear. How does this tone affect the meaning?

READING STRATEGY CHECK

WRITING A SUMMARY

The strategy Writing a Summary was presented after the Malcolm X selection. The application discussion showed the process of drafting a summary based on a markup of that article. You were advised to look for the main point and begin your summary by paraphrasing it. Then you were to provide the author's support for details. There is a built-in advantage in summarizing narrative material. In a story, the author provides you with characters, a setting, and a plot.

Summarizing argumentative and persuasive writing is different. Rather than having a person and a plot to follow, you are looking for an issue or idea and the arguments and evidence that develop the author's position on the issue. The following steps can be used in writing a summary of argumentative and persuasive writing:

1. Identify the issue or idea of concern to the author in an opening statement.

2. Determine the author's position on the issue or idea and paraphrase it.

3. Cite the major arguments and/or crucial evidence the author provides.

Be certain to accurately portray the author's ideas without adding your own opinion. Your judgment of an author's work is the appropriate subject of a critique or an interpretive essay and not a summary.

The Reading

Why We Should Read

by VINCE NOWELL

Y ou've asked me why we should read books. I can only answer your
question by sharing what books have meant for me over the past fifty-
plus years of living and working in various places, doing many kinds of jobs.
Maybe my experience will be similar to some of your feelings and needs,
now and in the future.

Books are my friends. They've always been loyal, consistent, available and   *consistent*
helpful to me. I've never encountered a book that:

• criticized me;

• hassled me or put me down;

• told me I had to do something I didn't want to do;

• deserted me for someone else.

Books are my companions. They've always kept me company under all circumstances. Every book I've met in my life has:

- traveled with me willingly if I wanted to go somewhere;

- remained usable even if the electricity failed;

- kept me entertained and informed, no matter where I was;

- been there for me even when no one else was around.

Books are part of my exercise. A great feature of every book is that it lets me:

- construct scenes in my mind as I think they should be;

- follow the action and get involved just as if I were there;

- stretch my imagination to the limits of the universe;

- perform mental workouts as often and for as long as I want.

Books have been my way to:

- fight—and settle—wars;

- probe the mysteries of the atom;   *probe*

- travel to places I only know as names on a world globe;

- see animals and spectacles that few others have even imagined;

- go back to ancient civilizations, even to prehistoric eras;

- zoom into the future to explore a world that may exist some day;

- visit every planet and most moons in the solar system;

- speed through space to far-flung stars and galaxies.

Books have made it possible for me to:

- be in places other than where I live;

- be someone besides myself;

- be something other than myself;

- be myself as I want to be.

2   What else other than a book can do all these things for me? What else can fire up my imagination, drive my ambitions, inspire my life—and all without needing batteries, electricity or any physical effort on my part other than turning pages and staying awake?

3   I can watch a television show once. I can rent a video more than once, paying a price for it each time. By its very nature a book gives me all the time I need to spend with it, rather than having to rush it back to the rental store in 24 hours. I can read a book over and over and over—and all for free if it's from the public library.

4   I was a slow learner and almost a nonreader until about third grade. Then someone showed me—using comic books—all I was missing by only looking at the picture in each frame. Suddenly, those magazines came to life. Ever since, I've been a fanatical reader. I discovered previously unknown   *fanatical* worlds that now were open to me.

5   Now I read everything: three newspapers every day, six to eight magazines each month, cereal boxes and packaged food labels, advertising and, of course, books.

6   I read technical books because that's part of my work as a writer. I read nonfiction in general because I learn things that make my life better, easier and more fun and because I can reach my own conclusions. I read novels for fun and recreation.

7   Books have helped make me what I am, and I'm pleased with that. Books have made me into a stronger person. Books make it possible for me to cope better with the future we all are racing toward.

8   So to you, the young person who wants to know why we should read books, let me say (borrowing a slogan from the U.S. Army's recruiting posters), that no matter who you are, what your background is, or how life is treating you, if you want to be all you can be, start reading now. There is nothing—nothing—that will ever give back to you so much more than what you put into it.

9   Enjoy your adventures. The world is yours through books.

QUESTIONS

1. The introduction to this unit (Unit One) contains the following statements: "Being literate lets us sample many experiences not possible in daily living. In books we find advice, information, satisfaction, escape, and challenge. We can enter another world or become deeply involved in our own." Explain the meaning of this quote and relate its content to the information presented by Vince Nowell. Would he agree or disagree with the quote? Support your answer by citing specific information given by the author.

2. The author suggests that books have certain advantages over other forms of media such as television or videos. Explain his reasoning.

3. The author notes that he reads a variety of materials and for different purposes. Explain.

EXTENDING YOUR VOCABULARY

consistent: I could see that his behavior was not consistent by the fact

                that ———————

probe: The detective decided to continue to probe the witness be-

                cause ———————

fanatical: At major sporting events, some fanatical fans tend to

                ———————

PROCESS GUIDE

Nowell's article takes the form of a letter that he writes to students in reply to their question: *Why should we read?* Many key ideas in the first half of this article are presented in **boldface** followed by bulleted • items. This is a common writing pattern when a major idea is followed by supporting statements. One way to both comprehend and recall this type of material is to create an idea map, a visual representation of the author's organization of major points together with relevant details. Below you will find one possible way of graphically organizing the ideas presented in the article. Key statements taken from the text have been surrounded in text frames. To help you begin the process, a paraphrased version of these key statements is provided. In the space beneath each paraphrased idea, add any supporting details that would clarify the author's major ideas.

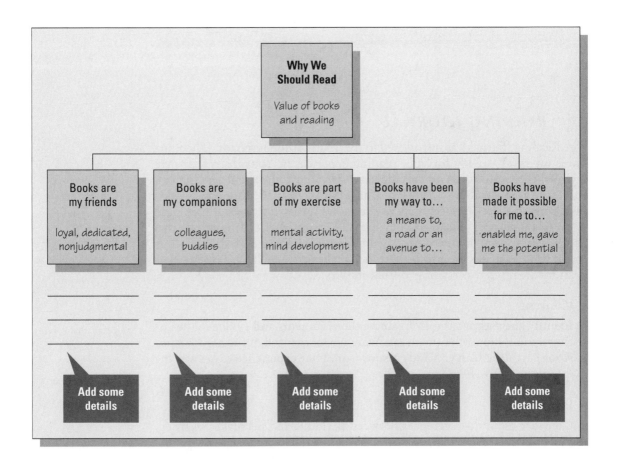

After the bulleted sections the author continues to support the value of reading. He mentions how reading is opposed to more mechanically based forms of information gathering, reveals how he got "hooked on books," and shares his reading preferences. Use the spaces that follow to summarize the author's ideas.

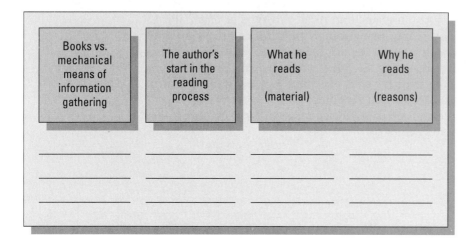

 READING JOURNAL

The Reading Journal was introduced in the To the Student section. The journal is intended as a log for your reading experiences. Your instructor may have asked you to focus on specific areas for your journal entries. Or you may have great flexibility in your responses. If you have a more open-ended task, some suggestions were made at the end of the narrative section on page 67 to give you some guidance and help you get started. We bring the journal assignment to your attention once again because you have now studied a different kind of material, argumentation and persuasion. The following suggestions are offered as reading journal starters.

- **Content**

  Identify the author's thesis. Evaluate the arguments and evidence the author used in support of the thesis. Were you convinced of the author's position? Explain. Can you add reasons from your experience to answer the question, "Why should we read?"

- **Process**

  Consider the style differences between narrative and persuasive writing. How did you find reading the persuasive material in comparison with the narrative? Did you approach this reading using the same techniques that you used in reading the narratives? Were you able to follow the author's logic and recognize his arguments? Evaluate the author's bias in his position. What arguments could be made for not reading?

- **Response**

  Did the author get you to change your attitude or feelings about the importance of reading? Was he able to reinforce existing beliefs and feelings? What might you say to him if you met him at a conference?

The Proficient Reader

IRA D. EPSTEIN and ERNEST B. NIERATKA

Ira Epstein and Ernest Nieratka are members of the Communication Skills Department of LaGuardia Community College of The City University of New York. They are actively involved in the field of college reading.

GEARING UP

1. Write your own definition of *reading* before you read the article.

2. Imagine that you completely lacked the ability to read. How would this affect your life?

3. What do you think makes some reading material difficult to understand?

4. Describe something you read that had a significant effect on you.

5. List the steps you can take to improve your reading ability.

6. What reading materials would be easy for you to understand but difficult for someone else?

 READING STRATEGY

READING EXPOSITION—PART I

The next article, "The Proficient Reader," is an example of expository writing. **Exposition** is material that presents information and teaches ideas. Textbooks, lectures, and informative articles and essays often use the expository mode; they present facts, ideas, theories, processes, and other information.

The language of exposition differs from the narrative language you encountered earlier in this unit. Narrative writing tends to be informal and familiar and uses a common framework of a plot with a beginning, a middle, and an end. Typically you are able to follow along, "get into" the story, and anticipate its outcome. Exposition, however, lacks the familiar story framework, and you must approach it with different expectations.

An example of exposition follows. As you read it, note the information presented and the way it is developed.

> Several reasons can be offered to explain why the Prime Minister's government was overthrown after a period of six years. First, the people were unhappy with her economic policies. Before she took office, most groups enjoyed a reasonable standard of living and employment was high. By her fourth year in office, however, the economy was no longer healthy. Workers' earnings fell, unemployment rose, and the cost of living soared. New taxes had to be imposed, which resulted in even larger-scale dissatisfaction from all parts of society.
>
> A second reason for the downfall of the Prime Minister can be found in her attitude toward religious groups. The government imposed harsh restrictions and tried to prohibit group worship. This policy angered religious groups who had up to this point enjoyed religious toleration. It resulted in the formation of a united religious opposition party that organized effective anti-government protests and succeeded in having the policy dropped even before it was implemented.
>
> Another factor that contributed to widespread indignation and unrest stemmed from the Prime Minister's notorious and infamous Censorship Laws. These laws were meant to . . .

When you read exposition, you must determine the topic and major ideas the author is presenting. In the preceding example, the opening sentence signals the topic: "Several reasons can be offered to explain why the Prime Minister's government was overthrown. . . ." When you see the phrase "several reasons," you can expect the author to present several factors responsible for the government's downfall. Each paragraph contains details to explain the general statement about the overthrow of the government:

First, the people were unhappy . . .

A second reason for the downfall . . .

Another factor that contributed to . . .

As you read each explanation, you need to follow the author's thought pattern and see how ideas are being developed. Expository texts use several writing patterns to signal the flow of ideas. These writing patterns include cause and effect, comparison and contrast, sequence or process, listing, analysis, example, and definition.

Cause and Effect

In using the pattern of *cause and effect*, the writer shows why something has happened. The reader is presented with reasons and results.

> *Example* The development of the printing press had a significant impact on the spread of literacy.

> **Cause**   **Effect**
>
> Development of printing press $\longrightarrow$ Spread of literacy

Comparison and Contrast

In using *comparison and contrast*, the writer shows how ideas are similar to or different from one another.

> *Example* Both the television and the telephone are devices for communication. But unlike a telephone conversation, a television program's message goes in only one direction: from the TV set to the audience. With the telephone, both parties send and receive information.

Sequence or Process

A writer uses *sequence* to demonstrate a particular order or arrangement of information. Often the writer is describing a *process*—an action that unfolds as a set of events.

> *Example* Before reading a text, you should survey or preview it. Look at the headings and subheadings. Read through it once without stopping to get a general idea of its contents. Then return to the text for a more careful, deliberate reading.

Listing

In *listing*, the writer organizes information in a series that may or may not have a particular order.

> *Example* The functions of the family can be grouped into four categories: (1) reproduction and socialization, (2) economic cooperation, (3) assignment of social roles, and (4) personal relationships.

Analysis

In using *analysis*, the writer breaks down material into its essential parts for examination and interpretation.

> *Example* The television industry is in many ways like any other business. It operates largely on the system of supply and demand. The more demand there is for commercial time on a particular program, the higher the price for use of that time. Advertisers want to reach as

many people as possible. Therefore, a very popular show is more attractive to advertisers than a program with few viewers. Accordingly, the price for commercial time is higher for popular shows.

Example

A writer uses *example* to illustrate an idea. The writer selects something as a sample to show the nature of the major point. The example serves as a "typical instance."

> *Example:* One finds evidence of increasing dissatisfaction with jobs, even among such traditionally privileged groups as the nation's 4.5 million middle managers. For example, whereas this group once represented the bulwark of company loyalty, today one out of three middle managers indicates some willingness to join a union. Another striking indicator of discontent is the increasing number of middle-aged managers seeking a mid-career change.

Definition

When a writer provides a *definition,* he or she states or explains the meaning of something.

> *Example:* CATV stands for "community antenna television." It is a TV reception system used mainly in rural locations where it is difficult for the homeowner to pick up a signal. A large central antenna is mounted in a strategic location, and people's TV sets are served by cable from this central facility.

Reading Exposition

If you reread the example of exposition on page 76, you will probably notice several patterns of expository writing. You already saw how a general statement is used, followed by a listing ("First, . . .," "A second reason . . .," "Another factor . . ."). You need to follow these reasons as the author explains and develops them.

Comparisons and contrast appear in the following statements: "Before she took office, most groups enjoyed a reasonable standard of living . . ."; "By her fourth year in office, however, the economy was no longer healthy."

Cause and effect occur in the following statement: "New taxes had to be imposed, which resulted in even larger-scale dissatisfaction from all parts of society."

Cause		**Effect**
New taxes imposed	$\longrightarrow$	Larger-scale dissatisfaction

Consider the following questions as you read expository material:

1. What idea(s) is the author presenting?

2. What information are you being asked to learn?

3. What important details are provided to support the major points?

4. How does the author develop the idea(s)?

READING STRATEGY CHECK

PREVIEWING

The strategy of "Previewing" was introduced in the "To the Student" section. Previewing was defined as a look ahead in a text to prepare for reading. By surveying the text before you read it carefully you are hoping to achieve some sense of the overall content and structure. After previewing you should be able to ask yourself some general questions about the material. Approaching a text with questions in mind helps you focus on comprehending it. Some material lends itself to previewing more readily in that it is set up with graphic features like headings and summary statements. These features are most helpful in the previewing process and should be used when present. The article "The Proficient Reader" has been written and structured with previewing application in mind. Try applying the "previewing strategy" on your own or follow the suggestions given here:

1. Note the title. Does the term *proficient* mean anything to you? If not, try to determine the meaning from the article before you look it up in the dictionary.

2. Study the subheads. Check those (√) that have reasonably clear meaning for you. Put a question mark (?) by those subheads that are unclear or have no meaning.

3. Choose two of the subheads and make one question for each of them. These questions will guide you in your careful reading. Try to answer your questions after you have finished reading the article.

The Reading

The Proficient Reader

by IRA D. EPSTEIN and ERNEST B. NIERATKA

1   Imagine waking up this morning to find that you completely lacked the ability to read. How would your life be different? Of course, you wouldn't be reading this article—but seriously, did you ever stop to think what a vital part reading plays in your everyday living? Many people take for

granted this ability unique to human beings. However, noted educator G. R.   *unique*
Carlsen said, "Learning to read is one of the most complex tasks that a human being accomplishes in a lifetime. The amazing thing is not that a few
people fail, but that so many succeed."

2   Like writing, listening, and speaking, reading is a process of communication using language. Reading is communication between the writer and the
reader. It is more than a mechanical process of moving your eyes across the
page and sounding out symbols. Reading is an active process of constructing
meaning from written texts. It requires interaction or transaction with a
written text. When you read, you try to understand the writer's message. To
do this, you must relate the author's message to your own knowledge. Consider the following example:

> He looked at his fuel gauge and saw it was almost empty. To make matters
> worse, he had passed the last gas station an hour ago and the next scheduled
> rest stop on the turnpike was 25 miles away.

To understand this scenario you would have to use information from the text
together with your own background knowledge to produce meaning. The
first sentence suggests that someone is driving a car on a highway and is
about to run out of fuel. Once this is understood the rest of the example is
easy to process because of the expectations that come from your background
knowledge. If you knew nothing about this subject or had no concept of
what is a fuel gauge, you could expect to learn very little. Reading therefore
involves mentally processing printed information in a meaningful way. In
your attempt to make meaning out of the text you read, you must get actively involved in it.

Processing Written Language and Reading

3 On the surface, it appears that when you are reading, you are simply looking at marks on a page—symbols that don't talk. Yet these marks on a page
can make you laugh, cry, shiver, cringe, smile, or reflect. Look at the following examples, and think about how you react:

1. The professor was so absent-minded that he often put on his coat with the
    hanger still in it.

2. We regret to inform you that your son has been taken prisoner by the
    enemy.

3. She locked the door and was about to switch on the light. Suddenly, she
    sensed something. Someone was in the room. Before she could even
    gather her thoughts, a hand reached out and grabbed her throat. She tried
    to scream, but . . .

4. Try our special steak dinner. For $10 you receive a thick, juicy, mouth
    watering grilled steak, smothered in fried onions, with golden French
    fried potatoes and creamy cole slaw.

5. They removed their clothes and lay down on the bed. Their bodies felt warm as their lips met. They embraced passionately, knowing that they might never see each other again.

6. I know a guy who was so ugly that when he was born, the doctor slapped his mother instead of him.

4   You probably reacted differently to each example. This can be explained in part by the experiences and knowledge that you bring to the printed page. Reading involves the "total you." It engages your mind in imagining and understanding, as well as your feelings and emotions.

5   What you see on this page is only ink marks; they have no meaning in themselves. Yet you are able to derive meaning and react. These marks signal some idea that is already in your mind. The most important part of reading is what you know before you begin to read and the connections you make while reading. "A text" according to Anderson, Hiebert, Scott and Wilkinson "is not so much a vessel containing meaning as it is a source of partial information that enables the reader to use already-possessed knowledge to determine the intended meaning." Thus, proficient reading is an active process. It can be thought of as a search for meaning. It is something that is not achieved overnight but rather is a lifelong endeavor.   *endeavor*

The Impact of the Written Word

6   Through the written word, writers convey meaning. Written words can stir our emotions, imaginations and intellect. They can inform, influence, enrage, plead, amuse and persuade. In short, written words have power. The writer and the reader—those who create and recreate the written word—have power. The writer has the power to communicate thoughts and ideas. The reader who takes in the writer's message has the power to know, evaluate and act. The English poet Lord Byron remarked:

> But words are things, and a small drop of ink,
> That which, makes thousands, perhaps millions, think

The following examples show the impact of the written word:

> We hold these truths to be self-evident, that all men are created equal; that
> they are endowed by their creator with certain inalienable rights. (Declaration   *inalienable*
> of Independence)

> Give me your tired, your poor,
> Your huddled masses yearning to breathe free,
> The wretched refuse of your teeming shore
> Send these, the homeless, tempest-tossed, to me;
> I lift my lamp beside the golden door! (Emma Lazarus)

> We, the people of the United States, in order to form a more perfect union . . .
> (Preamble to the Constitution)

> Free at last! Free at last! Thank God almighty, we are free at last! (Martin
> Luther King, Jr.)

> I can, therefore I am. (Simone Weil)

7   We are all accustomed to reacting to the writing of others. But written words may also be a product of our own hands and imaginations. Seeing them on paper may give us a great sense of pride and accomplishment. In addition, our words may have an impact on others.

8   In his autobiography *Growing Up, New York Times* columnist Russell Baker recalls how as a student he came to appreciate the power of the written word. He had composed an essay entitled "The Art of Eating Spaghetti," and his teacher, Mr. Fleagle, read it aloud to the class:

> . . . My words! He was reading *my words* out loud to the entire class. What's more, the entire class was listening. Listening attentively. Then somebody laughed, then the entire class was laughing, and not in contempt and ridicule, but with openhearted enjoyment. Even Mr. Fleagle stopped two or three times to repress a small prim smile.
>
> I did my best to avoid showing pleasure, but what I was feeling was ecstasy at this startling demonstration that my words had the power to make people laugh.

The Language Base for Reading

9   When did you begin to learn to read? Was it in kindergarten or first grade? Or did you learn at home with the help of your parents, a brother or sister, or perhaps television? Actually, the first step in the reading process occurred at birth when you entered the world of language with your first cry. Soon afterward you began to distinguish the human voice from all other sounds, and you produced sounds that eventually became meaningful speech. Before you entered school, you became quite adept at using language. You recognized and produced oral language and understood that it had meaning. Your grasp of language helped prepare you for the day you would read print.

10   Many individuals recall being read to as children and this plays an important role in introducing and promoting literacy. Writer and essayist Sven Birkerts commented on how oral reading on the part of a parent (himself) to a child (his daughter) helps promote an active search for meaning:

> Being read to, while not strictly reading, is nonetheless not an entirely passive absorption either, as any parent can tell you. The child fleshes out the narrative through imaginative projection, and questions the text constantly. "Why is he crying?" "Is she going to get hurt?" She also engages the book itself, looking at the illustrations, monitoring the momentum of the turning pages, and, with the increase of aptitude, noting the correlation between what is being read out and the placement of words on the page. I see my daughter, now five, hovering on the brink of literary independence. She still loves being read to, but she breaks the flow of the story constantly by fastening on some word and working to sound it out. I can almost see the cognitive machinery at work. My hope is that as my daughter acquires mastery over words and meanings she will also discover that specialized and self-directed inwardness that makes private reading so rewarding.

passive

correlation

It is clear that this early stage of oral reading helps promote literacy and the reading process.

Early Reading Development

11 Once you understood something about language on the basis of your speaking, listening, and visual perception abilities, you were ready to read and write. Although your experience in learning to read may differ from those of your friends, you and they most likely had common experiences. At one point, you had to learn that the English language

    tfel ot thgir morf daer dna nettirw ton si

but is written and read from left to right. (If you didn't understand that strange-looking line, start on the right and move left.) You also had to learn the alphabet and understand that it formed words which did not appear in print like

    this, but rather

like this.

The Developing Reader

12 As you grew older, progressed through school, and gained new experiences, you also had a chance to read more. You began to see that not everything could be read or understood in the same way. One thing that changed was the kind of material you were expected to read. Many of your initial experiences in learning to read at school or at home involved material that was narrative in form. In reading a narrative, you knew that a story was introduced and a plot developed. You came to expect a beginning, a middle, and an end. The popular fairy tales follow this pattern, and so did many of the first books you read. You were able to read and follow these narratives because you were accustomed to listening to, and being told, stories with a narrative structure. You were becoming sensitive to the tone and style of narratives. Often accompanying pictures helped you understand what you were reading. *initial*

13 The autobiographical accounts presented earlier are other examples of narrative material. In each excerpt, the author recounted some aspect of his or her life. Although the language was more sophisticated than that of fairy tales, the articles were similar to children's stories in that events were described and you could follow the story line. *recounted*

14 Not long after you entered elementary school, you realized that not everything you read was a story. As you progressed past the initial stages of reading, you began to encounter more complicated reading material. New ideas outside your range of experience were introduced together with unfamiliar vocabulary. The language you were exposed to was more involved than the conversational language you were accustomed to. You were moving from the stage of "learning to read" to "reading to learn." You were now expected to read expository materials. Expository texts presented facts,

ideas, and explanations rather than the stories you were accustomed to seeing in your first reading books. You were introduced to specific subjects,
each with its own vocabulary, concepts, and facts. You probably noticed that
the simple sentences you saw in beginning reading books were gone and
were replaced by longer, more complex sentences. You encountered new,
challenging forms of expression. You were "bombarded" with many facts
that often were squeezed into a few pages. Instead of following a story with
a beginning, middle, and an end, you were asked to understand relationships
such as cause and effect. You may have been asked to compare and contrast
different things. As you progressed through school, you had to learn a new
language: the language of the textbook.

Examples of Exposition

15   An example will help illustrate the preceding points. Here is a passage from
an American history textbook commonly used in the lower elementary
school grades. It deals with the early life of Abraham Lincoln.

> . . . The young man decided to be a lawyer. He borrowed law books and read
> them while he held other jobs. When he finished studying the books, he
> moved to Springfield, Illinois. There he opened an office and became a lawyer.
>   Abraham was chosen by the people of Illinois to be a member of the legis-
> lature. The legislature made laws for the state of Illinois. . . .

16   Now compare the preceding passage with the following one. This passage deals with the same topic, but it is taken from a textbook that would be
used in the middle grades.

> . . . He wanted to be a lawyer, but he knew he would need a better education,
> so he borrowed books, often walking the long miles between New Salem and
> Springfield for that purpose, "and went at it in good earnest." In 1836 he re-
> ceived a license to practice law. By this time he had blossomed into an affable   *affable*
> young politician and two years previously had been elected to the state legisla-
> ture. . . .

17   What differences do you notice between the versions? Which would you
consider easier to read and understand? Most people agree that the first version is simpler because the sentences are shorter, each sentence contains
fewer ideas, and the vocabulary is easier. In contrast, the first and last sentences of the second version are more complicated, each sentence contains
several ideas, and the vocabulary is generally more challenging.

18   Both excerpts mention that Lincoln became a lawyer. At this time in
your life, you have a fairly good idea of what a lawyer does. But were you
familiar with the occupation of lawyer when you were in second grade?
How did you form an understanding of what a lawyer does over the years?
As you grew, you had new experiences and gained background knowledge
that enabled you to develop a frame of reference for the profession of lawyer.
You may have read books describing the law profession. You may have met
a lawyer in person or via a television program (the often distorted picture of
attorneys on TV notwithstanding). If you ever needed the services of a

lawyer or studied law yourself, your understanding of the term *lawyer* would be even broader. With each type of reading you encounter, you must either have a frame of reference or build one. Without it, you will be unable to process information in a meaningful way.

Proficient Reading: A Never-Ending Quest

19   Of course, you cannot expect to reach a point in your life where you will fully understand everything you read. No one can read every piece of material with total comprehension. Some written passages are more difficult to understand than others.

20   One case arises when the words used are unfamiliar to you but express a common idea. An example of this occurs in the following sentence: "You can convey an equus to a compound of hydrogen and oxygen, but you cannot compel him to imbibe." The author could have expressed the idea more simply by saying, "You can lead a horse to water, but you can't make him drink." Putting it in the more complicated form is similar to using code: A translation must take place before you can make sense of it. Once the less familiar words are linked with the more common terms, the difficulty is cleared up.

21   A second problem occurs when familiar words are used to express an idea that is new and difficult to understand. Most adults know the ideas associated with the words *light* and *year*, but when these words are combined as in *light year*, they represent a difficult concept. The idea of a star so far away that we must measure its distance by the time it takes light to travel a year (moving at a speed of 186,000 miles per second) is hard to grasp.

22   A third difficulty occurs when unfamiliar words are used to express an unfamiliar idea. This is the most complicated problem because there is nothing familiar to rely on. The phrase "ionization potential of a compound" sounds completely foreign to a nonchemist.

23   One problem in reading comprehension, especially at the college level, is that you encounter so many terms, expressions, and concepts that are new to you. You can figure some of them out by using clues found in a sentence. You can predict others on the basis of clues that appear before or after the sentence that contains the unknown word. Of course, you can use a dictionary to make unfamiliar terms clearer and more understandable. In certain situations, however, you may have to read other material for more explanation or rely on someone to explain in terms you can comprehend.

24   As you encounter various written material in college, in the workplace, and elsewhere in your daily life, you should expect to come across some material that lies outside your frame of reference. Consider the next example, taken from an automobile service manual.

SHOCK ABSORBER AND SPRING MOUNTING

Direct double-acting shock absorbers are attached at the upper eye to a frame bracket and at the lower eye to the strut rod mounting shaft which incorporates a threaded stud for the shock absorber lower eye. The transversely mounted multi-leaf spring is clamp bolted at the center section to the lower mounting surface on the differential carrier cover. The outer ends of the main leaf are provided with a hole through which the spring is link bolted to the rear of the torque control arms. The spring assembly is provided with full length liners.

25   Are these instructions clear? Do they make sense to you? Some individuals with many years of schooling and advanced degrees would find these instructions incomprehensible. Although highly educated, these individuals have no frame of reference or background information to draw on. There is no interaction between the knowledge they possess and the information the directions contain. On the other hand, a teenager who spends time repairing cars might find these instructions quite clear and meaningful. This person would have a frame of reference based on practical, hands-on experience.

26   As another example, consider employment advertisements in the newspaper. It is likely that many advertisements make sense to you, whereas others seem to be written in a foreign language. What meaning does the following advertisement have for you?

FERMENTATION/CELL BIOLOGIST

This position requires a scientist with a broad knowledge of fermentation/bioreactor processes for producing recombinant proteins in microbial, yeast, and preferably other expression systems (e.g., insects or mammalian) at the plate, tube and 1–60 liter scale. The successful candidate will have experience in maintaining and adjusting lab fermentors/bioreactors and familiarity with downstream processing is desirable. A BS/MS degree in biology or related field is required along with at least 3 years of work experience in microbiology, fermentation, and/or large scale cell culturing.

27   If you had some background in biology, especially at the graduate school level, you probably would understand this advertisement. But how much meaning would you derive from this advertisement with no biology background? Many of the words would make sense if presented individually. But taken as a whole, the ad's message would be incomprehensible.

Steps to Proficient Reading: The Role of Effort

28 Although you no doubt will find some materials more difficult to read than others, you can take certain steps to minimize reading difficulties:

1. *Take an active role.* Reading requires interaction between the reader and the writer—that is, between you and the written text. Remember that reading is more than moving your eyes across the page. You must recreate the author's message, and this requires effort. You must try to put yourself into the text as you attempt to make sense of it.

2. *Read productively.* One reading usually is not enough to grasp the full message of the text. Be prepared to give the material a fairly rapid read-

ing to get the general idea of the text and then return for a careful, close reading.

3. *Ask questions as you read.* Framing questions gives you a purpose and a goal and promotes active reading on your part.

4. *Examine the writer's purpose in creating the text.* Is the writer trying to narrate, describe, argue, explain, persuade, or arouse? Knowing why the writer wrote the material often helps you in your initial effort to understand.

5. *Examine your purpose in reading a selection.* Are you reading for information or amusement? What level of understanding do you want to achieve? Is a superficial understanding sufficient, or are you seeking in-depth knowledge? What will you be expected to do with the reading? Will you have to answer questions? Will you perform a certain task?

    superficial

6. *Monitor your reading behavior as you read.* Think about what you need for effective performance. Check your understanding as you read. If you do not understand, ask yourself:
   a. What specifically do I not understand?
   b. What do I need to know to make sense of this material?
   c. What can I do to increase my comprehension?
   d. Can I use the parts of the material that I do understand to help me figure out what is not clear to me?
   e. Where can I go to get further help?

Remember, your text cannot tell you whether you understood its message. Nor should you expect your instructor to always recognize your level of understanding. Your awareness must begin with you. If you are not aware of your own actions, you are reading passively and can't take steps to help yourself. To be an effective reader, you must be an active reader.

A Final Word

29 In reading, you control the flow of ideas. You can read as quickly or as leisurely as you want. You can stop, think, question, and reread as many times as you wish. The act of reading is private, personal and self-controlled. As Patricia and Gordon Sabine noted in their text *Books That Made a Difference: What People Told Us,* . . . "in a time when identity is increasingly lost, even drowned, the reading of books may remain as one of the few truly personal acts left to us."

30   In conclusion, we present an excerpt from an advertisement. Although this ad was geared to promote a particular magazine, its message is powerful and easily applicable to reading in general.

    In the year 2075, when the travel-weary passenger on the moonshuttle has had his fill of: dinner on the anti-gravity magnetic tray, three dimensional TV, inter-galactic weather reports and conversational banter with the stewardess, as she floats by—he'll settle back in his contour couch, and return to that important, private activity each of us does alone.

Reading...

The act of reading is essentially a process of thinking. It has the scan and scope beyond any camera—as you have just demonstrated on the cosmic screen of your own mind. It is a concentratively individual act. An involvement. The reader makes the printed communication happen... releases the magic that causes words on a page to leap into living thoughts, ideas, emotions.

And no matter how many millions may be on the receiving end of the message, it is addressed to, and received by, *individuals,* one at a time—each in the splendid solitude of his or her mind. There, the silent language of print can whisper, rage, implore, accuse, burst into song, explode into revelation, stab the consciousness. Or work a healing faith. And so it will always be, come hell, high water, or McLuhan.

Aeschylus knew this when he called written words "physicians." And so did Hitler when he burned them. Because mobs roar, but individuals think. They think. They read. And they ask questions that alter the course of the world....

31   We could give numerous other examples of reading material to make certain points about reading or about how other people think about it. We could also present many more examples of material to demonstrate that even a lifetime of study would leave us short of understanding even a small portion of the total set of possibilities. But what is crucial is that we can read what is important to us—not only in our jobs, but also in the pursuits we choose to enrich our personal lives. For reading is a special medium with the power to stir us across time, distance, and culture.

QUESTIONS

1. The authors state, "Reading... is more than a mechanical process of moving your eyes across the page and sounding out symbols. Reading is an active process of constructing meaning from written texts.... Reading therefore involves mentally processing printed information in a meaningful way." Explain this statement.

2. Using an example that is not in the text, illustrate the saying "Literacy is a form of power."

3. Analyze the excerpt from Russell Baker's autobiography (page 82), and explain why it was included in the article.

4. Why do students typically find reading increasingly challenging and difficult as they progress from elementary school through junior and senior high school?

5. Explain the difference between narrative and expository texts.

6. The authors state, "With each type of reading... you must either have a frame of reference or build one. Without it, you will be unable to process information in a meaningful way." Explain this statement.

7. Identify three cases of potential difficulty with reading material.

8. Describe the reading strategies good readers use, according to the article.

9. Reread the passages about shock absorbers and the advertisement on pages 85–86. Circle the words that are unfamiliar to you. Why did you have difficulty understanding the passages? What would you need to know for this material to make sense to you?

10. Paraphrase the concluding sentence of the article.

EXTENDING YOUR VOCABULARY

unique: You may have seen other watches, but this is unique because
_____

endeavor: Helen Keller's endeavor to learn to read _____

inalienable: Rights that are inalienable cannot be _____

passive: I don't want to hire passive workers because _____

correlation: Researchers found a strong correlation between cigarette
smoking and _____

initial: My initial reaction to the candidate changed after I learned
_____

recounted: The witness recounted how _____

affable: Because of her affable nature, _____

superficial: A superficial reading of the contract is not recommended
because _____

 MARKED COPY*

The Reading

The Proficient Reader

by Ira D. Epstein and Ernest B. Nieratka

1   Imagine waking up this morning to find that you completely lacked the ability to read. How would your life be different? Of course, you wouldn't be reading this article—but seriously, did you ever stop to think what a vital part reading plays in your everyday living? <u>Many people take for granted this ability unique to human beings.</u> However, noted educator G. R.

Introduction

Reading as a special ability

---

*This is a partial marked copy. We encourage you to continue marking up this article on your own.

Carlsen said, "Learning to read is one of the most complex tasks that a human being accomplishes in a lifetime. The amazing thing is not that a few people fail, but that so many succeed."

2   Like writing, listening, and speaking, reading is a process of communication using language. Reading is communication between the writer and the reader. It is more than a mechanical process of moving your eyes across the page and sounding out symbols. Reading is an active process of constructing meaning from written texts. It requires interaction or transaction with a written text. When you read, you try to understand the writer's message. To do this, you must relate the author's message to your own knowledge. Consider the following example:

> He looked at his fuel gauge and saw it was almost empty. To make matters worse, he had passed the last gas station an hour ago and the next scheduled rest stop on the turnpike was 25 miles away.

*Reading defined

To understand this scenario you would have to use information from the text together with your own background knowledge to produce meaning. The first sentence suggests that someone is driving a car on a highway and is about to run out of fuel. Once this is understood the rest of the example is easy to process because of the expectations that come from your background knowledge. If you knew nothing about this subject or had no concept of what is a fuel gauge, you could expect to learn very little. Reading therefore involves mentally processing printed information in a meaningful way. In your attempt to make meaning out of the text you read, you must get actively involved in it.

Processing Written Language and Reading

3   On the surface, it appears that when you are reading, you are simply looking at marks on a page—symbols that don't talk. Yet these marks on a page can make you laugh, cry, shiver, cringe, smile, or reflect. Look at the following examples, and think about how you react:

We respond to marks on a page

1. The professor was so absent-minded that he often put on his coat with the hanger still in it.

2. We regret to inform you that your son has been taken prisoner by the enemy.

3. She locked the door and was about to switch on the light. Suddenly, she sensed something. Someone was in the room. Before she could even gather her thoughts, a hand reached out and grabbed her throat. She tried to scream, but . . .

A variety of reactions to written text

4. Try our special steak dinner. For $10 you receive a thick, juicy, mouth watering grilled steak, smothered in fried onions, with golden French fried potatoes and creamy cole slaw.

5. They removed their clothes and lay down on the bed. Their bodies felt warm as their lips met. They embraced passionately, knowing that they might never see each other again.

6. I know a guy who was so ugly that when he was born, the doctor slapped his mother instead of him.

4   You probably reacted differently to each example. This can be explained in part by the experiences and knowledge that you bring to the printed page. Reading involves the "total you." It engages your mind in imagining and understanding, as well as your feelings and emotions.

The mind and feelings are involved in reading

5   What you see on this page is only ink marks; they have no meaning in themselves. Yet you are able to derive meaning and react. <u>These marks signal some idea that is already in your mind.</u> The most important part of reading is what you know before you begin to read and the connections you make while reading. "A text" according to Anderson, Hiebert, Scott and Wilkinson "is not so much a vessel containing meaning as it is a source of partial information that enables the reader to use already-possessed knowledge to determine the intended meaning." Thus, proficient reading is an active process. It can be thought of as a search for meaning. It is something that is not achieved overnight but rather is a lifelong endeavor.

Getting meaning from printed symbols

The Impact of the Written Word

6   <u>Through the written word, writers convey meaning.</u> Written words can stir our emotions, imaginations and intellect. <u>They can inform, influence, enrage, plead, amuse and persuade.</u> <u>In short, written words have power.</u> The writer and the reader—those who create and recreate the written word— have power. The writer has the power to communicate thoughts and ideas. The reader who takes in the writer's message has the power to know, evaluate and act. The English poet Lord Byron remarked:

What written words can do

> But words are things, and a small drop of ink,
> That which, makes thousands, perhaps millions, think

The following examples show the impact of the written word:

> We hold these truths to be self-evident, that all men are created equal; that they are endowed by their creator with certain inalienable rights. (Declaration of Independence)

> Give me your tired, your poor,
> Your huddled masses yearning to breathe free,
> The wretched refuse of your teeming shore
> Send these, the homeless, tempest-tossed, to me;
> I lift my lamp beside the golden door! (Emma Lazarus)

> We, the people of the United States, in order to form a more perfect union . . . (Preamble to the Constitution)

> Free at last! Free at last! Thank God almighty, we are free at last! (Martin Luther King, Jr.)

> I can, therefore I am. (Simone Weil)

Examples of the power of words

7   We are all accustomed to reacting to the writing of others. <u>But written words may also be a product of our own hands and imaginations. Seeing them on paper may give us a great sense of pride and accomplishment. In addition, our words may have an impact on others.</u>

The power of our own writing

8   In his autobiography *Growing Up, New York Times* columnist Russell Baker recalls how as a student he came to appreciate the power of the written word. He had composed an essay entitled "The Art of Eating Spaghetti," and his teacher, Mr. Fleagle, read it aloud to the class:

> . . . My words! He was reading *my words* out loud to the entire class. What's more, the entire class was listening. Listening attentively. Then somebody laughed, then the entire class was laughing, and not in contempt and ridicule, but with openhearted enjoyment. Even Mr. Fleagle stopped two or three times to repress a small prim smile.

PROCESS GUIDE

1. The opening paragraph introduces the general subject, but the authors do not define reading until the second paragraph. Note, however, that the definition is not found in a single sentence; it must be gathered from several sentences and combined. One way to organize your ideas is to list the major points that define reading. Try it now:

   a. _____

   b. _____

   c. _____

2. Writers typically use examples to illustrate a point. Paragraph 3 gives six examples to highlight a key point. What is the major idea being proposed?

   _____

3. In paragraph 6, the authors quote from Lord Byron, Thomas Jefferson, Emma Lazarus, the Preamble to the Constitution, Martin Luther King Jr., and Simone Weill. Paragraph 8 gives a brief excerpt from Russell Baker's autobiography. What point do all these examples make?

   _____

4. In paragraph 9, the authors explain how language is the foundation on which we learn to read. When we learn to read, we build our knowledge and use of language sounds, words, and meaning. This paragraph uses the writing pattern known as time order, in which you are asked to follow an event or series of events over a period of time. What examples of this writing pattern can you find in this paragraph? List those words that signal time order.

   a. _____   b. _____

5. In the heading "The Developing Reader" (page 83), the word *developing* suggests growth or change. Paragraph 12 contains words that support the idea of change, progression, or development. List some of these words.

   a. _____   b. _____

6. In paragraphs 13 and 14, the authors describe the differences between *narrative* and *expository* writing. A narrative is a story, whereas exposition presents facts, information, and explanations.

   Paragraphs 15 and 16 present two excerpts from American history textbooks. What point do these passages illustrate?

   _____

7. Paragraph 18 briefly discusses the legal profession. What purpose does this example serve?

   _____

92

8. List the three reasons the authors give to explain why some readings are more difficult to understand than others.

a. _____

b. _____

c. _____

9. In paragraph 24, the authors state that everyone encounters reading material that falls outside his or her frame of reference. Reread the excerpt from the automobile service manual, and list some reasons why this example was either difficult (or easy) for you to read with understanding.

a. _____

b. _____

c. _____

10. Now read the advertisement in paragraph 26. List some reasons why this advertisement was difficult (or easy) to understand.

a. _____

b. _____

c. _____

Both of these examples illustrate the important role background knowledge and frame of reference play in reading with understanding. The more familiar you are with a subject, the easier it is for you to read about it.

11. The article concludes with a brief statement regarding the special nature of reading. What is the author's bias regarding reading?

_____

_____

History of Printing

Geoffrey Rubinstein

GEARING UP

1. Explain how it was possible for people to share information before the development of the printing press (that is, in the 1450s).

2. Refer to a dictionary and look up the term *manuscript*. This word is composed of two parts: *manu + script*. Explain the meaning of both parts of the word and the word as a whole.

3. Imagine a world in which printing did not exist. List several ways our society would be affected.

READING STRATEGY

READING EXPOSITION—PART II

The strategy of reading exposition was introduced on page 75 prior to the article "The Proficient Reader." Exposition is the most common writing pattern you experience in college. For this reason we will continue to introduce other aspects of exposition that will help you process this type of writing.

You may recall that expository writing presents facts and information and teaches ideas. The exposition strategy introduced you to several common writing patterns such as cause and effect, comparison and contrast, sequence, listing, example, and definition. When expository writers try to convey meaning, they often use signal or directional words. "The Proficient Reader" article contained many signal words:

for example	therefore	yet
the following examples	in short	but
in addition	actually	soon afterward
of course	although	also
as you grew	another example	not long after
as you moved	instead of	now compare
in contrast	one case	a second problem
a third difficulty	on the other hand	nor should you expect
in conclusion	but what is crucial	and so it will always be

By themselves, these words don't carry much meaning. But used in a paragraph they help alert the reader to the thought patterns the writer intends to follow. Consider the following examples with signal words italicized.

- Reading *therefore* is more than a mechanical process of moving your eyes across the page. Reading involves mentally processing printed information in a meaningful way.

- On the surface, it appears that when you are reading, you are simply looking at marks on a page—symbols that don't talk. *Yet* these marks on a page can make you laugh, cry, shiver, cringe, smile or reflect.

- *Although* your experiences in learning to read may differ from those of your friends, you and they most likely had common experiences.

- Most people agree that the first version is simple because the sentences are shorter, each sentence contains fewer ideas, and the vocabulary is easier. *In contrast,* the first and last sentences of the second version are more complicated, each sentence contains several ideas, and the vocabulary is generally more challenging.

You can expect writers to use several signal words within a paragraph, and the paragraph itself may contain more than one thought pattern.

A story was told about a science professor who was lecturing his class about the negative effects of drinking too much alcohol. The dialogue went something like this:

> I have before me 2 beakers. On my left is a beaker containing clear water whereas the beaker on my right contains alcohol. Also, please note that I have 2 small worms that are alive. Now watch what happens when I put the first worm into the clear water. Notice that the worm is wriggling about in the water and is fully alive. Next I'll place the second worm in the solution containing alcohol. In contrast to the behavior of the first worm in the water beaker please observe that this worm placed in the alcohol solution starts to shrivel up and finally lays motionless. Thus, what can we conclude from this experiment?

Our professor was of course expecting his students to come to the conclusion that drinking alcohol can have negative effects upon our body. After all the poor little worm lay motionless and lifeless in the beaker containing the alcohol. Therefore he was quite surprised by the response he received from one student: "If you drink alcohol, you won't get worms!"

We use this amusing anecdote to illustrate the use of signal words. Are you able to pick out the various examples of the signal words? Did you notice that the story uses several writing patterns? There is comparison and contrast to signal differences between the two beakers and the two worms. There is a listing of steps taken to carry out the procedure. And there is a conclusion that the professor was hoping his students would reach. Some of the signal words you may have noted include *on my left, whereas, please note, now watch, notice, next, in contrast, finally,* and *thus.* Pay attention to signal words because they provide a road map to the writer's thought process.

Consider the following two signal words: *although* and *because.* Used in a sentence they can dramatically affect meaning. For example, imagine that a student woke up later than planned and arrived late for an important final exam. How would you complete the following two sentences?

Because he came late to class, _____

Although he came late to class, _____

Would this make sense? *Because* he came late to class, he finished the exam on time.

You would not expect this to happen but rather would expect the sentence to read something like this: *Because* he came late to class, he could *not* finish the exam in the given time.

The word *because* signals a cause-and-effect pattern with a result. The person came late to class and the result was that he lacked the time to complete the exam.

If the sentence began with the word *although,* a different signal is suggested. In spite of what occurred, the reader is prepared for a shift in thought. In this case you could reasonably expect the following: *Although* he came late to class, he still managed to complete the exam in the allotted time.

The following list is provided to give you an overview of some of the signal words that you might encounter in your reading. Although there is no single way to categorize signal words, the following classifications should help you become more familiar with them. Please note that some signal words fall into more than one category.

Type of Signal	Purpose	Common Signal Words	Some Examples
Description/ characteristics or components	To present and detail features and components (order is not significant)	*several, many, also, last, such as, another*	• There are *several* ways to characterize families. • Advertisers use *many* techniques to get viewers to pay attention to their products.
Sequence	To present an order or progression (order is significant)	*first, last, then, next, before, later, finally, another*	• *Before* submitting your final draft, make sure to . . . • Assembling your new computer involves *several* steps. *First* carefully . . . , *next* plug your . . .
Cause	To present factors or reasons that produce something	*leads to, makes, brings about, determines, are factors in, influences*	• The number of viewers *determines* the rates that TV stations can charge advertisers. • Your educational level *influences* your earning potential.
Effect	To present outcomes or results	*results, thus, as a consequence of, therefore*	• Some researchers attribute aggressive behavior in children *as a consequence of* their viewing TV violence.
Comparison and contrast	To show similarities and differences	*like, but, or, on the other hand, conversely, both, neither*	• Television's messages are based primarily on pictures and emotional responses to graphics. *Conversely,* the classroom relies heavily on reading and the spoken word.

Type of Signal	Purpose	Common Signal Words	Some Examples
Change or reversal of thought	To develop an idea and then shift to another viewpoint	*however, on the other hand, in contrast, nevertheless, unlike, although, instead, conversely*	• *Although* some progress has been made in the fight against AIDS, much work lies ahead. • Some employers are in favor of monitoring their workers' phone calls. *On the other hand,* there are many individuals who oppose this practice.
Continuation and illustration of thought	To develop an idea with supporting evidence	*for example, for instance, also, similarly, such as, furthermore, moreover, for instance, likewise*	• The more knowledge children are able to gain at home, the greater their chance for success in reading. *For example,* children who have been read to will acquire background reading knowledge that will help in school.
Conclusion	To finish or conclude an idea (an important signal because it can serve to sum up a thought)	*thus, therefore, finally, consequently, hence*	• *In conclusion,* parents play a vital role in establishing the foundation for learning to read.

The article that follows, "The History of Printing," uses many signal words. Here are several examples.

In the following sentence the author describes how two events that occurred at about the same time influenced one another: "Rag paper became increasingly cheap and plentiful while literacy expanded; the processes accelerated, in part, by stimulating each other." Another way of looking at this writing style is to consider a sentence that uses the same style: "The price of home computers continued to drop while the Internet gained in popularity; the two events stimulated each other." In both sentences you have a cause-and-effect pattern. Two events took place at the same time that had an influence on one another.

Let's look at another excerpt:

Because their alphabet employs thousands of visually specific ideograms, the use of moveable type was much more labor-intensive for the Chinese. Consequently, it did not change production efficiency as dramatically as it did for the Europeans.

Now consider another text that uses a similar structure:

Because they didn't have modern farm equipment in the village, they had to rely on wooden plows and oxen to cultivate the land. Consequently, they produced _____ than the neighboring village that had obtained up-to-date farm machinery.

The word *consequently* signals a result. In this second example a blank has been left for you to complete the thought. What word would you insert that would support the thought pattern being developed?

Let's examine one additional sentence from the article: "Despite their rapid growth in numbers, secular scribes simply could not keep up with the current demand for books." This sentence makes use of the signal word *despite.*

Again let's consider a sentence that uses a parallel structure. "Despite their increase in numbers before the holiday season, factory workers could not produce enough of the popular doll to satisfy the demand."

Here is one way the sentence and its ideas can be broken down and analyzed: The public liked a new doll. There wasn't an adequate supply to meet the demand so more factory workers were hired. In spite of this fact (even with the hiring of extra workers), they (the workers) couldn't make enough of the dolls to satisfy the growing demand.

 # READING STRATEGY CHECK

MAKING ALL THE STRATEGIES WORK FOR YOU

If you have followed the Unit One sequence, you have been introduced to a number of strategies at this point. There is a lot to remember and perhaps you feel a bit overwhelmed. As we have pointed out before, time and practice will help make much of this task seem easier farther down the road. Before the process becomes fully automatic for any one strategy, you must have worked this activity into your reading behavior by conscious effort.

In an effort to collapse and simplify much of the reading advice we have given thus far, we offer the following points to consider:

1. Decide what you need to get out of a particular reading, such as answers for questions or information for a term paper.

2. Preview the text by looking for headings and questions at the end of the reading. Other features like outlines and summaries alert you to what the author thinks is important or worth asking about.

3. Read through without stopping to get a sense of the article.

4. Read the article carefully, applying the strategies that you are comfortable with.

5. Use other study aids such as Marked Copy and the Process Guide to assist you in comprehending the article.

6. Take stock of what you know and don't know about a reading. Try using your question marks from your markup as reference points. Seek the instructor's assistance to clarify points of confusion and difficulty.

The Reading

History of Printing
by GEOFFREY RUBINSTEIN

1 *Gutenberg's invention of the printing press is widely thought of as the origin of mass communication—it marked Western culture's first viable method of disseminating ideas and information from a single source to a large and far-ranging audience. A closer look at the history of print, however, shows that the invention of the printing press depended on a confluence of both cultural and technological forces that had been unfolding for several centuries. Print culture and technology also needed to go through centuries of change after Gutenberg's time before the "massification" of audiences could fully crystallize.*

viable
disseminating

confluence

[*Italicized words in the text signal hyperlinks in the Internet version of this article.*]

2 The story of print is a long and complex one. It may be too much to claim that print was the single cause of the massive social, political and psychological changes it is associated with. However, print did wield enormous influence on every aspect of European culture. Some historians suggest that print was instrumental in bringing about all the major shifts in science, religion, politics and the modes of thought that are commonly associated with modern Western culture.

instrumental

3 The key technological, cultural and psychological issues associated with the emergence of the printing press can be organized into the following areas:

China: The Technological Roots

- rag paper
- paper's migration to Europe
- ideographic alphabet

Gutenberg and the Historical Moment in Western Europe

- scribal hand-copying
- Church indulgences
- movable metal type

- Gutenberg Bibles
- the Protestant Reformation
- William Caxton and print in England

Print and Modern Thought

- scientific thinking
- the scientific community
- the rise of an intellectual class
- transformations: oral, written and print cultures
- privacy and individual rights

Print in the U.S.

- first colonial press in Cambridge
- the penny press: news for all

Advances in Print Technology

- innovations since the Linotype   *innovations*
- innovations in contemporary print culture

China: The Technological Roots

4   The invention of the printing press depended on the invention and refinement of *paper in China* over several centuries. The Chinese had developed "rag" paper, a cheap cloth-scrap and plant-fiber substitute for cumbersome *bark and bamboo strips* and for precious silk paper, by A.D. 105. Chinese prisoners passed a mature technology on to their Arab captors in the eighth century. The secrets of the craft that were revealed to *Europeans* in the twelfth and thirteenth centuries were substantially the same techniques the Chinese had passed to the Arabs several centuries earlier.   *cumbersome*

5   Long before the Gutenberg press, Chinese innovations in ink, block printing and movable clay type all fed the technological push toward expanding the written word's range of influence. Although the European innovations came much later, European culture certainly felt the impact of print more dramatically than the Chinese did. Because their alphabet employs thousands of visually specific ideograms, the use of movable type was much more labor-intensive for the Chinese. Consequently, it did not change production efficiency as dramatically as it did for Europeans. Some historians will also assert that the sequential, linear and standardized character of the printed word especially suited Western impulses toward progress and conquest—a disposition that favors quick and intense change.   *assert*

      disposition

Gutenberg and the Historical Moment in Western Europe

6   In the early 1450s rapid cultural change in Europe fueled a growing need for the rapid and cheap production of written documents. *Johannes Gutenberg,* a goldsmith and businessman from the mining town of Mainz in southern Germany, borrowed money to develop a technology that could address this serious economic bottleneck. From its European debut in the 12th century, *debut* paper gradually proved to be a viable alternative to the animal-skin vellum and parchment that had been the standard means of carrying written communication. Rag paper became increasingly cheap and plentiful while literacy expanded; the two processes accelerated, in part, by stimulating each other. The need for documentation continued to increase with expansions in trade and in governmental scope and complexity. *Scribal monks* sanctioned *sanctioned* by the Church had overseen the maintenance and hand-copying of sacred texts for centuries, but the secular world began to foster its own version of *foster* the scribal copyist profession. The many new *scriptoria,* or writing shops, that sprang up employed virtually every literate cleric who wanted work. Gutenberg foresaw enormous profit-making potential for a printing press that used movable metal type. Despite their rapid growth in numbers, secular scribes simply could not keep up with the commercial demand for books. Gutenberg also saw strong market potential in selling indulgences, the slips so paper offering written dispensation from sin that the Church sold to fund *dispensation* crusades, new buildings and other projects devoted to expanding its dominance. In fact, press runs of 200,000 indulgences at a time were common soon after the handwritten versions became obsolete.   *obsolete*

7   Gutenberg developed his press by combining features of existing technologies: textile, papermaking and wine presses. Perhaps his most significant innovation, however, was the efficient molding and casting of movable metal type. Each letter was carved into the end of a steel punch which was then hammered into a copper blank. The copper impression was inserted into a mold and a molten alloy made of lead, antimony and bismuth was poured in. *alloy* The alloy cooled quickly and the resulting reverse image of the letter attached to a lead base could be handled in minutes. The width of the lead base varied according to the letter's size (for example, the base of an "i" would not be nearly as wide as the base of a "w"). This emphasized the visual impact of words and clusters of words rather than evenly spaced letters. This principle lent an aesthetic elegance and sophistication to what seemed to many to be *aesthetic* the magically perfect regularity of a printed page. Gutenberg designed a Latin print Bible which became his signature work. He launched a run of some 300 two-volume *Gutenberg Bibles* which sold for 30 florins each, or about three years of a clerk's wage. Despite the dramatic success of his invention, Gutenberg managed to default on a loan and lost his whole printing *default* establishment. His techniques were made public and his creditor won the rights to the proceeds from the Gutenberg Bibles.

8   The clergy were eager to take advantage of the power of print. Printed indulgences, theological texts, even how-to manuals for conducting inquisitions became common tools for the spread of the Church's influence. But the   *theological / inquisitions*

Church had even more difficulty controlling the activities of printers than they had with the secular scribes. The production and distribution of an expanding variety of texts quickly became too widespread to contain. Printed copies of *Martin Luther's theses,* for example, were widely and rapidly disseminated. They prompted far-reaching discussions that became the foundation for mounting opposition to the Church's role as the sole custodian of spiritual truth. Bibles printed in vernacular languages rather than Latin *vernacular* fueled the Protestant Reformation based on the assertion that there was no need for the Church to interpret scripture—an individual's relationship with God could be, at least in theory, direct and personal.

9   In 1476, *William Caxton* set up England's first printing press. Caxton had been a prolific translator and found the printing press to be a marvelous *prolific* way to amplify his mission of promoting popular literature. Caxton printed and distributed a variety of widely appealing narrative titles including the first popular edition of Chaucer's *The Canterbury Tales.* Caxton was an enthusiastic editor and he determined the diction, spelling and usage for all the books he printed. He realized that English suffered from so much regional variation that many people couldn't communicate with others from their own country. Caxton's contributions as an editor and printer won him a good portion of the credit for standardizing the English language.

Print and Modern Thought

10   The scientific revolution that would later challenge the entrenched "truths" *entrenched* espoused by the Church was also largely a consequence of print technology. *espoused* The scientific principle of repeatability—the impartial verification of exper- *impartial / verification* imental results—grew out of the rapid and broad dissemination of scientific insights and discoveries that print allowed. The production of scientific knowledge accelerated markedly. The easy exchange of ideas gave rise to a scientific community that functioned without geographical constraints. This *constraints* made it possible to systematize methodologies and to add sophistication to the development of rational thought. As readily available books helped expand the collective body of knowledge, indexes and cross-referencing emerged as ways of managing volumes of information and of making creative associations between seemingly unrelated ideas.

11   Innovations in the accessibility of knowledge and the structure of human thought that attended the rise of print in Europe also influenced art, literature, philosophy and politics. The explosive innovation that characterized the *Renaissance* was amplified, if not in part generated by, the printing press. The rigidly fixed class structure which determined one's status from birth based on family property ownership began to yield to the rise of an intellectual middle class. The possibility of changing one's status infused the *infused* less privileged with ambition and a hunger for education.

12   Print technology facilitated a communications revolution that reached *facilitated* deep into human modes of thought and social interaction. Print, along with spoken language, writing and electronic media, is thought of as one of the markers of key historical shifts in communication that have attended social

and intellectual transformation. *Oral culture* is passed from one generation to the next through the full sensory and emotional atmosphere of interpersonal interaction. Writing facilitates interpretation and reflection since memorization is no longer required for the communication and processing of ideas. Recorded history could persist and be added to through the centuries. Written manuscripts sparked a variation on the oral tradition of communal story-telling—it became common for one person to read out loud to the group.

13   Print, on the other hand, encouraged the pursuit of personal privacy. Less expensive and more portable books lent themselves to solitary and silent reading. This orientation to privacy was part of an emphasis on individual rights and freedoms that print helped to develop. Print injected Western culture with the principles of standardization, verifiability and communication that comes from one source and is disseminated to many geographically dispersed receivers. As illustrated by dramatic reform in religious thought and scientific inquiry, print innovations helped bring about sharp challenges to institutional control. Print facilitated a focus on fixed, verifiable truth, and on the human ability and right to choose one's own intellectual and religious path.

Print in the U.S.

14   Religious, intellectual and political freedom served as rallying cries for the Europeans who were drawn to the American colonies. Stephen Daye, a locksmith whose son Matthew was a printer's apprentice, brought the con-   *apprentice* tinent's first press to Cambridge, Massachusetts in 1638. The Dayes printed a broadside and an almanac in their first year. In 1640 they produced 1700 copies of the first book printed in the colonies, the *Bay Psalm Book*. The printing press quickly became central to political and religious expression in the New World. Writers and printers like *Benjamin Franklin* were heroes of the time. Print was at the heart of the dissemination and defense of visionary ideas that shaped the *American Revolution*.

15   Until the 19th century Gutenberg's print technology had not changed dramatically. In the early 1800s the development of *continuous rolls of paper,* a steam-powered press and a way to use iron instead of wood for building presses all added to the efficiency of printing. These technological advances made it possible for newspaperman Benjamin Day to drop the price of his *New York Sun* to a penny a copy in 1833. Some historians point to this "penny press" as the first true mass medium—in Day's words, his paper was designed to "lay before the public, at a price well within the means of everyone, all the news of the day."

Advances in Print Technology

16   A number of dramatic technological innovations have since added a great deal of character and dimension to the place of print in culture. Linotype, a method of creating movable type by machine instead of by hand, was introduced in 1884 and marked a significant leap in production speed. The

typewriter made the production and "look" of standardized print much more widely accessible. The process of setting type continued to go through radical transformations with the development of photo-mechanical composition, cathode ray tubes and laser technologies. The *Xerox* machine made a means of disseminating print documents available to everyone. Word processing transformed editing and contributed dramatic new flexibility to the writing process. Computer printing has already moved through several stages of innovation, from the first daisy-wheel and dot matrix "impact" printers to common use of the non-impact printers: ink-jet, laser and thermal-transfer.

17   Both the *Internet* and interactive multimedia are providing ways of employing the printed word that add new possibilities to print's role in culture. The printed word is now used for real-time social interaction and for individualized navigation through interactive documents. It is difficult to gauge the social and cultural impact of new media without historical distance, but these innovations will most likely prove to signal another major transformation in the use, influence and character of human communication.

Related Resources (Hyperlinks)

- AEJMC visual communication division
- American Museum of Papermaking
- History of Media
- Marshall McLuhan
- Oxford Early Books Project
- Society for The History of Authorship, Reading & Publishing
- SPEED
- Harold Innis
- Interview with Marshall McLuhan
- scriptorium@christdesert
- *A Brief History of Scriptoria*

Sources

- Carter, T.F., *The Invention of Printing in China and Its Spread Westward* (Ronald Press: 1925).

- Eisenstein, Elizabeth, *The Printing Revolution in Early Modern Europe* (Cambridge University Press, 1983).

- Olmert, Michael, *The Smithsonian Book of Books* (New York: Wing Books, 1992).

- The Graphion Type Museum on the Internet

- "Printers" in the *Jones MultiMedia Encyclopedia* CD-ROM

QUESTIONS

1. According to the author, print culture and technology did not happen overnight, but rather evolved over time. List the major events that influenced the development of printing.

2. Discuss the Chinese contribution to the development of printing and explain why their efforts had less of an impact on print technology.

3. Analyze the economic, social, and religious conditions during Gutenberg's time that paved the way for the success of his printing press.

4. Discuss the impact of printing on the spread of scientific knowledge.

5. The author discusses how print, unlike oral culture, played a unique role in human communication, religious thought, and scientific inquiry. Explain.

EXTENDING YOUR VOCABULARY

viable: Can you suggest a viable solution to _____

disseminating: The mayor accused his opponent of disseminating

_____

confluence: The confluence of several ideas helped to _____

crystallize: The ideas began to crystallize in her mind after _____

_____

instrumental: My teacher was instrumental in getting me to _____

_____

innovations: Examples of some twentieth-century innovations are ___

_____

cumbersome: I try to avoid traveling with cumbersome luggage because

_____

assert: Sometimes you need to assert yourself in order to _____

_____

disposition: His disposition to drinking began to _____

debut: After the singer made her public debut on a radio show,

_____

sanctioned: Examples of behavior on public transportation that is not

sanctioned are _____

foster: To foster a good working environment, the teacher

_____

dispensation: The new recruits went to their commanding officer seek-
                   ing dispensation from _____

obsolete: Products often become obsolete when _____

alloy: The crime lab was able to determine that the metal was an
                   alloy by the fact that _____

aesthetic: His lack of an aesthetic sense was evident by _____
                   _____

default: After he defaulted on a loan, _____

theological: If you want to find theological texts, I suggest looking
                   _____

inquisitions: The teacher's frequent inquisitions caused the pupils to
                   _____

vernacular: I pray in the vernacular language because _____

prolific: He is a prolific composer. Just yesterday he _____
                   _____

entrenched: With both sides of the labor dispute entrenched in their
                   positions, the mayor _____

espoused: My grandfather espoused ideas that _____

impartial: In a trial it is crucial that the judge remain impartial be-
                   cause _____

verification: All evidence is subject to verification before the court can
                   _____

constraints: So many constraints were placed on the performer that
                   she decided to _____

infused: We became infused with hope after listening to _____
                   _____

facilitated: It was obvious that the new computer facilitated her
                   work by the fact that _____

apprentice: At an early age Benjamin Franklin served as an apprentice
                   to a printer in order to _____

PROCESS GUIDE

CONTENT		PROCESS

CONTENT

Keyword:
History
Events over time

The article "History of Printing" traces the events that led up to the development of printing in Europe and examines the role it played in shaping our world. It is written in an expository style and presents many facts and concepts.

PROCESS

Note title to set expectations of material type

To comprehend this article better, you'll need to read and study the material and research unknown or unfamiliar ideas. The author assumes that you are familiar with many of the historical references. The more you know about these ideas the greater your comprehension will be.

Paragraph #1
Thesis regarding
print history

The first paragraph introduces the thesis or major idea. One way to make sure that you understand the author's ideas is to try paraphrasing the central ideas, expressing them in your own language. This may help to break up the big chunks of new words and ideas into units you understand better. Paraphrasing also helps you focus on a small but important part of the larger text.

Paraphrasing as
an expression of
comprehension

Here is an example from the introductory paragraph where the author discusses the significance of Gutenberg's invention of the printing press.

author's thesis

. . . it [the printing press] marked Western culture's first viable method of disseminating ideas and information from a single source to a large and far-ranging audience.

A paraphrase of this might take the following form:

author's idea
paraphrased

The printing press was Western culture's (Europe's) first workable way of distributing ideas and information from one point (the press) to many people in different places.

Western culture
defined

The author uses the expression *Western culture* to explain how the development of printing affected a large part of society. When writers use the term *West* or *Western,* they are signaling more than a geographic location. Most often you will see the term *the Western world* (the Occident) mentioned in literature, music, art, or history courses. Used this way the term refers mostly to the ideas and customs of Western Europe and North America in contrast to those of countries like China or Japan, which represent the East or Orient. Sometimes you may read about an Eastern country (for example, Japan) that is becoming increasingly "Westernized" (being influenced, for example, by dress styles, music preferences, or food tastes).

A reference or
signal

1. Now try to paraphrase the next idea signaled by the author in the introductory paragraph. Pay close attention to the word *however* and what it does in the sentence:

Print history: printing events that have taken place over time

A closer look at the history, however, shows that the invention of the printing press depended on the confluence of both cultural and technological forces that had been unfolding for several centuries.

Paraphrasing as a comprehension check

Your paraphrase:

_____

_____

_____

_____

The word *however* is used to signal a change of thought from the previous sentence. Another way to think about this signal word is to substitute the word *but*. Putting together the ideas in the paragraph might look something like this:

Key transition word *however*

Many people think that Gutenberg's invention of the printing press started the process of mass communication.

BUT it should be realized that many forces were at work long before Gutenberg's time that helped pave the way for his invention.

IN ADDITION, many years had to go by since Gutenberg's time until print culture could really be considered a form of mass communication.

2. Following this brief overview, the author in the second paragraph continues to make a general statement about the history and influence of print. Note that once again the author uses the signal word *however* in the third sentence. Briefly paraphrase the major ideas presented here:

_____

_____

_____

_____

Before getting to the body of the article, the author outlines the points to be discussed. Note that the article is divided into five headings with several subsections in each. Studying this outline can be beneficial both as a prereading and postreading exercise. Previewing the heading gives you a road map that the author will be using. It may also alert you to new or unfamiliar terms or ideas that you will encounter. As a postreading exercise you can review the headings and check your understanding and recall of the key points.

Previewing reveals an outline. An outline reveals key points

3. Another study strategy that students use is to create questions based on the section headings: Look at the first heading: *China:*

The Technological Roots. You might pose the following question: What were the technological roots in China that prepared for the development of printing? or, using some of the subheads, what connections were there between the availability of rag paper and the development of printing?

Creating questions: a strategy for focusing attention

Try to compose questions using the other parts of the outline.

II. Gutenberg _____

III. Print and Modern Thought _____

IV. Print in the U.S. _____

V. Advances in Print Technology_____

China is first at print technology.

4. China: The Technological Roots—The title of this section signals a major idea. The author in the first paragraph of this section explains how events in China prepared for later developments in the evolution of print. In one or two sentences, summarize the author's major point(s).

_____

_____

_____

Before Gutenberg Press: reference to China

In the second paragraph the author shows how the Chinese developed the tools and technology for printing long before the Europeans. The first sentence "Long before the Gutenberg press, Chinese innovations in . . ." mentions the Gutenberg press, but at this point the author hasn't discussed or developed this idea. If, however, you previewed the article and examined his outline, you should have noted that the next major section of the reading will discuss Gutenberg's contribution to the development of printing.

Previewing article lets you see a reference that will be developed.

5. Although the author credits the Chinese with contributing to the early stages of the development of print, he explains why the impact of their work was not widely felt. Specifically, he claims that the impact of print technology was more widely felt in Europe than in China. Explain this point.

_____

_____

China: print technology impact is not great—WHY???

You need to understand that while the Chinese did invent a form of movable type, the complex characters that formed their written language made it too difficult and impractical to implement printing in a widespread manner.

The author states that the Chinese alphabet uses ideograms (characters representing an idea or thing) without expressing the pronunciation of a particular word or words for it.

fire

ice

moon

water

Written Chinese uses ideograms. Each ideogram corresponds to one syllable. Therefore, a one-syllable word in the spoken language would be expressed by one character. A two-syllable word would be depicted with two characters, and so on. Since there are thousands of different syllables in the spoken language, one has to know thousands of printed characters to be literate in Chinese. Gutenberg, on the other hand, worked with the much simpler Western phonetic alphabet.

Print history: the shift from China to Europe and Gutenberg

6. The next section focuses on Johannes Gutenberg and the impact of his work on Western Europe. In paragraph 6 the author writes that certain events paved the way for Gutenberg. That is, for him to succeed, prior conditions had to be in place. Explain how the following factors had an impact on Gutenberg's work. If necessary, reread the sections to make sure you understand the terms and/or consider using your dictionary for unfamiliar terms.

Factors that had an impact on the work of Gutenberg

• The need for rapid and cheap production of written documents

_____

_____

• Rag paper rather than animal-skin vellum and parchment

_____

_____

A list format is common in exposition and signals that more than one factor is involved.

- The commercial demand for books

  _____

  _____

- The work of scribes

  _____

  _____

- The potential for selling indulgences

  _____

  _____

Gutenberg's method of printing—expository writing

7. After presenting the social and economic conditions that helped prepare for printing, the author (in paragraph 7) turns to the technology of printing developed by Gutenberg. Much of this expository writing is similar to that which could be found in a science or technology textbook where the author is explaining a process. In this case the writer is illustrating Gutenberg's process of developing movable type. In your own words, explain Gutenberg's method of developing a printing press:

The writing style of process explanation is similar to science textbook writing.

_____

_____

_____

_____

The impact of print on religion

8. In paragraph 8 the author discusses the impact of printing on religion. At first printing supported the established Roman Catholic Church's goals. Later the spread of religious ideas through print was too difficult to control. New movements, personalities, and texts eventually began to challenge the established Church's authority. Specifically mentioned are the _Protestant Reformation_ and _Martin Luther's theses_. (To have the paragraph make sense, you need to gather some background information. A paperback desktop encyclopedia, a CD-ROM electronic encyclopedia, or an online Internet resource might be helpful.) After consulting one of these sources, discuss both of the references below.

Note references: Protestant Reformation & Martin Luther's theses

Protestant Reformation

_____

Understanding key references to follow author's discussion

Historical references in print history

_____

_____

_____

Martin Luther's theses

_____

_____

_____

_____

9. The next heading, "Print and Modern Thought," and its accompanying four paragraphs continue to explore how printing influenced society. Again the author assumes that his readers are familiar with two general historical events: *the scientific revolution* and the *Renaissance.* For the first event, you might have to look under related terms such as the *history of science* or the *scientific method.* The second term, *Renaissance,* should be easier to locate.

Scientific revolution

_____

Two additional   _____
key terms

_____

_____

Renaissance

_____

_____

_____

_____

10. As you examine this period of time in history, ask yourself: If the term *renaissance* literally means a rebirth or revival, what innovations (a term used by the author) took place, and how did printing further their development?

_____

_____

_____

_____

11. In paragraph 12 the author makes an important general statement about the influence of printing: "Print, along with spoken language, writing and electronic media, is thought of as one of the markers of key historical shifts in communication

Try breaking up this complex sentence into key points.

that attended social and intellectual transformation." Explain this statement. Be sure to compare and contrast print to oral culture and writing. In what ways is it similar and different?

_____

_____

Print in the U.S.

12. In the section labeled "Print in the U.S." the author shows how printing influenced religious and political thought. Give an example to support its influence.

_____

_____

_____

No major print technology developed for many years

13. In paragraph 15 the author says that for several hundred years little changed in the way printing was done. What nineteenth-century technological advances had an impact upon printing?

_____

_____

_____

14. The author refers to Benjamin Day's *New York Sun*'s "penny press" as the first true mass medium. Explain this point.

_____

_____

The Internet and interactive media

15. The concluding two paragraphs found under the heading "Advances in Print Technology" describe current technology such as the Internet and interactive multimedia. Explain the author's concluding statement: "It is difficult to gauge the social and cultural impact of new media without historical distance, but these innovations will most likely prove to signal another major transformation in the use, influence and character of human communication."

Paraphrasing as a measure of understanding

_____

_____

_____

READING JOURNAL

This is the last place we include a Reading Journal reminder in Unit One. Previous journal references occurred after the narrative section and the argument and persuasion article, "Why We Should Read." We intend that the journal assignment be open-ended and encourage you to explore your own reading behavior. The following questions are intended only as suggestions to help you examine some possibilities for journal entries. Comment on what is most helpful for you in your reading and study journey.

- **Content**

  Describe one idea you learned that will be helpful in your further study. Discuss the connections that you see between the two expository articles, "The Proficient Reader" and "History of Printing."

- **Process**

  Analyze your reading of one of the expository articles. Describe the techniques and strategies you used. Did you do anything different in your reading of this work than in your reading of the narratives or argumentative article? Explain. Describe any difficulties you may have had in reading one of the expository articles. What did you do about these problems? Cite an idea or concept that is still confusing to you.

- **Response**

  Expository readings found in textbooks are the most common kind of material you are likely to encounter in college. How do you react to this type of reading as compared to narratives? Explain.

8

A Summer's Reading

BERNARD MALAMUD

Bernard Malamud (1914–1986) was born in Brooklyn, New York. He taught literature at Bennington College in Vermont and was a renowned writer of novels and short stories. Themes of Jewish tradition dominate his writings, and his childhood neighborhood is the setting for many of his works. Malamud's 1966 novel The Fixer *won the Pulitzer Prize and a National Book Award.*

The following short story, "A Summer's Reading," originally appeared in Malamud's first collection of short stories, The Magic Barrel, *which won the National Book Award for fiction in 1958. It describes a young man's attempt to find a better life and relates how reading played a role in this effort.*

GEARING UP

1. How is someone who dropped out of school likely to regard education in general and reading in particular?

2. Sociologists define *significant others* as people who have a major impact on an individual's life. Identify a significant other in your life, and explain the influence this person has had on you.

The Reading

A Summer's Reading

by BERNARD MALAMUD

1   George Stoyonovich was a neighborhood boy who had quit high school on an impulse when he was sixteen, run out of patience, and though he was ashamed every time he went looking for a job, when people asked him if he had finished and he had to say no, he never went back to school. This summer was a hard time for jobs and he had none. Having so much time on his hands, George thought of going to summer school, but the kids in his classes would be too young. He also considered registering in a night high school, only he didn't like the idea of the teachers always telling him what to do. He felt they had not respected him. The result was he stayed off the streets and in his room most of the day. He was close to twenty and had needs with the neighborhood girls, but no money to spend, and he couldn't get more than an occasional few cents because his father was poor, and his sister Sophie, who resembled George, a tall bony girl of twenty-three, earned very little and what she had she kept for herself. Their mother was dead, and Sophie had to take care of the house.

2   Very early in the morning George's father got up to go to work in a fish market. Sophie left about eight for her long ride in the subway to a cafeteria in the Bronx. George had his coffee by himself, then hung around in the house. When the house, a five-room railroad flat above a butcher store, got on his nerves he cleaned it up—mopped the floors with a wet mop and put things away. But most of the time he sat in his room. In the afternoons he listened to the ball game. Otherwise he had a couple of old copies of the *World Almanac* he had bought long ago, and he liked to read in them and also the magazines and newspapers that Sophie brought home, that had been left on the tables in the cafeteria. They were mostly picture magazines about movie

stars and sports figures, also usually the *News* and *Mirror.* Sophie herself read whatever fell into her hands, although she sometimes read good books.

3   She once asked George what he did in his room all day and he said he read a lot too.

4   "Of what besides what I bring home? Do you ever read any worthwhile books?"

5   "Some," George answered, although he really didn't. He had tried to read a book or two that Sophie had in the house but found he was in no mood for them. Lately he couldn't stand made-up stories, they got on his nerves. He wished he had some hobby to work at—as a kid he was good in carpentry, but where could he work at it? Sometimes during the day he went for walks, but mostly he did his walking after the hot sun had gone down and it was cooler in the streets.

6   In the evening after supper George left the house and wandered in the neighborhood. During the sultry days some of the storekeepers and their wives sat in chairs on the thick, broken sidewalks in front of their shops, fanning themselves, and George walked past them and the guys hanging out on the candy store corner. A couple of them he had known his whole life, but nobody recognized each other. He had no place special to go, but generally, saving it till the last, he left the neighborhood and walked for blocks till he came to a darkly lit little park with benches and trees and an iron railing, giving it a feeling of privacy. He sat on a bench there, watching the leafy trees and the flowers blooming on the inside of the railing, thinking of a better life for himself. He thought of the jobs he had had since he had quit school—delivery boy, stock clerk, runner, lately working in a factory—and he was dissatisfied with all of them. He felt he would someday like to have a good job and live in a private house with a porch, on a street with trees. He wanted to have some dough in his pocket to buy things with, and a girl to go with, so as not to be so lonely, especially on Saturday nights. He wanted people to like and respect him. He thought about these things often but mostly when he was alone at night. Around midnight he got up and drifted back to his hot and stony neighborhood.

7   One time while on his walk George met Mr. Cattanzara coming home very late from work. He wondered if he was drunk but then could tell he wasn't. Mr. Cattanzara, a stocky, bald-headed man who worked in a change booth on an IRT station, lived on the next block after George's, above a shoe repair store. Nights, during the hot weather, he sat on his stoop in an undershirt, reading the *New York Times* in the light of the shoemaker's window. He read it from the first page to the last, then went up to sleep. And all the time he was reading the paper, his wife, a fat woman with a white face, leaned out of the window, gazing into the street, her thick white arms folded under her loose breast, on the window ledge.

8   Once in a while Mr. Cattanzara came home drunk, but it was a quiet drunk. He never made any trouble, only walked stiffly up the street and slowly climbed the stairs into the hall. Though drunk, he looked the same as always, except for his tight walk, the quietness, and that his eyes were wet. George liked Mr. Cattanzara because he remembered him giving him nick-

els to buy lemon ice with when he was a squirt. Mr. Cattanzara was a different type than those in the neighborhood. He asked different questions than the others when he met you, and he seemed to know what went on in all the newspapers. He read them, as his fat sick wife watched from the window.

9   "What are you doing with yourself this summer, George?" Mr. Cattanzara asked. "I see you walkin' around at nights."

10   George felt embarrassed. "I like to walk."

11   "What are you doin' in the day now?"

12   "Nothing much just now. I'm waiting for a job." Since it shamed him to admit he wasn't working, George said, "I'm staying home—but I'm reading a lot to pick up my education."

13   Mr. Cattanzara looked interested. He mopped his hot face with a red handkerchief.

14   "What are you readin'?"

15   George hesitated, then said, "I got a list of books in the library once, and now I'm gonna read them this summer." He felt strange and a little unhappy saying this, but he wanted Mr. Cattanzara to respect him.

16   "How many books are there on it?"

17   "I never counted them. Maybe around a hundred."

18   Mr. Cattanzara whistled through his teeth.

19   "I figure if I did that," George went on earnestly, "it would help me in my education. I don't mean the kind they give you in high school. I want to know different things than they learn there, if you know what I mean."

20   The change maker nodded. "Still and all, one hundred books is a pretty big load for one summer."

21   "It might take longer."

22   "After you're finished with some, maybe you and I can shoot the breeze about them?" said Mr. Cattanzara.

23   "When I'm finished," George answered.

24   Mr. Cattanzara went home and George continued on his walk. After that, though he had the urge to, George did nothing different from usual. He still took his walks at night, ending up in the little park. But one evening the shoemaker on the next block stopped George to say he was a good boy, and George figured that Mr. Cattanzara had told him all about the books he was reading. From the shoemaker it must have gone down the street, because George saw a couple of people smiling kindly at him, though nobody spoke to him personally. He felt a little better around the neighborhood and liked it more, though not so much he would want to live in it forever. He had never exactly disliked the people in it, yet he had never liked them very much either. It was the fault of the neighborhood. To his surprise, George found out that his father and Sophie knew about his reading too. His father was too shy to say anything about it—he was never much of a talker in his whole life—but Sophie was softer to George, and she showed him in other ways she was proud of him.

25   As the summer went on George felt in a good mood about things. He cleaned the house every day, as a favor to Sophie, and he enjoyed the ball games more. Sophie gave him a buck a week allowance, and though it still

wasn't enough and he had to use it carefully, it was a helluva lot better than just having two bits now and then. What he bought with the money—cigarettes mostly, an occasional beer or movie ticket—he got a big kick out of. Life wasn't so bad if you knew how to appreciate it. Occasionally he bought a paperback book from the news-stand, but he never got around to reading it, though he was glad to have a couple of books in his room. But he read thoroughly Sophie's magazines and newspapers. And at night was the most enjoyable time, because when he passed the storekeepers sitting outside their stores, he could tell they regarded him highly. He walked erect, and though he did not say much to them, or they to him, he could feel approval on all sides. A couple of nights he felt so good that he skipped the park at the end of the evening. He just wandered in the neighborhood, where people had known him from the time he was a kid playing punchball whenever there was a game of it going; he wandered there, then came home and got undressed for bed, feeling fine.

26   For a few weeks he had talked only once with Mr. Cattanzara, and though the change maker had said nothing more about the books, asked no questions, his silence made George a little uneasy. For a while George didn't pass in front of Mr. Cattanzara's house anymore, until one night, forgetting himself, he approached it from a different direction than he usually did when he did. It was already past midnight. The street, except for one or two people, was deserted, and George was surprised when he saw Mr. Cattanzara still reading his newspaper by the light of the street lamp overhead. His impulse was to stop at the stoop and talk to him. He wasn't sure what he wanted to say, though he felt the words would come when he began to talk; but the more he thought about it, the more the idea scared him, and he decided he'd better not. He even considered beating it home by another street, but he was too near Mr. Cattanzara, and the change maker might see him as he ran, and get annoyed. So George unobtrusively crossed the street, trying to make it seem as if he had to look in a store window on the other side, which he did, and then went on, uncomfortable at what he was doing. He feared Mr. Cattanzara would glance up from his paper and call him a dirty rat for walking on the other side of the street, but all he did was sit there, sweating through his undershirt, his bald head shining in the dim light as he read his *Times,* and upstairs his fat wife leaned out of the window, seeming to read the paper along with him. George thought she would spy him and yell out to Mr. Cattanzara, but she never moved her eyes off her husband.

27   George made up his mind to stay away from the change maker until he had got some of his softback books read, but when he started them and saw they were mostly story books, he lost his interest and didn't bother to finish them. He lost his interest in reading other things too. Sophie's magazines and newspapers went unread. She saw them piling up on a chair in his room and asked why he was no longer looking at them, and George told her it was because of all the other reading he had to do. Sophie said she had guessed that was it. So for most of the day, George had the radio on, turning to music when he was sick of the human voice. He kept the house fairly neat, and Sophie said nothing on the days when he neglected it. She was still kind and

gave him his extra buck, though things weren't so good for him as they had been before.

28   But they were good enough, considering. Also his night walk invariably picked him up, no matter how bad the day was. Then one night George saw Mr. Cattanzara coming down the street toward him. George was about to turn and run but he recognized from Mr. Cattanzara's walk that he was drunk, and if so, probably he would not even bother to notice him. So George kept on walking straight ahead until he came abreast of Mr. Cattanzara and though he felt wound up enough to pop into the sky, he was not surprised when Mr. Cattanzara passed him without a word, walking slowly, his face and body stiff. George drew a breath in relief at his narrow escape, when he heard his name called, and there stood Mr. Cattanzara at his elbow, smelling like the inside of a beer barrel. His eyes were sad as he gazed at George, and George felt so intensely uncomfortable he was tempted to shove the drunk aside and continue on his walk.

29   But he couldn't act that way to him, and, besides, Mr. Cattanzara took a nickel out his pants pocket and handed it to him.

30   "Go buy yourself a lemon ice, Georgie."

31   "It's not that time anymore, Mr. Cattanzara," George said, "I am a big guy now."

32   "No, you ain't," said Mr. Cattanzara, to which George made no reply he could think of.

33   "How are all your books comin' along now?" Mr. Cattanzara asked. Though he tried to stand steady, he swayed a little.

34   "Fine, I guess," said George, feeling the red crawling up his face.

35   "You ain't sure?" The change maker smiled slyly, a way George had never seen him smile.

36   "Sure I'm sure. They're fine."

37   Though his head swayed in little arcs, Mr. Cattanzara's eyes were steady. He had small blue eyes which could hurt if you looked at them too long.

38   "George," he said, "name me one book on that list that you read this summer, and I will drink to your health."

39   "I don't want anybody drinking to me."

40   "Name me one so I can ask you a question on it. Who can tell, if it's a good book maybe I might wanna read it myself."

41   George knew he looked passable on the outside, but inside he was crumbling apart.

42   Unable to reply, he shut his eyes, but when—years later—he opened them, he saw that Mr. Cattanzara had, out of pity, gone away, but in his ears he still heard the words he had said when he left: "George, don't do what I did."

43   The next night he was afraid to leave his room, and though Sophie argued with him he wouldn't open the door.

44   "What are you doing in there?" she asked.

45   "Nothing."

46   "Aren't you reading?"

47   "No."

48   She was silent a minute, then asked, "Where do you keep the books you read? I never see any in your room outside of a few cheap trashy ones."

49   He wouldn't tell her.

50   "In that case you're not worth a buck of my hard-earned money. Why should I break my back for you? Go on out, you bum, and get a job."

51   He stayed in his room for almost a week, except to sneak into the kitchen when nobody was home. Sophie railed at him, then begged him to come out, and his old father wept, but George wouldn't budge, though the weather was terrible and his small room stifling. He found it very hard to breathe, each breath was like drawing a flame into his lungs.

52   One night, unable to stand the heat anymore, he burst into the street at one A.M., a shadow of himself. He hoped to sneak to the park without being seen, but there were people all over the block, wilted and listless, waiting for a breeze. George lowered his eyes and walked, in disgrace, away from them, but before long he discovered they were still friendly to him. He figured Mr. Cattanzara hadn't told on him. Maybe when he woke up out of his drunk the next morning, he had forgotten all about meeting George. George felt his confidence slowly come back to him.

53   That same night a man on a street corner asked him if it was true that he had finished reading so many books, and George admitted he had. The man said it was a wonderful thing for a boy his age to read so much.

54   "Yeah," George said, but he felt relieved. He hoped nobody would mention the books anymore, and when, after a couple of days, he accidentally met Mr. Cattanzara again, *he* didn't, though George had the idea he was the one who started the rumor that he had finished all the books.

55   One evening in the fall, George ran out of his house to the library, where he hadn't been in years. There were books all over the place, wherever he looked, and though he was struggling to control an inward trembling, he easily counted off a hundred, then sat down at a table to read.

QUESTIONS

1. In one paragraph, summarize the plot of the story.

2. How does George feel about himself?

3. What is George's attitude toward reading?

4. Describe George's feelings about Mr. Cattanzara.

5. Discuss the moral, or lesson, of the story. What does the story teach you?

✦ **NOTE**   A technology connection comes at the end of each of the four units. We think that there are obvious connections between technology issues and the themes of *The Proficient Reader.* Each technology connection article is accompanied by Gearing Up and comprehension questions. Marked copies, process guides, target vocabulary, and other exercises are not included. ✦

 ## THE TECHNOLOGY CONNECTION

Technology has enabled humans to develop the tools and implements that promote reading and writing. The development of writing devices, parchment, paper, and later the printing press greatly affected the spread of literacy. More recently, computer-related technology such as word processors, desktop publishing programs, CD-ROMs, e-mail programs, and the Internet has continued to influence our reading and writing habits. Can the traditional book—like the one you are reading now—survive in our digital age? The following essay provides one view on this issue.

In His Book, The Printed Word Will Live On

MARY PURPURA and PAOLO PONTONIERE

Mary Purpura and Paolo Pontoniere are freelance writers from California who frequently contribute to the Los Angeles Times. *This is an interview with Geoffrey Nunberg on the future of the book.*

GEARING UP

1. Compare and contrast reading text in a book versus reading text on a computer.

2. Some people feel that electronic forms of text will replace the more traditional printed page. Explain your position on this issue.

Introduction

For years now, the popularity of computers and the Internet and other computer networks has fueled speculation about the future of the printed word. Pundits ponder whether newspapers, magazines, and books as we know them can survive beside their online counterparts.

A conference organized by Italian author Umberto Eco and Stanford University linguistics professor Geoffrey Nunberg in July 1994 at the University of San Marino in San Marino, Italy, sought to address this concern head-on by exploring the future of the book and reading. The conference proceedings generated the appropriately titled *The Future of the Book* (University of California Press, $14.95), which contains eleven essays from conference participants, as well as an afterword by Eco and an introduction by Nunberg, the book's editor.

The *Times* talked to Nunberg—who, in addition to teaching, works as principal scientist at the Xerox Palo Alto Research Center—about the recently published collection and his own views on the book's future.

The Reading

In His Book, The Printed Word Will Live On

Interview with GEOFFREY NUNBERG

Q: Has writing become trivialized since the introduction of the Net? That is, has it become more of a daily chore and less a reflection of a writer's soul?
A: No. One of the things about the technology that's interesting, and that Umberto Eco also points out in his afterword to this collection, is that the computer really does create a new environment for writing. We're actually in a world where the written word has more importance than ever before—even replacing many of the conversations that used to take place over the phone with written conversations via e-mail.

One thing that's striking is the degree to which people have had to re-learn the conventions of letter writing that were very familiar in the 19th century, when a major city like London might have as many as five mail deliveries each day and people thought nothing of writing 15 letters a day.

Q: Do you think the new technology affects the way writers express themselves?
A: In a certain sense, yes. You certainly read articles in print now and you say to yourself, "This was sent in by e-mail." You can just tell because there's a loose quality to the prose, and, at times, there's no connection between the opening sentence of the article and the following paragraphs.

On the other hand, when you go to the Web, you can see that a new form of writing is emerging there. It's very pert; it's very casual and informal; it's very brief. It's a sort of writing that's almost too ephemeral for print. But on the Web it works very well. In fact, it works better than attempts to move the traditional writing forms like the novel or the class print magazine onto the Web wholesale.

Q: Is this a transitional moment for the book, caught between old printing methods and new, digitized ways of recording information?
A: There's been so much concentration on the emergence of the digital media that people may tend to neglect the enormous importance of these technologies for the book itself, particularly for the sorts of publishing that have been relatively marginal in an economic sense but that bear a lot of the re-

sponsibility for print culture—literature, works of translation, poetry and small press and university press books.

Works of that sort are much easier to publish now than they used to be. That's partly because of digital printing, which eliminates the economies of scale that are associated with offset printing; partly because it's now possible to distribute books like that electronically and print them wherever they're wanted—in a bookstore or a library, for example—and partly because the Web itself makes available an apparatus of publicity.

You never really know what the essence of a medium is until it's in danger of being supplanted. In a certain sense, it wasn't until the introduction of photography that we knew what painting was about.

In the same way, I think we're beginning to learn what's essential to the book as a kind of presentation. We already know, for example, that many of the things that have been printed in book form really have no essential reason to live in that form. Directors and parts catalogs, even encyclopedias, are much more efficient when you put them online. On the other hand, other kinds of books—the novel, history, critical writing and, to my mind, the dictionary, can't be transformed to an electronic life without losing part of their essence.

Q: What do you think about the efforts of the MIT Media Lab and others to produce books that are made of super-thin, waterproof, flexible, electronic displays?

A: The idea is to create something essentially like paper that can bear a charge and display characters. My sense is that there are a lot of applications for which that kind of book would be very useful. But I think again, it's something that highlights certain properties of the traditional book that that sort of book wouldn't have.

For example, when you read an ordinary bound-paper book, you have a sense of where you are in the text according to the distance between your thumb and forefinger. If it's electronic paper, you only have a few pages.

That's a wonderful advantage if you're traveling on an airplane and you want to take 15 novels with you. But typically, when you're reading a novel, you want to have this sense of moving from the first page of the book to the last. You want to have an almost subconscious sense of your place in the narrative according to the relative weight of the pages to the left and to the right.

That's a crucial element of traditional reading that neither electronic paper nor an electronic screen can provide. This is not to say that we can't have books in both forms. For instance, I want to have a copy of all of Jane Austen's works online, so I can annotate them, or so I can efficiently search for a particular scene. But when it comes to sitting down and reading a Jane Austen novel from beginning to end, I want to have it in paper form.

You often hear it said that the book will vanish and be replaced by the screen. But it's very rare that one technology wholly supersedes another. New possibilities for expression emerge with a new medium, but I don't think there's anything wrong with the traditional book.

QUESTIONS

1. Summarize Nunberg's position regarding the future of the book.

2. Describe how technology has affected and is affecting written communication.

3. According to Professor Nunberg, how might technology promote reading and literacy?

MAKING CONNECTIONS

Reading and Literacy

1. The following passage by Holbrook Jackson appeared on page 3: "The time to read is any time: no apparatus, no appointment of time and place, is necessary. It is the only art which can be practiced at any hour of the day and night, whenever the time and inclination comes, that is your time for reading; in joy or sorrow, health or illness." Relate this quotation to Douglass, Keller, Malcolm X, and Nowell. Speculate on their possible responses; that is, write at least one sentence of reaction for each. Be sure to consider their circumstances.

2. Compare and contrast Helen Keller's attitude toward reading with that of George Stoyonovich in "A Summer's Reading."

3. Douglass, Keller, and Malcolm X all had different experiences in learning to read, but their literacy development had some similar characteristics. Compare and contrast their experiences.

4. In "The Proficient Reader" article, the authors state: "Reading . . . is more than a mechanical process of moving your eyes across the page. Reading involves mentally processing printed information in a meaningful way" (page 80). Apply this statement to the reading processes of Douglass, Keller, and Malcolm X.

5. In "A Summer's Reading," Mr. Cattanzara plays the role of the "significant other," the individual who motivates George to pursue reading. Identify an individual who played a similar role in the lives of Douglass, Keller, and Malcolm X. Then explain how that person fostered literacy development in the writer's life.

6. In the second excerpt from his autobiography, Douglass further develops his method of learning to read and discusses the consequences of his actions. Discuss the new information he presents in the second excerpt. Explain how it helps you understand Douglass's reading development.

7. If Douglass, Keller, Malcolm X, and Nowell had kept reading journals, what might a typical entry have been for each of them?

8. In his essay, Nowell explains what reading has meant for him during his lifetime. Imagine that Douglass, Keller, and Malcolm X read his essay. Discuss their probable reactions to his statements.

9. In the section titled "Print in the U.S." the "History of Printing" article states: "The printing press quickly became central to political and religious expression in the New World." Relate this statement to the lives of Douglass and Malcolm X.

10. Speculate how the lives of Douglass, Keller, Malcolm X, and Nowell might have been affected had the printing press never been developed.

11. Twentieth-century historian Barbara Tuchman once remarked:

    Without books, history is silent, literature dumb, science crippled, thought and speculation at a standstill. Without books, the development of civilization would have been impossible. They are engines of change, windows on the world, and "lighthouses erected in the sea of time." They are companions, teachers, magicians, bankers of the treasures of the mind. Books are humanity in print.

    How might Douglass, Keller, Malcolm X, and Nowell have reacted to these statements? Explain.

12. "The Proficient Reader" reports on the impact of the written word. "History of Printing" reports on the use of technology to spread the written word. State and analyze the central thesis in both of these articles and discuss the connections between these ideas.

13. The printed word has taken many forms throughout history, from hand-written letters through electronic displays on computer screens. The articles "History of Printing" and "In His Book, The Printed Word Will Live On" both reflect on the impact of these changes on communication styles. Compare and contrast the remarks of both authors.

LIBRARY ASSIGNMENT

The Week I Was Born

This library assignment will get you to use reading to gather information about your life and to make connections between your world of today and the world into which you were born. In this assignment, you will study both current issues of the *New York Times* (or another well-respected newspaper) and back issues containing news from your first week of life. To get the back issues, use a library that has newspapers available on microfilm (a special film on which the newspaper is photographed in reduced size). Many larger libraries have the *New York Times* and other major dailies in their microfilm collection.

It is relatively easy to find the content of many current daily newspapers on the Internet. However, at the time of this writing, it is difficult and expensive to locate a complete version of a newspaper from the time of your birth. Microfilm still provides the best solution to this task.

As you read both sets of newspapers, notice the changes that have taken place in your lifetime. At the same time, note what appears to have remained the same. To get a sense of what was happening during the week you have chosen, begin your research using the Sunday edition of the *New York Times.* The Sunday paper has a section titled "The Week in Review" that summarizes major events of the preceding week.

Start reading the daily newspapers from the Sunday on or before your selected date through the following Sunday. Begin with Sunday's "News of the Week in Review" to get an overview of the time period, and then explore the rest of the Sunday paper. Continue this procedure for the Monday through the following Sunday newspapers. If you need additional information, consult a weekly newsmagazine such as *Time, Newsweek,* or *U.S. News & World Report.* These may be available in print, on microfilm, or on CD-ROM. Again, many of these publications are available on the Internet, but at the present time archived issues are typically not available without a fee. You will need to take notes on your reading. Also, make photocopies of any pages that will help clarify your report.

To focus your research, study the questions that follow. These are the specific areas you will be looking for. You may find it helpful to take brief notes numbered to correspond with the numbered questions. Conduct your search so that you can write a complete answer for each of the questions. Several questions offer suggestions to help you. Respond in complete sentences and proofread your responses.

QUESTIONS

1. Note clothing styles as shown in pictures and advertisements. Compare the styles popular earlier to today's fashions. In what ways are they different and/or similar? *Hint:* Clothing styles vary with the season of the year. If you were born in a month that does not fall in the same season as the month in which you are doing this assignment, you can use issues from the same season when comparing clothing styles.

2. Describe the weather on the day you were born. What phase was the moon in? Try to determine the temperature and humidity at the hour of your birth.

3. What major events took place during the week you were born? Divide your answer into events that took place locally (in your metropolitan area), nationally (in the United States), and internationally (throughout the world). Next, do the same for the major events that occurred in the current week. How did the events from the past differ from those that occurred recently? How were they similar?

4. Identify some leaders of government—at the local, national, and international levels—during the week you were born. Are any of these people living today? If so, what are they doing? *Hint:* In addition to news stories, you may have to check some other reference sources (e.g., *Who's Who*) or a CD-ROM version of a popular encyclopedia to determine what has happened to the people who were leaders at the time of your birth.

5. Study some newspaper articles about current technology (e.g., cellular telephones, laser disks, laptop computers). What were some examples of "new" technology at the time of your birth? Pay particular attention to advertisements. *Hint:* Keep a list of products that you come across during your search. The Sunday paper usually has more advertisements than the daily edition. If you find it difficult to locate enough advertisements to study, consider looking at newspapers published before Christmas, since many ads appear at this time of year.

6. Look at the sports sections. How have the sports that were played on your birthday changed? How do players' salaries compare? How have league rules changed? What teams now play in different cities? How did your favorite team do on the date of your birth? *Hint:* As in question 1, compare newspapers from the same season.

7. Study the employment sections and locate a job or profession that interests you. How have salaries, working conditions, and educational requirements for that position changed over the years? What listings in the current newspaper didn't exist on the day of your birth? What job opportunities are now available for both men and women that traditionally were open to only one or the other?

8. Compare the advertisements that appeared on your birth date with those you see today. How have product and service offerings changed? How can you account for the changes you observe?

9. Examine the movie, television, and radio sections of the newspapers.
    a. What movies were featured on your birthday? Who were the popular stars, and what has become of them? (Consider using an Internet movie database or CD-ROM encyclopedias to help you.) What differences do you note between the types of movies shown today and the movies shown on the date of your birth?
    b. Which television and radio programs, if any, have remained on the air throughout your lifetime? How do you account for their continuing popularity? What kinds of TV and radio programs were featured during "prime time" (news, sports, variety, adventure, mystery)? How do they compare with today's programs?

10. Select a neighborhood in the real estate section, and go house or apartment hunting. Choose a similar type of dwelling in the same neighborhood, and compare prices and features available then and today. What conclusions do you reach?

If there is a particular question that you cannot answer, try to create one of your own after studying the newspaper. For example, one student created and then answered the following question: "What features do today's newspapers contain that did not exist on the day you were born? What features from the past have disappeared? How do you explain these changes?" Another student created the following question based on the Internet version of the *New York Times:* "How can the Internet version of the newspaper be compared to its traditional printed version? What are the benefits and drawbacks of each?"

Here are some other points to keep in mind:

- Write complete sentences and proofread your work.

- Develop your ideas, especially when you are asked to compare and contrast.

- You may want to photocopy parts of the newspaper to illustrate your ideas.

After you finish answering the questions, write a concluding section to your paper in which you summarize your overall conclusions about how things are similar to or different from the day you were born.

UNIT

TWO

Work and Careers

READINGS IN UNIT TWO

1. "McDonald's—We Do It All for You" by Barbara Garson

Garson interviews McDonald's employees about their work and what it means to them.

2. "So You Want to Be a Physician/ Ophthalmologist"

An ophthalmologist discusses her work.

3. "Solving the Job Puzzle" by Anne W. Clymer and Elizabeth McGregor

Clymer and McGregor examine factors that need to be considered when exploring career options.

4. "Tomorrow's Jobs" from the *Occupational Outlook Handbook*

This chapter highlights Bureau of Labor Statistics projections of industry and occupational employment and labor trends that are designed to help guide career plans.

5. "Looking for Work in All the Right Places" by Robert Lewis

Lewis shows how the Internet is changing the way job seekers, employees, and recruiters are addressing employment needs.

6. "Work to Make the World Work Better" by James Michener

Michener examines changing work values and suggests a new orientation to our work ethic.

7. "How It Feels to Be Out of Work" by Jan Halvorsen

Halvorsen speaks from personal experience about the devastation of being "let go" from a job.

8. "The Day the Mommies Went Home" by Anita Shreve

Shreve delivers a tongue-in-cheek description of the impact of women leaving the work force en masse.

9. "Managing Workforce Diversity in Organizations" by Ricky Griffin

Griffin explores the nature of workforce diversity and examines its impact on organizations.

10. "The Day's Work" by Barbara Holland

Why would a full-time mother and homemaker seek to work outside the home? This short story shows the meaning and challenges of work.

11. "Change and the Transformation of Work" from *Job Shift: How to Prosper in a Workplace Without Jobs* by William Bridges

Bridges examines how technology is affecting the work world.

INTRODUCTION

Most people need to work a large portion of their lives. The average person spends more of his or her life working at a job than in any other activity, except sleeping. How work is regarded, however, depends on the individual. Some people view work as the most important part of their lives, an activity from which they derive identity and great satisfaction. They may even regard family, friends, and recreation as secondary. For many other people, work is a means of survival only, or a way to earn money for things they need and want.

A Brief History of Work in America

In the United States, work historically had a different meaning for most people than it does today. People did not always expect work to be fulfilling and rewarding; they looked to their families and religious worship for satisfaction. Today, partly because of the decline of religious influence and the different role the family plays, many people expect both economic security and personal satisfaction from work. However, this desire may be frustrated by difficult conditions in the work world, such as unemployment cycles or the rapid changes brought about by technology.

In preindustrial America (the 1600s and 1700s), work was largely a matter of survival. People worked long hours, often from sunup to sundown. Almost 90 percent of the 4 million colonists were farmers (compared to the current figure of approximately 2 percent). Indentured servants usually were bound to labor for a period of five to seven years, often in return for their passage to the colonies. Slaves, on the other hand, were forced by those in power to work against their will for nothing.

Farmers did more than plant crops. Farmers and members of their families often had to hunt, fish, and build. Farm women commonly spun thread for wool, wove cloth, made soap and candles, and preserved meat, among other labor-intensive chores. Other colonists worked in occupations that required detailed skills such as carpentry, weaving, fishing, blacksmithing, shoemaking, and shipbuilding. Individual craftspeople took pride in the handmade objects they produced, objects that were often both useful and beautiful.

The development of the factory system in the 1800s changed the nature of work for much of the population. Men and women worked less at home and more in depersonalized surroundings, often doing repetitive tasks twelve or more hours a day, six days a week. By 1900, ours was an industrial society, with two out of five workers engaged in factory work. At the same time, the role of agriculture began to diminish as more people moved to cities seeking newly created jobs. Working on an assembly line did not demand specialized skills, nor did it require literacy. Because most jobs on a factory assembly line were broken down into simple operations, newly hired workers could be trained in a relatively short time. Workers were essentially interchangeable.

Work Today

As we move toward the twenty-first century, we are witnessing a shift in that factory workers are being replaced by what management expert Peter Drucker has termed "knowledge workers" whose positions require more sophisticated thinking skills, creativity, and a grasp of technology. Our postindustrial society needs fewer and fewer individuals to produce manufactured goods. Agricultural labor plays only a small role in our economy, and jobs that are purely mechanical in nature are rapidly disappearing. Our economy has shifted from producing goods to providing services. "Work," according to writer and consultant Price Prichett, "is becoming less physical and more mental . . . we do less with our hands and more with our heads." More and more, jobs can be done equally by men and women.

Today, having skills in a certain area no longer guarantees a job. Technology is changing the nature of work and employment and creating new opportunities and challenges unforeseen twenty-five years ago. Hospital workers now run tests that were once conducted by doctors, and truck drivers use computers to manage the delivery of goods. Unskilled workers are increasingly being displaced by automation, and technology will make certain jobs obsolete. Technology has progressed to such a point that even some people who have advanced skills and training are facing unemployment or underemployment. The job market is a challenge. Certain industries are contracting while others are expanding. We can probably expect to witness changing employment cycles and the creation of new and stimulating jobs brought about by technology. As the twentieth century comes to a close, we see women, older persons, and minority group members entering the job market in greater numbers. The workplace is becoming increasingly diverse. But experts also state that, after a period of improvement, circumstances could worsen again. During the last decade many workers have experienced the effects of downsizing in the form of layoffs and an increase in job insecurity as evidenced in the decline of health and pension benefits. Unlike their parents, today's workers cannot assume that they will keep their same job for life. In his monumental book *Future Shock*, Alvin Toffler argues that we must all be prepared to face the possibility of changing careers two or three times during our lives.

Career Planning

Despite these sobering facts, jobs are still available, and many new ones are constantly being created. One need only pick up the Sunday employment section of a major metropolitan newspaper to see this. But with people unemployed, why are so many job openings advertised? If you read the ads, you will quickly discover the answer: Most good jobs require considerable technical training. Many employers lament the fact that the supply of skilled workers is not keeping up with the demand. One challenge for today's workers is to keep abreast of technology, improve their education levels, and not let their skills become outdated.

These realities of today's job market make a very strong statement to students: The need to make informed decisions is crucial, and careful career planning is essential. In fact, career planning has become a field in itself, with professionals trained to help people plan their work future. Career planning requires the prospective job hunter to plan not only for the immediate future but also for his or her lifetime.

What You Can Expect in This Unit

This unit presents a variety of articles that examine issues related to work. Topics range from people's specific experiences in the work world, to how to begin researching and planning a career, to the larger meaning and role of work in our lives. The information you will find in these readings will help you formulate your own career plan.

After completing this unit, you should be able to do the following:

Content

- Describe the meaning of work as interpreted by various individuals
- Recognize the connection between education and literacy and success in the workplace
- Understand the changing nature of work

Process

- Collect and connect ideas within a unit and across units
- Evaluate and analyze information from diverse sources
- Synthesize ideas from various sources

Strategies

- Evaluate qualifications and sources
- Interpret graphs
- Analyze satire
- Determine an author's purpose
- Judge an essay's evidence
- Read argument and persuasion

Connecting Themes

In Unit One, Reading and Literacy, you were asked to make connections among the articles. You saw that you could use certain ideas—motivation and effort, the power of reading, and the process of reading—as frameworks for understanding and connecting many of the selections. When you completed the chart on page 30, in which you organized information about how the writers of the articles learned to read, you saw that the various reading selections addressed many of the same broad issues. In your personal and professional lives, you will often need to put information together from various sources. Doing so will allow you to understand and remember more. Not only can you relate ideas and make connections within one theme, such as literacy; you can also take ideas from the literacy unit and relate them to the unit on work. Several observations and questions follow to help guide your thinking as you read the selections in Unit Two.

COMPETENCY

One critical issue in the world of work is competency. To be *competent* in something means that you have the skill to do a particular task. Unfortunately, many Americans lack even minimum competency in reading, even though our technological age demands a great deal more than basic reading skills. What is the relationship between one's ability to read and one's job competency? Suppose you are an employer about to hire workers. What would happen if your staff consisted of only minimally competent readers? How would this affect your business? As a worker, how would you improve your reading ability?

THE ROLE OF EFFORT

In Unit One, you saw the importance of determination and effort in learning to read. The narratives by Frederick Douglass, Helen Keller, and Malcolm X—all individuals who valued reading—demonstrate that people with clear objectives and commitment can achieve their goals. What connection do you see between their efforts and those needed to build a career? What role do determination and effort play in a person's job? How clear must a person's goals be before she or he selects a particular career? Think about these questions and those in the preceding section as you begin studying Unit Two.

WORK AND CAREERS: A CONNECTING EXERCISE

You may already know the field you wish to enter, or you may be undecided. In any event, you probably have some definite ideas about what you hope to gain from your work. Do you want to work with people? Is money of primary importance? Do you prefer a steady, secure job or one that involves greater risks and possibly greater rewards?

Before you begin this unit, think about what you want to get out of work. Then, as you read the various articles, compare your goals with those that motivated the writers in their work lives. Even if the selection is not a narrative and does not include central characters, it may address the issue of work.

When you have finished the unit, consider what people want from their work. Note whether or not your own feelings and thoughts have changed in any way after studying this unit.

McDonald's—We Do It All for You

BARBARA GARSON

In addition to her book about work, The Electronic Sweatshop, *from which this excerpt is taken, Barbara Garson has written another text on labor,* All the Live-long Day. *She has also written several plays, including* MacBird!, Security, *and* The Dinosaur Door. *For her nonfiction, journalism, and playwriting, she was awarded a Guggenheim Fellowship, a National Endowment for the Arts Fellowship, and a National Press Club Citation.*

GEARING UP

1. What associations and memories come to mind when you hear the company name *McDonald's*? How did you form these impressions?

2. Based on your experiences with fast food restaurants—as a customer, worker, or both—describe the work environment and various tasks. Rate the fast food restaurant as a place to work.

READING STRATEGY

FRAMING AN ANSWER II

The Framing an Answer strategy was introduced in Unit One in relation to the Helen Keller article. Producing appropriate, accurate answers is crucial for academic success. As was pointed out then, constructing answers is a multipart process that includes the following steps:

1. Understanding the question (cue word and other key terms)

2. Rereading the text and/or searching your mind for related ideas

3. Selecting the relevant information and recreating it in your mind

4. Constructing the answer (paraphrasing, summarizing)

5. Editing your response (accuracy, grammar, mechanics, transitions)

Application

The McDonald's article is followed by a series of questions. The first question is "Discuss the positive and negative aspects of working at McDonald's according to the employees interviewed by the author." The following discussion is an effort to model the framing strategy in response to this question.

1. The first step is to make sure that you understand what is being asked. This includes taking note of the cue word, *discuss. Discuss* means to comment on, to talk about. What you are discussing is both the positive and negative aspects and so two parts are necessary to the discussion. Also note that you are limited to the views of the people interviewed by the author. Your opinion is not appropriate in this case even if you have information that contradicts what is reported.

2. The second step is rereading the text and/or searching your mind for related ideas. Although you are asked to report on what is stated in the text, you might well be guided by what you know from your experience. You have a preexisting frame of reference for work (see "The Proficient Reader" article for further discussion here) and are to note whether the McDonald's workers fit your general model. For example, the following list might apply to people holding jobs.

Positive Job Aspects	Negative Job Aspects
Pleasant working environment	Unpleasant working environment
Opportunity for challenge	Repetitious, routine tasks
Feeling of public service	Little or no contact with people
Sufficient pay	Inadequate pay

Each job potentially has certain pluses and minuses. If you randomly polled 1,000 McDonald's workers, you could no doubt come up with a list of positives and negatives that specifically apply to working at McDonald's. However, you are not asked to do this. You are to report on what specific workers have to say. Your pre-existing knowledge about work may help you understand why the four workers feel as they do.

3. The third step is selecting the relevant information. From your reading of the text, you pick out the information that relates to the question. In your second, careful reading you may find it helpful to underline the appropriate material and put the question number by it for quick reference. Making plus (+) and minus (−) signs next to your underlining will also help you keep track of which aspects of the job (the positive or negative) you have identified. You might also list the positives and negatives in two columns.

4. *The fourth step is constructing the answer (paraphrasing, summarizing).*
Instructors are interested in responses that are filtered through your own perspective and language. So avoid copying a text unless you are copying for a specific reason, like quoting a source to support a point. Instead, while aiming to retain the essentials of the author's message, try paraphrasing the text or putting the author's ideas in your own words.

A second concern is that you are selective in what you report: strive to summarize or condense the author's ideas. When textbook authors present information, they tend to include more than the basic message in order to give as full a picture as possible. Thus particularly troublesome concepts may be accompanied by a series of clarifying examples. All of these explanatory examples would not be reported in a summary.

To begin to answer the question the situation (an interview) is specified. Then the question is paraphrased as an introduction. A sample answer structure follows:

Begin by rephrasing the question as a lead-in.

"In this interview, a McDonald's worker stated that she liked these two things about her job [paraphrase of worker's statements]. She felt this way because [paraphrase of reasons]. However, she found these two things to be distressing [paraphrase of the negative job features]. She felt this way because [paraphrase of reasons]."

5. *The last step is editing your response for accuracy, grammar, mechanics, and transitions.*   Once you have constructed your answer, carefully proofread it and make corrections. The following questions should be useful in the proofing stage:

Accuracy

1. Does my statement reflect the ideas of the author?

2. Have I added anything that is not found in the text?

3. Have I changed the tone of the author's message through my presentation of it?

4. Have I omitted a key idea that alters the author's ideas or point of view?

Grammar

1. Have I written a complete thought that has a subject and a verb?

2. Is there agreement between my subject and verb?

3. Are irregular verbs correct?

4. Have I been consistent about tense?

Mechanics

1. Are all the words spelled correctly?

2. Does every sentence end with a punctuation mark?

3. Are possessives marked by an apostrophe correctly?

4. Are proper names capitalized?

Transitions

1. Are my thoughts logically connected to one another?

2. Have I used the appropriate transitional words? (See discussion of signal words on pages 94–98.)

3. Do my transitions accurately reflect the direction of the ideas they connect?

 # READING STRATEGY CHECK
PREVIEWING

"To the Student" introduced the strategy of previewing. As you may recall, previewing means looking through an article, chapter, or book to anticipate its structure and ideas. Anticipating ideas helps keep you active and involved with the material.

Some material is better structured for previewing than other types. For example, a textbook that includes many subheads and a chapter or section summary allows you to see the structure of the major points. A useful preview strategy is to examine these features before your first reading.

The "McDonald's—We Do It All for You" article does not have the usual features that aid previewing but nevertheless can be previewed. Refer to the reading as you work through this strategy check.

The article's title, "McDonald's—We Do It All for You," might suggest certain associations. What comes to mind when you read this title?

_____

_____

A quick skimming of the article should reveal four names of individuals. List the names:

1. _____   3. _____

2. _____   4. _____

Notice also in your quick once-over that the reading begins with quotation marks and that quotation marks are used throughout the article. What might this suggest about the reading?

_____

_____

The second sentence in the second paragraph provides the answer. The author reveals that this is an interview. You might predict that the four individuals are customers or perhaps employees. Your careful reading will allow you to confirm, alter, or reject your predictions.

Now read "McDonald's—We Do It All for You" through without stopping. Then return for a careful second reading.

The Reading

McDonald's—We Do It All for You

by BARBARA GARSON

Jason Pratt

1 "They called us the Green Machine," says Jason Pratt, recently retired McDonald's griddleman, "'cause the crew had green uniforms then. And that's what it is, a machine. You don't have to know how to cook, you don't have to know how to think. There's a procedure for everything and you just follow the procedures."

2 "Like?" I asked. I was interviewing Jason in the Pizza Hut across from his old McDonald's.

3 "Like, uh," the wiry teenager searched for a way to describe the all-encompassing procedures. "O.K., we'll start you off on something simple. You're on the ten-in-one grill, ten patties in a pound. Your basic burger. The guy on the bin calls, 'Six hamburgers.' So you lay your six pieces of meat on the grill and set the timer." Before my eyes Jason conjures up the gleaming, mechanized McDonald's kitchen. "Beep-beep, beep-beep, beep-beep. That's the beeper to sear 'em. It goes off in twenty seconds. Sup, sup, sup, sup, sup, sup." He presses each of the six patties down on the sizzling grill with an imaginary silver disk. "Now you turn off the sear beeper, put the buns in the oven, set the oven timer and then the next beeper is to turn the meat. This one goes beep-beep-beep, beep-beep-beep. So you turn your patties, and then you drop your re-cons on the meat, t-con, t-con, t-con." Here Jason takes two imaginary handfuls of reconstituted onions out of water and sets them out, two blops at a time, on top of the six patties he's arranged in two neat rows on our grill. "Now the bun oven buzzes [there are over a half dozen different timers with distinct beeps and buzzes in a McDonald's kitchen]. "This one turns itself off when you open the oven door so you just take out your crowns, line 'em up and give 'em each a squirt of mustard and a squirt of ketchup." With mustard in his right hand and ketchup in his left, Jason wields the dispensers like a pair of six-shooters up and down the lines of buns. Each dispenser has two triggers. One fires the premeasured squirt for ten-in-ones—the second is set for quarter-pounders.

4 "Now," says Jason, slowing down, "now you get to put on the pickles. Two if they're regular, three if they're small. That's the creative part. Then the lettuce, then you ask for a cheese count ('cheese on four please'). Finally the last beep goes off and you lay your burger on the crowns."

5 "On the *crown* of the buns?" I ask, unable to visualize. "On top?"

6   "Yeah, you dress 'em upside down. Put 'em in the box upside down too. They flip 'em over when they serve 'em."

7   "Oh, I think I see."

8   "Then scoop up the heels [the bun bottoms] which are on top of the bun warmer, take the heels with one hand and push the tray out from underneath and they land (plip) one on each burger, right on top of the re-cons, neat and perfect. [The official time allotted by Hamburger Central, the McDonald's headquarters in Oak Brook, Ill., is ninety seconds to prepare and serve a burger.] It's like I told you. The procedures makes the burgers. You don't have to know a thing."

9   McDonald's employs 500,000 teenagers at any one time. Most don't stay long. About 8 million Americans—7 per cent of our labor force—have worked at McDonald's and moved on. Jason is not a typical ex-employee. In fact, Jason is a legend among the teenagers at the three McDonald's outlets in his suburban area. It seems he was so fast at the griddle (or maybe just fast talking) that he'd been taken back three times by two different managers after quitting.

10   But Jason became a real legend in his last stint at McDonald's. He'd been sent out the back door with the garbage, but instead of coming back in he got into a car with two friends and just drove away. That's the part the local teenagers love to tell. "No fight with the manager or anything . . . just drove away and never came back. . . . I don't think they'd give him a job again."

11   "I would never go back to McDonald's," says Jason. "Not even as a manager." Jason is enrolled at the local junior college. "I'd like to run a real restaurant someday, but I'm taking data processing to fall back on." He's had many part-time jobs, the highest-paid at a hospital ($4.00 an hour), but that didn't last, and now dishwashing (at the $3.35 minimum). "Same as McDonald's. But I would never go back there. You're a complete robot."

12   "It seems like you can improvise a little with the onions," I suggested.   *improvise*
"They're not premeasured." Indeed, the reconstituted onion shreds grabbed out of a container by the unscientific-looking wet handful struck me as oddly out of character in the McDonald's kitchen.

13   "There's supposed to be twelve onion bits per patty," Jason informed me. "They spot check."

14   "Oh come on."

15   "You think I'm kiddin'. They lift your heels and they say, 'You got too many onions.' It's portion control."

16   "Is there any freedom anywhere in the process?" I asked.

17   "Lettuce. They'll leave you alone as long as it's neat."

18   "So lettuce is freedom; pickles is judgment?"

19   "Yeah but you don't have time to play around with your pickles. They're never gonna say just six pickles except on the disk. [Each store has video disks to train the crew for each of about twenty work stations, like fries, register, lobby, quarter-pounder grill.] What you'll hear in real life is 'twelve and six on a turn-lay.' The first number is your hamburgers, the

second is your Big Macs. On a turn-lay means you lay the first twelve, then you put down the second batch after you turn the first. So you got twenty-four burgers on the grill, in shifts. It's what they call a production mode. And remember you also got your fillets, your McNuggets. . . ."

20   "Wait, slow down." By then I was losing track of the patties on our imaginary grill. "I don't understand this turn-lay thing."

21   "Don't worry, you don't have to understand. You follow the beepers, you follow the buzzers and you turn your meat as fast as you can. It's like I told you, to work at McDonald's you don't need a face, you don't need a brain. You need to have two hands and two legs and move 'em as fast as you can. That's the whole system. I wouldn't go back there again for anything."

June Sanders

22   McDonald's french fries are deservedly the pride of their menu; uniformly golden brown all across America and in thirty-one other countries. However, it's difficult to standardize the number of fries per serving. The McDonald's fry scoop, perhaps their greatest technological innovation, helps to *innovation* control this variable. The unique flat funnel holds the bag open while it aligns a limited number of fries so that they fall into the package with a paradoxically free, overflowing cornucopia look.

23   Despite the scoop, there's still a spread. The acceptable fry yield is 400 to 420 servings per 100-lb. bag of potatoes. It's one of the few areas of McDonald's cookery in which such a range is possible. The fry yield is therefore one important measure of a manager's efficiency. "Fluffy, not stuffy," they remind the young workers when the fry yield is running low.

24   No such variation is possible in the browning of the fries. Early in McDonald's history Louis Martino, the husband of the secretary of McDonald's founder Ray Kroc, designed a computer to be submerged in the fry vats. In his autobiography, *Grinding It Out*, Kroc explained the importance of this innovation. "We had a recipe . . . that called for pulling the potatoes out of the oil when they got a certain color and grease bubbles formed in a certain way. It was amazing that we got them as uniform as we did because each kid working the fry vats would have his own interpretation of the proper color and so forth. [The word "kid" was officially replaced by "person" or "crew person" in McDonald's management vocabulary in 1973 in response to union organizing attempts.] Louis's computer took all the guesswork out of it, modifying the frying to suit the balance of water to solids in a given batch of potatoes. He also engineered the dispenser that allowed us to squirt exactly the right amount of catsup and mustard onto our premeasured hamburger patties. . . ."

25   The fry vat probe is a complex miniature computer. The fry scoop, on the other hand, is as simple and almost as elegant as the wheel. Both eliminate the need for a human being to make "his own interpretation," as Ray Kroc puts it.

26   Together, these two innovations mean that a new worker can be trained in fifteen minutes and reach maximum efficiency in a half hour. This makes

it economically feasible to use a kid for one day and replace him with an-   *feasible*
other kid the next day.

27   June Sanders worked at McDonald's for one day.

28   "I needed money, so I went in and the manager told me my hours would
be 4 to 10 P.M." This was fine with June, a well-organized black woman in
her early twenties who goes to college full time.

29   "But when I came in the next day the manager said I could work till 10
for that one day. But from then on my hours would be 4 P.M. to 1 A.M. And
I really wouldn't get off at 1 because I'd have to stay to clean up after they
closed. . . . Yes it was the same manager, a Mr. O'Neil.

30   "I told him I'd have to check first with my family if I could come home
that late. But he told me to put on the uniform and fill out the forms. He
would start me out on french fries.

31   "Then he showed me an orientation film on a TV screen all about
fries. . . . No, I still hadn't punched in. This was all in the basement. Then I
went upstairs, and *then* I punched in and went to work. . . . No, I was not
paid for the training downstairs. Yes, I'm sure."

32   I asked June if she had had any difficulty with the fries.

33   "No, it was just like the film. You put the french fries in the grease and
you push a button which doesn't go off till the fries are done. Then you take
them out and put them in a bin under a light. Then you scoop them into the
bags with this thing, this flat, light metal—I can't really describe it—scoop
thing that sits right in the package and makes the fries fall in place."

34   "Did they watch you for a while?" I asked. "Did you need more
instruction?"

35   "Someone leaned over once and showed me how to make sure the fry
scooper was set inside the opening of the bag so the fries would fall in right."

36   "And then?"

37   "And then, I stood on my feet from twenty after four till the manager
took over my station at 10:35 P.M.

38   "When I left my legs were aching. I knew it wasn't a job for me. But I
probably would have tried to last it out—at least more than a day—if it
wasn't for the hours. When I got home I talked it over with my mother and
my sister and then I phoned and said I couldn't work there. They weren't angry. They just said to bring back the uniform. . . . The people were nice, even
the managers. It's just a rushed system."

39   "June," I said, "does it make any sense to train you and have you work
for one day? Why didn't he tell you the real hours in the first place?"

40   "They take a chance and see if you're desperate. I have my family to stay
with. That's why I didn't go back. But if I really needed the money, like if I
had a kid and no family, I'd have to make arrangements to work any hours.

41   "Anyway, they got a full day's work out of me."

Damita

42   I waited on line at my neighborhood McDonald's. It was lunch hour and
there were four or five customers at each of the five open cash registers.

"May I take your order?" a very thin girl said in a flat tone to the man at the head of my line.

43   "McNuggets, large fries and a Coke," said the man. The cashier punched in the order. "That will be—"

44   "Big Mac, large fries and a shake," said the next woman on line. The cashier rang it up.

45   "Two cheeseburgers, large fries and a coffee," said the third customer. The cashier rang it up.

46   "How much is a large fries?" asked the woman directly in front of me.

47   The thin cashier twisted her neck around trying to look up at the menu board.

48   "Sorry," apologized the customer, "I don't have my glasses."

49   "Large fries is seventy-nine," a round-faced cashier with glasses interjected from the next register.

50   "Seventy-nine cents," the thin cashier repeated.

51   "Well how much is a *small* fries?"

52   As they talked I leaned over the next register. "Say, can I interview you?" I asked the clerk with glasses, whose line was by then empty.

53   "Huh?"

54   "I'm writing a story about jobs at fast-food restaurants."

55   "O.K. I guess so."

56   "Can I have your phone number?"

57   "Well . . . I'll meet you when I get off. Should be sometime between 4 and 4:30."

58   By then it was my turn.

59   "Just a large fries," I said.

60   The thin cashier pressed "lge fries." In place of numbers, the keys on a McDonald's cash register say "lge fries," "reg fries," "med coke," big mac," and so on. Some registers have pictures on the key caps. The next time the price of fries goes up (or down) the change will be entered in the store's central computer. But the thin cashier will continue to press the same button. I wondered how long she'd worked there and how many hundreds of "lge fries" she'd served without learning the price.

61   Damita, the cashier with the glasses, came up from the crew room (a room in the basement with lockers, a table and a video player for studying the training disks) at 4:45. She looked older and more serious without her striped uniform.

62   "Sorry, but they got busy and, you know, here you get off when they let you."

63   The expandable schedule was her first complaint. "You give them your availability when you sign on. Mine I said 9 to 4. But they scheduled me for 7 o'clock two or three days a week. And I needed the money. So I got to get up 5 in the morning to get here from Queens by 7. And I don't get off till whoever's supposed to get here gets here to take my place. . . . It's hard to study with all the pressures."

64   Damita had come to the city from a small town outside of Detroit. She lives with her sister in Queens and takes extension courses in psychology at New York University. Depending on the schedule posted each Friday, her McDonald's paycheck for a five-day week has varied from $80 to $114.

65   "How long have you worked at McDonald's?" I asked.

66   "Well, see I only know six people in this city, so my manager from Michigan . . . yeah, I worked for McDonald's in high school . . . my manager from Michigan called this guy Brian who's the second assistant manager here. So I didn't have to fill out an application. Well, I mean the first thing I needed was a job," she seemed to apologize, "and I knew I could always work at McDonald's. I always say I'm gonna look for something else, but I don't get out till 4 and that could be 5 or whenever."

67   The flexible scheduling at McDonald's only seems to work one way. One day Damita had arrived a half hour late because the E train was running on the R track.

68   "The assistant manager told me not to clock in at all, just to go home. So I said O.K. and I left."

69   "What did you do the rest of the day?" I asked.

70   "I went home and studied, and I went to sleep."

71   "But how did it make you feel?"

72   "It's like a humiliating feeling 'cause I wasn't given any chance to justify myself. But when I spoke to the Puerto Rican manager he said it was nothing personal against me. Just it was raining that day, and they were really slow and someone who got here on time, it wouldn't be right to send them home."

73   "Weren't you annoyed to spend four hours traveling and then lose a day's pay?" I suggested.

74   "I was mad at first that they didn't let me explain. But afterwards I understood and I tried to explain to my sister: 'Time waits for no man.'"

75   "Since you signed on for 9 to 4," I asked Damita, "and you're going to school, why can't you say, 'Look, I have to study at night, I need regular hours'?"

76   "Don't work that way. They make up your schedule every week and if you can't work it, you're responsible to replace yourself. If you can't they can always get someone else."

77   "But Damita," I tried to argue with her low estimate of her own worth, "anyone can see right away that your line moves fast yet you're helpful to people. I mean, you're a valuable employee. And this manager seems to like you."

78   "Valuable! $3.35 an hour. And I can be replaced by any [pointing across the room] kid off the street." I hadn't noticed. At a small table under the staircase a manager in a light beige shirt was taking an application from a lanky black teenager.

79   "But you know the register. You know the routine."

80   "How long you think it takes to learn the six steps? Step 1. Greet the customer, 'Good morning, can I help you?' Step 2. Take his order. Step 3.

Repeat the order. They can have someone off the street working my register in five minutes."

81   "By the way," I asked, "on those cash registers without numbers, how do you change something after you ring it up? I mean if somebody orders a cheeseburger and then they change it to a hamburger, how do you subtract the slice of cheese?"

82   "I guess that's why you have step 3, repeat the order. One cheeseburger, two Cokes, three . . ."

83   "Yeah but if you punched a mistake or they don't want it after you get it together?"

84   "Like if I have a crazy customer, which I do be gettin' 'specially in this city, and they order hamburger, fries and shake, and its $2.95 and then they just walk away?"

85   "I once did that here," I said. "About a week ago when I first started my research. All I ordered was some french fries. And I was so busy watching how the computer works that only after she rang it up I discovered that I'd walked out of my house without my wallet. I didn't have a penny. I was so embarrassed."

86   "Are you that one the other day? Arnetta, this girl next to me, she said, 'Look at that crazy lady going out. She's lookin' and lookin' at everything and then she didn't have no money for a bag of fries.' I saw you leaving, but I guess I didn't recognize you. [I agreed it was probably me.] O.K., so say this crazy lady comes in and orders french fries and leaves. In Michigan I could just zero it out. I'd wait till I start the next order and press zero and large fries. But here you're supposed to call out 'cancel sale' and the manager comes over and does it with his key.

87   "But I hate to call the manager every time, 'specially if I got a whole line waiting. So I still zero out myself. They can tell I do it by the computer tape, and they tell me not to. Some of them let me, though, because they know I came from another store. But they don't show the girls here how to zero out. Everybody thinks you need the manager's key to do it."

88   "Maybe they let you because they can tell you're honest," I said. She smiled, pleased, but let it pass. "That's what I mean that you're valuable to them. You know how to use the register. You're good with customers."

89   "You know there was a man here," Damita said, a little embarrassed about bragging, "when I was transferred off night he asked my manager, 'What happened to that girl from Michigan?'"

90   "Did your manager tell you that?"

91   "No, another girl on the night shift told me. The manager said it to her. They don't tell you nothing nice themselves."

92   "But, see, you are good with people and he appreciates it."

93   "In my other McDonald's—not the one where they let me zero out but another one I worked in in Michigan—I was almost fired for my attitude. Which was helping customers who had arthritis to open the little packets. And another bad attitude of mine is that you're supposed to suggest to the customer, 'Would you like a drink with that?' or 'Do you want a pie?'—

whatever they're pushing. I don't like to do it. And they can look on my tape after my shift and see I didn't push the suggested sell item."

94   McDonald's computerized cash registers allow managers to determine immediately not only the dollar volume for the store but the amount of each item that was sold at each register for any given period. Two experienced managers, interviewed separately, both insisted that the new electronic cash registers were in fact slower than the old mechanical registers. Clerks who knew the combinations—hamburger, fries, Coke: $2.45—could ring up the total immediately, take the cash and give change in one operation. On the new registers you have to enter each item and may be slowed down by computer response time. The value of the new registers, or at least their main selling point (McDonald's franchises can choose from several approved registers), is the increasingly sophisticated tracking systems, which monitor all the activity and report with many different statistical breakdowns.

95   "Look, there," said Damita as the teenage job applicant left and the manager went behind the counter with the application, "If I was to say I can't come in at 7, they'd cut my hours down to one shift a week, and if I never came back they wouldn't call to find out where I was.

96   "I worked at a hospital once as an X-ray assistant. There if I didn't come in there were things that had to be done that wouldn't be done. I would call there and say, 'Remember to run the EKGs.' Here, if I called and said, 'I just can't come by 7 no more,' they'd have one of these high school kids off the street half an hour later. And they'd do my job just as good."

97   Damita was silent for a while and then she made a difficult plea. "This might sound stupid, I don't know," she said, "but I feel like, I came here to study and advance myself but I'm not excelling myself in any way. I'm twenty years old but—this sounds terrible to say—I'm twenty but I'd rather have a babysitting job. At least I could help a kid and take care. But I only know six people in this city. So I don't even know how I'd find a babysitting job."

98   "I'll keep my ears open," I said. "I don't know where I'd hear of one but . . ."

99   Damita seemed a little relieved. I suppose she realized there wasn't much chance of babysitting full-time, but at least she now knew seven people in the city.

Jon DeAngelo

100   Jon DeAngelo, twenty-two, has been a McDonald's manager for three years. He started in the restaurant business at sixteen as a busboy and planned even then to run a restaurant of his own someday. At nineteen, when he was the night manager of a resort kitchen, he was hired away by McOpCo, the McDonald's Operating Company.

101   Though McDonald's is primarily a franchise system, the company also owns and operates about 30 percent of the stores directly. These McOpCo stores, including some of the busiest units, are managed via a chain of

command including regional supervisors, store managers and first and second assistants who can be moved from unit to unit. In addition, there's a network of inspectors from Hamburger Central who make announced and unannounced checks for QSC (quality, service, cleanliness) at both franchise and McOpCo installations.

102   Jon was hired at $14,000 a year. At the time I spoke with him his annual pay was $21,000—a very good salary at McDonald's. At first he'd been an assistant manager in one of the highest-volume stores in his region. Then he was deliberately transferred to a store with productivity problems.   *deliberately*

103   "I got there and found it was really a great crew. They hated being hassled, but they loved to work. I started them having fun by putting the men on the women's jobs and vice versa. [At most McDonald's the women tend to work on the registers, the men on the grill. But everyone starts at the same pay.] Oh, sure, they hated it at first, the guys that is. But they liked learning all the stations. I also ran a lot of register races."

104   Since the computer tape in each register indicates sales per hour, per half hour or for any interval requested, the manager can rev the crew up for a real "on your mark, get set, go!" race with a printout ready as they cross the finish line, showing the dollars taken in at each register during the race.

105   The computer will also print out a breakdown of sales for any particular menu item. The central office can check, therefore, how many Egg McMuffins were sold on Friday from 9 to 9:30 two weeks or two years ago, either in the entire store or at any particular register.

106   This makes it possible to run a register race limited to Cokes for instance, or Big Macs. Cashiers are instructed to try suggestive selling ("Would you like a drink with that?") at all times. But there are periods when a particular item is being pushed. The manager may then offer a prize for the most danish sold.

107   A typical prize for either type of cash register race might be a Snoopy mug (if that's the current promotion) or even a $5 cash bonus.

108   "This crew loved to race as individuals," says Jon of his troubled store, "but even more as a team. They'd love to get on a production mode, like a chicken-pull-drop or a burger-turn-lay and kill themselves for a big rush.

109   "One Saturday after a rock concert we did a $1,900 hour with ten people on crew. We killed ourselves but when the rush was over everyone said it was the most fun they ever had in a McDonald's."

110   I asked Jon how managers made up their weekly schedule. How would he decide who and how many to assign?

111   "It comes out of the computer," Jon explained. "It's a bar graph with the business you're going to do that week already printed in."

112   "The business you're *going* to do, already printed in?"

113   "It's based on the last week's sales, like maybe you did a $300 hour on Thursday at 3 P.M. Then it automatically adds a certain percent, say 15 percent, which is the projected annual increase for your particular store.... No, the person scheduling doesn't have to do any of this calculation. I just happen to know how it's arrived at. Really, it's simple, it's just a graph with

the numbers already in it. $400 hour, $500 hour. According to Hamburger Central you schedule two crew members per $100 hour. So if you're projected for a $600 hour on Friday between 1 and 2, you know you need twelve crew for that lunch hour and the schedule sheet leaves space for their names."

114   "You mean you just fill in the blanks on the chart?"

115   "It's pretty automatic except in the case of a special event like the concert. Then you have to guess the dollar volume. Scheduling under could be a problem, but over would be a disaster to your crew labor productivity."

116   "Crew labor productivity?"

117   "Everything at McDonald's is based on the numbers. But crew labor productivity is pretty much *the* number a manager is judged by."

118   "Crew labor productivity? You have to be an economist."

119   "It's really simple to calculate. You take the total crew labor dollars paid out, divide that into the total food dollars taken in. That gives you your crew labor productivity. The more food you sell and the less people you use to do it, the better your percentage. It's pretty simple."

120   Apparently, I still looked confused.

121   "For example, if you take an $800 hour and you run it with ten crew you get a very high crew labor percent."

122   "That's good?"

123   "Yes that's good. Then the manager in the next store hears Jon ran a 12 percent labor this week, I'll run a 10 percent labor. Of course you burn people out that way. But . . ."

124   "But Jon," I asked, "if the number of crew you need is set in advance and printed by the computer, why do so many managers keep changing hours and putting pressure on kids to work more?"

125   "They advertise McDonald's as a flexible work schedule for high school and college kids," he said, "but the truth is it's a high-pressure job, and we have so much trouble keeping help, especially in fast stores like my first one (it grossed $1.8 million last year), that 50 percent never make it past two weeks. And a lot walk out within two days.

126   "When I was a first assistant, scheduling and hiring was my responsibility and I had to fill the spots one way or another. There were so many times I covered the shifts myself. Times I worked 100 hours a week. A manager has to fill the spaces on his chart somehow. So if a crew person is manipulable they manipulate him."

127   "What do you mean?"

128   "When you first sign on, you give your availability. Let's say a person's schedule is weeknights, 4 to 10. But after a week the manager schedules him as a closer Friday night. He calls in upset, 'Hey, my availability isn't Friday night.' The manager says, 'Well the schedule is already done. And you know the rule. If you can't work it's up to you to replace yourself.' At that point the person might quit, or he might not show up or he might have a fight with the manager."

129   "So he's fired?"

130   "No. You don't fire. You would only fire for cause like drugs or steal-
ing. But what happens is he signed up for thirty hours a week and suddenly
he's only scheduled for four. So either he starts being more available or he
quits."

131   "Aren't you worried that the most qualified people will quit?"

132   "The only qualification to be able to do the job is to be able physically
to do the job. I believe it says that in almost those words in my regional
manual. And being there is the main part of being physically able to do the
job."

133   "But what about your great crew at the second store? Don't you want
to keep a team together?"

134   "Let me qualify that qualification. It takes a special kind of person to be
able to move before he can think. We find people like that and use them till
they quit."

135   "But as a manager don't you look bad if too many people are quitting?"

136   "As a manager I am judged by the statistical reports which come off the
computer. Which basically means my crew labor productivity. What else can
I really distinguish myself by? I could have a good fry yield, a low M&R
[Maintenance and Repair budget]. But these are minor."

137   As it happens, Jon is distinguished among McDonald's managers in his
area as an expert on the computerized equipment. Other managers call on
him for cash register repairs. "They say, 'Jon, could you look at my register?
I just can't afford the M&R this month.' So I come and fix it and they'll buy
me a beer."

138   "So keeping M&R low is a real feather in a manager's cap," I deduced.

139   "O.K., it's true, you can over spend your M&R budget; you can have a
low fry yield; you can run a dirty store; you can be fired for bothering the
high school girls. But basically, every Coke spigot is monitored. [At most
McDonald's, Coke doesn't flow from taps that turn on and off. Instead the
clerk pushes the button "sm," "med" or "lge," which then dispenses the premeasured amount into the appropriate-size cup. This makes the syrup yield
fairly consistent.] Every ketchup squirt is measured. My costs for every item
are set. So my crew labor productivity is my main flexibility."

140   I was beginning to understand the pressures toward pettiness. I had by
then heard many complaints about slight pilferage of time. For instance, as a
safety measure no one was allowed to stay in a store alone. There was a common complaint that a closer would be clocked out when he finished cleaning the store for the night, even though he might be required to wait around
unpaid till the manager finished his own nightly statistical reports. At other
times kids clocked out and then waited hours (unpaid) for a crew chief training course (unpaid).

141   Overtime is an absolute taboo at McDonald's. Managers practice every   *taboo*
kind of scheduling gymnastic to see that no one works over forty hours a
week. If a crew member approaching forty hours is needed to close the store,
he or she might be asked to check out for a long lunch. I had heard of a couple of occasions when, in desperation, a manager scheduled someone to stay

an hour or two over forty hours. Instead of paying time-and-a-half, he com-   *compensated*
pensated at straight time listing the extra hours as miscellaneous and paying
through a fund reserved for things like register race bonuses. All of this of
course to make his statistics look good.

142   "There must be some other way to raise your productivity," I suggested,
"besides squeezing it out of the kids."

143   "I try to make it fun," Jon pleaded earnestly. "I know that people like to
work on my shifts. I have the highest crew labor productivity in the area. But
I get that from burning people out. Look, you can't squeeze a McDonald's
hamburger any flatter. If you want to improve your productivity there is
nothing for a manager to squeeze but the crew."

144   "But if it's crew dollars paid out divided by food dollars taken in, maybe
you can bring in more dollars instead of using less crew."

145   "O.K., let me tell you about sausage sandwiches."

146   "Sausage sandwiches?" (Sounded awful.)

147   "My crew was crazy about sausage sandwiches. [Crew members are entitled to one meal a day at reduced prices. The meals are deducted from
wages through a computerized link to the time clocks.] They made it from a
buttered English muffin, a slice of sausage and a slice of cheese. I understand
this had actually been a menu item in some parts of the country but never
here. But the crew would make it for themselves and then all their friends
came in and wanted them.

148   "So, I decided to go ahead and sell it. It costs about 9¢ to make and I sold
it for $1.40. It went like hotcakes. My supervisor even liked the idea because
it made so much money. You could see the little dollar signs in his eyes when
he first came into the store. And he said nothing. So we kept selling it.

149   "Then someone came from Oak Brook and they made us stop it.

150   "Just look how ridiculous that is. A slice of sausage is 60¢ as a regular
menu item, and an English muffin is 45¢. So if you come in and ask for a
sausage and an English muffin I can still sell them to you today for $1.05. But
there's no way I can add the slice of cheese and put it in the box and get that
$1.40.

151   "Basically, I can't be any more creative than a crew person. I can't take
any more initiative than the person on the register."   *initiative*

152   "Speaking of cash registers and initiative," I said . . . and told him about
Damita. I explained that she was honest, bright and had learned how to zero
out at another store. "Do you let cashiers zero out?" I asked.

153   "I might let her in this case," Jon said. "The store she learned it at was
probably a franchise and they were looser. But basically we don't need
people like her. Thinking generally slows this operation down.

154   "When I first came to McDonald's, I said, 'How mechanical! These kids
don't even know how to cook.' But the pace is so fast that if they didn't have
all the systems, you couldn't handle it. It takes ninety seconds to cook a
hamburger. In those seconds you have to toast the buns, dress it, sear it, turn
it, take it off the grill and serve it. Meanwhile you've got maybe twenty-four
burgers, plus your chicken, your fish. You haven't got time to pick up a rack

of fillet and see if it's done. You have to press the timer, drop the fish and know, without looking, that when it buzzes it's done.

155   "It's the same thing with management. You have to record the money each night before you close and get it to the bank the next day by 11 A.M. So you have to trust the computer to do a lot of the job. These computers also calculate the payrolls, because they're hooked into the time clocks. My payroll is paid out of a bank in Chicago. The computers also tell you how many people you're going to need each hour. It's so fast that the manager hasn't got time to think about it. He has to follow the procedures like the crew. And if he follows the procedures everything is going to come out more or less as it's supposed to. So basically the computer manages the store."

156   Listening to Jon made me remember what Ray Kroc had written about his own job (head of the corporation) and computers:

> We have a computer in Oak Brook that is designed to make real estate surveys. But those printouts are of no use to me. After we find a promising location, I drive around it in a car, go into the corner saloon and the neighborhood supermarket. I mingle with the people and observe their comings and goings. That tells me what I need to know about how a McDonald's store would do there.

157   By combining twentieth-century computer technology with nineteenth-century time-and-motion studies, the McDonald's corporation has broken the jobs of griddleman, waitress, cashier and even manager down into small, simple steps. Historically these have been service jobs involving a lot of flexibility and personal flare. But the corporation has systematically extracted the decision-making elements from filling french fry boxes or scheduling staff. They've siphoned the know-how from the employees into the programs. They relentlessly weed out all variables that might make it necessary to make a decision at the store level, whether on pickles or on cleaning procedures.   *siphoned*
    relentlessly

158   It's interesting and understandable that Ray Kroc refused to work that way. The real estate computer may be as reliable as the fry vat probe. But as head of the company Kroc didn't have to surrender it. He'd let the computer juggle all the demographic variables, but in the end Ray Kroc would decide, intuitively, where to put the next store.

159   Jon DeAngelo would like to work that way, too. So would Jason, June and Damita. If they had a chance to use some skill or intuition at their own levels, they'd not only feel more alive, they'd also be treated with more consideration. It's job organization, not malice, that allows (almost requires) McDonald's workers to be handled like paper plates. They feel disposable because they are.   *malice*

160   I was beginning to wonder why Jon stayed on at McDonald's. He still yearned to open a restaurant. "The one thing I'd take from McDonald's to a French restaurant of my own is the fry vat computer. It really works." He seemed to have both the diligence and the style to run a personalized restaurant. Of course he may not have had the capital.   *diligence*

161   "So basically I would tell that girl [bringing me back to Damita] to find a different job. She's thinking too much and it slows things down. The way

the system is set up, I don't need that in a register person, and they don't need it in me."

162   "Jon," I said, trying to be tactful, "I don't exactly know why you stay at   *tactful*
McDonald's."

163   "As a matter of fact, I have already turned in my resignation."

164   "You mean you're not a McDonald's manager any more?" I was
dismayed.   *dismayed*

165   "I quit once before and they asked me to stay."

166   "I have had such a hard time getting a full-fledged manager to talk to me
and now I don't know whether you count."

167   "They haven't actually accepted my resignation yet. You know I heard
of this guy in another region who said he was going to leave and they didn't
believe him. They just wouldn't accept his resignation. And you know what
he did? One day, at noon, he just emptied the store, walked out, and locked
the door behind him."

168   For a second Jon seemed to drift away on that beautiful image. It was
like the kids telling me about Jason, the crewman who just walked out the
back door.

169   "You know what that means to close a McDonald's at noon, to do a zero
hour at lunch?"

170   "Jon," I said. "This has been fantastic. You are fantastic. I don't think
anyone could explain the computers to me the way you do. But I want to
talk to someone who's happy and moving up in the McDonald's system. Do
you think you could introduce me to a manager who . . ."

171   "You won't be able to."

172   "How come?"

173   "First of all, there's the media hotline. If any press comes around or anyone is writing a book I'm supposed to call the regional office immediately
and they will provide someone to talk to you. So you can't speak to a real
corporation person except by arrangement with the corporation.

174   "Second, you can't talk to a happy McDonald's manager because 98 percent are miserable.

175   "Third of all, there is no such thing as a McDonald's manager. The computer manages the store."

QUESTIONS

1. Discuss the positive and negative aspects of working at McDonald's according to the employees interviewed by the author. Be sure to include
   the following aspects of employment:

   • Job preparation
   • Initiative
   • Satisfaction
   • Lack of satisfaction

2. Analyze the author's choice of title for the article. What is she alluding to
   by saying "We Do It All for You"?

3. Jon, a McDonald's manager, speaks about "crew labor productivity." Explain this concept and illustrate its importance to the corporation.

4. Discuss the role that technology plays in McDonald's operation.

5. Has your perception of McDonald's been altered by reading this article? Explain.

EXTENDING YOUR VOCABULARY

improvise: Without pillows or a mattress we managed to improvise a
                  bed by using _____

innovation: Lighting by electricity was an innovation in 1890 because

                  _____

feasible: With her illness, we didn't know if airplane travel was fea-
                  sible because _____

deliberately: He deliberately left the door open so that _____

taboo: Some topics that are taboo in kindergarten are _____

                  _____

compensated: We expect to be fully compensated since _____

initiative: She showed a great deal of initiative when _____

siphoned: We siphoned off gasoline from my uncle's car because

                  _____

relentlessly: It rained relentlessly and so we had to _____

malice: Because they showed malice toward our children, we

                  _____

diligence: We worked with greater diligence after we learned that

                  _____

tactful: We need workers who are more tactful because _____

                  _____

dismayed: We were dismayed when we learned that _____

So You Want to Be a Physician/Ophthalmologist

"So You Want to Be" is a feature of the Web site Student/Center.com. *Informational interviews are conducted by Student Center staff members, who select industries informally, taking into account whether users have requested information about certain fields. Staff members try to maintain a balance between traditional fields (such as medicine and banking) and nontraditional fields (such as toy making and ski instruction). Interviewees are usually friends or friends of friends of staff members. Staff members look for people who are out of school long enough to have established themselves, but not so long that what they do is out of reach of college students. The person interviewed in this selection is Stephanie B.*

GEARING UP

1. Describe the factors that are motivating you to pursue your career.

2. Discuss the steps you could take to get a more realistic picture of your chosen career before you commit time, money, and energy in the process.

3. List the television shows or movies you have seen that feature doctors in lead roles. Illustrate how the occupation is portrayed. Describe the typical television or movie view of clinics and hospitals.

4. Compare and contrast your response to the above question with what you know about physicians, clinics, and hospitals based on personal experience.

READING STRATEGY

READING INTERVIEWS

An interview is a discussion between an interviewer (the person asking questions) and an interviewee (the person or persons responding to the questions). You may have already read a series of interviews conducted by Barbara Garson. Now you will be able to read about the work of a physician/ophthalmologist that was presented in a Web-based magazine titled *Insider Information*. This online publication presents informational interviews with real-world professionals.

Information presented in an interview can be very informative and instructive. Probing questions by the interviewer can get the interviewee to open up and share information with readers. However, as a source of information, data contained in interviews can differ in many ways from narrative autobiographical accounts, the types of reading that you most likely experienced in the first unit of this textbook.

Interviews involve a question-and-answer format in which the interviewer usually controls what is asked. In typical autobiographical accounts, on the other hand, the writer chooses what to discuss. There is no opportunity for someone to probe and challenge the subject.

Your reading of interviews may be more meaningful if you consider the following questions:

1. What information might have been included if the persons interviewed were instead given the opportunity to tell about themselves without question prompts, either by recording their voice or by writing their story?

2. Is the printed interview the full transcript of the discussion that took place? Or is the print version an excerpt from the face-to-face interview?

3. Did the interviewee have the opportunity to review the transcript before it was published?

4. Are some of the printed remarks ambiguous? Is it possible to give more than one interpretation to a statement?

5. If the transcript is as accurate and complete as possible, was there a significant omission in the interview? That is, was a question not asked that would have changed the overall message of the interview or caused certain aspects of it to be interpreted quite differently?

6. How representative is the person or persons interviewed? If the sample of interviewees were enlarged, would you find information that altered the basic message?

7. Who is asking the questions? Is the interviewer objective or subjective? Does the interviewer show any bias? Is the interviewer presenting a point, analyzing and interpreting, or merely asking a question?

Application

The previous article was entitled, "McDonald's—We Do It All for You." The questions posed above can be asked about this article. In her book, Garson asks, "How have computer related technologies transformed the workplace and the worker?" On one level, her book looks at how the new technologies will affect the centralization of control. Garson asks her readers to consider basic questions such as "What skills will future workers and management need to work in the office of the future?"; "What will the worker and office look like?"; and "Who will control the office?"

Garson not only interviews but also provides readers with comments and insights into the operation of McDonald's. Her writing style resembles that of a newspaper journalist conducting an investigative report. A straight question-and-answer format is not used; instead questions are integrated into the narrative. Garson sometimes "editorializes," for example: "The flexible scheduling at McDonald's only seems to work one way." This comment reveals Garson's attitude toward McDonald's treatment of workers. Considering the topic of her book, *The Electronic Sweatshop,* would it serve the purposes of the author to include an interview that featured happy or relatively content McDonald's workers? Despite the message of Garson's article, do you know of people who have worked or are working at McDonald's who feel contented with their work? If not, do you feel there are happy, contented McDonald's workers?

The next article is an interview with an ophthalmologist, Dr. Stephanie B. This doctor was interviewed for a Web site designed to help readers obtain advice and guidance regarding employment matters. This interview follows the more traditional format of the interviewer posing questions and the subject answering them. The doctor's responses fall into what physicians might reasonably say about their training and practice, with a few exceptions. As a probing reader, you need to ask yourself: "How representative is she of her profession?" Does Dr. Stephanie B.'s position on testing patients and billing strike you in any particular way? Lastly, are there questions that might have been asked that would change the tone of the interview?

 # READING STRATEGY CHECK

COLLECTING IDEAS

The strategy of collecting ideas was introduced with the narrative readings in Unit One. To restate the point made there, you will be expected to gather information from various sources in your college and work life. The strategy of collecting ideas is an organizational aid to help you do this. In the first unit, a chart was suggested to collect information from the readings on three issues. A chart may also be used for the issues in Unit Two, or you may put the information in outline form. The advantage of the chart is that it allows you to see many different ideas in one location. The limitation of the chart is that a block format restricts the amount of information that you can enter. If you need to make extensive notes for the different categories, you may wish to consider an outline.

Application

Two major issues of Unit Two are job satisfaction and job competence. These larger issues can be further divided. For example, job satisfaction can be broken down into pay, security, working conditions, advancement opportunity, human relations, meaningful work, and recognition from others.

Many of these issues are addressed directly or indirectly in both "McDonald's—We Do It All for You" and in the second reading of the unit, on Dr. Stephanie B. In addition to this information, you can add information about yourself. Even if you haven't worked, you can express your feelings concerning each of these issues.

To help you gather information from these sources as you are studying them, a chart may be constructed.

Personal Needs	Myself	McDonald's (Jason Pratt)	McDonald's (June Sanders)	McDonald's (Damita)	McDonald's (Jon DeAngelo)	Dr. Stephanie B.
Pay						
Security						
Good working conditions						
Advancement opportunities						
Human relations						
Meaningful work						
Recognition						

You may want to use this format for your chart but transfer it to a larger sheet of paper that will give you more space to write. Alternately, if you wish to make lengthy notes, you may wish to use an outline form. A sample structure follows:

Personal needs on the job

A. Pay
    1. Myself
    2. Jason Pratt
    3. June Sanders
    4. Damita
    5. Jon DeAngelo
    6. Dr. Stephanie B.

B. Security
    1. Myself
    2. Jason Pratt
    3. June Sanders

4. Damita
5. Jon DeAngelo
6. Dr. Stephanie B.

You may find, as have many of our students, that an efficient approach is to use both systems. The chart form helps you organize brief notes on first reading or in your effort to narrow the focus. Once you begin to do a careful study of the articles and decide on a particular topic, you move to the outline form, which accommodates more extensive note taking.

The Reading

So You Want to Be a Physician/Ophthalmologist

Q. What made you interested in becoming a doctor?

A. It's going to sound silly, but when I was little I used to watch *Marcus Welby* reruns on TV after school. I always thought it would be great to be Marcus Welby. He seemed to have every answer for every question. And then *Emergency*—you know, with the paramedics—came on after *Marcus Welby.* I thought *Emergency* looked really exciting.

So that's what spawned my interest. And then I had a really good science teacher in sixth grade. We did a lot of dissections, and we had a science fair, and I got to dissect cow eyes.

Q. And you didn't get grossed out, so you took that as a sign.

A. Actually, I was the kid whom the boys in the back of the room would pay a dollar to do their dissection! No, I never found it gross, or anything like that. I actually thought it was really cool to find out how things worked on the inside.

Q. Did you ever want to do anything else?

A. Not really. I have enjoyed other things; I really enjoy creative things. And at one point in my medical school career when I was incredibly miserable, I thought about quitting medical school and opening a flower shop. But in terms of professional goals, no, I never seriously considered anything else. I always knew what I wanted to do.

Q. Do you think that's important? Is being a physician one of those professions where you have to be "born" to do it?

A. Absolutely, because the process to get there is so uncomfortable.

Q. Tell me about the process.

A. Well, my experience was a little bit different because I did a six-year medical program were I was accepted into college and medical school from the beginning. So you're already a pre-selected group, but the competition for grades and placement breeds a little bit of nastiness among the students. And then the sheer volume of the work you have to do, and dealing with issues like, "Am I good enough to do this?" "Am I smart enough to do this?" "Can I really take care of people?" "What do you do when they die?" "How do you touch somebody?" "How do you deal with their naked body the first time without turning purple?" Those are really uncomfortable things at the same time that you're just overwhelmed with memorization and work. You say, "My God, maybe I should just quit and be a florist!"

Q. How did you come to terms with those issues?

A. I always knew I wanted to be a doctor, and I figured if my pediatrician could do it, and if all these other people I knew who didn't seem like rocket scientists could do it, then I could do it too. And it's just a matter of getting through that process, which, admittedly, is not fun. My analogy when my friends and I were in medical school was if you go to jail and you know your sentence, you just live out your time and do your best.

Q. For you college and med school was six years. How long is it usually?

A. Typically it's eight years: four years of college and four years of med school, and then you do your residency training program.

Q. How long is a residency?

A. Anywhere from three to five years. And then if you decide to do a fellowship and subspecialize, it's another couple of years after that.

Q. When would you need to do a fellowship?

A. Say, for example, I'm an ophthalmologist. I'm in general practice. So I did one year of internal medicine, because in certain specialties you have to do one year in general medicine so you have enough of a basis. Then I did three years of ophthalmology. So now I'm a general ophthalmologist. If I wanted to be a retina specialist and only do retinas, then I'd need to do two more years in a fellowship.

Q. So how old are most people before they're out on their own and practicing?

A. I'd say thirty-five and up. Because most people do four years of college, four years of medical school, five years of residency training, and then very often along the way they had to do a master's, or they didn't get into the residency they wanted, or they took some time off.

Q. Do a lot of people burn out and drop out?

A. Not really. I think if you're going to burn out, you do it in medical school. Although the suicide rate in residency is very high.

Q. Why do you think that is?

A. Pressure. You have a group of people who were used to being the smartest kids in their classes in high school and then again in college, and maybe they did really well in medical school. Then all of a sudden you're a resident, and it's not book smart anymore. It's practical smart, how well you do things with your hands and how well you relate to people. It's a very different game, and you're working thirty-six hour shifts, or at least it was thirty-six hours when I did my residency.

Q. Is it still?

A. Depends on the hospital. Sometimes it's twenty-four, sometimes it's thirty-six.

Q. So you're working twenty-four or thirty-six hour shifts, depending on the hospital.

A. Right.

Q. And you're working how many days a week?

A. Theoretically, you're not supposed to work more than eighty hours a week. All programs are different, and the extent to which they comply to the Bell Commission is different everywhere. It's really hard to enforce that limit, because you can't leave when there are things to be done. So especially now with decreased government support for medical training programs on the horizon, I'm not sure how those rules will be enforced. The other way hospitals cut back on doctor hours was by hiring ancillary staff to do things   *ancillary*
like starting intravenous lines and what we used to call "scut"—the busy work nobody really wants to do. Now with decreasing reimbursements   *reimbursements*
from HMO's and private insurance plans, how many of those people will be able to stay on payroll is unknown.

Q. So the scut work falls to the residents who now have even more work than they had before.

A. Right.

Q. Tell me what you like about being a doctor.

A. Oh, it's great. I wouldn't do it if I didn't really love it. It's great because you deal with people all day, and you're helping people all day. In my field, I get to diagnose, I get to treat, I get to do medical therapy and surgical ther-   *diagnose*
apy, and I do the follow-up care. I have long-standing relationships with people who have chronic problems. I also have patients who have emergen-   *chronic*
cies where they're in pain, they come to you, and they feel better. It's really gratifying. And curing blindness is the most gratifying thing that I can think of to do.

　　People appreciate you, they really do. And if you like to work with your hands, and you like science, if you enjoy that kind of stuff it's really great.

Q. So what's bad? What don't you like?

A. The bad parts are the other sides of the good things. You can't separate them even if you want to. The bad thing is the responsibility. The bad thing is that people's expectations are sometimes unrealistic. The bad thing is that if you're a surgeon and you operate, you'll have complications—there's a complication rate with everything, and it's devastating when you have a complication because you feel the weight of the world of curing humanity on your head. The downside is also the business aspect of running a small practice, when you realize you signed up to take care of people and you're actually running a small business.

Q. You're very young and you have your own independent practice. That's unusual, isn't it?

A. Yes it is. Most people generally get out at about thirty-five. I finished when I was about twenty-nine. Then people will usually sign up to work with an academic institution or they'll go on staff with a big, multi-specialty group in order to get their feet wet. I worked for somebody for a year, and I decided that I could do it better. I could do it my own way. Especially as a woman, in professional life I didn't feel I had to take someone else's abuse and be underpaid for the same work a man would do. So I said to hell with it and I opened my own business.

Q. How much of your time do you spend being a business person as opposed to being a doctor?

A. That's really hard to say. I'd say 100% of the time I'm both. It comes down to how much you want to delegate and how much do you want to pay a larger staff.

Q. So you can hire an office manager and a bookkeeper to do all that stuff.

A. Exactly. Originally I did a lot of it. Now I'd say I do about two hours worth of paper work and busy work on an average day. Then I do a full day every other week or so, catching up. But I also have a full-time office manager and a full-time biller who do a lot of the other stuff.

Q. How are changes in the health care system affecting your work?

A. It means I have to be busier to make the same kind of money I would make otherwise. In medicine you always want to be busy because it means you're successful. But now, since reimbursement is lower you have to do twice as much work to make the same amount of money. That's number one. It also means that I have to know what kind of insurance somebody has in order to decide when to proceed with a procedure or a test. If I feel the patient needs a test, I have to check and see what kind of insurance they have, because some plans say you have to come back on a separate visit or you need a referral form, and I have to write a consultation report to their primary doctor and make a phone call and ask to get it back.

Q. Do you ever find yourself in an ethical bind where there's a procedure you want to do but their insurance won't cover it?

A. Not really, because my theory is you do what's right for the patient and you worry about the money a different day. If you don't get paid you can still sleep with yourself at night. Luckily for me, my practice is successful enough that I can do that. We take charity patients the same way. And Medicaid patients are the same—we don't even bill Medicaid because it costs us more in secretary time than we get back. But we do it because it's the right thing, and you live with the consequences later.

Q. What's a typical day like for you?

A. On a typical office day, I'd say we schedule between forty and fifty patients. I'll get to my office between 7:30 and 8:00 and I'll do paperwork for about an hour. At 9:00 we start patients and they're scheduled every fifteen minutes until about 5:00. We double book post-op patients and follow-up patients two patients to a slot. So a post-op or follow-up patient is given seven and a half minutes. It's a roller coaster. We leave a couple of spaces in the middle of the day for emergencies, but . . .

Q. No lunch.

A. Lunch is not a thing we do. Lunch means I've got a period of time where I'm running on schedule and I can eat half my tuna fish sandwich standing up. By taking an hour out of the office, I decrease my productivity significantly, and I'd rather relax and eat after the office is done. I have a staff of eight, and office down time is expensive.

So that's, say, a typical Monday. We have late days in the office where we start a little later and we stay until 8:00 so people can come in after work. And on surgery days when I have eyelid cases I'll do those at 7:00 in the morning before office hours. A regular cataract surgery day also would begin at 7:00 in the morning, and I'll have five or six cases until we're done for the day. I don't go back to the office after those because I'm too tired, and I smell like rubber gloves, that kind of thing.

The hours are long.

Q. Do they ever get better? Do doctors decrease their hours as they move on in their careers?

A. Most no. Because what happens is you get busier and busier as you become more popular and prominent. You have more to do and hopefully you get more efficient at it. What ends up happening is you take on an associate, and then you spend forever trying to train them to be just like you, and then they get really busy too.

prominent

Q. What kinds of personality traits or skills do you think a person needs to have in order to be a doctor?

A. You have to have the patience of a saint. (Laughs) You have to able to sit and listen to people kvetch all day long, because that's what they do. Nobody ever comes in and says, "I'm so glad to see you!" They say, "It hurts!" You have to be able to smile and be nice no matter what, no matter what's happening in your personal life or if you had a fire in your wastebasket. Nobody can ever see you sweat, because people expect their doctor to be perfect and unruffleable.

Q. Nobody wants a nervous doctor.

A. No, not at all.

Q. So I guess you need a lot of self-confidence.

A. Self-confidence, yes. And you have to be stubborn; you have to be able to push yourself beyond the limits of what you thought you could do.

Because when an emergency happens in the middle of the night, you can't say, "Well, I'm sorry, I'm tired right now." You have to be able to be extremely disciplined and say, "Maybe I feel like going to the movies, but I have surgery tomorrow and I have to be up at 5:00."

Aside from that I think it takes good managerial skills, good people skills. You have to be able to run an office and make sure your staff doesn't kill each other and they're nice to the patients. A lot of that running a small business stuff is the same. Managing patient emotions is the same as managing customer service. But nobody talks to you about that in medical school. They just say if you're smart, it's good enough. But it's really not. There are plenty of smart people who have no bedside manner, and they can be brilliant and well-trained, but nobody wants to sit with them in an office.

Q. So they become surgeons so all their patients are unconscious.

A. No, they become anesthesiologists! But even so, it's hard to trust someone to put you to sleep or to operate on you if you can't stand being in the same room with them. Or if they don't empathize with what you're going   *empathize*
through. Even if you don't empathize, you have to sit and nod your head like you do. And you can't think of yourself as being fake for doing that. It's just part of the job.

Q. There are a lot of different things you can do in medicine, isn't that true?

A. There's a huge variety of things to do within medicine. An office practice in ophthalmology is really different from radiology, or being an OBGYN, or pathology, where you don't even see any live people. Some people find teaching and academics much more rewarding than private practice.

There are so many different areas within medicine, you just have to know what they are. If you can find a family friend who's a physician, or even your pediatrician, and ask their advice, or ask if you can observe them for a day, that's a good thing to do.

Q. Is it hard to find volunteer positions?

A. No, not at all. But remember that as a candy striper you're not going to see what it's really like. You have to get involved in a shadow program, or work in a lab, or work in the emergency room, or something like that. Then you see how it really works, and you can determine what's right for you.

Q. What does someone who's just starting college need to do to prepare for a medical career?

A. You have to know you want to do it; you have to know you're going to be good at it. When I was in high school I did a shadow program where I followed a doctor around for a while. It was great because then I knew I wouldn't pass out at the sight of blood. In college it's a good idea to try to get work programs or volunteer programs in a hospital where you can actually see the mechanics of what happens. It's quite different from what you expect it to be.

Q. What are the medical schools looking for?

A. Diversity. They're looking for a well-rounded person. We're not going *diversity* to talk about grades, because obviously your grades and MCAT scores have to be good. On top of that they want to know that you're human, that you can relate to other human beings and be caring. Also that you can juggle good grades with other stresses, because the grades alone aren't what's going to make you a doctor. It's being able to do other stuff at the same time.

Q. Having extra-curriculars that demonstrate those skills is important.

A. Absolutely. Being just a bookworm isn't going to do it. If you're on the debate team or something, that would be really favorable. Or if you've been successful in competitive sports or performances, that would do it. They want people with personality, people who can be dynamic and accomplished in the face of a difficult situation.

Q. Do you have any specific advice for someone considering this field?

A. It's the greatest field in the world—if you really want it. If it's not for you, it's not for you. When I was in college there were a bunch of kids in my class who were there because their parents wanted them to be doctors. They didn't last. You can't convince yourself it's something you want to do. Your life is a long period of time, and to train for fifteen or twenty years to do something you really weren't in the mood for is a huge sacrifice.

If you really want it, there's nothing more rewarding. You can't think of it in terms of the money—who knows what socialized medicine or health care reform is going to do. You have to do it because you enjoy taking care of people.

QUESTIONS

1. The doctor being interviewed, Stephanie B., specifies how she became interested in becoming a doctor. Summarize her thoughts on this matter.

2. Describe the medical school process and other training requirements for Dr. Stephanie B.

3. Discuss the pressures involved in becoming an ophthalmologist and running a daily practice.

4. According to the interviewee, what traits and characteristics are necessary to become a successful ophthalmologist?

5. Describe how changes in health organizations have affected Dr. Stephanie B's workload.

6. The interviewee mentions that much of what she does on a daily basis is not learned in medical school. Explain.

7. Dr. Stephanie B. runs her own practice. Analyze her reasons for choosing this path.

8. Summarize the positive and negative aspects of being an ophthalmologist according to the interviewee.

9. Cite the advice Dr. Stephanie B. offers to someone considering the field of medicine as a career.

EXTENDING YOUR VOCABULARY

ancillary: In many courses, instructors distribute ancillary materials because _____

reimbursements: We felt that we should have received the reimbursements because _____

diagnose: In trying to diagnose the problem, the doctor had to _____

chronic: I hope my back pain is not chronic because that would mean that _____

prominent: She is recognized as a prominent person in our community by the fact that she _____

empathize: How do you expect him to empathize with my problems since he _____

diversity: We never expected such diversity of opinion from the class considering _____

READING JOURNAL

The two articles that open Unit Two are both interviews. Both selections focus on people reporting about work. As you reflect on the two sets of interviews, keep the issues of job satisfaction and job competence in mind. Use your journal to keep track of your reading efforts. Remember that the assignment is intended to be informal and personal—make entries that are meaningful to you. The following points will help you get started.

- **Content**

  How has your knowledge of McDonald's or ophthalmology changed as a result of these readings?

  Based on what you know and have read, would you consider either as a career?

- **Process**

  Which of the two selections was the hardest and easiest for you to read? Explain.

Which strategies are you using comfortably in reading these narratives? Which strategies are causing some difficulty? Explain.

Comment on your use of the reading interviews strategy. What suggestions, if any, were helpful for you in reading the interviews?

• **Response**

How interesting was the information presented? How interested were you in the material? Elaborate.

React to the author's presentation of the material. Is there something that you would have wanted to know that was not included in the interview?

Try to place yourself in the world of the interviewees. Given the same circumstances, how do you think you might react to their situations?

If you meet one of the individuals who were interviewed, what might you say to him or her?

Choose one of the people interviewed. Based on what they said, what kind of person do you think he or she is? Would you consider having this person as a friend? Explain.

Solving the Job Puzzle

ANNE W. CLYMER AND ELIZABETH MCGREGOR

Anne W. Clymer and Elizabeth McGregor are economists in the Office of Employment Projections at the Bureau of Labor Statistics.

GEARING UP

1. Cite what you want to accomplish from your job.

2. List questions you have regarding your career.

3. Name the skills you believe to be of particular importance for your career.

READING STRATEGY

SUMMARIZING EXPOSITION

The strategy of summarizing was introduced in relation to the Malcolm X article in Unit One (see page 62). Summarizing a narrative has a built-in advantage in that you can anticipate the elements that will be present: a setting (a time and place where the story takes place), a plot (or set of events unfolding), characters (the people who act), and some kind of ending. Expository writing, on the other hand, does not present a plot and story line but rather contains explanation and information about ideas, concepts, experiences, and events. Instead of following a familiar story structure you need to process ideas, compare and contrast points, and understand relationships such as cause and effect. The structure of exposition differs from narration, but it does offer a set of features you can look for:

1. The topic—What subject area is the author addressing?

2. Main idea or thesis—What does the author want to say about the topic? What is the most important thing(s) the author wants the reader to know?

3. Development—How does the author elaborate on what is said about the topic? What information does the author provide to develop the thesis?

   You need to understand and master the material in order to write an effective summary. Before you try to summarize, see if you can form a clear mental picture of the essential ideas. For exposition we suggest that you do the following before you try to summarize.

1. Preview the article or chapter. Note the title of the chapter and examine the headings and subheadings for a sense of the overall message. Convert the headings into questions to give you something to look for in your reading. You should also examine such reading aids as a chapter summary or an outline of objectives.

2. Read the article through once without stopping. You would do the same for a short chapter in a textbook or the material contained under one chapter heading. Stopping your reading to look up words or puzzle over ideas will interrupt your concentration on the overall message.

3. Study the material carefully. Before you can summarize an article you must know what the author has said. Read with the writer's purpose in mind. "Listen" to what the author is saying. You need to determine the purpose(s) of the author—for example, to explain, illustrate, compare, or contrast. This requires a second reading at a minimum. Pay particular attention to the first and last several paragraphs. The opening paragraphs often introduce you to the topic and subject and state the purpose of the article. The final paragraphs often provide conclusions and may even summarize the major ideas presented. During your second reading you try to do the following:
   a. Predict vocabulary and confirm it as necessary.
   b. Mark the text with annotations and symbols. Focus on key or repeated words and phrases.
   c. Take note of the author's writing pattern, such as cause/effect or comparison/contrast, and use of signal words (see pages 75–79 and 94–98 in Unit One).
   d. Note the flow of ideas by paying attention to signal words.

   e. Distinguish the major ideas from the details that are less significant.

   f. Make a note of each important idea mentioned. These notes will later be combined to form your summary.

Summary Checklist

A well-formed summary should give someone who has not read the original article a good idea of what the author has said. IT SHOULD CERTAINLY INCLUDE THE AUTHOR'S MAIN POINTS OR THESIS. It should also include enough of the author's supporting documentation to make a case for the thesis.

   A summary should do the following:

1. Clearly state the author's main point in your own words. Paraphrasing is important.

2. Contain sufficient support or detail to allow a reader to follow the author's train of thought leading up to the main point. However, you must condense ideas and eliminate nonessential details.

3. Preserve the author's tone or attitude toward the subject as well as the order of ideas presented.

   A summary does not include the following:

1. Opinion, judgment, interpretation

2. Arguments or evidence that are not in the article

3. A shift in the author's tone

Application

In previewing "Solving the Job Puzzle," you will discover that there is a series of headings that break the article into sections. The quick read through should leave the impression that the article is giving advice about jobs. You will probably discover that you already know many of the ideas discussed based on your own work experiences and information found in the culture. To approach a summary of this kind of article, consider the following:

1. Start with a general introductory statement of the topic. Mention the author by name, refer to the title, and indicate his/her purpose in writing.

2. Paraphrase the author's main idea for each paragraph. Ignore minor points and focus on key ideas that support the author's thesis.

3. Take each of your paragraph summaries and combine them with the thesis statement that you provided in step 1.

4. Use transitions and connecting words to make your summary smooth.

5. Revise your first draft and check your summary for accuracy. Ask yourself:

- Does my summary make the same points as the author does?
- Does my summary remain faithful to the author's emphasis and interpretation?
- Have I omitted anything essential?
- Does my work read smoothly and have clear transitions between ideas?
- Can someone unfamiliar with the article read my summary and get an overall sense of the material?

Here is a sample summary beginning:

The article "Solving the Job Puzzle" is taken from the *Occupational Outlook Quarterly* and concerns the issue of _____. The authors stress the importance of job selection because _____. The authors provide advice in the form of a list of bulleted items. The first point is about interests. The authors suggest that the job seeker _____. The authors then address the topic of _____ and say that _____.

Try filling in the blanks and finishing the summary after you read the article. If you prefer, try your own summary.

 # READING STRATEGY CHECK
CONNECTING IDEAS

If you have proceeded with the "collecting ideas" strategy, you have some information entered under the job satisfaction categories for the people interviewed in the first two articles. If you are working or have been employed, you can furnish information in the "myself" block. For example, if we consider the first issue, "pay," you may have entered "minimum" or "inadequate" or maybe "okay" or "sufficient." (Actually, very few people feel they're adequately paid.) The chart is constructed so that short comments can be inserted as a kind of note. Your task in developing this issue is to take notes and turn them into a full discussion.

Personal Needs	Myself	McDonald's (Jason Pratt)	McDonald's (June Sanders)	McDonald's (Damita)	McDonald's (Jon DeAngelo)	Dr. Steph B.
Pay	First job—minimum wage Second job—better money	No information on money	Needed money but worked 1 day	Needed money and had no options	$21,000 and quit	Good money and options

It is sometimes useful to begin with yourself as a reference point. The following "bubble thinking" and written reflection is an effort to model the thinking-writing process as it connects different sources of material.

> I am thinking about my first job in a fast food restaurant. Two things stand out — the little check and my sore feet at the end of the shift. My current position makes me happy. I have responsibility and a skill that is rewarded with good pay.

✍ I worked in a fast food restaurant for minimum wage. I was not happy with the pay. Even working 35 hours per week brought in little money. Later I found a job in a paint store. I had some art background and had a real knack for mixing colors to match little pieces of material and wallpaper people brought in. I also had the good luck to hit it off with the biggest contractor in the area, who would only come to me for color matches. His company used a lot of paint, and I guess my boss quickly realized I was worth $10 an hour because of all the business coming to me. I only worked 20 hours per week but was taking home more money than my 35 hours at the restaurant.

> Now I can relate my experience to the other individuals. Of the four, the first three worked at entry level, minimum wage jobs such as counter and grill. I understand the work and the money situation because I have been there.

✍ The first four people worked at McDonald's. Jason Pratt does not say anything about how he views his wages. I might guess that he did not feel adequately

169

compensated because his wage could not be any lower. Both Pratt and Sanders have left McDonald's—Sanders after one day. Sanders and Damita were not thrilled about working at McDonald's but they "needed the money."

When the interviewer tries to convince Damita that she is a valuable employee, Damita responds, "Valuable! $3.35 an hour. And I can be replaced by any kid off the street." I can infer from Damita's comments that if she were truly valuable then she would not be making minimum wage.

The last person who works at McDonald's is Jon. Jon was paid $21,000 a year as a manager, which the interviewer reports is big money at McDonald's. We discover at the end that Jon has turned in his resignation. Jon doesn't mention money as a problem but complains about other nonmoney factors. I conclude that his pay was satisfactory or at least adequate.

Although I think pay is very important to people, it seems that it is not everything. I expect the minimum wage people to be frustrated with the little money they get, but the manager's bigger pay didn't make him happy either. The doctor is different than the other people. She seems to love her work and makes good money too!

Dr. Stephanie B.'s salary is not given. However, I think that she is making good money. Part of this inference is based on the fact that on average doctors make a good living. A second factor is that Dr. Stephanie employs a staff of eight, including a full-time biller. Obviously she has some options here. If things get tight for her she could work with fewer people in her office and thus less overhead expense.

In conclusion I, along with the other individuals interviewed, believe that pay is very important to people. But I also believe that pay is not everything. If you don't like your work then good pay doesn't mean much.

The Reading

Solving the Job Puzzle

by ANNE W. CLYMER and ELIZABETH MCGREGOR

1   I am myself reminded that we are not alike; there are diversities of na- | *diversities*
tures among us which are adapted to different occupations." These words, which Plato attributed to Socrates, are still true today. | *attributed*

2   Choosing a career is one of the hardest jobs you will ever have. You should devote extensive time, energy, and thought to make a decision with which you will be happy. Even though undertaking this task means hard work, view a career as an opportunity to do something you enjoy, not simply as a necessity or as a means of earning a living. Taking the time to thoroughly explore career options can mean the difference between finding a stimulating and fulfilling career or hopping from one job to the next in search of the right job. Finding the best occupation for you also is important because work influences many aspects of your life—from your choice of friends and recreational activities to where you live.

3   Choosing a career is work that should be done carefully. As you gain experience and mature, however, you may develop new interests and skills which open doors to new opportunities. Work is an educational experience

and can further focus your interests or perhaps change your career preferences. The choice you make today may not be your last. In fact, most people change occupations several times during their careers. With careful consideration of the wide range of occupations available, you should be able to find the right career.

4   There are many factors to consider when exploring career options and many ways to begin solving your job puzzle. Everyone has certain expectations of his or her job—these may include career advancement, self-expression or creativity, a sense of accomplishment, or a high salary. Deciding what you want most from your job will make choosing a career easier.

5   This article can assist you in your search for a suitable career. It discusses things to consider—personal interests, educational and skill requirements, and job outlook—and lists sources of additional information.

Interests

6   Identifying your interests will help in your search for a stimulating career. You might start by assessing your likes and dislikes, strengths and weaknesses. If you have trouble identifying them, consider the school subjects, activities, and surroundings that appeal to you. Would you prefer a job that involves travel? Do you want to work with children? Do you like science and mathematics? Do you need flexible working hours? Does a particular industry, such as health services, appeal to you? These are just a few questions to ask yourself. There are no right or wrong answers, and only you know what's important. Decide what job characteristics you require, which ones you prefer, and which ones you would not accept. Then rank these characteristics in order of importance to you.

assessing

7   Perhaps job setting ranks high on your list of important job characteristics. You may not want to work behind a desk all day. Many diverse occupations—from building inspectors, to surveyors, to real estate agents—require work away from an office. Or maybe you always dreamed of a job that involves instructing and helping others; in this case, child care workers, teachers, and physicians are among the occupations that might interest you.

8   Geographic location may also concern you. If so, it could influence your career decision because employment in some occupations and industries is concentrated in certain regions or localities. For example, aerospace jobs are concentrated in three states—California, Texas, and Washington—while advertising jobs are concentrated in large cities. If you choose to work in one of these fields, you probably will have to live in one of these states or in a large city. Or, if you live in Denver or the Southeast, for instance, you should learn which industries and occupations are found in those locations. On the other hand, many industries such as hotels and motels, legal services, and retail trade, as well as occupations such as teachers, secretaries, and computer analysts, are found in all areas of the country.

9   Earnings potential varies from occupation to occupation, and each person must determine his or her needs and goals. If high earnings are important to you, look beyond the starting wages. Some occupations offer

relatively low starting salaries, but earnings substantially increase with experience, additional training, and promotions. In the end, your earnings may be higher in one of these occupations. For example, insurance sales workers may have relatively low earnings at first; after years of building a clientele, however, their earnings may increase substantially.

10   Job setting, working with a specific group of people, geographic location, and earnings are just a few occupational characteristics that you may consider. Be open-minded. Consider occupations related to your initial interests. For example, you may be interested in health care, and certain qualities of nursing may appeal to you, such as patient care and frequent public contact. Exploring other health occupations that share these characteristics—including doctors, respiratory therapists, and emergency medical technicians—may stimulate your interest in a health field other than nursing.

11   Don't eliminate any occupation or industry before you learn more about it. Some occupations and industries invoke certain positive or negative images. For some people, fashion designers produce a glamorous image, while production occupations in manufacturing industries bring to mind a less attractive image. However, jobs often are not what they first appear to be, and misconceptions are common. Exciting jobs may have dull aspects, *misconceptions* while less glamorous occupations may interest you once you learn about them. For example, the opportunity to travel makes a flight attendant's job seem exciting, but the work is strenuous and tiring; flight attendants stand for long periods and must remain friendly when they are tired and passengers are unpleasant. On the other hand, many people consider automotive assembly work dirty and dull; however, production workers in the motor vehicle manufacturing industry are among the highest paid in the nation.

Skills

12   One way to choose an occupation is to examine the skills required to perform the job well. Consider the skills you already have, or your ability and interest in obtaining the skills or training required for specific occupations. Some occupations that require mechanical ability, for instance, include elevator installers and repairers and automotive mechanics. If you do not plan to attend college, consider occupations that require less formal education. If you are interested in engineering, for example, but do not want to pursue a college degree, drafters and engineering technicians are two occupations you can enter with 1 or 2 years of postsecondary training.

13   Some skills—analysis, persuading, and mechanical ability, for example— are specific to certain occupations. However, certain skills are needed, in varying degrees, in virtually all occupations, from factory workers to top executives.

Skills Common to All Jobs

14   As the marketplace becomes increasingly competitive, a company's ability to succeed depends upon its workers' skills—in particular, basic skills in reading, writing, and mathematics. These skills allow workers to learn and adapt

to rapid technological advances and changing business practices in their jobs. This adaptability is crucial to one's survival in the job market.

15   Reading skills are essential to perform most jobs. Workers must often read and understand text, graphs, charts, manuals, and instructional materials. Writing skills are necessary to communicate thoughts, ideas, and information in written forms such as memorandums, invoices, schedules, letters, or information requests. Many jobs require basic mathematical skills to take measurements and perform simple calculations. Lack of these skills can lead to many problems, including poor quality products and missed deadlines. These problems can then result in a decline in sales and increased customer complaints.

16   Reading, writing, and mathematical skills are as important for a research scientist as they are for occupations that require little formal education, such as a stockroom clerk at a manufacturing plant. Although a computer system may be designed to track inventory by electronically recording all transactions, the clerk is responsible for verifying the information. The clerk must   *verifying*
be able to read and do simple calculations to confirm that stockroom inventory matches what the computer registers. Any inaccuracies in counting, computing, or recording of this inventory could result in a slowdown in production.

17   Workers also need good listening and speaking skills to interact with others. Greater interaction among workers is evident in factories, offices, and laboratories. Problems often are solved through communication, cooperation, and discussion, and workers must be able to listen, speak, and think on their feet. When dealing with customers, workers must listen and understand customers' needs and communicate solutions and ideas. It is not good enough to merely take a customer's order; workers must provide customers with useful information.

18   The banking industry illustrates the importance of listening and speaking skills. Banks face competition from other industries—including insurance companies, credit unions, and investment houses—that offer a growing array of financial products. Tellers, customer service representatives, and bank managers need strong communication skills to explain, promote, and sell the bank's services to potential customers. Customer satisfaction can only be achieved by understanding what the customer wants and by providing that service as quickly as possible.

19   Good interpersonal skills are critical as the workplace becomes more team-oriented. Apparel plants, for instance, are replacing the traditional assembly line with modular manufacturing. On the traditional assembly line, workers performed a specific task independent of other workers and were compensated accordingly. Today, groups of workers, called modules, work   *compensated*
as a team to produce garments, solve problems as they occur, and make suggestions to improve production or working conditions. Group interaction is important because an individual's earnings are based upon the group's performance.

20   Workers at all levels must be willing to learn new techniques. Computers, for instance, were once found primarily in office settings; today,

computers are found in every work setting from factories to classrooms. The introduction of computers into the manufacturing process is transforming many craft and factory occupations; many of these jobs now require the use of computer-controlled equipment. For example, most elevators are computerized and electronically controlled. In order to install, repair, and maintain modern elevators, elevator repairers need a thorough knowledge of electronics, electricity, and computer applications. Even though a high school education is the minimum requirement for entering this field, workers with postsecondary training in electronics usually have better advancement opportunities than those with less training. As technological changes continue, retraining will be essential for workers in many fields.

Outlook

21   When matching your interests and skills to an occupation, you should also consider the employment outlook for that occupation or related industry. For instance, stiff competition is expected for jobs as advertising managers because the number of applicants greatly exceeds the number of job openings. On the other hand, job openings for preschool workers should be plentiful due to a rapidly growing demand for this occupation and relatively high turnover among preschool workers. Outlook is discussed in detail in the *Occupational Outlook Handbook* and *Career Guide to Industries,* which are revised every two years.

22   Information about job openings, supply-demand conditions, and susceptibility to layoffs indicate, in part, the ease or difficulty of landing a job. Many factors affect the demand for an occupation, including changes in consumer spending, demographics, and technology. Researching an occupation or industry will help you identify key factors and their impact on employment. For example, increased use of computers has contributed to the rapid growth of computer service technician jobs. On the other hand, the growing use of computers in offices has greatly reduced the demand for typists. This illustrates the diverse effects that technological advances can have on different occupations and emphasizes the importance of learning about specific occupations.   *susceptibility*   *diverse*

23   Job growth is a good indicator of favorable opportunities, but the fastest growing occupations do not always equate with the largest numbers of job opportunities. Most job openings result from the need to replace workers who leave their jobs. Consequently, larger occupations—which usually have the highest replacement needs—generally provide the most job openings. As a result of replacement needs, even occupations that are declining can provide employment opportunities.

24   Knowledge of the industries in which occupations are found also is important in looking for a job. Job opportunities generally are favorable in an occupation found in a wide range of industries, such as receptionists. On the other hand, employment prospects are likely to be unfavorable, and workers more subject of layoffs, in an occupation that is concentrated in a declining industry, such as machine operators in the textile industry. Some workers   *prospects*

also may be subject to layoffs because of the nature of the industry. For example, the demand for construction workers is cyclical—employment rises and falls with changes in construction activity—and motor vehicle manufacturing workers may be laid off during periods of slack sales.

Additional Information

25   Once you identify an interest in one or more occupations or industries, many sources of additional information are available. The specific sources may vary, depending on the fields which interest you. Use common sense and resourcefulness to learn about potential jobs. For example, local television or radio stations may be a good source of information and, perhaps, work experience if broadcasting interests you. The following sources may serve as starting points in your career search.

Libraries

26   A library is a great place to find information about jobs. Libraries have career guidance publications that present occupational information covering job duties, training requirements, working conditions, employment outlook, and earnings. Librarians can direct you to the information you need.

Career Centers

27   Many career centers have computerized job information systems that match jobs to your skills and interests. These systems generally are easy to use and generate a list of suggested occupations. Career centers often have career literature that may interest you. Also, career counselors at these centers can help you develop jobseeking skills, such as resume writing or interviewing.

State Employment Service Offices

28   State employment service offices can provide you with information concerning the industrial and occupational composition of specific areas. This is a good place to start if you need to find out what job opportunities a particular area offers.

Guidance Counselors

29   Counselors interview, test, and counsel students to help them discover their skills and interests and how these relate to career opportunities. If you have a particular aptitude for certain subjects, a counselor can direct you toward occupations that require these talents. If you are interested in art, your counselor might provide information on becoming a designer or graphic artist; if you are good at mathematics, a counselor may suggest that engineer or statistician might be a good occupational choice for you. Counselors may also direct students to career information centers or career education programs.

Informational Interviews

30   Interviewing individuals to gather information about their occupation or industry is a very effective way to find out about jobs that may interest you.

An informational interview is not a job interview. Rather, it's your opportunity to learn from a person who knows the pros and cons of an occupation or industry.

31   If you don't know someone in the occupation that interests you, network! Ask your parents, neighbors, teachers, or friends if they know someone in the occupation. Most people enjoy talking about their jobs and are pleased to have an audience. Your network could lead to internships, volunteer work, or other opportunities in your field of interest.

32   Before you talk to someone about a particular occupation, think about what you want to know. You may ask questions about job duties, educational or training requirements, advancement opportunities, and average wages. You may also ask for his or her opinion of your qualifications for a particular job.

Internships/Volunteer Work

33   There is no substitute for practical experience. Internship programs and volunteer work help students explore a field and develop career skills at the same time. For example, someone interested in politics may volunteer to help a local, state, or national campaign elect a candidate to office. Many local government planning offices offer internships to college and graduate students specializing in urban and regional planning. Through these programs, students gain planning experience that not only improves their chances of finding a full-time job after graduation but also helps them decide whether or not the field interests them.

Cooperative Education

34   This program is similar to internships; students gain practical experience by working in their chosen fields. Students enrolled in cooperative education programs divide their time between school and work, applying the knowledge and theory gained in class to practical situations on the job. Credit and grades are given for both the worksite learning and the related school instruction. Not all cooperative education programs are alike. In some programs, students switch from school to job each quarter or semester; in others, students may work for a couple of months a year. Through these programs, students earn money, gain experience, test their interest in particular careers, and learn how they fit into the world of work. Your counselor, financial aid office, or career center may have information on these opportunities.

Trade Unions and Associations

35   These organizations specialize in a particular field and are well informed on the issues affecting the employment of workers in occupations or industries that they represent. They can provide information about training and skill requirements. Local unions sponsor apprenticeships and formal training programs for many occupations.

QUESTIONS

1. Explain the meaning of the article's title. What is the "puzzle" that needs to be solved?

2. In the opening paragraph the authors quote Plato: "I am myself reminded that we are not alike; there are diversities of nature among us which are adapted to different occupations." Explain the meaning of this quote. Do you agree with the authors, who claim that these words, written long ago, are still true today? Explain.

3. Explain why one needs to look beyond starting wages to get a true picture of potential earnings.

4. The authors state: "Jobs are often not what they first appear to be, and misconceptions are common." Explain the meaning of this statement and discuss its implications for career exploration.

5. The authors state: "Certain skills are needed, in varying degrees, in virtually all occupations. . . ." Explain this statement and relate it to the occupation of your choice.

6. Explain the concept of "adaptability" and show why it is important for job market survival.

7. Illustrate how computers are becoming more common in all work settings.

8. Explain the concept of "outlook" and show why it needs to be considered when choosing an occupation.

EXTENDING YOUR VOCABULARY

diversities: In comparing and contrasting the three species of birds, we found diversities in their _____

attributed: He attributed his success to _____

assessing: The career counselor felt that it was worthwhile to begin assessing Joan's likes and dislikes in order to

_____

misconceptions: Because of the many misconceptions that teenagers have about pregnancy, the counselor decided to

_____

verifying: After verifying the information, the bank officer

_____

compensated: When the workers felt they weren't properly compensated, they decided to _____

susceptibility: Because of their child's susceptibility to colds, the par-
                   ents decided to _____

diverse: To cope with the diverse student body from many
                   countries, counselors _____

prospects: If you wish to improve your job prospects, it is recom-
                   mended that you _____

Tomorrow's Jobs

"Tomorrow's Jobs" is taken from the 22nd edition of the Occupational Outlook
Handbook, *published in 1996–1997 and produced in the Bureau of Labor Statistics under the general guidance and direction of Ronald E. Kutcher, associate
commissioner for employment projections, and Neal H. Rosenthal, chief, Division for Occupational Outlook. The handbook is widely used for counseling individuals about the world of work. Since 1966 it has been published biennially
in even numbered years and is also available on the Internet.*

GEARING UP

1. Based on your knowledge of the work world, list the jobs you would expect to have the greatest growth and the greatest decline in the next five
   years. Explain possible reasons for the projected growth or decline.

2. Describe the steps you would take to investigate the potential outlook for
   your job or career.

3. Interview someone who has worked at least twenty years. Ask that individual how the nature of work has changed in the past two decades.

 ## READING STRATEGY

READING AND INTERPRETING GRAPHS

With the approach of the millennium, the amount of information that we
must process continues to grow. Not only are we required to deal with written materials but increasingly we are also expected to handle all sorts of
visual data. Readers of newspapers and viewers of the nightly news on
television probably recognize that both forms of media make wide use of

graphics. Stock performance, employment data, and budget information are commonly expressed in the forms of graphs, charts, tables, and other diagrams. College textbooks use visual aids to communicate information. A business textbook might include a graph that compares and contrasts the performances of two corporations.

Some readers don't pay close enough attention to these visual aids and so miss important information. Sometimes, in a limited amount of space, a well-designed graphic can help communicate a great deal of information that might otherwise require many lines of text. Just as you are learning strategies to process written information from texts, so must you develop ways to effectively process information from visuals.

In reading and interpreting visual aids, you can use some of the text-reading strategies previously presented. Previewing a graphic can give you an overview of its purpose and its relationship to the text. The title, captions, and notes can provide valuable information. Just as you saw in a previous strategy that expository texts use paragraph patterns such as cause and effect or comparison and contrast, so do graphic designers use visual elements that seek to compare and contrast data or suggest a cause-and-effect relationship among data.

Among the more common graphics are tables, charts, diagrams, and graphs. There are certain common principles that need to be understood when preparing to deal with graphics.

1. *Recognize and interpret the elements that make up a visual.* Extract the basic information contained in the visual. Some preliminary questions need to be addressed:

    - What is the topic?

    - What is the source of the information?

    - Who prepared it?

    - What does it say?

    - Why was it included? (what does the author want me to learn?)

    - What is the relationship between what the author wants me to learn and the parts contained in the visual?

2. *Part of using graphics effectively involves making interpretations. Be prepared to do the following:*

    - Make comparisons of quantitative data

    - Look at part/whole relationships

    - Determine general trends or movements

    - Note cause and effect

    - Predict outcomes

    - Make generalizations

- Seek conclusions
- Look for deeper meaning

Application

Graphs are drawings or diagrams that show relationships between two sets of data. A well-designed graph can communicate a great deal of information that might take a writer several paragraphs to convey. Three common types of graphs are bar graphs, circle or pie graphs, and line graphs.

Bar Graphs

As their name implies, bar graphs use horizontal or vertical bars to compare quantities. This type of graph is useful for comparing sizes of several items or the size of a particular item at different times. Most graphs will include a title and a legend or key.

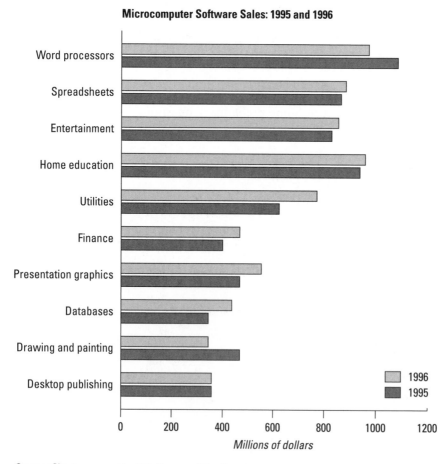

Microcomputer Software Sales: 1995 and 1996

Source: Chart prepared by U.S. Bureau of the Census.

In the example, microcomputer software sales data are provided for two different time periods: 1994 and 1995. To distinguish the two time periods, a light and a dark shading is employed, indicated in the legend located on the right side of the graph.

In reading a bar graph, examine the horizontal and vertical scales to note what is being measured or compared. In the example above, the vertical scale lists various categories of microcomputer software, such as word processors and spreadsheets. The horizontal scale presents the dollar amounts (in increments of 200 million dollars) that have been spent on microcomputer software in the years 1994 and 1995.

Data for each category of software are being presented for two years: 1994 and 1995. The color or shading of the bar reveals the year, and the size of the bar reveals the amount of money spent. Since not every bar falls exactly on an increment of 200 million dollars, some approximation is necessary. If you examine the bottommost entry, Desktop publishing, the 1994 bar seems to fall almost exactly on the 200 million mark. But the 1995 bar falls slightly past the 200 million dollar mark.

Even though no text accompanies this graph, certain conclusions can be drawn, and trends can be observed about software sales for the two years being studied. For example, examine the following three categories:

Word processors

Home education

Desktop publishing

For each of these categories, carefully study the bars representing 1994 and 1995.

What conclusions can be reached?

_____

_____

_____

The reading that follows this strategy makes use of several bar graphs or charts to highlight trends in the labor market. Most of these graphs have accompanying text that supports the message conveyed in the visual.

CIRCLE OR PIE GRAPHS

In order to show the relationships of individual parts to a whole, writers use circle or pie charts. These visuals are useful when you need to see the percentage of the whole that each individual part represents. Study the next example, which illustrates state government tax collections for the year 1994. By coincidence, sales and gross receipts amounted to 50 percent of the total revenue collected, or $373.8 billion. This can be seen by the diagonal line that cuts the pie in half. Although there is no legend or key provided, the graph

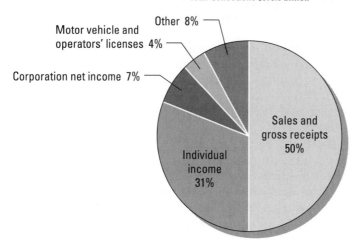

State Government Tax Collections, 1994
Total Collections $373.8 billion

Source: Chart prepared by U.S. Bureau of the Census.

is titled and labeled and each part or wedge of the pie is represented by a different color or shade.

Just as bar graphs can be used to show comparative data, pie charts can be used for the same purposes. To compare data, authors commonly use another pie chart to represent data from a different time period. Thus the above pie chart showing tax collections from 1994 can be compared and contrasted to the following chart that presents data from 1970.

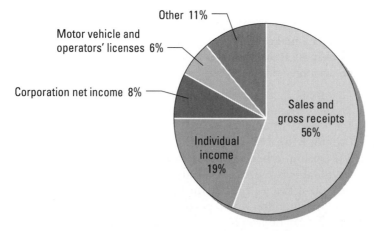

State Government Tax Collections, 1970
Total Collections $48.0 billion

Source: Chart prepared by U.S. Bureau of the Census.

Note that the total collections for 1970 amounted to 48.0 billion dollars, in contrast to the 373.8 billion dollars collected in 1994. But these graphs are presenting percentages of the total revenues. It is easy to note that the sales and gross receipts percentage collected in 1994 (50 percent) was proportionally less than what was collected in 1970 (56 percent). This can be seen in the 1970 pie chart, where the sales and gross receipts part of the total is slightly larger than half.

LINE GRAPHS

Line graphs usually are used to show changes in amounts over a period of time. These graphs also have horizontal and vertical scales, and points plotted on a line graph have a value on both scales. Line graphs are useful for representing the relation between two quantities or variables.

Consider two common objects that are used for measurement: a thermometer and a calendar.

April						
1	2	3	4	5	6	7
8	9	10	11	12	13	14
15	16	17	18	19	20	21
22	23	24	25	26	27	28
29	30					

Now add the idea of a variable—something that changes. The temperature reading can be considered a variable in that it is subject to fluctuation, and the purpose of the thermometer is to measure temperature variations. A calendar is used to record the days in a week, month, and year. Viewed by the week, month, and year, the calendar also records change. The information from both of these instruments can be combined and expressed in graphic form.

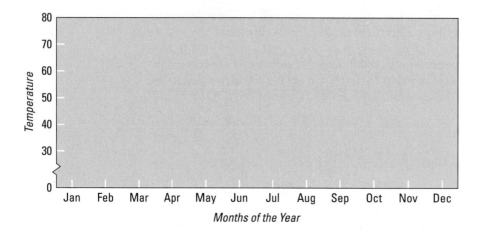

The above diagram is the beginning form of a graph that can measure temperature change during the course of a year. By plotting the average temperature (one variable) for each month (another variable), it is possible to see how temperature varies according to the seasons (assuming that this graph represents a geographic area that has seasonal variation).

This same graph can be used to compare average seasonal temperatures with actual measured temperatures. The expected average readings can be shown using one line style (such as the gray line in the graph), and the actual readings could be shown with a different line style (the black line shown in the graph).

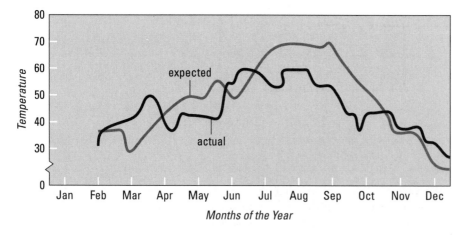

What can you conclude about the yearly temperature of this region? How did the expected temperature compare with the actual?

_____

_____

Now let's examine another line graph.

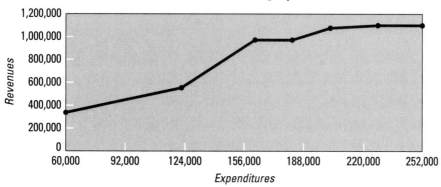

What conclusions can be drawn from the above data?

_____

_____

This graph shows the relationship between two sets of data, advertisement expenditures and sales revenue for a company. What happens when the company increases its advertising expenses? Revenues tend to rise, but not in a strictly linear fashion. This can be seen by examining the graph and doing some calculations. When the company spends $60,000, it generates revenues of around $380,000. When spending is more than doubled to approximately $122,000, the amount of revenue generated is approximately $580,000. But when an additional $32,000 is spent on advertising, the resulting revenue is close to $1,000,000. The steep slope of the line indicates this sharp increase in revenue.

Conclusion

Now you should be ready to apply these techniques to the next reading, "Tomorrow's Jobs." It contains a series of bar graphs that are designed to support the message of the text. As you examine these graphs, keep the following questions in mind:

- Is there a title, caption, or key provided?

- Can you tell how the graph is organized?

- Can you determine what relationship is being described or what data are being compared?

- Does the size, shape, or direction of the bars or lines (or for a circle graph, the size or percent of the circle part) suggest a pattern?

- Can you tell what all the details add up to?

- Can you conclude why the graph was included—what is the purpose?
- Can you connect the graph with any supporting text?

 # READING STRATEGY CHECK

SUMMARIZING TEXT

The strategy of summarizing text was first presented in relation to the Malcolm X article in Unit One and to "Solving the Job Puzzle" in this unit. It was pointed out that the ability to summarize is important in both your academic and professional life.

The article under consideration, "Tomorrow's Jobs," is an example of expository writing. It contains information in the form of statistics, data, and trends related to the occupational market. As a brief reminder on summarizing this type of article, consider the following:

1. Use the headings and subheadings to gather key ideas.

2. Look at the visuals presented because they also highlight important ideas.

3. Cite the main point of concern in your opening sentences.

4. Make sure that you include the key points that support your opening statement.

5. Report accurately but use your own words.

The Reading

Tomorrow's Jobs

1   Making informed career decisions requires reliable information about opportunities that should be available in the future. This chapter presents highlights of Bureau of Labor Statistics **projections** of industry and occupational employment and the labor force, that can help guide your career plans.

projections

2   **A slowdown in employment growth is expected.**

- Over the 1994–2005 period, employment is projected to increase by 17.7 million or 14 percent. This is slower than the 24-percent increase **attained** during the 11-year period, 1983–94, when the economy added 24.6 million jobs.

attained

- Wage and salary worker employment will **account** for 95 percent of this increase. In addition, the number of self-employed workers is expected to increase by 950,000, to 11.6 million in 2005, while the number of unpaid family workers will decline.

account

3   **Service-producing industries will account for most new jobs.** (See chart 1.)

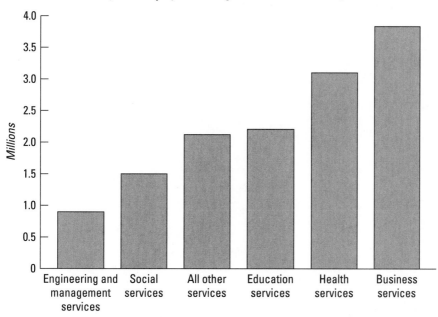

Chart 1. Projected Employment Change in Services Industries, 1994–2005

Source: Bureau of Labor Statistics, 1996.

- Employment growth is projected to be highly concentrated by industry. The services and retail trade industries will account for 16.2 million out of a total projected growth of 16.8 million wage and salary jobs.

- Business, health, and education services will account for 70 percent of the growth—9.2 million out of 13.6 million jobs—within services.

- Health care services will account for almost one-fifth of all job growth from 1994–2005. Factors contributing to continued growth in this industry include the aging population, which will continue to require more services, and the increased use of **innovative** medical technology for intensive *innovative* diagnosis and treatment. Patients will increasingly be shifted out of hospitals and into outpatient facilities, nursing homes, and home health care in an attempt to contain costs.

- The personal supply services industry, which provides temporary help to employers in other industries, is projected to add 1.3 million jobs from 1994 to 2005. Temporary workers tend to have low wages, low stability, and poor job benefits.

4 **The goods-producing sector will decline.** (See chart 2.)

- The goods-producing sector faces declining employment in two of its four industries—manufacturing and mining. Employment in the other two industries—construction, and agriculture, forestry, and fishing—is expected to increase.

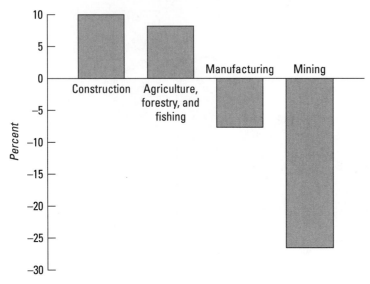

Chart 2. Projected Percent Change in Employment in Goods-Producing Industries, 1994–2005

Source: Bureau of Labor Statistics, 1996.

- Employment in manufacturing is expected to continue to decline, losing 1.3 million jobs over the 1994–2005 period. Operators, fabricators, and laborers, and precision production, craft, and repair occupations are expected to account for more than 1 million of these lost jobs. Systems analysts and other computer-related occupations in manufacturing are expected to increase.

5 **Job opportunities can arise in two ways—job growth and replacement needs.** (See chart 3.)

- Job growth can be measured by percent change and numerical change. The fastest growing occupations do not necessarily provide the largest number of jobs. Even though an occupation is expected to grow rapidly, it may provide fewer openings than a slower growing, larger occupation.

- Opportunities in large occupations are **enhanced** by the additional job openings resulting from the need to replace workers who leave the occupation. Some workers leave the occupation as they are promoted or change careers; others stop working to return to school, assume household responsibilities, or retire.   *enhanced*

- Replacement needs are greater in occupations with low pay and **status,** low training requirements, and a high proportion of young and part-time workers.   *status*

- Replacement needs will account for 29.4 million job openings from 1994 to 2005, far more than the 17.7 million openings projected to arise from employment growth.

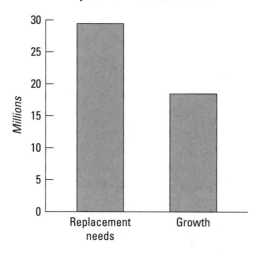

Chart 3. Total Job Openings Due to Growth and Replacement Needs, 1994–2005

Source: Bureau of Labor Statistics, 1996.

6   **Employment change will vary widely by broad occupational group.** (See chart 4.)

- Employment in professional specialty occupations is projected to increase at a faster rate than any other major occupational group.

- Among the major occupational groups, employment in professional specialty occupations is also projected to account for the most job growth from 1994–2005.

- Professional specialty occupations—which require high educational attainment and offer high earnings—and service occupations—which require lower educational attainment and offer lower earnings—are expected to account for more than half of all job growth between 1994 and 2005.

- Agriculture, forestry, fishing, and related occupations is the only major occupational group projected to decline. All job openings in this group will stem from replacement needs.

- Office automation is expected to have a significant effect on many individual administrative and clerical support occupations.

- Precision production, craft, and repair occupations and operators, fabricators, and laborers are projected to grow much more slowly than average due to continuing advances in technology, changes in production methods, and the overall decline in manufacturing employment.

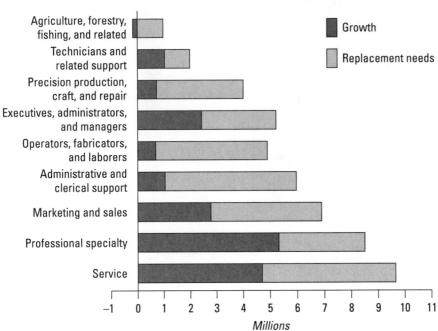

Chart 4. Projected Job Openings Due to Growth and Replacement Needs by Major Occupational Group, 1994–2005

Source: Bureau of Labor Statistics, 1996.

7 **Twenty occupations will account for half of all job growth over the 1994–2005 period.** (See chart 5.)

- The 20 occupations accounting for half of all job growth over the 1994–2005 period tend to be large in size rather than fast growing. Three health care occupations are in the top 10, and 3 education-related occupations are in the second 10.

8 **The fastest growing occupations reflect growth in computer technology and health services.** (See chart 6.)

- Many of the fastest growing occupations are concentrated in health services, which is expected to increase more than twice as fast as the economy as a whole. Personal and home care aides, and home health aides, are expected to be in great demand to provide personal and physical care for an increasing number of elderly people and for persons who are recovering from surgery and other serious health conditions. This is occurring as hospitals and insurance companies **mandate** shorter stays for recovery to contain costs.   *mandate*

- Employment of computer engineers and systems analysts is expected to grow rapidly to satisfy expanding needs for scientific research and applications of computer technology in business and industry.

Chart 5. Occupations Having the Largest Numerical Increase in Employment, 1994–2005

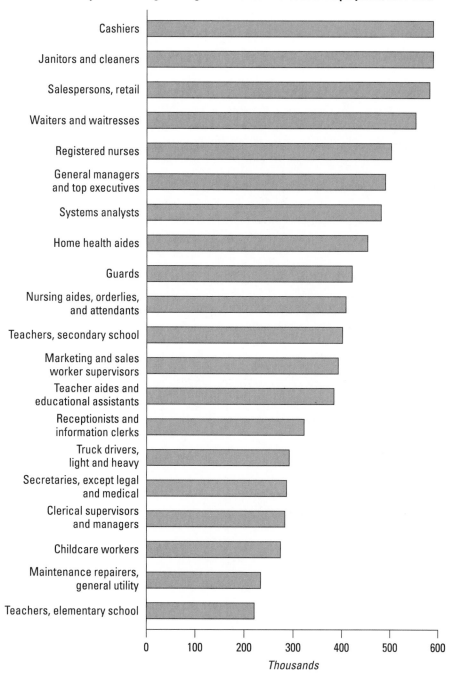

Source: Bureau of Labor Statistics, 1996.

Chart 6. Occupations Projected to Grow the Fastest, 1994–2005

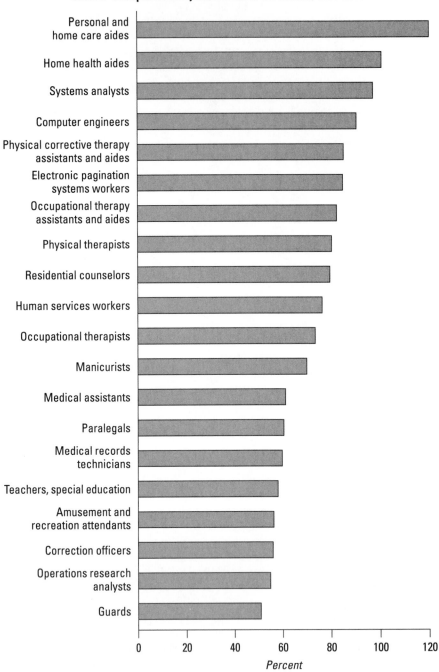

Source: Bureau of Labor Statistics, 1996.

Chart 7. Occupations with the Largest Projected Numerical Decreases in Total Employment, 1994–2005

- Farmers
- Typists and word processors
- Bookkeeping, accounting, and auditing clerks
- Bank tellers
- Sewing machine operators, garment
- Cleaners and servants, private household
- Computer operators, except peripheral equipment
- Billing, posting, and calculating machine operators
- Duplicating, mail, and other office machine operators
- Textile draw-out and winding machine operators and tenders
- File clerks
- Freight, stock, and material movers, hand
- Farm workers
- Machine tool cutting operators and tenders, metal and plastic
- Central office operators
- Central office and PBX installers and repairers
- Electrical and electronic assemblers
- Station installers and repairers, telephone
- Personnel clerks, except payroll and timekeeping
- Data entry keyers, except composing

−300   −250   −200   −150   −100   −50   0

Thousands

Source: Bureau of Labor Statistics, 1996.

Chart 8. Projected Percent Growth in Employment by Level of Education and Training, 1994–2005

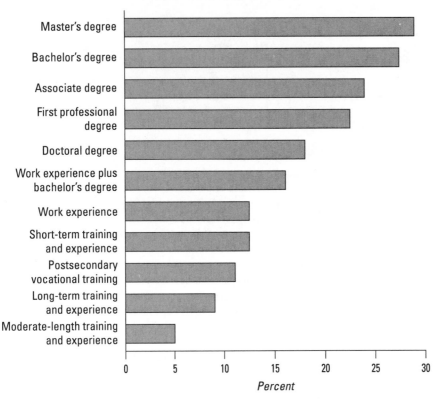

Source: Bureau of Labor Statistics, 1996.

9   **Declining occupational employment stems from declining industry employment and technological change.** (See chart 7.)

- Farmers, garment sewing machine operators, and private household cleaners and servants are examples of occupations that will lose employment because of declining industry employment.

- Many declining occupations are affected by structural changes, resulting from technological advances, organizational changes, and other factors that affect the employment of workers. For example, the use of typists and word processors is expected to decline substantially because of productivity improvements resulting from office automation, and the increased use of word processing equipment by professional and managerial employees.

10   **Education and training affect job opportunities.** (See chart 8 and table 1.)

- Workers in jobs with low education and training requirements tend to have greater occupational **mobility.** Consequently, these jobs will provide   *mobility* a larger than proportional share of all job openings stemming from re-placement needs.

- Jobs requiring the most education and training will grow faster than jobs with lower education and training requirements.

- Table 1 presents the fastest growing occupations and those having the largest numerical increase in employment over the 1994–2005 period, cat-egorized by level of education and training.

11 **Jobs requiring the most education and training will be the fastest grow-ing and highest paying.**

- Occupations which require a bachelor's degree or above will average 23 percent growth, almost double the 12-percent growth projected for occu-pations that require less education and training.

- Occupations that pay above average wages are projected to grow faster than occupations with below average wages. Jobs with above average wages are expected to account for 60 percent of employment growth over the 1994–2005 period. Jobs with higher earnings often require higher lev-els of education and training.

- Education is important in getting a high paying job. However, many oc-cupations—for example, registered nurses, blue-collar work supervisors, electrical and electronic technicians/technologists, carpenters, and police and detectives—do not require a college degree, yet offer higher than av-erage earnings.

- Groups in the labor force with lower than average educational attainment in 1994, including Hispanics and blacks, will continue to have difficulty obtaining a share of the high paying jobs that is consistent with their share of the labor force, unless their educational attainment rises. Although high paying jobs will be available without college training, most jobs that pay above average wages will require a college degree.

- Educational services are projected to increase by 2.2 million jobs and ac-count for 1 out of every 8 jobs that will be added to the economy between 1994 and 2005. Most jobs will be for teachers, who are projected to ac-count for about 20 percent of all jobs available for college graduates.

- Projected employment growth of the occupations whose earnings rank in the top quartile in the Nation was highly concentrated. Eight of the 146 occupations will account for about half of the new jobs: Registered nurses, systems analysts, blue-collar worker supervisors, general managers and top executives, and four teaching occupations—elementary school teachers, secondary school teachers, college faculty, and special education teachers.

12 **Jobs requiring the least education and training will provide the most openings, but offer the lowest pay.** (See chart 9.)

- The distribution of jobs by education and training, and earnings, will change little over the 1994–2005 period, with jobs requiring the least

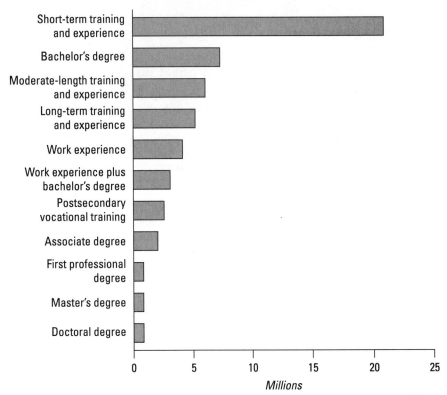

Chart 9. Projected Total Job Openings by Level of Education and Training, 1994–2005

Source: Bureau of Labor Statistics, 1996.

amount of education and training, and generally offering low pay, continuing to account for about 4 of every 10 jobs.

- Jobs which require moderate-length and short-term training and experience (the two categories requiring the least amount of education and training) will provide over half of total job openings over the 1994–2005 period.

13 **The labor force will continue to grow faster than the population.**

- **Spurred** by the growing proportion of women who work, the labor force will grow slightly faster than the population over the 1994–2005 period.   *Spurred*

14 **Women will continue to comprise an increasing share of the labor force.** (See chart 10.)

- Women, as a result of a faster rate of growth than men, are projected to represent a slightly greater portion of the labor force in 2005 than in 1994—increasing from 46 to 48 percent.

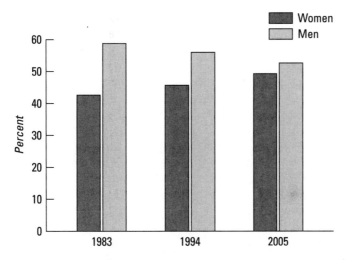

Chart 10. **Labor Force by Sex, 1983, 1994, and Projected 2005**

Source: Bureau of Labor Statistics, 1996.

- The number of men in the labor force is projected to grow, but at a slower rate than in the past, in part reflecting declining employment in good-paying production jobs in manufacturing, and a continued shift in demand for workers from the goods-producing sector to the service-producing sector. Men with less education and training may find it increasingly difficult to obtain jobs **consistent** with their experience.

consistent

15 **The labor force will become increasingly diverse.** (See chart 11.)

- The number of Hispanics, and Asians and other races, will increase much faster than blacks and white non-Hispanics. Blacks will increase faster than white non-Hispanics.

- Despite relatively slow growth, resulting in a declining share of the labor force, white non-Hispanics will still make up the vast majority of workers in 2005.

16 **Interested in more detail?**

- Readers interested in more information about projections and detail on the labor force, economic growth, industry and occupational employment, or methods and assumptions should consult the November 1995 *Monthly Labor Review: The Employment Outlook: 1994–2005*, BLS Bulletin 2472; or the Fall 1995 *Occupatoinal Outlook Quarterly.* Information on the limitations inherent in economic projections also can be found in these publications.

- For more information about employment change, job openings, earnings, unemployment rates, and training requirements by occupation, consult *Occupational Projections and Training Data, 1996 Edition*, BLS Bulletin 2471.

Chart 11. Distribution of the Labor Force by Race, 1994 and Projected 2005

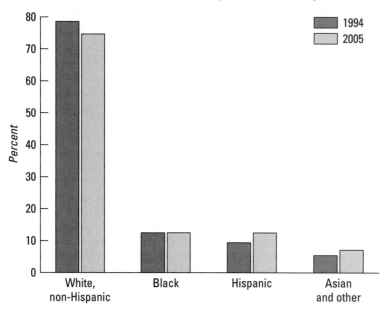

Source: Bureau of Labor Statistics, 1996.

Table 1. Jobs growing the fastest and having the largest numerical increase in employment from 1994–2005, by level of education and training	
Fastest Growing Occupations	**Occupations Having the Largest Numerical Increase in Employment**
First-professional degree	
Chiropractors	Lawyers
Lawyers	Physicians
Physicians	Clergy
Clergy	Chiropractors
Podiatrists	Dentists
Doctoral degree	
Medical scientists	College and university faculty
Biological scientists	Biological scientists
College and university faculty	Medical scientists
Mathematicians and all other mathematical scientists	Mathematicians and all other mathematical scientists

Fastest Growing Occupations	Occupations Having the Largest Numerical Increase in Employment
Master's degree	
Operations research analysts	Management analysts
Speech-language pathologists and audiologists	Counselors
Management analysts	Speech-language pathologists and audiologists
Counselors	Psychologists
Urban and regional planners	Operations research analysts
Work experience plus bachelor's degree	
Engineering, mathematics, and natural science managers	General managers and top executives
Marketing, advertising, and public relations managers	Financial managers
Artists and commercial artists	Marketing, advertising, and public relations managers
Financial managers	Engineering, mathematics, and natural science managers
Education administrators	Education administrators
Bachelor's degree	
Systems analysts	Systems analysts
Computer engineers	Teachers, secondary school
Occupational therapists	Teachers, elementary school
Physical therapists	Teachers, special education
Special education teachers	Social workers
Associate degree	
Paralegals	Registered nurses
Medical records technicians	Paralegals
Dental hygienists	Radiologic technologists and technicians
Respiratory therapists	Dental hygienists
Radiologic technologists and technicians	Medical records technicians
Postsecondary vocational training	
Manicurists	Secretaries, except legal and medical
Surgical technologists	Licensed practical nurses
Data processing equipment repairers	Hairdressers, hairstylists, and cosmetologists
Dancers and choreographers	Legal secretaries
Emergency medical technicians	Medical services
Work experience	
Nursery and greenhouse managers	Marketing and sales worker supervisors
Lawn service managers	Clerical supervisors and managers
Food service and lodging managers	Food service and lodging managers
Clerical supervisors and managers	Instructors, adult education
Teachers and instructors, vocational and nonvocational training	Teachers and instructors, vocational education and training

Fastest Growing Occupations	Occupations Having the Largest Numerical Increase in Employment
Long-term training and experience (more than 12 months of on-the-job training)	
Electronic pagination systems workers	Maintenance repairers, general utility
Correction officers	Correction officers
Securities and financial service sales workers	Automotive mechanics
Patternmakers and layout workers, fabric and apparel	Cooks, restaurant
Producers, directors, actors, and entertainers	Police patrol officers
Moderate-length training and experience (1 to 12 months of combined on-the-job experience and informal training)	
Physical and corrective therapy assistants and aides	Human services workers
Occupational therapy assistants and aides	Medical assistants
Human services workers	Instructors and coaches, sports and physical training
Medical assistants	Dental assistants
Detectives, except public	Painters and paper hangers, construction and maintenance
Short-term training and experience (up to 1 month of on-the-job experience)	
Personal and home care aides	Cashiers
Home health aides	Janitors and cleaners, including maids and housekeepers
Amusement and recreation attendants	Salespersons, retail
Guards	Waiters and waitresses
Adjustment clerks	Home health aides

QUESTIONS

1. Summarize the major conclusions of the article.

2. Explain the expected growth of service-producing industries, particularly the health care services.

3. Explain and give examples of job growth and replacement needs.

4. Discuss and give examples of how technology is expected to affect the job market.

5. Describe the major factors that are expected to contribute to declining occupational employment.

6. Analyze the relationship between education and job opportunities.

7. Agree or disagree with the following statement and justify your response based on information provided in the article:

   "The work force is expected to become more homogeneous and less diverse."

EXTENDING YOUR VOCABULARY

projections: The projections of voter turnout needed to be revised after
               it was learned that _____

attained: Researchers believe that members of the Smith family at-
               tained the age of 90 because _____

account: The lawyer asked him to account for his actions after it was
               discovered that _____

innovative: By the use of innovative techniques, the medical team was
               able to _____

enhanced: His chances of getting the job were enhanced by _____
               _____

status: Some people feel that their status in life can be improved by
               _____

mandate: In order to cut down on accidents, the government decided
               to mandate that _____

mobility: One reason for job mobility is _____

spurred: The team was spurred to victory by _____

consistent: It is advisable to find a spouse whose values are consistent
               with _____

 # PROCESS GUIDE

Unlike the readings you have encountered thus far, "Tomorrow's Jobs" is
taken from a government publication. The writing style is expository, with
little narration or description. The layout uses a headline followed by details
that are set off as bulleted items.

A slowdown in employment growth is expected.

- Over the 1994–2005 period, employment is projected to increase by 17.7
  million or 14 percent. This is slower than the 24-percent increase attained
  during the 11-year period, 1983–94, when the economy added 24.6 million jobs.

To process information of this kind, focus on the details provided and
see how they relate to the main point in the headline. In the example provided you need to process several pieces of information:

Over the 1994–2005 period, employment is projected to increase by 17.7 million or 14 percent. This is slower than the 24-percent increase attained during the 11-year period, 1983–94, when the economy added 24.6 million jobs.

The paragraph requires you to compare and contrast data from 1983–94 to 1994–2005. One way to do this is to outline the information in categories such as this:

1983–94	**1994–2005**
24-percent increase	Employment is projected to increase by 14 percent
Economy added 24.6 million jobs	Employment is projected to increase by 17.7 million

You are provided with numbers that represent total jobs (a numerical sum) and the same figure expressed as a percent. However you process the information, two time periods need to be examined and compared and contrasted.

Another feature that the writers of this document have provided is a series of bar graphs. Let's reexamine Chart 7.

1. The title alone suggests the area of focus. In one sentence, state the major point the graphic is trying to convey.

   _____

2. Notice also that the bar graph differs from the other ones that accompany the article in that the bars begin on the right and grow to the left. Also notice that the numbers on the bottom of the graph have a minus sign. Taken together, what does the graph want you to immediately notice?

   _____

   _____

3. Now compare the information found in the chart with the headline that accompanies the section in which the chart is found: **"Declining occupational employment stems from declining industry employment and technological change."** In what way does the graphic help you process this information?

   _____

   _____

4. The graph, however, cannot convey the possible reasons for the decline of certain industries. Examine the paragraphs that provide the details. What are some reasons for declining industries?

   _____

   _____

   _____

Chart 7. Occupations with the Largest Projected Numerical Decreases in Total Employment, 1994–2005

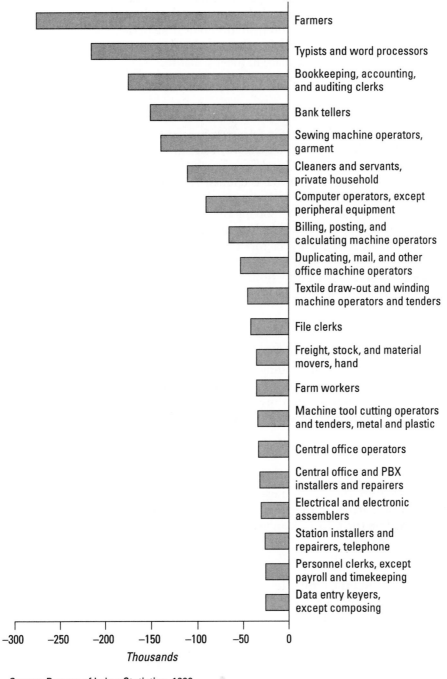

Source: Bureau of Labor Statistics, 1996.

Continue using these techniques as you process the article. Remember, focus on the boldfaced headline of each paragraph. Examine any accompanying graphic and make sure that its visual message supports what is expressed in the text. Read the details that are provided below each headline. Be prepared to compare and contrast information from different time periods and consider cause-and-effect explanations for changes that have occurred, are occurring, or are projected to take place in the job market.

 ## READING JOURNAL

The last Reading Journal exercise was linked to two interviews. You were asked to react to a number of people reporting on their work situations. The two preceding articles, "Solving the Job Puzzle" and "Tomorrow's Jobs," require a switch of gears. Instead of reading personal accounts, you are reading exposition.

Authors attempt to structure an article like "Solving the Job Puzzle" so that it can be helpful to as many people as possible. You may already know some of what the author says. Similarly, work factors that are new to you may not receive enough coverage to be helpful to you. "Tomorrow's Jobs," for example, might discuss your chosen profession only in very general terms. These are the kinds of issues we would like you to think about as you reflect on your reading of these articles.

- **Content**

   What did you find practical in these two readings? Was the information new, or did it merely reinforce facts that you have vaguely remembered? Explain how you might use this information in your career search. Did some items need more explanation? What should have been included in the discussion?

- **Process**

   What reading strategies or techniques did you use to keep track of the information? Did you read each article in the same way, or did you have to adjust your approach based on the information presented?

- **Response**

   Regardless of whether you found the information in the two articles useful or not, do you react differently to expository readings as opposed to narratives? How do you account for this?

Looking for Work in All the Right Places

ROBERT LEWIS

Robert Lewis is a senior editor of the AARP Bulletin, *a publication of the American Association of Retired Persons.*

GEARING UP

1. Imagine needing to find a job. List the steps you would take to begin exploring employment opportunities.

2. Based on your current knowledge of technology, describe how computers can be used to help prospective job seekers.

READING STRATEGY

EVALUATING INFORMATION ON THE INTERNET

The Internet—the world's largest computer network—enables us to travel the world and tap into a vast amount of information. The number of resources available is huge and growing daily. Our new information society is making demands on us that were unknown to our parents. President Clinton remarked: "In the information age, there can be too much exposure and too much information and too much sort of quasi-information."

One problem with the vast amount of information on the Internet is that there are relatively few quality controls. On any given topic users may find one site that contains accurate and reliable data while another site may hold data that are inaccurate, unreliable, or even worse, deliberately false. Users must prepare themselves to critically evaluate the information they find. The Internet has various resources that can help users become critically skilled consumers of data. One document that we found to be very informative and instructive was written by Elizabeth E. Kirk. Professor Kirk, Library Instruction Coordinator for the Milton S. Eisenhower Library at The Johns Hopkins University, is responsible for planning, developing, and managing the instructional activities of the library. Her text follows.

Evaluating Information Found on the Internet
by Elizabeth E. Kirk

The availability and growth of the Internet offers students, teachers and researchers the opportunity to find information and data from all over the world. In addition, the development of the World Wide Web has made the Internet easier to use, both for finding information and for publishing it electronically. Because so much information is available, and because that information can appear to be fairly "anonymous," it is necessary to develop skills to evaluate what you find. When you use a research or academic library, the books, journals and other resources have already been evaluated by a librarian or by a mechanism set up by a librarian. When you use an index or a database to find information on any given topic, the index or database is often produced by a professional or scholarly organization that selects the journals to be indexed on the basis of their quality. If the index or database is not produced by such an organization, it is usually the work of a commercial indexing and abstracting business that qualifies as part of the information industry. In other words, every resource you find has been evaluated in one way or another before you ever see it. When you are using the World Wide Web, none of this applies. There are no filters between you and the Internet. In addition, the ease of constructing Web documents results in information of the widest range of quality, written by authors of the widest range of authority, available on an "even playing field." Excellent resources reside along side the most dubious. The Internet epitomizes the concept of *Caveat lector: Let the reader beware.* This document discusses the criteria by which scholars in most fields evaluate print information, and shows how the same criteria can be used to assess information found on the Internet.

Basic criteria for evaluating all forms of information, and how they apply to the Internet

There are certain criteria that should be applied when evaluating all forms of information, be it in print, on film, or electronic. These criteria include the following:

- Authorship

- Publishing body

- Point of view or bias

- Referral to and/or knowledge of other sources

- Accuracy or verifiability

- Currency

Authorship is perhaps the major criterion used in evaluating information. Who wrote this? When we look for information with some type of critical value, we want to know the basis of the authority with which the author speaks. Here are some possible filters:

1. In your own field of study, the author is a well-known and well-regarded name you recognize.

2. When you find an author you do not recognize:

   - the author is mentioned in a positive fashion by another author or another person you trust as an authority;

   - you found or linked to the author's Web/Internet document from another document you trust;

   - the Web/Internet document you are reading gives biographical information, including the author's position, institutional affiliation and address;

   - biographical information is available by linking to another document; this enables you to judge whether the author's credentials allow him/her to speak with authority on a given topic;

   - if none of the above, there is an address and telephone number as well as an e-mail address for the author in order to request further information on his or her work and professional background. An e-mail address alone gives you no more information than you already have.

   The publishing body also helps evaluate any kind of document you may be reading. In the print universe, this generally means that the author's manuscript has undergone screening in order to verify that it meets the standards or aims of the organization that serves as publisher. This may include peer review. On the Internet, ask the following questions to assess the role and authority of the "publisher," which in this case means the server (computer) where the document lives:

1. Is the name of any organization given on the document you are reading? Are there headers, footers, or a distinctive watermark that shows the document to be part of an official academic or scholarly Web site? Can you contact the site Webmaster from this document?

2. If not, can you link to a page where such information is listed? Can you tell that it's on the same server and in the same directory (by looking at the URL)?

3. Is this organization recognized in the field in which you are studying?

4. Is this organization suitable to address the topic at hand?

5. Can you ascertain the relationship of the author and the publisher/server? Was the document that you are viewing prepared as part of the author's professional duties (and, by extension, within his/her area of expertise)? Or is the relationship of a casual or for-fee nature, telling you nothing about the author's credentials within an institution?

6. Can you verify the identity of the server where the document resides? Internet programs such as *dnslookup* and *whois* will be of help.

7. Does this Web page actually reside in an individual's personal Internet account, rather than being part of an official Web site? This type of information resource should be approached with the greatest caution. Hints on identifying personal pages are available in *Understanding and Decoding URLs.*

Point of view or *bias* reminds us that information is rarely neutral. Because data are used in selective ways to form information, they generally represent a point of view. Every writer wants to prove his point, and will use the data and information that assists him in doing so. When evaluating information found on the Internet, it is important to examine *who* is providing the "information" you are viewing, and what might be their *point of view* or *bias.* The popularity of the Internet makes it the perfect venue for commercial and sociopolitical publishing. These areas in particular are open to highly "interpretative" uses of data.

Steps for evaluating point of view are based on authorship or affiliation:

1. First, note the URL of the document. Does this document reside on the Web server of an organization that has a clear stake in the issue at hand?

   - If you are looking at a corporate Web site, assume that the information on the corporation will present it in the most positive light.

   - If you are looking at products produced and sold by that corporation, remember: you are looking at an advertisement.

   - If you are reading about a political figure at the Web site of another political party, you are reading the opposition.

   - Does this document reside on the Web server of an organization that has a political or philosophical agenda?

   - If you are looking for scientific information on human genetics, would you trust a political organization to provide it?

Many areas of research and inquiry deal with controversial questions, and often the more controversial an issue is, the more interesting it is. When looking for information, it is always critical to remember that everyone has an opinion. Because the structure of the Internet allows for easy self-publication, the variety of points of view and bias will be the widest possible.

Referral to and/or knowledge of the literature refers to the context in which the author situates his or her work. This reveals what the author knows about his or her discipline and its practices. This allows you to evaluate the author's scholarship or knowledge of trends in the area under discussion. The following criteria serve as a filter for all formats of information:

1. The document includes a bibliography.

2. The author alludes to or displays knowledge of related sources, with proper attribution.

3. The author displays knowledge of theories, schools of thought, or techniques usually considered appropriate in the treatment of his or her subject.

4. If the author is using a new theory or technique as a basis for research, he or she discusses the value and/or limitations of this new approach.

5. If the author's treatment of the subject is controversial, he or she knows and acknowledges this.

Accuracy or verifiability of details is an important part of the evaluation process, especially when you are reading the work of an unfamiliar author presented by an unfamiliar organization, or presented in a non-traditional way. Criteria for evaluating accuracy include:

1. For a research document, the data that were gathered and an explanation of the research method(s) used to gather and interpret it are included.

2. The methodology outlined in the document is appropriate to the topic and allows the study to be duplicated for purposes of verification.

3. The document relies on other sources that are listed in a bibliography or includes links to the documents themselves.

4. The document names individuals and/or sources that provided non-published data used in the preparation of the study.

5. The background information that was used can be verified for accuracy.

Currency refers to the timeliness of information. In printed documents, the date of publication is the first indicator of currency. For some types of information, currency is not an issue: authorship or place in the historical record is more important (e.g., T. S. Eliot's essays on tradition in literature). For many other types of data, however, currency is extremely important, as is the regularity with which the data are updated. Apply the following criteria to ascertain currency:

1. The document includes the date(s) at which the information was gathered (e.g., U.S. Census data).

2. The document refers to clearly dated information (e.g., "Based on 1990 U.S. Census data.").

3. Where there is a need to add data or update them on a constant basis, the document includes information on the regularity of updates.

4. The document includes a publication date or a "last updated" date.

5. The document includes a date of copyright.

6. If no date is given in an electronic document, you can view the directory in which it resides and read the date of latest modification.

If you found information using one of the search engines available on the Internet, such as AltaVista or InfoSeek, a directory of the Internet such as

Yahoo, or any of the services that rate World Wide Web pages, you need to know:

1. How that search engine looks for information, and how often their information is updated. An excellent Web document explaining this process was written by Terry A. Gray at Palomar College. Read "How to Search the Web."

2. How that rating service evaluates Web pages. Another excellent resource that includes information on this topic is "Finding Quality on the Net," by Hope Tillman of Babson College.

All information, whether in print or by byte, needs to be evaluated by readers for authority, appropriateness, and other personal criteria for value. *If you find information that is "too good to be true," it probably is. Never use information that you cannot verify.* Establishing and learning criteria to filter information you find on the Internet is a good beginning for becoming a critical consumer of information in all forms. "Cast a cold eye" (as Yeats wrote) on everything you read. Question it. Look for other sources that can authenticate or corroborate what you find. Learn to be skeptical and then learn to trust your instincts.

Application

When you use the World Wide Web as a research tool, you need to do so with a critical eye since, as you have just read, there is a great deal of information available from many sources. When you have found what you believe is useful information, stop for a moment and consider the following questions:

AUTHOR

- Does the author identify himself or herself?

- Is the information written or created by the author, or is it being presented secondhand?

- Is information provided about the author's qualifications, such as education, experience, or position?

- What motivated the author to place the information on the World Wide Web?

SUBJECT MATTER

- What is the purpose of the material—e.g., to inform, explain, persuade?

- Is the information factual or opinion-based?

- Is the material accurate and free from bias? Can it be checked against other sources?

- Does it cover the major aspects of the subject?

- When was the information created?

- When was it last updated?

- How does the information compare with that of other sources?

Host

- Who is supporting the information—a private individual, a company, a school, the government?

- Has anyone reviewed or filtered the information (e.g., an authority, an editor)?

- Could the author's affiliation with the hosting service possibly bias the information? (Could a writer about gun control be neutral if the host of the Web page is a manufacturer of hand guns?)

Conclusion

Although the World Wide Web presents what seems to be unlimited information, it has its drawbacks. Contrary to what some people believe, not everything of value to a researcher can always be found on the Web. In fact, there are many times when research questions can be answered more completely and accurately by using traditional library resources. When you investigate and seek information, consider using a variety of sources.

 ## READING STRATEGY CHECK

FRAMING AN ANSWER

Recall that framing an answer is a multipart process that includes the following:

1. Understanding the question (cue word and other key terms)

2. Rereading the text/and or searching your mind for related ideas

3. Selecting the relevant information/recreating it in your mind

4. Constructing an answer (paraphrasing/summarizing)

5. Editing your response (accuracy, grammar, mechanics, transitions)

   Responding to questions 1 and 3 in "Looking for Work in All the Right Places" involves several steps.

Question 1: The author claims that using the Internet for job-hunting has certain advantages as well as disadvantages. Summarize both aspects of the job search for employees as well as for employers.

To answer this question, you must organize your responses in several categories. Here is the question again with certain terms emphasized:

The author claims that using the Internet for job-hunting has certain *advantages* as well as *disadvantages*. *Summarize* **both** aspects of the job search for *employees* as well as for *employers*.

One way to make sure you are addressing all aspects of the question is to create a chart that categorizes the information.

Internet Job Hunting		
	Advantages	**Disadvantages**
For employees		
For employers		

The third question reads as follows:

Question 3: Describe the author's attitude toward the subject. Is he positive, negative, or neutral? Explain by citing specific references.

To answer this question you need first to DESCRIBE the author's attitude. Make sure you know what the word DESCRIBE calls for. In describing the author's attitude, you asked specifically to think in terms of three categories:

• Positive

• Negative

• Neutral

Make sure you understand the differences between these three categories. The last part of the question requires that you support your responses to the first part *by citing specific references*. This means that you must reread the article and quote or paraphrase information that supports your response.

The Reading

Looking for Work in All the Right Places

by ROBERT LEWIS

Cyberspace offers job opportunities

1   Need a job? Just sit down at your computer. That's what thousands of job-hunting Americans are doing every day, and getting sometimes amazing results, as Robert Thompson discovered recently to his delight.

2   When Thompson started his job search last fall he got no leads from newspaper want ads. Then an article about job sites on the Internet led him to post his résumé in cyberspace—and his phone wouldn't stop ringing.

3   "At least 70 companies called," says Thompson, 52, a computer engineer from Birmingham, Ala. He very quickly accepted an offer from Federal Express and in March moved to Castle Rock, Colo. "I found that most big companies are using recruiters to scan the Internet" to dig up new employees.

4   His experience was no quirk. From a modest start in the 1980s as a place for engineers to swap job tips, Internet job banks have grown into a huge, global employment exchange.

quirk

5   More than 1 million job openings are now advertised on 5,000 Internet sites, estimates John Sumser, editor of Electronic Recruiting News, an online newsletter. And the number of sites is growing "on the order of 20 to 50 new places a day," he says.

6   All kinds of jobs are on display, from bank tellers to bookkeepers, translators to truck drivers, nannies to nurses. Economics is driving the stampede into cyberspace. Employers can fill jobs faster and at less expense. Job-seekers can circulate résumés cost-free to employers across town or across the country.

7   No one knows how many jobs are being filled via cyberspace. But experts agree the Internet is a powerful new search tool that's changing the way the job market works.

8   "The amount of information [on the Internet] pertaining to career development and job recruiting has just exploded," says Larry Elliott, managing partner of executive recruiters Heidrick and Struggles.

9   Not all job-seekers are rushing into cyberspace. Some people dislike the impersonality of the Net, or are simply reluctant to put information about themselves on public display. Nor does the Internet, critics say, reveal the "hidden" job market (the world of unadvertised openings) any more fully than conventional information sources.

conventional
Caveats

10   Caveats aside, hundreds of major companies, including Boeing, IBM, Ford, Gannett and Citicorp, now list job openings on their Web sites.

11   With a few strokes at their keyboards, job-seekers can find employment tools ranging from job listings to career development aids. They can find lists organized by states, by occupations, by industries, by just about any category.

12   "You can find employment data bases for Asian Americans, Latino lawyers or Ivy League graduates," says Bob Stirling, vice president of Imcor, which uses the Internet to recruit executives for temporary assignments.

13   Employment sites work in different ways. Some invite people to "post" their résumé by filling out an online electronic form that is then submitted to a searchable data base. Some also provide job-search help, such as advice on résumé writing or interviewing.

14   Still others will automatically notify job-seekers when an opening in their field comes up. Of particular importance: Most job bank services are free; employers or recruiting firms usually pay job bank costs.

15   In the case of the largest service, America's Job Bank, taxpayers foot its $4.5 million annual tab. AJB is a service of the U.S. Labor Department and state employment agencies.

16   Moreover, using a job bank doesn't require technical expertise. Most job banks contain instructions for exploring their sites. Then, through "hyper-links," job-seekers can click their way through cyberspace from one employment bank to another.

17   Using the Internet to search for a job has other advantages.

18   Most employees can't hunt for a new job while at work. That's no problem for the Internet, which can be accessed 24 hours a day, 365 days a year.

19   Close study of Internet job sites gives insights into a prospective employer's needs. "You can discover what industry is really looking for," says Elliott. "You can get a feel for where the jobs are and what it takes to be qualified."   *prospective*

20   In preparing for a job interview, corporate home pages on the Internet can be a gold mine of information about a prospective employer. It allows a job applicant to walk into an interview armed with information about a company's goals and plans.

21   Because computer experience is an increasingly important job criterion, applying for work on the Internet shows at least some computer literacy. "The first thing you demonstrate when you apply for a job on the Internet," says Sumser, "is a knowledge and familiarity with computers. That's important."   *criterion*

22   Margaret Riley, author of "The Guide to Internet Job Searching" (NTC Publishing, 1996) recommends that beginners start by checking out the "Big Six" job banks. In addition to AJB, they are Career Mosaic, Career Path, E-Span, Monster Board and Online Career Center.

23   AJB boasts 600,000 job openings offered by 9,500 employers and recruiting firms and also provides direct hyperlinks to 1,354 employer Web sites, and 450 other job banks and private employment agencies on the Internet. This means that a job-seeker can jump from AJB directly into, say, IBM's job bank.

24   The Labor Department's Richard Hardin, an official of the U.S. Employment Service, says AJB averages 20,000 job searches a day. He has no way of knowing how many people find jobs through AJB, but he believes Ray Tennancour's experience is typical.

25   Caught up in a layoff, Tennancour, 47, of Phoenix, early this year applied for unemployment compensation and was given, among other forms, AJB's Internet address. "I did a few searches and within hours had over 25 openings in my field (servicing electronic equipment) in the six states I was interested in," Tennancour says.   *compensation*

26   "I sent my résumé to 20 [places] and got 12 responses. I called one in Colorado and was hired," he says.

27   The AJB, Hardin believes, has the potential to create a national job market, a development that could smooth out regional fluctuations in jobless rates.   *potential*

28   Because many job-seekers lack access to computers, Hardin's agency funds "Internet access zones" at universities, community colleges and some 1,800 state employment offices. Internet searches also can be conducted on computers at public libraries.

29   Federal and state employment agencies also are developing a résumé bank that will provide job-seekers a free site on the Internet to post their résumés. Called America's Talent Bank, it was scheduled to go online in Michigan in April and will spread to 25 states by Labor Day and to all states next year, Hardin says.

30   Among the other large job sites, Online Career Center [OCC] was founded five years ago by six corporations as a sort of Internet cooperative. Today nearly 2,500 employers advertise their job openings on OCC, including such companies as Marriott, Circuit City, Federal Express, Chrysler, McDonnell Douglas, Intel, Federal Reserve, Bell South, Union Carbide and the U.S. Army.

31   Career Path is unique in that it consists of the help-wanted ads from 28 major newspapers.

32   In the beginning, technical jobs, particularly those involving computers, dominated the Internet. But Riley, author of the Internet job guide, says this is changing. The ratio of technical to nontechnical jobs, she estimates, is now close to 50–50.

33   A random search of jobs posted on Online Career Center, for example, showed openings for 182 secretaries, 99 chemists, 94 attorneys, 171 editors, 600 assemblers, 189 nurses and 56 bus drivers.

34   Employers like the Internet for hiring because it's fast, efficient and, compared to newspaper advertising, inexpensive.

35   "Eighteen months ago I spent $5,000 a month on newspaper advertising," says Paula Watkins, who operates a recruiting firm in Anniston, Ala. "Now I spend $1,200 a year for an ad in Online Career Center and do no newspaper advertising at all."

36   For that, her recruiting message appears on the Internet 365 days a year. It generates 175 to 200 responses a week. In addition, she retrieves job applicants' résumés from the Internet and stores them in her own computer.

37   So many companies use this method to sift through résumés, in fact, that the rules for writing résumés are changing. Employers increasingly want résumés that are free of special graphics, such as boldface lines, italics, dashes and similar characters.

38   Words that express a skill or achievement are preferred over job titles. Some applicants include a keyword paragraph to help ensure that their résumés are noticed.

39   But job hunting on the Internet isn't without drawbacks. Chief among them is the loss of privacy. Sending a résumé into cyberspace places highly personal information in the hands of strangers. "Unless you're careful every Tom, Dick and Harry can look at your résumé," says Stirling, the recruiting executive.

40   People can post "blind" résumés, or have replies sent to an e-mail address. But Riley notes that this undercuts the effectiveness of a job search because recruiters may need to reach a job prospect quickly.

41   "You have to be careful," Riley says. "Use good common sense. Ask yourself, 'do I trust this site?' Be a selective consumer."

42   One thing missing from the electronic job search, at least in the initial   *initial*
stages, is the personal touch. "It's very impersonal," says Elliott, the executive recruiter. "People send out résumés and never hear anything back. You become just another batch of bits and bytes."

43   And the very size of the Internet employment market may make it difficult to find sites that will produce the best results. A few years ago Elliott did an Internet search for "executive jobs" and got 8,000 hits. Later the same search produced 20,000 hits and more recently, 1 million hits.

44   "A lot of it is garbage or duplicative listings," Elliott says. Still, he looks to the Internet to become a dominant forum for filling some kinds of jobs,   *dominant*
such as technical positions.

45   And he predicts that older workers, because their acquired job skills are readily recognized in job data searches, "increasingly will find the Internet is a good place to look for work."

46   But experts caution people not to overlook the value of two very traditional approaches to job hunting: personal contacts and networking in the "hidden" job market where positions are filled without being advertised. "That has always been important," Riley says, "and the Internet will never be a substitute."

QUESTIONS

1. The author claims that using the Internet for job hunting has certain advantages as well as disadvantages. Summarize both aspects of the job search for employees as well as for employers.

2. Explain how employment sites operate in cyberspace.

3. Describe the author's attitude toward the subject. Is he positive, negative, or neutral? Explain by citing specific references.

EXTENDING YOUR VOCABULARY

quirk: Finding this job was a quirk because _____

conventional: Rather than end her letter with a conventional closing,

                    she chose to _____

caveats: The park ranger related a number of caveats to the hikers

                    in order to _____

prospective: The prospective parents were delighted to find out that

                    _____

criterion: Memory alone is not an accurate criterion of intelligence
because _____

compensation: We sought proper compensation for our _____

_____

potential: When we saw that our child wasn't working to her fullest
potential, we decided to _____

initial: You must be careful with initial impressions since

_____

dominant: He became the dominant ruler in the region after successfully _____

 # PROCESS GUIDE

This article is largely descriptive in nature. It relates how employers and employees can use the Internet as part of the job-hunting process. Readers who have never used the Internet and the World Wide Web might be wondering what users see when they navigate to various job-related web sites. This Process Guide illustrates several key concepts of the article.

Background

The Internet is a vast collection of computers linked to one another. It stores and delivers a great amount of information and allows countless numbers of individuals on different computer systems to communicate with one another on a global scale. One major reason for the Internet's growing popularity is the World Wide Web. The World Wide Web (or WWW) is a network (or web) of files on computers all over the world that are connected with "links." The World Wide Web is the most widely used service for retrieving information on the Internet. It has become a multimedia environment that transmits text, full-color images, sound, and video. To access information on the Web, people use application software called a "browser." Web browsers provide users with either a text or graphical interface through which to view so-called homepages on the World Wide Web.

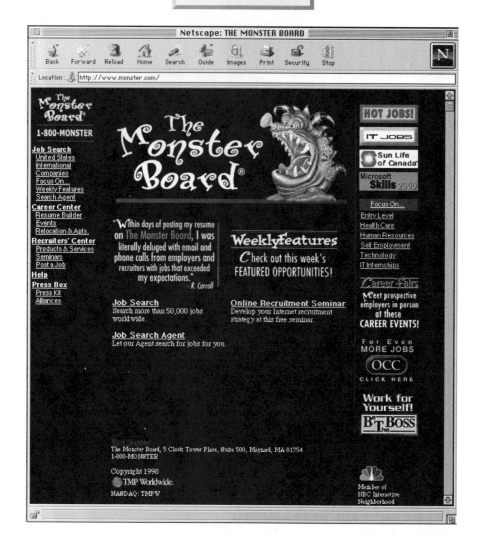

Using the Internet

The author informs you that many job-related resources are available on the Internet. Some of these are geared for a general audience, whereas others have a more narrow focus. Here are two examples geared for the general population. Note that each site presents users with various options. Monster

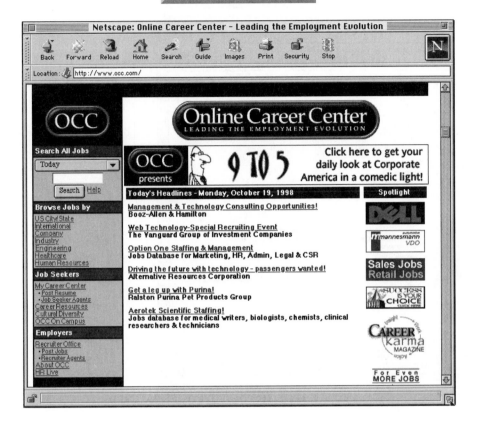

Board's Career Center provides suggestions for preparing a resume and strategies for dealing with job interviews. The Online Career Center has resources for both employers (recruiters) as well as prospective employees (job seekers). All the user has to do is select the appropriate category and follow the instructions or suggestions that are provided.

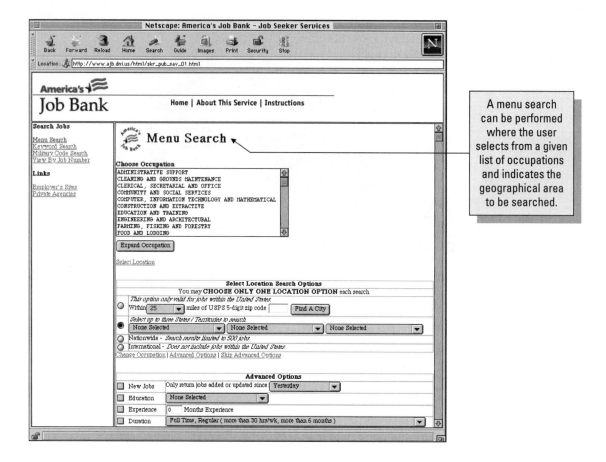

> A menu search can be performed where the user selects from a given list of occupations and indicates the geographical area to be searched.

America's Job Bank

America's Job Bank is a service of the U.S. Labor Department and state employment agencies. A user who navigates to its Internet address has several options.

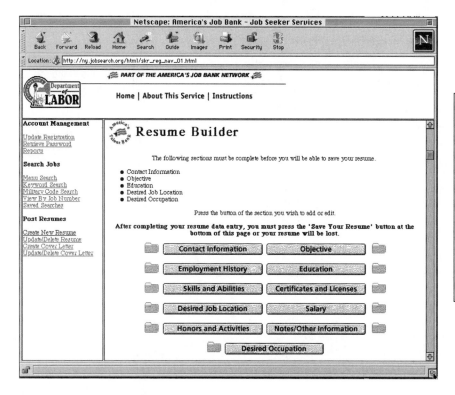

Job seekers can use a special form where they can key in their résumé and post it for prospective employers. They merely click the appropriate category and type in the space provided. The resulting "electronic" résumé is made available to numerous recruiters.

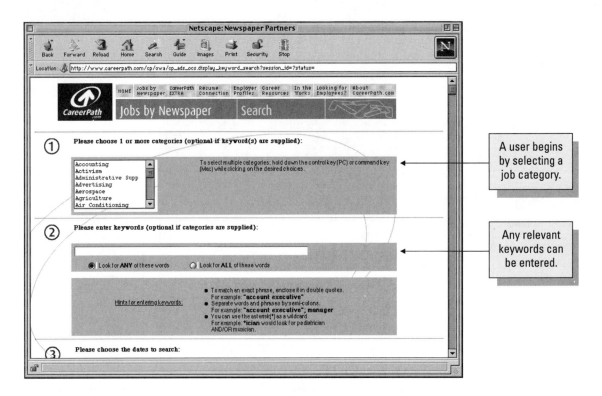

A user begins by selecting a job category.

Any relevant keywords can be entered.

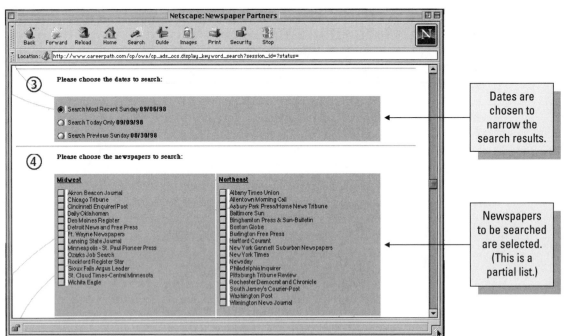

Dates are chosen to narrow the search results.

Newspapers to be searched are selected. (This is a partial list.)

Career Path

Career Path consists of the help-wanted ads from twenty-eight major news-papers. Rather than purchase each newspaper and scan the classified section, a job seeker can use computer technology.

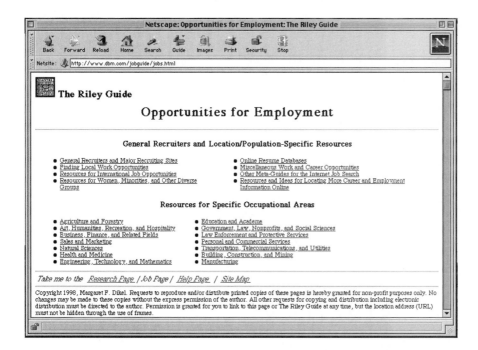

Margaret Riley, cited in the article as author of "The Guide to Internet Job Searching," has a popular Web site devoted to employment opportunities.

Conclusion

As the preceding screen shots have illustrated, numerous resources are available for prospective job seekers as well as for recruiters. The Internet and the World Wide Web provide job seekers and recruiters with an increasingly wide range of opportunities. Both groups report that using the Internet has made the job search more efficient and has significantly increased the range of opportunities for them.

Work to Make the World Work Better

JAMES A. MICHENER

James Michener was born in New York City in 1907 and died in 1997. As an author, his career spanned nearly fifty years, during which time he wrote over forty titles. The commercial success of his first work, Tales of the South Pacific, *was guaranteed after he won the Pulitzer Prize, and the work became the basis for* South Pacific, *a long-running Broadway musical and later a motion picture. This early achievement gave him the financial freedom to do in-depth research for his historical novels. Michener visited more than 100 countries and collected information for such works as* Hawaii *(1959),* Iberia *(1968), and* Poland *(1983). Michener was awarded the Presidential Medal of Freedom, America's highest civilian award. One year before his death his views on the problems facing America were published in* This Noble Land: My Vision for America. *He is one of the most read authors in modern-day America.*

GEARING UP

1. List several things today's young generation can learn about work from the older generation.

2. Discuss how people's views of work develop from their youth to their senior years.

READING STRATEGY

EVALUATING QUALIFICATIONS AND SOURCES

If you read the article "Looking for Work in All the Right Places" (page 205) you probably noted the attached strategy "Evaluating Information on the Internet." Although the Internet will probably continue to increase in importance for research purposes, many researchers still rely on printed materials found in libraries—books, journals, and documents.

Finding information is but one step. As a critical reader, you must evaluate the reliability of the material you read and determine the best and most appropriate sources. Three librarians from Cornell University prepared a guide entitled "How to Critically Analyze Information Sources" that is posted on the school's web site. We found the document to be well written and informative and were granted permission to reprint it. At the conclusion of the text we will apply the strategy to Michener's article, "Work to Make the World Work Better."

"How to Critically Analyze Information Sources"

Introduction

Evaluating a source can begin even before you have the source in hand. You can initially appraise a source by first examining the bibliographic citation. A bibliographic citation is a written description of a book, journal article, essay, or some other published material. Bibliographic citations characteristically have three main components: author, title, and publication information. These components can help you determine the usefulness of this source for your paper.

I. INITIAL APPRAISAL

A. Author

1. What are the author's credentials—educational background, past writings, or experience—in this area? Is the book or article written on a topic in the author's area of expertise? *Who's Who in America, Biography Index,* or the biographical information located in the publication itself can be used to determine the author's credentials.

2. Has your instructor mentioned this author? Have you seen the author's name cited in other sources or bibliographies? Respected authors are cited frequently by other scholars. For this reason, always note those names that appear in many different sources.

3. Is the author associated with an institution or organization? What are the basic values or goals of the organization or institution?

B. Date of Publication

1. When was the source published? This date is often located on the face of the title page below the name of the publisher. If it is not there, look for the copyright date on the reverse of the title page. On Web pages, the date of the last revision is usually at the bottom of the home page, sometimes every page.

2. Is the source current or out-of-date for your topic? Topic areas of continuing and rapid development, such as the sciences, demand more current information. On the other hand, topics in the humanities often require material that was written many years ago.

C. Edition or Revision

Is this a first edition of this publication or not? Further editions indicate a source has been revised and updated to reflect changes in knowledge, include omissions, and harmonize with its intended reader's needs. Also, many printings or editions may indicate that the work has become a standard source in the area and is reliable.

D. Publisher

Note the publisher. If the source is published by a university press, it is likely to be scholarly. Although the fact that the publisher is reputable does not necessarily guarantee quality, it does show that the publisher may have high regard for the source being published.

E. Title of Journal

Is this a scholarly or a popular journal? This distinction is important because it indicates different levels of complexity in conveying ideas. You may wish to check your journal title in the latest edition of *Katz's Magazines for Libraries* (Uris Ref Z 6941 .K21 1995) for a brief evaluative description.

II. CONTENT ANALYSIS

Having made an initial appraisal, you should now examine the body of the source. Read the Preface to determine the author's intentions for the book. Scan the Table of Contents and the Index to get a broad overview of the material it covers. Note whether bibliographies are included. Read the chapters that specifically address your topic.

A. Intended Audience

What type of audience is the author addressing? Is the publication aimed at a specialized or a general audience? Is this source too elementary, too technical, too advanced, or just right for your needs?

B. Objective Reasoning

Is the information covered fact, opinion, or propaganda? It is not always easy to separate fact from opinion. Facts can usually be verified; opinions, though they may be based on factual information, evolve from the interpretation of facts. Skilled writers can make you think their interpretations are facts.

   Does the information appear to be valid and well researched, or is it questionable and unsupported by evidence? Assumptions should be reasonable. Note errors or omissions.

   Is the author's point of view objective and impartial? Is the language free of emotion-rousing words and bias?

C. Coverage

Does the work update other sources, substantiate other materials you have read, or add new information? Does it extensively or marginally cover your topic? You should explore enough sources to obtain a variety of viewpoints.

   Is the material primary or secondary in nature? Primary sources are the raw material of the research process. Secondary sources are based on primary sources. For example, if you were researching Adenauer's role in rebuilding West Germany, Adenauer's own writings would be one of many primary sources available on this topic. Others might include relevant government documents and contemporary German newspaper articles. Scholars use this primary material to help generate historical interpretations—a secondary source. Books, encyclopedia articles, and scholarly journal articles about Adenauer's role are considered secondary sources. Choose both primary and secondary sources when you have the opportunity.

D. Writing Style

Is the publication organized logically? Are the main points clearly presented? Do you find the text easy to read, or is it stilted or choppy? Is the author's argument repetitive?

E. Evaluative Reviews

1. Locate critical reviews of books in a reviewing source, such as *Book Review Index* or *Book Review Digest.* Is the review positive? Is the book under review considered a valuable contribution to the field? Does the reviewer mention other books that might be better? If so, locate these sources for more information on your topic.
2. Do the various reviewers agree on the value or attributes of the book or has it aroused controversy among the critics?
3. For Web sites, consider consulting one of the *evaluation and reviewing sources on the Internet.*

Learning how to quickly determine the relevance and authority of a given resource for your research is one of the core skills of the research process. For more assistance with the research process, consult your instructor or a reference librarian.

Application

In applying the Cornell University document to Michener's article, we have chosen to focus on two broad areas: the author and the publication.

CREDIBILITY OF THE AUTHOR

In order to assess Michener's credentials, you will need some background information. One place to start is the brief biographical citation already given on pages 223–224. What facts suggest that the author is qualified to write a selection entitled "Work to Make the World Work Better"?

_____

_____

Although the brief biographical statement may give you some clue to Michener's qualifications, this information is somewhat limited. To get a more complete picture you would need to use reference sources such as _Who's Who in America_ and _Contemporary Authors._ Because Michener died in 1997, another source of information would be obituary columns. In addition, if you have access to the World Wide Web, you might be able to find several sites that contain _reliable_ information about the author, including an analysis of his legacy. We emphasize the world _reliable_ because, as was pointed out in a previous strategy (see page 205), you must be careful when you gather information from the Internet. When you consider that anyone can post a "James Michener" page, it becomes particularly important to know the source of the information.

At first you might wonder what qualifies Michener, a highly successful author, to comment about work. But reading his article and appreciating his lifelong pursuits make it easier to understand that he indeed can serve as a social commentator. He began working at assorted jobs at a young age. The great variety of odd jobs and experiences helped shape his attitude toward work. His personal experiences with work, his worldwide travels, and his research and teaching give him a unique perspective about social issues.

Michener spent his long life researching history and society and traveling to over one hundred countries. In _This Noble Land: My Vision for America,_ published a year before his death, he gives his views and perspectives on the problems and challenges facing America today and his recommendations for solutions. One review of this work noted: "Not all will agree with the specifics of Michener's arguments; still the author makes an admirable effort to define what has made our country great and how to preserve what is best about it."

THE PUBLICATION

"Work to Make the World Work Better" appeared in a 1976 publication of the IBM Corporation, *Think* magazine. This was a special issue of an IBM publication that had as its theme work in America. IBM is a respected corporation, and one might think that it would have a vested interest in publishing a theme-based magazine devoted to work in the hope that computers would be featured. But a careful reading of Mr. Michener's article reveals that computers are not mentioned at all. Apparently IBM gave free rein to its contributors to develop the theme as they saw fit.

The fact that the article was published in 1976 might lead you to think that the material is not relevant anymore. But again, think about the nature of the subject matter and consider several other readings in this unit. If anything, Michener foresaw trends that will shape our society as we approach the millennium. His statement "Today, America is experiencing a new trauma regarding work, and I suppose it will continue for the remainder of this century . . ." is one that many social scientists would agree with. Michener is not only reporting and analyzing work in America in 1976, but he is also prescribing a possible solution to the problems he presents. He does mix fact with opinion, but that is to be expected in such an article. Reasonable individuals might look at the same facts that Michener presents and come up with other conclusions.

READING STRATEGY CHECK

READING ARGUMENTATION AND PERSUASION

The Reading Argumentation and Persuasion strategy was introduced in Unit One (page 68) and applied to the "Why We Should Read" article. The point was made that in this form of writing, an author is attempting to convince a reader to think, feel, or react in a certain way. In order to do this, the author states a thesis (a belief about an idea) and uses a combination of logic and evidence to support the position that he or she is taking.

In this article, Michener is persuading you to view work in a new way. Most people work for the practical reason of making a living. Another reason people work is to feel personal satisfaction in the product or service they provide. Michener would not disagree with these two reasons but goes beyond these two usual responses to provide a third alternative. Identifying Michener's idea is not a problem as he gives it to you in the title, "Work to Make the World Work Better." In this case, the important tasks are to identify what leads Michener to make the statement he does about work and judge whether his logic and evidence are sound and convincing.

In reading argument and persuasion:

1. Identify the author's purpose. What motivates the writer to take a position on an issue?

2. Identify the author's thesis or idea. What does the author want you to believe?

3. Analyze the logic and the evidence. Is the support provided by the author clear and credible?

The Reading

Work to Make the World Work Better
by JAMES A. MICHENER

1   I was raised in an extremely poor family whose members had to work unceasingly if they wanted to survive. My widowed mother did sweatshop sewing of the cruelest kind, yet saved enough to send six children through high school and two through college.

2   From the age of 11, I worked six days a week every summer and delivered newspapers seven days a week during the winter, rising at four in the morning to do so. At age 14, I was apprenticed to a plumber and worked ten hours a day all summer, and four in the winter.

3   Instead of this turning me against work, it ingrained the attitude that sensible people work hard to attain sensible goals—a philosophy I still adhere to.

ingrained

4   My most crucial experience with work came when my family fell temporarily apart and I was moved into the local poorhouse. On two different occasions I lived with a group of memorable old men on the top floor of the poorhouse dormitory and there listened as these derelicts explained the specific disasters that had overtaken them. It was as harsh an introduction to life as a teen-age boy could have.

5   It was obvious, since the poorhouse was filled, that many people fail. I did my best to decipher why. From listening to scores of personal histories I concluded that a few suffered from the misdeeds of others, but that most failed because of their inability to work intelligently.

decipher

6   From this poorhouse experience I generated a positive reverence for work. I saw it as the principal means whereby people achieve what they want and avoid what they do not want. As a consequence, I became more addicted to work, perhaps, than was proper, and accorded it a greater respect than it deserved. I made myself a slave to the Puritan work ethic and have never been able to escape.

reverence

7   What song do I remember from our Sunday School? The one in which children were admonished:

admonished

> *Work till the last beam fadeth,*
> *Fadeth to shine no more.*

Work while the night is darkening,
When man's work is o'er.

8   Whenever I have watched luminous potentials destroy themselves through laziness, inattention to detail, or wastage of ability, I am content that if I erred in working too hard, it was an error in the right direction. I still believe hard work is the salvation for many of us and one of the principal agencies whereby our society achieves the goals it seeks.

9   At one time or another I have lived in most parts of the world. I have found no other society in which men and women work more diligently than in America. Some nations may demand more work on a more primitive level. Some today even bind their people like serfs to the bottom of the pile. But in total effort I believe our people work harder than any other. Our enviable standard of living derives primarily from our ability to operate in a society in which there is an opportunity for most of us to work most of the time. And an overriding feature of our society is that we have sponsored the idea that work can be ennobling as well as demanding.

diligently

10   At the same time, I think it commendable that today many of our best young people are questioning the assumptions of the Puritan work ethic and rejecting some of its manifestations. They are serious when they state, "I refuse to slip automatically into some routine job like my father's. I want something more relevant in life than that." Or, as a young woman told me recently, "I insist upon making some meaningful contribution."

commendable

manifestations

11   These are laudable goals, and I respect the young person who has the courage to keep casting about until he or she finds a kind of work that is meaningful. But in looking, one should also be learning, because the only way known to attain the goals of which the young speak is to acquire the necessary training to execute such work when it is found.

laudable

12   I have been much impressed by my experiences in the great art galleries of Europe. It is popular today to ridicule hard academic training, especially in the arts. But I recall a sequence of notable paintings in which Titian copied, in his own good style, the work of Giovanni Bellini; and Rubens copied Titian after making his personal adjustments; and Eugene Delacroix, a most individualistic painter, copied Rubens to probe his secrets; and Vincent van Gogh copied Delacroix in hopes of perfecting his own style.

13   These brilliant artists did not copy their betters to imitate them. They copied in order to learn, and in every instance the pupil went beyond the master. There is no way yet devised whereby a beginning artist can achieve a compelling style of his or her own without analyzing what great predecessors have done. The young must not slavishly ape the old—indeed, it is the responsibility of the beginner to move far beyond the master—but achievement without knowledge and hard work seems to me impossible.

predecessors

14   At the other end of the spectrum, the older I grow, the younger becomes the age at which I think people should retire. I had always suspected that as I approached my own retirement age I would chafe at the idea of quitting and would rail against the system that required me to do so. Now I believe

spectrum

chafe

that people should retire in their early 60s—or earlier. I mean retire from positions of management—not from work.

15   There are any number of jobs, in my view, that should be filled by younger men and women; heads of large corporations, presidents of universities, heads of labor unions, Congressmen with special emphasis on Senators, senior doctors in hospitals, presidents of banks, and heads of charities, television networks, newspapers, and most organizations. In such positions we need vigorous, imaginative, courageous leadership, and to get it we should look to younger men and women.

16   I do not mean the older worker should be cast aside. At 65, one is still capable of years of contribution, and the nation should find some way to utilize this talent. Raw energy diminishes, but sagacity increases. Daring subsides, but the ability to make prudent supportive decisions grows. Review, follow-through, and consolidation are the contributions that an older worker can offer, and these can be of value.   *sagacity*

17   The psychological value to the individual of work after 65 is obvious: It prolongs life. Even more important, however, is the economic contribution to our society. We simply cannot afford to squander the abilities of our older citizens, and imaginative new ways must be devised for utilizing them.   *squander*

18   Today, America is experiencing a new trauma regarding work, and I suppose it will continue for the remainder of this century: Our system can produce enough consumer goods to satisfy all the reasonable needs of our population, with enough left over to share with other nations. But we can produce these goods while using only part of our work force; we have found no really satisfactory way to provide for the unemployed.

19   As a consequence, we distribute relief and food stamps in a pattern that infuriates some of those who have to provide the funds and sometimes weakens the will of those who receive them. I concede that our system must help those who do not find jobs in normal channels, and I never complain when my tax dollars are used for this purpose. Taxes are the price we pay for the privilege of enjoying a stable society.   *concede*

20   Nevertheless, every function of our society creates work that cries to be done. We need millions of people to staff health services, to care for our children, to supervise apprenticeship programs. We need millions more to fill new jobs in caring for the elderly: nurses' aides, recreation guides, paramedics, drivers, food specialists, organizers of informal businesses in which the aged can work part-time, teachers who can satisfy the learning wants of those who are retired. We need workers to refurbish our villages, to restore our own towns and decaying cities; people to clean up, revitalize the slums, beautify our countryside, purify our polluted rivers, care for trees, and rehabilitate dilapidated houses. Most especially, we need a whole new cadre of workers willing to provide the services that so many families require and are ready to pay for.   *cadre*

21   Thus, America needs a whole new orientation to work. Our old-fashioned definition of work is something that a man or woman does in a factory or an office. I wish every willing worker might find such a job, but

this may be impossible. What we must do now is create a greater sense of pride in service-type jobs—jobs in which we literally serve one another—and encourage people to move into them.

22   The work ethic has served us well in the past. Our ships were sturdy.   *ethic*
Our automobiles functioned. Our refrigerator doors stayed closed. Our medicines were safe. And our stores became the envy of the world.

23   We could take pride in those accomplishments because the products were apparent, measurable, reputable. But in a service-oriented society, how shall we measure the value of a day without an identifiable product—a day spent, say, administering, expediting, organizing, no matter how skillfully?   *expediting*
What shall we take pride in when we tell our children what we have done?

24   The answer, I believe, lies in creating a world where we can all find genuine satisfaction in serving one another—not in a subservient sense, but in the helping, caring, sharing sense of a truly supportive society. We could take pride, then, in a world that really works.

25   That, indeed, would be something to tell our children about.

QUESTIONS

1. Why does Michener relate incidents from his past? How do these incidents relate to his subject and the point he is developing?

2. Paraphrase Michener's work philosophy.

3. What lessons(s) did Michener learn from his poorhouse experience?

4. The author states, "I made myself a slave to the Puritan work ethic and have never been able to escape." Explain.

5. State and explain Michener's views regarding retirement.

6. Describe the new trauma regarding work that the author discusses.

7. What solution(s) does the author propose to a work-related problem he describes?

8. According to Michener, in the past it was easier for workers to measure their accomplishments. Why? What problems does our present service-oriented society face with respect to measuring workers' accomplishments? What solution does the author propose?

EXTENDING YOUR VOCABULARY

ingrained: Childhood memories become ingrained if _____
                    _____

decipher: When we were able to decipher the message, we learned
                    that _____

reverence: We tend to show great reverence toward _____

_____

admonished: The children were admonished after they _____

_____

diligently: He worked diligently in order to _____

commendable: Commendable behavior deserves _____

manifestations: Examples of manifestations of poverty in our society

can be seen in _____

laudable: Because of the child's laudable behavior, the mayor de-

cided to _____

predecessors: President Clinton's and President Truman's prede-

cessors to the highest office were _____ and

_____

spectrum: In order to present a wide spectrum of music styles, the

promoter decided to _____

chafe: Understandably, she would chafe at the offer of less

money, considering _____

sagacity: Because I admired her sagacity, I decided to _____

_____

squander: If you squander your resources, you may find that

_____

concede: I was willing to concede only when I realized that _____

_____

cadre: From a small cadre of police officers, the commission

was able to _____

ethic: The recruiter was looking for someone with a strong

work ethic because _____

expediting: Without her help in expediting matters we probably

would still be _____

How It Feels to Be Out of Work

JAN HALVORSEN

At the time this article was written, Jan Halvorsen was an unemployed writer.
Subsequently, she was hired as an assistant editor at the Twin Cities Courier *in*
St. Paul, Minnesota.

GEARING UP

1. Briefly define *layoff, unemployment,* and *recession.*

2. List alternatives people can pursue when they become unemployed.

READING STRATEGY

DETERMINING THE AUTHOR'S PURPOSE

The critical reader seeks to determine the author's purpose for writing something. Does the author intend to inform, entertain, describe, or ridicule? For
example, the author's intent may be to satirize. If so, he or she may make a
number of statements about a local politician that are not technically true.
The outlandish nature of the ideas is meant to tip the reader that the objective is not only serious and factual but exaggerated and fun.

Authors may have a number of purposes for writing. Following are the
most common motives:

1. To inform.   If the author's purpose is to share information, that information must be reliable. Authors often use data and statistics in their discussions.
On the surface, numbers carry credibility. However, the critical reader must
be careful because they can be interpreted in various ways. For example, citing the mean or average income for a small, poor community may be misleading. If one wealthy person lives in this community and that individual's
income is incorporated into the mean, the result may distort the true picture
of the community. A more accurate way to determine the economic status of
this area would be to report the median income, or the midpoint—the income
level that lies exactly halfway between the lowest and the highest incomes.

Not all issues are supported with numbers. In such cases, you must
examine the logic of the author's argument. The article "The Proficient

Reader" in Unit One makes several statements about reading and books that are not supported with numbers. To determine whether this article has merit, you must carefully consider the ideas and arguments presented.

2. To persuade.   An author's intention may be to persuade you to believe or to do something. A very common use of persuasive writing is advertising. In this case, the writer's message is to convince you to buy a product or service.

In other instances, an author may wish you to believe or accept a certain point of view. This type of writing frequently occurs on the newspaper editorial page. Here you will find columns that offer the newspaper's position on a variety of issues. In the selection "Why We Should Read" in Unit One (page 70), Vince Nowell tries to persuade students that there is much to gain from reading books. In this unit, you will read articles with different perspectives on the meaning of work. The authors attempt to convince you of their position.

3. To satirize and/or entertain.   In writing satire, the author's intention is to make you laugh and provide a new and amusing perspective on current issues. There is much "truth" in the satiric form. Perhaps we can better see our own foibles when we are relaxed by humor. Writers like Russell Baker often satirize a person or idea but have a serious point to make as well. In this unit, Anita Shreve uses satire to depict women's relation to the workplace (see "The Day the Mommies Went Home" on page 244).

Application

In the article you will read next, Jan Halvorsen directly states her purpose in the title: she shares her feelings about being out of work. In the opening and ending paragraphs Halvorsen reports that her experience made her more sensitive to the plight of other unemployed people. The jobless were no longer a remote statistic in the media—she was one of them, and she knew how it felt. On one level, we may conclude that the author shares the information to make us more sensitive to this situation.

An author can have more than one purpose. A writer whose son was diagnosed as leukemic reported that he was able to release some of his anxiety through writing about what his family experienced in his son's battle with the disease. His moving journal, "A Family's Triumph over Tragedy," was subsequently published in a series of articles in the *Greensboro News.* The writer told his audience that sharing his story was a form of therapy. Perhaps Jan Halvorsen also had this motive.

Halvorsen's article originally appeared in *Newsweek.* Can you determine another purpose for an unemployed journalist writing for a national publication read by millions of people?

READING STRATEGY CHECK
EVALUATING SOURCES

The strategy of evaluating sources was introduced in the previous article, "Work to Make the World Work Better." The idea of credibility was discussed. Sources should be believable to those who read them. Certain factors make sources credible. First of all, the publication should be accurate. The *New York Times* and the *Washington Post* are considered reliable sources. That does not mean that these newspapers always get the facts correct. However, they do make a serious effort and print corrections when an error is brought to their attention. The tabloid newspapers found at the checkout counter of the supermarket stray greatly from accuracy and focus on the sensational aspects of a story. Accuracy is a much lesser concern than gaining a customer's attention and selling a paper. Understandably, they are not considered good sources of support.

Timeliness is also important in evaluating certain sources. Scientific publications and computer journals can easily become dated. On the other hand, a historical account of explorers from several centuries back can still provide us with timeless information.

Finally, the credentials of the author are important. It was suggested that authors have experience and education to make judgments on the topics they are addressing. An author's credibility has to be examined carefully. Having training and years of background in an area does not mean a person is always right.

Application

Jan Halvorsen has written about her feelings of being fired from a job. She is not citing sociological or psychological studies to support her reactions. She does not advertise herself as an expert on work-related matters. We surmise that she has not been fired a number of times in the past or she would have probably alluded to this in her remarks. The question might be asked, Why should we consider what Halvorsen has to say? We can believe her because she is a person with feelings. We can at least listen because we too are people with feelings. We read her because she captures in print frustrations shared by other people.

Halvorsen's essay originally appeared in *Newsweek* magazine, which has a credible reputation. Consequently we can conclude that the essay has passed before a number of critical eyes at that source. We can conclude from its appearance in the "My Turn" section of *Newsweek* that at least the editors thought Halvorsen had written something worth our consideration.

The Reading

How It Feels to Be Out of Work
by JAN HALVORSEN

1   Layoffs, unemployment and recession have always affected Walter Cronkite's tone of voice and the editorial page. And maybe they affected a neighborhood business or a friend's uncle. But these terms have always been just words, affecting someone else's world, like a passing ambulance. At least they were until a few weeks ago, when the ambulance came for me.

2   Even as I sat staring blankly at my supervisor, hearing, "I've got bad news: we're going to have to let you go," it all still seemed no more applicable to my daily life than a "60 Minutes" exposé. I kept waiting for the alternative—"but you can come back after a couple of months," or "you could take a salary cut, a different position," or even, "April fool." But none of these came. This was final. There was no mistake and no alternative. *alternative*

3   You find yourself going back over it in your idle moments. There wasn't so much as a "Thank you" for the long nights working alone, the "Sure, no problem, I'll have it tomorrow," the "Let me know if I can help," the "I just went ahead and did it this weekend" and, especially, for the "You forgot to tell me it changed? Oh, that's all right, I'll just do it over. No big deal." *idle*

4   No big deal. How it all echoes through your evenings and awakens you in the morning. The mornings are probably the worst—waking up with the habitual jar, for the first two weeks, thinking, "I'm late!" Late for what? The dull ache in your lower stomach reminds you: late for nothing.

5   *Depression:* Again, you face the terms. "Loss of self-esteem and security, fear of the future, stress, depression." You wonder dully if eating a dozen chocolate-chip cookies, wearing a bathrobe until 4, combing your hair at 5, cleaning behind the stove (twice) and crying in an employment-agency parking lot qualify as symptoms of stress or maybe loss of self-esteem. Fighting with your spouse/boyfriend? Aha—tension in personal relationships.

6   The loss of a job is rejection, resulting in the same hurt feelings as if a friend had told you to "bug off." Only this "friend" filled up 40 to 60 (or more) hours of your week. Constant references to the staff as "family" only accentuate the feeling of desertion and deception. You picture yourself going home to your parents or spouse and being informed, "Your services as our daughter/my wife are no longer required. Pick up your baby pictures as you leave." *accentuate*

7   Each new affirmation of unemployment renews the pain: the first trip to the employment agency, the first friend you tell, the first interview and, most dreaded of all, the first trip to the unemployment office. *affirmation*

8   Standing in line at the unemployment office makes you feel very much the same as you did the first time you ever flunked a class or a test—as if you had a big red "F" for "Failure" printed across your forehead. I fantasize myself standing at the end of the line in a crisp and efficient blue suit, chin up, neat and straight as a corporate executive. As I move down the line I start to come unglued and a half hour later, when I finally reach the desk clerk, I am

slouching and sallow in torn jeans, tennis shoes and a jacket from the Salvation Army, carrying my worldly belongings in a shopping bag and unable to speak.

9   You do eventually become accustomed to being unemployed, in the way you might accept a bad limp. And you gradually quit beating yourself for not having been somehow indispensable—or for not having become an accountant. You tire of straining your memory for possible infractions. You   *infractions* recover some of the confidence that always told you how good you were at your job and accept what the supervisor said: "This doesn't reflect on your job performance; sales are down 30 per cent this month."

10   But each time you recover that hallowed self-esteem, you renew a fight   *self-esteem* to maintain it. Each time you go to a job interview and give them your best and they hire someone else, you go another round with yourself and your self-esteem. Your unemployment seems to drag on beyond all justification. You start to glimpse a stranger in your rearview mirror. The stranger suddenly looks like a bum. You look at her with clinical curiosity. Hmmm. Obviously into the chronic stages. Definitely not employable.

11   We unemployed share a social stigma similar to that of the rape victim. Whether consciously or subconsciously, much of the work-ethic-driven public feels that you've somehow "asked for it," secretly wanted to lose your job and "flirted" with unemployment through your attitude—probably dressed in a way to invite it (left the vest unbuttoned on your three-piece suit).

12   *Satisfaction:* But the worst of it isn't society's work-ethic morality; it's your own, which you never knew you had. You find out how much self-satisfaction was gained from even the most simple work-related task: a well-worked letter, a well-handled phone call—even a clean file. Being useful to yourself isn't enough.

13   But then almost everyone has heard about the need to be a useful member of society. What you didn't know about was the loneliness. You've spent your life almost constantly surrounded by people, in classes, in dorms and at work. To suddenly find yourself with only your cat to talk to all day distorts your sense of reality. You begin to worry that flights of fancy might become one way.

14   But you always were, and still are, stronger than that. You maintain balance and perspective, mainly through resorting frequently to sarcasm and irreverence. Although something going wrong in any aspect of your life now seems to push you into temporary despair much more easily than before, you have some very important things to hang on to—people who care, your sense of humor, your talents, your cat and your hopes.

15   And beyond that, you've gained something—a little more knowledge and a lot more compassion. You've learned the value of the routine you scorned and the importance of the job you took for granted. But most of all, you've learned what a "7.6 per cent unemployment rate" really means.

QUESTIONS

1. At the end of paragraph 1, the author describes how "the ambulance came for me." Explain this statement.

2. Characterize the author's feelings about her dismissal.

3. What stigma does the author believe the unemployed share with a rape victim? Explain.

4. What satisfaction does the author say is found in the work situation?

5. In paragraph 15, the author claims that as an unemployed person, you gain something. List these gains and explain each briefly.

EXTENDING YOUR VOCABULARY

alternative: When we saw there was no alternative, we had to _____

_____

idle: The employer was upset to see idle machines because it

meant _____

accentuate: Standing next to the seven-foot basketball player served to

accentuate my _____

affirmation: The testimony of the three witnesses served as an affirma-

tion of _____

infractions: Repeated traffic infractions led to _____

self-esteem: A person with low self-esteem may _____

 PROCESS GUIDE

1. In this article, the author expresses her feelings about being fired from her job and her state of unemployment. Some people write as a form of therapy; that is, the process of describing a problem in print helps relieve some anxiety. Cite two examples of a situation you have read about in which the author shares a problem and expresses his or her frustration.

Problem	Author's Negative Responses	Author's Positive Responses
1.		
2.		

2. In paragraph 3, the author expresses bitterness about a number of instances in her job when she felt unrewarded and unappreciated. List three of these instances.

    a. _____

    b. _____

    c. _____

3. List two other situations that could cause people to feel unrewarded and unappreciated at work.

    a. _____

    b. _____

4. In paragraph 5, the author states that the loss of a job has a negative effect on an individual. Cite the examples she gives in paragraphs 6 through 10, and briefly explain each.

    Paragraph 6:

    _____

    Paragraph 7:

    _____

    Paragraph 8:

    _____

    Paragraph 9:

    _____

    Paragraph 10:

    _____

5. Halvorsen describes one reaction of the working public to the unemployed as "blaming the victim." Some people believe the unemployed deserve their situation because of poor job performance. Some also attribute the inability to find a new job to a lack of initiative. Cite another instance in which society's typical response to a problem is to blame the victim.

    _____

    _____

6. In paragraph 12, Halvorsen examines the work ethic she discovered within herself. Analyze her statements. Does she accurately reflect society's work ethic? Has she left anything out of her analysis? Explain.

    _____

    _____

7. According to the author, how does one maintain a psychological balance in the face of unemployment?

    _____

    _____

8. What strategies or resources are available to help people cope with unemployment?

_____

_____

 ### *READING JOURNAL*

In "How It Feels to Be Out of Work," Halvorsen analyzes her emotional reaction to being laid off.

- **Content**

  Aside from learning about layoffs and unemployment from reading newspapers or from viewing television, what new issues did Halvorsen raise
  that are of significance to you? If these issues are not new to you, did she
  make you examine the issues in a new light? Discuss.

- **Process**

  Halvorsen raises a number of issues related to being unemployed. She
  doesn't make use of subheadings or bulleted items. How were you able to
  keep track of the issues?

- **Response**

  Analyze your feelings toward Halvorsen's situation. Can you place yourself in her shoes? Can you empathize? Is there any particular sentence that
  caused you to have an emotional reaction?

The Day the Mommies
Went Home

ANITA SHREVE

*Anita Shreve lives in Massachusetts and writes both fiction and nonfiction. Her
novels include* The Pilot's Wife *(1998),* The Weight of Water *(1997),* Resistance
(1995), Where or When *(1993),* Strange Fits of Passion *(1991), and* Eden Close
*(1989). In addition to many articles, she has written several nonfiction books,
including* Women Together, Women Alone *(1989) and* Remaking Motherhood
*(1987). Her short stories and nonfiction writing have appeared in publications
such as* Esquire, Cosmopolitan, *and the* New York Times Magazine.

GEARING UP

1. Women are forming an increasingly important segment of the work force. Imagine that women decided to leave work en masse (in one group). Explore and discuss the many consequences of such a move.

2. Some people claim that women have particularly legitimate grievances about work. Identify some of these complaints and assess their validity.

 # READING STRATEGY

READING SATIRE

"The Day the Mommies Went Home" is an example of satire. The term *satire* refers to any work in prose or verse that uses wit to ridicule or expose vice or folly. Satire contains both humor and criticism. Virtually all satire uses exaggeration and distortion to arouse the reader's attention. The writer uses persuasion to get the reader to examine habitual assumptions and look beneath the surface. The author also uses ridicule to draw the reader's attention to foolishness, corruption, or excess. However, if you notice only the humorous element, you have missed the big picture. Behind the humor, the author is attempting to make an important point. Therefore, in reading satire it is necessary to determine the author's tone. The satirist may use a variety of approaches to attack a topic, including mockery, sarcasm, exaggeration, understatement, and parody (a humorous, satirical imitation of a person, event, or piece of literature).

The appeal of satire is timeless in Western civilization. Over the years satirists have selected from a wide range of subjects, such as government, religion, politics, schools, the armed forces, and nuclear war. One noted satirist was Aristophanes, who lived in the Greece of Socrates (450–388 B.C.). In a series of satirical dramas, Aristophanes targeted Cleon, a noted despot, attacked the war policy of his city-state, and ridiculed Socrates, among other subjects. Historically, satire found outlets in essays, plays, novels, poems, works of art, and, since the 1800s, newspaper articles.

Jonathan Swift, the author of *Gulliver's Travels,* is recognized as one of the greatest satirists. In his works he attacked the major institutions of his time. In his 1729 essay, *A Modest Proposal,* Swift lashed out at England's brutal treatment of the Irish. *A Modest Proposal* is presented as a letter of advice in which a public-spirited citizen suggests a remedy to Ireland's overpopulation and desperate economic conditions. In simple terms the writer suggests selling the children of the poor to be cooked as food by the rich, thereby providing the poor Irish with a source of income while at the same time adding variety to the diet of the wealthy.

Today satire is not restricted to print form. Television, radio, and the movies all feature satirical material. The movie and television show *M*A*S*H* satirizes army life. The motion picture *Animal House* pokes fun at various aspects of college life, including fraternity houses and pompous college offi-cials. Comedians often use satire in their monologues.

Cartoons have been an enduring vehicle for satire. Thomas Nast, a noted cartoonist of the late 1800s, dealt with the social issues of his day through cartoons. He lambasted slavery and moved Abraham Lincoln to call him "our best recruiting sergeant." Nast is perhaps most known for his attacks on the corrupt Tammany Hall political machine in New York City. His bit-ing satire helped bring about the downfall of "Boss" William Tweed's orga-nization.

In his text *Introduction to Satire* Professor Leonard Feinberg stated:

> Perhaps the most striking quality of satiric literature is its freshness, its originality of perspective. We are shown old things in a new way. Satire rarely offers original ideas. Instead, it presents the familiar in a new form. Satirists do not offer the world new philosophies. What they do is look at familiar condi-tions from a perspective which makes these conditions seem foolish, harmful or affected. Satire jars us out of complacence into a pleasantly shocked realiza-tion that many of the values we unquestioningly accept are false.

Application

In reading satire, keep in mind the following questions:

1. What is the author's target for the satire?

2. What style or method does the author use (mockery, understatement, exaggeration)?

3. What person, issue, institution, or policy is the author exposing?

4. What is the author's purpose in using satire? That is, what changes does the author hope to bring about in the subject being satirized? (Note: Of-ten you must infer the author's purpose.)

5. What might the author gain by writing the satire? Does the author have a personal ax to grind—that is, does the writer have a selfish or subjective aim?

READING STRATEGY CHECK
MARKING TEXT

The Marking Text strategy was first presented in relation to the Sam Leven-son article in Unit One (page 48). In one of his articles, Mortimer Adler, a noted philosopher and author, says that annotating a text is like conversing with the author. In fact, he says that is why he won't lend out his books, since most people would not lend out their diaries. Adler is obviously passionate about the value of annotation, and so are we. By annotation we do not mean just underlining. The object of marking is to capture the interaction of the text and your mind in a brief note. While this process takes more time than merely highlighting, you end up with a document that is able to signal your memory on not just what you considered important, but why you thought it to be so. As a brief review, consider the following in marking text:

1. A mark-up is your written record. It should be meaningful to you. Develop a scheme of marking that will help you with your reading efforts. You may wish to adopt some or all of the suggestions we have made. However, the important thing is to begin.

2. We consider the question mark (?) to be a valuable symbol because if it is used to signal points of confusion and uncertainty it quickly helps you locate areas for class discussion.

3. Circle key words and phrases in the text. In the reading under consideration, the author describes a mass walkout by American working women. The fourth paragraph begins,

> "Working women have had it" said the spokeswoman . . .

It would be useful to circle this phrase because it gives the reason for the walkout.

The Reading

The Day the Mommies Went Home
by ANITA SHREVE

1   New York City, Nov. 28 (IP)—at 11 A.M. yesterday, women across the country simultaneously stood up and left their places of work.

simultaneously

2   The mass walkout, believed to be the biggest single action taken by a special-interest group in American history, literally rocked the nation as 60 million women left office buildings, filled buses and subways, and clogged major traffic arteries for more than three hours in most areas.

3   The move appears to have been the work of a coalition of women's organizations, spearheaded by the group Women Will Walk (WWW).

coalition
spearheaded

4   "Working women have had it," said spokeswoman Mary Fedup from her Washington, D.C., home. "They're sick of inadequate day care, of too little flexibility in the workplace, of having to do more at home and on the job than men and not getting paid equally for it. And they're sick of employers' refusal to take their needs and requests seriously."

5   The exodus brought businesses to a halt, and by day's end the Dow Jones industrial average had plummeted 750 points. The sheer size of the walkout caused seismic activity measuring 5.2 on the Richter scale; aftershocks were felt in Halifax, Nova Scotia, and Mexico City.

exodus
plummeted

6   "I thought it was nuclear war," said a shaken Burt Smith, the CEO of Crumble, America's largest cereal manufacturer, which is headquartered just outside New York City. The walkout "crippled" his company, he added. Almost 75 percent of his employees participated, including more than half of the management staff.

7   "It's chaos here," said Smith in a telephone interview from his office, where he was working well after midnight. "Chaos. They just up and left."

8   Fedup claims that working mothers' groups began discussing the action several years ago. They soon won the support of single and childless women frustrated at the bleak future facing female workers, and WWW was formed in September of last year. During the past 14 months the group disseminated information, guidelines, and updates to women throughout the American workplace.

disseminated

9   The action, Fedup stressed, is a *walkout,* not a strike. "Calling it a strike implies that we're open to negotiation," she said. "If we see a real commitment to change on the part of employers, government, and husbands, many of us *will* return. But a lot of women are tired of empty promises. They may never go back."

10 Over the past year, she added, millions of women contributed generously to the WWW walkout fund. As a result of astute investment and the long-term pledges of a few wealthy contributors, the group estimates that it will be able to provide financial assistance to any walkout participant for the next 15 years.

astute

Schools, Hospitals Close

11 Though urban businesses were the hardest hit, women also walked off their jobs in schools, hospitals, and police and fire departments. By midnight most state governments had declared a state of emergency, and Cabinet members met with the president to discuss the crisis. But the absence of female personnel from key positions in the nation's capital hampered progress significantly, reported a White House spokesman.

hampered

12 Telephone service nationwide was interrupted for most of yesterday and last night. Most schools closed, many grocery stores and supermarkets never opened, and in hospitals everywhere male medical personnel worked around the clock to keep emergency wards functioning.

13 Last night the governor of New York, speaking from Albany, called for any available manpower to relieve the emergency staffs of hospitals and police and fire departments. He is reportedly considering a statewide curfew, but he made no mention of it during his statement. He did, however, issue a plea to the women of New York, asking them to return to their jobs in the morning. But without female anchor and production personnel, many TV and radio stations were off the air.

Day-Care Centers Shut Down

14 Day-care centers were jammed shortly after 11 A.M. yesterday as women flooded in to retrieve their children. "I think this means we're going out of business," said Eric Jones, director of the Kiddy Care Center in Burlington, Vermont.

15 Similar concerns were expressed by owners and employees of commercial enterprises that depend on working women for most of their business. "I'm out of a job," said Julio Hernandez, a cook at a Pizza Hut franchise in

Des Moines, Iowa. "Most of our customers are working mothers who don't have time to cook. Now they'll be home. What are they going to need us for?"

16   Tremors also reached the fashion industry as designers scurried to their drawing boards and tore up next season's designs for women's business wear. According to one industry spokesman, the look for the immediate future will be leisure wear. But, he added, "if women don't get back to work in the factories and sales offices, well, there won't be any new clothes for anybody."

tremors / scurried

On the Home Front

17   Suburban neighborhoods reported a rise in noise levels as children abandoned after-school classes and played on their blocks instead.

18   "There are kids playing tag in the yards and in the streets," said one dazed father, emerging from his car. "I haven't seen anything like this since my childhood."

19   Other husbands expressed panic at the thought of being the sole financial support for their families. "She told me she was going to do this if I didn't start helping out more, but I didn't believe her," said Fred White, a father of three who lives in Park Ridge, Illinois. "I don't think I can hack it." White, speaking from the Crazy Horse Bar and Grill on Third Avenue in Chicago, said he was on his third martini and was feeling "shell-shocked." "She made more money than I do," he added. "We'll have to give up the house."

Women Cautious

20   WWW has reportedly urged women not to talk publicly about the walkout until its short-term effects can be assessed. But many participants were willing to speak off the record, and a number of these cautioned that the action does not herald a return to the 1950s, when women devoted themselves entirely to hearth and home, only to wind up feeling isolated and oppressed.

assessed

21   "I plan to get in a lot of tennis," said a former high school teacher in Des Moines. "I won't be cleaning the windows. I'm going to relax, talk to my kids. I've been taking it on the chin for five years now, trying to keep my job, trying to take care of the family, commuting three hours a day. Now it's my husband's turn."

22   "You won't find me in an apron," said a former Pennsylvania attorney, who added that she was still feeling giddy at having walked out in the middle of a criminal trial. "I'm going to join a gym, get in shape."

23   "I'm going to read," said a former waitress in San Francisco. "As soon as my kids are on the bus, I'm going to sit in a hot tub and soak and read a good book."

24   Other women also expressed joy at the prospect of spending more time with their children, of no longer feeling torn between the home and the workplace. "It's the best thing I ever did," said the former editor of a weekly national newsmagazine. "Oh, I may go back if things change. But I haven't had a vacation in 10 years. I plan to enjoy myself for a while."

prospect

Uncertain Future

25 Experts are cautious in analyzing the short- and long-term effects of the walkout. Dr. Morgan Peters, a Harvard sociologist, expressed concern for society as a whole. "Apart from the severe blow to the economy," he said, "it is inconceivable that American society can continue to function without women in the key positions they have filled."   *inconceivable*

26   Peters added that no one could fail to be affected by the walkout. And he asked, "Whatever did we do before women were in the work force?"

QUESTIONS

1. The author begins paragraph 1 by listing a city and date and inserting the letters *IP* in parentheses. Explain why she does this.

2. Comment on the author's choice of title for this essay. Is it appropriate? Explain.

3. In one or two sentences, summarize the author's major points.

4. The author uses humor and exaggeration to raise a serious issue. List several examples of her use of humor and/or exaggeration.

5. The author presents the readers with a "what-if" scenario (an imaginary event and its consequences). List several potential effects of a mass walkout by women.

6. Discuss the message presented in the last two paragraphs. How does it relate to the author's overall purpose in writing the article?

EXTENDING YOUR VOCABULARY

simultaneously: No one expected Marie and Susan to give birth simultaneously because _____

coalition: The workers formed a coalition in order to _____
_____

spearheaded: Once Jenkins spearheaded the annual blood drive
_____

exodus: There was a mass exodus at the concert after it was discovered that _____

plummeted: The price of airline tickets plummeted because _____
_____

disseminated: The principal became concerned when he learned that students disseminated _____

astute:	One astute investment can result in _____
hampered:	Rescuers were hampered by _____
tremors:	Tremors were felt on the stock exchange by the news that _____
scurried:	Workers scurried about the office when it was learned that _____
assessed:	After the flood damage was assessed, the insurance company _____
prospect:	The prospect of winning a full scholarship became apparent after _____
inconceivable:	What is inconceivable to me is _____

◆▶ PROCESS GUIDE

1. This article is a satirical piece. Satire uses humor to ridicule a subject. The format and style of this article follow those of a newspaper. What characteristics of this piece make it resemble a newspaper article?

   _____

   _____

2. Many newspaper and magazine articles begin with a *byline* that gives the author's name, the place where the article was written, the source of the information provided, and sometimes a date. This article contains the byline: "New York City, Nov. 28 (IP)." What do you think the initials *IP* mean?

   _____

   _____

✦ NOTE In addition to their own reporters, most newspapers use wire services to obtain their stories. Many smaller newspapers have limited staffs and rely on these news agencies more heavily. The two largest wire services are AP (Associated Press) and Reuters (a British news organization). Originally these organizations sent their stories to their newspaper subscribers via telegraph wire (hence the term *wire service*). Then telephone and eventually satellite technology replaced the telegraph. AP is the nation's largest newsgathering agency, with reporters in every major city throughout the world. The next time you read a newspaper, observe which wire services it uses. In this article, the author uses a fictitious wire service, *IP*. ✦

3. Recall from the discussion of the reading satire strategy that satire has at least two purposes: to entertain and to provoke. The writer wants the reader to be amused but also wants to draw the reader's attention to a serious issue. In reading "The Day the Mommies Went Home," look for both kinds of statements. Then list them as follows:

   a. Statements intended to amuse or entertain

      1. _____

      2. _____

   b. Statements intended to stimulate thought

      1. _____

      2. _____

✦ **NOTE**   Shreve deals with some serious issues regarding women in the workplace. People often engage in protest to bring issues into the public light. Forms of protest include boycotts, strikes, sit-ins, and demonstrations. Usually the protest is intended not to change the entire social order but to address a specific need. A movement to overthrow the existing order (i.e., change the government in power) is not a specific objective and would be deemed revolutionary. Although we usually think of revolution as lying on the violent end of the continuum and a picket line as being a more peaceful form of protest, there are no absolutes. The kind of mass walkout Shreve describes may be peaceful, but it has the potential to effect revolutionary change because of the number of people involved and the consequences that would follow. ✦

4. Aristophanes' play *Lysistrata* also describes a mass movement by women. Locate some basic information about this topic in reference books at your library. Then answer the following questions:

   a. What were the women protesting?

   _____

   b. What form of protest did the women use?

   _____

   ## *READING JOURNAL*

"The Day the Mommies Went Home" is a style of writing not previously found in this text. The reading satire strategy noted that in satire an author is purposely exaggerating an idea in a comedic or sensational way with the purpose of making a serious point. Tone is thus very important in satire. You can expect to find dramatic, outrageous, or funny statements that are not intended to be taken as true but are written to have an effect on you. We include the following list of prompts to get you started in your journal entries.

- **Content**

  Can you recall ever reading satire before? Were you able to recognize the author's techniques and approach in communicating her message? Did she make you look at the issues in a new way?

  Choose one statement that is not intended to be taken as literally true but is an obvious exaggeration or distortion. Write down this sentence. Explain the nature of the exaggeration. Give a literal interpretation of the sentence. If taken at face value, what is the author saying? It may help to paraphrase the author's idea. Describe what makes the sentence a distortion or exaggeration of reality.

- **Process**

  Did you find yourself reading the article in your usual way, or did you need to reread and reconsider the material? Describe your approach to understanding the author's message.

- **Response**

  Describe your reaction to this type of writing. Were you amused, bored, upset, entertained? Characterize your feelings. Is this a writing style that you might enjoy and seek to find in the future? Explain.

Managing Workforce Diversity in Organizations

RICKY GRIFFIN

Ricky Griffin is a professor of management at Texas A & M University and serves on the Board of Directors of the Southern Management Association. In addition to contributing to numerous journals in his profession, Professor Griffin is the coauthor of Organizational Behavior *(with George Moorhead) and* International Business: A Managerial Perspective *(with Michael Pustay).*

GEARING UP

1. Describe the university or college you currently attend in terms of diversity. Discuss the differences between student population versus faculty.

2. List possible advantages and disadvantages of diversity in organizations such as schools and workplaces.

READING STRATEGY

STUDYING A TEXTBOOK CHAPTER
AND PREPARING FOR AN EXAM

Because of the detail involved in this strategy we recommend that you read through the textbook chapter first before you work through this section. Then return for study of the strategy in relation to the chapter. After finishing the chapter there is a sample exam. This is followed by question analysis and sample answers.

The purpose of this strategy is to bring together many of the strategies that have been previously introduced and applied with the goal of studying a textbook chapter in preparation for an exam. We have selected a major excerpt of Chapter 14—"Managing Workforce Diversity in Organizations"—from a textbook entitled *Management* by Ricky Griffin. We chose this reading for the following reasons:

- The topic fits thematically with the work/careers unit.

- The chapter examines a very important issue in today's workplace.

- The chapter has an abundance of study features.

- The chapter is clearly written and accessible.

Up to this point, strategies were introduced purposely one at a time. We wanted to give you the opportunity to focus on one technique rather than concern yourself with many strategies. Our assumption is that you now have become somewhat comfortable with the strategies and are ready to apply a number of them to a textbook chapter. Our goal is to provide you with a comprehensive plan to use in your reading and study of textbooks and also to help you prepare for exams. We will explain the steps involved in this task and show its application to the chapter.

Textbook Chapter Characteristics

Textbook chapters tend to be longer than newspaper or magazine articles, which give you the essential information on a single idea or issue. A textbook chapter, by contrast, introduces and analyzes a number of concepts in depth. This lengthier explanation requires enough supporting material so that even complicated concepts are accessible to most readers. Student reactions to a chapter will be as varied as the number of students who approach it. Three patterns do emerge from all the possible reactions:

Situation	Solution
You are overwhelmed by the amount of material. You don't know where to begin or what to do.	*You need a reading/study plan to size up the situation at hand.*

You seem to understand much of the material as you are reading it. The problem largely arises because of the amount of material, so that when you have finished you retain little in relation to the time you have spent.	*You need a plan for retaining the material.*
You do not prepare adequately for exams. Your approach is haphazard and lacks systematic exam-taking strategy.	*You need an organized plan for exam preparation.*

A Reading/Study Plan

Our intent is to use Chapter 14 in the Griffin textbook and develop it as a general model that you can apply in your reading and studying environment. You can adapt this model to the specifics of the chapter you are studying. Our model has three components:

- Sizing up the task

- The reading/study process

- Exam preparation and practice

SIZING UP THE TASK

A necessary first step is to reasonably estimate the situation before you jump into it. This means that you will consider the factors involved in the successful study of the chapter and prepare a plan. We believe that there are always at least three factors to consider.

1. Previous preparation.   Previous experience with a subject area is invaluable. A student with long-standing work experience in a business office is at an advantage in reading a book about business. If you do not have this first-hand experience, you must be prepared to learn the business procedures described and the terminology that refers to them.

2. Instructor/time parameters.   The instructor will set the tone for how a chapter is to be studied. For example, an instructor may view the chapter as useful for general background information but may not be concerned that you have comprehensive knowledge of the particulars. Therefore, the in-depth techniques that we will be discussing will not apply in every situation. The instructor may alert you to a specific section of a chapter that will be the focus of careful study. You will have to adopt our suggestions based on what your instructor is telling you plus a realistic assessment of how much time you have. Specific suggestions for time allotment and management will be made in the reading/study process section.

3. The chapter itself. Authors would like to believe that they are successfully communicating with their audience. However, they must make assumptions about the students who will be using their text. Many of the most recent textbooks attempt to supply much in the way of background information so that previous study and experience are less crucial.

In sizing up the chapter you will want to concern yourself with the following:

- *The chapter topic.* Is the title of the chapter familiar? Do you understand the terms in the title even though you have not seen them used in this way before?

- *The chapter length.* Length is an indication of the number of concepts covered, the depth of analysis used, and/or the amount of support material the author has used to clearly explain concepts. A long chapter is not necessarily a difficult one. But a long chapter means that you will need to devote sufficient time to process all of the material.

- *Chapter features.* Long and careful study has gone into the preparation of textbooks, and various support features are provided for students. Here is a list of the kind of features you will find in textbooks. Not every text will have all of them. Also you will discover that the author may use different terminology to refer to the same feature.

1. Chapter objectives (also referred to as Goals or Guide Questions). The chapter objectives are statements that occur at the beginning of the chapter that serve as guideposts to what the author thinks is important. Often you will see the statement introduced by a cue word that tells you the specific approach the author expects you to take in answering questions after you have studied the chapter.

APPLICATION

Chapter objectives occur on the first page of Chapter 14. Note that the objectives are introduced by cue words. The first objective appears as follows:

After studying this chapter, you should be able to:

- Discuss the nature of workforce diversity, including its meaning and reasons for its increase.

The author is signaling you that you should learn enough about the topic of workforce diversity to carry on an enlightened conversation in writing that includes reporting what diversity means and why there is more diversity in the workplace in recent years.

---

2. Chapter outline.   A chapter outline lists the points and subpoints the author will discuss. Often the chapter outline is a listing of the headings and subheadings found in the chapter with an additional phrase of explanation. The outline may be placed both at the beginning and end of the chapter, so look for it.

APPLICATION

The management text is accompanied by an outline on the right side of the first page of the chapter. The outline is an ordered listing of the points that will be discussed. In this case, the outline lists the headings and subheadings of the chapter. Note the first section of the outline:

The Nature of Workforce Diversity
    The Meaning of Diversity
    Reasons for Increasing Diversity

The outline listing tells you that the author will address this topic first and that it corresponds exactly to the first objective. Thus you know where to look for the answer.

---

3. Headings and subheadings.   Almost all textbooks have headings and subheadings. The headings serve as a quick way to preview the chapter. When you have finished studying the material, the headings again serve as a quick review. If you have understood the material, mental connections will take place as you read the heading. If you read a heading and draw a blank, you need to restudy the section.

APPLICATION

The management text is ordered by headings and subheadings. These heads are found in the same order and with the same wording in the outline. When you are given a chapter with heads but no outline you may wish to construct an outline by assembling the headings into a single, continuous list. The headings begin on the second page of the article. The first page includes the chapter title, a list of objectives, and an outline. The second page features an opening incident that will be discussed further on. Thus the author has devoted two pages of the book to getting you ready to read the chapter. The second page begins the text proper. The first two paragraphs that are not headed serve two purposes. They link the opening incident to the chapter and serve as a brief introduction to the material. The first bold heading is, **The Nature of Workforce Diversity.** It corresponds to the first listing on the outline. The heading is followed by two subheads in somewhat smaller print, **The Meaning of Diversity** and **Reasons for Increasing Diversity.** Once again these subheads correspond to the order of points in the outline.

---

4. Visuals/graphics.   Textbook writers are aware that it is helpful to provide visual support to readers with inserts, pictures, charts, graphs, tables, diagrams, and marginal notations. These visuals break up the text into smaller units to process and help to clarify and expand the discussion.

- *Inserts.* A development in the modern textbook is the frequent use of inserts. Inserts take two basic forms: extended examples or case studies and insets. Extended examples are frequently of the case study variety. They are inserted throughout the chapter and are intended to show a concrete model of the theory or concept the author is discussing. Insets are boxed-off material that is sometimes enlarged or color-coded that highlights an idea considered particularly important by the author and/or editor.

APPLICATION

Chapter 14 has both extended examples and insets. The author of the textbook chooses to call the extended examples "incidents." The incident is used to set the stage for the forthcoming discussion and give it immediate application. Chapter 14 discusses diversity, and the incident highlights the diversity issue at two corporations, Xerox and Avon. The author also uses this beginning example as a touchstone in later discussion. The inset on the second page of the chapter highlights a quote by the CEO at Xerox stating its affirmative action policy.

- *Pictures, charts, graphs, tables, diagrams, and marginal notations.* At major publishing houses, the author works closely with editors, designers, and reviewers to create a highly readable text. As was stated earlier, textbook research has shown that students more readily learn textbooks that use graphics. Thus this type of material is included to be helpful to you.

APPLICATION

Chapter 14 has much in the way of visual/graphic support for the reader. There are pictures, graphs, and diagrams that support the written text. Furthermore, inserts occur that expand on the ideas. Marginal notations are used to bring key words and definitions to your attention.

---

5. Chapter summaries.   Many textbooks feature summaries at the end of the chapter. The summary is a condensed version of the major points covered. Ideas are represented in short form. Chapter summaries are an excellent way to review for an exam. If, after studying the chapter, the summary makes complete sense to you, then you have learned the essentials of the chapter. You may wish to try to read the summary before you begin your careful reading of the material. Although you may have difficulty, the summary is one more guide to where you will be going.

APPLICATION

The management text has a summary at the end of the chapter. In five short paragraphs (about 250 words) the author has capsulized the issues found in the chapter. This particular summary follows the order of points addressed.

---

6. *Questions/projects.* Virtually all textbooks have a series of questions at the ends of chapters, units, or articles. These questions were written by the author to check your understanding of the concepts. You may find various question types. Sometimes these types are grouped into different categories:

- *Comprehension questions* (also called questions, comprehension checks, discussion questions, chapter checks, and questions for review). These questions check your literal understanding of the text. They require that you respond to the material in the text in some way. The answer can be found in the chapter and does not require going beyond what is written.

- *Inference questions* (also called extending concepts, chapter challenges, applying concepts, extending ideas, and questions for analysis). These questions go beyond the literal level of the text and require that you show your knowledge of concepts in the chapter by applying them to situations that were not covered in the chapter.

- *Chapter projects* (also called research questions and for further study questions). These questions require extended thought and writing and often involve consulting outside sources. These are the types of activities that can be the focus for a term paper.

- *Recognition questions* (also called multiple choice, fill-in-the-blank, matching, and true-false questions). These questions do not require that you construct an answer. All the answers are there. Your task is to select the best choice among the alternatives.

- *Idiosyncratic questions.* These are question types that appear infrequently and are very much determined by the nature of the subject matter. Authors are always looking for new ways to test and extend your knowledge of the material. A case study question is an example of this type.

APPLICATION

Chapter 14 includes four pages of material to test your knowledge of the chapter. The first section is called "Discussion Questions." The first category of question is called "Questions for Review." These are comprehension questions. Three of the four questions are introduced by cue words. Thus you will be asked to identify, discuss, and summarize certain ideas from the chapter. The second category of questions is termed "Questions for Analysis." These questions require that you go beyond the text. The last grouping under the Discussion Question heading is called "Questions for Application." These questions require extended thought, writing, and activity. For example, the first question asks you to visit the registrar's office at your college. Obviously, a question of this type will take some time and thought. Your instructor is not likely to ask everyone in class to do this same question. Various students may be assigned to different questions individually or in groups. It is also possible that these types of questions will be omitted altogether.

The second grouping is called "Skill Self-Assessment." In this particular exercise, the author is asking you to respond to a survey that attempts to get at your feelings and beliefs about diversity in the workplace. You are asked to read a number of statements about "Managing Diversity" and then indicate whether you strongly agree, somewhat agree, somewhat disagree, or strongly disagree. In an exercise of this type there are no right or wrong answers. Rather, the author is attempting to get you to bring your feelings about the diversity issue to the conscious level and in this way further stimulate your thinking.

The last two pages are devoted to case studies. The author presents you with two situations from real companies facing diversity issues. Each example is followed by discussion questions.

SIZING UP CONCLUSIONS

By sizing up the chapter, you should have a good idea of what time you will need to succeed with the chapter. As an example, let us say that your instructor assigns one chapter per week plus an additional supplementary handout of between five and ten pages. Your class meets four hours per week. A general rule is that the student should expect to spend two hours of outside study for each hour spent in class. Eight hours of preparation is what your instructor would expect as a minimum. You may spend more or less time depending on your related background and reading efficiency. We cannot give you an exact figure required for study time but can tell you that if you expect to master a textbook chapter like Chapter 14 and a handout in one hour of study time you are being unrealistic. The following time frame may be helpful:

- Sizing up the task   ½ hour
- First quick reading, use of question marks   ½–1 hour
- Second careful reading, including marking   1–2 hours
- Question answering   ½–1 hour
- Review   1 hour

The Second Stage: The Reading/Study Process

We find it useful to divide the reading/study process into three parts:

- The strategies you apply before you begin your careful reading of the text
- The strategies you apply during your careful reading of the text
- The strategies you apply after you have completed reading

BEFORE YOU READ

1. Gearing up.   We have also included gearing up as part of what you should do before you begin your reading. As we explained previously, gearing up is an effort to stimulate the existing related knowledge that you have on a particular topic. Learning is a matter of connecting new information to what you already have. This is a much more efficient process if you are conscious of your knowledge base. However, not many textbooks have this feature. We suggest that you make the effort to gear up before you begin reading the material.

APPLICATION

Even if you have had no previous formal training with management concepts, you are aware of how people interact with bosses and others in the workplace on the basis of experience and conversation with others. List two things that you know about either management or diversity in the workplace:

1. _____

2. _____

---

2. Previewing.   If you have invested time in sizing up the task, then you have essentially taken the first steps in previewing. As we pointed out before, the important aspect of previewing is to get a sense of what is coming in the text. Note the topics and the chapter features. Focus on some aspects of the chapter that you will be searching for in your reading. The proficient reader is an active, searching reader. Convert headings and subheads into questions.

This may be your approach in a number of textbooks. Ask yourself questions and then search for the answers.

APPLICATION

The management text converts the headings into questions for you in the statement of objectives. The objectives are questions directly related to the headings and subheadings. Therefore it would very useful to focus on the objectives before you begin reading the material. In reading the chapter you will be searching for the answers to the questions listed as objectives.

Once you discover the organizational format of a text, use it to your advantage. Since you know that each of the objectives corresponds to a heading, you may wish to focus on a single objective and the portion of the text that answers it. This keeps you from loading up your short-term memory. Then once you have finished reading this text section, return to the objectives and study the second one and the related material from the chapter.

List two questions that will be guiding you in your reading of the chapter.

1. _____

2. _____

---

3. The read through.   One more technique to consider before your careful reading of the material is the quick read through. In this stage, you are actually reading all the material in the chapter but at a rapid pace. You are not concerned with words that you do not know or the ideas that escape you. You will attend to these items in your careful reading. The purpose of the read through is to give you overall familiarity with the features and ideas of the chapter. If you constantly interrupt yourself to look up a word or puzzle over an idea you will lose the flow of the meaning.

DURING THE READING/STUDY PROCESS

You are now ready for the careful reading of the chapter. There are four strategies that can be applied as you are processing the information:

- Marking text
- Predicting vocabulary
- Reading exposition
- Periodic assessment

1. Marking text.   As we have pointed out before, marking a text is your written record of the comprehension process. Thus things which are somewhat confusing should be marked with a question mark (?). Ideas that you do not understand at all may be marked with a double question mark (??). Circle words that are new to you. Most importantly, attempt to capture the gist of the material in brief notes in the margin. This method of marking text is more time consuming than underlining or highlighting, but it has greater rewards. A good marginal note captures your thinking at the time you are reading the text. If you merely underline, you are only alerted that a particular section of text was worth noting. You will again have to read and process this section to determine why. The marginal note, by contrast, tells you why the section was important.

APPLICATION

The first thirteen paragraphs of the chapter after the objective and opening incident page are marked for you. We encourage you to continue marking the text after this point. A well-placed question mark is invaluable for seeking clarification in class.

---

2. Predicting vocabulary.   In the Marking Text strategy we suggested that you circle words that are new to you. We do not suggest that you go through all of the Predicting Vocabulary steps in the careful reading stage. We do suggest that you attempt to predict something that allows you to go on with your reading. You can check your predictions later in the dictionary. Consider the following sentence:

> The axolotys strategy was considered to be the most useful by the reading experts present.

The term *axolotys* must be new for you because we invented it to make a point. Predict a word for *axolotys* that makes sense in the context.

Your prediction _____

Your reasoning _____

The sentence gives you some helpful context. You know, for example, that *axolotys* is some kind of strategy. The sentence informs you that it was reading experts who judged the strategy to be the most helpful. So the strategy is some kind of reading strategy. A good prediction would be a term that described strategy in some way and was related to reading. Consider the following possible predictions:

- The scientific strategy

- The new strategy

- The metacognitive strategy

The three examples would be reasonable predictions because they make some sense in the context. The important thing is that you not get bogged down with one word and lose track of the overall meaning of what you are reading.

APPLICATION

After a brief introduction, the chapter begins by giving a meaning for *diversity*. *Diversity* is boldface in the margin and is clearly a key word in the chapter. It is not a candidate for the Predicting Vocabulary strategy. Words appearing in the title of a chapter must be known before you begin with your reading. The paragraph begins:

> Diversity exists in a group or organization when its members differ from one another along one or more important dimensions.

The term *dimensions* may be somewhat unfamiliar to you as it is used in this context, and in this sense it is a target word. Write a synonym or short phrase for *dimensions.* If you are not certain about it, make a prediction but do not look it up in the dictionary.

Your synonym or definition _____   OR

Your prediction _____

The sentence is saying that a group is diverse when the members of the group are different from one another. Thinking about how people can be different brings you to the notion of "dimensions." In what way are people different from one another?

_____

Based on your experience, you are aware that people are different in age, gender, size, and ethnicity. These factors are the dimensions or physical properties of diversity.

---

3. Reading exposition. "Managing Workforce Diversity in Organizations" is a textbook chapter and a typical example of the textbook writing style called exposition. Exposition reports information such as facts, data, formulas, processes, and techniques. This material is accompanied by description, explanation, graphics, and other supporting detail. Two approaches to reading exposition were introduced in Unit One. Reading Exposition I (page 75) focused on identifying and understanding an author's writing patterns as a means to comprehension. Exposition II examined the use of the signal word as an indicator of idea shift and development. You will want to apply these strategies to this article and in your future work with textbooks.

- *Writing patterns.* Determining an author's writing patterns will help you follow the development of ideas. The patterns include cause and effect, comparison and contrast, sequence or process, listing, analysis, example, and definition. For example, in the cause-and-effect pattern, the author illustrates why something has occurred. You are presented with an event or factor that causes something else to happen (the effect). For a discussion of this and the other patterns, see "The Proficient Reader" article (page 79).

APPLICATION

Chapter 14 claims that organizations have become increasingly diverse. This is the effect or the result of something occurring. You can expect that the author will provide a set of reasons (causes) to account for the increase in diversity. In your study, you will want to look for more than a set of facts (current assessment of the state of things), such as increased diversity in the workplace. For if there is validity in the author's cause/effect relationship, when causes change so will the effects. Thus if one or more of the reasons that brought about more diversity in the workplace changes, then a change in this reason may cause a decline in diversity.

- *Signal words.* Another way to follow an author's discussion is to consider signal words. It is not necessary or efficient to focus on every signal word. If the meaning of the text is clear as you read, then you are already processing the signal words as a part of the unfolding meaning of the text. It is when you experience difficulty with a particular section or idea that you will want to pick up your head from the reading and see where you are. The signal words function as location markers in the author's explanation of an idea.

APPLICATION

In Chapter 14, you will find the signal word *therefore* in the last sentence of paragraph 4. In this instance the use of *therefore* is a signal that the author is concluding his thought on the topic. The term serves as a signal that previous statements have led up to this last thought.

---

4. Periodic assessment.   Textbook chapters can be quite long. There is a lot of information to process and retain. It would be inefficient to try a careful reading of the entire chapter without stopping periodically to assess what is happening in your reading. You are putting the task of reading the chapter on hold while you step back to see what you have learned and how you have learned it.

APPLICATION

The management chapter is twenty-four pages long in the original version, including the objective and question pages. It would be wise to stop at convenient intervals to examine what is going on in your reading. The natural places in Chapter 14 are after the major headings. The first bold-face heading is "The Nature of Workforce Diversity." The next boldface headline, "Dimensions of Diversity," signals the end of the first section and announces that a new topic is to be discussed. This is a good place to stop and reflect. What are you going to ask yourself?

Focusing on the first objective gives you a ready-made question to answer. The first objective is "Discuss the nature of workforce diversity, including its meaning and the reasons for its increase." If you are able to respond to this question, then you can feel confident that you comprehend the ideas in this section. You should also check in with the reading strategies that you are using. Have you been marking the text for key ideas? Have you written brief marginal notes that capture the author's definition of diversity and the reasons for it increasing? Have you been predicting for unknown vocabulary? Have you circled the new terms? Or you may want to get into the habit of using heads and subheads in your review, since some textbooks do not feature objectives to guide you. The key words here are *diversity, meaning of,* and *reasons for diversity.*

Exam Preparation

PRE-EXAM STRATEGIES

From the syllabus and your instructor's comments, you should try to determine the topics that will be stressed. It is quite possible that an Introduction to Business course has furnished you with the knowledge of the first topics covered in a Management course, thus easing your introduction into the new material.

There are a number of steps that can be taken either before the class or early on in the term.

1. Check the reading load.

- Locate the readings assigned for the course, particularly the major textbook and/or novel. Instead of making an immediate purchase you may wish to do some reading in the bookstore or in the library. Most colleges require that texts used for classes be kept on reserve in the library. You won't be able to check out these books, but you should be able to make a reasonable assessment in a short time in the library.

- Read the first page of the introduction again. The introduction should tell you about the subject of the text, what topics will be covered, and the approach of the book. Does this make sense to you? If it makes only a little sense or not at all, then get focused and try again.

- Now read the first page of the first three chapters. There will be new words and ideas. However, you are not reading for complete understanding. You are trying to pick up the general sense of the text. If you are picking up very little and it looks like a tough challenge, we suggest the following:

2. Arrange your schedule so that you have sufficient time for preparation. This may mean dropping a course or two or cutting back on your work schedule.

3. Look for outside help such as tutoring and study groups.   The department that houses the course is a useful place to start. Many have bulletin board listings of study groups and/or graduate students looking for tutoring work.

4. Consult outside sources.   Virtually every introductory course in college (sociology, history, psychology, and biology) is supported by dozens of textbooks. Each book has some merit if it continues to be used. A text that is clear on some topics may not be as helpful on others. Knowing that there are dozens of textbook alternatives gives you options when you are stuck.

5. Plan weekly/prepare daily.   Construct a reading and study schedule for each week of the course. This means setting up a schedule for the daily preparation required by lectures and homework as well as extra time for exams and term papers or projects that span stretches of time.

PREPARING THE MATERIAL

You can't remember everything you are told or have read, nor should you want to. You are striving to understand the key concepts of the course. This is a compilation of the ideas advanced by the text and the instructor. A Venn diagram may help (see facing page).

A good portion of what happens in a classroom is support discussion. Explanations are provided in class with additional examples to make key concepts clear. Once you understand a concept, then you may dispense with the additional examples and explanations. You will want to narrow the sum total of key ideas to a manageable set for class study. Thus it is important to know the key concepts. The Venn diagram shows that some ideas thought significant by the instructor will not be in the book. Correspondingly, the authors of the book will have ideas that are important to them but not regarded as such by the instructor.

You may have heard students say, "The exam was hard; there was stuff on it that was not mentioned in class." In this case the student missed some key concepts introduced earlier. The student may have done an excellent job

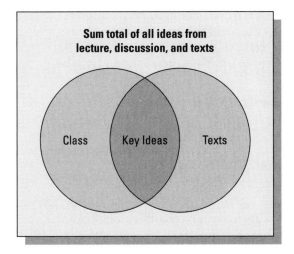

of preparing all the reading material but was tripped up by things covered in class that he or she missed because of absence.

As was mentioned before, one way to determine a list of key concepts is to study the instructor's syllabus. At a minimum, each topic area or subheading in the text has one key concept. Many textbooks have a summary of key ideas listed at the end of the chapter. This summary is well worth your time, for two reasons. First, examine it before your careful reading as a preparation exercise. Second, read it carefully after your study of the chapter as a check of your understanding.

EVALUATION

The vast majority of classes are evaluated in part or in whole by quizzes and exams. Let us say a business management instructor has established the following grading scheme:

%	Assignment
10	Class discussion
10	Project/paper of 3–5 pages
40	Two exams, one hour each
40	Final exam
100%	TOTAL

The point spread in the above example clearly favors exam performance. However, it is still important to do well in the discussion and paper categories. Getting most of these points will also give you some breathing room on the exams. Furthermore, instructors may be more likely to round up a point or two for students who make substantial class contributions and write good papers.

Determine the nature of the exam you will be taking. This includes the material to be covered, the date of the exam, and the question types. If in a fifteen-week semester the first hourly exam is given during the fifth week, you will have five weeks of material to prepare. Your preparation may take the following form:

1. Reduce lecture notes to one $5 \times 7''$ card per class.

2. Reduce textbook chapters to one $5 \times 7''$ card and/or use a marked version of the text.

3. Prepare a card for each handout or other supplementary material.

EXAM TYPE

Exams may be totally objective, totally subjective, or a combination of both. Your instructor may have you do only essay questions or only objective questions. A frequent combination is to have some of both types of questions. Different forms of questions will appear regarding the same content. It is wise then to prepare for both the current and the different form in which the content may be tested.

1. Objective tests.   In an objective exam, there is one expected correct response. The following are objective question formats:

- Multiple choice

- Matching

- Fill-in-the-blank

- True/false

2. Subjective tests.   Subjective tests are essay and short-answer formats where you are required to frame a response to a question. They are called subjective because no two responses will be exactly alike unless they are copied. The instructor must judge the merit of your answer against an abstract standard.

SIZING UP THE EXAM AND PLANNING YOUR TIME

Before you begin an exam, spend a moment looking over the test to get a sense of what you are facing and to budget your time. Consider the following exam analysis.

Management I—first hourly exam

Points	Task
10 pts.	5 short-answer questions
10 pts.	10 multiple-choice items
80 pts.	2 (40 pts. each) essay questions (a choice of two of three questions)

In this example, most points are found in the essays, so it would not be efficient to spend the first half hour on the short-answer and multiple-choice questions. By nature, multiple-choice questions are tricky because the correct answer needs to be disguised and planted in the midst of other reasonable possibilities. Therefore, it is quite possible that you could puzzle over a few multiple-choice possibilities far beyond the time that should be given them. Time budgeted solely on points yields the following distribution for the one-hour exam:

10 pts. 5 short answer questions	(6 minutes or 72 seconds per question)
10 pts. 10 multiple choice questions	(6 minutes or 36 seconds per question)
80 pts. 2 essay questions	(48 minutes or 24 minutes per question)

In an exam situation, you certainly do not want to spend time calculating exact numbers as we have done. Rather you need to quickly determine what you are facing on the exam and approximate how to allot time. Thus, noting that the short-answer and multiple-choice questions together are worth 20 percent of the points, allocating them about 20 percent of the time (12 minutes) would be a reasonable plan.

Flexibility is an exam virtue. You may discover that one of the essays is very easy to write and only takes you ten minutes. Obviously, you will have more time to devote to the rest of the exam.

TEST QUESTION STRATEGIES

Writing Essay Questions

Composing answers for essay questions on exams is a similar process to that of framing an answer for homework questions, with some exceptions. The differences relate to the circumstances of the test situation, where you will not be able to use your text and notes. Furthermore, there is time pressure in most testing situations. We will review the Framing-an-Answer strategy introduced previously and then suggest some alterations to apply it to an exam situation.

1. Understand the question

2. Reread the text and/or search your mind for related ideas

3. Select the appropriate information

4. Construct an answer

5. Edit your response

For both homework and exam questions, begin by spending sufficient time analyzing the question before you begin writing. It seems obvious that you should clearly understand what you are writing about. However, students tend to rush to write in an exam situation because they are time conscious. Too often they discover later on (or afterwards) that they have not answered what was asked. Therefore spend as much or more time analyzing the question as you do in actually responding to it.

- *Step 1—Understand the question.* This step remains the same for both homework and exams. Reviewing the list of cue words is a good first step in exam preparation. You will want to be very clear on the distinctions between what it means to define, describe, or critique, among other possibilities. The cue words are listed on pages 6–8. Another strategy in understanding a question is to paraphrase it. Try rewriting the question in your own words.

- *Step 2—Reread the text and/or search your mind for related ideas.* An open book test makes rereading selected text a possibility. However, in most cases you will need to rely on what you have remembered from your study. After you have previewed the exam and noted what is being asked for in the essays, you may wish to quickly write down in abbreviated note form everything you remember that generally relates to the topic of the essay. You are not concerned with grammar, style, or spelling but are simply giving yourself a list to work from as a starting point.

- *Step 3—Select the appropriate information.* If you have constructed a rough list as suggested in step 2, you now edit your list to only those items that specifically relate to the essay. In this process you may think of other things to add. You don't want to take the time to write another list. Cross out things that do not seem to apply with a single line. Do not erase or white out this entry since you may discover in the actual writing process that you will include something that was previously rejected. In short, you are constructing a working outline to guide you. Before you begin writing, read through the points in your outline, filling in around them mentally to determine whether you have a response that makes sense and answers the question.

- *Step 4—Construct an answer.* Organization is the key to an appropriate answer. To merely list related ideas haphazardly will not convince your instructor that you know the topic well even if you do! If you are uncertain of where to start, you may wish to paraphrase the instructor's question as a beginning sentence and add to it. For example, consider the question, "Discuss the three major factors that have caused the great change in management strategies in the last fifty years." The start to an essay answer might read as follows:

Management policies are subject to many factors, but the three biggest influences in the last half century have been the following: X, Y, and Z.

Your next sentence will focus on factor X, explaining it and defining it if necessary. Your essay might continue this way:

> Technology has changed the face of management, particularly the use of computers in the workplace. Heretofore many of the functions that needed to be monitored by people, such as inventory and quality control, are now handled routinely by computers.

Make sure you skip a line for ease of reading and to make corrections. If you might run out of time before recopying your essay, then write as neatly as possible.

- *Step 5—Edit your response.* Even the best of information is not compelling if it is poorly constructed. Instructors are aware that you are under time pressure on an exam, but they also do not wish to struggle to read your answer. Read through your remarks to make sure that you have stated things as well as you can. If you do not know what you've written, neither will your instructor. Gauge your time. Decide whether you will have enough time to copy over your essay before you begin your careful editing. If you have plenty of time, then you will not need to take as much care in making corrections. If time is a problem, make your corrections neatly by striking out the words or sections that you are changing and clearly indicating with the use of insert marks called carats (^) where the new material is to be inserted. Note: Essays are constructed for the sample exam and appear after the article (see page 302).

Multiple-Choice Questions

This type of question format is frequently used by instructors. It permits a vast amount of content to be covered and it can be scored in short time. Because the correct answer is given to you, it must be cleverly imbedded among other possible choices that may seem very close in meaning. The usual multiple-choice exam has either three or four choices for each question. Exams with five choices are harder to construct, and you will rarely see them unless you are taking a standardized exam. Here is a list of some multiple-choice strategies:

1. Plan your time.   You will want to use your time wisely as it relates to the point distribution on an exam. In the sample exam given, the multiple-choice questions made up a small percentage of the total exam points and therefore should be given an appropriately small amount of time. If the entire test is made up of multiple-choice questions, then most likely each will be worth the same amount. For the sake of math convenience, let us say that you are to answer 60 multiple-choice items in one hour. That means you have one minute for each question.

2. Keep moving in a first pass.   In most cases, all answers count equally on multiple-choice tests. If so, then the object is to get as many right as quickly as you can. You may as well skip the questions that cause you difficulty or are impossible. Make a first pass through to answer the questions that come quickly to you. You will discover that not all are of the same difficulty. Lingering is a mistake. You can always come back, but certainly get through the entire test first. There is an additional reason for taking this approach. Questions or possible answers later in the exam may tip you off on an earlier question that you didn't immediately recognize. The instructor may use just the right word or refer to an idea that brings some needed information to mind. If you didn't get to that point because you stalled over difficult questions, you will not be able to use these hints.

Caution: There is a drawback in using a first pass approach. You will be skipping around on your answer sheet. Take care that you are entering your answers next to the correct number.

3. Note your thinking.   In your first pass you may have been able to reduce the number of possibilities to two or three by eliminating certain choices. Put a small, light mark by these choices as a reference for your next pass. Doing this allows you to recapture the thinking that caused you to discard certain items without going through the whole process again.

4. The second pass fill-in.   In the second pass through you are trying to fill in some of the answers you skipped on the first round. If you have marked your answers as we suggested in step 3, then you can quickly locate the points at which you can resume your analysis. At this time, you may have additional information that is useful for moving through the rest of the exam. If you are forced to guess, do so wisely. Each time you eliminate a wrong answer from those remaining increases your chances of guessing correctly. Blindly guessing from four possibilities is only a 25 percent chance, and eliminating two choices raises your chances to 50 percent. Look for patterns in your answers. For example, you are uncertain of question 17. You are reasonably sure that the choice is either a (B) or a (C). Consider your work before and after 17. What if you have marked (B) as the correct choice three times in a row before 17, for 14, 15, and 16? Our bet is that the correct answer for 17 is (C) because it is unlikely that you will see 4 (Bs) in a row. Does this work all the time? Of course not, but it is a way to proceed when you are only guessing.

5. Additional tips.

- Make sure you read every answer choice carefully. Sometimes a "good" wrong answer is placed first to throw you off.

- Answers that include all-inclusive words like *"every* town," *"never* happens," or *"always* responds" are usually wrong because it means that there are no exceptions to the rule, and life doesn't work that way. You would only need to find one example that is an exception to prove the statement false.

- If you have eliminated the wrong choice and are only guessing, there is a way to proceed. Often the correct answer is the longest, most information-packed statement. This is so because the test maker must make this option a full, exact answer and needs enough words to qualify it.

- Be wary of negatives because they can throw you off. Consider the italicized words in the contexts given. ("All of the following characterize a multicultural institution *except* . . ." or "Which of the following characteristics is *not* found in a multicultural institution . . . ?" The wording in both cases means that three of the four choices fits with the stem. You are looking for the one option that does not fit with it.

- Many times, your first reaction is the right answer. Don't throw yourself off track by trying to read too much into the question. If you have to work hard at making up an elaborate reason for why your answer works, it is probably wrong.

Matching Questions

Matching becomes easier if there is an exact number correspondence between the choices in column A and those in column B. If there are twelve choices in A and only ten in B, then there is no exact fit. You will end up with two choices in A that are not linked to B. Unlike with multiple choice, where you usually have a 25 percent or better chance of a correct answer by guessing, it is possible to get everything wrong, even though it is not likely. We suggest the following plan:

1. Make a first pass in which you match the items of which you are sure.

2. In a second pass, guess wisely. If one A option seems to match two B options well but another A option seems somewhat good but still reasonable, choose on the basis of matching up as many items as possible.

Fill-in-the-Blank

The reason that fill-ins can pose a problem is that they are but one sentence lifted from a larger context. They are usually set up to omit a single word that the instructor is looking for. However, if you can provide a good answer that requires two or more words, then do this. Instructors prefer a short paraphrased reasonable answer to a single word answer that is wrong. Leave fill-ins until the end of the exam because the word or idea may be used in other questions or come to you as you are constructing an essay.

True/False Questions

The best guessing odds lie with true/false questions, since you have a 50 percent chance of being correct. Because the odds are high for guessing, you will see some cleverly disguised statements. The most common ploy is to have a statement that contains a true element but also a false one. A statement has to be fully true to be considered true. A false statement can be fully false or partially false. A few suggestions follow:

1. Guess on true/false questions if you are unsure. You have a 50 percent chance of being right even if you have no clue as to the correctness of your response.

2. As with multiple-choice questions, all-inclusive words like *every* and *never* are flags that the statement is probably false. Few statements are true without exception, and one example makes the "never" option wrong or false.

3. A lengthy, information-packed statement is likely to be false because every part of it must be true in order for it to be considered a true answer.

EXAM CHECKLIST

1. Plan for the exam.   Know in advance the kind of exam that you are facing and how long it will be. Listen carefully for directions. Must you bring pencils? Do you need a bluebook? You can save yourself much anxiety by being prepared about details in advance.

2. Prepare for the exam regularly.   You've heard it before and here it is again. There is no better strategy for an exam than daily preparation. Daily preparation will allow you to build your knowledge base over time so that the new information you have learned can be integrated with what you already know. You will be more confident going into an exam situation having prepared on a regular basis all term.

3. Cramming doesn't work.   Actually it works a little, but it has a big drawback. The human mind has almost an unlimited capacity for learning, but it takes time for the material to be learned and assimilated. If you have ever tried to cram by staying up all night to learn a term's work you know there is a point where you hit the wall. You simply cannot pack any more information in your head. And the results of cramming can be disastrous. A cramming session leaves you exhausted for the exam and for the next few days. If you are taking additional exams it compounds the problem.

4. Review early.   Reviewing is going over things that you have already learned. If you have waited until the night before to review and learn new material, you are asking for trouble. Ideas that are puzzling cannot be properly learned and remembered in one night. Furthermore, by doing this, you are taking away from your review time. In your review, you will want to go over your lecture notes, your marked copies of the texts, and any supplementary materials furnished by the instructor.

5. Stay with your routine.   Upsetting your usual personal routine regarding such things as sleeping, eating, and travel has the potential for exam stress. Do what you usually do with one exception: plan to arrive a few minutes early for school even if the test is not scheduled in your first class. Planning an early arrival will avoid the typical transit problems such as a late bus or no parking places.

6. *Preview the exam.* Before you begin writing, look over the whole exam to get a feel for it. Plan your time based on point distribution and what you know best and feel is your strength. Don't get distracted by extremely difficult questions, particularly if they have few points attached to them.

7. *Use the exam as a learning experience.* Consider the content of the exam as well as the strategy you may have used and could use in the future. An exam can be a good opportunity for a journal entry labeled, "reading exams." The following might act as prompts:

- What content was on the exam?

- What was the format of the questions?

- Was the content and format what you expected?

- How would you alter your study strategy for the next exam?

- Did you get the grade you deserve?

READING STRATEGY CHECK
APPLYING THE STRATEGIES

You will have been introduced to a number of reading strategies depending on the number of selections you have studied thus far. If you are studying the article "Managing Workforce Diversity in Organizations," you will see a number of the strategies reintroduced and applied as part of a larger composite strategy of reading textbooks. There are many strategies to remember. Here is another approach to using a number of strategies.

1. *Set the goal for reading a particular selection.* How you approach a particular reading will depend on your purpose. For example, if you are looking for material for a research paper, you will be doing a quick reading from a number of sources to determine if the material is appropriate. It would be inefficient to do a close reading, and you certainly would not want to take the time to mark up the article. On the other hand, if you are studying a textbook chapter for a midterm exam, then you will apply as many strategies as possible and read the material several times to fill in the gaps.

2. *Set your expectations for what to look for based on the material type.*

- *Narrative material.* Determine the basic story line. What is the author telling you through the story? Is there a message?

- *Argumentation.* Determine the author's argument. What does the author want you to consider? What is the author's purpose in having you examine your beliefs on a particular issue?

- *Exposition.* Determine the topic and major support. What information, ideas, and processes is the author describing?

3. *Ready yourself for the task.* If no gearing up exercise is part of the task, then provide your own. Bring to mind information that you already know that relates to the topic. Think about what you have seen, heard, and read.

4. *Preview the material.* Apply the previewing strategies to give yourself an overview of the reading material. Try to connect what you see will be coming with what you already know about the topic (the gearing up exercise). Frame at least two questions to provide a guide for your reading.

5. *Read the material through once quickly.* Do not stop for unknown words or ideas. Stay focused on what is making sense. You are reading through to get a feel for the whole selection. If you have a good idea of what to expect, you can better fill in meaning on your next careful reading.

6. *Apply the appropriate strategy depending on the material type.* If you are reading narrative, then look for the setting, characters, plot, and message.

7. *Apply other strategies as they seem appropriate.*

8. *After the careful reading, assess what you have learned and what seems unclear or confusing.* You should try to read the troublesome areas again before consulting other sources or taking questions to class.

Chapter 14 Managing Workforce Diversity in Organizations

OBJECTIVES

After studying this chapter, you should be able to:

- Discuss the nature of workforce diversity, including its meaning and reasons for its increase.
- Identify and describe the major dimensions of diversity in organizations.
- Describe diversity in different contexts.
- Discuss the primary impact of diversity on organizations.
- Describe individual and organizational strategies and approaches to coping with diversity.
- Discuss the six characteristics of the fully multicultural organization.

OUTLINE

The Nature of Workforce Diversity
    The Meaning of Diversity
    Reasons for Increasing Diversity

Dimensions of Diversity
    Age Distributions
    Gender
    Ethnicity
    Other Dimensions of Diversity

Diversity in Different Contexts
    Diversity in Other Countries
    Diversity as a Force for Social Change

The Impact of Diversity on Organizations
    Diversity as Competitive Advantage
    Diversity as a Source of Conflict

Managing Diversity in Organizations
    Individual Strategies for Dealing
        with Diversity
    Organizational Approaches to
       Managing Diversity

Toward the Multicultural Organization

OPENING INCIDENT

MORE AND MORE organizations are recognizing the importance of workforce diversity. Two of today's most successful firms in the areas of workforce diversity are Avon Products and Xerox Corp. Avon, headquartered in New York, is the largest cosmetics firm in the United States. For many years the firm sold its fragrances and cosmetics door-to-door through a cadre of thousands of saleswomen. The firm's slogan, "Avon calling," was widely recognized throughout the United States. Avon still earns almost 95 percent of its revenues from its direct sales operations.

In 1987 Avon entered the retail cosmetics business by acquiring the line of Giorgio fragrances. Giorgio's Red was the top-selling fragrance in the United States in 1990. Avon is also concentrating more and more on foreign markets; it recently entered markets in Eastern Europe and China.

For years, Avon has had an effective affirmative action program that allowed the firm to identify and hire qualified minority employees. But recently, the firm learned that despite its hiring many minority employees, they were not advancing quickly in the organization; many of them were leaving for better opportunities elsewhere.

To help address this problem, Avon created networks of black, Hispanic, and Asian employees. Each network meets regularly, publishes a newsletter for the employees it represents, and presents their interests to top management. So far, Avon's approach is paying off. Its retention rate has improved, and several minority group members have been promoted. But perhaps most important, white male managers in the firm say that they are developing a better understanding of what others value and how to work better with minority group members for the benefit of everyone.

Xerox has pursued a similar strategy. It calls its networks caucuses and finds that they help promote better communication and understanding throughout the organization. Unlike Avon, however, Xerox has been forced to balance its diversity programs against a workforce reduction plan that eliminated ten thousand jobs between 1994 and 1996. The challenge was to balance the need to reduce the number of employees while maintaining diversity among those employees that remain.

> *"Diversity is no fad for us. We remain aggressively affirmative on diversity in tough times as well as good times."*

To carry out this balancing act, Xerox fully involved all of its minority caucuses in its workforce reduction plan. Each caucus was informed of what was happening and what was planned, and each was asked to make suggestions and offer advice regarding the fairest way to eliminate employees.[1]

---

1   Like most other organizations in the world today, Avon and Xerox have seen tremendous changes in the composition of their workforces during the last several decades. Once dominated by white male managers, each firm now employs people at a variety of organizational levels from a diverse set of backgrounds. And like other organizations today, Avon and Xerox have encountered more than a few challenges along the way as they have sought to address the variety of issues, opportunities, and problems that their increasingly diverse workforces have created.

2   This chapter is about workforce diversity in organizations. We begin by exploring the meaning of diversity and reasons for its increase. We then identify and discuss several common dimensions of diversity and discuss diversity in different contexts. The impact of diversity on the organization is then explored. We next address individual strategies and organizational approaches for managing diversity. Finally, we characterize and describe the fully multicultural organization.

The Nature of Workforce Diversity

3   Workforce diversity has become a very important issue in many organizations, both in the United States and abroad. A logical starting

---

Source of Quotation: Paul Allaire, CEO of Xerox, quoted in *Fortune*, August 8, 1994, p. 84.

point, then, is to establish the meaning of diversity and then examine why such diversity is increasing today.

The Meaning of Diversity

4 **Diversity** exists in a group or organization when its members differ from one another along one or more important dimensions.[2] Thus diversity is not an absolute phenomenon wherein a group or organization is or is not diverse. Instead, diversity can be conceptualized as a continuum. If everyone in the group or organization is exactly like everyone else, there is no diversity whatsoever. If everyone is different along every imaginable dimension, total diversity exists. In reality, of course, these extremes are more hypothetical than real. Most settings are characterized by a level of diversity somewhere between these extremes. Therefore, diversity should be thought of in terms of degree or level of diversity along relevant dimensions.

diverse

hypothetical

- **diversity**
Exists in a group or organization when its members differ from one another along one or more important dimensions such as age, gender, or ethnicity

5   These dimensions of diversity might include gender, age, ethnic origin, or any of several others. A group comprising five middle-aged white male U.S. executives has relatively little diversity. If one member is replaced by a young white female executive, the group becomes a bit more diverse. If another member is replaced by an older African American executive, diversity increases a bit more. And when a third member is replaced by a Japanese executive, the group becomes even more diverse.

Reasons for Increasing Diversity

6 As we note earlier, organizations today are becoming increasingly diverse along many different dimensions. Although several different factors account for these trends and changes, four of the more important ones are illustrated in Figure 14.1.

Figure 14.1 *Reasons for Increasing Diversity*

Cultural diversity is increasing in most organizations today for four basic reasons. These reasons promise to make diversity even greater in the future.

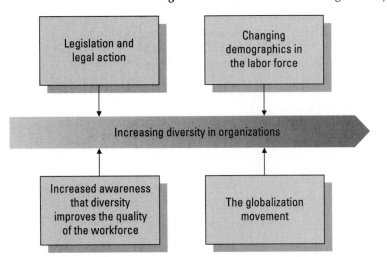

7   One factor contributing to increased diversity is changing demo-   *demographics*
graphics in the labor force. As more women and minorities enter the
labor force, for example, the available pool of talent from which
organizations hire employees is changing in both size and composition. If talent within each segment of the labor pool is evenly distributed (for example, if the number of very talented men in the workforce
as a percentage of all men in the workforce is the same as the number
of very talented women in the labor force as a percentage of all women
in the workforce), it follows logically that, over time, proportionately more women and proportionately fewer men will be hired by an
organization.[3]

8   A related factor contributing to diversity is the increased awareness by organizations that they can improve the overall quality of their
workforce by hiring and promoting the most talented people available.
By casting a broader net in recruiting and looking beyond traditional
sources for new employees, organizations are finding more broadly
qualified and better qualified employees from many different segments
of society. Thus these organizations are finding that diversity can be a
source of competitive advantage.[4]

9   Another reason for the increase in diversity is that legislation and
legal actions have forced organizations to hire more broadly. In earlier
times, organizations in the United States were essentially free to discriminate against women, blacks, and other minorities. Thus most organizations were dominated by white males. But over the last thirty
years or so, various laws have outlawed discrimination against these
and other groups. As we detail in Chapter 13, organizations must hire
and promote people today solely on the basis of their qualifications.

10   A final factor contributing to increased diversity in organizations
is the globalization movement. Organizations that have opened offices
and related facilities in other countries have had to learn to deal with
different customs, social norms, and mores. Strategic alliances and foreign ownership also contribute, as managers today are more likely to
have job assignments in other countries and/or to work with foreign
managers within their own countries. As employees and managers
move from assignment to assignment across national boundaries, organizations and their subsidiaries within each country thus become more
diverse.

Dimensions of Diversity

11   As we indicate earlier, many different dimensions of diversity can characterize an organization. In this section we discuss age, gender, ethnicity, and other dimensions of diversity.

Age Distributions

12   One important dimension of diversity in any organization is the age
distribution of its workers. The average age of the U.S. workforce is

Figure 14.2 *Age Distribution Trends in the U.S. Workforce*

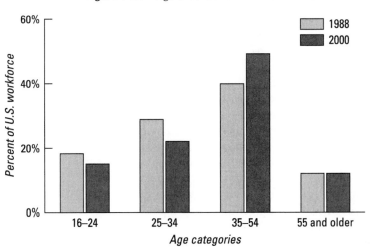

The U.S. workforce is gradually growing older. For example, by the year 2000 almost one-half of the U.S. workforce will be between the ages of 35 and 54. These younger workers will have different experience and values and will want different things from their work than their older colleagues.

Source: Occupational Outlook Handbook (U.S. Bureau of Labor Statistics: Washington D.C., 1990–1991), pp. 8–12.

gradually increasing and will continue to do so for the next several years. Figure 14.2 presents age distributions for U.S. workers in 1988 and projected age distributions for the year 2000.

13   Several factors are contributing to this pattern. For one, the baby-boom generation (a term used to describe the unusually large number of people who were born in the twenty-year period after World War II) continues to age. Declining birth rates among the post–baby-boom generations simultaneously account for smaller percentages of new entrants into the labor force. Another factor that contributes to the aging workforce is improved health and medical care. As a result of these improvements, people are able to remain productive and active for longer periods of time. Combined with higher legal limits for mandatory retirement, more and more people are working beyond the age at which they might have retired just a few years ago.[5]

simultaneously

mandatory

14   How does this trend affect organizations? Older workers tend to have more experience, to be more stable, and to make greater contributions to productivity than younger workers. On the other hand, despite the improvements in health and medical care, older workers are nevertheless likely to require higher levels of insurance coverage and medical benefits. And the declining labor pool of younger workers will continue to pose problems for organizations as they find fewer potential new entrants into the labor force.[6]

Gender

15   As more and more women have entered the workforce, organizations have subsequently experienced changes in the relative proportions of male and female employees. In the United States, for example, the percentage of male employees will shrink from 55 percent in 1988 to 53

subsequently

279

percent by the year 200. Simultaneously, the percentage of female employees will increase from 45 percent in 1988 to 47 percent by the year
2000.[7]

16   These trends aside, a major gender-related problem that many organizations face today is the so-called glass ceiling. The **glass ceiling**
describes a barrier that keeps women from advancing to top management positions in many organizations.[8] This ceiling is a real barrier
that is difficult to break, but it is also so subtle as to be hard to see. Indeed, whereas women comprise almost 45 percent of all managers,
there are only two female CEOs among the one thousand largest businesses in the United States. Similarly, the average pay of women in
organizations is lower than that of men. Although the pay gap is gradually shrinking, inequalities are present nonetheless.[9]

17   Why does the glass ceiling exist? One reason is that some male
managers are still reluctant to promote female managers.[10] As a result,
many talented women choose to leave their jobs in large organizations
and start their own businesses. Recall from Chapter 9, for example, that
most new U.S. businesses today are started by women. Another factor
is that some women choose to suspend or slow their career progression
to have children.[11]

- **glass ceiling**
A barrier that exists in some
organizations that keeps
women from advancing to
top management positions

Ethnicity

18 A third major dimension of cultural diversity in organizations is ethnicity. **Ethnicity** refers to the ethnic composition of a group or organization. Within the United States, most organizations reflect varying
degrees of ethnicity comprising whites, African Americans, Hispanics,
and Asians. Figure 14.3 shows the ethnic composition of the U.S.
workforce in 1988 and as projected for the year 2000 in terms of these
ethnic groups.[12]

19   The biggest projected changes involve whites and Hispanics. In
particular, the percentage of whites in the workforce is expected to
drop from 79 percent to 74 percent. At the same time, the percentage
of Hispanics is expected to climb from 7 percent to 10 percent. The
percentage of African Americans and Asians and others are expected to
climb only about 1 percent each.

20   As with women, members of the African American, Hispanic, and
Asian groups are generally underrepresented in the executive ranks of
most organizations today. And their pay is similarly lower than might
be expected. But also as is the case for women, the differences are gradually disappearing as organizations fully embrace equal employment
opportunity and recognize the higher overall level of talent available to
them.[13]

- **ethnicity**
The ethnic composition of a
group or organization

Other Dimensions of Diversity

21 In addition to age, gender, and ethnicity, organizations are also con-
fronting other dimensions of diversity. Country of national origin is a

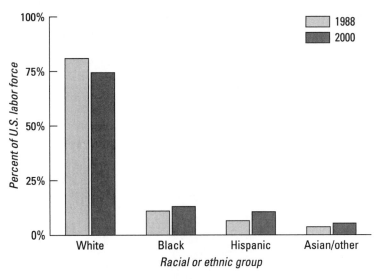

Source: Occupational Outlook Handbook (U.S. Bureau of Labor Statistics: Washington D.C., 1990–1991), pp. 8–12.

Figure 14.3 *Racial and Ethnicity Trends in the U.S. Labor Force*
The U.S. workforce is becoming ever more diverse along most dimensions of race and ethnicity. The most important trend suggests that whites will comprise a significantly smaller percentage of the workforce by the year 2000 than was the case as recently as 1988. Most growth is in the Hispanic sector. Modest growth in the percentage of black and Asian workers is also expected. Managers will have to become ever more sensitive to the needs, expectations, and aspirations of a multicultural workforce.

dimension of diversity that can be especially important for global organizations. This dimension can be particularly important when different languages are involved. Handicapped and physically challenged employees are increasingly important in many organizations.[14] Single parents, dual career couples, gays and lesbians, people with special dietary preferences (e.g., vegetarians), and people with different political ideologies and viewpoints also represent major dimensions of diversity in today's organizations.[15]

The Impact of Diversity on Organizations

22 There is no question that organizations are becoming ever more diverse. But what is the impact of this diversity on organizations? As we see, diversity provides both opportunities and challenges for organizations. Diversity also plays a number of important roles in organizations today.

Diversity as Competitive Advantage

23 Many organizations are also finding that diversity can be a source of competitive advantage in the marketplace. In general, six arguments

281

Figure 14.4 *How Diversity Promotes Competitive Advantage*

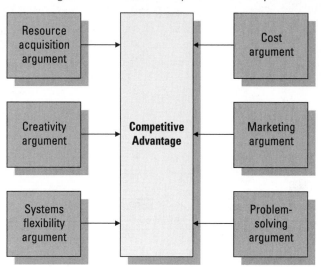

Many organizations today are finding that diversity can be a source of competitive advantage. A variety of arguments have been developed to support this viewpoint. For example, a black sales representative for Revlon helped that firm improve its packaging and promotion for its line of darker skin tone cosmetics.

have been proposed for how diversity contributes to competitiveness.[16] These are illustrated in Figure 14.4.

24   The *cost argument* suggests that organizations that learn to cope with diversity generally have higher levels of productivity and lower levels of turnover and absenteeism. Those organizations that do a poor job of managing diversity, on the other hand, suffer from problems of lower productivity and higher levels of turnover and absenteeism. Because each of this factors has a direct impact on costs, the former organization remains more competitive than the latter. Ortho Pharmaceutical Corporation estimates that it has saved $500,000 by lowering turnover among women and ethnic minorities.[17]

25   The *resource acquisition argument* for diversity suggests that organizations who manage diversity effectively become known among women and minorities as good places to work. These organizations are thus better able to attract qualified employees from among these groups. Given the increased importance of these groups in the overall labor force, organizations that can attract talented employees from all segments of society are likely to be more competitive.

26   The *marketing argument* suggests that organizations with diverse workforces are better able to understand different market segments than are less diverse organizations. For example, a cosmetics firm like Avon that wants to sell its products to women and blacks can better understand how to create such products and effectively market them if women and black managers are available to provide inputs into product development, design, packaging, advertising, and so forth.[18]

27   The *creativity argument* for diversity suggests that organizations with diverse workforces are generally more creative and innovative than are less diverse organizations. If an organization is dominated by

innovative

282

one population segment, it follows that its members generally adhere to norms and ways of thinking that reflect that segment. Moreover, they have little insight or stimulus for new ideas that might be derived from different perspectives. The diverse organization, in contrast, is characterized by multiple perspectives and ways of thinking and is therefore more likely to generate new ideas and ways of doing things.

perspectives

28   Related to the creativity argument is the *problem-solving argument.* Diversity carries with it an increased pool of information. In virtually any organization, there is some information that everyone has and other information that is unique to each individual. In an organization with little diversity, the larger pool of information is common and the smaller pool is unique. But in a more diverse organization, the unique information is larger. Thus, because more information can be brought to bear on a problem, there is a higher probability that better solutions can be identified.[19]

29   Finally, the *systems flexibility argument* for diversity suggests that organizations must become more flexible as a way of managing a diverse workforce. As a direct consequence, the overall organizational system also becomes more flexible. As we discuss in Chapter 3 and 11, organizational flexibility enables the organization to better respond to changes in its environment. Thus, by effectively managing diversity within its workforce, an organization simultaneously becomes better equipped to address its environment.[20]

Diversity as a Source of Conflict

30   Unfortunately, diversity in an organization can also become a major source of conflict. This conflict can arise for a variety of reasons. One potential avenue for conflict is when an individual thinks that someone has been hired, promoted, or fired because of her or his diversity status.[21] For example, suppose that a male executive loses a promotion to a female executive. If he believes that she was promoted because the organization simply wanted to have more female managers rather than because she was the better candidate for the job, he will likely feel resentful toward both her and the organization itself.

31   Another source of conflict stemming from diversity is through misunderstood, misinterpreted, or inappropriate interactions between people of different groups. For example, suppose that a male executive tells a sexually explicit joke to a new female executive. He may intentionally be trying to embarrass her, he may be clumsily trying to show her that he treats everyone the same, or he may think he is making her feel like part of the team. Regardless of his intent, however, if she finds the joke offensive she will justifiably feel anger and hostility. These feelings may be directed at only the offending individual or more generally toward the entire organization if she believes that its culture facilitates such behaviors. And of course, sexual harassment is both unethical and illegal.

facilitates

32   Conflict can also arise as a result of other elements of diversity. For example, when a U.S. manager publicly praises the work of a Japanese employee for his outstanding work, the action stems from the dominant cultural belief in the United States that such recognition is important and rewarding. But because the Japanese culture places a much higher premium on group loyalty and identity than on individual accomplishment, the employee will likely feel ashamed and embarrassed. Thus a well-intended action may backfire and result in unhappiness.

33   Conflict may also arise as a result of fear, distrust, or individual prejudice. Members of the dominant group in an organization may worry that newcomers from other groups pose a personal threat to their own position in the organization. For example, when U.S. firms have been taken over by Japanese firms, U.S. managers have sometimes been resentful or hostile to Japanese managers assigned to work with them. People may also be unwilling to accept people who are different from themselves. And personal bias and prejudices are still very real among some people today and can lead to potentially harmful conflict.[22]

Managing Diversity in Organizations

34   Because of the tremendous potential that diversity holds for competitive advantage, as well as the possible consequences of diversity-related conflict, much attention has been focused in recent years on how individuals and organizations can better manage diversity.[23] In the sections that follow we first discuss individual strategies for dealing with diversity and then summarize organizational approaches to managing diversity.

Individual Strategies for Dealing with Diversity

35   One important element of managing diversity in an organization consists of things that individuals themselves can do. The four basic attitudes that individuals can strive for are understanding, empathy, tolerance, and willingness to communicate.[24]

empathy

36   *Understanding*   The first of these is understanding the nature and meaning of diversity. Some managers have taken the basic concepts of equal employment opportunity to an unnecessary extreme. They know that, by law, they cannot discriminate against people on the basis of sex, race, and so forth. Thus in following this mandate they come to believe that they must treat everyone the same.

mandate

37   But this belief can cause problems when translated into workplace behaviors among people after they have been hired because people are not the same. Although people need to be treated fairly and equitably, managers must understand that differences among people do, in fact, exist. Thus any effort to treat everyone the same, without regard to their fundamental human differences, will only lead to problems. Man-

agers *must* understand that cultural factors cause people to behave in different ways and that these differences should be accepted.

38   *Empathy*   Related to understanding is empathy. People in an organization should try to understand the perspective of others. For example, suppose a woman joins a group that has traditionally comprised white men. Each man may be a little self-conscious as how to act toward the new member and may be interested in making her feel comfortable and welcome. But they may be able to do this even more effectively by empathizing with how she may feel. For example, she may feel disappointed or elated about her new assignment, she may be confident or nervous about her position in the group, and she may be experienced or inexperienced in working with male colleagues. By learning more about her feelings the group members can further facilitate their ability to work together effectively.

39   *Tolerance*   A third related individual approach to dealing with diversity is tolerance. Even though managers learn to understand diversity, and even though they may try to empathize with others, the fact remains that they may still not accept or enjoy some aspect of others' behavior. For example, one organization recently reported that it was experiencing considerable conflict among its U.S. and Israeli employees. The Israeli employees always seemed to want to argue about every issue that arose. The U.S. managers preferred to conduct business more harmoniously and became uncomfortable with the conflict. Finally, after considerable discussion it was learned that many Israeli employees simply enjoy arguing and just see it as part of getting work done. The firm's U.S. employees still do not enjoy the arguing, but they are more willing to tolerate it as a fundamental cultural difference between themselves and their colleagues from Israel.[25]

40   *Willingness to Communicate*   A final individual approach to dealing with diversity is communication. Problems often get magnified over diversity issues because other people are afraid or otherwise unwilling to openly discuss issues that relate to diversity. For example, suppose that a young employee has a habit of making jokes about the age of an elderly colleague. Perhaps the young colleague means no harm and is just engaging in what she sees as good-natured kidding. But the older employee may find the jokes offensive. If the two do not communicate, the jokes will continue and the resentment will grow. Eventually, what started as a minor problem may erupt into a much bigger one.

41   For communication to work, it must be two way. If a person wonders if a certain behavior on her or his part is offensive to someone else, the curious individual should just ask. Similarly, if someone is offended by the behavior of another person, he or she should explain to the offending individual how the behavior is perceived and request that it be stopped. As long as such exchanges are friendly, low key, and

nonthreatening, they will generally have a positive outcome. Of course, if the same message is presented in an overly combative manner or if a person continues to engage in offensive behavior after having been asked to stop, problems will only escalate. At this point, third parties within the organization may have to intervene. And in fact, most organizations today have one or more systems in place to address questions and problems that arise as a result of diversity. We now turn our attention to various ways that organizations can indeed better manage diversity.

Organizational Approaches to Managing Diversity

42   Whereas individuals are important in managing diversity, the organization itself must play a fundamental role.[26] Figure 14.5 summarizes several of the more common business initiatives regarding diversity. Through its various policies and practices, people in the organization come to understand what behaviors are and are not appropriate. Diversity training is an even more direct method for managing diversity. The organization's culture is the ultimate context from which diversity must be addressed. *The Environment of Management* box discusses how IBM is managing its diversity.

Figure 14.5   *Corporate Diversity Initiatives*

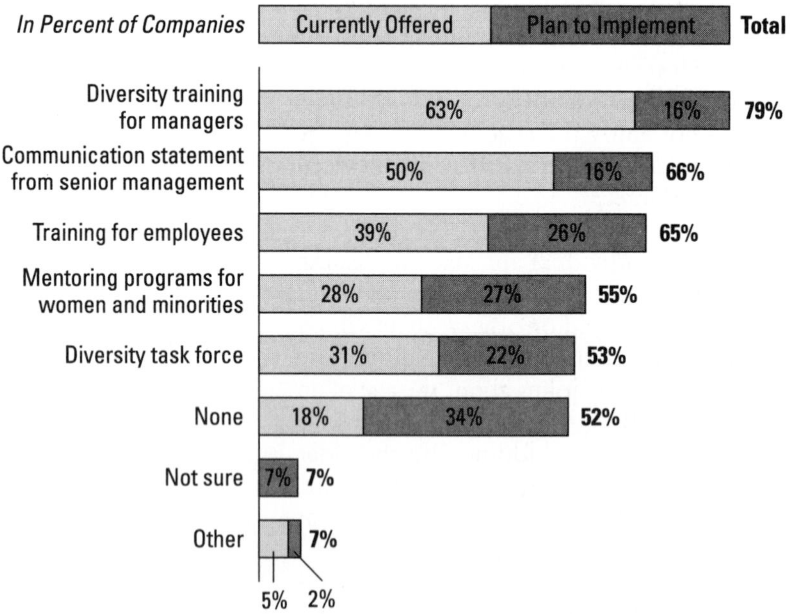

As the figure shows, diversity training for managers and communication statements from senior management are currently the most popular initiatives. Several other initiatives are also expected to become more widespread in the future.

Note: Percentages do not add up to 100 because many organizations undertake multiple initiatives at the same time.

Source: "Challenges of Retaining a Diverse Workforce," *Working Together, Boston Globe,* March 7, 1994, p.15.

Managing Diversity at IBM

 To derive the most benefit from its diversity management program, IBM expanded the meaning of *diversity* to go beyond race and gender. In doing so, it linked diversity more closely to its business objectives. While it could have done so without a special position to deal with it, IBM felt the need for such a position, a diversity director. Whoever held that job would need extensive knowledge of IBM's organizational culture and structure as well as its management style and philosophy. The diversity director then, would need to use that knowledge to get people to adopt the new perspective and manage diversity to the benefit of the organization.

No hard research evidence exists that diverse workforces perform better, but the diversity of both its customers and its labor market kept IBM pushing its effort. IBM says that its marketplace consists of people from all races, religions, and sexual orientations; therefore, its diversity effort must reflect that makeup. In San Jose, for instance, the diversity of the workforce is suggested by the fact that thirty-three languages are spoken by the populace. IBM's Systems Storage Division in San Jose makes special efforts to recognize that diversity. There's a diversity day during which employees dress in ethnic costumes, a monthly bulletin identifying diversity events in the city, and a series of videos featuring different cultures.

IBM's diversity training is designed to mirror company objectives. It translates its training goals into curricula that reflect the performance requirements established for every major job category in the company. That way IBM can accomplish its diversity goals while at the same time accomplishing its overall organizational objectives.

In support of its diversity effort, IBM spends a great deal of money on various human resource benefits and work-life programs. Work-life programs include a work-at-home program in which IBM furnishes the computer; flextime work schedules; a child care referral service; parenting, child-care, and elder care seminars; leaves of absence with full benefits; and funds for employees' children who have emotional or physical problems. These programs are designed to help employees meet family and workplace demands and to help managers relate to work and family problems. IBM also strongly supports the communities in which its facilities are located and supports employees who volunteer their time outside the company.

References: "Taking Adversity Out of Diversity," *Business Week,* January 31, 1994, pp. 54–55; Faye Rice, "How to Make Diversity Pay," *Fortune,* August 8, 1994, pp. 78–86; Barbara Love, "Is There a Diversity Director in Your Future?" *Folio: The Magazine for Magazine Management,* November 15, 1993, p. 10; Julie A. Cohen, "Managing Tomorrow's Workforce Today," *Management Review,* January 1991, p. 17–21; and Julie Cohen Mason, "IBM at the Crossroads," *Management Review,* September 1991, pp. 10–14.

43   *Organizational Policies*   The starting point in managing diversity is the policies that an organization adopts that directly or indirectly affect how people are treated. Obviously, for instance, the extent to which an organization embraces the premise of equal employment opportunity will to a large extent determine the potential diversity within an organization. But the organization that follows the law to the letter and practices only passive discrimination differs from the organization that actively seeks a diverse and varied workforce.

44   Another aspect of organizational policies that affects diversity is how the organization addresses and responds to problems that arise from diversity. For example, consider the example of a manager charged with sexual harassment. If the organization's policies put an excessive burden of proof on the individual being harassed and invoke only minor sanctions against the guilty party, it is sending a clear signal as to the importance of such matters. But the organization that has a balanced set of policies for addressing questions like sexual harassment sends its employees a message that diversity and individual rights and privileges are important.

45   Indeed, perhaps the major policy through which an organization can reflect its stance on diversity is its mission statement. If the organization's mission statement articulates a clear and direct commitment to diversity, it follows that everyone who comes into contact with that mission statement will grow to understand and accept the importance of diversity, at least to that particular organization.

46   *Organizational Practices*   Organizations can also help manage diversity through a variety of ongoing practices and procedures. Avon's creation of networks for various groups represents one example of an organizational practice that fosters diversity. In general, the idea is that because diversity is characterized by differences among people, organizations can more effectively manage that diversity by following practices and procedures that are based on flexibility rather than rigidity.

47   Benefits packages, for example, can be structured to better accommodate individual situations. An employee who is part of a dual-career couple and who has no children may require relatively little insurance (perhaps because his spouse's employer provides more complete coverage) and would like to be able to schedule vacations to coincide with those of his spouse. An employee who is a single parent may need a wide variety of insurance coverage and prefer to schedule his vacation time to coincide with school holidays.

48   Flexible working hours are also a useful organizational practice to accommodate diversity. Differences in family arrangements, religious holidays, cultural events, and so forth may each dictate that employees have some degree of flexibility in when they work. For example, a single parent may need to leave the office every day at 4:30 to pick up the children from their day care center. An organization that truly values diversity will make every reasonable attempt to accommodate such a need.

49   Organizations can also facilitate diversity by making sure that its important committees and executive teams are diverse. Even if diversity exists within the broader organizational context, an organization that does not reflect diversity in groups like committees and teams implies that diversity is not a fully ingrained element of its culture. In contrast, if all major groups and related work assignments reflect diversity, the message is a quite different one.

50   *Diversity Training*   Many organizations are finding that diversity training is an effective means for managing diversity and minimizing its associated conflict. More specifically, **diversity training** is training that is specifically designed to better enable members of an organization to function in a diverse workplace. This training can take a variety of forms. For example, many organizations find it useful to help people learn more about their similarities to and differences from others. Men and women can be taught to work together more effectively and can gain insights into how their own behaviors affect and are interpreted by others. In one organization, a diversity training program helped male managers gain insights into how various remarks they made to one another could be interpreted by others as being sexist. In the same organization, female managers learned how to point out their discomfort with those remarks without appearing overly hostile.[27]

- **diversity training** Training that is specifically designed to better enable members of an organization to function in a diverse workplace

51   Similarly, white and black managers may need training to better understand each other. Managers at Mobil Corporation noticed that four black colleagues never seemed to eat lunch together. After a diversity training program, they came to realize that the black managers felt that if they ate together, their white colleagues would be overly curious about what they might be talking about. Thus they avoided close associations with one another because they feared calling attention to themselves.[28]

52   Some organizations even go so far as to provide language training for their employees as a vehicle for managing diversity. Motorola, for example, provides English language training for its foreign employees on assignment in the United States. At Pace Foods in San Antonio, with a total payroll of 350 employees, staff meetings and employee handbooks are translated into Spanish for the benefit of the company's 100 Hispanic employees.[29]

53   *Organizational Culture*   The ultimate test of an organization's commitment to managing diversity is its culture.[30] Regardless of what managers say or put in writing, unless there is a basic and fundamental belief that diversity is valued, it cannot ever become truly an integral part of an organization. An organization that really wants to promote diversity must shape its culture so that it clearly underscores top management commitment to and support of diversity in all of its forms throughout every part of the organization. With top management support, however, and reinforced with a clear and consistent set of organizational policies and practices, diversity can become a basic and fundamental part of an organization.

Toward the Multicultural Organization

54   Many organizations today are grappling with cultural diversity. We note back in Chapter 5 that whereas many organizations are becoming increasingly global, no truly global organization exists. In similar fashion, although organizations are becoming ever more diverse, few are

truly multicultural. The **multicultural organization** has achieved high levels of diversity, is able to fully capitalize on the advantages of diversity, and has few diversity-related problems.[31] One recent article described the six basic characteristics of such an organization.[32] These characteristics are illustrated in Figure 14.6.

55   First, the multicultural organization is characterized by *pluralism.* This means that every group represented in an organization works to better understand every other group. Thus black employees try to understand white employees, and white employees try just as hard to understand their black colleagues. In addition, every group represented within an organization has the potential to influence the organization's culture and its fundamental norms.

56   Second, the multicultural organization achieves *full structural integration.* Full structural integration suggests that the diversity within an organization is a complete and accurate reflection of the organization's external labor market. If around half of the labor market is female, then about half of the organization's employees are female. Moreover, this same proportion is reflected at all levels of the organization. There are no glass ceilings or other subtle forms of discrimination.

• **multicultural organization**
An organization that has achieved high levels of diversity, is able to fully capitalize on the advantages of diversity, and has few diversity-related problems

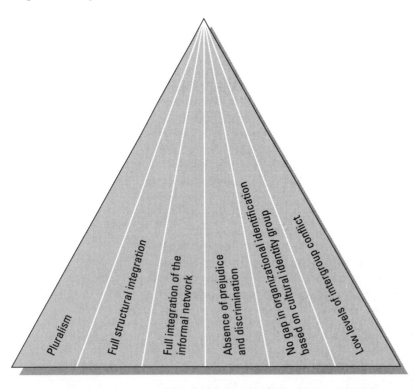

Figure 14.6
The Multicultural Organization
Few, if any, organizations have become truly multicultural. At the same time, more and more organizations are moving in this direction. When an organization becomes multicultural, it reflects the six basic characteristics shown here.

Source: Reprinted with permission of Academy of Management, PO Box 3020, Briar Cliff Manor, NY 10510-8020. "The Multicultural Organization," Taylor H. Cox, *Academy of Management Executive,* May 1991. Reproduced with permission of the publisher via Copyright Clearance Center, Inc.

57   Third, the multicultural organization achieves *full integration of the informal network.* This characteristic suggests that there are no barriers to entry and participation in any organizational activity. For example, people enter and exit lunch groups, social networks, communication grapevines, and other informal aspects of organizational activity without regard to age, gender, ethnicity, or other dimension of diversity.

58   Fourth, the multicultural organization is characterized by an *absence of prejudice and discrimination.* No traces of bias exist, and prejudice is eliminated. Discrimination is not practiced in any shape, form, or fashion. And discrimination is nonexistent not because it is illegal but because of the lack of prejudice and bias. People are valued, accepted, and rewarded purely on the basis of their skills and what they contribute to the organization.

59   Fifth, in the multicultural organization there is no *gap in organizational identification based on cultural identity group.* In many organizations today people tend to make presumptions about organizational roles based on group identity. For example, many people walking into an office and seeing a man and woman conversing tend to assume that the woman is the secretary and the man is the manager. No such tendencies exist in the multicultural organization. People recognize that men and women are equally likely to be managers and secretaries.

60   Finally, there are *low levels of intergroup conflict* in the multicultural organization. We note earlier that conflict is a likely outcome of increased diversity. The multicultural organization has evolved beyond this point to a state of virtually no conflict among people who differ. People within the organization fully understand, empathize with, have tolerance for, and openly communicate with everyone else. Values, premises, motives, attitudes, and perceptions are so well understood by everyone that any conflict that does arise is over meaningful and work-related issues as opposed to differences in age, gender, ethnicity, or other dimensions of diversity.

SUMMARY OF KEY POINTS

61   Diversity exists in a group or organization when its members differ from one another along one or more important dimensions. Diversity is increasing in organizations today because of changing demographics, the desire by organizations to improve their workforce, legal pressures, and increased globalization.

62   There are several important dimensions of diversity. Three of the more important ones are age, gender, and ethnicity. The overall age of the workforce is increasing. More women are also entering the workplace, although there is still a glass ceiling in many settings. In the United States, more Hispanics are also entering the workplace as the percentage of whites gradually declines.

CASE 14.1

Hoechst

 Hoechst (pronounced "herxt") AG is one of three German chemical and pharmaceutical world leaders (the other two are Bayer and BASF). Founded in the city of Hoechst in 1863 to make dyes, the company moved into pharmaceuticals in the late 1800s when its researchers developed a diphtheria vaccine. In 1923 they isolated insulin. Hoechst moved into fibers, plastics, and petrochemicals in the 1950s. It also began to establish extensive foreign subsidiaries, acquiring the Celanese corporation in the late 1980s. Hoechst Celanese Corporation, then, became Hoechst's U.S. subsidiary.

Ernest H. Drew, CEO of Hoechst Celanese, became interested in workforce diversity in 1990. He was taking part in a conference with top executives and some lower-level personnel; participants included women and minorities. During the conference, the large group broke up into small problem-solving groups. Drew noted that the best solutions came from the more diverse groups. Realizing that diversity could be a strength, he set out to attract, retain, and promote women and ethnic minorities in Hoechst Celanese's ranks.

Productivity has gone up at Hoechst Celanese plants where diversity has become the norm. For example, the polyester textile filament division in Shelby, North Carolina, had been losing money for eighteen years. In the late 1980s an African American, who was director of polyester filament, put together a diverse group of women, white men, and people of color to work on the problem. They came up with a strategy to change the focus of operations from commodity production to niche markets. They advocated cutting costs and improving quality to ensure that those markets,

such as automotive upholstery, would be satisfied with the products. In 1992 the filament division earned a profit and has maintained it since then.

Hoechst Celanese provides ample evidence that top management commitment is vital to the success of any diversity program. The company had made some efforts but had not been successful until Drew, as the CEO, demonstrated commitment at the top. He made workforce diversity one of four performance criteria on which managers' salaries and bonuses are based. In addition he set a specific, challenging objective: at least 34 percent representation of women and minorities at all levels of the company by the year 2001. These moves made diversity a business objective for everyone, not just a legal requirement to satisfy legislation.

Hoechst Celanese has tried to make sure that there is no backlash among its white male employees and that everyone will have equal opportunities to succeed in the organization. Part of that assurance comes from scrutinizing compensation and career pathing to be certain that all groups, including white men, are treated fairly.

To further his efforts, Drew required that the top twenty-six officers of the company join two organizations in which they were minorities. This was designed to help them understand and better appreciate the feelings of minorities. A side benefit, of course, has been to widen the visibility of the company within its community and to groups with which it had previously had limited exposure. Because many of the organizations involved are minority organizations, this activity also helps Hoechst Celanese with another part of its diversity program—increasing its supply of diverse workers.

CASE 14.1 (continued)

Discussion Questions

1. What definition of diversity does Hoechst seem to employ? Why?

2. What general guidance does Hoechst Celanese's experience with diversity suggest to other companies that wish to develop a more diverse workforce?

3. Is it likely that the experiences of the U.S. subsidiary, Hoechst Celanese, will be successfully transferred to other parts of the Hoechst organization? Why or why not?

References: Andrew Wood, "Dormann Kicks Off First Round of Changes at Hoechst," *Chemical Week,* May 11, 1994, p. 18; Faye Rice, "How to Make Diversity Pay," *Fortune,* August 8, 1994, pp. 78–86; and Elisabeth Kirschner, "Hoechst Celanese's Engelman: A Proactive Visionary," *Chemical Week,* September 9, 1992, pp. 30–31.

63   Diversity can impact an organization in a number of different ways. For example, it can be a source of competitive advantage (i.e., cost, resource acquisition, marketing, creativity, problem solving, and systems flexibility arguments). On the other hand, diversity can also be a source of conflict in an organization.

64   Managing diversity in organizations can be done by both individuals and the organization itself. Individual approaches to dealing with diversity include understanding, empathy, tolerance, and willingness to communicate. Major organizational approaches are through policies, practices, diversity training, and culture.

65   Few, if any, organizations have become truly multicultural. The major dimensions that characterize organizations as they eventually achieve this state are pluralism, full structural integration, full integration of the informal network, an absence of prejudice and discrimination, no gap in organizational identification based on cultural identity group, and low levels of intergroup conflict attributable to diversity.

DISCUSSION QUESTIONS

Questions for Review

1. Why is diversity increasing in many organizations today?

2. Identify the major dimensions of diversity and discuss recent trends for each.

3. Summarize the basic impact of diversity on organizations.

4. Discuss the four basic individual approaches and the four basic organizational approaches to managing diversity.

Questions for Analysis

5. The text outlines many different advantages of diversity in organizations. Can you think of any disadvantages?

6. What are the basic dimensions of diversity that most affect you personally?

7. When you finish school and begin your career, what should you be prepared to do to succeed in a diverse workforce?

Questions for Application

8. Visit the registrar's office or office of admissions at your college or university. Using their enrollment statistics, determine the relative diversity on your campus. Is the student population more or less diverse than the faculty?

9. Assume that you are starting a new organization that is likely to grow rapidly. Develop a diversity plan for becoming a multicultural organization.

10. Assume that you work for a large multinational organization. You have just learned that you are being transferred to India. You also know that you will be the first person of your ethnicity to work there. What steps might you take before you go to minimize diversity-related problems that your presence might cause?

SKILL SELF-ASSESSMENT

Managing Diversity

Introduction: As organizations become more diverse, managing diversity takes on increasing importance. The following assessment surveys your beliefs and values about the management of diversity.

Instructions: You will agree with some of the statements and disagree with others. In some cases, you may find making a decision difficult, but you should force a choice. Record your answers next to each statement according to the following scale:

Strongly Agree   =   +2
Somewhat Agree   =   +1
Somewhat Disagree   =   −1
Strongly Disagree   =   −2

Managing diversity

_____ 1. Means approaching diversity at three levels simultaneously: individual, interpersonal, and organizational.

_____ 2. Is synonymous with civil rights.

_____ 3. Involves a *management* perspective.

_____ 4. Is a new term for what used to be called equal employment opportunity programs.

_____ 5. Requires managers to spend less time "doing" work and more time enabling employees to do the work.

_____ 6. Should be done because of all the wrongs done to minorities throughout the years.

_____ 7. Defines diversity broadly, going beyond race and gender.

_____ 8. Is the same thing as affirmative action.

_____ 9. Assumes that adaptation is a mutual process between the individual and the organization.

_____ 10. Is synonymous with women's rights.

_____ 11. May take years to implement.

_____ **12.** Is required by federal legislation.

_____ **13.** Means getting from employees not only everything you have a right to expect, but everything they have to offer.

_____ **14.** Is a program or an orchestrated set of actions to "do" something.

Source: Adapted from *Beyond Race and Gender* (New York: AMACOM, a division of American Management Association, 135 West 50th Street, New York, New York 10020) by R. Roosevelt Thomas, Jr., pp. 326–327. Copyright 1991 by R. Roosevelt Thomas, Jr.

CASE 14.2

Grand Metropolitan

At the age of sixteen, Maxwell Joseph went to work for a real estate company in London. Five years later in 1931, he formed his own company and became probably the youngest real estate agent in England at that time. After World War II, he began to buy rundown hotels in Great Britain and abroad. In 1962 he named his company Grand Metropolitan Hotels because hotels so dominated his holdings. By 1972, however, the hotels no longer dominated so he shortened the name to simply Grand Metropolitan, or Grand Met.

After Joseph's death in 1982, Grand Met continued to buy and sell other corporations at a furious pace. It quickly became an international organization dealing in a variety of food, liquor, and retailing operations. Its international Distillers and Vintners unit is number-one in wine and spirits. Its eye-care retailer, Pearle Vision Centers, is the largest in its field. And Burger King, which it obtained when it bought Pillsbury Co. in 1989, is number-two in hamburgers.

In the early 1990s Grand Met participated in a strategic management study that revealed that its executives had bought and sold companies with seemingly little interest in long-term corporate strategy. The company was geared toward tangible investments instead of intangible ones such as its workforce. It used short-term financial tools to cope with the uncertainty of the environment with little thought about the long-term consequences of its actions. As a result of that study, however, Grand Met decided to change: it's using advertising and product development to try to build international brand names and market shares in more focused food, beverage, and retailing businesses.

Grand Met has long been known as a socially responsible company. In Britain it supports rebuilding efforts in inner cities and youth training programs. It belongs to the Per Cent Club, whose members donate a minimum of one-half of one percent of pretax profits to the community. It also has a policy of requiring its overseas subsidiaries to act with the highest integrity: the company must not only obey laws, but, more importantly, must also work in harmony with the economic and social aims of the society in which it operates.

Arising from that commitment to social responsibility is Grand Met's commitment to having a diversified workforce. It has invested heavily in education and training to change senior and middle management's behavior regarding attitudes, stereotyping, language, and everything that goes along with those. It has also worked to change the culture of the company itself so that everyone truly values diversity. Even in the face of downsizing and restructuring, rising hostilities among some ethnic groups, and intense competition, Grand Met has stuck to its diversity effort.

CASE 14.2 (continued)

One aspect of that commitment is its family responsibility policy. That policy includes the option to take a three-year maternity career break. Policies such as that have helped Grand Met attract and retain skilled women in its workforce. As it pushes its diversity effort, Grand Met plans to develop other policies to try to see that its workforce reflects the diversity of its customers around the world.

Discussion Questions

1. In what ways are Grand Met, Hoechst (see Case 14.1), and IBM (see *The Environment Management* box in this chapter) similar in their approaches to diversity? In what ways are they different?

2. What approach to managing diversity does Grand Met take? Try to use specific examples to support your response.

3. Why might a company as far ranging in its holdings as Grand Met develop a high degree of social responsibility, including a strong commitment to diversity?

References: M. Greenslade, "Getting Diversity on the Agenda," *Across the Board,* January 1994, p. 56; Faye Rice, "How to Make Diversity Pay," *Fortune,* August 8, 1994, pp. 78–86; "A Grand Design for Grand Met," *Business Week,* December 20, 1993, pp. 58–59; and "'Family Responsibility' Policy Helps Grand Met to Hold on to Skilled Women Employees," *Personnel Management,* February 1993, p. 4.

CHAPTER NOTES

1. Gary Hoover, Alta Campbell, and Patrick J. Spain (Eds.), *Hoover's Handbook of American Business 1995* (Austin, Tex.: The Reference Press, 1994), pp. 1130–1131; "Firms Address Workers' Cultural Variety," *Wall Street Journal,* February 10, 1989, p. B1; and Faye Rice, "How to Make Diversity Pay," *Fortune,* August 8, 1994, pp. 78–86.

2. Marlene G. Fine, Fern L. Johnson, and M. Sallyanne Ryan, "Cultural Diversity in the Workplace," *Public Personnel Management,* Fall 1990, pp. 305–319.

3. Badi G. Foster, Gerald Jackson, William E. Cross, Bailey Jackson, and Rita Hardiman, "Workforce Diversity and Business," *Training and Development Journal,* April 1988, pp. 38–42.

4. Sam Cole, "Cultural Diversity and Sustainable Futures," *Futures,* December 1990, pp. 1044–1058.

5. Walter Kiechel III, "How to Manage Older Workers," *Fortune,* November 5, 1990, pp. 183–186.

6. Louis S. Richman, "The Coming World Labor Shortage," *Fortune,* April 9, 1990, pp. 70–77.

7. *Occupational Outlook Handbook* (Washington, D.C.: U.S. Bureau of Labor Statistics, 1990–1991).

8. Gary Powell and D. Anthony Butterfield, "Investigating the 'Glass Ceiling' Phenomenon: An Empirical Study of Actual Promotions to Top Management," *Academy of Management Journal,* 1994, Vol. 37, No. 1, pp. 68–86.

9. Jaclyn Fierman, "Do Women Manage Differently?" *Fortune,* December 17, 1990, pp. 115–118.

10. Jaclyn Fierman, "Why Women Still Don't Hit the Top," *Fortune,* July 30, 1990, pp. 40–62.

11. "Paternal, Managerial Roles Often Clash," *Wall Street Journal,* September 12, 1991, pp. B1, B4.

12. *Occupational Outlook Handbook* (Washington, D.C.: U.S. Bureau of Labor Statistics, 1990–1991).

13. Taylor H. Cox, Sharon A. Lobel, and Poppy Lauretta McLeod, "Effects of Ethnic Group Cultural Differences on Cooperative and Competitive Behavior on a Group Task," *Academy of Management Journal,* December 1991, pp. 827–847.

14. See Barry Culhane and Jack Clarcq, "Deaf and Capable," *HR Magazine,* August 1994, pp. 81–88, for one interesting perspective.

15. Michael Chisholm, "Cultural Diversity Breaks the Mold," *Geographical Magazine,* November 1990, pp. 12–16.

16. Based on Taylor H. Cox and Stacy Blake, "Managing Cultural Diversity: Implications of Organizational Competitiveness," *The Academy of Management Executive,* August 1991, pp. 45–46.

17. Cox and Taylor, "Managing Cultural Diversity: Implications for Organizational Competitiveness."

18. For an example, see "Get to Know the Ethnic Market," *Marketing,* June 17, 1991, p. 32.

19. C. Marlene Fiol, "Consensus, Diversity, and Learning in Organizations," *Organization Science,* August 1994, pp. 403–415.

20. Douglas Hall and Victoria Parker, "The Role of Work-place Flexibility in Managing Diversity," *Organizational Dynamics,* Summer 1993, pp. 5–14.

21. "As Population Ages, Older Workers Clash With Younger Bosses," *Wall Street Journal,* June 13, 1994, pp. A1, A8.

22. Patti Watts, "Bias Busting: Diversity Training in the Workforce," *Management Review,* December 1987, pp. 51–54.

23. See Stephanie Overman, "Managing the Diverse Work Force," *HRMagazine,* April 1991, pp. 32–36.

24. Lennie Copeland, "Making the Most of Cultural Differences at the Workplace," *Personnel,* June 1988, pp. 52–60.

25. "Firms Address Workers' Cultural Variety," *Wall Street Journal,* February 10, 1989, p. B1.

26. Sara Rynes and Benson Rosen, "What Makes Diversity Programs Work?" *HRMagazine,* October 1994, pp. 67–75.

27. "Learning to Accept Cultural Diversity," *Wall Street Journal,* September 12, 1990, pp. B1, B9.

28. "Firms Address Workers' Cultural Variety."

29. "Firms Grapple With Language," *Wall Street Journal,* November 7, 1989, p. B1.

30. Anthony Carnevale and Susan Stone, "Diversity—Beyond the Golden Rule," *Training and Development,* October 1994, pp. 22–27.

31. Dinesh D'Souza, "Multiculturalism 101," *Policy Review,* Spring 1991, pp. 22–30.

32. This discussion derives heavily from Taylor H. Cox, "The Multicultural Organization," *The Academy of Management Executive,* May 1991, pp. 34–47.

QUESTIONS

1. Explain the term *diversity* and discuss its relevance to the world of business.

2. Explain why organizations are becoming increasingly diverse.

3. Although many organizations are becoming increasingly diverse, challenges remain. Discuss some of the problems and challenges associated with age, gender, and ethnicity in the increasingly diverse business world.

EXTENDING YOUR VOCABULARY

diverse: The diverse customs of the two immigrant groups became apparent when _____

hypothetical: The doctor could only respond to the lawyer with a hypothetical answer because _____

demographics: The mayor referred to the city's changing demographics to show that _____

simultaneously: When the explosions occurred simultaneously, we realized that _____

mandatory: They wanted to change the mandatory seat belt law after they learned that _____

subsequently: She subsequently won the race after she was able to

_____

innovative: Because of her innovative solution to the problem, we were able to _____

perspectives: Joining the workers on the assembly line gave the three

                                             managers new perspectives on _____

facilitates: The advertisement claims that this device facilitates my

                                             work, but I have found that _____

empathy: I appreciate your display of empathy at this time

                                             because _____

mandate: The election results gave the president a clear mandate

                                             to _____

◈ MARKED COPY*

1 Like most other organizations in the world today, Avon and Xerox have seen tremendous changes in the composition of their workforces during the last several decades. Once dominated by white male managers, each firm now employs people at a variety of organizational levels from a diverse set of backgrounds. And like other organizations today, Avon and Xerox have encountered more than a few challenges along the way as they have sought to address the variety of issues, opportunities, and problems that their increasingly diverse workforces have created.

Introduction
Relates opening incident to chapter objectives

2 This chapter is about workforce diversity in organizations. We begin by exploring the meaning of diversity and reasons for its increase. We then identify and discuss several common dimensions of diversity and discuss diversity in different contexts. The impact of diversity on the organization is then explored. We next address individual strategies and organizational approaches for managing diversity. Finally, we characterize and describe the fully multicultural organization.

The (Nature) of Workforce Diversity

Definitions
—Why?

3 Workforce diversity has become a very important issue in many organizations, both in the United States and abroad. A logical starting point, then, is to establish the meaning of diversity and then examine why such diversity is increasing today.

The Meaning of Diversity

4 (Diversity) exists in a group or organization when its members differ from one another along one or more important dimensions.[2] Thus diversity is not an absolute phenomenon wherein a group or organization is or is not diverse. Instead, diversity can be conceptualized as a continuum. If everyone in the group or organization is exactly like everyone else, there is no diversity whatsoever. If everyone is different along every imaginable dimension, total diversity exists. In reality, of course, these extremes are more hypothetical than real. Most settings are characterized by a level of diversity somewhere between these extremes. Therefore, diversity should be thought of in terms of degree or level of diversity along relevant dimensions.

• * **diversity**—Key
Exists in a group or organization when its members differ from one another along one or more important dimensions such as age, gender, or ethnicity

*Partial marked copy

5   These dimensions of diversity might include gender, age, ethnic origin, or any of several others. A group comprising five middle-aged white male U.S. executives has relatively little diversity. If one member is replaced by a young white female executive, the group becomes a bit more diverse. If another member is replaced by an older African American executive, diversity increases a bit more. And when a third member is replaced by a Japanese executive, the group becomes even more diverse.

Examples of diversity:
—gender
—age
—ethnic origin, etc.

Reasons for Increasing Diversity

6   As we note earlier, organizations today are becoming increasingly diverse along many different dimensions. Although several different factors account for these trends and changes, four of the more important ones are illustrated in Figure 14.1.

Why the increase?

—four factors

7   One factor contributing to increased diversity is changing demographics in the labor force. As more women and minorities enter the labor force, for example, the available pool of talent from which organizations hire employees is changing in both size and composition. If talent within each segment of the labor pool is evenly distributed (for example, if the number of very talented men in the workforce as a percentage of all men in the workforce is the same as the number of very talented women in the labor force as a percentage of all women in the workforce), it follows logically that, over time, proportionately more women and proportionately fewer men will be hired by an organization.[3]

factor #1
changing demographics

8   A related factor contributing to diversity is the increased awareness by organizations that they can improve the overall quality of their workforce by hiring and promoting the most talented people available. By casting a broader net in recruiting and looking beyond traditional sources for new employees, organizations are finding more broadly qualified and better qualified employees from many different segments of society. Thus these organizations are finding that diversity can be a source of competitive advantage.[4]

factor #2
*   improved workforce*

9   Another reason for the increase in diversity is that legislation and legal actions have forced organizations to hire more broadly. In earlier times, organizations in the United States were essentially free to dis-

factor #3
*   legal action*

Figure 14.1 *Reasons for Increasing Diversity*

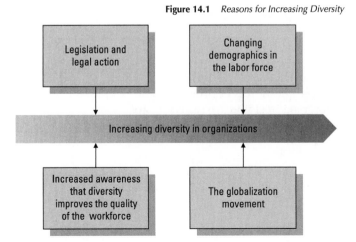

Cultural diversity is increasing in most organizations today for four basic reasons. These reasons promise to make diversity even greater in the future.

four factors graphed out

criminate against women, blacks, and other minorities. Thus most organizations were dominated by white males. But over the last thirty years or so, various laws have outlawed discrimination against these and other groups. As we detail in Chapter 13, organizations must hire and promote people today solely on the basis of their qualifications.

10   A final factor contributing to increased diversity in organizations is the globalization movement. Organizations that have opened offices and related facilities in other countries have had to learn to deal with different customs, social norms, and mores. Strategic alliances and foreign ownership also contribute, as managers today are more likely to have job assignments in other countries and/or to work with foreign managers within their own countries. As employees and managers move from assignment to assignment across national boundaries, organizations and their subsidiaries within each country thus become more diverse.

factor #4
globalization—
companies expand
all over the world

Dimensions of Diversity

11   As we indicate earlier, many different dimensions of diversity can characterize an organization. In this section we discuss age, gender, ethnicity, and other dimensions of diversity.

2 key terms

—examples of "dimensions"

Age Distributions

12   One important dimension of diversity in any organization is the age distribution of its workers. The average age of the U.S. workforce is gradually increasing and will continue to do so for the next several years. Figure 14.2 presents age distributions for U.S. workers in 1988 and projected age distributions for the year 2000.

age

age of workers increasing?
why?

13   Several factors are contributing to this pattern. For one, the baby-boom generation (a term used to describe the unusually large number of people who were born in the twenty-year period after World War II) continues to age. Declining birth rates among the post–baby-boom generations simultaneously account for smaller percentages of new entrants into the labor force. Another factor that contributes to the aging workforce is improved health and medical care. As a result of these improvements, people are able to remain productive and active for longer

general improvement means people
live longer

Sample Exam

The following model applied to Chapter 14, "Managing Workforce Diversity in Organizations," presents the most common question types for an exam. When you have completed reading the chapter and feel you are ready, try to take this exam. After the sample exam, a discussion of content and strategy follows.

Essay

1. Describe the potential impact of diversity on a company. Cite the conflicts and opportunities that may arise. How might a company face these challenges?

2. Discuss the reasons for increased workplace diversity in today's society.

Objective Questions

1. According to the chapter, all of the following are contributing factors to increased diversity except
   a. changing demographics.
   b. legislative and legal action.
   c. the globalization movement.
   d. rising minimum wages.

2. A multicultural organization
   a. recruits personnel from every country in the world.
   b. seeks to increase diversity and tolerance in the company.
   c. has full structural integration of workers but not of management.
   d. concerns itself with multicultural issues when a conflict arises.

3. The barrier that keeps women from advancing to top management positions is known as the
   a. ethnic factor.
   b. glass ceiling.
   c. pluralism effect.
   d. Avon rule.

Matching   Match one item from column A with one from column B.

A	B
1. glass ceiling	the policy of being as ethnically inclusive as possible
2. diversity	the barrier that keeps minorities from management positions
3. multicultural	the differences among the personnel in a company

Fill-in-the-Blank

1. Two of the features mentioned for a multicultural company are _____ and _____.

2. A glass ceiling refers to the _____ experienced by women and other minorities in the quest for top management positions.

3. Including workers of all ages is one measure of the _____ of a company.

True-False Questions

1. _____ Most major corporations are truly multicultural today.

2. _____ Age, gender, and ethnicity distribution are three measures of diversity.

3. _____ Diversity has only a positive impact on an organization.

Question Analysis

Essay Question 1

The first essay question reads as follows:

Describe the potential impact of diversity on a company. Cite the conflicts and opportunities that may arise. How might a company face these challenges?

1. Clearly understand what the question is asking for.   In this case the question has three parts. To respond to only one or two parts of the question is not a complete answer. The first part is introduced by the cue word *describe.* This cue word is defined in "The Proficient Reader" as "to give an account that presents a picture or story to the person who reads or hears it." Thus your answer must go beyond a simple sentence and give a reasonably full account of diversity. The next part of the question asks you to cite the conflicts and opportunities that may arise. *Cite* is another cue word. It is defined as "to give a series or number of." Unlike the first part of the question, this section is not requiring a full discussion but rather a listing of items. The last part of the question ties into the second part and asks you to discuss how a company can cope with the challenges that may arise from the conflicts and opportunities of increased diversity.

2. Reread the text and/or search your mind for related issues.   Quickly capture your mental connections in a rough list. This list will be further amended. The idea is to get something on paper without committing yourself at the full sentence level. The following points are numbered for ease of reference. The numbering does not refer to rank or order of the items.

   1—different people in the workplace have different needs

   2—attracting a diverse workforce

   3—the problems of promotion, layoffs

   4—new markets

   5—sensitivity to differences

   6—workplace spirit

   7—competitive advantage—six arguments given in text

   8—workplace resentment over increased diversity

   9—cultural difference conflicts as a result of more diversity

   10—managing diversity in organizations involves tolerance, communication, training, etc.

3. Organize and structure your work.   Step 3 involves organizing your list into a workable form by selecting the appropriate information and beginning to structure it. It would be easiest to follow the order of the question as a way to keep on track. Because of the structure of the question, you may wish to take the list and break it up by question part. In the following out-

line points from the original list are numbered and newer ideas have the ^
symbol next to them.

Describe the potential impact of diversity

#1 from list—different people and different backgrounds, experiences

#6 from list—workplace spirit

^ the change of a company's face

Cite the conflicts and opportunities

Conflicts
    #3 from list—resentment over promotions, layoffs
    ^ misunderstandings and culture clash

Opportunities
    #4 from list—new markets
    ^ broader source of information
    ^ a company's reputation

Company response

1. Individual response
    a. #10 tolerance
    b. ^ empathy
2. Company response
    a. ^ policies
    b. ^ practices
    c. #10 diversity training

4. Construct your answer.   You may wish to begin by paraphrasing the
question as a statement and then aligning your answer to the three parts of
the question.

Paraphrase the questions as a beginning.

I will begin the essay by describing the effect that diversity may have on a company.
I will then name the problems and advantages that may come to a company as a
result of more diversity. Finally, I will explain how a company can respond to these
challenges and opportunities.

Then move into a discussion of the first part of the question.

A company in today's society sees a more diverse workforce than in years past. The
change of the workforce will bring to the company people from different cultures and
with different backgrounds than the company has traditionally hired. As workers
reflect more differences in such things as age, race, and physical challenges, the
"face" of the company changes.

The increase in diversity presents the company with both opportunities and challenges. Some people argue that the purpose of a more diverse workforce is a competitive advantage. For example, they argue that the knowledge base expands because people from different perspectives are able to make contributions. Furthermore, people from various sectors can help companies break into new markets. Diversity also presents a company with potential problems. For example, in the interest of hiring and keeping more women employees, a company may look to expand their role in management as quickly as possible. A male passed over for promotion becomes resentful of the woman's promotion and potentially a disgruntled worker. This mentality is not healthy for the spirit or productivity of the company.

A company can move to handle difficulties that arise because of an increase in diversity. It can encourage individuals to practice tolerance of others' differences and can model this behavior. It can also embark on official company programs. For example, it can have a strong official policy statement regarding discrimination and prejudice. The company can also make its practices fit with its policy statement. A strongly worded sexual harassment policy is of little value unless complaints are handled quickly and fairly. Finally, a company can seek to enlighten all of its employees with diversity training. In these sessions, people learn to empathize and better communicate despite differences of age, race, gender, and nationality, among other things.

ESSAY QUESTION 2

The second essay question reads as follows:

Discuss the reasons for increased workplace diversity in today's society.

The first step is to focus on the cue word *discuss*. Discuss means "to talk about." It would be insufficient to list the reasons for diversity without further explanation. Note that "reasons" is plural, which means that there are two or more factors that need to be discussed. The remainder of the question gives you the *what* that is to be discussed (diversity), the *when* (today), and the *where* (the workplace in society).

The second step is to search your mind for the related information and make a list of reasons for increased diversity:

- Changing demographics
- Globalization movement
- Legislation and legal action
- Workforce quality awareness

You may not remember all four of the factors listed in the chapter for increased diversity. However, reporting two or three factors well will certainly be to your credit and show that you are familiar with the topic.

The third step is to select the appropriate information or organize your material. In this case the order of the reasons is not crucial. Several factors have an impact on a company, but one factor does not necessarily depend on another. In the first essay question, in contrast, it is necessary to specify the conflicts and opportunities brought about by increasing diversity before you discuss a company's response to them.

The fourth step is to construct an answer. We have suggested that you begin by rephrasing the question into a statement as in the following:

There are four factors that cause an increase in diversity in today's workplace. The four are: changing demographics, the globalization movement, legal action, and an awareness of workforce quality.

You may wish to omit the list and simply discuss each factor in a separate paragraph. We prefer the list because it becomes an organizer for your reader. Each paragraph should begin with a statement of the factor. For such a question, another good organizing strategy is to enumerate within the paragraphs as in the following.

The first factor that contributes to increased diversity is the change in the workforce. More women and minorities have entered the labor pool and hence make talent available from a broader range of people. The text makes the observation that over time more women will be hired than men if the percentage of talented women in relation to all women is the same as the percentage of talented men in relation to all men.

A transition or connection between paragraphs makes your writing smoother and easier to read. By enumerating your paragraphs you are setting up an easy way to make a transition. Thus your next paragraph can use "second factor" as the lead in as in the following:

A second factor that contributes to diversity is globalization. As companies expand overseas, they will be hiring local people as part of the workforce. Some of the people will be brought back to the states for other job responsibilities. As businesses expand, there is a greater likelihood that the workforce will become more and more diverse.

The essay continues in the third paragraph using the number connection, "a third factor."

A third factor that increases diversity is legal action. A variety of laws have been passed to thwart discrimination in the workplace. Thus some companies that might be slow to recognize the advantages of diversity for other reasons are prompted to make changes in the order of business to comply with the law.

The last reason may be listed as fourth or last.

The last reason that diversity has increased is that companies have become more aware that the overall quality of their workforce increases when they "cast a broader net" and look to the talents and contributions of an increasingly diverse group. People from different cultures and with different experiences can provide a company with a different perspective regarding their services and products. In this way, certain companies have come to view diversity as a means to enhance their competitive advantage in the marketplace.

In this particular case, a concluding statement is not crucial because the question is basically asking you to report a set of reasons and explain them. You are not being asked to argue a point or analyze a situation where a concluding statement would be expected. However, a general conclusion can be effective.

Thus we can see from the four reasons cited that there is a tendency for increasing diversity in the workplace. However, it is possible that changes in these causes could also have an effect on the direction that diversity takes in the future.

MATCHING

We have included three matching items in our sample test. Usually there are at least ten, which makes the task harder. As we suggested, make a quick pass through to see which items leap out at you. Say, for example, you remember from the chapter the definition of glass ceiling. This gets matched up with the second definition listed, "the barrier that keeps minorities from management positions." This leaves the other two possibilities. If you recognize one of the two, then the remaining item and the definition must be correct, even though you didn't recognize it. Leave matching items not recognized until the end of the exam. Additional information that you pick up may help you.

MULTIPLE CHOICE

Multiple-choice tests are objective tests. The usual format is a statement that is divided into two parts. The first part is called the stem. The stem portion is followed by a number of options. The stem leads or opens the statement and one of the options ends it. You are to select the option that best completes the stem.

Question 1

Consider the stem from the first question:

According to the chapter, all of the following are contributing factors to increased diversity except

The stem includes the qualifier *except*. This is a common way that the structure of the question may mislead you. Keep this term and other negating words in mind as you are reading stems. You are looking for the one choice that does *not* fit with the stem. Because the question is focusing on very specific details, it is difficult to get to the correct answer without remembering the information from the text. However, there is another approach. You are looking to link three of the options together in some way. In this case, the first three options contain specific technical language that is not likely to occur in everyday conversation. The last option that mentions "minimum wages" is an example from common experience and therefore stands apart from the other three choices. Approaching it in this way would result in a correct answer without you knowing the exact meaning of the other three options.

Question 2

The stem gives us the subject "the organization" (group or business) modified by the word *multicultural* (many cultures). It is reasonable to conclude that the option will make a statement about multiculturalism. Remember that the discussion in the book on multiculturalism is on an ideal situation and not reality. There are some catches among the choices on this question. Each of the options has a true part; however, three of the four also include something that is not true. For example, in option (a) it would be very unlikely that personnel could be recruited from so many places. Option (b) is the correct choice. It is the most reasonable in that it states that an effort is being made rather than that an ideal state (reaching complete diversity in an organization) has been reached. The first part of (c) "has full structural integration of workers" is indeed one of the characteristics cited for a multicultural organization. This phrase could easily mislead you unless you carefully read the rest of the option, "but not management." The text makes clear that the goal of multiculturalism extends through management, and indeed this has been where the bigger problem exists. Option (d) also begins with a true statement, "concerns itself with multicultural issues." However, the time element, "when a conflict arises," tells you that the organization responds to crisis. Paraphrased this option might be, "The company does nothing about multicultural issues unless a serious problem develops." Then they do something. This choice is not in the spirit of the textbook's discussion of multiculturalism.

Question 3

Question 3 is structured in such a way as to potentially throw you off track. As was mentioned previously, test makers often put a "good" wrong answer first. They will include an option in which you are likely to see a connection, although not the connection they have in mind as the "right answer." Ethnicity (a person's national identity) has been and can be a barrier to promotion in a company. However, the stem specifies "women." Thus the option needs to be gender-related. *Glass ceiling* is the correct answer. The various contexts in which this term appears can help in establishing its meaning.

FILL-IN-THE-BLANK

1. We suggested in our discussion earlier that unknown fill-ins be left until the end of the exam. Considering your questions might provide you with the memory prompt or the right word or thought to complete these questions. In this case it is only necessary to remember two of the five features listed. Also note that the size of the space left for the answer is misleading, and in fact you might think that a single word is called for. The following would be possibilities:
   a. Seeking to increase its diversity
   b. Characterized by an absence of discrimination and prejudice

2. The second question has been written this way so that if you were uncertain of the choice, consulting the previous matching question would help you get both questions right. If you were having trouble coming up with the word to be included, one of the options uses the term *barrier*. Placed in the context of the phrase, this may tip you off on the right choice, "glass ceiling."

3. Finishing the third question requires the word *diversity*. This term has also been used previously on the exam in other contexts. Use the language of the entire exam to help you with specific questions.

TRUE/FALSE QUESTIONS

Guess on true/false questions if you are uncertain of the correct answer. You have a 50 percent chance of being right.

1. The first statement is false. The textbook says that only a very few corporations can claim this distinction. The terms that should flag you are *most* and *today*. *Most* is not an all-inclusive word, but it is close to one. It suggests that the overwhelming majority is multicultural, and that would almost be as hard to achieve as "every." The other key question is *today*. As you may recall from the chapter, there is a trend for companies to move in a multicultural direction. In the future this may mean that most will have arrived at a multicultural state. *Today*, however, means a current assessment.

2. The statement is true. The text discusses this point, but you can also deduce it from your general knowledge. Diverse means different, and age, gender, and ethnicity are three differences.

3. Three contains the flag word *only.* Yes, diversity has a positive impact on companies, according to the text. But the chapter also claims that there are problems and conflicts that arise. You wouldn't need to know the specifics of this question, because the use of *only* tells you that there are no exceptions. When you see this type of term, it is telling you that the statement is false.

 ### READING JOURNAL

- **Content**
  What information do you learn from the chapter?

- **Process**
  What strategies did you use? If you discovered difficulties with the material, how did you resolve them? Describe how your reading may have changed as a result of reading the chapter and using some strategies.

- **Response**
  Were your feelings about your preparation realistic? How confident are you about your reading ability?

The Day's Work

BARBARA HOLLAND

Before becoming a freelance writer, Barbara Holland worked in an advertising office. The following essay first appeared in Ms. magazine in 1977.

GEARING UP

1. "Men and women do not work for the same reasons. They each have their own special needs for seeking employment." Agree or disagree with this statement and explain your reasons.

2. Discuss the problems and difficulties faced by a working parent with family responsibilities.

The Reading

The Day's Work

by Barbara Holland

1   After the first year, husbands don't put the seat back down any more. However, there are compensating advantages. I forget their names.

2   He slinks out into the dawn before the rest of us get up. He kisses me as I lie there fighting off the day with a pillow over my head. In fact, that's almost the only time he kisses me now. Maybe I look safer asleep. Maybe horizontal with my eyes shut I still look like a woman. As soon as I stand up I run around like a battery toy; push a button and it smacks the kids and burns the stew, screaming. So, for all the good it does us at that hour, he kisses me and is gone.

3   The alarm rings and I turn it off. Children come stand in the doorway, cautiously, and then go away whispering, "She's still asleep." I hunch under the covers, ripe with potential rages, a great rumpled sulky Gulliver. How did I get here? Can I leave? Am I held prisoner by little whispering people?

4   I am.

5   What brown eyes all my children have. It seems to give their stare a kind of weight. My sisters and brothers are all blue-eyed, and my mother; I have left a family where people's looks were light and clear and translucent, and found one where they stare at me opaquely, like chocolate drops; my life has dropped into an ominous key. They have been sent to get me.

6   They eat enormous breakfasts. When I was a child I suffered tortures over breakfast. A single bite of toast stuck in my chest like a fist all morning. Liquids gagged me. I whined, vomited, anything. I swore that my own children would never have to eat breakfast, not even juice.

7   They bang their spoons and call for oatmeal, eggs, toast, bacon, milk, juice, sausages, fruit. I run back and forth. "More juice!" they cry. "Can I have another egg?" "Is there any grapefruit?" "She's eating my toast!" "Well, you weren't eating it." "I was too!"

8   "Hush up, all of you!"

9   "But she took a big bite of my toast. I want another piece." "All right, give him another piece, I'll finish this one." "Mommy, I said I want oatmeal!"

10   *"Shut up or I'll slaughter you! I mean it! I will!"*

11   I talk like that a lot, and it worries me. I don't think parents should say things like that to their children.

12   The kitchen looks as if armies had fought in it. Oh, quick, quick, the hairbrush, where is it? I zipper jackets and give each child an extra hug because of shouting at them. Am I forgiven? I can't see through their brown eyes. Do they hate me? Do I frighten them? Worse, are they hardened, callus, and insensitive?

13   Guilt, the Mommy's monster.

14   They leave. Silence in the ears chiming like an overdose of quinine.

15   I make the bed, our bed, battleground and flower garden and sanctuary; it is my one concession. I always make the bed. Having made it I feel efficient. Good housekeeper. Wife. Mother. Advertising person. Shower. Dress. The dog whines: is it never my turn? Brother, can you spare a pat? A kind word? A harsh word, even? No. Look at the clock, the clock, the clock. Oh, boy, am I late.

16   The kitchen. Could I simply drop a bomb on it? Or have I already? Some of the mess is stale mess, yesterday's mess, looking much worse, more reproachful, than fresh mess. I could clean up. I'm so late already I might as well.

17   I do the frying pans and put the dog into the backyard. Backyard. Hah. Back toilet, dog latrine. This weekend I have to do something about it, scoop it all up. Unless I do something about the kids' rooms. No, forget it, Allie and Chris are coming for dinner; I have to do something about the living room. In my mind I always call it vaguely "doing something," which doesn't commit me to actually cleaning. Something; anything. Pick up the newspapers and take the children's sneakers off the mantelpiece.

18   I walk to work. Six and a half blocks of peace and noise. I stare around politely at the buildings. We know each other, they wish me a happy day. Whatever the weather I love this walk. Transition between home and office, lovely filthy streets full of blowing trash about which I need do nothing. Just passing through, just browsing, thank you. Passive, I browse like a cow on traffic and shop windows and plastic geraniums in the window boxes.

19   I like my office too, especially when I first come in and see my desk waiting for me like a patient child. I feel so much stronger and braver at work, where I know what I'm doing. Competent, like a man, an executive, glancing at papers and crumpling them up and tossing them toward the wastebasket. Real difference between men and women, home and work: here, if I miss the wastebasket, someone else must ultimately pick the papers up. Exhilarating.

20   "Dorney was looking all over for you." Ellen's secretary. "He was burned up. I said you'd gone to the little girls' room, but Art told him you weren't in yet."

21   "What did he want?" Why can't they simply get used to my being late? Why can't I get used to it? Then we could all stop fussing about it. There's no way, *there is absolutely no way* I can be here by nine; can't we all resign ourselves to it?

22   I leave early too. I always have. They can't get used to that either, and keep looking for me, in desk drawers and file cabinets after I'm gone.

23   Begin on a stack of radio commercials for a menswear shop.

24   Peace is an office.

25   Whistle without attempting a tune. Commercials proceed automatically from brain to fingers, without thought. Time was, back when I was a skittery slip of a lass in a ponytail, I used to have to time the things. Whisper them to myself, e-nunc-i-a-ting clearly, watching the second hand on the clock. Now the shapes of a sixty-second commercial, thirty-second, ten-second spot have sunk down into the dream-deep centers of the folded brain

and seeped from there to the finger muscles. I am never wrong. Curious things we pick up on the Road of Life. Not like a rolling stone but like rolling Play-Doh; junk embedded forever, the names of the Presidents, and how to make paper airplanes, and what to do for croup.

26   "Mr. Dorney wants you in his office."

27   Wants me in his office, does he? Wants my fair white body? Bent backward over the duplication machine, "Ooh, Mr. Dorney, please, somebody might come in!" Down, down, to the soft white carpet with that irritating abstract pattern like inkblots. "Mr. Dorney, you're tearing my dress!"

28   Nope. Not me, not Mr. Dorney. He's younger than I am and a whole lot dumber and we worked together once years before, at Mayburn & Atherton, when he was just a pockmarked kid and I was already somebody. Now he's a very large deal and I'm still just somebody. Story of a life. A lady's life.

29   He'll be bald as a stone, though, before he's forty-five.

30   "I want to talk to you about your hours. Now, I realize you have other responsibilities . . ."

31   Oh, why not bend me over the duplicating machine instead? Who taught you to talk that mush-mouth executive stuff? Me, that's who.

32   " . . . certain responsibility to us here."

33   Jerk.

34   "Like to give you some additional, uh, status around here. To tell you the truth, we have a new account coming in, not absolutely firmed up yet, keep this in strictest confidence . . . require more, uh, punctuality on your part . . ."

35   "I'm afraid I can't promise anything, Jack, I mean, Mr. Dorney. I move as fast as I can. And I don't think you have any complaints about my work once I get here."

36   I hitch my bottom rudely onto the corner of his desk, which he hates, he wants people to stand at attention, that's why the chairs are kept way over in the corner unless a client comes in. I slunch comfortably. Lovely feeling. This is the other side of the lady's life. I am irreplaceable at the nasty salary he pays me. Go on, fire me. Give my job to two guys and an English major. Besides that, I'm married. My husband works. Look at me cross-eyed, you jumped-up junior bookkeeper, and I can be gone before lunchtime. Just let me get my boots from the bottom drawer. Write your own commercials.

37   In a way you have to feel sorry for the married men around here. Take Art. He never misses a chance to double-cross me, but I can't blame him. He doesn't make much more than I do and his wife doesn't have a job, and they have two kids and a bouncing-baby mortgage, and when Mr. Dorney talks to *him* about being late he sweats pints of pure blood.

38   "Really would like you to take this on, sure you could handle it. However, it would mean . . ."

39   "No way." I smile cheerfully at him. He really hates me sometimes. I go out of my way to be pally with him and it drives him berserkers.

40   "Quite a substantial increase in salary."

41   Isn't it lovely to be grown up finally, after all these years? To know what

you want, to say no? Oh, there used to be a time: ecstasy, praise, raise, he thinks I can do it! I can, I can, just try me, chief! And oh, horrors, despair, I was late again this morning, what can I do? Maybe if I got up at five instead of six. Or four, or three, or never went to bed at all . . .

42 "Nope. I don't need any more responsibility any more than I need more money."

43 " . . . make a decision just now, want you to think it over; by the way the series for the Bluebell account . . ."

44 "You'll have it by two. Scout's honor." And I leave without being dismissed, switching my tail at him.

45 Back to work. Occasionally people come in to chat, and sit on *my* desk, not because I hide the chairs but because Jack Dorney doesn't like chatting. Nobody has chairs for visitors; if you chat, he thinks you're not working. We aren't, of course, but I told him to try to think of it as interdepartmental communications and he'd like it better. I believe he tries, but it's not easy, we giggle a lot.

46 The phone. Curses, oh, curses, the school nurse. Childish impulse to disguise my voice, pretend to be dead or somewhere else.

47 "Spots?" I say. All innocent, as if spots were as normal to my child as to any leopard's, any giraffe's kid.

48 "You don't seem to have returned the medical certificate, and we were wondering if he had had his measles vaccination . . ."

49 I join her in wondering. Somebody did, but I think it was Number 2; I remember cornering her under the examining table, and she bit the doctor. Unless that was tetanus.

50 We're old buddies, me and the nurse. I send my kids to school on a *stretcher* if necessary. She calls me a lot.

51 So I have to consult, this time with Ellen, avoiding Dorney. Ellen is the underboss.

52 "But you *can't,* not today. Mr. Warren is coming in at two-thirty about the Bluebell series. You'll just have to get someone else to take care of the child."

53 "Who? You?"

54 She laughs. "A neighbor or someone. There must be *someone.*"

55 People always think that. People's ideas of child care are frozen in the rural nineteenth century, when there were all those servants and helpful neighbors and resident aunts and decaying cousins, and dear old nursie up in the attic sewing smocks. It is hard for people to realize that nowadays there is *no one to take care of that child but you.* It's hard for me to realize too.

56 "You'll just have to bring him here, then."

57 "But he's *sick.*"

58 "Which one is it? 3-B? Sure, bring him in; I haven't seen the twins in ages." Childless Ellen. "Not since they had flu. They were great fun that time."

59 They sure were. You should have heard Dorney on the subject, after what they did to the adding machine.

60 Although in a way the twins do seem to belong to the office. They were born on a Friday (I took the day off) and popped into incubators, and on

Monday I came in to work. It was pretty childish, a gag, and they were horrified. I brought cigars, and said it was two boys and my husband was resting comfortably. "But we sent you a *card,*" Dorney's secretary kept wailing. "I just mailed it last night. To the *hospital.*"

61   Ellen says, "I don't see how you manage without a housekeeper. Or a cleaning woman, or anything. I think it's fantastic."

62   Shrug modestly. Nothing, really. I can walk on my hands, too, and whistle the overture to *Call Me Madam.*

63   "I don't know what I'm going to do without mine. She quit last week, simply walked out and never even said she was leaving, and the house is a perfect shambles. Howard and I have been eating out every night. I've been interviewing like mad, but it isn't easy to find someone these days."

64   Poor lamb.

65   "Did Dorney talk to you about the new account?"

66   "I turned it down. I haven't got the time."

67   "But there would be a raise," she cries, genuinely upset. "You know, with more money, you could hire someone to help around the house. You wouldn't have to work so hard."

68   I blush dark red at the real concern on the nice lady's face. Sister. Sister, kind sister, you don't understand, that's you but not me. Household help feels to me like three more children and another dog; someone else to bump into and apologize to. Someone with problems to hear. Someone to try to explain to, how I want things done, choking with guilt at having her do them when I could, and then not telling her after all. Someone to remember to praise: "Gee, that's nice, the way you dusted that cabinet. Really looks nice." Someone to notice where the syrup spilled on the kitchen shelf, a new relative with a husband who beats her and no-good kids.

69   Ellen is different, she enjoys command.

70   In the taxi, I inspect 3-B.

71   "Is it measles?" he asks eagerly.

72   I try to peer at the spots with professional interest. Your really proper mother these days is supposed to be a kind of barefoot doctor with shoes, shaking down thermometers and administering mouth-to-mouth at every turn. I'm not very good at it. Even my Band-Aids fall off, and when I look into somebody's sore throat all I can see is the soft palate and a couple of silver fillings.

73   "Is it?"

74   "Looks like mosquito bites to me. How do you feel?"

75   "Fine."

76   Oh, dear. If he's sick, really sick, with a fever, he will sit quietly in the art department and play with Magic Markers all day. If he isn't . . .

77   "If it's measles, how long do I get to stay out of school? Can I come to the office every day?"

78   I groan. A week? *Two weeks?* And then feel guilty. Did he have his shots? Oh, my poor neglected babies, my motherless lambs. I grab him and lay my cheek against his silky rumpled unwashed hair and he fights free. "Will they let me use the duplicator if I draw some pictures?"

79   All the women are glad to see him. Something about a kid in the office brightens up the ladies because it scares the men. Help, help, a child, anarchy and unreason, random destruction and tears, the opposite of what men hope for from their offices. What I hope for too, I guess.

80   He sits on Ellen's lap itching to get his hands on the interoffice phone.

81   "How are you doing in school, 3-B? My, you've certainly grown since I saw you last. You know how long it's been since you've come in to see me?"

82   If she catches measles from him, can they fire me for it, do you think?

83   "Now listen to me, young man." His eyes drift to the water cooler, how can he listen to me? My voice is a roaring sound in his world, like traffic. I drop it to a whisper: *"Ecoutes-moi, mon petit."* He hears; the head turns.

84   "I have to go to a meeting and I don't know how long it's going to last. You are going to sit here, *right here at my desk,* and draw me some pictures. If you draw a specially nice one, maybe we can put it through the duplicator. But don't touch anything else. Are you listening?"

85   "Can I get a drink from the water cooler?"

86   "Just one."

87   I have a morbid obscure passion for meetings. How *important* we all feel, with all those sharpened pencils and the phones shut off, and the awful twaddle we talk. I talk it too. As long as I don't lose my temper. Dorney keeps watching me, fiddling with his pen. Trouble with having all those children: tendency to haul off and holler at clients as if they'd forgotten to hang up their jackets.

88   Attention floating away a little. Tune out the client, tune in to the partition and sounds beyond. Art, far away, shouting "Stop ringing my phone!" Oh, dear. Well, I don't see how he can *hurt* the phones, and even if he does the phone company fixes them free. I think.

89   Dorney loves a meeting too. "According to statistical research obtaining optimum saturation of the area, readership-wise," he says. "Median per capita income as per the demographic charts."

90   A muffled crash. Out in the streets maybe? No. Better wind this up quick. No, no way, not with Dorney off and running, not when he sinks his teeth into per capitas, and drags out *Standard Rate and Data* and starts reading us percentages. Poor baby, we all like to feel smart. What the hell could that crash have been?

91   Muffled sound of running feet.

92   "Maximize the potential," says Dorney.

93   My eyes glaze over, I fidget uncontrollably. Two thirds of me rushes into the other room to whack my kid.

94   The client unrolls himself, says, "Well," and "Let's keep our eye on the ball here," and it's *his* turn to be important. Blast, I've been drawing spiderwebs on my note pad again. Guiltily write "Eye on the ball."

95   Over at last.

96   Water oozing out of my office to greet me, water and the sound of tears. Dorney's secretary mopping, mopping furiously, and lots of curly chunks of broken glass. Ellen comforting 3-B, who is soaked, bloody, weeping. One of

the big spare jars for the water cooler, tipped over to crash and smash. But why? And how? Those things are heavy.

97   Soppy litter of paper cups half-opened to make boats. Water creeps toward file cabinets, closer, closer; desperate mopping. Those are the temporary files, made of cardboard. Dorney's precious records, how he loves them, paid printing bills from 1962, carbons of letters saying "Enclosed please find proofs of your ad of January 11, 1971."

98   "He's hurt," says Ellen. She's glad to see me, offers me 3-B in a lump like wet laundry.

99   "Serves him right." 3-B howls convincingly. Ah, the poor chick, of course he's unruly and wicked, his mother works.

100   I step on a curl of glass and it wraps around my foot to pierce stocking and flesh. Blood. The world floats in tears. Why do I do it, why do I live like this? I can't do it any longer. I can't, nobody could. *It isn't fair.* I won't, I cannot go on any longer like this. Apologize, apologize, apologize to 3-B for bringing him here, apologize to Dorney for bringing him here. Sorry, the sitter was late. Sorry, darling, dinner isn't ready. Sorry, lambs, you have to wear yesterday's socks. Sorry, Mrs. McHenry, I couldn't come to school for the conference. Sorry, sweetie, I missed the class play. Not tonight, honey, I'm *so* tired. Sorry, Ellen, I have to leave early, I won't be in till noon, I can't make the sales meeting."

101   I won't do it any longer. I will not live this way.

102   My typewriter is buzzing angrily; its keys are jammed. I turn off the switch. Move stiffly, limping; say nothing. My phone is off the hook and its red lights twitch like nerves.

103   3-B's wounds are slight. He can hurt himself worse than that lying flat in bed.

104   Down in the elevator. 3-B nervous; I don't usually say nothing. "Are you mad? Mom?"

105   "I think I must be."

106   But he enjoys the walk home. We stop for coffee and peanut butter and at the drugstore for notebook paper, three-ring. It is trash day, the sidewalk is heaped with treasure, wealth beyond the dreams of avarice dribbles from every can, shining like emeralds. 3-B collects a broken hand mirror, a headless doll, a publicity shot of a television actor in a cowboy hat, most of a string of beads. "Wait, wait! Mom!" 3-B loves his world. For him life's an Egyptian tomb waist-deep for wallowing in curious and precious things.

107   Our own street. Alley, really. Our own neighbor, Mrs. Cavallo, who waits daily to take the bloom from my homecoming, lurking to spring. She has a petition for me to sign.

108   "It's a menace to health, that's what it is, and I've called city hall and called them, and the police too, and they absolutely refuse to do anything about it. All those dogs doing their business here in our street where the decent people live and pay taxes, too, and what for? Just to step in some dog's business? I was watching out the window this morning and that girl came by again, the one I spoke to, with the Great Dane, and let him do his business right smack in front of my house. There it is right there."

109   Exhibit A, buzzing with flies.

110   "Well, they have to go somewhere," I say weakly. "It's because it's a side street. They take them off the main drags, where there's so much traffic."

111   "I want every single person on this street to sign this, and then just let them try to laugh it off. I want *police action.*"

112   A squadron of our finest, sirens moaning, revolvers drawn, holding a poodle at bay. "One step closer, dog!" I sign, though.

113   "I should think you'd be angry especially, and you with them kids." There's a threat in her voice. I had just better be angry, or maybe she'll report me too. What kind of a mother am I?

114   What kind of a mother am I?

115   "Mrs. Cavallo, I'm too busy to be angry. Excuse me. Come on, kiddo."

116   There are cereal bowls all over the table and I forgot to put the milk away. The dog sobs with joy to see us. What is there in the freezer that will melt in time for dinner? I put the wash in the dryer and turn it on. Another section of the day begins, and miles to go before I sleep.

117   In five minutes they'll be home, all of them, a solid block of noise saying, "Mom, listen, I have to have a new gym suit and I have to have it by tomorrow, shut up, *I'm* talking, my teacher *said*—" . . ."and I hate school and I'm never going back!" "Can I have a cookie? Can Rob come over and play? Can you walk him over? Can I tell him?" "One hundred on the spelling test and I was the only one in the room!" "Look, I made it in Art, you're not *looking*!"

118   They close in on me, pulling at bits of my flesh and clothing for attention. One of these days I will come apart in their hands, and each child will have a little scrap of me to shout at.

119   I won't do it any more. I can't live like this.

120   Dinner. Sometimes little bits of dinner, burned or raw or still in the cracked saucers from the refrigerator, but on time; sometimes, guiltily, a real dinner, seasoned and sauced, made from recipes that mysteriously stretch out longer and later until my husband has a headache and the children quarrel and drowse over their plates. But always dinner.

121   The red marks on 3-B's chest fade peacefully.

122   My husband says, "Why do you insist on reading them a story every night? You're tired, you have all these dishes to do. Can't they watch television instead? You're just making more work for yourself."

123   "My mother always read to us."

124   Who'd believe we *owned* so many dishes? If I smashed half of them, would life be easier?

125   I can't live this way. He's right, I'm making work for myself, I have built myself into a *completely impossible situation.* I won't do it any more. Am I a victim of the Protestant work ethic? Am I trying to sweat off some buried guilt and in the process knocking more and more guilt down on my head? Am I that disgusting new word they keep using, a workaholic? I will stop it.

126   Stop what?

127   What is there to give up? I stare wildly around me, and see the dog. He

sees me seeing him, from the floor close to my ankles. If I gave up the dog, it would be one less thing to feed, one less dish to wash, one less scrap of attention to hand out. His ears flatten to his head and he slaps his tail on the floor; this was what he was waiting for, all day, me to look at him. It is enough, he says. Just see me, every two or three days. I'll wait. My throat chokes with sentimental tears. Give up such inexpensive love?

128   Not the dog. What, then? Which of my brown-eyed children shall I stop putting Band-Aids on? Give them all away to passing strangers, maybe Ellen? Or shall I give up my husband, the other adult around here, whom I greet occasionally as we pass each other in the shouting chaos, signal to, like people passing in a fire or a shipwreck?

129   The job, then. Stay home, make do, watch from the windows for dogs to poop? No, the job is mine. I clutch it fiercely, it is the thing I do for *me*, the place where I feel grown up and nobody calls me Mom; it is my self-indulgence, my bubble bath. They pay me money and call me a human being, and I spend the money and no man may question it, or say it was extravagant, buying those ice skates for Number One. It was extravagant, *my* extravagance. I won't give up my job, I need not to be Mom sometimes.

130   I could hire someone to clean the house. But the house is my flesh and blood, my second skin. Would I hire someone to wash my neck? I want to be alone here with my bellowing horde, my private mess. Remember that nurse I had for the 3's, she scared the liver out of everyone, including me; Number 2 sleeps with a light on since then.

131   There is nothing to give up. *All* these things are self-indulgences. Even the brown-eyed kids, even the dirty dishes. I do them for me, because I want to.

132   I stop stirring tomorrow's orange juice and look at the wall with my mouth open. For a moment it seems so terribly simple. Tomorrow it will seem complicated again, but for this instant I seem to see it so clearly. I can have everything, do everything I want. All I have to do is work, and it seems for one blinding moment such a small price to pay for such a lovely life; seems such a simple thing to do.

QUESTIONS

1. The main character describes both positive and negative feelings about her work in advertising. Describe both aspects and account for her feelings.

2. Explain the meaning of the story's title.

3. Discuss the dilemma the main character faces in trying to work, manage a household, and be a mother and wife.

4. The author suggests that women are not receiving the same treatment and given the same opportunities as men. Explain how this is made clear to the reader.

5. The main character has a certain degree of independence that is shown to the reader on several occasions. Analyze this statement, agree or disagree

with its premise, and support your position by citing specific references in the text.

6. The main character states: "I won't do it any longer. I will not live this way." Why then does she refuse to quit work or allow herself to hire a housekeeper to assist in daily chores? Explain.

7. The author uses two terms to describe the main character's attitude to work and her position in society: *workaholic* and *a victim of the Protestant work ethic*. Explain the meaning of these two terms and evaluate whether these terms appropriately reflect on her character and behavior. Support your answer by specific references in the story.

8. This story was written in 1977. If it were written today, would you expect the author's experiences to be the same? Explain.

 # THE TECHNOLOGY CONNECTION

Technology has transformed and continues to change the nature of work. From the wheel, which made hauling loads easier, to the computer, each advance in technology has made physical labor easier and faster. But these advances come at a price. Goods that were formerly handmade by many people are now made faster and at lower cost by machines. This move from manual labor to machine labor has displaced millions of workers. Technology develops exponentially—that is, developments come ever quicker because of thousands of related discoveries, and inventions increase the body of knowledge upon which to draw and simultaneously solve problems that had halted further progress. What impact will the burgeoning wave of technology have on the workers of the future? In the following excerpt from his text, William Bridges explores how technology is affecting the nature of work.

Change and the Transformation of Work

WILLIAM BRIDGES

William Bridges, Ph.D., is a business consultant, lecturer, and authority on change and managing change. A former professor at Mills College, California, he is currently president of William Bridges and Associates and the originator of transitions seminars on the West Coast. He is the author of Creating You &

Co. *(1997),* Job Shift *(1994),* Managing Transitions *(1991), and* Transitions *(1980).*

GEARING UP

1. Every generation experiences changes. Many people feel that our present generation is experiencing greater changes than in the past. Do you agree or disagree? Explain.

2. Interview someone who is at least twice your age to determine if there is a product that they once used that is now obsolete or has been replaced by another improved version. Report your findings.

The Reading

Change and the Transformation of Work
by William Bridges

1   We all know that change is more frequent today than in the past, but the reason why is not widely understood. Anyone who thinks about the speedup of change must sense that it has a lot to do with modern technology. You can see the link when you notice how short the new high-tech-product life cycles are becoming and how whole new industry sections appear almost overnight. An example: Watchmaking changed relatively little for more than a century, and timepieces were sold in watch and jewelry shops. But new technology created this rapid sequence of events:

- Timex turned the watch into a tiny electric motor and shifted watch sales to drugstores.

- Casio made the watch into an information-generating piece of electronic equipment and moved the watch business into electronics stores and departments.

- And Swatch reinvented the watch as a piece of designer clothing, to be sold (where else?) in clothing stores.

2   We also read that scientific discoveries are coming along so fast now, that most of what we now know was discovered only in the past decade. And the big new discoveries have the power to change whole sectors of the economy. Who knows, for example, what the pharmaceutical business will look like when the potentials of genetic engineering have been realized? Who knows what digitized images will do to our communication, or what video telephones will do to our need for travel? When such possibilities are widely capitalized upon, what will that do to the airline business, or to airplane manufacturers? What will it do to the hotel and restaurant business, and to the construction industry and equipment makers that serve it?

3   But such effects notwithstanding, if new products were the only way that technology affected the world of work, the job would be relatively safe:

jobs lost in one sector of the economy would be added in another. Technology affects jobs more directly in the way it changes how work is actually done. Those effects fall into three primary clusters.

Technology and Change 1: "Informating" the Workplace

4   Shoshana Zuboff coined the verb *to informate,* to describe the way information technology inserts "data" in between the worker and the product. The factory worker no longer manipulates the sheet of steel; he manipulates the data about the steel. Work that has been informated is no longer physical but is, instead, a sequence or pattern of information that can be handled and changed almost as if it were tangible. An order, once entered into a salesperson's laptop in a customer's office, becomes simply data, and it automatically triggers a chain of data events with a minimum of further human intervention.

- in the purchasing department, where necessary materials and components are ordered;

- at the suppliers' sites, where those orders are received and a comparable chain of electronic events initiates the preparation and shipment of what has been ordered;

- at the receiving dock, where the ordered goods arrive and where the finished product is later sent out to the market;

- in the factory, where the product specifications are coded into the computer-aided manufacturing (CAM) system and the product is turned out by largely automated machinery;

- at the accounts payable and receivable departments, where payment is made for the materials and an invoice is sent for the products;

- and at a dozen other points along the production-delivery route, such as the salesperson's electronic file, which will calculate the commission due on the sale, and the factor's production records, which will dictate everyone's bonus at the end of the year.

At each step along the way, people who used to fill out and file papers are made redundant. (Seeing how Mazda Motors had informated its accounts-payable system woke Ford Motor Company up to its possible savings. Mazda, which is admittedly a good deal smaller than Ford, did with five—yes *five!*—employees what Ford was using four hundred to accomplish.) Obviously, informated work needs fewer people.

5   We knew that automation would change how work was done, but until recently we still saw the future as an extension of the past. We pictured the twenty-first-century workplace as inhabited by dozens of little robots, humming around the floor doing humanoid things with their mechanical little arms. Instead of simply making products robotically, informated systems provide us with services—like ATM that gives us cash we need at all hours of the day and night. Instead of rooms full of R2D2s dashing around

retrieving things from files and mailing them to new locations, we have a computer network that gives employees a continent away access to the data in our electronic database. Instead of electronic brains making enormously complex decisions (like, should we send up the rocket or not?), computer programs make ordinary decisions (like, should we loan the customer $100,000 or $150,000?). Instead of "smart machines" replacing all the manual labor on the factory floor, they are replacing the mental labor in the middle-management offices. (No wonder that middle managers made up more than one in five of the layoffs in the current round of downsizing, even though they make up only one in ten workers.)

6   In showing how informated systems transform white-collar work, I don't want to leave the impression that informating has not changed how products are manufactured or that, in the process, it has not caused job losses in manufacturing. It has. At the Charlottesville, Virginia, GE Fanuc Automation plant, the production of circuit boards has doubled without an increase in employees. Wilson Chen, president of another circuit-board maker, Santa Clara, California's Solectron, has said, "If I had to produce this year's run with the old machinery, I would have had to nearly double my work force to 8,000 people."

7   We have hardly scratched the surface of the way informated work will affect our lives. Consider what the "smart card" (a card with an embedded programmable chip, already widely used in France and Japan) will do to clerical work at your bank. You hand your card to the cashier at a restaurant and she runs it through a scanner. The system not only records a charge—the way your present credit card does—but also instantaneously deducts the appropriate amount of money from your account, credits it to the restaurant account, and records your new balance on the card's embedded chip. Just like that.

8   There is no list of charges at the end of the month (and no workers to prepare that list), no processing the check you write to pay your credit card bill (and no workers to handle that check), no payment from the credit card company to the restaurant (there go more workers at both ends of that transaction). One has to wonder how far the process will go. Will this electronic wizardry end up transforming wealth so completely into credit data that money too will finally disappear (and with it all the workers who used to manufacture it and handle it)?

9   But don't stop there. What happens to jobs when similar cards—or enhanced ones, based on optical-disk technology—can be encoded with your whole medical history, the medication you currently take, your ten most recent blood-pressure readings, the image of your last chest X ray, and all the details of your medical insurance policy? All that record keeping and file storage at your doctor's office and the insurance company and the hospital will be unnecessary, and so will the jobs of the people who ran those departments. In a decade or so, we'll consider today's medical-data practices as archaic as the hand-copying of medieval manuscripts.

10   It's not just the clerical jobs that are being replaced by computer-driven systems. WHDH-TV in Boston now does all its studio filming with six

robotic cameras, coordinated by one technician seated in front of a touch-screen PC. Standard shots (those of news anchors, for example) are pro-grammed into a database. But the station's computers do much more. Virtually every activity—from budgeting to videotape editing—is integrated into a computer network. In the process, the station has become very prof-itable. Not coincidentally, it has only half as many employees as it did in 1988.

11   The process of informating our labors goes on everywhere. Colombian drug lord Pablo Escobar, describing the primitive conditions in the prison from which he subsequently escaped, was quoted by *Fortune* as saying, "We were fifteen prisoners, and there were only three computers."

Technology and Change 2: The Business of Data

12   Technology also renders jobs obsolete by replacing the relatively slowly changing world of "things" with the much more mercurial world of "data." Things have to be assembled or processed from raw materials by teams of workers; data are typed into a terminal by a single worker—or even hand-written on or spoken into tomorrow's computers. Things require space for storage; we need staffed stockrooms to maintain an inventory. Data take up almost no space, can be maintained by users, and can be duplicated as needed. We hear a lot today about "information workers" and how different they are from the old-style workers of the mechanical age. No wonder.

13   Peter Drucker estimates that the new workers, who work with data in-stead of things, "already number at least one-third and more likely two-fifths of all employees." This figure is significant, because our assumptions about jobs—the very concept of job itself—fitted the task-patterns dictated by the labor divisions necessary to run a mechanistic system. Long produc-tion runs, extended chains of command, fixed job descriptions—all these things made sense in the slower-moving factories and offices of the pre-electronic world. But today these things are too rigid. The structures, proce-dures, and roles of the past are too slow for a world driven and networked by electronic data, for as Safi Quereshy, the cofounder and CEO of AST Re-search, said recently, "The computer business is changing so quickly these days that sometimes we feel as if we're in the fresh-produce business." (If the recent genetically altered tomato lives up to its promise, vegetables may start having a longer shelf life than laptops.)

14   We still picture production on the model of a General Motors factory or a Chevron oil refinery, but such thinking is outmoded. As Nuala Beck has recently pointed out, the center of economic gravity has already moved from those "old" industries to the "new" ones of computers, biotechnology, and other data-based industries. Drawing on recent U.S. Census and Depart-ment of Labor statistics, she demonstrates conclusively that

> a fact of life today is that more Americans work in the computer industry as a whole (equipment, semiconductors and computer services) than in the auto, auto parts, steel, mining and petroleum-refining industries combined. . . .
> More Americans work in biotechnology than in the entire machine-tool

industry. . . . Twice as many Americans make surgical and medical instruments as make plumbing and heating products.

More evidence for the same extraordinary shift is found in the fact that in 1970, American corporations spent 11 percent of their durable-equipment outlays on information-processing equipment. In 1989 that figure had risen to 51 percent, and it is certainly higher still today.

15   Located along the growing edge of the economy and driven by the fastest-changing elements in modern technology, these "new" organizations have moved furthest away from traditional jobs. We'll see how they got their work done in the next chapter, but as a foretaste of their style and substance, consider this explanation (by a Silicon Valley manager to Rosabeth Moss Kanter) of how his job was defined.

> In my position, the nature of the duties can change a lot depending on the ex-
> pertise and interest of the individual. For example, if I were really anxious to
> travel and instruct, I could look around for some topics that aren't well docu-
> mented and make myself an expert on those topics, and tell management that
> someone needed to go out and teach a course in that. In general, there's more
> work to do than people to do it, so you look at your position and you say,
> there are lots of things that would be appropriate for me to do. I have a con-
> science, I'll do what needs to be done. If I'm selfish, I'll do what I want to do.
> So there is a lot of flexibility.

That's not a job description in the conventional sense.

Technology and Change 3: Communications Technology as "Multiplier"

16   In 1815, on the eve of American industrialism, the United States fought the Battle of New Orleans even though a peace treaty had already been signed to end the War of 1812. At that time, it took so long for information to move from one place to another that change could spread only slowly. Steam engines might be used to pump water out of coal mines in England, but in America it would still be buckets for a long time. A crop could fail in Canada, a king could be executed in France, a war could erupt in Asia, and a famine could ravage Africa—while elsewhere things went along unaffected and unchanged.

17   But today the weather predictions for drought-ravaged Africa, the morning's gold price in Tokyo, the latest hitch in negotiations in the Middle East, the new unemployment figures from Washington, and the announcements of job cuts at a European multinational corporation and of new software from a small American startup—they all reach us simultaneously. Now add to those events all the changes made *in reaction to* those primary changes (and also communicated everywhere at once). Of course, those secondary changes in turn create changes in reaction.

18   In this way technology, and particularly communications technology, introduces a "multiplier effect" that interlocks the whole world such that time and distance no longer buffer us against the effects of change. In the

past, if there were a thousand change events worldwide during any given period, only four or five of them would have been experienced in any one
place. But today's world is a great, electronic spider web, where footsteps
anywhere are felt by individuals everywhere, so that today we experience
hundreds of those thousand changes. No wonder we say that there is more
change today.

QUESTIONS

1. "The big new discoveries have the power to change whole sectors of the
   economy." Explain.

2. Discuss how technology affects jobs. Cite one example from the reading.

3. Explain the concept of "informating" the workplace. Discuss how this
   development is affecting the workplace.

4. The author cites researchers who claim that workers who work with
   "data" instead of "things" are a growing part of the employee pool. Explain and discuss the implications of this finding.

5. The author claims that in today's age of rapid communication, technology introduces a multiplier effect, and "time and distance no longer
   buffer us against the effects of change." Explain this concept and illustrate
   how this applies to our times.

MAKING CONNECTIONS

Work and Careers

1. Career counselors cite several issues that prospective job seekers need
   to consider when they are investigating a job. Among the issues are the
   following:

   - Job satisfaction
   - Pay
   - Working conditions
   - Human relations
   - Recognition

   - Job alienation
   - Job security
   - Advancement opportunities
   - Meaningful work
   - Need to serve others

   Relate any five of these issues to the McDonald's workers, Dr. Stephanie
   B., Jan Halvorsen, and the main character in Barbara Holland's story.

2. From the various issues and concerns raised in this unit, which ones
   do you think will be of greatest significance to you in your career?
   Explain.

3. Halvorsen relates how it feels to be unemployed and speaks about her own work ethic morality. How is this issue related to Michener's observations?

4. The author James Michener asked: "What shall we take pride in when we tell our children what we have done?" Select at least three individuals you encountered in this unit. How would they respond to this question?

5. "Tomorrow's Jobs" and "Managing Workforce Diversity in Organizations" share some similar conclusions about the changes taking place in the labor market. Select at least one issue that is discussed in both readings and explain the changes that we are experiencing and can expect to experience in the coming years. Support your answer by citing data presented in both readings.

6. Relate Shreve's messages about the role of women in the workplace to the ideas developed in "Tomorrow's Jobs," "Managing Workforce Diversity in Organizations," and "The Day's Work."

7. To succeed in today's job market, individuals need to be educated and literate. Agree or disagree with this statement based on your reading of "So You Want to Be a Physician/Ophthalmologist," "Solving the Job Puzzle," "Tomorrow's Jobs," and "Change and the Transformation of Work."

8. "Tomorrow's Jobs" identifies several factors that will affect the work force of the future. Select one individual from this unit and predict how three of these factors would affect the person and his or her profession.

9. Trace the issue of job satisfaction through the following articles: "McDonald's—We Do It All for You," "So You Want to Be a Physician/Ophthalmologist," "How It Feels to Be Out of Work," and "The Day's Work." Begin by defining the term and stating a thesis. If you use material directly from any of the articles, be sure to quote and give credit.

10. Technology continues to affect the job market. Agree or disagree with this statement by citing information from the unit's introduction as well as from the following readings: "Solving the Job Puzzle," "Tomorrow's Jobs," and "Change and the Transformation of Work."

LIBRARY ASSIGNMENT

Career Exploration

Purpose

The purpose of this activity is to give you an opportunity to explore and then prepare a report on a career of your choice. By gathering basic information on your chosen career, you will be able to plan more wisely for your future. You can use various materials to complete this assignment, but the *Occupational Outlook Handbook* (available online at *http://stats.bls.gov/ocohome. htm*) and *The Encyclopedia of Careers and Vocational Guidance* will be especially useful. Both of these reference texts are available in many libraries.

In addition to the *Occupational Outlook Handbook* that is now available online, the Internet has many resources available for career exploration. It is important to realize, however, that many Internet sites change and that some of the resources that follow might not be current or may have ceased to exist. As of May 1997, here are the Internet addresses and brief descriptions of some of the most popular career resource sites:

http://www.ajb.dni.us

America's Job Bank, run by the U.S. Department of Labor, is updated weekly and lists about 250,000 jobs. Most are in the private sector, with 5 percent of the jobs in government. You can apply for jobs online.

http://www.careermosaic.com

Career Mosaic maintains a vast job placement and job search engine, as well as areas devoted solely to health care jobs and international jobs. The site also has some special sections: "Career Resources" offer tips on résumé writing and salaries, and "Online Job Fairs" tell you where career fairs are being held near you.

http://www.CareerPath.com

CareerPath contains classified ads taken from twenty-five U.S. newspapers. Users can search under several categories and titles to locate many potential job offers.

http://www.monster.com

In addition to listing thousands of jobs, Monster Board also offers a customized job search agent. Other features are career advice from career counselor Joyce Kennedy, employer profiles, and communities such as College & Entry Level.

http://www.occ.com

OCC claims to post over 40,000 job listings and provides users with the option to post their own résumés. In addition, you can research a particular company or get outplacement assistance.

http://www.aboutwork.com/career/index.html

About Work lets you search numerous careers and obtain information about career profiles and major employers.

http://www.espan.com

E-Span pioneered online recruiting in 1991 and posts approximately 10,000 jobs. Candidates can post their résumés for free.

http://www.jobtrak.com/jobguide/

Margaret Riley, author of *The Guide to Internet Job Searching*, has an excellent online resource: *The Riley Guide: Employment Opportunities and Job Resources on the Internet*. This site has numerous links to a variety of job and career resources.

Report Requirements

Your report should contain the following:

1. Job or career title—a specific name or title

2. Description—the nature of work, duties and responsibilities, working conditions, and places of employment

3. Qualifications—the skills and special training required

4. Wage and salary structure—the income range that can be anticipated

5. Advancement and growth opportunities—how one can move ahead and develop

6. Outlook—the employment outlook and future prospects of the career or job

7. Conclusion—why this career is right for you and why it might satisfy you

   Write as much as necessary to describe each of these areas. Your answers should be brief but accurate and complete. Use full sentences.

   In addition, write and then send a letter to one professional organization in which you request information related to your career. (Both reference books mentioned above provide the names and addresses of professional organizations.) Attach a copy of your letter to your report.

   By completing this assignment, you should be able to answer the following questions:

- What kind of work would you do?

- What skills and abilities are required?

- How do you know if you would like this work?

- How do you know if you could learn to do this type of work?

- What must you do to prepare to enter this field?

UNIT

THREE

Mass Media

READINGS IN UNIT THREE

1. "Television Changed My Family Forever" from *Move On: Adventures in the Real World* by Linda Ellerbee

Ellerbee recalls the impact television had on her family and the changes it brought about.

2. "Only Good If You Can Trust It" by Tom Brokaw

Brokaw maintains that throughout history the value of any medium was dependent on whether its message was trustworthy.

3. "Introduction to the Mass Media" from *Media Impact* by Shirley Biagi

Biagi explores how the mass media have revolutionized the way we communicate and discusses their impact on society.

4. "Television" from *The Read-Aloud Handbook* by Jim Trelease

An advocate of reading examines what watching television does to youngsters.

5. "Don't Blame TV" by Jeff Greenfield

A television commentator cautions us to examine our reasoning and evidence before we condemn television for a host of problems.

6. "Can Your Students Read TV?" by Kathleen Tyner

Tyner suggests a method whereby students can be taught to critically evaluate what they view on television.

7. "The Language of Advertising Claims" by Jeffrey Schrank

Schrank instructs readers on how to critically examine advertising claims.

8. "The Evolution of the Newspaper of the Future" by Christine Lapham

Lapham explores how computer technology and the Internet are likely to affect the newspaper industry.

9. From *Bullet Park* by John Cheever

A father and son argue about excessive television viewing.

10. "Too Much Information, Too Little Time" by Joe Saltzman

Saltzman argues that new forms of media are overloading us with too much information.

INTRODUCTION

We live in an age of mass media. We are bombarded by daily messages transmitted to us via radio, television, newspapers, magazines, motion pictures, advertisements, and newer channels of communication like the Internet and World Wide Web. It is difficult to imagine a world devoid of radios, television sets, videocassette recorders, newspapers, and magazines. Consider the following statistics that suggest how much the media are part of our lives:

- 98% of American households have a television set.
- 98% of American households have a radio.
- 65% have cable television.
- 87% of American households have a VCR.
- Americans spent $10 billion on music in 1994.
- There are more than 10,000 radio stations in the U.S.
- U.S. movie box office receipts totaled $5.5 billion in 1995.
- Total U.S. advertisement spending in 1996 approached $60 billion.

The table on page 335 presents additional data from the 1997 edition of the *U.S. Statistical Abstracts* that highlight media usage and consumer spending from 1989 through 1999 (projected). One can see how newer technologies such as cable television and consumer online and Internet services are beginning to assume a major part of the media picture.

We are witnessing a change in the mass media as communications and information technologies converge to support our information-based society. At one time the media were seen as separate entities with their own production and distribution systems. New technologies are helping to blur the distinctions between traditional forms of media. Today a newspaper story can be prepared on a word processor and sent by satellite or high-speed modem on fiber-optic cable to an editor, who arranges to have it "published" on the World Wide Web for mass circulation while it is still being distributed via the traditional newsstand and home delivery channels. We can turn on our television news programs and receive up-to-the-minute dispatches from correspondents all over the globe equipped with portable cellular telephones, satellite transmission devices, fax machines, and laptop computers hooked up to high-speed modems. With appropriate equipment, many of these broadcasts can also be received via the Internet.

Johannes Gutenberg, known for his invention of the printing press in the fifteenth century, would be amazed at the speed with which the printed word is transmitted in our time. The ability to reach millions of people simultaneously through telecommunication technology is based largely on innovations that have emerged only in the last one hundred years. In 1963, most Americans received news of President Kennedy's assassination within thirty minutes. By contrast, in 1865, it took several months for news of President Lincoln's assassination to spread throughout the country. Fifty years ago television was the revolutionary medium that let us see and hear beyond our living rooms. During the past half century the medium has developed and evolved to incorporate newer forms of technology such as cable, satellite transmission, and now HDTV (high-definition television). By contrast, the Internet is developing and changing even more rapidly. Some researchers claim that the Internet is creating its own unique blend of media that doesn't fit neatly into our more traditional models of print or broadcast media. Although it differs from radio, television, newspapers, and magazines, it offers some of the same information but often in unique ways. For example, it is possible to receive radio and television broadcasts via the World Wide Web or participate in an online town meeting with a presidential candidate. Rarely a week goes by without some announcement of a new technology that will revolutionize the World Wide Web.

Assessing the Impact of the Media

We are so accustomed to obtaining information from the mass media that we sometimes fail to consider them from a broader perspective. In this unit we will explore various issues related to mass media and their impact on us. Because of their widespread presence in our lives, it is important that we reflect on how they are influencing our views, values, expectations, and behaviors—in short, how they are shaping our society. The questions that follow should help you focus on the mass media's impact.

- What role do the media play in our lives? How do they affect us?

- How do the media influence or persuade us? What values are being communicated to us?

- Are the mass media flooding us with too much information? Can we process all of this information and distinguish between what is real and not real, important and not important?

- Are we shifting away from a print culture to a visually oriented society? Do we spend more time watching TV than reading? Do we get our news from TV or from newspapers? How does television news differ from news derived from the press? Are we more influenced by a candidate's image in a thirty-second commercial than by his or her written statements on various complex policy issues?

- How much time do we spend watching television compared with other activities? What would we do if we weren't watching television? Does television stimulate or inhibit our thinking? Does it open our eyes to new worlds and ideas, or does it dull our imaginations? Does television make us withdraw from the outside world or become more active participants?

- How much control do the mass media have over us? How does the violence so prevalent in the media affect children's attitudes and beliefs? Do the media help shape our opinion or our view of the world? Do we choose our role models from the media?

- Are we losing our individuality by becoming part of a "mass culture" influenced by the same messages, or will newer technologies offer us more choices, provide greater diversity, and promote individuality by allowing viewers to choose what they want to see?

- Are we able to differentiate between real life and life portrayed in the media? Should the media, particularly television and the movies, be responsible for accurately representing the world?

- Do radio, television, and print advertisements give us valuable information, or do they merely promote our desire for material goods of questionable value?

- Are we "critical" viewers? Can we make critical judgments of the media—to question, analyze, challenge, and evaluate information?

CONNECTING THEMES

As you study this unit, it should become clear that it can be connected to the previous two units, "Reading and Literacy" and "Work and Careers," and to the next unit, "The Family." Here are some broad issues posed as questions to consider as you begin to work with this unit and relate it to the other units.

"MASS MEDIA" AND "READING AND LITERACY"

How can television and reading be compared and contrasted? Does one medium influence the other? Can television stimulate people to read and become more literate? Or does it promote antireading attitudes and foster lower literacy levels? Does television viewing require the same effort as reading a book? With the availability of so much news via the Internet, do we have time to filter and process important information?

"MASS MEDIA" AND "WORK AND CAREERS"

Do mass media present an accurate view of the working world? What types of occupations and careers are portrayed on television, in the movies, and in advertisements? Are certain careers and occupations overrepresented in the mass media in proportion to their true numbers in the real world? What work values are emphasized in the mass media? What kinds of work-related decisions are people shown making? Are women seen as gainfully employed? Are union members represented on shows? What picture of work and careers emerges from most television shows, movies, and advertisements?

"MASS MEDIA" AND "THE FAMILY"

How have mass media's portrayal of families changed over the years? Do the media present an accurate picture of the American family today? Which family values are stressed, and which are not? Are the families that you see on the TV screen, in the movies, and in advertisements similar in behavior to yours, or are they different? Do you expect or want your family life to resemble the life of families portrayed in the media? What role should parents play in controlling children's use of media?

What You Can Expect in This Unit

In this unit you will study a number of articles related to mass media and learn strategies to process text efficiently and effectively. After completing this unit, you should be able to do the following:

Content
- Cite the various mass media and define each.
- Discuss the positive and negative effects of mass media on society.
- Recognize various forms of advertising claims.
- Compare and contrast the effect of television and reading on youngsters.
- Understand how the newspaper industry is changing.

Process
- Analyze an ad for truthfulness.
- Critically examine information in table form.
- Demonstrate the ability to view television critically.
- Compare and contrast different views on a media issue.

Strategies
- Read and analyze tables.
- Understand allusions.
- Recognize connotation and denotation.
- Analyze conflicting opinion.

Mass Media: A Connecting Exercise

In reading and studying, it is important both to recall the major points an author is making and to connect this information to your prior learning. But as a proficient reader, you must go beyond this: You should determine the author's purpose and bias, evaluate the source(s) of information, and form an opinion about what the author says. In short, a proficient reader reads critically.

In this unit, you will read about various concerns related to the mass media. You will find that certain key issues appear in several articles. The purpose of the exercise that follows is to help you keep track of specific information found in the articles and to allow you to formulate your critical reactions to these issues.

One way to study the mass media is to examine both their positive and negative aspects. Some of the articles you are about to read focus primarily on this question, whereas others address the issue indirectly. The follow-ing chart will help you record information related to this question. You can use it in the form given or adapt it as you see fit.

1. Article	2. Positive Aspects	3. Negative Aspects	4. Critical Reaction

Before reading each article in the unit, record its title in column 1 of the chart. After reading, list the positive aspects of the mass media mentioned in the article in column 2 and the negative aspects in column 3. Do *not* express your opinion or offer any evaluation in these two columns; simply record your findings. If a particular article does not address this issue, leave a blank space. In column 4, enter your critical reaction to the positive and/or negative aspects identified in the article. This step requires that you evaluate the author's ideas and decide whether or not you accept them. You must examine the evidence the author presents. Be prepared to explain the reasons for your evaluation.

Here are some questions to keep in mind as you formulate your critical reaction.

1. Is the author presenting facts or opinions?

2. Does the fact that something is published necessarily make it true?

3. What evidence is offered in support of the author's points? Are there other sides that are not being presented? Does the author show bias?

4. What is the purpose of the article—to present factual information or to persuade us to believe a particular idea?

5. Are the author's conclusions reasonable on the basis of the information presented?

This chart is offered as a sample. As you continue to develop your own learning and studying techniques, you should design your own charts to help organize and record your ideas.

Media Usage and Consumer Spending: 1989 to 1999

[Estimates of time spent were derived using rating data for television and radio, survey research and consumer purchase data for recorded music, newspapers, books, home video, admissions to movies, and consumer on-line/Internet access services. Adults 18 and older except for recorded music where estimates include persons 12 and older.]

| YEAR | Total[1] | TELEVISION | | | | Recorded music | Daily newspapers | Consumer magazines | Consumer books | Home Video[4] | Consumer on-line/Internet access services |
		Network stations	Independent stations[2]	Basic Cable[3]	Pay Cable						
HOURS PER PERSON PER YEAR											
1989	3,278	835	345	210	95	220	175	90	96	39	(Z)
1990	3,267	780	340	260	90	235	175	90	95	42	1
1991	3,257	838	227	340	90	219	169	88	98	43	1
1992	3,329	914	159	359	78	233	172	85	100	46	2
1993	3,302	920	162	375	78	248	170	85	99	49	2
1994	3,402	919	172	388	81	294	169	84	102	52	3
1995 proj.	3,434	913	185	398	84	317	164	82	101	53	5
1996 proj.	3,457	909	205	408	78	323	163	81	100	54	8
1997 proj.	3,489	896	221	420	78	343	161	80	101	56	11
1998 proj.	3,528	899	224	435	77	365	160	80	103	57	13
1999 proj.	3,560	884	231	449	81	387	159	80	105	58	14
CONSUMER SPENDING PER PERSON PER YEAR (dollars)											
1989	331.65	–	–	77.86	(5)	32.25	45.71	31.49	61.24	50.71	2.22
1990	365.43	–	–	87.90	(5)	36.64	47.55	33.14	63.90	56.35	2.93
1991	378.77	–	–	94.44	(5)	37.73	46.56	33.45	68.18	58.69	3.61
1992	403.15	–	–	101.28	(5)	43.05	48.54	34.26	71.37	63.23	4.39
1993	428.19	–	–	108.54	(5)	47.42	48.25	35.27	74.90	68.42	5.35
1994	456.26	–	–	110.00	(5)	56.35	49.28	36.36	79.22	72.97	7.44
1995 proj.	492.35	–	–	117.84	(5)	62.36	52.67	38.79	84.20	78.19	11.23
1996 proj.	525.74	–	–	128.65	(5)	65.07	55.78	40.53	88.89	81.47	16.34
1997 proj.	563.32	–	–	137.16	(5)	70.76	58.08	42.12	93.91	86.47	21.82
1998 proj.	601.55	–	–	145.75	(5)	77.29	60.61	43.75	100.03	89.85	27.03
1999 proj.	639.17	–	–	154.30	(5)	83.92	62.76	45.53	107.19	93.56	29.95

– Represents zero. (Z) means less than 1 hour. [1]Includes other media, not shown separately. [2]Affiliates of the Fox network are counted as network affiliates for part of 1991 and all latter years, but as independent stations in earlier years. [3]Includes TBS beginning in 1992. [4]Playback of prerecorded tapes only. [5]Included with basic cable.

Source: Veronis, Suhler & Associates Inc., 350 Park Avenue, New York, NY, 10022. (212)935-4990.

READING STRATEGY

READING TABLES

In Unit Two (see page 178) the general strategy of reading visual information was introduced and applied specifically to reading graphs. Now we will examine another type of visual—a table that is commonly found in college textbooks. The introduction to the media unit that appears on the preceding pages has some facts and statistics related to the use of media in our society. A table was included that presented information about media usage and consumer spending (see page 335).

Why are tables included in so many texts? Basically, tables use numbers, data, and statistics and present them in some organized manner. They help the reader make comparisons and note trends. Reading a table takes time and effort and is a skill that develops with practice. Unlike bar graphs and pie graphs, which are highly visual and attractive in nature, tables can look dense and be challenging to read. Here is a table taken from the 1997 *U.S. Statistical Abstracts.*

Lottery Sales—Type of Game, 1980 to 1995 and Use of Proceeds, 1964–1995
[In millions of dollars. For fiscal years]

Game	1980	1985	1990	1992	1994	1995	Use of Profits, 1964–1995	Cumulative[1]
Total ticket sales	2,393	9,035	20,017	22,069	28,514	31,931	TOTAL	92,922
Passive[2]	206	88	(NA)	(NA)	(NA)	(NA)	Education	52,061
Instant[3]	527	1,296	5,204	6,104	9,681	11,511	General fund	21,133
Three-digit[4]	1,554	3,376	4,572	4,767	5,294	5,737	Cities	9,013
Four-digit[4]	55	693	1,302	1,637	1,872	1,941	Senior citizen programs	8,708
Lotto[5]	52	3,583	8,563	8,506	10,024	10,594		
Other[6]	(NA)	(NA)	409	1,055	1,642	2,148	Economic development	1,385
State proceeds (net income)[7]	978	3,735	7,703	8,118	9,977	11,100	Environment	485
							Other	137

NA Not available. [1]Cumulative profits tracks lottery revenue to government from March 12, 1964–June 30, 1995 [2]Also known as draw genre or ticket Player must match his ticket to winning numbers drawn by lottery. Players cannot choose their numbers [3]Player scratches a latex section on ticket which reveals instantly whether ticket is a winner. [4]Players choose and bet on three or four digits, depending on game with various payoffs for different straight order or mixed combination bets. [5]Players typically select six digits out of a large field outnumbers. Varying prizes are offered for matching three through six numbers drawn by lottery. [6]Includes breakopen tickets, spiel, keno, video lottery, etc. [7]Sales minus prizes and expenses equal net government income.

Source: TLF Publications Inc., BoyUs, MD, 1996 World Lottery Almanac annual; LaFleur's Fiscal 1995LotterySpecialReport; and LaFleur's Lottery World Government Profits Report (copyright).

From the 1997 *U.S. Statistical Abstracts,* "Lottery Sales—Type of Game and Use of Proceeds: 1980 to 1995." Reprinted by permission.

Let's examine how this table is arranged and see how it can be studied.

Title ➤

Lottery Sales—Type of Game, 1980–1995 and Use of Proceeds, 1964–1995
[In millions of dollars. For fiscal years] ◀─────────── Headnote

Game	1980	1985	1990	1992	1994	1995	Use of Profits, 1964–1995	Cumulative[1]
Total ticket sales	2,393	9,035	20,017	22,069	28,514	31,931	TOTAL . . .	92,922
Passive[2] . . .	206	88	(NA)	(NA)	(NA)	(NA)	Education . . .	52,061
Instant[3] . . .	527	1,296	5,204	6,104	9,681	11,511	General fund . . .	21,133
Three-digit[4] . . .	1,554	3,376	4,572	4,767	5,294	5,737	Cities . . .	9,013
Four-digit[4] . . .	55	693	1,302	1,637	1,872	1,941	Senior citizen programs . . .	8,708
Lotto[5] . . .	52	3,583	8,563	8,506	10,024	10,594		
Other[6] . . .	(NA)	(NA)	409	1,055	1,642	2,148	Economic development . . .	1,385
State proceeds (net income)[7] . . .	978	3,735	7,703	8,118	9,977	11,100	Environment . . .	485
							Other . . .	137

The title should give the first clue to the contents of the table. What does the table title suggest about its focus?

_____

_____

Below the title some additional information is provided in the form of a headnote. In this case the reader is told that the revenues presented in the table are expressed in millions of dollars and that certain fiscal (financial) years are being considered.

Most tables present information horizontally and vertically. Typically, categories are listed horizontally and items in each category are listed vertically. The table that indicates that two issues concerning the lottery will be addressed:

a) type of game and b) use of proceeds

Game	1980	1985	1990	1992	1994	1995	Use of Profits, 1964–1995	Cumulative[1]
Total ticket sales	2,393	9,035	20,017	22,069	28,514	31,931	TOTAL	92,922
Passive[2]	206	88	(NA)	(NA)	(NA)	(NA)	Education	52,061
Instant[3]	527	1,296	5,204	6,104	9,681	11,511	General fund	21,133
Three-digit[4]	1,554	3,376	4,572	4,767	5,294	5,737	Cities	9,013
Four-digit[4]	55	693	1,302	1,637	1,872	1,941	Senior citizen programs	8,708
Lotto[5]	52	3,583	8,563	8,506	10,024	10,594		
Other[6]	(NA)	(NA)	409	1,055	1,642	2,148	Economic development	1,385
State proceeds (net income)[7]	978	3,735	7,703	8,118	9,977	11,100	Environment	485
							Other	137

Also, note that the under game category, there are a series of small numbers (superscripts) attached to certain games such as Passive[2] or Lotto[5]. These numbers refer to information found in fine print in the table's footnotes.

Let's enlarge the footnotes a bit so that they are more readable.

NA Not available. [1]Cumulative profits tracks lottery revenue to government from March 12, 1964–June 30, 1995 [2]Also known as draw genre or ticket Player must match his ticket to winning numbers drawn by lottery. Players cannot choose their numbers [3]Player scratches a latex section on ticket which reveals instantly whether ticket is a winner. [4]Players choose and bet on three or four digits, depending on game with various payoffs for different straight order or mixed combination bets. [5]Players typically select six digits out of a large field outnumbers. Varying prizes are offered for matching three through six numbers drawn by lottery. [6]Includes breakopen tickets, spiel, keno, video lottery, etc. [7]Sales minus prizes and expenses equal net government income.

Source: TLF Publications Inc., BoyUs, MD, 1996 World Lottery Almanac annual; LaFleur's Fiscal 1995LotterySpecialReport; and LaFleur's Lottery World Government Profits Report (copyright).

Sometimes neglecting to read the fine print can limit one's understanding of a table. In the example, the footnotes explain the meaning of some games (e.g., passive) and clarify what is meant by "State proceeds (net income)." Also, note that on the right side of the table (in the last column) the word *cumulative* is explained in the first footnote. After the footnotes comes the source of the data.

Having done this preliminary work, you are ready to study the table in detail. Survey the rows and columns. Look for similarities, differences, and sudden or unexpected changes. Pay attention if totals or differences are provided (e.g., increases, decreases, percentage changes). Ask yourself:

- What information is contained in each column?

- What type of data is presented?

- What do the data represent?

- What is the unit of measurement?

- How are the data classified or organized?

- What point of time do the data represent?

- What conclusions can be drawn?

- What predictions can be made?

Here are some questions to test your comprehension:

- What type of lottery game saw the greatest increase in the time period studied?

- What type of lottery game saw the greatest decrease in the time period studied?

- What segment of government benefited most from lottery revenues?

- What conclusion(s) can be drawn regarding the lottery sales in the time period studied?

Application

Return to the table on page 335, "Media Usage and Consumer Spending: 1989 to 1999" and answer the following questions:

- What conclusions can be drawn regarding the number of hours spent per person on media during the time period presented?

- What conclusions can be drawn with respect to the dollar amount spent per person on media during the time period presented?

- Why is the letter "Z" placed under the "Consumer on-line/Internet access services" for the year 1989?

- What trends can be noted in the television category? (Be sure to include network, independent stations, and cable.)

- What type(s) of media saw the greatest growth?

- What type(s) of media saw the greatest decline?

Television Changed My Family Forever

LINDA ELLERBEE

Linda Ellerbee has been involved in mass media as a television producer, writer, anchor, and host. She established Lucky Duck Productions, *which has produced award-winning news programs for children, as well as a variety of specials for television, including programs on breast cancer (ABC), unsafe sexual practices (MTV), and addiction (HBO). Her book about television,* And So It Goes, *remained on the* New York Times *best-seller list for eighteen weeks. The following article is taken from her second book,* Move On: Adventures in the Real World *(1991).*

GEARING UP

Describe how television may affect your family. Imagine your family suddenly had to give up television. Consider the impact of such a change on your family's day-to-day functioning (relaxation, coping with stress, mealtime conversation, etc.).

READING STRATEGY CHECK
READING NARRATIVES

If you began this textbook with Unit One, you may have read one or more of the autobiographical accounts in which the writers describe how reading affected their lives. This excerpt is also autobiographical and follows a narrative and descriptive writing style; that is, it tells a story and uses details. In this excerpt, the writer relates how television affected her in her formative years. She tells a story and uses words that describe emotions, feelings, and impressions. As you read this selection, focus on the following questions:

1. Who are the characters in the account? How would you describe their personalities?

2. Where and when does the story take place (the setting and time period)? Does the historical period or the location have any special significance?

3. How does the story line develop?

4. Does the author express a particular mood (happiness, sadness, anger, frustration, amusement)?

5. What does the author want you to remember from this excerpt? How does the excerpt relate to the author's feelings about television?

6. What conflicts or problems, if any, make up the major action of the story (for example, humans versus humans, humans versus society, humans versus nature)? Are these conflicts resolved in the story? If so, how?

7. How relevant is the theme of the work and the issues discussed in today's world?

8. What have you learned from the excerpt about life in general (values, the role of the family, etc.)? Has the excerpt encouraged you to reexamine any of your values or beliefs? Does it support or contradict your own values?

9. How well did you relate to the feelings of the central character?

When you have completed the reading and are thinking about the above questions, you may find the following scheme helpful in organizing your thinking.

Setting	Characters	Plot	Conclusion
Time/place	People in key roles	Major events	Message(s)

The Reading

Television Changed My Family Forever

by LINDA ELLERBEE

1   Santa Claus brought us a television for Christmas. See, said my parents, television doesn't eat people. Maybe not. But television changed people. Television changed my family forever. We stopped eating dinner at the dining-room table after my mother found out about TV trays. We kept the TV trays behind the kitchen door and served ourselves from pots on the stove. Setting and clearing the dining-room table used to be my job; now, setting and clearing meant unfolding and wiping our TV trays, then, when we'd finished, wiping and folding our TV trays. Dinner was served in time for one program and finished in time for another. During dinner we used to talk to one another. Now television talked to us. If you had something you absolutely had to say, you waited until the commercial, which is, I suspect, where I learned to speak in thirty-second bursts. As a future writer, it was good practice in editing my thoughts. As a little girl, it was lonely as hell. Once in a while, I'd pass our dining-room table and stop, thinking I heard our ghosts sitting around talking to one another, saying stuff.

2   Before television, I would lie in bed at night listening to my parents come upstairs, enter their bedroom and say things to one another that I couldn't hear, but it didn't matter, their voices rocked me to sleep. My first memory, the first one ever, was of my parents and their friends talking me to sleep when we were living in Bryan and my bedroom was right next to the kitchen. I was still in my crib then. From the kitchen I could hear them, hear the rolling cadence of their speech, the rising and falling of their voices and the sound of chips.

cadence

3   "Two pair showing."

4   "Call?"

5   "Check."

6   "Call?"

7   "Call." *Clink.*

8   "I raise." *Clink clink.*

9   "See your raise and raise you back." *Clink clink clink.*

10   "Call," *Clink Clink.*

11   "I'm in," *Clink.*

12   "I'm out."

13   "Let's see 'em."

14   It was a song to me, a lullaby. Now Daddy went to bed right after the weather and Mama stayed up to see Jack Paar (later she stayed up to see Steve Allen and Johnny Carson and even Joey Bishop, but not David Letterman). I went to sleep alone, listening to voices in my memory.

15   Daddy stopped buying Perry Mason books. Perry was on television and that was so much easier for him, Daddy said, because he could never remember which Perry Mason books he'd read and was always buying the wrong ones by mistake, then reading them all the way to the end before he realized he'd already read them. Television fixed that, he said, because although the stories weren't as good as the stories in the books, at least he knew he hadn't already read them. But it had been Daddy and Perry who'd taught me how fine it could be to read something you liked twice, especially if you didn't know the second time wasn't the first time. My mother used to laugh at Daddy. She would never buy or read the same book again and again. She had her own library card. She subscribed to magazines and belonged to The Book-of-the-Month Club. Also, she hated mystery stories. Her favorite books were about doctors who found God and women who found doctors. Her most favorite book ever was *Gone With the Wind,* which she'd read before I was born. Read it while she vacuumed the floor, she said. Read it while she'd ironed shirts. Read it while she'd fixed dinner and read it while she'd washed up. Mama sure loved that book. She dropped Book-of-the-Month after she discovered *As the World Turns.* Later, she stopped her magazine subscriptions. Except for *TV Guide.* I don't know what she did with her library card. I know what she didn't do with it.

16   Mom quit taking me to the movies about this time, not that she'd ever take me to the movies very often after Mr. Disney let Bambi's mother get killed, which she said showed a lack of imagination. She and Daddy stopped going to movies, period. Daddy claimed it was because movies weren't as much fun after Martin broke up with Lewis, but that wasn't it. Most movies he cared about seeing would one day show up on television, he said. Maybe even Martin & Lewis movies. All you had to do was wait. And watch.

17   After a while, we didn't play baseball anymore, my daddy and me. We didn't go to baseball games together, either, but we watched more baseball than ever. That's how Daddy perfected The Art of Dozing to Baseball. He would sit down in his big chair, turn on the game and fall asleep within five minutes. That is, he appeared to be asleep. His eyes were shut. He snored. But if you shook him and said, Daddy, you're asleep, he'd open his eyes and tell you what the score was, who was up and what the pitcher ought to throw next. The Art of Dozing to Baseball. I've worked at it myself, but have never been able to get beyond waking up in time to see the instant replay. Daddy never needed instant replay and, no, I don't know how he did it; he was a talented man and he had his secrets.

18   Our lives began to seem centered around, and somehow measured by, television. My family believed in television. If it was on TV, it must be so. Calendars were tricky and church bells might fool you, but if you heard Ed Sullivan's voice you *knew* it was Sunday night. When four men in uniforms sang that they were the men from Texaco who worked from Maine to Mexico, you *knew* it was Tuesday night. Depending on which verse they were singing, you knew whether it was seven o'clock or eight o'clock on Tuesday night. It was the only night of the week I got to stay up until eight o'clock.

My parents allowed this for purely patriotic reasons. If you didn't watch Uncle Milty on Tuesday nights, on Wednesday mornings you might have trouble persuading people you were a real American and not some commie pinko foreigner from Dallas. I wasn't crazy about Milton Berle, but I pretended I was; an extra hour is an extra hour, and if the best way to get your daddy's attention is to watch TV with him, then it was worth every joke Berle could steal. Later I would find another solution, far more bizarre but ten times as effective.

19   Television was taking my parents away from me, not all the time, but enough, I believed. When it was on, they didn't see me, I thought. Take holidays. Although I was an only child, there were always grandparents, aunts, uncles and cousins enough to fill the biggest holiday. They were the best times. White linen and old silver and pretty china. Platters of turkey and ham, bowls of cornbread dressing and sweet potatoes and ambrosia. Homemade rolls. Glass cake stands holding pineapple, coconut, angel food and devil's food cakes, all with good boiled icing. There was apple pie with cheese. There were little silver dishes with dividers for watermelon pickles, black olives and sliced cranberry jelly. There was all the iced tea you'd ever want. Lord, it was grand. We kids always finished first (we weren't one of those families where they make the kids eat last and you never get a drumstick). After we ate, we'd be excused to go outside, where we'd play. When we decided the grown-ups had spent enough time sitting around the table after they'd already finished eating, which was real boring, we'd go back in and make as much noise as we could, until finally four or five grown-ups would come outside and play with us because it was just easier, that's all. We played hide-and-seek or baseball or football or dodge ball. Sometimes we just played *ball*. Sometimes we just played. Once in a while, there would be fireworks, which were always exciting ever since the Christmas Uncle Buck shot off a Roman candle and set the neighbor's yard on fire, but that was before we had a television.

20   Now, holiday dinners began to be timed to accommodate the kickoff, or once in a while the halftime, depending on how many games there were to watch; but on Thanksgiving or New Year's there were always games so important they absolutely could not be missed under any circumstances, certainly not for something as inconsequential as being "it" and counting to ten while you pretended not to see six children climb into the backseat of your car.

21   "Ssshhh, not now, Linda Jane. The Aggies have the ball."

22   "But you said . . . you promised . . ."

23   "Linda Jane, didn't your daddy just tell you to hush up? We can't hear the television for you talking."

patriotic

bizarre

accommodate

inconsequential

QUESTIONS

1. Analyze the author's attitude toward television. Support your response by citing specific references from the narrative.

2. Contrast the author's feelings about television with those of her parents.

3. Discuss television's impact on Ellerbee's parents' reading behavior.

4. List and describe at least five ways television changed the author's family life.

5. The author states, "Our lives began to seem centered around, and somehow measured by, television." Explain this statement based on the article.

EXTENDING YOUR VOCABULARY

cadence: The cadence of the waves breaking on the shore was interrupted by _____

patriotic: Patriotic songs are usually sung when _____

bizarre: We were puzzled by his bizarre behavior because

_____

accommodate: In order to accommodate the president's schedule, the manager of the show decided to _____

inconsequential: Don't bother me with inconsequential matters because

_____

Only Good If You Can Trust It

TOM BROKAW

Tom Brokaw, anchor and managing editor of NBC Nightly News with Tom Brokaw, has been sole anchor for NBC Nightly News since 1983. He is a recipient of the Peabody Award and numerous Emmy's, and has written essays for the New York Times, the Washington Post, and Sports Illustrated.

GEARING UP

1. What methods are available to keep in touch with others that were not available to our parents?

2. How can the accuracy of information received through the mass media be checked?

READING STRATEGY CHECK
DETERMINING THE AUTHOR'S PURPOSE

The strategy of Determining the Author's Purpose was first introduced in relation to the Jill Halvorsen article, "How It Feels to Be Out of Work" on page 234. Learning the author's purpose helps you understand the text. In the Halvorsen piece we learn that the author was unemployed at the time she wrote the article, and thus you can expect that she will list a number of personal reactions to this situation. Furthermore, we can assume that a well-written essay in a national publication might lead to a job.

In the Brokaw article, might he feel compelled to defend the TV news against charges of inadequate coverage and sensationalistic reporting? Furthermore, network news is a business. If Brokaw can instill in the reader's mind that at least he is concerned about fair, accurate news, then viewers might choose his program over the other news choices. How would this help the network?

The Reading

Only Good If You Can Trust It

by TOM BROKAW

1   WHEN I BEGAN TO GET INVOLVED in broadcasting and journalism as a teenager, I lived in a world of AM-only radio, rotary-dial telephones, long-distance operators, black-and-white televisions (one set per household), and really only two networks, NBC and CBS.

2   Now I work for one of five networks, competing against tenacious cable systems offering news all the time or music all the time or sports all the time or history all the time. I send email to my colleagues and download editorial information from one of three PCs in my home, office, and traveling backpack. I make telephone calls from airplanes, cars, and street corners.   *tenacious*

3   Whenever anything happens almost anywhere in the world, we can count on getting a signal and a picture via a portable satellite that can be set up in a camping tent or on the back of a pickup truck—as they were in Somalia. Moreover, even if we don't have our own camera crew at the site, it's likely someone will have a home video camera with broadcast quality tape.

4   Mass media have never been more mass. We're all better for it if we always keep in mind one fundamental truth: Ultimately, information is useful   *fundamental*
only if you can trust it. Is it factual? What's the source? How does it fit with other information?

5   Technology alone cannot provide those critical tests. Mass media work best when they have intelligent, curious people of independent judgment examining and testing information in a raw, shapeless form before it lands on your television set, computer screen, or radio.

6   That was true when news was passed by word of mouth, from cave to cave. It is especially true now that all of the computers in the world have the capacity to be hooked together via the Internet. That technology has so swiftly widened the universe of information and communication that even the founding geniuses of cyberspace struggle to define its magnitude and dis-   *magnitude*
cover its applications.

7   My crystal ball is not flawless, but I strongly believe that in the future   *flawless*
we'll have a mix of all of the various media: over the air, satellite, cable, and the Internet. They will complement one another. Indeed, in some cases they   *complement*
will be combined by enterprising visionaries. As information consumers we'll shift easily from the large screen to the small screen and back again, downloading, uploading, surfing, browsing, printing, and emailing to our heart's content.

8   Maybe even one day I'll be able to spend the early morning hours fly-fishing, rock climbing, or horseback riding in my beloved American West, and then boot up my cell-powered computer and work on the production of NBC Nightly News until it's time to mosey over to the satellite truck parked streamside and go on the air.

9   All of that is possible, if not practical. What is neither practical nor possible is my ability to explain to you how the picture gets from where I work to where you watch it.

10   Trust me. It's a miracle. Leave it at that.

QUESTIONS

1. Explain the author's choice of title for this selection. Discuss the relationship of the title to the content of the selection.

2. Brokaw compares mass media today to his teenage years. Describe the changes he notes and explain why he chose to contrast the two time periods.

3. Analyze the author's tone. Is he critical, optimistic, or pessimistic? Explain.

EXTENDING YOUR VOCABULARY

tenacious: Because of her tenacious courage, she was able to

_____

fundamental: A fundamental right provided to us in the Constitution is

_____

magnitude: People didn't realize the magnitude of the situation until

      _____

flawless: Because of the lawyer's flawless reasoning, _____

      _____

complement: She thought that a bright scarf would complement her

dress because _____

➡ PROCESS GUIDE

Brokaw begins the article by giving you some background on his career in journalism. He reports on the technology of his youth.

1. Some articles do not contain the author's main point in the first paragraph. Rather, the author chooses to lead you into the main idea through background or a story. Brokaw has given you some introductory material but does not introduce the main point of the article until paragraph 4. Paraphrase his idea.

_____

_____

2. Brokaw tells us that the major concern in any kind of news is whether it can be trusted. How does Brokaw suggest that we test the trustworthiness of news?

_____

_____

3. From the issue of trust, Brokaw moves on to speculate on the news of the future. What form does Brokaw see for the news of the future, and how does he see himself in the process?

_____

_____

4. The final sentence begins with "Trust me." Note the connection with the article's title. In what regard is Brokaw asking you to trust him?

_____

_____

Introduction to the Mass Media

SHIRLEY BIAGI

Shirley Biagi is professor of journalism at California State University, Sacramento, and has served as guest faculty at other institutions. She is the author of Interviews That Work *and has written numerous magazine articles.*

GEARING UP

1. How would our daily lives differ if we lacked mass media?

2. The mass media (e.g., newspapers, magazines, television, radio, books, recordings, movies) are a big business designed to make a profit. How do they generate revenue and income?

3. What mass media are available today that did not exist one hundred years ago?

READING STRATEGY

MAPPING INFORMATION

This text has emphasized the importance of being an active reader. By previewing text, activating prior knowledge by answering gearing-up questions, and by creating marked copies of readings, you have seen how a reader and text can interact. Postreading questions, the various Process Guide activities, and the selected charts and tables that you were asked to complete are other examples of how a reader can engage the text. Information mapping is another strategy that you can use to become a more active and ultimately a proficient reader. As its name implies, information mapping involves the creation of a visual representation of text. You are providing a map or picture of how ideas are organized, presented, and related to one another. Creating a map of how information is presented can help your comprehension and recall. In fact, you could even use this strategy as a prereading activity to explore what you already know or would like to know about a topic.

There is no single way to visualize information, and not all textual material lends itself to mapping. Usually you start your map by focusing on the key concept or main idea and then work your way down to the details. As you proceed, you provide connectors that show the relationship between the major points and the details. Here are just two of many possibilities to present the process:

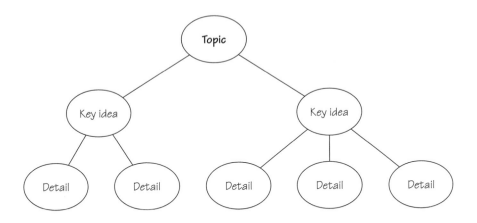

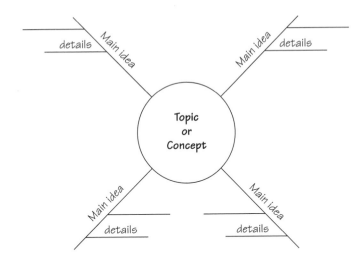

Consider the following outline dealing with the topic of "Technology" taken from the *World Book Encyclopedia.*

Technology

I. Benefits of technology
   A. Increased production
   B. Reduced labor
   C. Easier labor
   D. Higher living standards

II. Undesirable effects of technology
   A. Environmental pollution
   B. The depletion of natural resources
   C. Technological unemployment

II. The challenge of technology
   A. Combating undesirable effects
   B. Preventing undesirable effects
   C. Spreading the benefits of technology

This same information could be mapped to appear as follows:

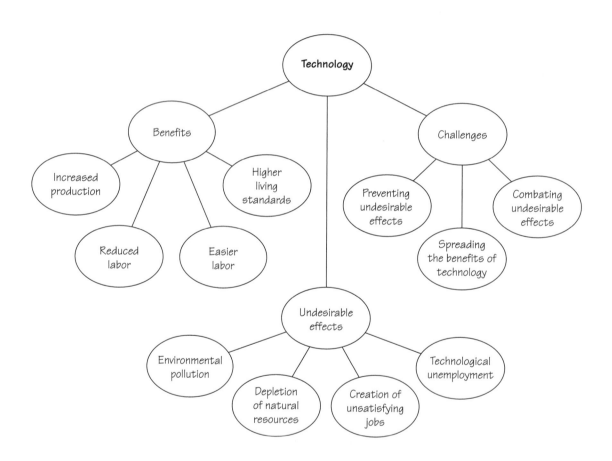

Application

In the chapter "Introduction to the Mass Media," Shirley Biagi discusses the media as business and shows that there are basically five forms of concentration of ownership. One way to "map" this information might be the following:

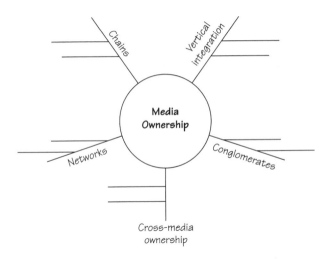

Next to each form of ownership you will find two blank lines. Read this portion of the article (see pages 357–359) and add one or two key details.

Try your hand at mapping information. Beginning on page 363, Biagi discusses "Three Communications Revolutions." Create an information map that lists the major points and supporting details.

 # READING STRATEGY CHECK

READING TEXTBOOK CHAPTERS

The strategy of reading textbook chapters and studying for exams was introduced in connection with the "Managing Workforce Diversity in Organizations" chapter in Unit Two (page 251). There are a number of things to keep in mind before you approach a reading assignment the length of a textbook chapter.

1. First, size up the task. This includes noting what the instructor expects you to learn from the chapter as well as the amount of time you have to prepare the material. Additionally, be aware of features in the chapter to help you, such as headings, objectives, questions, and a summary. These should be noted and used to your advantage.

2. Second, have a reading and study plan. We suggested the following approach, which is described in detail in Unit Two.

   A. Strategies before you read carefully
      1. Gearing up
      2. Previewing
      3. The read through
   B. Strategies during the careful reading
      1. Marking text
      2. Predicting vocabulary
      3. Reading exposition I and II
      4. Periodic assessment
   C. Strategies after you read
      1. Checking comprehension
      2. Reviewing ideas
      3. Discussing ideas/revising understanding
      4. Synthesizing ideas

3. Third, have a plan for taking an exam. The following was suggested:

   A. The exam time frame
   B. Preparation
      1. Preparing the material
      2. Preparing the question type
      3. Preparing yourself
   C. Exam practice
   D. Sizing up the exam
   E. Exam strategy

The Reading

Chapter 1

INTRODUCTION TO THE MASS MEDIA

There's hardly anything you could conceive of today in the information and entertainment field that you can't try. It's that kind of world.
John Malone, Chief Executive Officer, Tele-Communications Inc. (TCI)

1 **W**hen was the last time you spent 24 hours without the media? From the moment you get up in the morning until the time you go to bed at night, the media are waiting to keep you company. Radio news gives you headlines in the shower and traffic reports on the freeway; the newspaper offers you national and local news and helps you keep up with the latest college bas-

ketball standings and Garfield's attempts to steal another piece of lasagne; magazines describe new computer software for work, and during your lunch hour they keep you current with the latest fashions; after work, the newest novel competes with your videocassette recorder, beckoning you to spend an evening with the hottest video release.

2　　According to industry estimates, the average adult spends more than half of his or her waking life with the media. This is the breakdown of the way Americans divide their time watching, listening, and reading:

- About 62 percent of all adults read a daily newspaper, 75 percent of all adults read a newspaper at least once a week.

- Adults read an average of ten magazines a month.

- On weekdays adults listen to the radio an average of 3 hours and 20 minutes a day.

- Each household leaves the TV set turned on for an average of 7 hours and 15 minutes a day; adults watch TV an average of 4 hours a day.

- One out of four adults goes to the movies once a month; adults with a VCR rent an average of one videocassette a week.

- Each American spends an average of $55 per year on recorded music.

- Half of all Americans buy at least one book a year; the average library user borrows fifteen items a year.

3　　Some form of mass media touches nearly every American every day—economically, socially, or culturally. The mass media can affect the way you vote and the way you spend your money. They sometimes influence the way you eat, talk, work, study, and relax. This is the *impact* of mass media on American society.

4　　This wide-reaching presence distinguishes American media from the media in other countries. In no other country do the mass media capture so much of people's time and attention. In no other country do the media affect so many aspects of the way people live. And in no other country do the media collect so much money for delivering information and entertainment. The American mass media industries earn about $175 billion a year (see Figure 1.1).

5　　Today's American society has inherited the wisdom and the mistakes of the people who work in the mass media and the society that regulates and consumes what the mass media produce. Consider these situations:

- You are a newspaper publisher in a small New England town in the 1700s. You publish an article that angers the local council, and they throw you in jail. Yet, you want to continue to publish the newspaper. What would you do?

- You have just bought a computer and you want to stay current with new developments in software. You subscribe to *PC World* and *Mac-World*. How does your choice of magazines reflect the changes in the magazine industry?

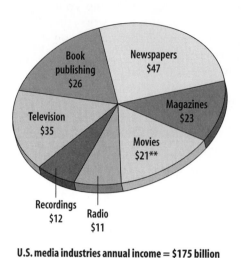

FIGURE 1.1
**Relative Size of the U.S.
Media Industries, 1994**

U.S. media industries annual income = $175 billion

Source: Data from *The Veronis, Suhler & Associates Communications
Industry Forecast,* 1994–1998.

- You are in a bookstore with $10 to spend. You can't decide whether to buy a novel by Stephen King, a book of poems by Maya Angelou, a travel guide to Mexico, or a collection of "Calvin & Hobbes" cartoons. What are the economic consequences of these decisions by book buyers for the publishing industry?

- You have just bought a small radio station in a big-city market and you need programming. How can you program your station cheaply and quickly?

- You believe you have been misquoted and misrepresented in a major magazine story written by a freelance journalist, so you sue the author and the magazine. The case eventually reaches the U.S. Supreme Court. What implications will the court decision have on the media's liability for the stories they print and broadcast?

implications

6   People who work in the media industries and people who watch, listen to, read, and govern what the media offer make choices like these every day. The future of American mass media will be determined by these choices.

The Communication Process

7 To understand the mass media, first it is important to understand the process of communication. Communication is the act of sending ideas and attitudes from one person to another. Writing and talking to each other are only two ways human beings communicate. We also communicate when we gesture, move our bodies, or roll our eyes.

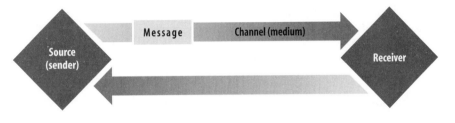

Message   Channel (medium)   Source (sender)   Receiver

FIGURE 1.2
Elements of Mass Communication
The process of mass communication: A sender (source) puts a message on a channel, which is the medium that delivers the message to the receiver. Feedback occurs when the receiver responds, and that response changes subsequent messages from the source.

8   Three terms that scholars use to describe how people communicate are *intrapersonal communication, interpersonal communication,* and *mass communication.* Each communication situation involves different numbers of people in specific ways.

9   If you are in a grocery store and you silently discuss with yourself whether to buy a package of chocolate chip cookies, you are using what scholars call *intrapersonal communication:* communication within one person.

10   To communicate with each other, people use many of the five senses—sight, hearing, touch, smell, and taste. Scholars call this direct sharing of experience between two people *interpersonal communication.*

11   **Mass communication** is communication from one person or group of persons through a transmitting device (a medium) to large audiences or markets. In MEDIA/IMPACT you will study mass communication.

12   To describe the process of mass communication, scholars draw charts and diagrams to convey what happens when people send messages to one another. This description begins with five easily understood terms: *sender, message, receiver, channel,* and *feedback* (see Figure 1.2).

13   Pretend that you're standing directly in front of someone and that you say, "I like your hat." In this simple communication, you are the sender, the message is "I like your hat," and the person in front of you is the receiver (or audience). This example of interpersonal communication involves the sender, the message, and the receiver.

14   In the mass communication, the **sender** (or **source**) puts the message on what is called a **channel.** The sender (source) could be your local cable company, for example. The channel delivers the *message.* The channel could be the cable line that hooks into the back of your TV set. A **medium** is the means by which a message reaches an audience. (The plural of the word *medium* is *media;* when scholars discuss more than one medium they refer to **media.**) Your television set is the medium that delivers the message simultaneously to you (and many other people).

15   **Feedback** occurs when the receivers process the message and send a response back to the sender (source). Using a very crude example, say that the cable company (sender/source) sends an advertisement for pizza (the message) over the cable line (channel) into your TV set (medium). If you (the receiver) use the controls on your interactive TV set to order a pizza, the order you place will ultimately bring you a pizza (feedback).

crude

ultimately

This entire loop between sender and receiver, and the resulting response (feedback) of the receiver to the sender, describes the process of mass communication.

16   Using a very general definition, mass communication today shares three characteristics:

1. A message is sent out using some form of mass media (such as newspapers or television).

2. The message is delivered rapidly.

3. The message reaches large groups of different kinds of people simultaneously or within a short period of time.   *simultaneously*

Thus, a telephone conversation between two people would not qualify as mass communication, but a message from the president of the United States, broadcast simultaneously by all of the television networks, would qualify.

17   Mass media deliver messages to large numbers of people at once. The businesses that produce the mass media in America—newspapers, magazines, radio, television, movies, recordings, and books—are mass media industries.

Understanding the Mass Media Industries: Three Key Themes

18   This book uses the term **mass media industries** to describe the seven types of American mass media businesses: newspapers, magazines, radio, television, movies, recordings, and books. The use of the word *industries* underscores the major goal of mass media in America—financial success.

19   But the media are more than businesses: They are key institutions in our society. They affect our culture, our buying habits, and our politics, and they are in turn affected by changes in our beliefs, tastes, interests, and behavior. To help organize your thinking about the mass media and their impact, this section introduces three key themes that will recur in the chapters to come: The media are profit-centered businesses; technology changes the media; and the media both reflect and affect the political, social, and cultural institutions in which they operate.

1. The Media as Businesses

20   What you see, read, and hear in the American mass media may cajole, entertain, inform, persuade, provoke, and even perplex you. But to understand the American media, the first concept to understand is that the central force driving the media in America is the desire to make money: *American media are businesses, vast businesses.* The products of these businesses are information and entertainment.   *cajole*

21   Other motives shape the media in America, of course: the desire to fulfill the public's need for information, to influence the country's governance, to disseminate the country's culture, to offer entertainment, and to   *disseminate*

provide an outlet for artistic expression. But American media are, above all, profit-centered.

22   **WHO OWNS THE MEDIA?**   To understand the media, it is important to know who owns these important channels of communication. In America, all of the media are privately owned except the Public Broadcasting Service and National Public Radio, which survive on government support and private donations. The annual budget for public broadcasting, however, is less than 3 percent of the amount of money advertisers pay every year to support America's commercial media.

23   Many family-owned media properties still exist in the United States, but today the trend in the media industries, as in other American industries, is for media companies to cluster together in groups. The top ten newspaper chains, for example, own one-fifth of the nation's daily newspapers. This trend is called concentration of ownership, and this concentration takes five different forms.

24   *1. Chains.*   Benjamin Franklin established America's first newspaper chain. This tradition was expanded by William Randolph Hearst in the 1930s. At their peak, Hearst newspapers accounted for nearly 14 percent of total national daily circulation and nearly 25 percent of Sunday circulation. Today's newspaper chain is Gannett, with more than 80 daily newspapers, including *USA Today.*

25   Broadcast companies also own chains of stations, called networks. But the **Federal Communications Commission (FCC)** regulates broadcast ownership. Today one company can own up to 12 TV stations, 20 AM radio stations, and 20 FM radio stations, as long as the total number of stations doesn't reach more than 25 percent of the national audience.

26   *2. Networks.*   A network operates in the same way as a newspaper chain. It is a collection of radio or television stations that offer programs, usually simultaneously throughout the country, during designated program times. The four major networks are ABC (American Broadcasting Company), NBC (National Broadcasting Company), CBS (Columbia Broadcasting System), and Fox Broadcasting. NBC, the oldest network, was founded in the 1920s. This network and the two other older ones (CBS and ABC) were established to deliver radio programming across the country, and the network concept continued with the invention of television. Networks can have as many affiliates as they want, but no network can have two affiliates in the same broadcast area. (Affiliates are stations that use network programming but that are owned by companies other than the networks.)

27   Fox is the youngest network, founded in 1986, and serves only television. Time Warner and Paramount Communications launched fifth and sixth networks in 1995.

28   *3. Cross-Media Ownership.*   Many media companies own more than one type of media property: newspapers, magazines, radio and TV stations, for example. Gannett, which owns the largest chain of newspapers,

also owns television and radio stations. Among the properties of Capital Cities/ABC are the *Kansas City Star, Modern Photography* magazine, San Francisco's KGO radio, KGO-TV, and the ABC network. Rupert Murdoch's News Corporation owns newspapers, television stations, magazines, 20th Century-Fox Film, and Fox Broadcasting.

29 *4. Conglomerates.*   When you go to the movies to watch a Columbia picture, you might not realize that Sony owns the film company. Sony is a *conglomerate*—a company that owns media companies as well as companies unrelated to the media business. Media properties can be attractive investments, but some conglomerate owners are unfamiliar with the idiosyncrasies of the media industries.

30 *5. Vertical Integration.*   The most noticeable trend among today's media companies is **vertical integration**—an attempt to control several related aspects of the media business at once, each part helping the other. Besides publishing magazines and books, Time Warner, for example, owns Home Box Office (HBO), Warner movie studios, and various cable TV systems throughout the United States. The Japanese company Matsushita owns MCA Records and Universal Studios and manufactures broadcast production equipment. Viacom owns TV stations, movie theaters, and cable networks as well as the book publishing company Simon & Schuster.

31   To describe the financial status of today's media is also to talk about acquisitions. The media are buying and selling each other in unprecedented numbers and forming media groups to position themselves in the marketplace to maintain and increase their profits. In 1986, the first time a broadcast network had been sold, *two* networks were sold that year— ABC and NBC.

acquisitions / unprecedented

32   Media acquisitions have skyrocketed since 1980 for two reasons. The first is that most conglomerates today are publicly traded companies, which means that their stock is traded on one of the nation's stock exchanges. This makes acquisitions relatively easy.

33   A media company that wants to buy a publicly owned company can buy that company's stock when the stock becomes available. The open availability of stock in these companies means that anybody with enough money can invest in the American media industries, which is exactly how CBS Board Chairman Laurence Tisch joined the media business.

34   The second reason for the increase in media alliances is that beginning in 1980, the Federal Communications Commission (FCC) gradually deregulated the broadcast media. Before 1980, for example, the FCC allowed one company to own only five TV stations, five AM radio stations, and five FM radio stations; companies also were required to hold onto a station for three years before the station could be sold. The post-1980 FCC eliminated the three-year rule and raised the number of broadcast holdings allowed for one owner. This trend of media acquisitions is likely to continue throughout the 1990s, as changing technology expands the market for media products.

35   The issue of media ownership is important. If only a few corporations direct the media industries in this country, the outlets for differing political viewpoints and innovative ideas could be limited.

36   **WHO PAYS FOR THE MASS MEDIA?**   Most of the $175 billion a year in income that the American mass media industries collect comes directly from advertisers. Advertising directly supports newspapers, radio, and television. (Subscribers pay only a small part of the cost of producing a newspaper.) Magazines receive more than half of their income from advertising and the other portion from subscriptions. Income for movies, recordings, and books, of course, comes from direct purchases and ticket sales.

37   This means that most of the information and entertainment you receive from television, radio, newspapers, and magazines in America is paid for by people who want to sell you products. You support the media industries *indirectly* by buying the products that advertisers sell.

38   Advertising pays most of the bills. One full-page black-and-white ad in *The Wall Street Journal,* for example, costs about $120,000. To place a full-page color ad in *Rolling Stone* magazine costs about $50,000. A 30-second television commercial in prime time (8 P.M. to 11 P.M.) costs about $120,000. Multiply the prices for all of these ads in all media, and you can understand how easily American media industries accumulate the $175 billion they collect annually.

39   You also pay for the media *directly* when you buy a book or a compact disc or go to a movie. This money buys equipment, underwrites company research and expansion, and pays stock dividends. Advertisers and consumers are the financial foundation for American media industries. (See Figure 1.3.)

40   **HOW DOES EACH MEDIA INDUSTRY WORK?**   Books, newspapers, and magazines were America's only mass media for 250 years after the first American book was published in 1640. The first half of the 20th century brought four new media—movies, radio, recordings, and television—in less than 50 years.

41   To understand how this happened and where each medium fits in the mass media industries today, it is important to examine the individual characteristics of each medium. (For a pie chart showing income in the media industries, see Figure 1.1.)

42   *Newspapers.*   There are about 1,600 daily newspapers in the United States. Evening papers outnumber morning papers 3 to 1, but the number of evening papers is declining. Papers that come out in the morning are growing in circulation, and papers that come out in the afternoon are shrinking. The number of weekly newspapers is also declining. Advertising makes up about two-thirds of the printed space in daily newspapers. Newspaper income is expected to remain steady over the next decade, with very little growth.

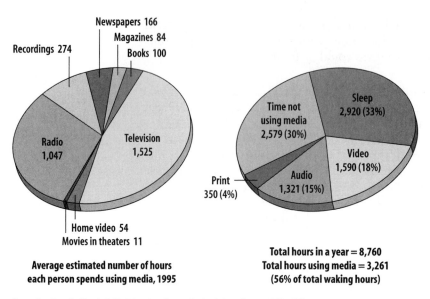

FIGURE 1.3
Yearly Time Each Person Spends Using Media, 1996 (Projected)

Recordings 274
Newspapers 166
Magazines 84
Books 100
Radio 1,047
Television 1,525
Home video 54
Movies in theaters 11

Average estimated number of hours each person spends using media, 1995

Time not using media 2,579 (30%)
Sleep 2,920 (33%)
Video 1,590 (18%)
Audio 1,321 (15%)
Print 350 (4%)

Total hours in a year = 8,760
Total hours using media = 3,261
(56% of total waking hours)

Source: Data from *The Veronis, Suhler & Associates Communications Industry Forecast, 1994–1998.*

43 ***Magazines.***   According to the Magazine Publishers of America, about 11,000 magazines are published in the United States. This number is remaining steady. To maintain and increase profits, magazines are raising their subscription and single-copy prices and fighting to maintain their advertising income. The number of magazines people buy by subscription is going up, but newsstand sales are going down. Magazine income is expected to decline slightly in the next decade.

44 ***Radio.***   More than 11,000 radio stations broadcast programming in the United States, about evenly divided between AM and FM stations. About 1,500 of these stations are noncommercial, most of them FM. The average American household owns five radios. Radio revenues are expected to grow slightly in the next decade.

45 ***Television.***   About 1,500 television stations are operating in the United States; one out of four stations is noncommercial. Many of the stations are affiliated with one of the four major networks—NBC, CBS, ABC, or FOX—although an increasing number of stations, called *independents,* are not affiliated with any network.

46   Ted Turner launched Cable News Network (CNN) in 1980 to serve cable companies. About 60 percent of the homes in the United States are wired for cable, and half of the nation's viewers receive 33 or more channels. Cable receives about 10 percent of the overall money spent on television advertising. Network income is declining, while income to independents and cable operators is going up. Total industry revenue is projected to grow slightly in the next decade.

47 *Movies.*   Nearly 25,000 theater screens exist in the United States. The major and independent studios combined make about 500 pictures a year. The industry is collecting more money because of higher ticket prices, but the number of people who go to the movies is declining.

48   The major increase in income to the movie industry in the past decade came from video sales. The year 1986 marked the first time that number of videotape rentals was higher than the number of movie ticket purchases. Industry income is expected to remain stable.

49 *Recordings.*   Compact discs account for more than half of the recordings sold. Another 30 percent of sales comes from prerecorded cassettes. Most recordings are bought by people who are under 30. The industry is expected to grow slightly, boosted by sales of compact discs.

50 *Book Publishing.*   Publishers issue about 40,000 titles a year in the United States, although some of these are reprints and new editions of old titles. Retail bookstores in the United States account for one-third of all money earned from book sales. The rest of the income comes from books that are sold through book clubs, in college stores, to libraries, and to school districts for use in elementary and high schools. Book publishing income is expected to remain stable.

51   Overall, media industries in the United States are prospering. The division of profits is shifting, however, as different media industries expand and contract in the marketplace to respond to the audience. For example, if the population's interest shifts away from the print media to video entertainment, fewer people will buy newspapers, magazines, and books, which means that these industries could suffer. (For recent trends in consumers' media spending, see Figure 1.4.) Understanding the implications of these changes is central to understanding the media as businesses.

52 2. The Media and Communications Technology

The second theme that you will encounter throughout this book is *the effect of technological change on the mass media.* The development of communications technology directly affects the speed with which a society evolves. An entire country with one telephone or one radio may be impossible for people in the United States to imagine, but there are still many countries today where ten families share a single telephone and people consider a television set to be a luxury.

53   In the United States and other countries such as Japan that have encouraged technological advancements, communications changes are moving faster than ever before. For the media industries, this means increasing costs to replace old equipment. For consumers, this means a confusing ar-   *array* ray of products that seem to be replaced as soon as they are marketed— compact discs overcoming audio cassettes, for example.

54   By today's standards, the earliest communications obstacles seem unbelievably simple: for instance, how to transmit a single message to several people at the same time, and how to share information inexpensively.

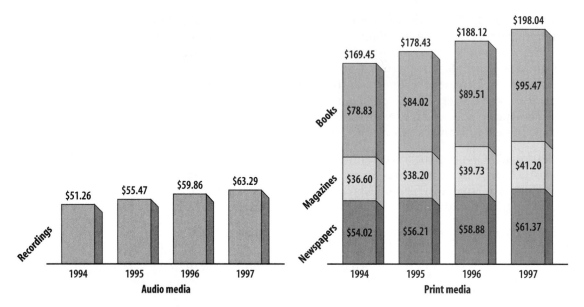

Source: Data from *The Veronis, Suhler & Associates Communications Industry Forecast,* 1994–1998.

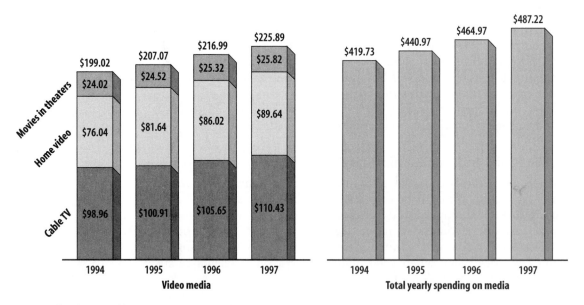

Source: Data from *The Veronis, Suhler & Associates Communications Industry Forecast,* 1994–1998.

FIGURE 1.4

How People Spend Their Media Dollars

Projected amount each person in the United States spends each year for audio media, print media, and video media.

Yet, it has taken nearly 5,500 years to achieve the capability for instant communication that we enjoy today.

55   **THREE COMMUNICATIONS REVOLUTIONS.**   The channels of communication have changed dramatically over the centuries, but the idea that a society will pay to stay informed and entertained is not new. In imperial Rome, people who wanted to know the news paid professional speakers a coin (a *gazet*) for the privilege of listening to the speaker announce the day's events. Many early newspapers were called gazettes to reflect this heritage.

56   The first attempt at written communication began modestly with pictographs. A pictograph is a symbol of an object that is used to convey an idea. If you have ever drawn a heart with an arrow through it, you understand what a pictograph is. The first known pictographs were carved in stone by the Sumerians of Mesopotamia in about 3500 B.C.

57   The stone in which these early pictographic messages were carved served as a medium—a device to transmit messages. Eventually, messages were imprinted in clay and stored in a primitive version of today's library. These messages weren't very portable, however. Clay tablets didn't slip easily into someone's pocket.

58   In about 2500 B.C., the Egyptians invented papyrus, a type of paper made from a grasslike plant called sedge. The Greeks perfected parchment, made from goat and sheep skins, in about 200 B.C. By about A.D. 100, before the use of parchment spread throughout Europe, the Chinese had invented paper, which was much cheaper to produce than parchment, but Europeans didn't start to use paper until more than a thousand years later, in about A.D. 1300. The discovery of parchment and then paper meant that storing information became cheaper and easier.

59   *The First Information Communications Revolution.*   Meanwhile, pictographs as a method of communication developed into phonetic writing, using symbols for sounds. Instead of drawing a representation of a dog to convey the idea of a dog, scholars could represent the sounds d-o-g with phonetic writing. The invention of writing has been called the *first information communications revolution.* "After being stored in written form, information could now reach a new kind of audience, remote from the source and uncontrolled by it," writes media scholar Anthony Smith. "Writing transformed knowledge into information."

60   The Greek philosopher Socrates anticipated the changes that widespread literacy would bring. He argued that knowledge should remain among the privileged classes. Writing threatened the exclusive use of information, he said: "Once a thing is put in writing, the composition, whatever it may be, drifts all over the place, getting into the hands not only of those who understand it, but equally of those who have no business with it."

61   As Socrates predicted, when more people learned to write, wider communication became possible because people in many different societies

could share information among themselves and with people in other parts of the world. But scholars still had to painstakingly copy the information they wanted to keep, or pay a scribe to copy it for them. In the 14th century, for example, the library of the Italian poet Petrarch contained more than 100 manuscripts that he had copied individually himself.

62   In Petrarch's day, literate people were either monks or members of the privileged classes. Wealthy people could afford tutoring, and they could also afford to buy the handwritten manuscripts copied by the monks. Knowledge—and the power it brings—belonged to very few people.

63   *The Second Information Communications Revolution.*   As societies grew more literate, the demand for manuscripts flourished, but a scribe   *flourished* could produce only one copy at a time. What has been called the *second information communications revolution* began in Germany in 1455, when Johannes Gutenberg printed a Bible on a press that used movable type.

64   More than 200 years before Gutenberg, the Chinese had invented a printing press that used wood type, and the Chinese also are credited with perfecting a copper press in 1445. But Gutenberg's innovation was to line up individual metal letters that he could ink and then press with paper to produce copies. Unlike the wood or copper presses, the metal letters could be reused to produce new pages of text, which made the process much cheaper. The Gutenberg Bible, a duplicate of the Latin original, is considered the first book printed by movable type (47 copies survive).

65   As other countries adopted Gutenberg's press, the price for Bibles plummeted. In 1470, the cost of a French mechanically printed Bible was one-fifth the cost of a hand-printed Bible. This second revolution—printing—meant that knowledge, which had belonged to the privileged few, would one day be accessible to everyone. This key development was one of the essential conditions for the rise of modern governments, as well as an important element of scientific and technological progress.

66   Before the Gutenberg press, a scholar who wanted special information had to travel to the place where it was kept. But once information could be duplicated easily, it could travel to people beyond the society that created it. The use of paper instead of scribes' bulky parchment also meant that books could be stacked end to end. For the first time, knowledge was portable and storable. Libraries now could store vast amounts of information in a small space. And because these smaller lightweight books could be carried easily, classical works could be read simultaneously in many cities by all different kinds of people. Another benefit of the development of printing was that societies could more easily keep information to share with future generations.

67   This effort to communicate—first through spoken messages, then through pictographs, then through the written word, and finally through printed words—demonstrates people's innate desire to share information   *innate* with one another. **Storability, portability,** and **accessibility** of information are essential to today's concept of mass communication. By definition, mass communication is information that is available to a large audience quickly.

The Third Information Communications Revolution. Today's age of communication has been called the *third information communications revolution* because computers have become the storehouses and transmitters of vast amounts of information that previously relied on the written word. Computer technology, which processes and transmits information much more efficiently than mechanical devices, is driving the majority of changes affecting today's media. This means that changes in today's media industries happen much faster than in the past. Satellite broadcasts, digital recordings, and the international computer network called the Internet are just three examples of the third information communications revolution.

68   Although each medium has its own history and economic structure, today all of the media industries compete for consumers' attention. Before the century ends, satellite and microchip technology will transform the media business more than we can foresee—enabling faster transmission of more information to more people than ever before.

69   **3. The Media and Political, Social, and Cultural Institutions**

The media industries, as already discussed, provide information and entertainment. But media also can affect the political, social, and cultural institutions.

70   This is the third theme of this book—the *impact* of mass media on the society in which they operate. Although the media can actively influence society, they also mirror it, and scholars constantly strive to delineate the differences.   *delineate*

71   When the advertising industry suddenly marched to patriotic themes by using flags and other patriotic logos in ads following the United States's claim of victory in the 1991 gulf war, was the industry pandering,   *pandering* or were advertisers proudly reflecting genuine American sentiment, or both? Did the spread of patriotic themes silence those who felt that the United States had overreacted in the Persian Gulf? If you were a scholar, how would you prove your arguments?

72   This is an example of the difficulty that scholars face when analyzing the media's political, social, and cultural effects. Early media studies analyzed the message in the belief that, once a message was sent, it would be received by everyone the same way. Then studies proved that different people perceived messages differently—a phenomenon described as **selective perception.** This occurs because everyone brings many variables—family background, interests, and education, for example—to each message.

73   Complicating the study of the media's political, social, and cultural effects is the recent proliferation of media outlets. These multiplying   *proliferation* sources for information and entertainment mean that today very few people share identical mass media environments. This makes it much more difficult for scholars to determine the specific or cumulative effects of mass media on the general population.

74   Still, the attempts by scholars to describe media's political, social, and cultural roles in society are important because, once identified, the effects can be observed. The questions should be posed so we do not become

complacent about media in our lives, so we do not become immune to the   *complacent / immune*
possibility that our society may be cumulatively affected by the media in   *cumulatively*
ways we cannot yet define.

How MEDIA/IMPACT Works

75   The effects of media are so interwoven in American society that isolating
their influence is difficult. But to help you understand how the American
media work together, MEDIA/IMPACT first talks about the development of each medium separately. Then MEDIA/IMPACT expands the
discussion to important media effects and media issues.

76   Chapter 2 describes the new communications network proposed for
the 21st century. Within the next decade, the media industries will be developing strategies to cope with the rapid changes in the nation's communications, computer, telephone, and electronics industries. This new
network, commonly known as the information superhighway, promises
to be as important, and as controversial, for U.S. media as the development of the nation's transportation system was at the turn of the century.

77   Chapters 3 through 9 cover each of the seven types of media in America. These chapters explain the historical development of each type of media business and describe how each business works today. The discussion
of the media industries is divided into print media (newspapers, magazines, and books); audio media (radio and recordings); and video media
(television and movies). Each of these chapters includes an Industry Window feature to give you a graphic overview of how each media industry
works.

78   Chapters 10 and 11 cover two media-support industries: advertising
and public relations. Because advertising pays for most of the American
mass media, understanding how the advertising business works is important. A discussion of public relations is included to help you understand
how advertising and public relations companies sometimes work together
and the role that public relations companies play in garnering media attention for their clients.

79   The discussion expands in Chapters 12 through 15 to cover critical arguments about the overall effects of media today and the economic, social, cultural, and political consequences of the American media system
on American society. Recent studies of these effects pose many provoca-
tive questions: Do the owners and the members of the media have too
much power? Why must political candidates spend so much money on
campaign advertising, and does it help get them elected? Should high
school principals have the power to censor student newspapers? Are reporters too insensitive to people's privacy?

80   Chapter 16 covers the expanding role of the global media marketplace.

81   Section VI, the last section in this text, is a Student Resource Guide.
It contains a Glossary of Media Terms to help you remember new terminology. It also includes a Media Research Directory, which suggests
books and magazines to read and lists organizations that compile infor-

mation about each type of media business. The directly also lists on-line databases that track media information and articles.

82   Throughout the chapters are sections called Impact/Perspectives and Impact/Profiles to focus attention on particularly interesting persons or events or to expand on important debates about the mass media.

83   Once you understand the media separately, you can consider their collective effects. After you understand how each type of media business works, you can examine why the people who work in the media make the decisions they do. Then you can evaluate the impact of these decisions on you and on society.

In Focus

INTRODUCTION TO THE MASS MEDIA

According to industry estimates, the average adult spends more than half of his or her waking life with the media.

The mass media industries in the United States earn about $175 billion a year.

Communication is the act of sending ideas and attitudes from one person to another. Intrapersonal communication means communication within one person. Interpersonal communication means communication between two people. Mass communication is communication from one person or group of persons through a transmitting device (a medium) to large audiences or markets.

Many motives shape the American media, including the desire to fulfill the public's need for information, to influence the country's governance, to disseminate the country's culture, to offer entertainment, and to provide an outlet for creative expression. But, above all, the major goal of the American media is to make money.

Three key themes can be used to study American media:
1. American media operate as a profit-centered businesses.
2. The media are greatly affected by technological changes.
3. The mass media are political, social, and cultural institutions that both reflect and affect the society in which they operate.

Although many media businesses are still family-owned, the main trend in the United States today is for media companies to cluster together in groups. This trend is called concentration of ownership and can take five forms: chains, networks, cross-media ownership, conglomerates, and vertical integration.

Media acquisitions in the United States have skyrocketed because most conglomerates today are publicly traded companies and because, beginning in 1980, the federal government deregulated the broadcast industry. This trend is expected to continue in the late 1990s as changing technology expands the market for media products.

U.S. media industries continue to prosper, but the share of profits is shifting among the industries; different media expand and contract in the market-place to respond to the audience.

The communications revolution occurred in three stages. The invention of written symbols was considered the first communications revolution, the invention of movable type marked the second communications revolution, and the invention of computers ushered in the third communications revolution.

Storability, portability, and *accessibility* of information are essential to today's concept of mass communication. By definition, mass communication is information that is available to a large audience quickly.

Review Questions

1. Cite three major landmarks in the historical development of mass media from pictographs to today. What did each development contribute to the mass media's evolution?

2. Give an example of your own to demonstrate each of the following types of communication:
   a. interpersonal communication
   b. intrapersonal communication
   c. mass communication

3. Identify the three communications revolutions and describe how each one drastically changed the world's mass media.

4. Explain what vertical integration means. Give a specific example.

5. Explain what the sender, message, receiver, and channel are and how they form the process of mass communication.

QUESTIONS

1. "Some form of mass media touches nearly every American every day—economically, socially, or culturally." Based on your reading of this chapter, agree or disagree with this statement. Support your answer.

2. Explain the process of mass communication. Be sure to discuss the following elements: sender (source), channel, medium, and feedback.

3. As profit-centered businesses, a major goal of the mass media is financial success. Explain.

4. Discuss media ownership in America. Include and explain the following: chains, networks, cross-media ownership, conglomerates, and vertical integration.

5. Explain the role of technology in the development of mass media.

6. The author describes three communication revolutions that the world has experienced. Cite each one and provide a brief explanation.

7. Explain the process of "selective perception" and discuss its application to the study of media effects.

EXTENDING YOUR VOCABULARY

implications: The implications of dropping out of high school must be considered because _____

crude: Because early man had only crude tools available, _____

_____

ultimately: I began my trip in California but ultimately _____

_____

simultaneously: Using several telephones, my sister can simultaneously

_____

cajole: They tried every trick they knew to cajole their child to

_____

disseminate: In order to disseminate the information quickly, the government had to _____

acquisitions: His company made so many acquisitions in a short period of time that _____

unprecedented: Because of the unprecedented number of college applicants, the authorities had to _____

array: The sophisticated array of weapons that the police captured proved that _____

flourished: Their new store flourished after _____

innate: Innate feelings come from _____

delineate: The mayor wanted to delineate his proposals to the press because _____

pandering: Some people accuse advertisers of pandering to the masses in order to _____

proliferation: We were surprised by the proliferation of coffee shops in our neighborhood because _____

complacent: The coach was upset by his team's complacent attitude because _____

immune: The leader thought for sure that he would be immune

                   from criticism because _____

cumulatively: At first the drug had no noticeable effect; by looking at

                   the picture cumulatively, we saw _____

➡ PROCESS GUIDE

This textbook chapter is taken from a book entitled *Media Impact: An Introduction to Mass Media.* The chapter is the first in the book. The term *introduction* suggests that you are not expected to know much about the topic and that the author will familiarize you with ideas and terminology from the mass media subject area.

The first paragraph says that media are ever present in our lives. Some data are presented to show how much time we spend with different forms of media. For example, it says that "adult read on average ten magazines per month." Does this mean that every adult reads ten per month? It is important to keep in mind the meaning of average.

1. Define average: _____

2. Biagi amasses the data to demonstrate the impact of mass media on America. List three areas that she claims can be affected by contact with the media.

   _____   _____   _____

3. Biagi then cites a series of examples related to media and choices. Discuss the reason for these various examples.

   _____

   _____

The Communication Process

4. Biagi states that to understand media it is important to know how the process of communication works. Paraphrase her discussion.

   _____

   _____

5. The author's explanation of communication is followed by a series of key technical terms used to refer to elements in the process. It is necessary to know these terms to be able to follow her discussion. Briefly define each of these key terms:

   intrapersonal communication _____

   interpersonal communication _____

mass communication _____

sender _____

medium _____

channel _____

receiver _____

feedback _____

6. Briefly describe a spoken communication between two people using the key technical terms that you have defined above.

_____

_____

Understanding the Mass Media Industries: Three Key Terms

7. *Mass media* refers to seven different businesses. List them:

a. _____ b. _____ c. _____

d. _____ e. _____ f. _____

g. _____

8. What is the goal of the mass media industry?

_____

9. Paragraph 2 under the "Understanding Mass Media" heading states that the media are important institutions in our society. They affect society and are affected by what happens in society. Biagi notes that themes will be introduced to help in organizing thoughts about mass media. (Recall that the notion of themes and thematic material was discussed in the "To the Student" section.) List the themes:

a. _____ b. _____ c. _____

10. The first theme examined is the media as business. Biagi notes that it is important to realize that the goal of media businesses is to make money. There are other reasons to be in the business, such as _____ and _____, but the primary focus is profit.

11. To understand the media as businesses it is important to know who owns them. It is reported that there are only two publicly owned media in the country. Name them.

a. _____ b. _____

12. All other media, including all newspapers and magazines, are privately owned. A number of families own media, but the trend is toward concentration of ownership—that is, ownership of a large number of media

businesses by a group. List the five different forms of ownership and briefly describe each:

       Form   **Description**

a. _____

b. _____

c. _____

d. _____

e. _____

Who Pays for the Mass Media?

13. You probably were aware before reading the article that advertisers paid for much of the cost of the media. This section tells you how much and gives examples. Cite an instance in which you pay for the media directly. Explain.

_____

_____

How Does Each Media Industry Work?

14. The mass media have changed the country dramatically in the last fifty years. What media have existed from 1460 to the present?

_____ _____ _____

15. What media have come about in the last fifty years?

_____ _____ _____ _____

16. Biagi claims that to understand how the media industries fit together into the mass media business as a whole, it is useful to examine each part. List the seven media and in a brief statement summarize each medium's audience and popularity. The first example, newspapers, is done for you.

a. Newspapers—1,600 daily papers. The number of afternoon, evening, and weekly papers is declining. Revenue will remain the same with small growth.

b. _____

_____

c. _____

_____

d. _____

_____

e. _____

_____

f. _____

_____

g. _____

_____

17. This section concludes with a statement about profits. Note that profits are increasing overall, but Biagi introduces an important qualifier in the word *shifting*. Define this term and note the implications for the media industry.

Definition:_____

Implication:_____

The Second Theme: The Media and Communications Technology

18. The point is made that technology has an impact on mass media. In fact, the claim is made that the development of communications technology "directly affects the speed with which a society evolves." Interpret this statement.

_____

_____

Three Communications Revolutions

19. Before discussing the three revolutions, the author introduces the notion that people have always been interested in staying informed but it was not easy to do so in the past. Cite an example of the earliest method of getting the news in ancient Rome.

_____

_____

20. The first communications revolution, the use of phonetic writing to represent an idea, belonged to only a few people. Explain why this type of communication was restricted.

_____

_____

The Second Information Communications Revolution

21. The invention of the printing press marks the beginning of the second revolution. (If you studied the article "History of Printing" in the first unit, you should have some background information on this

development.) The printing press allowed multiple copies of a text to be printed, thus cutting down on the labor and ultimately the cost of producing a document. Biagi discusses some of the advantages of the printing press. Briefly paraphrase her remarks.

_____

_____

The Third Information Communications Revolution

22. The coming of computers marks the beginning of the third revolution. Computers can efficiently store and rapidly transmit a great amount of information. Biagi notes that computers are behind most of the changes in media. What is Biagi's prediction for the computer's impact on media in the future?

_____

_____

The Third Theme: The Media and Political, Social, and Cultural Institutions

23. The third theme of the book is the impact of media on society. Biagi notes that media can play the role of both cause and effect in social change. That is, the media has an effect on what occurs in society, but also society has an impact on the direction and content of the media. The author notes that scholars have difficulty assessing the impact of the media's effect on political, social, and cultural phenomena. State the nature of this supposed problem.

_____

_____

How MEDIA/IMPACT Works

The final section is a preview of what is forthcoming in the book. The topics mentioned in the first chapter have been further explained later on. In your subsequent study of other books, keep in mind that such a preview section is a feature to look for and use.

 READING JOURNAL

• **Content**

There is a great deal of information presented in this introductory chapter. List what you remember from the reading without consulting the text. Can you summarize the main points? Were you able to grasp and retain the most important points?

- **Process**

   How did you process all the information presented? What strategies and
   techniques did you use—did you take notes, mark the text, develop an information map, create an outline? Did you use headings and subheadings?
   Did visuals help you? Were you able to keep your focus, or did you tend
   to drift? Why were certain points more easily remembered than others?
   Cite one reading strategy that was the most helpful to you in reading the
   chapter. Analyze your use of this strategy.

- **Response**

   What did you find interesting in this assignment? Summarize the point of
   interest and explain why it appealed to you. What did you find boring in
   this assignment? What could the writer have done to make the material
   more enjoyable?

Television

JIM TRELEASE

Writer and lecturer Jim Trelease is known for his best-seller The Read-Aloud
Handbook. *In this book, Trelease encourages parents and teachers to introduce
children to the pleasures of reading by reading aloud to them from interesting
books. He lists recommended read-aloud books grouped according to categories. In the following excerpt, Trelease discusses television's negative impact
on children and the implications this impact has for literacy.*

GEARING UP

1. Why are children in particular attracted to television? What makes this
   medium so appealing to youngsters?

2. Some individuals believe television has a positive influence on children,
   whereas others think it has a negative impact. Discuss both the beneficial
   and harmful influences of this medium.

3. Television and reading can be compared and contrasted. Mention several
   ways that they are alike and different.

4. What impact, if any, has television had on your reading?

READING STRATEGY
DETECTING AND EVALUATING BIAS

Bias refers to a viewpoint that is not open to information and evidence but is decidedly in favor of or opposed to an idea or issue. As a critical reader, it is important that you determine whether an author is biased. For example, former surgeon general Dr. Everett Koop was clearly against cigarette smoking. Koop based his case against tobacco on numerous scientific studies. He cited considerable evidence that smoking could be directly linked to 400,000 deaths a year in the United States and 20,000 deaths of nonsmokers who passively inhaled cigarette smoke. Through advertising and legislation, Koop waged a vigorous campaign against smoking. Clearly Koop's position was unshakable. Can we say he was biased regarding this issue? Certainly the tobacco industry thought he was. They presented another side of the story based on a different interpretation of the data—that smoking is not as bad as the critics claim. Now suppose the tobacco companies introduced a new filter that independent studies proved could trap all the harmful by-products of cigarette smoke. Had Koop or other government officials refused to change their position and acknowledge the new data, they indeed would have exhibited bias.

The following questions should help you detect bias in the material you read:

1. What is the issue? Has the author accurately described the situation under discussion?

2. Is the evidence presented accurate and verifiable? Has the author examined various viewpoints and conflicting evidence, if any?

3. Does the author stand to lose or gain something from the issue under consideration? For example, does the author work for a company that provides a service or product that the article endorses?

4. Does the author tell you directly that he or she is biased, or is the bias disguised with an aura of objectivity?

In the article you are about to read, the author takes a position against current practices by the television industry, particularly their implications for reading and literacy. The author presents evidence to support his position. Is he biased? Read the arguments and evidence and make a judgment. Also, try putting yourself on the other side. As an employee in the TV industry, such as an executive in charge of programming, how would you present the pro-TV side of the issue? What arguments would you make? What evidence would you provide to show television's worth, particularly with regard to literacy?

READING STRATEGY CHECK
MARKING TEXT

The strategy of marking text was introduced in the first unit in relation to the Sam Levenson article (page 48). A well-done marking allows you to keep track of the ideas in an article and the points of uncertainty. There are two parts to the marking scheme, the symbols and the notes.

1. *The symbols.* The symbols are the consistently used notations such as the asterisk (*) and question mark (?) that signal you on your reading comprehension decisions. The asterisk is suggested for your main point. The question mark indicates places of confusion and uncertainty.

2. *The notes.* The notes capture your thinking in short form. Underlining alone does not allow you to qualify an idea except within the general category of "important." A note can signal *why* something is important. In addition, the process of converting the text into short notes keeps you actively involved.

The marking procedure becomes even more important when studying longer selections like textbook chapters. The markup can serve as a chapter review for exams and term papers. As with any new task, it takes time to develop proficiency. In the "Television" article by Trelease, work toward adding to the marking efforts you have made thus far.

As a minimum goal we suggest:

1. Use one asterisk (*) to mark the main point of each text section. Accompany it with one brief note in the margin.

2. Circle words and phrases that are new to you that need to be checked later.

3. Use the question mark (?) to signal points of uncertainty or confusion that can be further studied or clarified in class.

The Reading

Television

by JIM TRELEASE

"I believe television is going to be the test of the modern world, and that in this new opportunity to see beyond the range of our vision we shall discover either a new and unbearable disturbance of the general peace or a saving radiance in the sky. We shall stand or fall by television—of that I am quite sure."

—E. B. White
from "Removal from Town,"
Harper's (October, 1938)

1   My first job in the business community was selling television sets. I was nine years old and living in Union, New Jersey, when a Philco television store opened at the corner of my street. To the astonishment of the neighborhood kids the store manager immediately told us, "You kids are welcome to come by and watch TV any time you want." Those of us who were used to being thrown out of the five-and-dime store for reading comics were further astounded when he provided us with chairs! The result was a daily late-afternoon and early-evening caucus of ten normally rambunctious children tranquilized into passivity.   *caucus / rambunctious*

2   It wasn't until years later that my father explained the man's generosity: We were being used as demonstration models for prospective customers, living testimonials to an electronic Pied Piper who would solve parenting and babysitting woes the world over. "Take a look at these kids, folks. Would you believe they've been here for an hour. Not one peep out of them, not one fight, and no one's even had to go to the bathroom," the salesman announced.   *testimonials*

3   Since then, television has become the most pervasive and powerful influence on the human family and, at the same time, the major stumbling block to literacy in America. The A. C. Nielsen Company reports the average television set ran for four hours, thirty-five minutes each day in 1950; by 1987, the daily total had risen to seven hours.[1] (Adding daily VCR use to that figure would bring it to seven hours, thirty minutes.)   *pervasive*

4   But fear not—I am not one of those purists urging you to throw out your television set. I am a realist who recognizes both the enormous potential *and* the liabilities of the medium. As a teacher, television could be unparalleled. Consider how well it educated the public during the two great struggles of the last thirty years: civil rights and Vietnam. Had the network cameras not been in Selma and Saigon, who knows how long the public might have been forced to tolerate those conflicts.

5   The elitists who dismiss television as vacuous must have their heads buried in the sand. How do they explain the rebel forces engaged in life-and-death struggles throughout the globe who make the government's television station their first objective, or the opposition party in Nicaragua that demands its own television channel as part of the peace process? These instances exemplify television's potential—its ability to instruct a vast audience for change.   *vacuous*

6   Most Americans, however, use television as entertainment, not for instruction or information. Informational programming like news shows has such a small audience that only one such program turns a profit—"Sixty Minutes"; the rest lose money and are outdrawn by game shows.

7   There is nothing wrong, of course, with entertainment. To my way of thinking, we all need a daily dose of entertainment to break the routine in our lives. It's like dessert, something to look forward to. The danger comes

---

1. Television Bureau of Advertising (477 Madison Avenue, New York, NY 10022), January 1988 report for 1987 viewing.

when you allow it to become the main course. And over the last thirty years, entertainment, which is television, has become the main course in children's and families' intellectual lives. Both children and adults average nearly four hours a day passively letting someone else do all the thinking, speaking, imagining, and exploring. The result has been an unprecedented negative impact on American reading and thinking habits.

unprecedented

8   I want to suggest a method for dealing with television. This approach was used in my own home and in countless others, and proved to be a reasonable and workable solution to the problem of what to do about television. In order to make it work, however, parents must believe in it, must understand fully why they are using it, and what the consequences are to family and child if it is not used.

9   It is just as important for teachers to understand because television, as the main preoccupation of adults and children, is the prime teacher. Children spend more time in front of television than in front of parents or teachers. Like it or not, television is the prime competition for every teacher and parent and it is here to stay. The challenge is to make it work *for* us instead of *against* us.

10   We have to recognize its power fully. I've already stated its potential for good, but what about its negatives? Two decades ago when author Marie Winn called TV the "plug-in-drug," it was not without reason. Its psychological control of humans is demanding and extensive. Prison officials at the maximum-security prison in Erie County, New York, found that the most effective threat against even the most incorrigible inmates was to deny them television privileges. In 1986, the inmates voted unanimously to give up their right to receive packages from outside the prison (the prime source for drugs) in exchange for the option to buy personal televisions for their cells.[2]

11   Children are even more susceptible to the influence it has over their appetites, attention, and loyalties. It will largely determine what they wear and won't wear, what they eat and won't eat, what they play and won't play, what they read and won't read. If there were a medicine that had as much influence on child behavior, it would be strictly monitored, would it not? Yet only 36 percent of parents set any limits on their children's television viewing.[3]

12   An important step toward teaching children to cope with television is to put the same controls on your television that you already have on your medicine cabinet.

13   The first serious alarm was sounded by a small cluster of educators in 1964 when the scores were computed for that year's college admission tests. That year's high-school seniors, born in the late 1940s, were the first generation to be raised on a steady television diet. Their Scholastic Aptitude Test

---

2. "Incentives for Inmates: Television Sets in Cells," *The New York Times,* April 4, 1988, p. B3.
3. According to 1981 Gallup Poll on TV viewing on school nights.

(SAT) scores showed an unprecedented decline from previous years. From an average verbal score of 478 in 1963, U.S. students dropped to a low of 424 in 1981. By 1988 they had risen slightly, to 428.[4] . . .

14   Naturally there are those in the television industry who claim that these lower standards have nothing to do with their medium. Social scientists, educators, and psychologists respond loudly that there is every connection between the two. Television, they declare, interrupts the largest and most instructive class in childhood: life experience.

15   Paul Copperman, president of the Institute of Reading Development and author of *The Literacy Hoax*, sees the interruption in these terms: "Consider what a child misses during the 15,000 hours (from birth to age seventeen) he spends in front of the TV screen. He is not working in the garage with his father, or in the garden with his mother. He is not doing homework, or reading, or collecting stamps. He is not cleaning his room, washing the supper dishes, or cutting the lawn. He is not listening to a discussion about community politics among his parents and their friends. He is not playing baseball or going fishing, or painting pictures. Exactly what does television offer that is so valuable it can replace these activities that transform an impulsive, self-absorbed child into a critically thinking adult?"[5] . . .

impulsive

16   What it offers is a steady stream of entertainment based on daily social and business values that would qualify most people for prison terms! Parents regularly use television as a babysitter—yet how many would hire a sitter who systematically taught children to solve most of their problems violently, to desire things they didn't need, and to lie and cheat because most of the time you'd never be punished. Farfetched? Read on.

17   A New York University dean recently spent eight hours with twenty-four public high school students from diverse socioeconomic and ethnic groups; their conversations focused on several shows portraying corrupt businessmen. To the dean's dismay, the student consensus was not only that such practices are the norm in business; they are also acceptable, even admirable. Asked if they would dump chemicals into a town sewer system in order to save their business, the students' pragmatic response was they would do it as long as they made enough money and it didn't hurt their own relatives.

pragmatic

18   The dean's conclusions were alarming: The continuous unethical and unpunished behavior of *heroes* from "Dallas," "Knots Landing," and "Dynasty," fed into children's unformed consciences, does not portend good things for tomorrow's society. His *New York Times* recounting[6] of those student discussions should be studied by all concerned educators, par-

portend

---

4. "National Report on College-Bound Seniors, 1988," The College Board, 888 Seventh Avenue, New York, NY 10106.
5. Paul Copperman, *The Literacy Hoax: The Decline of Reading, Writing, and Learning in the Public Schools and What We Can Do About It* (New York: Morrow, 1980), p. 166.
6. Herbert London, "What TV Drama Is Teaching Our Children," *The New York Times*, August 23, 1987, p. 23.

ents, and clergy interested in exploring American ethics with classes of children.

19   Research offers cause for both alarm and hope. In 1980, California's Department of Education administered a standard achievement exam and survey to all the state's sixth- and twelfth-graders (half a million students). When they correlated each child's grade with the number of hours the student spent watching television, the findings were conclusive: The more time in front of TV, the lower the scores; the less time, the higher the scores. The statistics proved true regardless of the child's IQ, social background, or study practices.[7]

20   Tannis Macbeth Williams of the University of British Columbia came to similar conclusions when she studied three Canadian towns—two with television and one without. Children in the community without television had higher reading scores—until television was introduced to the town. Not surprisingly, the scores then declined. Such research speaks directly to the need for limits on family TV viewing and for children to discover the pleasures of books before the pleasures of television.[8]

21   The parents who are always asking me, "What about 'Sesame Street'? How about 'Mr. Rogers'?" can take heart from a recent two-year study of 326 five- and seven-year-olds that showed viewing of educational television has a positive effect on children's reading while noninformative shows (situation comedies) have a detrimental effect.[9] A distinction should be made as to the *kinds* of television programs children watch, though even educational programs hurt when they become substitutes for play or socializing or when viewed to excess—more than fourteen hours a week. That same long-term project concluded that the biggest influence on children's reading development and skills was parent attitudes about reading and the availability of books in their homes. On the subject of educational TV, it is my opinion (and shared by many) that "Mr. Rogers," with its civil, value-oriented focus on children through conversation, is the finest programming for children today and proves you can hold their attention without car chases or violent robotics.

detrimental

22   "Reading Rainbow," the award-winning PBS series on children's books, shows what can be accomplished when the industry makes up its mind to educate and entertain. Conceived by producer Twila Liggett as a way to encourage reading during summer vacations, the series' sixty shows boast a

7. California Department of Education, "Student Achievement in California Schools, 1979–80 Annual Report" (P.O. Box 271, Sacramento, CA 96802).

8. M. Morgan and L. Gross, "Television and Educational Achievement and Aspiration," in *Television and Behavior: Ten Years of Scientific Progress and Implications for the Eighties*, ed. D. Pearl, L. Bonlithilet, and J. Lazar (Rockville, MD: NIMH, 1982).

9. Rosemarie Truglio, Aletha Huston, and John Wright, "The Relation Between Children's Print and Television Use to Early Reading Skills," Center for Research on the Influences of Television on Children, Department of Human Development, University of Kansas, 1988.

unique power: Once a book is spotlighted on the show, libraries and book-stores report an immediate positive response among children and their parents. It is not unusual for a book that normally sells 1,200 copies to sell 20,000 after appearing on "Reading Rainbow."

23   "Reading Rainbow" is the programming exception, rather than the rule. Most of today's programming is a serious impediment to children's growth because of both what it offers and what it does *not* offer.

impediment

24   *1. Television is the direct opposite of reading.*   In breaking its programs into eight-minute commercial segments (shorter for shows like "Sesame Street"), it requires and fosters a short attention span. Reading, on the other hand, requires and encourages longer attention spans in children. Good children's books are written to hold children's attention, not interrupt it. Because of the need to hold viewers until the next commercial message, the content of television shows is almost constant action. Reading also offers action but not nearly as much, and reading fills the considerable space between action scenes with subtle character development. Television is relentless; no time is allowed to ponder characters' thoughts or to recall their words because the dialogue and film move too quickly. The need to scrutinize is a critical need among young children and it is constantly ignored by television. Books, however, encourage a critical reaction; the reader moves at his own pace as opposed to that of the director or sponsor. The reader can stop to ponder the character's next move, the feathers in his hat, or the meaning of a sentence. Having done so, he can resume where he left off without having missed any part of the story.

relentless

scrutinize

25   The arrival of remote control is only exacerbating the attention span problem: the average family "zaps" once every three minutes, twenty-six seconds, versus those who have no remote (once every five minutes, fifteen seconds); and higher-income families zap three times more often than poorer families.[10]

exacerbating

26   *2. For young children television is an antisocial experience, while reading is a social experience.*   The three-year-old sits passively in front of the screen, oblivious to what is going on around him. Conversation during the program is seldom if ever encouraged by the child or by the parents. On the other hand, the three-year-old with a book must be read to by another person—parent, sibling, or grandparent. The child is a participant as well as a receiver when he engages in discussion during and after the story. This process continues to an even greater degree when the child attends school and compares his own reactions to a story with those of his classmates.

oblivious

27   *3. Television deprives the child of his most important learning tool: his questions.*   Children learn the most by questioning. For the thirty-three hours a week that the average five-year-old spends in front of the set, he can neither ask a question nor receive an answer.

---

10. "Zapping of TV Ads Appears Pervasive," *Wall Street Journal,* April 25, 1988, p. 29.

28   *4. Television interrupts the child's most important language lesson: family conversation.*   Studies show the average kindergarten graduate has already seen nearly 6,000 hours of television and videos before entering first grade, hours in which he engaged in little or no conversation. And with 30 percent of all adults watching TV during dinner and 36 percent of teenagers owning their own sets (and presumably watching alone in their rooms), the description of TV as "the great conversation stopper" has never been more appropriate.

29   *5. Much of young children's television viewing is mindless watching, requiring little or no thinking.*   When two dozen three- to five-year-olds were shown a "Scooby Doo" cartoon, the soundtrack of which had been replaced by the soundtrack from a "Fangface" cartoon, only three of the twenty-four children realized the soundtrack did not match the pictures.[11]

30   *6. Television presents material in a manner that is the direct opposite of the classroom's.*   Television's messages are based almost entirely on moving pictures and our emotional response to them. Conversely, the classroom relies *Conversely* heavily on reading the printed word, and a critical response to those words, not just on raw emotion. School also requires large amounts of time to be spent on a task. The minutes spent doing things like multiplication tables and spelling are often boring and repetitious when compared with "Family Ties." Whereas the classroom pursues subjects in depth, television treats nearly all areas superficially. The networks' nightly newscasts contain ap- *superficially* proximately 3,500 words—only slightly more than you find on *half* a newspaper front page; yet more than half the adults in the U.S. now depend entirely on TV for their daily news information.

31   *7. Television is unable to portray the most intelligent act known to man: thinking.*   In 1980 Squire Rushnell, vice-president in charge of ABC's children's programming, said that certain fine children's books cannot be adapted for television. Much of the character development in these books, Rushnell noted, takes place inside the character's head. He said, "You simply can't put thinking on the screen." As a result, a child almost never sees a TV performer thinking through a problem.[12]

32   *8. Television encourages deceptive thinking.*   In *Teaching as a Conserving Activity,* educator Neil Postman points out that it is implicit in every one of *implicit* television's commercials that there is no problem which cannot be solved by

---

11. Donald Hayes and Dana Birnbaum, *Development Psychology* 16:5 and 17:2. See also: *Psychology Today,* June 1982, pp. 78–79.
12. Meg Schwartz, "Broadcasting Books to Young Audiences," *RE:ACT,* Spring/Summer 1980, p. 19. Mr. Rushnell's remarks were made at a symposium co-sponsored by Action for Children's Television (ACT) and the Library of Congress Center for the Book. *RE:ACT* is a nonprofit journal published by ACT.

simple artificial means.[13] Whether the problem is anxiety or common diarrhea, nervous tension or the common cold, a simple tablet or spray solves the problem. Seldom is mention ever made of headaches being a sign of more serious illness, nor is the suggestion ever made that elbow grease and hard work are viable alternatives to stains and boredom. Instead of thinking through our problems, television promotes the "easy way." The cumulative effect of such thinking is enormous when you consider that between ages one and seventeen the average child is exposed to 350,000 commercials (four hundred a week) promoting the idea that solutions to life's problems can be purchased. Moreover, alcohol, the number-one form of drug abuse in America, is promoted as a pleasureful form of recreation with 100,000 beer commercials viewed by children between ages two and eighteen.[14]   *viable*
cumulative

33 *9. Television, by vying for children's time and attention with a constant diet of unchallenging simplistic entertainment, stimulates antischool and anti-reading feeling among children.*   A 1977 study showed that the majority of the preschool and primary school students examined felt that school and books were a waste of time.[15] Offered the same story on television and in book form, 69 percent of the second-grade students chose television. That figure increased to 86 percent among the third-grade pupils—the grade where national reading skills begin to decline.   *vying*

34 *10. Television has a negative effect on children's vital knowledge after age ten, according to the Schramm study of 6,000 schoolchildren.*[16]   It does help, the report goes on to say, in building vocabulary for younger children, but this stops by age ten. This finding is supported by the fact that today's kindergartners have the highest reading-readiness scores ever achieved at that level and yet these same students tail off dismally by fourth and fifth grades. Since television scripts consist largely of conversations that contain the same vocabulary words these students already know, few gains are made. Moreover, a study of the scripts from eight programs favored by teenagers showed a sentence averaged only seven words (versus eighteen words in my local newspaper), and 72 percent of the language in the shows consisted of simple sentences or fragments.[17]

35 *11. Television stifles the imagination.*   A study of 192 children from Los Angeles County showed children *hearing* a story elicited greater imaginative   *elicited*

---

13. Neil Postman, *Teaching as a Conserving Activity* (New York: Delacorte, 1980), pp. 77–78.
14. "Myths, Men, & Beer," booklet available from AAA Foundation for Traffic Safety.
15. Jackie S. Busch, "TV's Effects on Reading: A Case Study," *Phi Delta Kappan,* June 1978, pp. 668–71.
16. Wilbur Schramm, Jack Lyle, and Edwin B. Parker, *Television in the Lives of Our Children* (Stanford, CA: Stanford University Press, 1961).
17. Michael Liberman, "The Verbal Language of Television," *The Journal of Reading,* April 1983, pp. 602–609.

responses than did their seeing the same story on film.[18] Consider for a moment this single paragraph from Eric Knight's classic, *Lassie-Come-Home:*

> Yet, if it were almost a miracle, in his heart Joe Carraclough tried to believe in that miracle—that somehow, wonderfully, inexplicably, his dog would be there some day; there, waiting by the school gate. Each day as he came out of school, his eyes would turn to the spot where Lassie had always waited. And each day there was nothing there, and Joe Carraclough would walk home slowly, silently, stolidly as did the people of his country.

stolidly

36   If a dozen people were to read or hear those words, they would have a dozen different images of the scene, what the boy looked like, the school, the gate, the lonely road home. As soon as the story is placed on film there is no longer any room for imagination. The director does all your imagining for you.

37   *12. Television overpowers and desensitizes a child's sense of sympathy for suffering, while books heighten the reader's sense of sympathy.*   Extensive research in the past ten years clearly shows that television bombardment of the child with continual acts of violence (18,000 acts viewed between the ages of three and seventeen) makes the child insensitive to violence and its victims—most of whom he is conditioned to believe die cleanly or crawl inconsequently offstage.[19]

desensitizes

38   Though literature could never be labeled a nonviolent medium, it cannot begin to approach television's extreme. Frank Mankiewicz and Joel Swerdlow noted in *Remote Control: Television and the Manipulation of American Life* that you would have to watch all thirty-seven of Shakespeare's plays in order to see the same number of acts of human violence (fifty-four) that you would see in just three evenings of prime-time television.

39   Television and sponsors have found the one sure way to hold audience attention (and prevent zapping) while at the same time solving story dilemmas is violence, at the rate of 13.3 incidents per prime-time hour. Nearly half the videos on MTV (Music Television) portray violence of one form or another.[20] In one week in 1986, the University of Pennsylvania's Annenberg School of Communications counted a combined 168 acts of violence during just the "family hour" (8:00–9:00 P.M.) on the three major networks.[21]

40   The addition of cable television and VCRs has only increased the amount of violence to which children of all ages are exposed. Librarians in

---

18. Patricia Greenfield and Jessica Beagles-Roos, "Radio and Television: Their Cognitive Impact on Children of Different Socioeconomic and Ethnic Groups," *Journal of Communication,* Spring 1988, pp. 71–91.
19. Frank Mankiewicz and Joel Swerdlow, *Remote Control: Television and the Manipulation of American Life* (New York: Times Books, 1978), pp. 6, 15–72.
20. "Why TV Won't Let Up on Violence," *The New York Times,* January 13, 1985, Section 2, H-1, 25.
21. "TV 'Family Hour' Rated Most Violent," *USA Today,* September 11, 1986, p. 1.

Panama City, Florida, told me of the day-care class that visited the children's room one morning in 1987 where the librarian announced excitedly that the day's stories were going to be about "monsters!" This prompted the dozen four-year-olds to cheer, "Ohhhhhh—Freddy Krueger!" referring to the psychotic killer with the razor-clawed gloves from *A Nightmare on Elm Street*, which many of these preschoolers had been allowed to view that week when it was a late-night cable channel selection. This was a far cry from the storybook monsters the librarian was going to read about in *There's a Nightmare in My Closet*, by Mercer Mayer, and *Harry and the Terrible Whatzit*, by Harry Gackenbach. One can only wonder what these preschoolers will be ready for in adolescence.

41   **13. Television is a passive activity and discourages creative play.**   The virtual disappearance of neighborhood games like I spy, kick the can, spud, hopscotch, Johnny-jump-the-pony, stickball, red light, Simon says, flies up, giant steps, and statue attests to that.

42   Compared to reading, television is still the more passive of the two activities. In reading, educators point out, a child must actively use a variety of skills involving sounds, spelling rules, blendings, as well as constructing mental images of the scene described in the book. Television requires no such mental activity.

43   **14. Television is psychologically addictive.**   In schools and homes where students voluntarily have removed themselves from TV viewing, their subsequent class discussions and journals report the addictive nature of their attachment to television: It draws upon their idle time and there is an urgency to watch it in order to fulfill peer and family pressure. I recall the Oregon elementary school principal and father of five who told me he and his wife had refused to have a television until the children were grown. During all those years, he explained, he read an average of two books a week. Three months before I spoke with him, his wife bought their first television and, he sheepishly confessed, he hadn't read a book since the day it arrived.

44   **15. Television has been described by former First Lady Betty Ford as "the greatest babysitter of all time," but it also is reported to be the nation's second largest obstacle to family harmony.**   In a 1980 survey by the Roper Organization, 4,000 men and women listed money as the most frequent subject of fights between husband and wife. Television and children tied for second, and produced three times as many arguments as did sex.

45   **16. Television's conception of childhood, rather than being progressive, is re-**   *regressive*
gressive—a throwback, in fact, to the Middle Ages.   In *Teaching as a Conserving Activity*, Postman points to Philippe Ariès's research, which shows that until the 1600s children over the age of five were treated and governed as though they were adults.[22] After the seventeenth century, society devel-

---

22. Postman, *Teaching as a Conserving Activity*, p. 208.

oped a concept of childhood which insulated children from the shock of instant adulthood until they were mature enough to meet it. "Television," Postman declares, "all by itself, may bring an end to childhood." Present-day TV programming offers its nightly messages on incest, murder, abortion, rape, moral and political corruption, and general physical mayhem to 85 million people—including 5.6 million children between ages two and eleven who are still watching at 10:30 P.M.[23] The afternoon soap operas offer a similar message to still another young audience. Of the twenty-one children (ages seven to nine) in my wife's second-grade class one year, all but four of them were daily soap opera viewers. The Center for Population Options in Washington, D.C., pointing to a survey of midwestern teenagers who said television was their major source of sexual information, estimates the average viewer will see more than 9,000 instances of "sexually suggestive comments or suggested sexual intercourse," each year.

46   **17. Television presents a continuous distortion of physical and social realities, thus reinforcing false stereotypes.**   Extensive studies by major research firms[24] point out these misrepresentations:

- TV shows are populated by three times as many men as women, and men are usually ten years older than women. (In reality, women outnumber men, 52 percent to 48 percent, with a median age two years older than men's.)

- Children make up only one-tenth of the TV population. (In reality, 27 percent.)

- Only 4 percent of TV characters suffer from obesity. (In reality, 30 percent.)   *obesity*

- Only 6 to 10 percent of TV characters hold blue-collar or service jobs. (In reality, 60 percent.)

- TV characters seldom wear glasses. Fifty percent of the population wears them.

- Two out of every three TV businessmen are portrayed as foolish, greedy, or criminal.

- TV characters seldom wear seat belts, yet never sustain crippling injuries from TV car crashes.

- Murder is 200 percent more prevalent as a TV crime than it is in reality.

47   Children's television is just as heavily distorted. A study funded by the Ford and Carnegie foundations showed thirty-eight hours of Boston

---

23. Mankiewicz and Swerdlow, *Remote Control*, p. 6.
24. Linda S. Lichter and S. Robert Lichter, *Crooks, Conmen and Clowns* (Washington, DC: Media Institute of Mental Health, 1982); Earle Barcus, *Images of Life on Children's Television: Sex Roles, Minorities, and Families* (New York: Praeger, 1983).

children's programming contained these misleading statistics: Of the 1,145 characters, 3.7 percent were black; 3.1 percent were Spanish-speaking; only 16 percent were women. In reality, the following statistics hold true: blacks—11 percent; Spanish-speaking—6 percent; women—52 percent.

48   **18. Some *books are simple-minded;* most *television is simple-minded.***
When Grant Tinker was chairman of NBC, he admitted the industry's philosophy of gearing programs to the lowest possible denominator in the audience and placed the blame squarely on a viewing public that swallows unflinchingly much of the worst programming it is fed. "They are such a dis-   *unflinchingly*
appointment," he said. "I had to watch a pilot of a new program awhile ago and we made the decision: It's a little too good. That's a terrible decision to make."[25] It is also either a scathing indictment of American education or an   *scathing*
insult to the intelligence of its alumni.

49   Bob Keeshan, most often seen and heard in his role as Captain Kangaroo, places the prime responsibility for television's negative influence upon the parent. "Television is the great national babysitter," Keeshan says. "It's not the disease in itself, but a symptom of a greater disease that exists between parent and child. A parent today simply doesn't have time for the child, and the child is a very low priority item, and there's this magic box that flickers pictures all day long, and it's a convenient babysitter. I'm busy, go watch television. . . . The most direct answer to all our problems with television and children is the parent, because if the parent is an effective parent, we're not going to have them."[26]

50   Keeshan's call for parental control of the television set is more easily said than done, as any parent can tell you who has ever tried it.

51   It would be naïve, however, to assume that even half the parents will   *naïve*
avail themselves of such awareness programs. Thus the best hope for changing America's television habits rests with the classroom teacher who is educating tomorrow's parents sitting in the classroom today. We're spending a great deal of time and money educating children to the dangers of alcohol and drug abuse, teenage pregnancy, and AIDS, but so far we've done *nothing* to teach them how to cope with television.

52   As long as Americans spend more time watching than reading, educators must address the need for critical *viewing* as well as critical *reading*. If readers are trained to read interpretively, so too must viewers be taught to look critically at TV. And if we succeed with this teaching, we'll have changed the present pattern in which 70 percent of what Americans hear in a political

---

25. "NBC's Head Says TV Viewers Spurn Quality Shows," *The New York Times,* September 30, 1984, p. 1.
26. Bob Keeshan's remarks were made during an interview on September 24, 1979, with John Merrow for *Options in Education,* a co-production of National Public Radio and the Institute for Educational Leadership of George Washington University.

campaign consists of thirty- and sixty-second commercials consisting of half-truths and innuendo. The whole country benefits if we teach the next gener-   *innuendo*
ation to know when the TV evangelist is talking about Almighty God and
when he's talking about the almighty dollar, and how to spot the hidden commercials on talk shows ("Don, tell us about this clip from your special coming up this Thursday night . . ."). And they will also have a better chance of
knowing when a congressional committee witness is acting instead of testify-
ing, when he is manipulating the audience with grins and macho posturing.

53   As E. B. White noted a half century ago, television is "the test of the
modern world." Used correctly, it can inform, entertain and inspire. Used
incorrectly, television will control families and community, limiting our language, dreams, and achievements. It is our "test" to pass or fail.

QUESTIONS

1. Describe the author's attitude toward television and toward reading.
   Cite specific information to support your answer.

2. What do you think was the author's purpose in writing this excerpt?

3. To make his point, the author uses statistics and refers to various reports
   and studies. Cite several research studies mentioned, and explain how
   Trelease uses them to support his argument.

4. According to the author, how are television and reading similar? How
   do they differ?

5. The author claims that viewing violence on television makes children insensitive to violence and its victims. Yet, some critics claim, children's
   storybooks have their share of violence (a girl is poisoned by an apple, a
   child pushes a witch into a hot oven, a pig boils a menacing wolf in a ket-
   tle of water). These people believe that reading stories containing violence is just as harmful as watching a violent episode on television. Do
   you agree or disagree with this position? Explain.

6. According to the author, how does television encourage deceptive
   thinking?

7. The author quotes Neil Postman: "Television, all by itself, may bring an
   end to childhood." Explain how this might occur.

8. Explain what the author means by this statement: "Television presents a
   continuous distortion of physical and social realities, thus reinforcing
   false stereotypes."

9. What role does the author suggest parents should play in directing their
   children's television viewing?

10. Discuss the relationship between critical reading and critical viewing as
    put forth by the author.

EXTENDING YOUR VOCABULARY

caucus: Upon learning the court's decision, committee members
                     decided to caucus in order to _____

rambunctious: The children at the party became rambunctious when

                     _____

testimonials: After hearing the many testimonials on his behalf, the
                     senator remarked: "_____"

pervasive: The storm's pervasive damage became evident when

                     _____

vacuous: We were surprised by the speaker's vacuous comments
                     since _____

unprecedented: The unprecedented rainfall amazed forecasters espe-
                     cially since _____

impulsive: We became concerned with his impulsive behavior after
                     he _____

pragmatic: Because of her pragmatic ideas, we decided to _____

                     _____

portend: After the weather forecaster realized that conditions
                     portended disaster, he advised listeners _____

detrimental: Lack of sleep can have a detrimental effect on your body
                     by _____

impediment: Despite her speech impediment, she managed to _____

                     _____

relentless: Because of the relentless pounding of the waves on its
                     foundation, the beach house began to _____

scrutinize: Airport officials were told to scrutinize each and every
                     passenger after it was learned that _____

exacerbating: Because giving their child more candy was only exacer-
                     bating the problem, they decided to _____

oblivious: Walking down the street oblivious to your surround-
                     ings can be dangerous because _____

conversely: Under dry conditions walking is not that dangerous; conversely, _____

superficially: After the doctor examined my family superficially, I decided to _____

implicit: Although she didn't directly state it, it was implicit that

_____

viable: When they realized that there was no viable solution, they decided to _____

cumulative: It was difficult to dispute all the cumulative evidence, especially since _____

vying: Having a classroom full of children vying for your attention can make you _____

elicited: After her jokes elicited laughter from the audience, the speaker felt _____

stolidly: The accused accepted the sentence stolidly, looked at the camera, and _____

desensitizes: Researchers claim that watching TV violence desensitizes us because _____

regressive: The president stated that his opponent's regressive proposals would _____

obesity: In order to combat obesity, many people decide to _____

_____

unflinchingly: His ability to deal unflinchingly with his opponents' attacks earned him a reputation as _____

scathing: We were surprised by the minister's scathing reply, especially since _____

naïve: We often say that children are naïve because _____

_____

innuendo: Don't just accept every innuendo you hear or read, because _____

 PROCESS GUIDE

Jim Trelease has specific feelings about television. As you read the article, list those statements the author makes about television that are positive and those that are negative.

Positive	Negative
_____	_____
_____	_____
_____	_____
_____	_____
_____	_____
_____	_____
_____	_____
_____	_____
_____	_____
_____	_____

You will probably find that you list most statements in the negative column, because the author has mainly negative things to say about television. Even the few positive statements he makes are qualified; that is, he notes some potential benefits, but goes on to say that they are limited. In paragraph 4, for example, he says, "I am a realist who recognizes both the enormous potential *and* the liabilities of the medium. As a teacher, television could be unparalleled." He provides a few examples in paragraph 5 and concludes, "These instances exemplify television's potential—its ability to instruct a vast audience for change." But in paragraph 6, Trelease qualifies his preceding comments: "Most Americans . . . use television as entertainment, not for instruction or information." As you read the article, you probably noticed similar examples.

The author devotes a large part of the text to comparing and contrasting television and reading. Not every paragraph contains information on this topic. On the other hand, a single paragraph may present several ideas; you will have to search those portions of the text that apply. The following chart will help you organize this information. In columns 1 and 2, list the page and paragraph. In columns 3 and 4, list the author's ideas. The first answer is provided for you.

Page(s)	Paragraph	Television	Reading
382	24	Fosters short attention span	Encourages longer attention span

Don't Blame TV

JEFF GREENFIELD

Jeff Greenfield is an Emmy award–winning CNN News *political and media analyst. Before moving to CNN in 1988, he worked at* ABC News *beginning in 1983, appeared regularly on* Nightline, *and provided weekly commentaries for* World News Sunday. *In addition to his television work, Greenfield has written or coauthored ten books, including* Television: The First 50 Years, Playing to Win, *and* The Real Campaign. *His first novel, the 1995 best-seller* The People's Choice, *was named by the* New York Times Book Review *as one of the notable books of the year. He is a contributing columnist for* Time *magazine and has written articles for publications ranging from* Harper's *to* National Lampoon.

GEARING UP

1. Some people argue that television can have both positive and negative influences on people's behavior. List examples of both types of influences.

2. List some things you have learned from watching television that you probably would not have learned otherwise.

 # READING STRATEGY
READING COMPARATIVELY

The strategy of reading comparatively is the practice of reading two or more articles and looking for agreement and disagreement regarding specific ideas and issues. The strategy also involves your judgment on the merits of the arguments and evidence. You are determining which arguments are sounder and which evidence is more compelling.

Among their collections, many libraries have anthologies that focus upon controversial issues and contain articles that take opposing viewpoints. A topic is stated as it might be in a debate, for example: "Should children be spanked for bad behavior?" Authors are asked to respond to the topic either affirmatively or negatively and present evidence to support their position. Occasionally, the authors are invited to review each other's work before publication and write a rebuttal that is also published. To illustrate, the following pairing of articles might appear in a book devoted to the question of punishing children.

Article 1:   Yes, children should be spanked for bad behavior.
Article 2:   No, children should not be spanked but counseled about their inappropriate behavior.

The value of these anthologies is that the issues are often presented in a clear, pro-con fashion. Editors usually select authors with different views to contribute their perspective about a controversial topic. However, you cannot depend on finding these types of anthologies for every controversial issue. It is more likely that when investigating an issue with many possible viewpoints you will find articles that compare and contrast to another piece on but one or two points. The authors of these works are not writing with another article in mind. Using the example above of punishing children, a set of these somewhat less-related articles (found in unrelated journals) might look like the following:

Article A: Children should be disciplined for bad behavior.
Article B: A history of corporal punishment practices in colonial America.

You might indeed be able to find points of contrast in these articles, but you may have to work harder.

As you are researching controversial issues, keep an open mind and be willing to consider points of view that differ from yours. Sometimes novice researchers examine the literature to find sources that support their point of view and ignore evidence that seems to support the other side. But ignoring the other side of an idea actually weakens the credibility of your work. People who will be evaluating the quality of your work are generally aware of counterarguments and evidence and will expect to see contrary evidence mentioned. You are not endorsing contrary arguments by citing them, but you are expected to be able to argue why they have less merit.

The procedure for looking for and examining opposing viewpoints in two articles can be illustrated in the following manner:

• Consider each article and look for a common issue or concern.

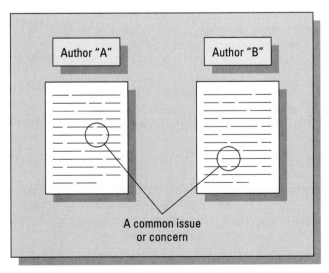

The Issue or Concern		
As seen by author "A"	*As seen by author "B"*	*As seen by me*
		My understanding My reaction My conclusion

- Critically evaluate the issue from each author's perspective and then give your reaction.

Application

The articles written by Trelease and Greenfield were not written with each other in mind. Each of the writers has a point of view and argues to support a particular stand on an issue. Therefore, in making connections between these articles, do not go beyond the bounds of what the author is saying just to make a link. To do so is to misrepresent the views of one author or both.

Writers like Trelease and Greenfield strive for balance. Both authors are aware of the arguments on the other side of the issue. Neither author uses a simplistic approach that claims television viewing is either totally positive or completely negative. Rather they make claims that are qualified. For example, Trelease says that television is the major stumbling block to literacy in this country, but he also says that television's potential as a teacher is unmatched. Greenfield does not say that television has no negative influence on viewers, but he says that its impact seems to make little difference in serious matters. In your comments, keep the balanced efforts of the authors in mind.

In analyzing readings like "Television" by Trelease and "Don't Blame TV" by Greenfield, you should not expect to see all the ideas discussed in one article considered in the other. Instead, focus on those ideas addressed directly or indirectly by both authors. The chart on page 397 identifies issues that are addressed in both articles.

After you have completed both articles and are reasonably sure that you understand each author's major points (refer to the process guides for Trelease and Greenfield for additional assistance), organize key ideas and issues and see where the authors agree or disagree. In addition, examine your own position on these concerns. We provide you with a chart and suggest some common issues in the first column. Next, record Trelease's and Greenfield's position in the appropriate column. Finally, note your responses to the author's statements. If you agree with a position, briefly state your reasons for doing so. If you disagree, state your stand on that issue. After reading both articles and thinking about a particular concern, you may find that you have a view that is different from either author. If so, indicate it and your reasons for feeling as you do.

Topic/Issue	Trelease	Greenfield	My Response
TV influence (+)			
TV influence (−)			
TV and test scores			
TV education versus entertainment			

 # READING STRATEGY CHECK

SUMMARIZING

The strategy of summarizing was introduced in relation to the Malcolm X article in Unit One. A summary contains these things:

1. A paraphrased main point

2. Condensed, paraphrased support statements or detail

3. The author's tone preserved

A summary does not contain opinion or interpretation. Nor does it add or take away from the author's argument. Try to remain faithful to the spirit of the author's work and not shift the tone. This becomes particularly important in viewing a piece like Greenfield's article. The title is somewhat misleading: "Don't Blame TV." You might expect that Greenfield is absolving TV from the things it is usually blamed for, like stirring violent emotions in young people. But he doesn't attempt to make TV blameless. Rather, he carefully qualifies the blame by arguing it is less or partial in particular situations. His careful reasoning must be reflected in a summary of the article. Overstating his argument (TV is blameless) or understating it (TV is to blame for most bad social behavior) violates the most important rule in summarizing—the author's ideas must come through fairly.

The Reading

Don't Blame TV

by JEFF GREENFIELD

1   One of the enduring pieces of folk wisdom was uttered by the 19th-century humorist Artemus Ward, who warned his readers: "It ain't what you don't know that hurts you; it's what you know that just ain't so."

2   There's good advice in that warning to some of television's most vocif-erous critics, who are certain that every significant change in American so-cial and political life can be traced, more or less directly, to the pervasive influence of TV.

    vociferous

    pervasive

3   It has been blamed for the decline of scores on scholastic achievement tests, for the rise in crime, for the decline in voter turnout, for the growth of premarital and extramarital sex, for the supposed collapse of family life and the increase in the divorce rate.

4   This is an understandable attitude. For one thing, television is the most visible, ubiquitous device to have entered our lives in the last 40 years. It is a medium in almost every American home, it is on in the average household some seven hours a day, and it is accessible by every kind of citizen from the most desperate of the poor to the wealthiest and most powerful among us.

    ubiquitous

5   If so pervasive a medium has come into our society in the last four decades, and if our society has changed in drastic ways in that same time, why not assume that TV is the reason why American life looks so different?

6   Well, as any philosopher can tell you, one good reason for skepticism is that you can't make assumptions about causes. They even have an impres-sive Latin phrase for that fallacy: *post hoc, ergo propter hoc.* For instance, if I do a rain dance at 5 P.M. and it rains at 6 P.M., did my dance bring down the rains? Probably not. But it's that kind of thinking, in my view, that charac-terizes much of the argument about how television influences our values.

7   It's perfectly clear, of course, that TV does influence some kinds of be-havior. For example, back in 1954, *Disneyland* launched a series of episodes on the life of Davy Crockett, the legendary Tennessee frontiersman. A song based on that series swept the hit parade, and by that summer every kid in America was wearing a coonskin cap.

8   The same phenomenon has happened whenever a character on a prime-time television show suddenly strikes a chord in the country. Countless women tried to capture the Farrah Fawcett look a decade ago when *Char-lie's Angels* first took flight. Schoolyards from Maine to California picked up—instantly, it seemed—on such catch phrases as "Up your nose with a rubber hose!" (*Welcome Back, Kotter*), "Kiss my grits!" (*Alice*) and "Na-nunanu!" (*Mork & Mindy*). Today, every singles bar in the land is packed with young men in expensive white sports jackets and T-shirts, trying to em-ulate the macho looks of *Miami Vice*'s Don Johnson.

    emulate

9   These fads clearly show television's ability to influence matters that do

not matter very much. Yet, when we turn to genuinely important things, television's impact becomes a lot less clear.

10   Take, for example, the decline in academic excellence, measured by the steady decline in Scholastic Aptitude Test scores from 1964 to 1982. It seemed perfectly logical to assume that a younger generation spending hours in front of the TV set every day with Fred Flintstone and Batman must have been suffering from brain atrophy. Yet, as writer David Owen noted in a recent book on educational testing, other equally impassioned explanations *impassioned* for the drop in scores included nuclear fallout, junk food, cigarette smoking by pregnant women, cold weather, declining church attendance, the draft, the assassination of President Kennedy and fluoridated water.

11   More significant, SAT scores stopped declining in 1982; they have been rising since then. Is TV use declining in the typical American home? On the contrary, it is increasing. If we really believed that our societal values are determined by new media, we might conclude that the birth of MTV in 1981 somehow caused the test scores to rise.

12   Or consider the frequently heard charge that the increase in TV violence is somehow responsible for the surge in crime. In fact, the crime rate nationally has been dropping for three straight years. It would be ludicrous to "credit" television for this; explanations are more likely to be found in the shift of population away from a "youth bulge" (where more crimes are committed) and improved tracking of career criminals in many big cities.

13   But why, then, ignore the demographic factors that saw in America an *demographic* enormous jump in teen-agers and young adults in the 1960s and 1970s? Why *assume* that television, with its inevitable "crime-does-not-pay" morality, somehow turned our young into hoodlums? The same kind of problem be- *bedevils* devils those who argue that TV has triggered a wave of sexually permissive behavior. In the first place, television was the most sexually conservative of all media through the first quarter-century of its existence. While Playboy began making a clean breast of things in the mid-1950s, when book censorship was all but abolished in the "Lady Chatterly's Lover" decision of 1958, when movies began showing it all in the 1960s, television remained an oasis—or desert—of twin beds, flannel nightgowns and squeaky-clean dialogue and characters.

14   In fact, as late as 1970, CBS refused to let Mary Tyler Moore's Mary Richards character be a divorcée. The audience, they argued, would never accept it. Instead, she was presented as the survivor of a broken relationship.

15   Why, then, do we see so many broken families and divorces on television today? Because the networks are trying to denigrate the value of the nuclear *denigrate* family? Hardly. As *The Cosby Show* and its imitators show, network TV is only too happy to offer a benign view of loving husbands, wives and children.

16   The explanation, instead, lies in what was happening to the very fabric of American life. In 1950, at the dawn of television, the divorce rate was 2.6 per 1000 Americans. By 1983, it had jumped to five per thousand; nearly half of all marriages were ending in divorce. The reasons range from the

increasing mobility of the population to the undermining of settled patterns   *undermining*
of work, family and neighborhood.

17   What's important to notice, however, is that it was not television that
made divorce more acceptable in American society; it was changes in American society that made divorce more acceptable on television. (Which is why,
in her new sitcom, Mary Tyler Moore can finally play a divorced woman.)
In the mid 1980s, divorce has simply lost the power to shock.

18   That same argument, I think, undermines much of the fear that television has caused our young to become sexually precocious. From my in-   *precocious*
creasingly dimming memory of youthful lust, I have my doubts about
whether young lovers really needed the impetus of *Dallas* or *The Young and*   *impetus*
the Restless to start thinking about sex. The more serious answer, however,
is that the spread of readily available birth control was a lot more persuasive
a force in encouraging premarital sex than the words and images on TV.

19   We can measure this relative impotence of television in a different way.   *impotence*
All through the 1950s and early 1960s, the images of women on TV were
what feminists would call "negative"; they were portrayed as half-woman,
half-child, incapable of holding a job or balancing a checkbook or even running a social evening. (How many times did Lucy burn the roast?) Yet the
generation of women who grew up on television was the first to reject force-
fully the wife-and-homemaker limitations that such images ought to have
encouraged. These were the women who marched into law schools, medical
schools and the halls of Congress.

20   The same was true of the images of black Americans, as TV borrowed
the movie stereotypes of shiftless handymen and relentlessly cheerful maids.   *stereotypes*
We didn't begin to see TV blacks as the equal of whites until Bill Cosby
showed up in *I Spy* in 1966. Did the generation weaned on such fare turn out
to be indifferent to the cause of black freedom in America? Hardly. This was
the generation that organized and supported the civil-rights sit-ins and freedom rides in the South. Somehow, the reality of second-class citizenship was
far more powerful than the imagery of dozens of television shows.

21   I have no argument with the idea that television contains many messages
that need close attention; I hold no brief for shows that pander to the ap-   *pander*
petite for violence or smarmy sexuality or stereotyping. My point is that
these evils ought to be fought on grounds of taste and common decency. We
ought not to try and prove more than the facts will bear. Television, powerful as it is, has shown precious little power over the most fundamental values of Americans. Given most of what's on TV, that's probably a good thing.
But it also suggests that the cries of alarm may be misplaced.

QUESTIONS

1. Analyze the author's attitude toward television. Support your response
   with specific examples found in the article.

2. According to Greenfield, why has television received so much criticism?

3. Greenfield argues against those critics who blame television for changes in American society. List the arguments of the critics in one column and next to their arguments list Greenfield's response.

4. At the conclusion of his article the author states: "We ought not to try and prove more than the facts will bear." Explain this statement in light of his position.

EXTENDING YOUR VOCABULARY

vociferous: We could tell the debate had become vociferous by the fact that _____

pervasive: The storm's pervasive effects were hard to measure because _____

ubiquitous: Today computers seem to be ubiquitous, so much so that _____

emulate: I would like to emulate my sister's accomplishments because _____

impassioned: Her impassioned plea for justice caused people to _____ _____

demographic: The advertiser wanted a demographic profile of the audience because _____

bedevils: This problem bedevils us so much that _____

denigrate: When they tried to denigrate my accomplishments, I became _____

undermining: She accused her husband of undermining her authority when he _____

precocious: Her daughter was said to be very precocious because she _____

impetus: Her impetus to succeed came from _____

impotence: The armies' impotence was due to _____

stereotypes: Many television stereotypes are misleading because _____ _____

pander: Some politicians believe it is smart to pander to _____ _____

PROCESS GUIDE

1. A writer will often begin an article with a maxim. A maxim is a saying about people's behavior that seems to ring true. For example, a maxim used often is Santayana's "Those who cannot remember the past are condemned to repeat it." Paraphrase the maxim reported by the author: "It ain't what you don't know that hurts you; it's what you know that just ain't so." Then discuss how it is used as a reference point to introduce the idea in paragraph 2.

   Paraphrase _____

   _____

   Discussion _____

   _____

2. In paragraph 3, cite the social ills that have been blamed on TV.

   _____

3. Do you believe that television is the cause of these problems? Explain.

   _____

4. In paragraphs 4–6, the author examines the logic that has prompted people to blame TV for problems. He specifically examines the idea of "causes." What does he share that cautions us about supposed cause-and-effect relationships?

   _____

   _____

5. In paragraphs 7 and 8 the author claims that he would be skeptical about a strong cause-and-effect relationship between TV and bad social behavior. Nevertheless, he points out that there is good evidence to suggest that TV does influence some social behavior. What examples does he cite?

   _____

   _____

6. In paragraph 9, what does he conclude about the influence of TV on behavior?

   _____

7. In paragraph 10, the author discusses the possible connection between the decline in test scores and television watching. What does he say

might be a reasonable expectation of the result of young people spending many hours a day in front of the TV?

_____

8. He then points out that other causes have been suggested for the decline in test scores. From the list provided, which factors do you feel are the most reasonable? Explain.

_____

_____

9. Paragraph 11 presents a counterargument to the TV-test score, cause-effect relationship. What argument is given?

_____

_____

10. What would you need to know to assess the validity of Greenfield's argument? (Hint: Check the publication date of this article.)

_____

_____

11. Paragraphs 12–16 examine some purported TV/social problems, cause-effect relationships that the author questions. Select one issue and analyze it. What is the problem? Why does the author feel we can't totally blame TV for it? Evaluate his argument.

_____

_____

12. In paragraphs 17–20, the author argues that TV mirrors the changes occurring in American life rather than the other way around. In other words, he reverses the cause-effect relationship. Cite two of the examples he gives and analyze them. Evaluate his arguments for logic and evidence.

_____

_____

13. Paraphrase the author's closing argument in paragraph 21. Analyze and evaluate it. Based on what the author has presented, have you altered your view of television's influence on society? Explain your position.

_____

READING JOURNAL

"Television" by Trelease and "Don't Blame TV" by Greenfield share the common theme of television, but each author approaches the topic differently.

- **Content**

  What new information did you gain about television? What details stand out in your mind? Why do you think these were ones you remembered?

  Were parts of the readings unclear? Copy a sentence that you don't understand and pose questions to the author.

- **Process**

  You probably came across information and ideas that challenged you either because they were difficult to comprehend or they were unfamiliar. What strategies did you use to help you process the information? Which elements of the reading argumentation strategy did you use? If you had difficulty with any of the allusions made by the authors, how did you resolve your uncertainty? Did the length of Trelease's article pose any challenges? How did you retain so much information? Were you able to compare and contrast both readings?

- **Response**

  Did either Trelease's or Greenfield's style of writing appeal to you? Were you personally affected by either writer's message? Have you changed your mind regarding television as a result of reading these articles?

Can Your Students Read TV?

KATHLEEN TYNER

Kathleen Tyner is an educator, author, and founding director of Strategies for Media Literacy, Inc., a San Francisco–based organization that promotes media education in the United States. This article first appeared in the January 1991 issue of Cable in the Classroom *and is reprinted with permission of the author. It is available online at the following address:* http://interact.uoregon.edu/MediaLit/FA/MLArticleFolder/read.html

GEARING UP

1. Some people claim that watching television is a passive activity and others feel that it is not. List several points each side could make to support its claim.

2. What role, if any, should schools play in instructing students to think critically about television? Discuss your position.

READING STRATEGY

ALLUSIONS

If you read a newspaper account describing a dispute between a small bookstore and a giant bookstore, the headline might state: "Battle of the Books—David versus Goliath." A television program showing the romantic involvement of the main character might say she was "struck by Cupid's arrow." Both of these examples use allusions. An allusion (not to be confused with illusion) is an indirect reference in which the source is not specifically identified. In the David versus Goliath example, a reference is being made to two biblical characters. David was a young Israelite shepherd boy who challenged the mighty Philistine giant Goliath and was victorious. In the second example, a reference is being made to the Roman god of love. He is commonly portrayed as a winged infant carrying a bow and a quiver of arrows. When his victims are wounded, love or passion is aroused.

Writers use many sources for allusions—art, religion, mythology, science, literature, music, and psychology, as well as current events, sports, and popular culture. Allusions add meaning and richness to writing. In addition, they serve as shorthand for writers, who presume their audience will identify with the subject of the allusion. Writers often assume that their readers share the same frame of reference and background information, but this is not always so. Not everyone is well read, and certain allusions become more obscure with the passage of time. Occasionally writers or their editors provide footnotes that explain the allusion, but this is not commonly done. Sometimes readers may require guidance to interpret the author's allusions. One way is to ask the instructor, but first consult reference books such as dictionaries, encyclopedias, or specialized books devoted to allusions. Two useful sources are the following:

- *Common Knowledge: A Reader's Guide to Literary Allusions* by David Grote

- *Allusions—Cultural, Literary, Biblical and Historical: A Thematic Dictionary* by Laurence Urdang and Frederick G. Rufner, Jr.

When you encounter an allusion, make note of it. If you are unfamiliar with the allusion, use a reference book to locate and define the term. Once you understand the meaning of the allusion, ask yourself: "Why did the author choose to include it?" "Why was it mentioned?" "In what way does it help me to understand the text?"

The more you read, the greater your chances of recognizing the allusions that you encounter. Your reading experiences will be more rewarding and you'll derive greater pleasure from being able to share a common experience with the writer.

In the next article, "Can Your Students Read TV?", the author refers to *Socratic discourse* and the *Socratic method*. Socrates was a Greek philosopher and teacher who taught by asking questions, thereby leading others to reach conclusions by themselves. Today writers who refer to the *Socratic method* assume that readers are familiar with it.

In Jim Trelease's article on television, he refers to the medium as "an electronic Pied Piper" (page 378). This is an allusion to a legendary flute player who offers the residents of Hamelin, Germany, a solution to their rat problem. In return for payment he will lead the rats out of the town by charming them with his flute playing. When he is refused payment, he seeks revenge by charming the children and leading them out of the town. The reference to television as an electronic Pied Piper suggests a device that offers viewers strong yet seductive charms.

Another allusion that appears in several places in this textbook is the name *Gutenberg*. His contribution to the development of print was discussed in the Unit One article "History of Printing" (page 101) and again in this unit in Biagi's chapter from *Media Impact* (page 364). Often, you will encounter the term *Gutenberg Bible* because this was considered the first book printed by moveable type. Sometimes writers take an allusion and add to or expand it. You may recall an excerpt from "The Proficient Reader" article in Unit One (page 82) in which author Sven Birkerts discussed reading aloud to his daughter. This excerpt was taken from his book, *The Gutenberg Elegies: The Fate of Reading in an Electronic Age*. It is interesting to note how he uses Gutenberg in his title. In his book Birkerts makes the following statement: "We are in the midst of an epoch-making transition; that the societal shift from print-based to electronic communications is as consequential for culture as was the shift instigated by Gutenberg's invention of movable type" (p. 192).

Application

Now it is your chance to identify some common allusions. In the leftmost column of the table on the facing page you will find examples of allusions. Use reference books to find background information about each example and record your response in the background column. Finally, in the last column write the meaning of the allusion.

Allusion	Background	Meaning
He's my **Romeo.**		
Can **Hercules** lift Walt Disney's stock?		
This is a modern **Horatio Alger** story.		
They met their **Waterloo.**		
He has **Samson**-like qualities.		
A bank robber was labeled **Robin Hood.**		
She is noted for her **quixotic** behavior.		
We've finally discovered his **Achilles heel.**		
"Hong Kong amounts to a colossal **Trojan Horse:** a prize so glorious that China's Communists cannot leave it outside the gates but which, once inside, will destroy those in power." (Headline in the *New York Times*—July 1997)		

READING STRATEGY CHECK
USING CUE WORDS

The Cue Word strategy was first introduced in the introduction to Unit One and has reappeared as strategy checks in Units One and Two. Cue words are specific verbs that frequently begin questions that you are asked to answer on homework and exams. It is important that you know the exact meaning of these terms so that you will answer appropriately. We encourage you to consult the chart listing cue words on pages 6–8 to resolve uncertainty. The next article, "Can Your Students Read TV?" includes the following cue words in the questions: *explain, list, summarize,* and *describe.*

The Reading

Can Your Students Read TV?

by KATHLEEN TYNER

1 Plato disliked the printed word. He was afraid that reading and writing would destroy oral culture and memory—and he was probably right. Of course, only an elite few could read and write in ancient Greece. It wasn't until at least two centuries after the invention of the printing press, a scant 500 years ago, that ordinary people began to make sense of the printed page. This awareness of print caused tremendous social, economic and cultural upheaval.

elite

2 We are currently in a similar communication revolution so far-reaching that we have yet to fully understand its significance. We still read books, but information bombards us from films, television, radio and advertising, too.

3 A recent Roper poll indicates that over 80% of North Americans get their news and information from television. As television becomes the communication form of choice, teachers are beginning to extend their definition of literacy to include electronic forms of communication. They are teaching their students to read TV.

4 Of course, students already know how to read the highly emotional and symbolic language of television. They learned it informally by clocking in an average of 5000 hours in front of the set before they reach school age—the same amount of time it takes to jet around the world 148 times, or orbit the moon 30 times. But just because students are sitting slack-jawed and motionless in front of the set, it doesn't mean their minds aren't hard at work. Contrary to popular wisdom, television watching is not a passive activity.

passive

5 It takes concentration to make sense of contemporary television. Narratives are broken by commercials, flying graphics, rolls and crawls, fast cuts and fades to black. Students may not have the vocabulary to articulate to adults how they make a story out of this hodge-podge of images, but on a rudimentary level, they already have a firm grasp on the grammar of television. In order for them to be fully aware that television is carefully constructed with specific codes and conventions, someone has to talk to them about the way TV works.

rudimentary

6 The television teacher brings this fast-paced, symbolic and emotional language into the realm of rational discourse so that students can learn to talk about the programs they see in an active and articulate way. This doesn't take a special class in media, or expensive equipment. It can be done every time television is used in the classroom. Since students are saturated with media messages throughout life, teachers practice a formal and structured program of critical thinking about media until students begin to question media on their own. The goal of media education is to make students lifelong learners and critical questioners when the teacher is not around.

rational / discourse

saturated

7 Media education can begin at an early age. Minneapolis writer Lyn Lacy teaches Grades 1–3 at Cooper Elementary in Minneapolis. She creates me-

dia education exercises for her students that stress visuals and are akin to reading readiness. "Students in lower elementary grades can begin to learn about media languages, how television is put together, and how to distinguish the different kinds of television. Older students can understand more of the social and political elements around television." "Students are reading television like they used to read textbooks," says Michigan teacher Russ Gibb. "This idea that print is superior to television is just plain snobbery. Yes, print is important. The spoken word is important, but so is television. Reading and writing are not the only ways to communicate." His media education classes reach 100 Dearborn High School students every semester.

8   While some teachers might prefer their students turn off the television and read books, they recognize the futility of blocking a surging wave of electronic communication. Television has been blamed for everything from a rising crime wave to a drop in reading scores, but there is no evidence that students would spend their leisure time reading, if the television were indeed turned off.

9   Media teachers realize that information is only powerful if students know what to do with it. As students are inundated with media messages, the   *inundated* challenge is not to amass more information, but to access, organize and eval-   *amass* uate useful information from a variety of print and electronic sources. Critical thinking and good, old-fashioned research skills are essential for tunneling through the information glut.   *glut*

10   Dave Master teaches 200 students every semester in his media program at John Rowland High School in Rowland Heights, California. "Today's students are citizens of the computer-video age and we have a responsibility to prepare young people for their electronic future. The aware and creative citizen of the future must be an active media viewer and a capable media doer. There is nothing inherently evil about modern technology any more than   *inherently* there is something inherently evil about a pencil. Creative, artistic, critical-thinking young people will help society realize the full potential of new technologies. It's up to them."

11   If television's increased popularity as a teaching tool is any indication, teachers do not want to turn it off. They want to use it to their students' best education advantage. Teachers of media see television as an opportunity to open up the whole curriculum. Media education teaches students to think critically about all media information, from textbooks to television. As Lyn Lacy remarks, "I don't think in terms of 'bad' or 'good' TV. I only object to television that scares little kids. The rest of it, even ads, are opportunities for critical viewing." Russ Gibb comments, "We watch all kinds of TV and tear it apart to see how they did it. Not all television is great, but TV is a cultural phenomenon, so all of it is useful for other purposes."

12   Teachers who teach about television note that television exercises work best in tandem with traditional reading and writing skills. Robert Gipe, Education Director at Appalshop in Whitesburg, Kentucky, has found that teaching about television can improve students' storytelling and writing skills. He shows elementary students documentaries and asks them to speculate about the questions that must have been asked to elicit the answers they see on the

tape. "I tell them that I don't know the real questions, but that they can figure them out by listening to the answers on the tape. They learn good interviewing skills, but also begin to question editing decisions—what was left out
of the interview and why." The Kentucky students go on to use their interview skills by questioning each other's compositions in group work. "I remember teaching composition before and people had no idea how to help
each other. I think this works. They just don't know what questions to ask
unless you guide them. Using video interview techniques are the catalyst."   *catalyst*

13   Ironically, the method of questioning teachers use to teach about television is not new. It harkens back to ancient Greece. By using Socratic
discourse, teachers practice a set of questions with their students until the
students begin to question media on their own—every time it appears in the
environment. Questions like "Who produced the program? How was it
made? What values were reflected in this television show? How did the director represent the characters? What kind of program is it?" can be practiced with students until they begin to question television on their own,
without teacher prompting.

14   Socratic method is not comfortable for every teacher. It implies that
there are no right answers—only good questions. It does not speak to a standardized test. It takes concentration and focus to guide students to think.
Since students often know more about media than their teachers, it works
best if students and teachers work together as co-investigators of media. "It
is important for students to understand that not all questions have a 'correct'
answer," says Dave Master. "Many times the quest is for the best answer,   *quest*
given need, tastes and conditions. In media education, the process is more
important than the product."

QUESTIONS

1. Explain the title of the article, "Can Your Students Read TV?" What does
   the author mean by "read"?

2. The author states: "Contrary to popular wisdom, television watching is
   not a passive activity." List the arguments she makes to support this point.

3. Summarize the role educators should play in preparing their students to
   deal effectively with media, according to the author.

4. Explain the term *Socratic discourse.* Describe the role it can play in helping students to learn to "read TV."

EXTENDING YOUR VOCABULARY

elite: To be considered part of society's elite, you need to

               _____

passive: The parents became concerned with their children's pas-

               sive behavior when _____

rudimentary: A person with a rudimentary understanding of law must
                  be careful when _____

rational: We could tell that his behavior wasn't rational by the fact
                  that _____

discourse: While engaging in discourse with her students, the in-
                  structor _____

saturated: My shirt became saturated with water after _____
                  _____

inundated: After becoming inundated with requests for free samples,
                  the advertiser decided to _____

amass: After we were able to amass a great deal of data, we needed
                  to _____

inherently: I find nothing inherently wrong with his behavior because
                  _____

glut: To deal with the glut of information, we had to
                  _____

catalyst: The catalyst that brought about a change in leadership was
                  _____

quest: In her quest for the truth, the lawyer _____

 PROCESS GUIDE

Consider the title again. We usually don't think of *reading* TV but as watching it. In *The Read-Aloud Handbook*, Trelease distinguishes between reading a book, which he claims is active, and watching TV, which he says is
passive. Given the choice of title, it is likely that the author is hoping students can do more with TV than be passively entertained by it.

1. The strategy of Reading Allusions was introduced before this article.
   Note that the author begins by alluding to Plato and mentioning his views
   on the printed word. Authors cite particular people who give credibility
   to an argument. Who was Plato, and why was he mentioned here?

   _____

2. The author claims that once people were reading after the invention of the
   printing press, a kind of revolution took place. She argues that we are in

a similar revolution today but that the sources of information have been expanded. What are the sources of information?

_____

_____

3. In paragraph 5, Tyner qualifies her earlier statement about TV literacy. In paragraph 6, what does she suggest should happen to expand student awareness?

_____

_____

4. In paragraphs 7–12, Tyner cites examples of teachers reflecting on a TV literacy program. List two teachers and their suggestions regarding the reading of TV. Give your opinion on their ideas. Do their views agree? Is there disagreement? Is there overlap in their ideas? Make notes of your ideas on the chart that follows.

Teacher	TV Reading Suggestion	Your Reaction	Comparison/Contrast

5. In paragraph 13, the author mentions Socratic dialogue as the method used by teachers to explore television. Despite what seems to be a useful approach to a very important part of our culture, Tyner suggests that some teachers are reluctant to use Socratic dialogue as a teaching strategy. What reason does she cite for this reaction?

_____

6. The article ends with a quote from Dave Master: "In media education, the process is more important than the product." Interpret this statement in light of the author's arguments. Cite other instances in education where

the primary focus is on process. That is, the goal is not on the product, but on the skill it takes to be able to make the product.

The Language of Advertising Claims

JEFFREY SCHRANK

Jeffrey Schrank is a free-lance writer and served as a contributing editor to Media and Methods. *He is the author of* Understanding Mass Media *and* Teaching Human Beings.

GEARING UP

1. What are some techniques used by advertisers in commercials to persuade viewers to buy their products?

2. You have just seen a commercial advertising the benefits of a certain product. As a wise consumer, what are some questions you should be asking yourself before you buy the product?

 # READING STRATEGY

CONNOTATION AND DENOTATION

If you were to look up the word *lemon* in a dictionary, you would probably find a definition similar to this: a small citrus fruit with a yellow skin and a juicy sour pulp. Yet if your friend told you that he bought a used car and it was a lemon, he is not suggesting that the car is a citrus fruit but rather that it is defective. The dictionary definition is an example of **denotation**—a direct, specific, nonemotional meaning of lemon. The used car example of the word *lemon* is an example of **connotation**—the meaning and association suggested by a word. This would include its emotional overtones, colorings, and implications.

Being aware of connotative meanings is of particular importance when reading advertisements or propaganda. Ad writers commonly make use of the connotative powers of language. They look for words that will evoke a response from their audience. The choice of brand names undergoes a great deal of thought because advertisers expect the public to have an automatic reaction and equate the name of the product with the product itself. Many products that are associated with colors are given exotic or alluring names that have connotative meanings. Here are some examples of names given to red lipstick. Next to each name write the meaning and association that the advertiser or manufacturer wants to convey.

Name	Connotation
Rosegarden	_____
Nightlife	_____
Hollywood Red	_____
Uptown Red	_____
Scarlet	_____
Apple Butter	_____

Consider another example of names given to green paint. As with the previous set of names, write the meaning and association that the advertiser or manufacturer wants to convey.

Name	Connotation
Adirondack	_____
Everglade	_____
Christmas Green	_____
Meditation	_____
Caribbean	_____

Although advertisers would love us to buy their products, they rarely use the word *buy* and instead use terms like *try, use, get,* or *ask for.* Why? Because the word *buy* carries with it the unpleasant connotation of parting with your money!

In his poem "The Garden," the English poet Andrew Marvell (1621–1678) describes someone looking to a society for peace, contentment, and innocence and finding it amongst the garden greens.

Annihilating all that's made
To a green thought in a green shade.

The poet is using the color green to suggest images of grass, trees, growth, and tranquility. Such words can suggest feelings of hope, contentment, desire, and expectation.

Images as well as words are rich in connotative meaning. What pictures would an advertiser use to suggest relaxation, serenity, and optimism? Cigarette advertisers make use of colors and images to suggest just such an atmosphere. Often a young couple can be seen near a brook or waterfall, picnicking on a green lawn surrounded by blossoming green trees. Green represents growth, renewal, and refreshment.

Of course, in other contexts the word *green* can carry other meanings. Someone can be described as "green with envy," or a new, inexperienced worker can be called "green under the collar." Telling someone that he looks like a million bucks may seem like a compliment until you add the line: "green and crumpled." In this case, *green* suggests a sickly color, as in Shakespeare's Act 1, Scene 7 of Macbeth: "to look so green and pale."

An advertisement for a weight control product might promise to help make you look slender (and perhaps thin) but not skinny because of the negative connotation associated with *skinny.* Advertisers must consider how their audience will respond to word choice. Why does a skin product claim to give you skin like peaches and cream rather than pineapples and ketchup? If you wish to sell a product and emphasize that it's economical and not outrageously priced, would your ad read "inexpensive" or "cheap"? *Cheap* often connotes poor quality. As a restaurant owner, would you advertise that you have a world famous cook or a world famous chef? Many words have fairly similar meanings yet different connotations.

Application

In the article that follows this strategy, Jeffrey Schrank describes several techniques advertisers use to sell their merchandise. In particular, he focuses on the language and words they use to promote their products. Although he doesn't discuss connotation and denotation, several of his examples of product names have connotative meanings. Next to each name, describe the mood or association the manufacturer or advertiser wants you to remember.

Product Name	Function	Connotation
Supergloss	Paint	_____
Cougar	Automobile	_____
Lipsaver	Lip balm	_____
Wonder bread	Bread	_____
Easy off	Oven cleaner	_____

Consider the following words that are used as part of several products. What ideas or images are suggested?

Golden   _____

Sunrise   _____

Crystal   _____

Imagine you are the head of advertising for a cigar manufacturer. Given the terms *odor, fragrance, smell,* and *aroma,* which would you use to promote your product? Explain. Now imagine you head an advertising campaign designed to ban cigar smoking in public places. Given these previous four terms, which would you use to promote your product? Explain. If you were a perfume manufacturer, which of the four terms would you use, and why?

Finally, here are some words that are rich in connotative meaning. They are also used by manufacturers as part of product names. In the space provided, write the meaning and association suggested by the names.

Hug	Huggies diapers	_____
Sunny	Sunny Delight fruit drink	_____
Secret	Secret deodorant	_____
Miracle	Miracle Whip spread	_____
Love	Luv's diapers	_____
Cheer	Cheer laundry detergent	_____
Taboo	Tabu cologne	_____

READING STRATEGY CHECK

ALLUSIONS

In the previous reading you were introduced to the strategy of reading allusions—indirect references that authors use to add richness and meaning to their writing. You may recall that writers draw upon a wide range of materials for allusions, including mythology, literature, science, and religion, as well as elements of popular culture. In Schrank's article, "The Language of Advertising Claims," the author uses several allusions.

There are several sources that can be used to help you understand the meaning and significance of an allusion. A library will usually contain a number of reference books devoted to allusions. In addition, an Internet search can also provide valuable information. There are World Wide Web sites devoted to advertising and literature that can also help.

In the first paragraph Schrank refers to Vance Packard and his "hidden persuaders" while discussing the persuasive appeals of advertising. This is an allusion to writer and sociologist Vance Packard, whose book *The Hidden Persuaders* became a best-seller in 1957. In his text Packard discussed the psychological techniques used by advertisers to sell their products. He presented many examples and details to show how ad campaigns are designed to exploit our fears, needs, and insecurities. As in other allusions, Schrank does not provide the information about Packard that you are given in this strategy check. He assumes that you will know this reference. If you cannot make a connection here, you will miss some of the historical context that Schrank is providing. In other words, he is showing that a published description of advertising deception has a forty-year history.

Schrank provides another allusion in the sixth paragraph when he states:

"The first rule of parity claims involves the Alice in Wonderlandish use of the words 'better' and 'best.' In parity claims, 'better' means 'best' and 'best' means 'equal to.'" He is referring to *Alice's Adventures in Wonderland,* the Lewis Carroll children's classic tale first published in 1865. In the tale, Alice chases a rabbit and falls into a magical madcap world of Wonderland with characters that include Tweedledee and Tweedledum, the Cheshire Cat, and the Mad Hatter and March Hare, who invite her to a memorable tea party. Wonderland is a place of crazy logic where the absurd and surreal are the norm. Riddles have no answers, songs turn into nonsense, and Alice is constantly challenged to reevaluate her words. Logic and common sense no longer apply in Wonderland. It is a place where everything changes constantly and nothing is exactly as it appears to be.

Here is a sample from the seventh chapter of Lewis Carroll's book. Notice how the author plays with language and keeps us looking for the deeper meaning of words. This excerpt includes Schrank's reference to the words *better* and *best* that are commonly used in advertising.

"Come, we shall have some fun now!" thought Alice. "I'm glad they've begun asking riddles.—I believe I can guess that," she added aloud.

"Do you mean that you think you can find out the answer to it?" said the March Hare.

"Exactly so," said Alice.

"Then you should say what you mean," the March Hare went on.

"I do," Alice hastily replied; "at least—at least I mean what I say—that's the same thing, you know."

"Not the same thing a bit!" said the Hatter. "You might just as well say that 'I see what I eat' is the same thing as 'I eat what I see'!"

"You might just as well say," added the March Hare, "that 'I like what I get' is the same thing as 'I get what I like'!"

"You might just as well say," added the Dormouse, who seemed to be talking in his sleep, "that 'I breathe when I sleep' is the same thing as 'I sleep when I breathe'!"

"It IS the same thing with you," said the Hatter, and here the conversation dropped, and the party sat silent for a minute, while Alice thought over all she could remember about ravens and writing-desks, which wasn't much.

The Hatter was the first to break the silence. "What day of the month is it?" he said, turning to Alice: he had taken his watch out of his pocket, and was looking at it uneasily, shaking it every now and then, and holding it to his ear.

Alice considered a little, and then said "The fourth."

"Two days wrong!" sighed the Hatter. "I told you butter wouldn't suit the works!" he added looking angrily at the March Hare.

"It was the BEST butter," the March Hare meekly replied.

"Yes, but some crumbs have got in as well," the Hatter grumbled: "you shouldn't have put it in with the bread-knife."

The March Hare took the watch and looked at it gloomily: then he dipped it into his cup of tea, and looked at it again: but he could think of nothing better to say than his first remark, "It was the BEST butter, you know."

The Reading

The Language of Advertising Claims

by JEFFREY SCHRANK

1 Students, and many teachers, are notorious believers in their immunity to advertising. These naive inhabitants of consumerland believe that advertising is childish, dumb, a bunch of lies, and influences only the vast hordes of the less sophisticated. Their own purchases are made purely on the basis of value and desire, with advertising playing only a minor supporting role. They know about Vance Packard and his "hidden persuaders" and the adman's psychosell and bag of persuasive magic. They are not impressed.

immunity

2 Advertisers know better. Although few people admit to being greatly influenced by ads, surveys and sales figures show that a well-designed advertising campaign has dramatic effects. A logical conclusion is that advertising works below the level of conscious awareness and it works even on those who claim immunity to its message. Ads are designed to have an effect while being laughed at, belittled, and all but ignored.

3 A person unaware of advertising's claim on him is precisely the one most defenseless against the adman's attack. Advertisers delight in an audience which believes ads to be harmless nonsense, for such an audience is rendered defenseless by its belief that there is no attack taking place. The purpose of a classroom study of advertising is to raise the level of awareness about the persuasive techniques used in ads. One way to do this is to analyze ads in microscopic detail. Ads can be studied to detect their psychological hooks, they can be used to gauge values and hidden desires of the common man, they can be studied for their use of symbols, color, and imagery. But perhaps the simplest and most direct way to study ads is through an analysis of the language of the advertising claim.

rendered

4 The "claim" is the verbal or print part of an ad that makes some claim of superiority for the product being advertised. After studying claims, students should be able to recognize those that are misleading and accept as useful information those that are true. A few of these claims are downright lies, some are honest statements about a truly superior product, but most fit into the category of neither bold lies nor helpful consumer information. They balance on the narrow line between truth and falsehood by a careful choice of words.

5 The reason so many ad claims fall into this category of pseudo-information is that they are applied to parity products, a product in which all or most of the brands available are nearly identical. Since no one superior product exists, advertising is used to create the illusion of superiority. The largest advertising budgets are devoted to parity products such as gasoline, cigarettes, beer and soft drinks, soaps, and various headache and cold remedies.

pseudo

parity

superiority

6 The first rule of parity claims involves the Alice in Wonderlandish use of the words "better" and "best." In parity claims, "better" means "best" and

"best" means "equal to." If all the brands are identical they must all be equally good, the legal minds have decided. So "best" means that the product is as good as the other superior products in its category. When Bing Crosby declares Minute Maid Orange Juice "the best there is" he means it as good as the other orange juices you can buy.

7   The word "better" has been legally interpreted to be a comparative and therefore becomes a clear claim of superiority. Bing could not have said that Minute Maid is "better than any other orange juice." "Better" is a claim to superiority. The only time "better" can be used is when a product does indeed have superiority over other products in its category or when the better is used to compare the product with something other than competing brands. An orange juice could therefore claim to be "better than a vitamin pill," or even "the better breakfast drink."

8   The second rule of advertising claim analysis is simply that if any product is truly superior, the ad will say so very clearly and will offer some kind of convincing evidence of the superiority. If an ad hedges the least about a *hedges* product's advantage over the competition you can strongly suspect it is not superior—maybe equal to but not better. You will never hear a gasoline company say "we will give you four miles per gallon more in your car than any other brand." They would love to make such a claim, but it would not be true. Gasoline is a parity product, and, in spite of some very clever and deceptive ads of a few years ago, no one has yet claimed one brand of gaso- *deceptive* line better than any other brand.

9   To create the necessary illusion of superiority, advertisers usually resort to one or more of the following ten basic techniques. Each is common and easy to identify.

The Weasel Claim

10   A weasel word is a modifier that practically negates the claim that follows. *negates* The expression "weasel word" is aptly named after the egg-eating habits of weasels. A weasel will suck out the inside of an egg, leaving it appear intact to the casual observer. Upon closer examination, the egg is discovered to be hollow. Words or claims that appear substantial upon first look but disintegrate into hollow meaninglessness on analysis are weasels. Commonly used weasel words include "helps" (the champion weasel); "like" (used in a comparative sense); "virtual" or "virtually;" "acts" or "works;" "can be;" "up to;" "as much as;" "refreshes;" "comforts;" "tackles;" "fights;" "comes on;" "the feel of;" "the look of;" "looks like;" "fortified;" "enriched;" and "strengthened."

Samples of Weasel Claims

11   "*Helps control* dandruff *symptoms* with *regular use*." The weasels include "helps control," and possibly even "symptoms," and "regular use." The claim is not "stops dandruff."

12   "Leaves dishes *virtually* spotless." We have seen so many ad claims that we have learned to tune-out weasels. You are supposed to think "spotless," rather than "virtually" spotless.

13   "Only half the price of *many* color sets." "Many" is the weasel. The claim is supposed to give the impression that the set is inexpensive.

14   "Tests confirm one mouthwash *best* against mouth odor." "Hot Nestlés' cocoa is the very *best.*" Remember the "best" and "better" routine.

15   "Listerine *fights* bad breath." "Fights," not "stops."

16   "Lots of things have changed, but Hershey's *goodness* hasn't." This claim does not say that Hershey's chocolate hasn't changed.

17   "Bacos, the crispy garnish that *tastes* just *like* its name."

The Unfinished Claim

18   The unfinished claim is one in which the ad claims the product is better, or has more of something but does not finish the comparison.

Samples of Unfinished Claims

19   "Magnavox gives you more." More what?

20   "Anacin: Twice as much of the pain reliever doctors recommend most." This claim fits in a number of categories but it does not say twice as much of what pain reliever.

21   "Supergloss does it with more color, more shine, more sizzle, more!"

22   "Coffee-mate gives coffee more body, more flavor." Also note that "body" and "flavor" are weasels.

23   "You can be sure if it's Westinghouse." Sure of what?

24   "Scott makes it better for you."

25   "Ford LTD—700% quieter." When the FTC asked Ford to substantiate   *substantiate* this claim, Ford revealed that they meant the inside of the Ford was 700% quieter than the outside.

The "We're Different and Unique" Claim

26   This kind of claim states simply that there is nothing else quite like the product advertised. For example, if Schlitz would add pink food coloring to its beer they could say "There's nothing like new pink Schlitz." The uniqueness claim is supposed to be interpreted by readers as a claim to superiority.

Samples of "We're Different and Unique" Claim

27   "There's no other mascara like it."

28   "Only Doral has this unique filter system."   *unique*

29   "Cougar is like nobody else's car."

30   "Either way, liquid or spray, there's nothing else like it."

31   "If it doesn't say Goodyear, it can't be polyglas." "Polyglas" is a trade name copyrighted by Goodyear. Goodrich or Firestone could make a tire exactly identical to the Goodyear one and yet couldn't call it "polyglas"—a name for fiberglass belts.

32   "Only Zenith has chromacolor." Same as the "polyglas" gambit. Admiral has solarcolor and RCA has accucolor.

The "Water Is Wet" Claim

33 "Water is wet" claims say something about the product that is true for any brand in that product category (e.g., "Schrank's water is really wet."). The claim is usually a statement of fact, but not a real advantage over the competition.

Samples of "Water Is Wet" Claim

34 "Mobil: the Detergent Gasoline." (Any gasoline acts as a cleaning agent.)

35   "Great Lash greatly increases the diameter of every lash."

36   "Rheingold, the natural beer." Made from grains and water as are other beers.

37   "SKIN smells differently on everyone." As do many perfumes.

The "So What" Claim

38 This is the kind of claim to which the careful reader will react by saying "So what?" A claim is made which is true but which gives no real advantage to the product. This is similar to the "water is wet" claim except that it claims an advantage which is not shared by most of the other brands in the product category.

Samples of the "So What" Claim

39 "Geritol has more than twice the iron of ordinary supplements." But is twice as much beneficial to the body?

40   "Campbell's gives you tasty pieces of chicken and not one but two chicken stocks." Does the presence of two stocks improve the taste?

41   "Strong enough for a man but made for a woman." This deodorant claim says only that the product is aimed at the female market.

The Vague Claim

42 The vague claim is simply not clear. This category often overlaps with others. The key to the vague claim is the use of words that are colorful but meaningless, as well as the use of subjective and emotional opinions that defy verification. Most contain weasels.

*defy
verification*

Samples of the Vague Claim

43 "Lips have never looked so luscious." Can you imagine trying to either prove or disprove such a claim?

44   "Lipsavers are fun—they taste good, smell good and feel good."

45   "Its deep rich lather makes hair feel new again."

46   "For skin like peaches and cream."

47   "The end of meatloaf boredom."

48   "Take a bite and you'll think you're eating on the Champs Elysées."

49   "Winston tastes good like a cigarette should."

50   "The perfect little portable for all around viewing with all the features of higher priced sets."

51   "Fleischman's makes sensible eating delicious."

The Endorsement or Testimonial

52   A celebrity or authority appears in an ad to lend his or her stellar qualities to the product. Sometimes the people will actually claim to use the product, but very often they don't. There are agencies surviving on providing products with testimonials.

Samples of Endorsements or Testimonials

53   "Joan Fontaine throws a shot-in-the-dark party and her friends learn a thing or two."

54   "Darling, have you discovered Masterpiece? The most exciting men I know are smoking it." (Eva Gabor)

55   "Vega is the best handling car ever made in the U.S." This claim was challenged by the FTC, but GM answered that the claim is only a direct quote from *Road and Track* magazine.

The Scientific or Statistical Claim

56   This kind of ad uses some sort of scientific proof or experiment, very specific numbers, or an impressive sounding mystery ingredient.

Samples of Scientific or Statistical Claims

57   "Wonder Bread helps build strong bodies 12 ways." Even the weasel "helps" did not prevent the FTC from demanding this ad be withdrawn. But note that the use of the number 12 makes the claim far more believable than if it were taken out.

58   "Easy-Off has 33% more cleaning power than another popular brand." "Another popular brand" often translates as some other kind of oven cleaner sold somewhere. Also the claim does not say Easy-Off works 33% better.

59   "Special Morning—33% more nutrition." Also an unfinished claim.

60   "Certs contains a sparkling drop of Retsyn."

61   "ESSO with HTA."

62   "Sinarest. Created by a research scientist who actually gets sinus headaches."

The "Compliment the Consumer" Claim

63   This kind of claim butters up the consumer by some form of flattery.

Samples of "Compliment the Consumer" Claims

64   "We think a cigar smoker is someone special."

65   "If what you do is right for you, no matter what others do, then RC Cola is right for you."

66   "You pride yourself on your good home cooking. . . ."

67   "The lady has taste."

68   "You've come a long way, baby."

The Rhetorical Question

69 This technique demands a response from the audience. A question is asked and the viewer or listener is supposed to answer in such a way as to affirm the product's goodness.

Samples of Rhetorical Questions

70 "Plymouth—isn't that the kind of car America wants?"

71   "Shouldn't your family be drinking Hawaiian Punch?"

72   "What do you want most from coffee? That's what you get most from Hills."

73   "Touch of Sweden: could your hands use a small miracle?"

Suggestions for a Unit on Advertising Interpretation

1. Collect, categorize, and analyze advertising claims according to the ten techniques presented in this article. Remember that there may be other types of claims and that some are difficult to classify completely in any one category. Look for advertising claims that fit category 11—honest and useful consumer information.

2. Compare product claims with the product. Construct a series of tests to verify the claims made about a particular product.

3. Rewrite ad claims so they give information that would help a customer make a wise buying decision. Write honest ads that correct ads you consider misleading.

4. Write manufacturers and ask them to back up the claims they present in their corporate advertising. A college class in marketing tried this and found that many companies did not respond and very few took up the challenge.

5. Find the emotional hooks in ads. This would include appeals to status, security, acceptance, patriotism, happiness, etc. Vance Packard is still a most useful source of ideas.

6. Select some parity product and write advertising claims for it, illustrating each of the ten techniques explained in this article. For example, if you select a mousetrap as your parity product (not the "better" mousetrap, just an ordinary one) your ad claims might include:

   a. Weasel   "Often helps control your rodent problem"
   b. Unfinished   "Kills rats better and faster"
   c. We're Unique   "Only Imperial mousetraps have that unique Imperial craftsmanship behind them."
   d. Water is wet   "Spring action mousetrap"
   e. So what?   "Made with the finest knotty pine and tempered steel. Uses any kind of cheese as bait and comes in a variety of sizes."

f. Vague claim	"Imperial mousetraps are easy to operate, effective, and can make you feel like a new person again without that annoying gnawing fear of being eaten alive by a hungry mouse."
g. Endorsement	"None of my friends will ever go near an Imperial mousetrap. Believe me."—Mickey Mouse
h. Scientific claim	"Works 33% faster than another popular brand under normal conditions."
i. Compliment	"For the man whose time is too important to spend hunting mice."
j. Rhetorical question	"Shouldn't your family have the feeling of Imperial safety?"

QUESTIONS

1. There is an expression that says: "Let the buyer beware!" Interpret this expression in light of what you have read in this article regarding advertising claims.

2. Explain the following advertising claims discussed in the article and give an example of each:

   • The endorsement or testimonial

   • The rhetorical question

   • The unfinished claim

3. The author states that "advertising is used to create the illusion of superiority." Explain this statement and give examples to support your response.

4. Analyze the following claim for toothpaste: "Now with ZD-70, New Ultra Nocav toothpaste helps fight cavities and helps get your teeth whiter and cleaner." What types of claims are being made? How are the claims misleading?

EXTENDING YOUR VOCABULARY

immunity: As a diplomat, his immunity protects him from _____

_____

rendered: The tear gas rendered the large crowd _____

pseudo: I don't trust the work of a pseudo scientist because

_____

parity: In the labor contracts the firefighter demanded parity with

the police because _____

superiority: In order to demonstrate the superiority of one product

over another, you must _____

hedges: If a salesperson hedges about the quality of his or her prod-

uct, I _____

deceptive: You must be careful in reading a deceptive advertisement

because _____

negates: Her statement negates his testimony because she claims

that _____

substantiate: In order to substantiate her theory, the researcher decided

to _____

unique: This product is unique in that _____

defy: If you defy the order of the king _____

verification: After examining the verification of his claim, it was discov-

ered that _____

 # PROCESS GUIDE

1. The author begins by stating that students and teachers alike believe that they are not fooled by the tricks of advertisers. If this is true, according to Schrank, how do they feel they make their purchases?

_____

Schrank counters this "naive view" of teachers and students by suggesting that advertising has a considerable effect on people, even on those who say it is "harmless nonsense." He says that the purpose of the classroom study of advertising is to raise the level of awareness about the techniques used in ads.

2. In paragraph 3, Schrank notes that ads can be studied in a variety of ways in "microscopic" (very close attention) detail. But perhaps the simplest way is to study the language of claims. Paragraph 4 tells us that *claim* is a key word. How does the author define it, and what does he suggest you should be able to do with a claim?

Claim definition _____

Student claim skill _____

In paragraph 5, Schrank states that most claims, by selecting words carefully, fall in between truth and lies. This practice is referred to as hedging. He focuses on product parity. *Parity* means that products have the same basic ingredients and of course the same basic results (toothpaste and aspirin are examples). Naturally a company wants you to buy its brand even though it is identical to that of the competition. The company must therefore create the illusion that its product is superior in some way.

3. In paragraphs 6–8, Schrank claims that there are two basic rules in analyzing parity claims. List each and briefly discuss them.

Parity rule #1 _____

Discussion _____

Parity Rule #2 _____

Discussion _____

To create the illusion that their product is superior to that of competing companies, companies use the techniques demonstrated in the ten examples in the article.

Of the claims listed, our experience is that the weasel claim is the most common. Schrank states that the weasel word is a term that qualifies the claim in such a way that it is almost meaningless. In the example given, "Helps control dandruff," *helps* is the weasel. The ad does not say that it cures dandruff or stops it, but strongly implies that it does. This is what the advertisers want you to think. What the ad really says is that the product makes dandruff less severe. You can understand why advertisers dodge the truest statements that can be made about their products. Would you buy a dandruff product that "helps make your dandruff problem less severe"? Therefore consumers become victims of the implication.

4. Schrank provides a list of common weasel words such as *helps, like,* and *virtual.* Can you add to this list? Consult some ads in magazines and select additional weasel words.

 READING JOURNAL

"The Language of Advertising Claims" is meant to help you read and examine advertisements. Since you are so familiar with advertising, the author argues that you overlook its impact on your purchases.

- **Content**

  What did you know about the topic before reading the article? Did you learn anything new, or did the author make you reexamine familiar information in a new light? Can you apply this information to your daily experiences? Do you consider this information practical or useful? Select one of Schrank's claim descriptions. You may wish to pick the one that was most surprising to you. Analyze this claim. Now that you are aware of it, do you think that it will affect how you view commercials that use this approach?

- **Process**

  Schrank presents ten techniques that advertisers use in creating their messages. Were you able to read and process each technique in the same way, or did some points require further clarification? Did reading the examples help you grasp the author's main points? What strategies did you use in reading the article? Cite areas of difficulty. How did you resolve these problems?

- **Response**

  Describe your reaction to this type of writing. Did you find yourself agreeing with what the author said based on your experiences with advertisements? Do you take issue with anything he said regarding the way advertisers try to get the public to buy their products? Can you cite an example of a highly effective advertisement? What makes this so, in your opinion? Cite an example of an ineffective commercial and justify your response.

The Evolution of the Newspaper of the Future

CHRISTINE LAPHAM

Christine Lapham, chief correspondent for CMC magazine, is an online content consultant and free-lance writer who lives in the capital region of New York. She received her master's degree from Rensselaer Polytechnic Institute in Troy, New York.

GEARING UP

1. Discuss the role newspapers play in helping people understand the world around them.

2. Many of today's leading newspapers are available online via the computer. Describe the advantages and disadvantages of reading the news online versus reading the paper version. (If necessary, consult someone who is familiar with reading online news.)

READING STRATEGY

READING JOURNAL ARTICLES

Your college reading material will involve textbooks, but that will not be the only source of your information. Increasingly, instructors are requiring students to read journal articles that report on research and trends in a particular field. Apart from reading and studying this type of material, you probably will have to write reports on certain subjects. Paying attention to the structure and format of journal articles can help you with your reading as well as writing. Some writers are turning to the Internet and publishing their research in on-line journals. The next article, "The Evolution of the Newspaper of the Future," appeared in the *Computer-Mediated Communication (CMC)* magazine, a magazine that is available only via the Internet.

Whether a publication is published in the traditional print format or is only available electronically, it has certain features. Here are some points to consider as you read journal articles:

Thesis statement	Does the writer take a stand, adopt a point of view, have a central theme, maintain a focus, or provide relevant background information?
Organization	Are the materials organized and presented in a logical fashion?
Presentation of evidence	Are the author's conclusions based on facts and logical deductions drawn from facts and the opinions of experts? Does the author show a firm grasp on the subject matter?
Citations and references	Is the reader guided to other sources of information where the author found information? Are footnotes or endnotes provided? Are the sources listed recognized authorities?
Synthesis	Is the author able to draw together diverse points of information to show patterns and relationships?
Analysis	Is the author able to examine arguments for evidence and logical errors?
Conclusion	Does the author adopt a clear point of view or an opinion or judgment after investigating the topic?

Application

Many of the steps you can take to read journal articles are the same approaches you would use if you were reading other types of expository material.

TITLE

Using the article that follows as an example, study the title,

"The Evolution of the Newspaper of the Future."

What predictions can be made regarding the title?

_____

_____

What is the significance of the word *evolution*?

_____

_____

THESIS STATEMENT

An author's thesis statement may be found in more than one place. It may appear in the opening paragraph, but not always. Sometimes a thesis statement may be repeated in the middle of the article to further develop a key point or at the conclusion of the essay to summarize major ideas.

Consider parts of sentences that appear in the first paragraph:

- Two powerful forces have emerged to *change* the mass communication model.

- By juxtaposing the best of the *new model* . . . with the best of the *old model* . . . a better *hybrid model* that combines the best of both worlds is created.

Add to these sentences one found in the second sentence of paragraph 2.

- We are actually experiencing a natural step in *the evolutionary progression* of communication from orality and literacy to computers.

HEADINGS

These examples begin to illustrate how an author develops a thesis. Another way to understand the development of an author's ideas is to consider the title, headings, and subheadings. You can create questions that you expect would be answered by the text that follows. Four sample questions are provided. After you have studied the article, try composing questions for the remaining headings.

Heading	Question(s)
CMC Is the Natural Next Step	What does CMC stand for, and what does it mean when it says it's the natural step—to what?
Emergence of the Many-to-Many Model	What is the many-to-many model? What is its significance?
Newspapers Must Redefine Their Mission	Why must newspapers redefine their mission?
Using Technology to Improve Content	How can technology improve newspaper content?
Journalism Returns to Its Roots	
The Creation of a New Hybrid Model	
Innovative Solutions	

 # USING THE STRATEGIES

PUTTING IT ALL TOGETHER

At the end of Unit Two we presented a strategy summary called "Making the Strategies Work for You" (page 273). Once again, we are presenting a summary strategy as a guide to help you in your reading. In the Introduction, we observed that a goal of this textbook was to help you become a self-monitoring reader. This means that you are aware of your role in the reading process. You know what you need to get from a particular reading. You prepare yourself for the reading task ahead of time by overviewing the material. We called this prereading strategy *previewing*. Other texts call it *surveying*. The idea is to establish a kind of mental road map before you start. Even though the reading journey is a new one, you can still expect to see familiar signposts such as a title and headings.

A proficient reader also reads through a text quickly to get a flavor for the major points. Even though you may miss major ideas and considerable detail in this quick read, you will have begun to get a sense of the article. The quick read also helps to locate areas where you will have trouble.

The next step is a careful or close reading. The quick read has helped establish where difficulty may be expected. At these points you slow down and use various strategies. In the careful reading, you keep track of what you understand and what you don't. We suggested the strategy of *marking text.* A brief note in the margin allows you to keep track of your thoughts as you are reading. Ideas that are confusing can be marked with a question mark. A good marking of a text leaves you with a record of what you understand and what you need to find out.

As a proficient reader, don't be overly strategy conscious. That is, don't approach a reading task with a dozen reading strategies that you are seeking to apply. Rather, stay focused on the meaning of the text. When you hit a trouble spot, seek to apply a strategy that seems appropriate. For example, in reading a newspaper editorial that seems confusing it is often useful to determine the author's purpose. By concentrating on what the writer seeks to accomplish in the article, you can fill in some of the problem areas in the logic or the evidence.

After completing a reading, you should be aware of what you know and what you need to find out. Certainly a second reading of a text is a bare minimum requirement. The second reading will allow you to begin filling in gaps in your understanding and reinforce those concepts that are clear and/or familiar to you.

Finally, sometimes the problem is not lack of comprehension but keeping track of all the information. We suggest periodic assessment. In reading a textbook chapter, check your progress at the end of each section between major headings. To check yourself, list in point form the major ideas of the text and briefly note what they mean. You may also wish to try an idea map or a short summary. Try to convert the text language into your own words. If you are not able to translate the ideas comfortably, you don't understand the concept well. This is a signal to apply additional strategies.

In short:

1. Concentrate on what you seek to accomplish.

2. Preview the text to establish a mental framework (a set of questions) to approach the material.

3. Read through quickly to get a general impression of the material.

4. Read carefully, marking the text for knowns (brief notes) and unknowns (question marks).

5. Apply strategies at trouble points (e.g., for an unknown word use *predicting vocabulary*).

6. Read carefully a third time to fill in gaps in your understanding.

7. Assess what you know at regular intervals; condense ideas and use your own words.

The Reading

The Evolution of the Newspaper of the Future

by CHRISTINE LAPHAM

1 As we approach the end of the twentieth century, two powerful forces have emerged to change the mass communication model. The first is the use of computers as a means of processing, analyzing, and informing. The second is the constantly accelerating capacity of that technology to enhance communication so it is almost unbounded by time and space. Because older communication technology required a huge investment of capital, a one-to-many model dominated, with those owning the broadcasting equipment or newspaper presses disseminating information to the masses. *disseminating* Current technology, specifically the digital transmission of text, audio, and video, has altered the traditional one-to-many communication model; instead, audiences are becoming producers as well as consumers of information, and a new many-to-many communication model has emerged. Today anyone with a modem, personal computer, and a telephone line can become a publisher, as we now know the term. But it is a mistake to eliminate totally the old model in favor of the new. By juxtaposing the best of the new *juxtaposing* model—computerized access, delivery, and packaging of information—with the best of the old model—insightful reporting in a well written story—a better hybrid model that combines the best of both is created. *hybrid*

CMC Is the Natural Next Step

2 Because this change in the mass communication model is occurring so rapidly, some are calling it a "technological" or "information" revolution. However, we are actually experiencing a natural step in the evolutionary progression of communication from orality and literacy to computers. If we can accept that writing is a form of technology (Ong 80), then it follows that computer-mediated communication (CMC) is simply another way of technologizing the word. While many squawk in alarm and anxiety, the millions of people using the Internet illustrate that society is now ready for this next stage in the evolution of communication. In fact, computer-mediated communication may return to human exchanges what the process of writing removed. In his text, *Orality and Literacy: The Technologizing of the Word,* Walter Ong describes the limitations of writing as a form of communication:

> "Writing is in a way the most drastic of the three technologies (speech, writing, computers). It initiated what print and computers only continue, the reduction of dynamic sound to quiescent space, the separation of the word from the living present, where alone spoken words can exist." (82)   *initiated*

3 As the appropriate next step on an evolutionary continuum, CMC can return to language (the word) the immediacy lost in writing and give it a

real-time presence. In fact, this is the very reason that the most popular form of CMC is electronic mail, fondly referred to as e-mail. People around the world have embraced CMC and instinctively formed "virtual communities" of like-minded individuals. Communication theorist *Marshall McLuhan* anticipated this warm response to the technological changes in communication more than 30 years ago. He predicted the formation of a "global village," which in many ways is coming true in the form of the Internet. The network has experienced astronomical growth—475 percent over the last year and 31,155 percent over the last three years (Rutkowski 7).

Emergence of the Many-to-Many Model

4   As people all over the world begin to produce and then share information within McLuhan's prophetic "global village," they naturally depend less and less on the information that flows from more traditional sources. *Howard Rheingold*, who describes himself as a high-tech social historian, explained this phenomenon at a Canadian writers conference:

> "A tremendous power shift is underway, and despite the obscure or phony terminology used to describe it, this power shift is about people, and our ability to connect with each other in new ways much more than it is about fiber optic cable and multimedia appliances. The revolution triggered by the printing press was about literacy, and what literate populations are capable of doing (eg: governing themselves), long after it had anything to do with the mechanics of moveable type. The technology enabled the power shift, but the power shift was created by the people who used the tool to educate themselves." (127)

5   As Rheingold aptly states, this new communication revolution is shifting power to the people. This power shift seriously threatens the dominance *dominance* of traditional mass media forms, specifically television, radio stations, magazines, and newspapers, which were built from the one-to-many communication model. Newspapers, which currently print and then deliver information on paper, are particularly vulnerable. Astute editors and pub- *vulnerable* lishers have recognized the threat digital delivery poses to the nation's estimable "Fourth Estate," and in an effort to reach today's "wired" audiences, they are creating new, electronic publications. But so far, creating a successful, futuristic model has eluded most publishers. Many outlets have opted *eluded* simply to put the content of the "paper" product online, only to discover that the online world has its own, often mysterious ethos. Writing in *Wired Magazine*, Jon Katz, a media critic and former executive producer of the *CBS Evening News*, succinctly summarizes the dilemma facing newspaper *succinctly* publishers:

> "So far, at least, online papers don't work commercially or conceptually. With few exceptions, they seem to be just what they are, expensive hedges against onrushing technology with little rationale of their own. They take away what's best about reading a paper and don't offer what's best about being online. That's the point of a newspaper . . . to filter the worthwhile information, then print it. . . . The newspaper needs to reinvent itself. . . . The object is not to

replace, or put into a different format, but to gain a toehold in cyberspace and even absorb some of its values."

Newspapers Must Redefine Their Mission

6 Reinventing itself is a tall order for an industry that works under a constant deadline to produce a new product each day. How can the industry begin to construct a new model that takes advantage of state-of-the-art technology? Paradoxically, the answer comes from reflecting on the past. By analyzing and paring down the essentials of journalism as a craft and a profession, the real essence of the industry will emerge and a predictive model will begin to take shape. To its credit, the newspaper industry has conducted research and written and thought a great deal about what to do in the future. In *Come the Millennium: Interviews on the Shape of our Future,* a project of the American Society of Newspaper Editors, *Michael Hooker,* former president of the University of Massachusetts, says this is a pivotal moment in the history of newspaper publishing.

> "The challenge for you will be perhaps your greatest ever. As a producer of newspapers, what you must do first is determine how you conceive yourself. Are you an organization that supplies newspapers or are you an organization that supplies information? Remington and Underwood saw themselves as being in the typewriter business. IBM saw itself as being in the word-processing business. The rest is history." (49)

7 This self-analysis is being conducted in turbulent times when conflicting forces threaten to pull the industry apart. Reading a daily newspaper is a habit of millions of middle-age and older Americans. However, today's young people often prefer more sophisticated media to the daily ritual of the morning newspaper. We are also experiencing what some call an information explosion that threatens to bury even the most avid reader and intellectual. *avid* Ironically, it is the glut of information that holds the key to the survival of *glut* the newspaper industry. The digitizing of information has created a vast expansion in the amount of information that is readily available to audiences. Books and manuscripts that previously consumed libraries and other physical spaces are now contained in digital bytes that can move with great speed over vast distances. Quite simply, more information is available to more people more quickly than ever before.

8 Mass media evolved because people from all walks of life needed help to understand the world around them. Throughout history, newspapers have excelled at collecting, recording, and distributing information at many different levels and geographic locales. As they evolve in light of technological change, newspapers need to embrace that mission anew. In fact, defining what is news is now more critical than ever. And it is their ability to do this within the context of new technology that is the key to newspapers' survival. Writing in a recent *New York Times Magazine* column, veteran journalist Max Frankel prognosticates: *prognosticates*

"The newspapers that prosper in the next century will be the ones that offer the best journalism, that master the subjects about which they write and acquire the talent and expertise to appraise and explain an infinite variety of events. . . . Newspapers can trust the fermenting computer industry to perfect the technologies that will gradually replace their presses and delivery trucks. It's talent that they will need to survive in the digital age—gifted editors, reporters, and image artists who can find meaning in the approaching information glut." (38)

Using Technology to Improve Content

9   In addition to improving the delivery of news, computer and telecommunications technology can improve the research and news gathering processes of newspapers. Unlike the one-to-many model where information came from the top, news on the Internet bubbles up from the bottom and meanders its way upward. The daily reality of the many-to-many model means that the journalist now has a chance to really know and interact with his or her audience that goes way beyond traditional letters to the editor. This closer interaction should ideally lead to a better knowledge of the audience, and writing and reporting that more closely reflects readers' values and interests.

meanders

10   In today's more competitive information delivery environment, better research, better reporting, and better analysis are critical. Of the three, research is the priority. Speaking at a *Neiman Foundation* conference, J.T. Johnson explained the importance of the pre-reporting process:

"The quality of the information out can only be as good as the data flowing in. . . . Hence because of this shift in the data environment, educators and journalists must immediately turn more attention to the left side of the equation, the research, reporting, and analysis aspects if we are to improve the quality of the data in analysis components." (21)

11   The value of research and analysis in creating the newspaper of the future may best be illustrated by one of the industry's leaders, the *News and Observer* (N&O) in Raleigh, North Carolina. While the paper has attracted attention for its World Wide Web site, Nando Land electronic service for children, and multimedia forays, the newspaper's real muscle comes from its research prowess. Nora Paul of the *Poynter Institute,* a journalism think-tank, claims that Raleigh's research operations are unparalleled. Writing in the *American Journalism Review,* Philip Moeller identified the N&O's real strengths:

prowess
unparalleled

" . . . what sets Raleigh apart is the fact that digitized information skills—for using computers, databases, online services—are becoming standard for nearly everyone in the newsroom." (43)

12   He outlines what sets Raleigh's operation apart from the norm in the industry: a 21-person research department with a network of databases; staffers who write software to create research pathways to access databases;

the creation of a database to track state legislation that was turned into an online service; and three generations of hypertext software that enable writers to search their own notes. These developments were the precursors of other innovative ventures, such as a multimedia series in collaboration with a local television station, and an electronic version of the newspaper.

precursors

Journalism Returns to Its Roots

13   In building a successful digital enterprise, Raleigh's N&O is a good model because it uses the new technology to improve its primary product at a grassroots level. This is a good lesson for the industry as a whole, which is now being called upon to turn information into knowledge—the ultimate goal. In her essay, "Writing for the Third Millennium," Beth Agnew talks about a return to the historical and literary roots of journalism:

> "Writers have always been society's visionaries. We now have too much information to rationally deal with on a daily basis, and we need skilled professional help to turn that information into the currency of the next millennium— knowledge." (1)

14   Along with its muckraking and investigative roots, there is a long history of the newspaper reporter as a writer of literature. In fact, the first newspapers in this country were partisan reports of events. It was the organization of the Associated Press in 1848 that introduced the requirement of objectivity in reporting, and reporters have been walking a tightrope ever since trying to be both observer and participant.

15   The insightful reporter interpreting reality ultimately has the same goals as McLuhan's highly intuitive "artist," who is capable of understanding the present as well as the future.

> "The artist is the man in any field, scientific or humanistic, who grasps the implications of his actions and of new knowledge in his own time. He is the man of integral awareness. . . . The artist picks up the message of cultural and technological challenge decades before its transforming impact occurs." (65)

The Creation of a New Hybrid Model

16   The real beauty of the new technology is its ability to enable newspapers to not only enhance their researching and reporting capabilities, but also to deliver a better, more audience-aware product in an immediate and inexpensive way. Digital delivery is greatly improved by publication on the World Wide Web, the fastest growing part of the Internet. One of the main attractions of the Web is hypertext, a system that seamlessly links computers and files continents apart. For example, a story about a poll on the performance of a government official could include color-highlighted links that readers simply click on to get more in-depth information about his or her voting record, recent speeches, or a news story about campaign promises. Using the hypertext capabilities of the Web totally eliminates the proverbial "news hole" and opens up an unlimited amount of "space" for presenting the news product.

George Gilder neatly summarizes the marriage of the computer and the newspaper:

> "The computer is a perfect complement to the newspaper. . . . [It] enables the existing news industry to deliver its product in real time. It hugely increases the quantity of information that can be made available, including archives, maps, charts and other supporting material. It opens the way to upgrading the news with full screen photography and videos, while hugely enhancing the richness and timeliness of the news. The computer empowers readers to use the "paper" in the same way they do today—to browse and select stories and advertisements at their own time and place." (10)

17   By using computer technology to produce and deliver a new product, newspapers have welded both the old (literacy-print) with the new (computers-digital delivery) and created a better model. McLuhan explains this process as the creation of a hybrid which blends the old and the new to create a superior medium.

> "The hybrid or the meeting of two media is a moment of truth and revelation from which new form is born. For the parallel between two media holds us on the frontiers between forms that snap us out of the Narcissus-narcosis. The moment of the meeting of media is a moment of freedom and release from the ordinary trance and numbness imposed by them on our senses." (55)

Innovative Solutions

18   The priority of this new model will be listening to the audience and creating innovative opportunities for ongoing communication. *The WELL,* which stands for Whole Earth 'Lectronic Link, recently became the first online service to offer self-publishing on the Web. The WELL, which is based in Sausalito, California, helped nurture author Howard Rheingold and the *Electronic Frontier Foundation.* The organization celebrated its 10th anniversary in April of 1995 by creating a Community Page that provides an index to the individual home page publishing efforts of its members.

19   One of the many newspapers embarking on an electronic future is the *Arizona Daily Star.* The *Star* is working on a new service called *StarNet* that offers a comprehensive mix of features and services. Some of those features include Internet access, news from the paper edition, local discussion groups, and access to the paper's archives. The *Star* is attempting to become an electronic home base for its readers and will give nonprofit organizations (with a budget of less than $1 million) space on their service to publish local newsletters. While this service may be too ambitious for some publishers just beginning to venture into cyberspace, the concept of the newspaper as the community's electronic publishing hub is a critical component of the newspaper of the future.

20   While many are searching for the yet elusive answer, the only certainty now is that there is no one right way to do things: each newspaper must discover its niche and provide insightful and innovative content in a format its readers want. And that format may range from a hand-held tablet to a

personalized newspaper created by an intelligent agent searching the Internet for customized news. Living the many-to-many model means that the flow of information is fluid with readers responding to and creating information and ideas. In addition to providing access to information, the newspaper publisher is now a facilitator of public discussion. By building community discussion, what is reported in the news takes on new meaning, and people come to better understand not only the world around them, but themselves as well.

References

- Agnew, B. (1994, June). Writing for the third millennium. *Writers' Retreat on Interactive Technology & Equipment Conference.* University of Vancouver, Vancouver, British Columbia.

- Frankel, M. (1995). The Daily Digital. *The New York Times Magazine.* 9 April 1995: 38.

- Gilder, G. F. (1994). Fidler's Electronic News Panel is a better bet for the future than home shopping. *ASNE Bulletin.*

- Hooker, M. (1994). Interview. *Come the Millennium: Interviews on the Shape of Our Future.* Kansas City: Andrews and McMeel.

- Johnson, J.T. and Markoff, J. (1994). What skills does the journalist require to take advantage of new technology? *Neiman Report.*

- Katz, J. (1994, September). Online or not, newspapers suck. *Wired.*

- McLuhan, M. (1994). *Understanding Media: The Extensions of Man.* Cambridge: MIT Press.

- Moeller, P. (1994) The age of convergence. *American Journalism Review,* 22–28.

- Ong, W. (1982). *Orality and Literacy: The Technologizing of the Word.* London: Methuen.

- Reingold, H. (1994, June). The electronic landscape: A writer's perspective. *Writers' Retreat on Interactive Technology & Equipment Conference.* University of Vancouver, Vancouver, British Columbia.

- Rutkowski, A. (1995, May). Statistics on the growth of the Internet. *Web Week.*

QUESTIONS

1. The author chose to title the article "The Evolution of the Newspaper of the Future." Explain the meaning of the term *evolution* as it relates to the article.

2. Compare and contrast the "one-to-many" model of communication versus the "many-to-many" model.

3. The author writes: "We are also experiencing what some call an information explosion that threatens to bury even the most avid reader and intellectual. Ironically, it is the glut of information that holds the key to the survival of the newspaper industry." Explain this statement. How can an excess of information help newspapers to endure? What role can journalists play to deal with this problem?

4. The author speaks of "the creation of a new hybrid model." Describe this model and explain how it will function.

EXTENDING YOUR VOCABULARY

dissemination: In some countries, disseminating information is illegal because _____

juxtaposing: By juxtaposing the two documents, we were able to _____

hybrid: In order to produce a hybrid model, they needed to _____

initiated: Contact was initiated with the other party only after _____

dominance: The dominance of the political party was threatened when _____

vulnerable: The police officer was vulnerable because _____

eluded: The criminal's identity eluded the police because _____

succinctly: The instructor wanted summaries that were succinctly written because _____

avid: You could tell she was an avid basketball fan by the fact that _____

glut: The glut of used cars caused the prices to _____

prognosticates: He prognosticates that _____

meanders: Because she chose to take the path that meanders, she arrived _____

prowess: The military's prowess was proven by _____

unparalleled: Their unparalleled discovery was significant because

_____

precursors: Precursors of today's computers were _____

from

Bullet Park

JOHN CHEEVER

John Cheever (1912–1982) was born in Quincy, Massachusetts. His works in-clude seven collections of short stories and four novels. His first novel, The Wapshot Chronicle, *won the National Book Award in 1958. Cheever also won other awards, including a Pulitzer Prize. The following excerpt is taken from Cheever's third novel,* Bullet Park *(1969). The Nailles family lives in "Bullet Park," a fashionable suburban community outside New York. The excerpt con-cerns a family argument over the son's excessive television viewing.*

GEARING UP

1. Describe how television viewing could have both a positive and a nega-tive effect on schoolwork.

2. How could a child's excessive television watching lead to an argument be-tween the child and the parents?

3. What control, if any, should parents exercise over children's television viewing?

4. "Limiting children's television viewing is an effective means of disci-pline." Do you agree or disagree? Why?

The Reading

from Bullet Park

by JOHN CHEEVER

1   He had no way of judging his worth as a father. They had quarreled. When Tony was nine. He had suddenly given up all his athletics and friendships and settled down in front of the television set. The night of the quarrel was rainy. Nailles came into the house by the kitchen door. Nellie was cooking. Nailles kissed her on the back of the neck and raised her skirts

but she demurred. "Please darling," she said. "It makes me feel as if I were in a burlesque skit. Tony's report card is on the table. You might want to take a look at it." Nailles mixed a drink and read the report. The marks were all C's and D's. Nailles walked through the dining room, crossed the dark hall to the living room where Tony was watching a show. The tube was the only light, shifting and submarine, and with the noise of the rain outside the room seemed like some cavern in the sea.

2   "Do you have any homework," Nailles asked.

3   "A little," Tony said.

4   "Well I think you'd better do it before you watch television," Nailles said. On the tube some cartoon figures were dancing a jig.

5   "I'll just watch to the end of this show," Tony said. "Then I'll do my homework."

6   "I think you'd better do your homework now," Nailles said.

7   "But Mummy said I could see this show," Tony said.

8   "How long has it been," said Nailles, "that you've asked permission to watch television?" He knew that in dealing with his son sarcasm would only multiply their misunderstandings but he was tired and headstrong. "You never ask permission. You come home at half past three, pull your chair up in front of the set and watch until supper. After supper you settle down in front of that damned engine and stay there until nine. If you don't do your homework how can you expect to get passing marks in school?"

9   "I learn a lot of things on television," Tony said shyly. "I learn about geography and animals and the stars."

10   "What are you learning now?" Nailles asked.

11   The cartoon figures were having a tug of war. A large bird cut the rope with his beak and all the figures fell down.

12   "This is different," Tony said. "This isn't educational. Some of it is."

13   "Oh leave him alone, Eliot, leave him alone," Nellie called from the kitchen. Her voice was soft and clear. Nailles wandered back into the kitchen.

14   "But don't you think," he said, "that from half past three to nine with a brief interlude for supper is too much time to spend in front of a television set?"

15   "It is a lot of time," Nellie said, "but it's terribly important to him right now and I think he'll grow out of it."

16   "I know it's terribly important," Nailles said. "I realize that. When I took him Christmas shopping he wasn't interested in anything but getting back to the set. He didn't care about buying presents for you or his cousins or his aunts and uncles. All he wanted to do was to get back to the set. He was just like an addict. I mean he had withdrawal symptoms. It was just like me at cocktail hour but I'm thirty-four years old and I try to ration my liquor and my cigarettes."

17   "He isn't quite old enough to start rationing things," Nellie said.

18   "He won't go coasting, he won't play ball, he won't do his homework, he won't even take a walk because he might miss a program."

19   "I think he'll grow out of it," Nellie said.

20   "But you don't grow out of an addiction. You have to make some exertion or have someone make an exertion for you. You just don't outgrow serious addictions."

21   He went back across the dark hall with its shifty submarine lights and outside the noise of rain. On the tube a man with a lisp, dressed in a clown suit, was urging his friends to have Mummy buy them a streamlined, battery-operated doll carriage. He turned on a light and saw how absorbed his son was in the lisping clown.

22   "Now I've been talking with your mother," he said, "and we've decided that we have to do something about your television time." (The clown was replaced by the cartoon of an elephant and a tiger dancing the waltz.) "I think an hour a day is plenty and I'll leave it up to you to decide which hour you want."

23   Tony had been threatened before but either his mother's intervention or Nailles's forgetfulness had saved him. At the thought of how barren, painful and meaningless the hours after school would be the boy began to cry.

24   "Now crying isn't going to do any good," Nailles said. The elephant and the tiger were joined by some other animals in their waltz.

25   "Skip it," Tony said. "It isn't your business."

26   "You're my son," Nailles said, "and it's my business to see you do at least what's expected of you. You were tutored last summer in order to get promoted and if your marks don't improve you won't be promoted this year. Don't you think it's my business to see that you get promoted? If you had your way you wouldn't even go to school. You'd wake up in the morning, turn on the set and watch it until bedtime."

27   "Oh please skip it, please leave me alone," Tony said. He turned off the set, went into the hall and started to climb the stairs.

28   "You come back here, Sonny," Nailles shouted. "You come back here at once or I'll come and get you."

29   "Oh please don't roar at him," Nellie asked, coming out of the kitchen. "I'm cooking veal birds and they smell nice and I was feeling good and happy that you'd come home and now everything is beginning to seem awful."

30   "I was feeling good too," Nailles said, "but we have a problem here and we can't evade it just because the veal birds smell good."

31   He went to the foot of the stairs and shouted: "You come down here, Sonny, you come down here this instant or you won't have any television for a month. Do you hear me? You come down here at once or you won't have any television for a month."

32   The boy came slowly down the stairs. "Now you come here and sit down," Nailles said, "and we'll talk this over. I've said that you can have an hour each day and all you have to do is to tell me which hour you want."

33   "I don't know," Tony said. "I like the four-o'clock show and the six-o'clock and the seven-o'clock show . . ."

34   "You mean you can't confine yourself to an hour, is that it?"

35   "I don't know," Tony said.

36   "I guess you'd better make me a drink," Nellie said. "Scotch and soda."

37   Nailles made a drink and returned to Tony. "Well if you can't decide," Nailles said, "I'm going to decide for you. First I'm going to make sure that you do your homework before you turn on the set."

38   "I don't get home until half past three," Tony said, "and sometimes the bus is late and if I do my homework I'll miss the four-o'clock show."

39   "That's just too bad," Nailles said, "that's just too bad."

40   "Oh leave him alone," Nellie said. "Please leave him alone. He's had enough for tonight."

41   "It isn't tonight we're talking about, it's every single night in the year including Saturdays, Sundays and holidays. Since no one around here seems able to reach any sort of agreement I'm going to make a decision myself. I'm going to throw that damned thing out the back door."

42   "Oh no, Daddy, no," Tony cried. "Please don't do that. Please, please, please. I'll try. I'll try to do better."

43   "You've been trying for months without any success," Nailles said. "You keep saying that you'll try to cut down and all you do is to watch more and more. Your intentions may have been good but there haven't been any noticeable results. Out it goes."

44   "Oh please don't, Eliot," Nellie cried. "Please don't. He loves his television. Can't you see that he loves it?"

45   "I know that he loves it," Nailles said. "That's why I'm going to throw it out the door. I love my gin and I love my cigarettes but this is the fourteenth cigarette I've had today and this is only my fourth drink. If I sat down to drink at half past three and drank steadily until nine I'd expect someone to give me some help." He unplugged the television set with a yank and picked the box up in his arms. The box was heavy for his strength, and an awkward size, and in order to carry it he had to arch his back a little like a pregnant woman. With the cord trailing behind him he started for the kitchen door.

46   "Oh, Daddy, Daddy," Tony cried. "Don't, don't, don't," and he fell to his knees with his hands joined in a conventional, supplicatory position that he might have learned from watching some melodrama on the box.

47   "Eliot, Eliot," Nellie screamed. "Don't, don't. You'll be sorry, Eliot. You'll be sorry."

48   Tony ran to his mother and she took him in her arms. They were both crying.

49   "I'm not doing this because I want to," Nailles shouted. "After all I like watching football and baseball when I'm home and I paid for the damned thing. I'm not doing this because I want to. I'm doing this because I have to."

50   "Don't look, don't look," Nellie said to Tony and she pressed his face into her skirts.

51   The back door was shut and Nailles had to put the box on the floor to open this. The rain sounded loudly in the yard. Then, straining, he picked up the box again, kicked open the screen door and fired the television out into the dark. It landed on a cement paving and broke with the rich, glassy music

of an automobile collision. Nellie led Tony up the stairs to her bedroom, where she threw herself onto the bed, sobbing. Tony joined her. Nailles closed the kitchen door on the noise of the rain and poured another drink. Fifth, he said.

52   All of this was eight years ago.

QUESTIONS

1. Summarize the incident presented in the excerpt.

2. Interpret the actions of each character.

3. Do you agree or disagree with the father's actions? Explain.

4. Considering the other articles you have read in this unit, what other alternatives were available to members of the Nailles family to solve the problem?

5. In what way do Eliot and Tony share a similar problem?

 # THE TECHNOLOGY CONNECTION

Technology has helped bring about the so-called information age, in which data flow to us from multiple sources. According to media analyst David Shenk, one by-product of technology is that "information is moving faster and becoming more plentiful, and people everywhere are benefiting from this change." But he notes that the price we pay for this technology is information overload. "We are bathing in information, and while this is often a very good thing, there is the danger of drowning in it." The rock group The Police characterized the problem as follows:

> Too much information, runnin' through my brain.
> Too much information, drivin' me insane.

Is the pace at which we produce information exceeding our ability to digest it? In the following article, media critic Joe Saltzman examines the consequences of too much information.

Too Much Information, Too Little Time

JOE SALTZMAN

Joe Saltzman, producer-writer, won multiple Emmy Awards for his documentary work at Channel 2, the CBS-owned television station in Los Angeles. He also received the Alfred L. duPont–Columbia University Broadcast Journalism Award. Saltzman writes a regular column for USA Today, *on which he serves as associate mass media editor. He is a professor and associate director of the School of Journalism at the University of Southern California.*

GEARING UP

1. What news sources are available to the public today that were not available fifty years ago?

2. What does a person need to do to be well informed?

The Reading

Too Much Information, Too Little Time

by JOE SALTZMAN

1   Let's admit it. If we're going to go into the 21st century of new technology, the Internet, the World Wide Web, and other information delivery systems, then we all should be given a 25th hour to explore the new media. There just isn't enough time in the normal daily cycle to do the job. So suppose you had that extra hour to do nothing but become informed courtesy of the new technology. What would you do?

2   Timer in hand, you would probably go directly to the AJR newslink (http://www.newslink) courtesy of the *American Journalism Review*, where you can find 4,500 links to newspapers, magazines, broadcasters, and worldwide news services. Everyone in the media seems to agree that this is an essential resource, the best media index available. So skip your Yahoo and go directly to AJR newslink to at least give yourself a fighting chance at getting the information you need and want to know in less than an hour.

3   One problem with the new technology is the incredible array of options available. It's like going to one of those sumptuous smorgasbords at a good

hotel—except the subsequent ache won't be in your stomach: it will be in your brain.

4   Consider this. If you choose newspapers, you can go to major metropolitan newspapers, national newspapers, state newspapers, daily newspapers, non-daily newspapers, alternative newspapers, business newspapers, special newspapers, limited newspapers, promotional newspapers, and inactive newspapers: non-United States newspapers in Canada, the Caribbean, Central America, Africa, Asia, the Mideast, Europe, Oceania, and South America; and campus newspapers (dailies, non-dailies, experimentals, and non-U.S.).

5   If you choose magazines, 23 of the 50 largest U.S. popular ones and seven of the 25 largest Canadian magazines are available. Also at your service are news and opinion magazines, business and professional magazines, computing magazines, entertainment magazines, and lifestyle-people-activities magazines. If you choose broadcasters, you get nationwide U.S. radio and television networks, regional and virtual networks, and non-U.S. networks, as well as broadcast stations from all over the country. And if you choose news services, you get everything from weather services to journalism organizations to new-media newsletters to e-mail forums.

6   All you have is an extra hour, though, so skip all of that and take a look at the top 50 Web sites for information. That way you can go directly to CNN interactive or the *Washington Post* or the *Wall Street Journal* or the *Los Angeles Times.* What about the *Jerusalem Post* or the *San Jose Mercury News*? Tired yet? There's Reuters, the *Times of London,* the *Sacramento Bee,* the *Christian Science Monitor,* the *Las Vegas Sun,* the *Irish Times,* and 38 other popular sites.

7   It takes more than an hour just to consider the options, so here is a suggestion: Get your computer Web-friendly by subscribing to a service that enables you to get on the Web as quickly as possible. Then zip over to AJR newslink. Scan the "front pages" of your favorite news sources. CNN, the *Washington Post, The New York Times,* the *Los Angeles Times,* the *Wall Street Journal, Time,* and *Newsweek* are among the most reliable sources. Print out anything of interest for old-fashioned reading in places where the computer is not yet available (the bathroom, elevators, subways, the park).

8   Spend another 15 minutes browsing through the periodicals you like the best, looking at the rest of the news sections. Pick out three stories that particularly interest you. Print those stories out.

9   Now you've covered your basic information needs for the day, so it's time to check out other sites to flesh out what's going on in your world. When it comes to broadcasting, CNN, ESPN, MSNBC, and Fox News are the best, but, depending on your interests, you might want to glance at the Discovery Channel, Sci-Fi Channel, and the Weather Channel.

10   The problem is there is so much information out there and so little time to figure out what is important and what isn't. It may be heresy to say this, but some may long for that long-ago day when, in the early morning dew, a loud thud on the porch brought a package of printed paper that summed up everything you had to know in the day ahead.

11   The wonderful thing about the newspaper was that all the work was done

for you. There was nothing to turn on, nothing to search for, nothing between you and information. Somebody else had categorized, organized, edited, and condensed the information for you in a form easily handled and assimilated.

12   The newspaper also brought the family together. Different sections of the paper would be parceled out to members of the family in a politically incorrect order. There was something wonderful about the habit of a family reading and digesting the daily newspaper. Ideas were shared, opinions voiced, lives and deaths verified.

13   Today, fewer and fewer people read the newspaper. The buzzword is online journalism, and there is something miraculous in the concept of being able to peruse 4,500 newspapers and periodicals from around the world simply by punching them up on your computer screen. But are we better informed as a people? Probably not. News junkies always know more than anyone else and they are becoming news-obese by devouring everything in site. Infoguts are becoming a national disaster. But for the rest of us, it may all be too much. Getting information on the Internet is hard work. It takes diligence, a firm hand on the mouse, and a rough idea of how all of this works. For many, a slip of the finger and chaos ensues.

14   Digital sound and pictures, color and moving video, snazzy art, searches, and megabytes be damned. Maybe the best idea for some of us might be to use that 25th hour simply to digest an old-fashioned newspaper the way many of us used to do in the pre-new technology era when the printed word, in simple black and white, was all we needed to tell us all we wanted to know about the world around us.

QUESTIONS

1. Describe the problem the author is presenting.

2. Describe the solution he proposes.

3. Agree or disagree with his solution and explain your position.

4. Technology can be seen to have its positive as well as negative aspects when it comes to keeping abreast of the latest news. Explain.

MAKING CONNECTIONS

Mass Media

1. Ellerbee in her autobiographical account and Cheever in his fictional narrative describe the effects of TV on family members. Compare and contrast their views. In what way are their experiences similar to your own?

2. Schrank addresses aspects of advertising in the media. Summarize and interpret his remarks. Relate his advice regarding analyzing advertisements to the information found in the following strategies: Reading Argument and Persuasion (page 68) and Connotation and Denotation (page 413).

3. Technology has affected and continues to affect mass media. Cite information from the introduction to the unit as well as the remarks of Brokaw, Biagi, Lapham, and Saltzman concerning this issue.

4. "In today's society, people need to become media literate." Interpret this statement with respect to the comments of Tyner and Schrank.

5. Some critics have argued that television is a powerful threat to education. Others have taken a more neutral view. Cite information from Trelease, Greenfield, and Tyner concerning this topic.

6. Biagi examines the principle of selective perception. How is the principle addressed in the remarks of Schrank?

7. Brokaw's article deals with trust in the media. How do you view his cautionary note given what Lapham has to say about the evolution of the newspaper of the future?

8. Biagi considers the principle of selective perception. How is this principle addressed in Schrank's remarks?

9. Saltzman and Lapham discuss changes in the delivery of news. What common concerns do they share?

LIBRARY ASSIGNMENT

Exploring an Issue in Television

Throughout your college experience and afterward, you will use the library for various research purposes. You will be required to locate information and examine issues. The purpose of this library assignment is to let you explore a specific topic in one area of mass media: television. Of all the mass media, television has the most widespread impact on our society.

You are to locate at least three articles on a topic of your choice related to television and write an essay in which you do the following:

1. State and explain the issue or topic you have selected.

2. Summarize the contents of each article.

3. React to the position(s) of the authors.

Step 1: State and Explain the Issue or Topic You Have Selected

In this introductory section of your paper, you should state the topic and discuss the focus of your essay. The general nature of your topic and the specific subject matter you will deal with should be clear to your readers.

Students often find it difficult to choose a specific topic. Often they do not narrow the focus of their research and end up with a topic that is too broad. For example, your intention should not be to write a paper about "television." Because television is such a broad topic, you should focus on a specific issue related to a particular aspect of television. One way to do this is to familiarize yourself with television-related concerns that you frequently encounter in magazines and newspapers.

To get started, consider the following list of topics related to television that have appeared in various magazine indexes. This is only a partial list, but it should give you an idea of some possibilities. If you study the indexes, you will get a broader sampling of topics, issues, and concerns.

- *Television advertising:* selling techniques, types of persuasion, effects on the audience
- *Television and children:* effects of viewing, violence, time spent, quality of programs
- *Television and politics:* use of TV to influence voters, coverage of issues
- *Moral and religious concerns:* sex, violence, censorship
- *Television news:* coverage of stories, fairness, quality
- *Psychological aspects:* heavy versus light viewing, reality versus make-believe
- *Social aspects:* home, society, culture, lifestyles
- *Sports coverage:* games, salaries, use of videotape
- *Television soap operas:* attraction, message, positive and negative aspects

When you find a topic that interests you, try to formulate it into a question. For example, you can narrow the issue of television advertising by composing the following questions:

1. What are some selling techniques used by advertisers on television?
2. What are the various forms of persuasion? How do they affect the audience?
3. How do children respond to commercials shown on television?

If you cannot find three articles that deal with the issue you have selected, consider changing to a topic about which you are likely to find enough information.

Step 2: Summarize the Contents of Each Article

For each article you select, list the title, the author(s), the magazine from which it is taken, the date of publication, and page references. Next, write a brief summary of the article. Be sure to include the essential points. Limit yourself to the information the author(s) presents; do not offer your personal opinion or reaction. Express ideas in your own words. Use quotation marks if you cite material verbatim (word for word) from the article. But don't overdo quotations; use quotes only to emphasize specific points.

Step 3: React to the Position(s) of the Authors

After you have completed your summaries, present your opinion about each article. Indicate whether you agree or disagree with the author(s), and justify your views. You may have mixed feelings about a particular author's views and find that you agree with some ideas and disagree with others. You may also find that you cannot arrive at a firm position despite the information presented.

Using Indexes

The most widely available resource for locating articles is *The Readers' Guide to Periodical Literature.* This reference indexes publications in numerous fields. It is published twice a month. Indexes are also compiled quarterly and annually. *The Readers' Guide* indexes according to author, title, and subject.

Another resource, available in some libraries, is the *Magazine Index.* This is a cumulative electronic index of over 350 popular American magazines, with issues dating back four years. The index is stored on tape and, more recently, compact disk. Like *The Readers' Guide,* the *Magazine Index* can be searched according to title, author, or subject. The compact disk version also lets you do cross-referencing. For example, if you request articles that deal with television, violence, and children, the index will search for articles that fall into all three categories.

More recently, several companies that deal with CD-ROM databases now provide access to various databases containing a broad range of articles that can be searched electronically and accessed via the World Wide Web. H.W. Wilson's *Wilson Web,* InfoTrac's *Search Bank, EBSCOhost, Lexus/ Nexus,* and *SIRS Researcher* are some current companies providing these services. Ask your college or local librarian if such a service is available to you.

There are several advantages to conducting electronic searches:

- In most cases you can read an abstract of an article to see if it is relevant to your needs.

- You may be able to read the full text of an article and obtain a printout, thereby saving valuable time.

- Databases often store articles dating back several years. Rather than search year by year with the printed version, you can conduct a more comprehensive and efficient search by using an electronic version.

- Many information providers offer search engines that allow users to narrow their search to a key word, topic, or concept.

Reminder: Titles may sound very appealing. But only after you actually see the article can you determine whether it is suitable. Make sure your article contains enough information to be useful. Check to see which magazines are available in your school or public library. Use more than one library if necessary.

UNIT FOUR

The Family

READINGS IN UNIT FOUR

1. "The New Traditional Family" by Jacquelyn Mitchard

According to the author, traditions, rituals, and values are essential elements that help bind families.

2. "Family" from *Society: A Brief Introduction* by Ian Robertson

An expository chapter from a sociology textbook that examines the family and explores its transformation.

3. "The Way We Weren't: The Myth and Reality of the 'Traditional' Family" by Stephanie Coontz

Coontz maintains that the American family is both as strong and as fragile as it ever was and that attempts to reproduce any type of family outside of its original socioeconomic context are doomed to fail.

4. "The Second Shift: Working Parents and the Revolution at Home" by Arlie Hochschild with Anne Machung

An interview with a married couple reveals the family tensions created by the need to work outside the home.

5. "Put Family First" by Dr. Benjamin Spock

Despite the changes the family has undergone over time, Dr. Spock offers timely advice on what is needed to sustain it.

6. From *Keeping Families Together: The Case for Family Preservation* by Maya Angelou

Angelou argues that our society must find ways to preserve families as healthy, functioning units.

7. "Quality Time" by Barbara Kingsolver

Kingsolver portrays the inner workings of a single parent family and relates the pressures and the pleasures that each member experiences.

8. "Technology's Coming . . . Technology's Coming" by Erma Bombeck

Bombeck presents an amusing tale of how technology affected one family.

INTRODUCTION

The family is our oldest social institution and, according to some thinkers, the only natural one. A *family* can be defined as a group of people who are together because of marriage, blood ties, or adoption, who usually share a residence, and who have common goals. We usually think of a family as a mother, father, and children, but this "nuclear family," as sociologists call it, is only one possible combination. In fact, some of the articles in this unit argue that this definition of *family* is too narrow. The original meaning of the term (from the Latin *familias*) encompassed everyone in the household, including servants.

Recorded history clearly shows that the family was consistently important to both personal and communal lifestyles. Artifacts such as fossils and cave drawings indicate the dominance of a familylike structure from the very early days of humankind. Although its form and function (or roles) have changed over time, the family continues to be an important social institution.

At one time, families were commonly "extended"; that is, they consisted of parents, children, grandparents, and other relatives who shared a residence and had considerable social interaction. This type of family structure remains, but it is less widespread than it once was. In the 1940s and 1950s, there was a trend toward the nuclear or conjugal family. Recently other family patterns have evolved, such as the single-parent family, the childless family, and individuals who choose to live together but do not formally marry. Current data indicate that these nonnuclear living combinations now outnumber what was once considered a "typical" family.

Some critics view the rapidly changing family structure as social dynamite. A number of commentators even predict the end of our present-day society because of the disintegration of the traditional family in the face of rising divorce rates. Others suggest, however, that although the form of the family may be changing, its functions are remaining intact. For example, sociologists note a strong tendency for divorced parents to remarry and form a second family. Even though unmarried persons who live together may not meet the strict definition of the nuclear family, they are a family unit in terms of their structure and the roles they perform. If remarried individuals, single-parent families, unmarried couples, and experimental families are added to the number of nuclear families, a strong trend in favor of some type of family structure becomes clear. Sociologists attribute the persistence of the family to the needs that a family fulfills.

In a sense, we are all experts on the family—at least on our own families. The family is a complex subject, however, and there is much to consider and learn about this familiar institution.

What You Can Expect in This Unit

There are no marginal vocabulary terms, marked copies, or process guides for the readings in this unit. The Gearing Up questions and Questions continue, however. You now have a chance to apply on your own the reading strategies you have been developing throughout this book.

Connecting Themes

This unit, "The Family," was preceded by units on "Reading and Literacy," "Work and Careers," and "Mass Media." These interrelated topics were chosen because you already know something about them and can bring some prior knowledge to the material. Studying the first three units should have increased your knowledge of these topics and enabled you to relate what you learned about literacy, work, and mass media to this unit on the family. Even if you haven't studied all of the previous units, your general knowledge should allow you to see relationships between their content and the ideas explored in "The Family."

"The Family" and "Reading and Literacy"

Unit One presented three issues for focused study: the power of literacy, the effort put into reading, and how reading is learned. You know firsthand the powerful influence the family has on its members. What role might the family play in a child's learning to read? What effects could the family's lifestyle and recreation patterns have on the reading habits of its members? Some critics claim that our nation has lost its respect for literacy. What role might the family play in this development? What influence have members of your family had on your own reading, studying, and attitude toward learning?

"The Family" and "Work and Careers"

At one time, families had a strong effect on the work their children pursued. Children of farmers grew up to be farmers themselves. Families engaged in a trade (such as baking or tailoring) passed these skills on to their offspring, both to prepare them to earn a living and to gain more helping hands. Does this trend continue today? If not, what factors do you think are changing this pattern? Some authorities claim that the family, once the highest priority in individuals' lives, is now losing its dominant role to work and careers. What effect do you think such a trend will have on the family of the future?

Economic pressures have forced both parents to work full time in many families, even though they would prefer that one parent remain at home or work only part time. What impact have these circumstances had on the children and parents? Might positive as well as negative effects result from this situation? Parents in single-parent families bear the double burden of work and full-time family responsibilities. What effect might this heavy workload have on the children and the single parent?

"The Family" and "Mass Media"

Before the development of mass media, interaction with family members and neighbors was an individual's principal source of news and entertainment. Even as newspapers became commonplace, they did not compare to today's. For example, the *New York Times* of the 1850s was a single page. Then, in less than a hundred years, technological advances made possible paperback books, radio, phonographs, motion pictures, and television. Today computers, fax machines, VCRs, satellite and cable broadcasting, and the Internet provide even more alternatives for transmitting information. Virtually every American family is affected by media.

It is reasonable to expect that the mass media have an influence on the dynamics of the modern family. In what ways is this evident? How does today's family spend time together? Do interactions among family members differ from those in the past? Are the families portrayed in the mass media representative of real-world families? What problems can arise when individuals use fictional families as role models?

These questions are only a sampling of those you will consider as you read this unit and attempt to make connections with ideas and issues in other units.

The Family: A Connecting Exercise

In this unit, you will read articles dealing with various aspects of family life. You will see that certain issues form a common thread among several articles. The first three units provided a structured exercise to help you tie such issues together. In this unit, however, you will select the issues concerning the family on the basis of your reading. Then you will devise a chart showing how each issue is addressed in the articles you study. After completing the unit, you will be asked to state your own opinion on the issues. Your opinion will reflect your prior experience, reading, and judgment.

The following questions are intended to stimulate your thinking and to help you select some issues for study. These questions are only suggestions. Feel free to use issues of your own choice.

- Either directly or indirectly, each article in Unit Four addresses the question "What is a family?" An issue in a number of the articles is "What constitutes a healthy family?" Families are social institutions, and as such they fulfill some needs for their members. What needs does the family address, and how does the family work to meet those needs?

- The outside world is often a source of stress. How can the family help its members cope with outside pressures?

- The careers of family members and the family's leisure habits are another source of influence. How do these factors alter family relationships?

The New Traditional Family

JACQUELYN MITCHARD

Jacquelyn Mitchard is a contributing editor to Parenting *and* TV Guide *and is the author of* Mother Less Child *(1985),* The Deep End of the Ocean *(1996),* The Rest of Us: Dispatches from the Mother Ship *(1997), and* The Most Wanted *(1998).*

GEARING UP

1. Cite some customs that are carried on by your family. Explain or speculate on how they originated.

2. Identify a custom or rite followed by a family other than your own. Would you like to have this custom in your own family? Explain your reasons.

The Reading

The New Traditional Family

by JACQUELYN MITCHARD

1   It's one of those TV-hip phrases that make my teeth hurt: "untraditional family." If it appeared in the dictionary, you might very well find my family's picture right next to the definition.

2   We didn't start out that way. Not too long ago, we looked like poster people for the much extolled nuclear family: Mom. Dad. Kids. Jobs. Tension. Coffee. Laughter. Mortgage.

3   But in recent years, my family has faced almost every demographic risk that society has to offer. I've experienced single motherhood in one of the most wrenching ways possible—rocked by the death of my still-young husband. Left with four children to raise, I went on to adopt an infant, making us a multicultural family, too.

4   You name the pothole, and we've had at least one wheel in it. Underemployment. Rubber checks. Second (and third and fourth) jobs. School failure. Counseling for one of the older children about his rage over being left with the "wrong" parent. Learning the literal meaning of the phrase "The roof fell in." Even a visit from Social Services, after a concerned acquaintance interpreted kite-string burns on my son's shoulder as a sign of abuse.

5   It all sounds fairly grim and, in fact, parts of it were. But now, nearly four years after my husband's death, we live a family life that is ordered,

successful, noisy, active, social, noisy, healthy, prudent—did I say noisy?—
and economically stable. Luck played a part in that. So did determination.
But one of the most critical elements in the survival of this family has been
our sense of tradition. We count on our traditions, but the key word is *our.*

6   They may not be the kinds of rituals and values that government leaders
like to refer to in speeches—speeches in which "the way it used to be" really
means "the way it should be." In truth, those idyllic times barely deserve
their enduring reputation.

7   I know, because I grew up in a traditional family of the sixties—and not
an unhappy one. I knew what tradition sounded like. It sounded like
"Streets of Laredo," my mother's favorite song, as she sang it over and over.
But it was also the sound of my parents bickering in the car as they hashed
over the dinner we'd just endured with my father's relatives.

8   I knew how tradition smelled—like candles guttering in pumpkins at
Halloween and the genuine greasepaint our mother let us slather on our
faces for trick or treat. It also smelled like half-empty cans of beer stuffed
with stale cigarette butts, abandoned by my various uncles when too much
alcohol turned a Saturday-night card game into a Saturday-night fight.

9   I began to think of tradition as something best endured, subdued, and if
possible, ignored. But when I started my own family, I was haunted by a
sense that we needed more to rely on, something to represent our presence
as links in a long chain. We needed ritual, but not the kind perpetuated for
no real purpose.

10   In the saddest way, I learned how to forge new traditions. Following a
short and merciless illness, my husband, Dan, died just after our youngest
child's fourth birthday. Some relatives demanded a high mass, others an out-
door memorial for an outdoorsy guy. But I had to choose what was right for
our family: a service in the Unitarian Meeting House, conducted by a former
rabbi and a Catholic priest, with music that ranged from gospel to the Beach
Boys to "Danny Boy."

11   And from that first heartbreaking and nerve-racking debut, we kept
right on creating, blending the best gleanings from our history with the best
of our current reality—a reality in which moms work and even little boys
learn how to change diapers.

12   In my untraditionally traditional family, we go to church every Sunday,
at the same Meeting House where we gathered for that sad first parting
among us. It was there, too, that the newest member of our family became
the first to be welcomed with a naming dedication instead of a baptism.

13   And for the second time in my life, I've discovered how tradition
sounds. Whenever we drive farther than a few miles, we all sing the old
Marty Robbins song "El Paso." Every night before bed, I still quote from
Madeline. "Goodnight, little ones! Thank the Lord you are well!"

14   I know how tradition smells. Like beans and rice, which my children
prepare on Wednesday nights—"Mom night," when we watch my favorite
TV show all twined up on the couch like a nest of rabbits. I know how tradition tastes. Like homemade birthday cakes, never made with the low-fat
alternative directions.

15   It's our custom to celebrate holidays with a glass of champagne—one glass, and everyone, even children, takes a sip. Then we put away the alcohol and get out the board games. We still visit relatives, just more briefly.

16   Not all our traditions involve festivity. Ask any one of my kids about the family custom that requires every child to learn to read music. Or the rule that everyone's grounded until the siblings sort out which one really drew on the fabric shade.

17   Children in our house need to respect their elders. But they also need to respect one another. Big-brother bullying is not tolerated as "boys being boys." Kids who swear get a dot of soap on the tongue, but they administer it themselves, not under threat of hammerlock as it was in my childhood. We have to give away some of whatever we earn or have, to the point where it pinches. But we don't have to hide, as my father did, when the priest came around to discuss the building-fund pledge. We forgive everyone their trespasses, but they have to make restitution, myself included.

18   Some days it all works better than other days. But even on the bad days, our traditions bind us close—closer, perhaps than some families who look a lot more unified, families who "match" because no one was adopted, families with younger, bouncier mothers, families with fathers.

19   I guess I'm supposed to think that in a perfect world, things would be the way they used to be: a nuclear family with one parent on the home front, and couples nicely paired according to gender, race, and religion.

20   Except I don't believe that.

21   I think that in a perfect world, the perfect family would look all kinds of ways. Yearning single fathers could adopt and raise happy babies, and three women could pool their resources to buy a big house for themselves and their kids, and we would be tolerant of their beliefs and not threatened by them. And each one of those families would be a nuclear family—with the nucleus a glowing core of commitment and tenderness.

22   Honoring rituals and values we believe in, whether we inherited or created them, really does matter. That's what makes even the most eccentric-seeming family, at least in the truest sense of the word, traditional. Just like mine.

QUESTIONS

1. The author begins by describing some difficult times faced by her family. Briefly summarize her comments.

2. State the author's reasons for the usefulness of traditions.

3. Name two traditions the author follows with her children. How do these traditions help to bring her family close together?

4. Discuss the techniques the author uses with her family when things don't go the way they are supposed to.

Family

IAN ROBERTSON

Ian Robertson is an educator and author with wide teaching experiences. He completed his undergraduate studies at the University of Natal and went on to finish graduate studies at Oxford, Cambridge, and Harvard universities. He is the author of Race and Politics in South Africa *(1978),* Social Problems *(1980),* Sociology *(1987), and* Society: A Brief Introduction *(1988), from which the following excerpt is taken.*

GEARING UP

1. Without using a dictionary or any other text, write your own definition of *family.*

2. What needs do families provide for their members?

3. How do you think the family of the future (a hundred years or more from now) will differ from today's families?

The Reading

Family

by IAN ROBERTSON

The Family Institution

1 What exactly is a family? Our ideas on the subject may tend to be ethnocentric, for they are often based on the middle-class "ideal" family so relentlessly portrayed in TV commercials, one that consists of a husband, a wife, and their dependent children. This particular family pattern, however, is far from typical. A more accurate conception of the family must take account of the many different family forms that have existed or still exist both in America and in other cultures. Such a conception would have to include, for example, a Kenyan union consisting of one husband and several wives—or an American unmarried mother with her dependent children. To cover all the possibilities, we say that the family is a relatively permanent group of people related by ancestry, marriage, or adoption, who live together, form an economic unit, and take care of their young. If this definition seems a little cumbersome, it is only because it has to include such a great variety of family forms.

2 Most of us spend our lives in two families in which we have quite

different statuses and roles: a **family of orientation,** the one into which we are born as son or daughter, and a **family of procreation,** the one which we create ourselves as father or mother. In every society, a family is expected to be formed through **marriage,** a socially approved mating arrangement between two or more people. Social recognition of a marriage is usually marked through some culturally prescribed ritual, such as a wedding by a religious official, a registration of the union by a judge or other government servant, or a formal exchange of gifts between the families of the partners. The partners in a marriage are expected to have a sexual relationship, and are also expected to honor the economic rights and duties involved in the sharing of a household.

3   Every society distinguishes between offspring born in wedlock and those born out of wedlock. **Legitimate birth** is birth to a mother and father who are married to each other; **illegitimate birth** is birth to a mother who is not married to the father. All societies encourage legitimacy, because it enables them to automatically allocate the social roles of mother and father to specific persons who are then responsible for the care and protection of the young. Illegitimacy, on the other hand, can present a social problem, because although the mother is known, there may be nobody to take on the social role of father.

4   The family is a unit within a much wider group of relatives, or kin. **Kinship** is a social network of people related by common ancestry, adoption, or marriage. A kinship network is a highly complicated affair, as you will know if you have ever tried to construct your own family tree. If you include distant relatives such as in-laws and second cousins, it can easily run into hundreds of people. In many traditional societies, kinship is the basis of social organization, but in modern societies the family tends to become isolated from all but the closest kin. Many of us do not even know the names of our second cousins or similarly distant relatives. Frequently, even close kin gather only for a few ceremonial occasions such as Thanksgiving or funerals.

The Family: A Functionalist View

5 As functionalists emphasize, the family institution is a universal one because it performs vital functions in all societies.

1. *Regulation of sexual behavior.* No society allows people to mate at random. The marriage and family system provides a means of regulating sexual behavior by specifying who may mate with whom and under what circumstances they may do so.

2. *Replacement of members.* A society cannot survive unless it has a system for replacing its members from generation to generation. The family provides a stable, institutionalized means through which this replacement can take place.

3. *Socialization.* People do not become fully human until they are socialized, and the primary context for this socialization is the family, starting at birth. Although in modern society many socialization functions have

been taken over by other institutions, the family remains the earliest and most significant agency of socialization.

4. *Care and protection.* People need warmth, food, shelter, and care. The family provides an environment in which these needs can be met. In particular, the productive members of the family can take care of those who, by reason of their youth, age, or infirmity, are unable to take care of themselves.

5. *Social placement.* Our family background is the most significant single determinant of our place in society. We inherit from our family of orientation not only material goods but also our social status. We belong to the same racial or ethnic group and usually to the same religion and social class that our parents belong to.

6. *Emotional support.* Human beings have a need for affection, nurturance, intimacy, and love. The family is the primary social context in which emotional needs can be fulfilled and the deepest personal feelings can be expressed. In this sense the family may function as "a haven in a heartless world," the place of ultimate emotional refuge and comfort (Lasch, 1977).

6   All these functions are necessary. Of course, the family is not the only conceivable means through which they could be fulfilled. Yet the family fulfills them so effectively that it takes primary responsibility for them in every culture.

The Family: A Conflict View

7 While conflict theorists do not dispute that the family has important social functions, they believe that the functionalist analysis does not tell the whole story. In particular, they note that the family is the principal institution in which the dominance of men over women has been expressed.

8   In many societies women have been treated for practical and legal purposes as the property of their husbands (or, if unmarried, of their fathers). As recently as the late 1960s, many American statutes made married women legally incompetent to enter into contracts, rent cars, or get credit without their husband's signature—in much the same way that minors cannot exercise certain privileges without the approval of a parent or guardian. Even more strikingly, husbands had absolute sexual rights over their spouses, and it is only recently that some states have made it illegal for a husband to rape his wife. Traces of the old traditions are also to be found in our contemporary wedding ceremony: in the standard form of vows, the bride solemnly promises to "obey" the groom, and it is her father who "gives her away" to her new husband, as though some piece of property were being transferred. (We can see the implications of this symbolic interaction more clearly if we imagine its opposite—the mother of the groom giving him away to the bride, and he then vowing to obey his wife for the rest of his life.) Male dominance is still very much the pattern in most societies, but in the Western postindustrial societies, these traditional inequalities are now steadily diminishing.

9   Conflict theorists also point out that the sociological research of the past two decades has revealed an astonishing amount of family violence—between spouses, between parents and offspring, and among the offspring themselves. About a fifth of all murders in the United States are committed by a relative of the victim—in half of the cases, by the spouse. The police detest "disturbance calls"—usually family fights—because of the vicious and dangerous nature of so many of these conflicts; indeed, more police are killed intervening in these disputes than in almost any other type of situation they face. Surveys suggest that each year around 7 million couples go through a violent episode in which one spouse tries to cause the other serious pain or injury. Wives assault their husbands as often as husbands assault their wives, and spouses are equally likely to kill each other. Although wives are rarely a match for their husbands in a fistfight, they are more likely to use lethal weapons (notably kitchen knives). In most nonfatal physical violence between the spouses, however, wives are very much the victims, for wife-beating is a widespread and very serious problem. Child abuse—involving such acts as burning children with cigarettes, locking them up in closets, tying them up for hours or days, or breaking their bones—is alarmingly common, and probably causes many of the 2 million runaways that happen each year. And the sexual abuse of children—now recognized as a national epidemic—is rarely a matter of molestation by a stranger. It is usually perpetrated by one family member on another (Gelles and Cornell, 1983, 1985; Gelles, 1987; Finkelhor, 1983, 1984; Russell, 1984, 1986).

10   One source of this violence may lie in the dynamics of the family as an intimate environment: close relationships are likely to involve more conflict than less intimate ones, since there are more occasions for tension to arise and more likelihood that deep emotions will be provoked. Another source may lie outside the family, for violence is frequently a response to frustration. If the person affected cannot strike back at the source of the problem—the arrogance of an employer, say, or the lack of a job—the aggression may be readily redirected at family members. Perhaps most important, violence between husband and wife takes place in a general social context that has traditionally emphasized male dominance and female subservience (Straus and Hotaling, 1980).

Family Patterns

11   Each society views its own patterns of marriage, family, and kinship as self-evidently right and proper, and usually as God-given as well. Much of the current concern about the fate of the modern family stems from this kind of ethnocentrism. If we assume that there is only one "right" family form, then naturally any change in that particular form will be interpreted as heralding the doom of the whole institution. It is important to recognize, therefore, that there is an immense range in marriage, family, and kinship patterns; that each of these patterns may be, at least in its own context, perfectly viable; and above all, that the family, like any other social institution, must inevitably change through time, in our own society as in all others.

A Cross-Cultural Perspective

12   The family patterns of other cultures challenge many of our assumptions about the nature of marriage, family, and kinship (Murdock, 1949; Ford and Beach, 1951; Stephens, 1963; Fox, 1965; Murstein, 1974).

13   As we saw in Chapter 7 ("Sexuality and Society"), every society has an **incest taboo,** a powerful moral prohibition against sexual contact between certain categories of relatives. However, different societies have quite different ideas about who the incest taboo should apply to. In the United States, all fifty states prohibit marriage between a person and his or her parent, grandparent, uncle or aunt, brother or sister, and niece or nephew; an additional twenty-nine states regard marriage between first cousins as incestuous, but the remainder do not. Many societies, however, do not make any distinction between siblings (brothers and sisters) and cousins. In these societies there are usually no separate words for "brother" and "cousin": they are regarded as the same kind of relative, and the incest taboo is therefore extended to first, second, third, and even more distant cousins as well. And, although certain societies consider it incestuous to marry a child of one's mother's sister, or of one's father's brother, they may expect—or even require—that one should marry a child of one's mother's brother, or of one's father's sister.

14   In modern, industrialized societies it is generally assumed that marriage is founded on romantic love between the partners and that the choice of a mate should be left to the individual. But this concept of romantic love is entirely unknown in many societies and is considered laughable or tragic in many others. In most traditional societies, marriage is regarded as a practical economic arrangement or a matter of family alliances, not a love match. In these societies, therefore, marriage is negotiated by the parents of the partners, often with little or no consideration of their children's wishes. If love is a feature of these marriages at all, it is expected to be a result and not a cause of the union. The economic aspect of these marriages is especially apparent in those societies in which an intending groom must pay a bride-price to his prospective father-in-law. This practice is especially widespread in sub-Saharan Africa, where nearly all the tribes expect a groom to exchange cattle for the bride.

15   In all Western nations, the law insists on **monogamy,** a marriage involving one spouse of each sex. However, this ideal is held by a minority of the societies of the world. In a survey of evidence from 238 mostly preindustrial societies, George Murdock (1949) found that only 43 prohibited **polygamy,** a marriage involving a spouse of one sex and two or more spouses of the opposite sex. In 4 of the remaining societies a woman was permitted to have more than one husband, and in all the rest a man was allowed to have more than one wife, a ratio that reflects the superior power and privileges of the male partner in the family institution.

16   In modern industrialized societies, we generally assume that married partners should be adults of much the same age, although certain exceptions are made for an older man and a younger woman. Some societies offer strikingly contrasting patterns. The Kadara of Nigeria marry infants to one an-

other. The Chuckchee of Siberia, believing that parental care is the best way of cementing the marriage bond, allow adult women to marry males of only two or three years of age; the new wives then look after the boys until they are old enough to assume their husbandly duties. And among the Tiwi of Australia, adult males marry females even before they are conceived, annulling the marriage if the newborn turns out to be the wrong sex.

17   In most traditional, preindustrial societies, the family system takes the form of the **extended family,** one in which more than two generations of the same kinship live together, either in the same house or in adjacent dwellings. The head of the entire family is usually the eldest male, and all adults share responsibility for child-rearing and other tasks. The extended family can be very large: sometimes it contains several adult offspring of the head of the family, together with their spouses and children. We are more familiar with the **nuclear family,** one in which the family group consists only of the parents and their dependent children, living apart from other relatives. The nuclear family occurs in some preindustrial societies, and is the usual type in virtually all modern industrialized societies. In fact, the growing dominance of the nuclear family is transforming family life all over the world.

The Transformation of the Family

18   As one society after another has industrialized over the course of the past two centuries, there has been a major, global change in family patterns—a change that involves a fundamental shift in people's loyalties. Essentially, people have come to focus less on their responsibilities toward their extended kin and more on their own needs and those of their family of procreation. Marriage is now viewed less as an economic arrangement or a kinship alliance, and more as a companionship based on the emotional commitment of two individuals. This shift in loyalties has had dramatic effects on family life. In particular, the extended family has tended to be replaced by the nuclear family (Laslett, 1971, 1977; Laslett and Wall, 1972; Shorter, 1975; Stone, 1977; Gordon, 1983).

19   Why has the nuclear family become the dominant type? The answer is that the extended family is well suited to the conditions of preindustrial society, where every able-bodied family member is an economic asset. But the nuclear family is far better adapted to the conditions of the modern world, for several reasons.

1. *Geographic mobility.* Life in a modern society offers and sometimes requires geographic mobility—workers are expected to go where the jobs and promotions are. They cannot do so if obligations to various kin tie them to a particular area and prevent prolonged separation from relatives.

2. *Social mobility.* Unlike the traditional, preindustrial societies, modern societies offer people the chance to achieve new and often higher social statuses. As a result of social mobility, various family members may eventually come to have lifestyles that are quite different from one another. Consequently, the bonds of common interests and shared experience that

once bound the extended family together are loosened or, in some cases, even shattered.

3. *Loss of family functions.* In an industrialized, urban environment, formal organizations and institutions—corporations, schools, hospitals, welfare agencies, day-care centers, and the media—take over many of the functions that were once the prerogative of the extended family. People no longer have to rely on the support network provided by their kin, and instead seek a new foundation for married life—close companionship with a single spouse.

4. *Advantages of small families.* In a modern society, children become an economic liability rather than an asset. The parents get no financial benefits to compensate for the vast expense of clothing, feeding, and educating their offspring. People therefore find it convenient to restrict the size of their households, preferring to live in independent units away from other relatives.

5. *Individualism.* An outstanding feature of industrial societies, and especially of the emerging postindustrial societies, is individualism. As we noted in Chapter 2 ("Culture"), people in these societies are increasingly concerned with self-fulfillment as a personal goal. Individual desires become more important than traditional obligations. Whether the issue is marriage or divorce, they ask: "What's in it for me?" rather than "What does my kin group expect me to do?" As Betty Yorburg (1983) observes:

> Married women will go out to work even against opposition from their husbands. They will leave unhappy marriages, sometimes without their children, especially in the middle or upper classes. Husbands will leave their economically dependent wives. . . . The presence of children no longer preserves marriages. . . . The oldest child will no longer give up educational or other personal goals to support needy brothers and sisters or aged parents and grandparents. Young people will choose marital partners or live together in heterosexual or homosexual relationships with or without the approval of parents.

20   Yet although the nuclear family is functional in modern society, it suffers from a number of dysfunctions as well—and this is the key to understanding some of its present difficulties. In the extended family, the individual could turn for support to an array of relatives. Today the married partners can turn only to each other, and sometimes demand more from one another than either can provide. If members of an extended family were for some reason unable to play their roles, other members could take them over. In the nuclear family, on the other hand, the death, prolonged illness, or unemployment of a breadwinner can throw the entire family into severe crisis. In the extended family, people rarely had expectations of romantic love with their spouses; marriage was a practical, common-sense affair. In the nuclear family, far higher expectations exist, and if they are not fulfilled—and often they cannot be—discontent and unhappiness may result.

Marriage and Family in America

21   "Love and marriage," an old popular song tells us, "go together like a horse and carriage." A compelling assumption in American society is that everyone will fall in love, will marry, will have children, and will have an emotionally satisfying lifetime relationship with the chosen partner. It is probably true that most of us fall in love at some point; it is certainly true that nearly all of us marry and have children; but it is likely that a great many of us—perhaps the majority—find that married life falls below our expectations. To find out what can go wrong and why, we must look in more detail at romantic love, courtship, marriage, and marital breakdown and divorce.

Romantic Love

22   The American family, like those in modern industrialized societies, is supposed to be founded on the romantic love of the marital partners. Happily enough, romantic love defies a clinical definition. It is a different kind of love, though, from the love you have for your parents or your dog. It involves physical symptoms, such as pounding heart and sexual desire, and psychological symptoms, such as obsessive focus on one person and a disregard for any resulting social or economic risks. Our culture encourages us to look for this love—to find that "one and only," perhaps even through "love at first sight." Behavior of this kind is portrayed and warmly endorsed throughout American popular culture, by books, magazines, comics, records, popular songs, movies, and TV.

23   Romantic love is a noble ideal, and it can certainly help provide a basis for the spouses to "live happily ever after." But since marriage can equally well be founded on much more practical considerations, why is romantic love of such importance in the modern world? The reason seems to be that it has the following basic functions in maintaining the institution of the nuclear family (Goode, 1959):

1. *Transfer of loyalties.* Romantic love helps the young partners to loosen their bonds with their family of orientation, a step that is essential if they are to establish an independent nuclear family. Their total absorption in one another facilitates a transfer of commitment from existing family and kin to a new family of procreation.

2. *Emotional support.* Romantic love provides the couple with emotional support in the difficulties that they face in establishing a new life on their own. This love would not be so necessary in an extended family, where the relatives are able to confront problems cooperatively.

3. *Incentive to marriage.* Romantic love serves as bait to lure people into marriage. In the modern world, people have considerable choice over whether they will get married or not. A contract to form a lifelong commitment to another person is not necessarily a very tempting proposition, however: to some, the prospect may look more like a noose than like a

bed of roses. Without feelings of romantic love, many people might have no incentive to marry.

24   To most of us, particularly to those who are in love, romantic love seems to be the most natural thing in the world, but as we saw earlier, it is a purely cultural product, arising in certain societies for specific reasons. In a different time or in a different society, you might never fall in love, nor would you expect to.

Courtship and Marriage

25   A courtship system is essentially a marriage market. (The metaphor of the "market" may seem a little unromantic, but, in fact, the participants do attempt to "sell" their assets—physical appearance, personal charms, talents and interests, and career prospects.) In the matter of mate selection, different courtship systems vary according to how much choice they permit the individual. The United States probably allows more freedom of choice than any other society. In this predominantly urban and anonymous society, young people—often with access to automobiles—have an exceptional degree of privacy in their courting. The practice of dating enables them to find out about one another, to improve their own interpersonal skills in the market, to experiment sexually if they so wish, and finally to select a marriage partner.

26   Who marries whom, then? Cupid's arrow, it turns out, does not strike at random. Despite the cultural emphasis on love as something mysterious and irrational, the selection of marital partners is actually fairly orderly and predictable. In general, the American mate-selection process produces **homogamy,** marriage between partners who share similar social characteristics. In general, spouses tend to be of similar age, social class, religious affiliation, and educational level, and they are also much more likely to marry within their own racial or ethnic group than outside it. The reason is not hard to find, for there is considerable parental and peer pressure for young people to restrict their social contacts to those who are "suitable"—which usually means "similar."

27   Of course, homogamy provides only the general framework in which specific people choose their specific mates. In selecting their partners, people are influenced by psychological as well as social factors. Some researchers claim that people want partners whose personalities match their own in significant respects. In this "birds of a feather" view, conservatives may be attracted by other conservatives, or alcoholics may tend to seek out other alcoholics. But other researchers claim that people look for partners whose personality traits are different from, but complementary to, their own. In this "opposites attract" view, dominant people may look for passive mates, or those who love to eat may link up with those who love to cook. Both views are probably valid, depending on the psychological "chemistry" of the couple in question—a chemistry that may well change over the course of the relationship.

Marital Breakdown

28   The divorce rate in the United States is believed to be the highest in the world, and statistics on the subject are often quoted as conclusive evidence of the decay of the family. This evidence indicates that about 50 percent of recent marriages will end in divorce, the average duration of these ill-fated unions being around 7 years.

29   Divorce constitutes official social recognition that a marriage has failed, and it can be a traumatic experience for all concerned. Most states now offer a "no fault" divorce on grounds of simple incompatibility, but there is still room for fierce resentment over the custody of offspring and child-support payments. Children are present in over 70 percent of the families that break up through divorce: more than a million children are involved every year. The children inevitably suffer through the divorce of their parents—particularly during the first year or two—but many people believe that it may be even more emotionally disturbing for them to remain in a home where the marriage is deeply unhappy. Both divorcing parties may also be in for a difficult time emotionally. Divorce ruptures one's personal universe; it is no coincidence that men are much more likely to be fired from their jobs after divorce, nor that the death rate for divorced people is significantly higher than that for married people, at all age levels (Weiss, 1975; Emery et al., 1984).

30   The ex-wife may face severe economic problems, especially if she has to raise young children. In the past, when most wives were not expected to work outside the home, courts frequently awarded alimony to divorced women; but now that women are considered capable of earning their own living, they receive alimony in only about 15 percent of divorce settlements. Courts award child custody to mothers rather than fathers in 90 percent of cases, however, and usually require that the fathers provide child support. But many divorced women find that they have low earning power—particularly if they have spent their entire married lives as housewives and have no job skills or experience—and a majority of divorced fathers default on their child-support payments. More than half of American children in families where the father is absent live below the poverty line, and many single mothers become long-term welfare recipients.

31   Who gets divorced? The social characteristics of divorce-prone partners have been well established. Divorces are especially common among urban couples, among those who marry very young, among those who marry after only short or shallow acquaintance, and among those whose relatives and friends disapprove of the marriage. In general, the people who are most likely to get divorced are those who, statistically, would be considered the least likely to marry. And the greater the wife's ability to support herself, the more likely she is to leave an unhappy marriage. Partners who have been married before are more likely to become involved in subsequent divorce. Most divorces take place within the first few years of marriage—and the longer a marriage has lasted, the less likely it is to end in divorce (Carter and Glick, 1976; Goode, 1982; Fisher, 1987).

Marriage and Divorce Rates: 1940–1987
Per 1,000 population

Source: U.S. Bureau of the Census, 1988.

Figure 11.5 As this chart shows, from the 1940s to the 1980s, the rate of divorce increased steadily, while the rate of marriage fluctuated during this time. The divorce rate is now one-half the marriage rate. This ratio is distorted, however, by the fact that the population that is eligible for divorce is a huge one, containing everybody who is married, while the population that is eligible for marriage is much smaller, consisting primarily of unmarried people between the ages of eighteen and thirty. The ratio is therefore not as alarming as it seems to be.

Different social factors influence the marriage and divorce rate. The divorce rate may be pushed up, for example, by laws that make divorce easier to get, or by better employment opportunities for women. The marriage rate, on the other hand, may be influenced by such factors as the proportion of young adults in the population, or by current social attitudes toward alternatives to marriage, such as living together.

Causes of Marital Breakdown

32 There are many causes for the collapse of modern American marriages, but
the following seem to be the main ones.

1. *Stress on the nuclear family.* As we have seen, the nuclear family is highly
    vulnerable if the breadwinner is for any reason unwilling or unable to
    meet economic obligations. In addition, the spouses in a nuclear family
    have a very strong mutual dependency and may make heavy demands on
    one another for emotional support. The failure of one partner to meet the
    expectations of the other jeopardizes the marriage in a way that would
    hardly be possible under the extended family system.

2. *The fading of romantic love.* Americans are thoroughly socialized into
    the expectation that romantic love will "conquer all" and make their mar-
    riage happy ever after. But the heady joys of romantic love are usually
    short-lived, and the excitement of the earlier relationship is lessened or
    even lost in the daily routines of job and housework, diapers and dish-
    washing, mortgages and bills. This does not mean that the partners no
    longer love one another; it is just that their love is likely to be of a differ-
    ent kind. It can be mature, companionable, intimate, committed, and
    deeply fulfilling—but Americans are not socialized to recognize or ap-
    preciate this change, and may start looking for romance elsewhere.

3. *The changing role of women.* In the past, the role of the wife in an Amer-
    ican marriage was assumed to be that of housekeeper, child-rearer, and
    nurturant supporter of a husband who was active in the world beyond the
    home. More and more American women are rejecting this role, and in do-
    ing so are challenging the established structure of the nuclear family. The
    average family now has only two children, and the average woman now
    has her last child in her late twenties. Traditional family norms make lit-
    tle provision for the woman who wants an independent career, and even
    less for the family in which the wife earns more than the husband and be-
    comes the primary breadwinner. The growing economic independence of
    women makes it much easier for them to divorce their mates, and it chal-
    lenges the role relationship on which the nuclear family has been based
    (Kanter, 1977; Rubin, 1979).

4. *Sexual permissiveness.* The development and widespread availability of
    contraceptives have potentially separated two quite different functions of
    sexual relations—procreation and recreation. In the days when intercourse
    was likely to lead to pregnancy, there was a strong practical incentive for sex
    to be restricted to marital partners, for our society makes little provision for
    the proper care of children born to unmarried mothers. But if the prospect
    of pregnancy is removed, many of the inhibitions against the use of sex for
    recreation disappear also. The nuclear family is founded on an assumption
    of monogamous fidelity, but permissiveness encourages many people to
    look outside their marriages for sexual satisfaction. Changing sexual norms
    inevitably threaten a family system based on the assumption that the part-
    ners will have an exclusive and mutually gratifying sexual relationship.

The Future of the Family

33   The alterations that the American family is undergoing cannot be halted by laws or sermons, for they are the products of much more encompassing social and economic developments. The changes in the family are perhaps even more extensive than is generally realized. For example, not only is the family consisting of a husband who works and a wife who stays home to care for their two dependent children no longer the norm; it exists in fewer than one of every ten households in the United States.

34   In this climate of change, what may become of the American family? We can gain some insights into its future by looking at trends in the institution, and particularly at some alternatives to the established nuclear pattern that already exist. Some of these alternatives are relatively frequent; some are quite rare; and several overlap one another.

35   SINGLE-PARENT FAMILIES   The single-parent family is now emerging as the most common alternative to the nuclear unit. In 1960, 8 percent of families had one parent; in 1970, 13 percent; in 1980, 21 percent; in 1985, 26 percent. High divorce and illegitimacy rates are likely to push this figure up even further, and it is expected that half the children born in the 1980s will spend part of their childhood living with one parent. The main source of the rapid increase in single-parent families is a soaring illegitimacy rate, which has leaped from 4 percent of all births in 1950 to over 20 percent today—representing some 700,000 babies annually. The percentage of black children living in homes with a single parent (usually the mother) rose from 36 percent in 1970 to 51 percent in 1980 and then to 59 percent in 1985. In that year, just over half of the black births in the United States were illegitimate, and in some ghetto areas the rate was much higher. Overall, about three-quarters of unmarried women are now sexually active—and most do not regularly practice birth control. Not too surprisingly, one in every four American women gets pregnant by the age of nineteen, and 80 percent of these pregnancies are premarital—a statistic without parallel in the modern world. If current trends persist in the future, half of all the households in America could be headed by a single parent by the end of this century.

36   COHABITATION   Although it might have caused a minor neighborhood scandal a few decades ago, cohabitation, or openly "living together," is now a relatively common type of domestic and sexual arrangement, particularly among young people. The number of unmarried people of opposite sex sharing a household has more than tripled during the past two decades and now comprises nearly 2.6 million adults, 60 percent of them under thirty-five years of age. In some cases cohabitation seems to be a modern form of "going steady"; in others it is more like a "trial marriage," in which the partners explicitly decide to test their compatibility before taking the plunge into married life. Actually, about a third of cohabiting couples eventually do marry; most of the rest separate within two or three years (Simenauer and Carroll, 1982; Blumstein and Swartz, 1983).

37   **SERIAL MONOGAMY** A growing number of people marry more than once; in fact, nearly 80 percent of divorced partners marry someone else within a few years of divorcing (Glick and Lin, 1986). Now that divorces are easier to get and provoke less social disapproval than ever before, many people embark on a career of "serial" marriages, marrying, divorcing, remarrying, perhaps divorcing again. Indeed, the more often people have been divorced, the more likely it is that their subsequent marriage will end in the same way. Jessie Bernard (1982) has suggested that serial marriage makes having several spouses more common in America than polygamy does in other societies. Serial monogamy allows the partners to maintain a commitment to marriage, if not to one spouse.

38   **RECONSTITUTED FAMILIES** Divorce and remarriage may create a "reconstituted family"—one that is put together, as it were, from the fragments of previous families. These families, which are becoming increasingly common, face special difficulties, most obviously that of establishing appropriate relationships among step-parents and step-children, between the children of one spouse and the children of the other spouse, and, eventually perhaps, between various new half-brothers and half-sisters and the existing children. With a certain effort of the imagination, we can see that serial monogamy, leading to two or even more reconstituted marriages of two or more different sets of partners, can produce a very complex family tree indeed, and can create classes of relatives for which our language does not even have words (Cherlin, 1981).

39   **CHILDLESS COUPLES** An increasing number of married couples are deliberately choosing not to have children. On the whole, these couples are more likely than other couples to be first-born, highly educated, and career-oriented. Often they have married late, or have been married before, and are less traditional about sharing household chores. It seems that the decision not to have children is usually a gradual one, rather than a firm commitment at the time of marriage. A series of postponements ends with a final determination that having children would interfere too much with other goals and interests. Currently, about 5 percent of the married women in the United States have decided not to have children. Many more couples, of course, are childless because of infertility (Yorburg, 1983).

40   **"OPEN" MARRIAGE** Some spouses want to make many of the mutual commitments implied by marriage, but are unwilling to accept certain of the obligations that marriage traditionally imposes. Their response is the "open" marriage—essentially, one in which the partners agree to certain flexible arrangements, sometimes including the right of each to have extramarital sexual relationships. In some cases the spouses draw up a formal contract specifying what the various rights and responsibilities of the partners are to be—a self-consciously "do-it-yourself" approach to the problem of how to modify existing family patterns to meet the needs of changing lifestyles (Murstein, 1978a; Knapp and Whitehurst, 1978).

41 GAY COUPLES AND GAY-PARENT FAMILIES   About 10 percent of the population is believed to be predominantly homosexual, although most of the people also have some heterosexual experience and many actually marry and have children. Additionally, the great majority of gay men and lesbian women form stable, long-lasting relationships with a person of the same sex at some time in their lives. In some cases, families with two gay adults are created, usually when a divorced lesbian mother with custody of her children forms a relationship with another woman. Additionally, social welfare agencies in some large cities sometimes place orphaned or runaway gay teenage boys—who are unwelcome in heterosexual foster homes—in the custody of gay males, usually couples (Tanner, 1978; Bell and Weinberg, 1978; Bozett, 1987).

42 REMAINING SINGLE   A growing number of people are choosing to remain single. By 1988, more than a quarter of all American households consisted of people living alone or with nonrelatives. Nearly 22 million people now live alone, more than double the number of two decades ago. A major reason for this increase, in addition to the divorce rate, is a growing tendency for young adults to postpone marriage. The average age of first marriage is now 25.8 for men—the highest age since the turn of the century—and 23.6 for women—the highest age on record. Although a majority of single adults will eventually marry or remarry, it seems likely that there will be an increase in the proportion of the population remaining single throughout life, from about 5 percent today to perhaps 10 percent or more by the end of the century (P. Stein, 1981; Cargan, 1982).

43   What conclusions can we draw from our survey of the American family? The existence of alternative patterns does not mean that the nuclear family is about to disappear. After all, three-quarters of the population aged 25 to 65 is married, and about 90 percent of all Americans are expected to marry at some time. Even the divorced are still deeply committed to marriage—their marriage rates at all ages are higher than that for single or widowed persons. Four out of five children are still born in wedlock, and four out of five still live in a two-parent nuclear family. Divorce rates seem to have stopped rising, and birth rates seem to have stopped dropping. Clearly, the nuclear family is not about to disappear.

44   What is happening, though, is that the United States is increasingly tolerating a variety of alternative marriage and family styles. The reasons are linked, primarily, to the nature of modern America as a postindustrial society. As we noted in Chapter 3 ("Society"), a hallmark of such a society is its economic and cultural diversity, combined with a highly developed sense of individualism. In this environment, many Americans are modifying the family system to suit their individual needs.

45   Yet the family in the sense that we defined it earlier—a relatively permanent group of related people, living together, forming an economic unit, and sharing responsibility for the offspring—is here to stay as a permanent part of human society. Of the 91 million households in America, 71 percent contain families of one kind or another. As the social and economic factors that

affect all institutions continue to change, the nuclear family will doubtless respond with further adaptations, but it seems destined to remain the preferred and dominant system in the societies of the modern world.

Summary

1. The family is the most basic of all social institutions. It consists of a relatively permanent group whose members are related by ancestry, marriage, or adoption, who live together and form an economic unit, and whose adult members assume responsibility for the young. The family is expected to be formed through a marriage which legitimates any offspring. The family is part of a wider network of relatives, or kin.

2. The family is universal partly because it is highly functional. The main functions of the family are the regulation of sexual behavior, the replacement of members, socialization, care and protection, social placement, and emotional support.

3. Conflict theorists emphasize that the family is the main institution in which male dominance of females is expressed, and they argue that the extraordinary degree of violence in the family is a symptom of its underlying tension.

4. Family patterns vary widely from one society to another. Industrialism and urbanization have been accompanied by a worldwide transformation of the family; the extended family is dysfunctional in the modern environment and has given way to the nuclear form. The nuclear family, however, experiences distinctive problems resulting from the intense reliance that the husband and wife have on one another.

5. Americans place high emphasis on romantic love, which is functional for a nuclear family system. American marriage tends to be homogamous: people generally marry others with similar social characteristics.

6. The American divorce rate is very high; the partners most likely to get divorced are those whose social characteristics differ markedly. The main causes of divorce are stress on the nuclear family, the fading of romantic love after marriage, the changing role of women, and certain effects of sexual permissiveness.

7. There are a number of existing alternatives to traditional marriage and family arrangements, such as single-parent families, cohabitation, serial monogamy, reconstituted families, childless couples, "open" marriage, gay couples and gay-parent families, and remaining single. Even so, the nuclear family seems to be here to stay.

References

Bell, Alan, P., and **Martin S. Weinberg.** 1978. *Homosexualities: A Study of Diversity Among Men and Women.* New York: Simon and Schuster.

Bozett, Frederick W. (ed.). 1987. *Gay and Lesbian Parents.* New York: Praeger.

Cargan, Leonard. 1982. *Singles: Myths and Realities.* Beverly Hills, Calif.: Sage.

Carter, Hugh, and **Paul C. Glick.** 1976. *Marriage and Divorce: A Social and Economic Study.* Cambridge, Mass.: Harvard University Press.

Finkelhor, David. 1984. *Child Sexual Abuse: New Theory and Research.* New York: Free Press.

_____, et al. (eds.). 1983. *The Dark Side of Families.* Beverly Hills, Calif.: Sage.

Fisher, Helen. 1987. "The four-year itch." *Natural History,* 96, pp. 22–23.

Ford, Clellan S., and **Frank A. Beach.** 1951. *Patterns of the Sexual Behavior.* New York: Harper & Row.

Fox, Thomas, G., and S. M. Miller. 1965. "Inter-country variations: Occupational stratification and mobility." *Studies in Comparative International Development*, 1, pp. 3–10.

Gelles, Richard J. 1987b. *Family Violence*. 2nd ed. Newbury Park, Calif.: Sage.

_____, and Claire Pedrick Cornell (eds.). 1983. *International Perspectives on Family Violence*. Lexington, Mass.: Lexington Books.

Glick, Paul C., and Sung-Ling Lin. 1986. "Recent changes in divorce and remarriage." *Journal of Marriage and the Family*, 48, pp. 737–748.

Goode, William J. 1959. "The theoretical importance of love." *American Sociological Review*, 24, pp. 38–47.

_____. 1982. *The Family*. 2nd ed. Englewood Cliffs, N.J.: Prentice-Hall.

Gordon, Michael. 1983. *The American Family in Social-Historical Perspective*. 3rd ed. New York: St. Martin's Press.

Kanter, Rosabeth Moss. 1977. *Work and Family in the United States*. New York: Russell Sage Foundation.

Knapp, Jacquelyn J., and Robert N. Whitehurst. 1978. "Sexually open marriages and relationships: Issues and prospects," in Bernard I. Murstein (ed.), *Exploring Intimate Life Styles*. New York: Springer.

Laslett, Peter. 1971. *The World We Have Lost*. 2nd ed. New York: Scribner's.

_____. 1977. "Characteristics of the Western family considered over time." *Journal of Family History*, 2:2, 89–115.

_____, and Richard Wall (eds.). 1972. *Household and Family in Past Time*. Cambridge, Eng.: Cambridge University Press.

Murdock, George P. 1949. *Social Structure*. New York: Macmillan.

Murstein, Bernard I. 1974. *Love, Sex, and Marriage Through the Ages*. New York: Springer.

_____. 1978a. "Swinging," in Bernard I. Murstein (ed.), *Exploring Intimate Life Styles*. New York: Springer.

Rubin, Lillian. 1979. *Women of a Certain Age*. New York: Harper & Row.

Russell, Diana E. H. 1984. *Sexual Exploitation: Rape, Child Sexual Abuse, and Workplace Harassment*. Beverly Hills, Calif.: Sage.

_____. 1986. *The Secret Trauma: Incest in the Lives of Girls and Women*. New York: Basic Books.

Shorter, Edward. 1975. *The Making of the Modern Family*. New York: Basic Books.

Stein, Peter J. (ed.). 1981. *Single Life: Unmarried Adults in Social Context*. New York: St. Martin's Press.

Stone, Lawrence. 1977. *The Family, Sex, and Marriage in England, 1500–1800*. New York: Harper & Row.

Straus, Murray A., and Gerald T. Hotaling. 1980. *The Social Causes of Husband-Wife Violence*. Minneapolis: University of Minneapolis Press.

Tanner, Donna M. 1978. *The Lesbian Couple*. Lexington, Mass.: D. C. Heath.

Weiss, Robert S. 1975. *Marital Separation*. New York: Basic Books.

Yorburg, Betty. 1983. *Families and Societies: Survival or Extinction?* New York: Columbia University Press.

QUESTIONS

1. Robertson implies that a simple, uniform definition of *family* applicable to all societies is not easy to formulate. Explain why this is so.

2. State the definition of marriage provided by Robertson.

3. Cite the differences between a *family of orientation* and a *family of procreation*.

4. Robertson claims that all societies encourage legitimacy. State the reasons and evidence that he provides to support this assertion.

5. Robertson provides two different views of the family, the functionalist and the conflict view. Briefly summarize the main features of each.

6. Robertson claims that the interpretation of family patterns is ethnocentric. Explain.

7. Discuss the variety of marriage patterns practiced in other cultures.

8. Paraphrase the Robertson explanation for the decline of the extended family and its replacement by the nuclear family.

9. Analyze Robertson's reason for the importance of romantic love in our society.

10. Robertson claims that many marriages fail in America. The rate approaches 50 percent for new, first-time marriages. Briefly state the reasons given for this breakdown and describe how the circumstances differ from those of the past.

11. Robertson analyzes the current patterns of family living and finds that a number of changes are taking place. Describe what he sees as the future alternatives to the nuclear family.

The Way We Weren't: The Myth and Reality of the "Traditional" Family

STEPHANIE COONTZ

Stephanie Coontz teaches history and family studies at Evergreen State College in Olympia, Washington, and serves on the advisory board to the national family index of Family Circle. *Her articles have been featured in the* New York Times, *the* Washington Post, Newsweek, Harper's, *the* Wall Street Journal, *and other national publications and academic journals. She is the author of* The Way We Never Were: American Families and the Nostalgia Trap *(1992) and* The Way We Really Are: Coming to Terms with America's Changing Families *(1997).*

GEARING UP

1. You may have heard your parents or grandparents say that "things were better in the old days." Cite an example of the things that they were referring to.

2. From what you may recall from history classes or from books or movies, in what way is family life today different from the past?

The Reading

The Way We Weren't: The Myth and Reality of the "Traditional" Family

by STEPHANIE COONTZ

1   Families face serious problems today, but proposals to solve them by reviving "traditional" family forms and values miss two points. First, no single traditional family existed to which we could return, and none of the many varieties of families in our past has had any magic formula for protecting its members from the vicissitudes of socioeconomic change, the inequities of class, race, and gender, or the consequences of interpersonal conflict. Violence, child abuse, poverty, and the unequal distribution of resources to women and children have occurred in every period and every type of family.

2   Second, the strengths that we also find in many families of the past were rooted in different social, cultural, and economic circumstances from those that prevail today. Attempts to reproduce any type of family outside of its original socioeconomic context are doomed to fail.

Colonial Families

3   American families always have been diverse, and the male breadwinner-female homemaker, nuclear ideal that most people associate with "the" traditional family has predominated for only a small portion of our history. In colonial America, several types of families coexisted or competed. Native American kinship systems subordinated the nuclear family to a much larger network of marital alliances and kin obligations, ensuring that no single family was forced to go it alone. Wealthy settler families from Europe, by contrast, formed independent households that pulled in labor from poorer neighbors and relatives, building their extended family solidarities on the backs of truncated families among indentured servants, slaves, and the poor. Even wealthy families, though, often were disrupted by death; a majority of colonial Americans probably spent some time in a stepfamily. Meanwhile, African Americans, denied the legal protection of marriage and parenthood, built extensive kinship networks and obligations through fictive kin ties, rit-

ual co-parenting or godparenting, adoption of orphans, and complex naming patterns designed to preserve family links across space and time.

4   The dominant family values of colonial days left no room for sentimentalizing childhood. Colonial mothers, for example, spent far less time doing child care than do modern working women, typically delegating this task to servants or older siblings. Among white families, patriarchal authority was so absolute that disobedience by a wife or child was seen as a small form of treason, theoretically punishable by death, and family relations were based on power, not love.

The Nineteenth-Century Family

5 With the emergence of a wage-labor system and a national market in the first third of the nineteenth century, white middle-class families became less patriarchal and more child-centered. The ideal of the male breadwinner and the nurturing mother now appeared. But the emergence of domesticity for middle-class women and children depended on its absence among the immigrant, working class, and African American women or children who worked as servants, grew the cotton, or toiled in the textile mills to free middle-class wives from the chores that had occupied their time previously.

6   Even in the minority of nineteenth-century families who could afford domesticity, though, emotional arrangements were quite different from nostalgic images of "traditional" families. Rigid insistence on separate spheres for men and women made male-female relations extremely stilted, so that women commonly turned to other women, not their husbands, for their most intimate relations. The idea that all of one's passionate feelings should go toward a member of the opposite sex was a twentieth-century invention—closely associated with the emergence of a mass consumer society and promulgated by the very film industry that "traditionalists" now blame for undermining such values.

Early Twentieth-Century Families

7 Throughout the nineteenth century, at least as much divergence and disruption in the experience of family life existed as does today, even though divorce and unwed motherhood were less common. Indeed, couples who marry today have a better chance of celebrating a fortieth wedding anniversary than at any previous time in history. The life cycles of nineteenth-century youth (in job entry, completion of schooling, age at marriage, and establishment of separate residence) were far more diverse than they became in the early twentieth-century. At the turn of the century a higher proportion of people remained single for their entire lives than at any period since. Not until the 1920s did a bare majority of children come to live in a male breadwinner-female homemaker family, and even at the height of this family form in the 1950s, only 60 percent of American children spent their entire childhoods in such a family.

8   From about 1900 to the 1920s, the growth of mass production and emergence of a public policy aimed at establishing a family wage led to new ideas about family self-sufficiency, especially in the white middle class and a privileged sector of the working class. The resulting families lost their organic connection to intermediary units in society such as local shops, neighborhood work cultures and churches, ethnic associations, and mutual-aid organizations.

9   As families related more directly to the state, the market, and the mass media, they also developed a new cult of privacy, along with heightened expectations about the family's role in fostering individual fulfillment. New family values stressed the early independence of children and the romantic coupling of husband and wife, repudiating the intense same-sex ties and mother-infant bonding of earlier years as unhealthy. From this family we get the idea that women are sexual, that youth is attractive, and that marriage should be the center of our emotional fulfillment.

10   Even aside from its lack of relevance to the lives of most immigrants, Mexican Americans, African Americans, rural families, and the urban poor, big contradictions existed between image and reality in the middle-class family ideal of the early twentieth century. This is the period when many Americans first accepted the idea that the family should be sacred from outside intervention; yet the development of the private, self-sufficient family depended on state intervention in the economy, government regulation of parent-child relations, and state-directed destruction of class and community institutions that hindered the development of family privacy. Acceptance of a youth and leisure culture sanctioned early marriage and raised expectations about the quality of married life, but also introduced new tensions between the generations and new conflicts between husband and wife over what were adequate levels of financial and emotional support.

11   The nineteenth-century middle-class ideal of the family as a refuge from the world of work was surprisingly modest compared with emerging twentieth-century demands that the family provide a whole alternative world of satisfaction and intimacy to that of work and neighborhood. Where a family succeeded in doing so, people might find pleasures in the home never before imagined. But the new ideals also increased the possibilities for failure: America has had the highest divorce rate in the world since the turn of the century.

12   In the 1920s, these contradictions created a sense of foreboding about "the future of the family" that was every bit as widespread and intense as today's. Social scientists and popular commentators of the time hearkened back to the "good old days," bemoaning the sexual revolution, the fragility of nuclear family ties, the cult of youthful romance, the decline of respect for grandparents, and the threat of the "New Woman." But such criticism was sidetracked by the stock-market crash, the Great Depression of the 1930s, and the advent of World War II.

13   Domestic violence escalated during the Depression, while murder rates were as high in the 1930s as in the 1980s. Divorce rates fell, but desertion

increased and fertility plummeted. The war stimulated a marriage boom, but by the late 1940s one in every three marriages was ending in divorce.

The 1950s Family

14   At the end of the 1940s, after the hardships of the Depression and war, many Americans revived the nuclear family ideals that had so disturbed commentators during the 1920s. The unprecedented postwar prosperity allowed young families to achieve consumer satisfactions and socioeconomic mobility that would have been inconceivable in earlier days. The 1950s family that resulted from these economic and cultural trends, however, was hardly "traditional." Indeed, it is best seen as a historical aberration. For the first time in 100 years, divorce rates dropped, fertility soared, the gap between men's and women's job and educational prospects widened (making middle-class women more dependent on marriage), and the age of marriage fell—to the point that teenage birth rates were almost double what they are today.

15   Admirers of these very nontraditional 1950s family forms and values point out that household arrangements and gender roles were less diverse in the 1950s than today, and marriages more stable. But this was partly because diversity was ruthlessly suppressed and partly because economic and political support systems for socially-sanctioned families were far more generous than they are today. Real wages rose more in any single year of the 1950s than they did in the entire decade of the 1980s; the average thirty-year-old man could buy a median-priced home on 15 to 18 percent of his income. The government funded public investment, home ownership, and job creation at a rate more than triple that of the past two decades, while 40 percent of young men were eligible for veteran's benefits. Forming and maintaining families was far easier than it is today.

16   Yet the stability of these 1950s families did not guarantee good outcomes for their members. Even though most births occurred within wedlock, almost a third of American children lived in poverty during the 1950s, a higher figure than today. More than 50 percent of black married-couple families were poor. Women were often refused the right to serve on juries, sign contracts, take out credit cards in their own names, or establish legal residence. Wife-battering rates were low, but that was because wife-beating was seldom counted as a crime. Most victims of incest, such as Miss America of 1958, kept the secret of their fathers' abuse until the 1970s or 1980s, when the women's movement became powerful enough to offer them the support denied them in the 1950s.

The Post-1950s Family

17   In the 1960s, the civil rights, antiwar, and women's liberation movements exposed the racial, economic, and sexual injustices that had been papered over by the Ozzie and Harriet images on television. Their activism made older kinds of public and private oppression unacceptable and helped create the incomplete, flawed, but much-needed reforms of the Great Society.

Contrary to the big lie of the past decade that such programs caused our current family dilemmas, those antipoverty and social justice reforms helped overcome many of the family problems that prevailed in the 1950s.

18   In 1964, after fourteen years of unrivaled family stability and economic prosperity, the poverty rate was still 19 percent; in 1969, after five years of civil rights activism, the rebirth of feminism, and the institution of nontraditional if relatively modest government welfare programs, it was down to 12 percent, a low that has not been seen again since the social welfare cutbacks began in the late 1970s. In 1965, 20 percent of American children still lived in poverty; within five years, that had fallen to 15 percent. Infant mortality was cut in half between 1965 and 1980. The gap in nutrition between low-income Americans and other Americans narrowed significantly, as a direct result of food stamp and school lunch programs. In 1963, 20 percent of Americans living below the poverty line had never been examined by a physician; by 1970 this was true of only 8 percent of the poor.

19   Since 1973, however, real wages have been falling for most Americans. Attempts to counter this through tax revolts and spending freezes have led to drastic cutbacks in government investment programs. Corporations also spend far less on research and job creation than they did in the 1950s and 1960s, though the average compensation to executives has soared. The gap between rich and poor, according to the April 17, 1995, *New York Times,* is higher in the United States than in any other industrial nation.

Family Stress

20   These inequities are not driven by changes in family forms, contrary to ideologues who persist in confusing correlations with causes; but they certainly exacerbate such changes, and they tend to bring out the worst in all families. The result has been an accumulation of stresses on families, alongside some important expansions of personal options. Working couples with children try to balance three full-time jobs, as employers and schools cling to policies that assume every employee has a "wife" at home to take care of family matters. Divorce and remarriage have allowed many adults and children to escape from toxic family environments, yet our lack of social support networks and failure to forge new values for sustaining intergenerational obligations have let many children fall through the cracks in the process.

21   Meanwhile, young people find it harder and harder to form or sustain families. According to an Associated Press report of April 25, 1995, the median income of men aged twenty-five to thirty-four fell by 26 percent between 1972 and 1994, while the proportion of such men with earnings below the poverty level for a family of four more than doubled to 32 percent. The figures are even worse for African American and Latino men. Poor individuals are twice as likely to divorce as more affluent ones, three to four times less likely to marry in the first place, and five to seven times more likely to have a child out of wedlock.

22   As conservatives insist, there is a moral crisis as well as an economic one in modern America: a pervasive sense of social alienation, new levels of vio-

lence, and a decreasing willingness to make sacrifices for others. But romanticizing "traditional" families and gender roles will not produce the changes in job structures, work policies, child care, medical practice, educational preparation, political discourse, and gender inequities that would permit families to develop moral and ethical systems relevant to 1990s realities.

23   America needs more than a revival of the narrow family obligations of the 1950s, whose (greatly exaggerated) protection for white, middle-class children was achieved only at tremendous cost to the women in those families and to all those who could not or would not aspire to the Ozzie and Harriet ideal. We need a concern for children that goes beyond the question of whether a mother is waiting with cookies when her kids come home from school. We need a moral language that allows us to address something besides people's sexual habits. We need to build values and social institutions that can reconcile people's needs for independence with their equally important rights to dependence, and surely we must reject older solutions that involved balancing these needs on the backs of women. We will not find our answers in nostalgia for a mythical "traditional family."

QUESTIONS

1. Coontz claims that the traditional family ideal existed in history for only a short time. By contrast, describe other family structures that existed in colonial America.

2. Characterize the family structure of the nineteenth century according to Coontz.

3. Describe the 1950s family characteristics that are often considered the standard.

4. Coontz finds that the pressures of modern life stress the family. Cite some of the pressures and describe how they are manifested in family life.

5. The author claims: "Attempts to reproduce any type of family outside of its original socioeconomic context are doomed to fail." Explain why she believes this is so.

The Second Shift: Working Parents and the Revolution at Home

ARLIE HOCHSCHILD with ANNE MACHUNG

Arlie Hochschild is a professor of sociology at the University of California at Berkeley. She is the author of The Time Bind: When Work Becomes Home and Home Becomes Work *(1997) and* The Second Shift: Working Parents and the Revolution at Home *(1989), from which the following article is taken.*

GEARING UP

1. "In today's family of two working parents, domestic tasks are shared equally." Agree or disagree with this statement and explain your position by citing specific examples.

2. What tensions might arise regarding household responsibilities in a marriage where both couples work outside the home?

The Reading

The Second Shift: Working Parents and the Revolution at Home

by ARLIE HOCHSCHILD with ANNE MACHUNG

Behind the Footsteps

1   Between 8:05 A.M. and 6:05 P.M., both Nancy and Evan are away from home, working a "first shift" at full-time jobs. The rest of the time they deal with the varied tasks of the second shift: shopping, cooking, paying bills; taking care of the car, the garden, and yard; keeping harmony with Evan's mother who drops over quite a bit, "concerned" about Joey, with neighbors, their voluble baby-sitter, and each other. And Nancy's talk reflects a series of second-shift thoughts: "We're out of barbecue sauce.... Joey needs a Halloween costume.... The car needs a wash...." and so on. She reflects a certain "second-shift sensibility," a continual attunement to the task of striking and restriking the right emotional balance between child, spouse, home, and outside job.

2   When I first met the Holts, Nancy was absorbing far more of the second shift than Evan. She said she was doing 80 percent of the housework and 90 percent of the childcare. Evan said she did 60 percent of the housework, 70 percent of the childcare. Joey said, "I vacuum the rug, and fold the dinner napkins," finally concluding, "Mom and I do it all." A neighbor agreed with Joey. Clearly, between Nancy and Evan, there was a "leisure gap": Evan had more than Nancy. I asked both of them, in separate interviews, to explain to me how they had dealt with housework and childcare since their marriage began.

3   One evening in the fifth year of their marriage, Nancy told me, when Joey was two months old and almost four years before I met the Holts, she first seriously raised the issue with Evan. "I told him: 'Look, Evan, it's not working. I do the housework, I take the major care of Joey, *and* I work a full-time job. I get pissed. This is *your* house too. Joey is *your* child too. It's not all *my* job to care for them.' When I cooled down I put to him, 'Look, how about this: I'll cook Mondays, Wednesdays, and Fridays. You cook Tuesdays, Thursdays, and Saturdays. And we'll share or go out Sundays.'"

4   According to Nancy, Evan said he didn't like "rigid schedules." He said he didn't necessarily agree with her standards of housekeeping, and didn't like that standard "imposed" on him, especially if she was "sluffing off" tasks on him, which from time to time he felt she was. But he went along with the idea in principle. Nancy said the first week of the new plan went as follows. On Monday, she cooked. For Tuesday, Evan planned a meal that required shopping for a few ingredients, but on his way home he forgot to shop for them. He came home, saw nothing he could use in the refrigerator or in the cupboard, and suggested to Nancy that they go out for Chinese food. On Wednesday, Nancy cooked. On Thursday morning, Nancy reminded Evan, "Tonight it's your turn." That night Evan fixed hamburgers and french fries and Nancy was quick to praise him. On Friday, Nancy cooked. On Saturday, Evan forgot again.

5   As this pattern continued, Nancy's reminders became sharper. The sharper they became, the more actively Evan forgot—perhaps anticipating even sharper reprimands if he resisted more directly. This cycle of passive refusal followed by disappointment and anger gradually tightened, and before long the struggle had spread to the task of doing the laundry. Nancy said it was only fair that Evan share the laundry. He agreed in principle, but anxious that Evan would not share, Nancy wanted a clear, explicit agreement. "You ought to wash and fold every other load," she had told him. Evan experienced this "plan" as a yoke around his neck. On many weekdays, at this point, a huge pile of laundry sat like a disheveled guest on the living-room couch.

6   In her frustration, Nancy began to make subtle emotional jabs at Evan. "I don't know *what's* for dinner," she would say with a sigh. Or "I can't cook now, I've got to deal with this pile of laundry." She tensed at the slightest criticism about household disorder; if Evan wouldn't do the housework, he had absolutely *no* right to criticize how she did it. She would burst out angrily at Evan. She recalled telling him: "After work *my* feet are just as tired

as *your* feet. I'm just as wound up as you are. I come home. I cook dinner. I wash and I clean. Here we are, planning a second child, and I can't cope with the one we have."

7   About two years after I first began visiting the Holts, I began to see their problem in a certain light: as a conflict between their two gender ideologies. Nancy wanted to be the sort of woman who was needed and appreciated both at home and at work—like Lacey, she told me, on the television show "Cagney and Lacey." She wanted Evan to appreciate her for being a caring social worker, a committed wife, and a wonderful mother. But she cared just as much that she be able to appreciate *Evan* for what *he* contributed at home, not just for how he supported the family. She would feel proud to explain to women friends that she was married to one of these rare "new men."

8   A gender ideology is often rooted in early experience, and fueled by motives formed early on and such motives can often be traced to some cautionary tale in early life. So it was for Nancy. Nancy described her mother:

> My mom was wonderful, a real aristocrat, but she was also terribly depressed being a housewife. My dad treated her like a doormat. She didn't have any self-confidence. And growing up, I can remember her being really depressed. I grew up bound and determined not to be like her and not to marry a man like my father. As long as Evan doesn't do the housework, I feel it means he's going to be like my father—coming home, putting his feet up, and hollering at my mom to serve him. That's my biggest fear. I've had *bad* dreams about that.

9   Nancy thought that women friends her age, also in traditional marriages, had come to similarly bad ends. She described a high school friend: "Martha barely made it through City College. She had no interest in learning anything. She spent nine years trailing around behind her husband [a salesman]. It's a miserable marriage. She hand washes all his shirts. The high point of her life was when she was eighteen and the two of us were running around Miami Beach in a Mustang convertible. She's gained seventy pounds and she hates her life." To Nancy, Martha was a younger version of her mother, depressed, lacking in self-esteem, a cautionary tale whose moral was "if you want to be happy, develop a career and get your husband to share at home." Asking Evan to help again and again felt like "hard work" but it was essential to establishing her role as a career woman.

10   For his own reasons, Evan imagined things very differently. He loved Nancy and if Nancy loved being a social worker, he was happy and proud to support her in it. He knew that because she took her caseload so seriously, it was draining work. But at the same time, he did not see why, just because she chose this demanding career, *he* had to change *his own* life. Why should her personal decision to work outside the home require him to do more inside it? Nancy earned about two-thirds as much as Evan, and her salary was a big help, but as Nancy confided, "If push came to shove, we could do without it." Nancy was a social worker because she loved it. Doing daily chores at home was thankless work, and certainly not something Evan needed her to appreciate about him. Equality in the second shift meant a loss in his stan-

dard of living, and despite all the high-flown talk, he felt he hadn't *really* bargained for it. He was happy to help Nancy at home if she needed help; that was fine. That was only decent. But it was too sticky a matter "committing" himself to sharing.

11   Two other beliefs probably fueled his resistance as well. The first was his suspicion that if he shared the second shift with Nancy, she would "dominate him." Nancy would ask him to do this, ask him to do that. It felt to Evan as if Nancy had won so many small victories that he had to draw the line somewhere. Nancy had a declarative personality; and as Nancy said, "Evan's mother sat me down and told me once that I was too forceful, that Evan needed to take more authority." Both Nancy and Evan agreed that Evan's sense of career and self was in fact shakier than Nancy's. He had been unemployed. She never had. He had had some bouts of drinking in the past. Drinking was foreign to her. Evan thought that sharing housework would upset a certain balance of power that felt culturally "right." He held the purse strings and made the major decisions about large purchases (like their house) because he "knew more about finances" and because he'd chipped in more inheritance than she when they married. His job difficulties had lowered his self-respect, and now as a couple they had achieved some ineffable "balance"—tilted in his favor, she thought—which, if corrected to equalize the burden of chores, would result in his giving in "too much." A certain driving anxiety behind Nancy's strategy of actively renegotiating roles had made Evan see agreement as "giving in." When he wasn't feeling good about work, he dreaded the idea of being under his wife's thumb at home.

12   Underneath these feelings, Evan perhaps also feared that Nancy was avoiding taking care of *him*. His own mother, a mild-mannered alcoholic, had by imperceptible steps phased herself out of a mother's role, leaving him very much on his own. Perhaps a personal motive to prevent that happening in his marriage—a guess on my part, and unarticulated on his—underlay his strategy of passive resistance. And he wasn't altogether wrong to fear this. Meanwhile, he felt he was "offering" Nancy the chance to stay home, or cut back her hours, and that she was refusing his "gift," while Nancy felt that, given her feelings about work, this offer was hardly a gift.

13   In the sixth year of her marriage, when Nancy again intensified her pressure on Evan to commit himself to equal sharing, Evan recalled saying, "Nancy, why don't you cut back to half time, that way you can fit everything in." At first Nancy was baffled: "We've been married all this time, and you *still* don't get it. Work is important to me. I worked *hard* to get my MSW. Why *should* I give it up?" Nancy also explained to Evan and later to me, "I think my degree and my job has been my way of reassuring myself that I won't end up like my mother." Yet she'd received little emotional support in getting her degree from either her parents or her in-laws. (Her mother had avoided asking about her thesis, and her in-laws, though invited, did not attend her graduation, later claiming they'd never been invited.)

14   In addition, Nancy was more excited about seeing her elderly clients in tenderloin hotels than Evan was about selling couches to furniture salesmen with greased-back hair. Why shouldn't Evan make as many compromises

with his career ambitions and his leisure as she'd made with hers? She couldn't see it Evan's way, and Evan couldn't see it hers.

15   In years of alternating struggle and compromise, Nancy had seen only fleeting mirages of cooperation, visions that appeared when she got sick or withdrew, and disappeared when she got better or came forward.

16   After seven years of loving marriage, Nancy and Evan had finally come to a terrible impasse. Their emotional standard of living had drastically declined: they began to snap at each other, to criticize, to carp. Each felt taken advantage of: Evan, because his offering of a good arrangement was deemed unacceptable, and Nancy, because Evan wouldn't do what she deeply felt was "fair."

17   This struggle made its way into their sexual life—first through Nancy directly, and then through Joey. Nancy had always disdained any form of feminine wiliness or manipulation. Her family saw her as "a flaming feminist" and that was how she saw herself. As such, she felt above the underhanded ways traditional women used to get around men. She mused, "When I was a teen-ager, I vowed I would *never* use sex to get my way with a man. It is not self-respecting; it's demeaning. But when Evan refused to carry his load at home, I did, I used sex. I said, 'Look, Evan, I would not be this exhausted and asexual every night if I didn't have so much to face every morning.'" She felt reduced to an old "strategy," and her modern ideas made her ashamed of it. At the same time, she'd run out of other, modern ways.

18   The idea of a separation arose, and they became frightened. Nancy looked at the deteriorating marriages and fresh divorces of couples with young children around them. One unhappy husband they knew had become so uninvolved in family life (they didn't know whether his unhappiness made him uninvolved, or whether his lack of involvement had caused his wife to be unhappy) that his wife left him. In another case, Nancy felt the wife had "nagged" her husband so much that he abandoned her for another woman. In both cases, the couple was less happy after the divorce than before, and both wives took the children and struggled desperately to survive financially. Nancy took stock. She asked herself, "Why wreck a marriage over a dirty frying pan?" Is it really worth it?

Upstairs-Downstairs: A Family Myth as "Solution"

19   Not long after this crisis in the Holts' marriage, there was a dramatic lessening of tension over the issue of the second shift. It was as if the issue was closed. Evan had won. Nancy would do the second shift. Evan expressed vague guilt but beyond that he had nothing to say. Nancy had wearied of continually raising the topic, wearied of the lack of resolution. Now in the exhaustion of defeat, she wanted the struggle to be over too. Evan was "so good" in *other* ways, why debilitate their marriage by continual quarreling. Besides, she told me, "Women always adjust more, don't they?"

20   One day, when I asked Nancy to tell me who did which tasks from a long list of household chores, she interrupted me with a broad wave of her hand and said, "I do the upstairs, Evan does the downstairs." What does that mean? I asked. Matter-of-factly, she explained that the upstairs included the

living room, the dining room, the kitchen, two bedrooms, and two baths. The downstairs meant the garage, a place for storage and hobbies—Evan's hobbies. She explained this as a "sharing" arrangement, without humor or irony—just as Evan did later. Both said they had agreed it was the best solution to their dispute. Evan would take care of the car, the garage, and Max, the family dog. As Nancy explained, "The dog is all Evan's problem. I don't have to deal with the dog." Nancy took care of the rest.

21   For purposes of accommodating the second shift, then, the Holts' garage was elevated to the full moral and practical equivalent of the rest of the house. For Nancy and Evan, "upstairs and downstairs," "inside and outside," was vaguely described like "half and half," a fair division of labor based on a natural division of their house.

22   The Holts presented their upstairs-downstairs agreement as a perfectly equitable solution to a problem they "once had." This belief is what we might call a "family myth," even a modest delusional system. Why did they believe it? I think they believed it because they needed to believe it, because it solved a terrible problem. It allowed Nancy to continue thinking of herself as the sort of woman whose husband didn't abuse her—a self-conception that mattered a great deal to her. And it avoided the hard truth that, in his stolid, passive way, Evan had refused to share. It avoided the truth, too, that in their showdown, Nancy was more afraid of divorce than Evan was. This outer cover to their family life, this family myth, was jointly devised. It was an attempt to agree that there was no conflict over the second shift, no tension between their versions of manhood and womanhood, and that the powerful crisis that had arisen was temporary and minor.

23   The wish to avoid such a conflict is natural enough. But their avoidance was tacitly supported by the surrounding culture, especially the image of the woman with the flying hair. After all, this admirable woman also proudly does the "upstairs" each day without a husband's help and without conflict.

24   After Nancy and Evan reached their upstairs-downstairs agreement, their confrontations ended. They were nearly forgotten. Yet, as she described their daily life months after the agreement, Nancy's resentment still seemed alive and well. For example, she said:

> Evan and I eventually divided the labor so that I do the upstairs and Evan does the downstairs and the dog. So the dog is my husband's problem. But when I was getting the dog outside and getting Joey ready for childcare, and cleaning up the mess of feeding the cat, and getting the lunches together, and having my son wipe his nose on my outfit so I would have to change—then I was pissed! I felt that I was doing *everything*. All Evan was doing was getting up, having coffee, reading the paper, and saying, "Well, I have to go now," and often forgetting the lunch I'd bothered to make.

25   She also mentioned that she had fallen into the habit of putting Joey to bed in a certain way: he asked to be swung around by the arms, dropped on the bed, nuzzled and hugged, whispered to in his ear. Joey waited for her attention. He didn't go to sleep without it. But, increasingly, when Nancy tried it at eight or nine, the ritual didn't put Joey to sleep. On the contrary,

it woke him up. It was then that Joey began to say he could only go to sleep in his parents' bed, that he began to sleep in their bed and to encroach on their sexual life.

26 Near the end of my visits, it struck me that Nancy was putting Joey to bed in an "exciting" way, later and later at night, in order to tell Evan something important: "You win, I'll go on doing all the work at home, but I'm angry about it and I'll make you pay." Evan won the battle but lost the war. According to the family myth, all was well: the struggle had been resolved by the upstairs-downstairs agreement. But suppressed in one area of their marriage, this struggle lived on in another—as Joey's Problem, and as theirs.

Nancy's "Program" to Sustain the Myth

27 There was a moment, I believe, when Nancy seemed to *decide* to give up on this one. She decided to try not to resent Evan. Whether or not other women face a moment just like this, at the very least they face the need to deal with all the feelings that naturally arise from a clash between a treasured ideal and an incompatible reality. In the age of a stalled revolution, it is a problem a great many women face.

28 Emotionally, Nancy's compromise from time to time slipped; she would forget and grow resentful again. Her new resolve needed maintenance. Only half aware that she was doing so, Nancy went to extraordinary lengths to maintain it. She could tell me now, a year or so after her "decision," in a matter-of-fact and noncritical way: "Evan likes to come home to a hot meal. He doesn't like to clear the table. He doesn't like to do the dishes. He likes to go watch TV. He likes to play with his son when he feels like it and not feel like he should be with him more." She seemed resigned.

29 Everything was "fine." But it had taken an extraordinary amount of complex "emotion work"—the work of *trying* to feel the "right" feeling, the feeling she wanted to feel—to make and keep everything "fine." Across the nation at this particular time in history, this emotion work is often all that stands between the stalled revolution on the one hand, and broken marriages on the other.

How Many Holts?

30 In one key way the Holts were typical of the vast majority of two-job couples: their family life had become the shock absorber for a stalled revolution whose origin lay far outside it—in economic and cultural trends that bear very differently on men and women. Nancy was reading books, newspaper articles, and watching TV programs on the changing role of women. Evan wasn't. Nancy felt benefited by these changes; Evan didn't. In her ideals and in reality, Nancy was more different from her mother than Evan was from his father, for the culture and economy were in general pressing change faster upon women like her than upon men like Evan. Nancy had gone to college; her mother hadn't. Nancy had a professional job; her mother never had. Nancy had the idea that she should be equal with her husband; her mother

hadn't been much exposed to that idea in her day. Nancy felt she should share the job of earning money, and that Evan should share the work at home; her mother hadn't imagined that was possible. Evan went to college, his father (and the other boys in his family, though not the girls) had gone too. Work was important to Evan's identity as a man as it had been for his father before him. Indeed, Evan felt the same way about family roles as his father had felt in his day. The new job opportunities and the feminist movement of the 1960s and '70s had transformed Nancy but left Evan pretty much the same. And the friction created by this difference between them moved to the issue of second shift as metal to a magnet. By the end, Evan did less housework and childcare than most men married to working women— but not much less. Evan and Nancy were also typical of nearly forty percent of the marriages I studied in their clash of gender ideologies and their corresponding difference in notion about what constituted a "sacrifice" and what did not. By far the most common form of mismatch was like that between Nancy, an egalitarian, and Evan, a transitional.

31   But for most couples, the tensions between strategies did not move so quickly and powerfully to issues of housework and childcare. Nancy pushed harder than most women to get her husband to share the work at home, and she also lost more overwhelmingly than the few other women who fought that hard. Evan pursued his strategy of passive resistance with more quiet tenacity than most men, and he allowed himself to become far more marginal to his son's life than most other fathers. The myth of the Holts' "equal" arrangement seemed slightly more odd than other family myths that encapsulated equally powerful conflicts.

32   Beyond their upstairs-downstairs myth, the Holts tell us a great deal about the subtle ways a couple can encapsulate the tension caused by a struggle over the second shift without resolving the problem or divorcing. Like Nancy Holt, many women struggle to avoid, suppress, obscure, or mystify a frightening conflict over the second shift. They do not struggle like this because they started off wanting to, or because such struggle is inevitable or because women inevitably lose, but because they are forced to choose between equality and marriage. And they choose marriage. When asked about "ideal" relations between men and women in general, about what they want for their daughters, about what "ideally" they'd like in their own marriage, most working mothers "wished" their men would share the work at home.

33   But many "wish" it instead of "want" it. Other goals—like keeping peace at home—come first. Nancy Holt did some extraordinary behind-the-scenes emotion work to prevent her ideals from clashing with her marriage. In the end, she had confined and miniaturized her ideas of equality successfully enough to do two things she badly wanted to do: feel like a feminist, and live at peace with a man who was not. Her program had "worked." Evan won on the reality of the situation, because Nancy did the second shift. Nancy won on the cover story; they would talk about it as if they shared.

34   Nancy wore the upstairs-downstairs myth as an ideological cloak to protect her from the contradictions in her marriage and from the cultural and economic forces that press upon it. Nancy and Evan Holt were caught

on opposite sides of the gender revolution occurring all around them. Through the 1960s, 1970s, and 1980s masses of women entered the public world of work—but went only so far up the occupational ladder. They tried for "equal" marriages, but got only so far in achieving it. They married men who liked them to work at the office but who wouldn't share the extra month a year at home. When confusion about the identity of the working woman created a cultural vacuum in the 1970s and 1980s, the image of the supermom quietly glided in. She made the "stall" seem normal and happy. But beneath the happy image of the woman with the flying hair are modern marriages like the Holts', reflecting intricate webs of tension, and the huge, hidden emotional cost to women, men, and children of having to "manage" inequality. Yet on the surface, all we might see would be Nancy Holt bounding confidently out the door at 8:30 A.M., briefcase in one hand, Joey in the other. All we might hear would be Nancy's and Evan's talk about their marriage as happy, normal, even "equal"—because equality was so important to Nancy.

QUESTIONS

1. Identify the problem stated by the author.

2. Explain what the author means by "second shift."

3. Analyze the situation of the Holts. Do you feel they are typical or atypical of married couples? Be sure to consider the age factor in your response.

4. What factors seemed to keep Evan Holt from changing his behavior? Are these factors typical of other married men? Explain.

5. Describe the solution achieved by the Holts. Evaluate the solution as far as being an equitable compromise.

Put Family First

Dr. Benjamin Spock

Widely known as America's foremost baby doctor, Dr. Benjamin Spock was a physician, educator, and author of the widely read Baby and Child Care. *He wrote or collaborated on fifteen other books, including (with his wife, Mary Morgan) an autobiography,* Spock on Spock: A Memoir of Growing up with the Century *(1989). He died in 1998 at the age of 94.*

GEARING UP

1. What support mechanisms are available to working parents with young children?

2. What circumstances might cause people to give priority to factors other than their families?

The Reading

Put Family First

by Dr. Benjamin Spock

1   The time demands of our jobs are just one of the changes causing the American family to be eroded in small, subtle ways. For instance, the simple ceremony of sitting down to eat dinner together has been abandoned in many families; overworked fathers tend to lose contact with their children and with their wives; and family members are busy with so many outside activities that they don't have time for one another. Because of this, I worry that children are feeling less connected to their parents and, ultimately, less confident and less prepared to find their way in the world.

2   The real problem is that many mothers and fathers take their work more seriously than they do their families. I believe we have to decide that family comes first and to make it clear to our children that they're more important than anything else in our lives. Even friendships, neighborhood activities, and cultural interests should take higher priority than jobs, because these are what humanize us and show our children what matters most.

3   I don't want to get into an argument about whether or not Einstein's work should have been his first priority, but I am suggesting that during the childrearing years, parents shift their career into the background and bring the family into the foreground. This may be easy for me to say, but I think parents should make whatever sacrifices are necessary for that to happen—whether it means getting by on less income for several years or temporarily postponing certain goals and pursuits.

4   If parents do make financial sacrifices to be at home with their children, they should be offered subsidies—from the government or from their employers. It's crazy for mothers and fathers who prefer to care for their children to pay someone else to do it. Of course, most of us still have to work, and subsidies are a long way off. So for many parents, it's a serious challenge to find the best care for their children.

5   High-quality daycare is not only hard to find, it's also expensive. Childcare workers are miserably paid and make their own sacrifices to go into those occupations. We should be raising their salaries, but families on modest incomes just can't afford to pay more for childcare. It's going to have to be paid for by the government and industry, as it is in many European countries.

6   We need to acknowledge that poor-quality daycare is a real deprivation that a child may never outgrow. I think we're going to pay seriously in future generations for the lack of good daycare that's being provided today. We'll pay for it in emotional insecurity and in crime. That's why we need daycare workers who are thoroughly trained and who know that what children need most isn't policing and disciplining but stimulation and kindness. Only by reevaluating priorities such as these, and by reconsidering our notion of family, will we really be putting family first as a nation.

QUESTIONS

1. Spock states that children today are feeling less connected to their families. Identify the major factor he cites that contributes to this situation.

2. Spock suggests that people who wish to care for their children in the midst of their working lives should do so. How is this possible if they need to work to support the family? Analyze his plan.

3. The day care situation is an important factor in Spock's plan. In examining day care, what does Spock conclude? Evaluate his proposals for changing day care.

from

Keeping Families Together: The Case for Family Preservation

MAYA ANGELOU

Author, poet, actress, and playwright Maya Angelou is perhaps most famous for her best-selling autobiographical account of her youth, I Know Why the Caged Bird Sings. *In addition to producing several books of prose and poetry, she has been involved in stage and screen as a producer, director, singer, and actress, and in 1977 received an Emmy nomination for her performance in the television series* Roots. *She lectures throughout the United States and abroad and has been Reynolds Professor of American Studies at Wake Forest University in North Carolina since 1981. At the request of President Clinton, she wrote and delivered a poem at his 1993 presidential inauguration. The following selection is taken from* Keeping Families Together: The Case for Family Preservation *(1985), published by the Edna McConnell Clark Foundation.*

GEARING UP

1. What potential disadvantages does a child face who is not growing up in a nuclear family?

2. Describe some possible programs and policies that society could provide to help children whose nuclear families have disintegrated because of death, divorce, or separation.

The Reading

from Keeping Families Together: The Case for Family Preservation

by MAYA ANGELOU

1   Having tried, like most people, so desperately to grow up, and like most people, having failed miserably and miserably often, I am convinced that emerging from the chrysalis of youth as a whole loving adult is the first and greatest challenge which faces the human being. Even when the child's environment is natural, healthy and supportive, the act of growing up is almost impossible.

2   Masses of information have to be internalized, and at least in part understood, and while the growing body wrestles with a variety of imperatives, codes are introduced which constrain those urges. The child is introduced to the family's values and through observation of the family's actions learns to repeat the enactment. This process is rarely easy, for the child, out of rebellion natural to the age and a lack of understanding of the tenets' importance, often resists being acculturated. Without quite knowing what he is doing or why he is doing it, the young person fights for his individuality, as a drowning person struggles for breath. Parents, incensed by the child's resistance, often retaliate with punishment, inordinately harsh, or withdraw into their bruised feelings, shutting out the child and further confusing an already muddled circumstance. A loving family teaches by encouragement and persuasion, and in the best of circumstances the child grudgingly accedes to the mores of its group.

3   It is known that the struggle, which can continue for years, has the power to destroy the family or reknit it together with stronger bonds. In any outcome, the child feels the dual burden of developing as a distinct person, and being the uniting force of its family.

4   How much more strain is put upon the child who is uprooted and thrust among strangers with whom he has no mutual history? How is it possible to convince a child of his own worth after removing him from a family which is said to be unworthy, but with whom he identifies?

5   When any child, vulnerable as the season's first snowflake, is handed into a strange atmosphere, even into a rare, sensitive and caring environment,

the question which afflicts the newcomer is always, "If I wasn't good enough for my own family, which they say is no good, how can I be accepted here, before strangers?" Tragically, the question is unanswerable and perseveres under the skin, in the viscera through the days, hours, and years into adulthood.

6   I know by sad experience that in the company of other children, the child who has been forcibly separated from parents becomes the "other" and considers itself only partially alive, only partially adequate, in fact, only partially human. These companions, who live in natural (family) groups, become to the separated child paragons of beauty, intelligence and obviously the very object of God's love. Even children who live with strict parents who inhibit their movements and chastise them physically, are regarded as lucky beyond any real comprehension.

7   Embarrassment at one's own obvious inadequacies becomes the "other" child's unhealthy but constant companion. Separation is hard to accommodate, even when it is caused by natural phenomena. The actor, the late James Dean, remarked angrily, "My mother died on me when I was nine years old. What did she expect me to do? Do it all alone?"

8   A bereft child tries in varying ways to cope. In amenable circumstances, she might become painfully timid and introvertedly obedient, reasoning that by keeping the lowest possible profile she will not be visible, and thereby avoid further dislocating experiences. Another child, confused by dislocation and stunned by what he considers as his family's rejection, turns against his immediate world. Resentment seethes in his mind, building with anger into fury and finally that combustible mixture becomes hate. First, hate of himself, and then hate of and for the entire world.

9   In the child, ungifted with the arts of dissembling, the rage is overt, obvious and self-destructive. And, quoting the poet Arna Bontemps, it is "small wonder" that he "gleans in fields he has not sown, and feeds on bitter fruit." Thus we see some of the breeding areas for our overcrowded penal and mental institutions, the persons who become the perpetrators or victims of homicidal attacks. We observe the beginnings of those who threaten violation of our homes and who lie in wait for us along perilous streets to threaten our very lives.

10   This is not to say that each social psychopath was once a child abused by family neglect and/or dislocation, nor that each non-disrupted family will produce healthy and stable offspring. Rather, the suggestion [here] . . . is that it is simply that much more difficult for a child to find and identify with stability after an early separation from its nuclear family.

11   G. P. Murdock, in *Social Structure*, states, "The nuclear family is universal and has four functions: sexual, economic, reproductive and educational," adding that "no society has succeeded in finding an adequate substitute for the nuclear family to which it might transfer these functions."

12   The first three functions may not be of immediate relevance to the child but the last function, education, is crucially significant. Extending the usual meaning of education to include the showing and teaching of love, the giving and accepting of affection and tenderness, and the sharing and demon-

stration of humor, good and bad, one is quick to see why the family offers, to its young, clear lessons in modes of survival. The family is undeniably the greatest force of informing the young of possibilities and prohibitions. The young child, seeing the repetition of social acts within a group which he resembles, is acculturated into the ways of his folk. Authority is observed, conclusions are reached, and thus the lessons of tradition are internalized because within the kinship group there is a usually unstated but obvious understanding that all members' actions are made for the group's welfare.

13   I have been both the child sent away from parents and the parent who was advised that I should give my child up for his own welfare. I survived the first condition by love and luck, and resisted the second by the same interventions.

14   Although my father and mother divorced and sent me a few thousand miles away, at six years old I arrived at my paternal grandmother's home in a small Arkansas village to find a world of strangeness kept mostly at bay by grandmother's lap of love.

15   I was 22 years old and my son was six when a school psychologist informed me that my cabaret singing jobs were bad for my son. I was told he was hyperactive and would be better left with a foster family, for he needed security. I decided that wherever I was, I would be his security, and although we traveled from Hawaii to New York to Cairo to West Africa over the next ten years, we were together and neither of us was seriously the worse for our perambulations. We shared tears, frustrations, anger, love and laughter.

16   Of course, there are some families and family situations which are more destructive to the life of their young than if they were abandoned in a jungle of hungry, wild beasts. In dealing with those cases, our courts are correct in taking the children out of danger and placing them as soon as possible into safer, even if strange, environs.

17   Yet, when practical, the preference should be for family. And a family is more than a group living together. A family differs from a group by its shared experience and memories. Each family is so complex as to be known and understood only in part even by its own members. And families struggle with contradictions more massive than Everest, as fluid and changing as the Mississippi, and through those struggles character can be built or defeated, and souls and intellects can be enlivened or crushed.

18   The poet/philosopher who described our species as the Family of Man (and Woman) might have gone further to explain us as the Man and Woman of Family. Often, in our desperate attempts to achieve security for our continuation, we endanger the very goal we seek to achieve. . . .

19   Lucky was the child who years ago had the good fortune to be cradled by a kinship family within an extended family group, for that child received a benefit of an abundance of love and support. A vastly changed society has seen the disappearance of the extended family and even the weakening of the natural family. As a result of those changes, the society's structure has been weakened and the children must bear the weight of shoring up a system which has made them victims.

20   Since the first humans became self-conscious enough to develop modesty and clothed themselves with animal skins and laces, and the perfume of Araby, we have known that we stay alive not for our individual selves alone. The idea of peace did not stem from fear for one's own individual safety, nor did that still unmanageable concept of love emanate from wherever great concepts are born, to arrive with the intent of serving only one individual. At our best level of existence, we are parts of a family, and at our highest level of achievement we work to keep the family alive.

21   There is a West African proverb which states, "The trouble for the thief is not how to steal the chief's bugle, but where to blow it." Our organizations can take a child from a non-supportive nuclear family, but to what end? Wouldn't we show our intelligence and concerns more effectively if, rather than removing the child, we worked together with the entire family in order to create a healthy unit?

22   Alone is unutterable loneliness.

QUESTIONS

1. Paraphrase Angelou's reasons for the difficulty she says is part of growing up.

2. State the dual burden suffered by the child who is uprooted and placed with strangers.

3. Cite two strategies foster children use to cope with their situation.

4. Describe the strengths Angelou sees in the nuclear family.

5. Angelou is able to bring her own experiences to bear on this article. What life situations qualify her to speak on the topic with authority?

6. Explain the West African proverb Angelou cites. How does she apply the proverb to her message about the family?

Quality Time

BARBARA KINGSOLVER

Barbara Kingsolver is an American novelist, short story writer, poet, and nonfiction writer. She is the author of The Bean Trees *(1988),* Holding the Line *(1989),* Homeland *(1989),* Animal Dreams *(1990),* Pigs in Heaven *(1993),* High Tide in Tucson *(1995), and* The Poisonwood Bible *(1998). Barbara Kingsolver came to fiction writing through her career as a scientific writer and journalist. Her short stories have appeared in* Mademoiselle, Redbook, *the* Virginia Quarterly Review, *and elsewhere. She grew up in eastern Kentucky and now lives in Tucson, Arizona. The following work appears in her collection of short stories,* Homeland.

GEARING UP

1. Discuss the challenges of being a single parent from the parent's perspective.

2. Discuss the challenges of being a single parent from the child's perspective.

The Reading

Quality Time

by BARBARA KINGSOLVER

1   Miriam's one and only daughter, Rennie, wants to go to Ice Cream Heaven. This is not some vision of the afterlife but a retail establishment here on earth, right in Barrimore Plaza, where they have to drive past it every day on the way to Rennie's day-care center. In Miriam's opinion, this opportunistic placement is an example of the free-enterprise system at its worst.

2   "Rennie, honey, we can't today. There just isn't time," Miriam says. She is long past trying to come up with fresh angles on this argument. This is the bland, simple truth, the issue is time, not cavities or nutrition. Rennie doesn't want ice cream. She wants an angel sticker for the Pearly Gates Game, for which one only has to walk through the door, no purchase necessary. When you've collected enough stickers you get a free banana split. Miriam has told Rennie over and over again that she will buy her a banana split, some Saturday when they have time to make an outing of it, but Rennie acts as if this has nothing to do with the matter at hand, as though she has asked for a Cabbage Patch doll and Miriam is offering to buy her shoes.

3   "I could just run in and run out," Rennie says after a while. "You could wait for me in the car." But she knows she has lost; the proposition is half-hearted.

4   "We don't even have time for that, Rennie. We're on a schedule today."

5   Rennie is quiet. The windshield wipers beat a deliberate, ingratiating rhythm, sounding as if they feel put-upon to be doing this job. All of southern California seems dysfunctional in the rain: cars stall, drivers go vaguely braindead. Miriam watches Rennie look out at the drab scenery, and wonders if for her sake they ought to live someplace with ordinary seasons—piles of raked leaves in autumn, winters with frozen streams and carrot-nosed snowmen. Someday Rennie will read about those things in books, and think they're exotic.

6   They pass by a brand-new auto mall, still under construction, though some of the lots are already open and ready to get down to brass tacks with anyone who'll brave all that yellow machinery and mud. The front of the mall sports a long row of tall palm trees, newly transplanted, looking frankly mortified by their surroundings. The trees depress Miriam. They were

probably yanked out of some beautiful South Sea island and set down here in front of all these Plymouths and Subarus. Life is full of bum deals.

7   Miriam can see that Rennie is not pouting, just thoughtful. She is an extremely obliging child, considering that she's just barely five. She understands what it means when Miriam says they are "on a schedule." Today they really don't have two minutes to spare. Their dance card, so to speak, is filled. When people remark to Miriam about how well organized she is, she laughs and declares that organization is the religion of the single parent.

8   It sounds like a joke, but it isn't. Miriam is faithful about the business of getting each thing done in its turn, and could no more abandon her orderly plan than a priest could swig down the transubstantiated wine and toss out wafers like Frisbees over the heads of those waiting to be blessed. Miriam's motto is that life is way too complicated to leave to chance.

9   But in her heart she knows what a thin veil of comfort it is that she's wrapped around herself and her child to cloak them from chaos. It all hangs on the presumption that everything has been accounted for. Most days, Miriam is a believer. The road ahead will present no serious potholes, no detour signs looming sudden and orange in the headlights, no burning barricades thrown together as reminders that the world's anguish doesn't remain mute—like the tree falling in the forest—just because no one is standing around waiting to hear it.

10   Miriam is preoccupied along this line of thought as she kisses Rennie goodbye and turns the steering wheel, arm over elbow, guiding her middle-aged Chevy out of the TenderCare parking lot and back onto the slick street. Her faith has been shaken by coincidence.

11   On Saturday, her sister Janice called to ask if she would be the guardian of Janice and Paul's three children, if the two of them should die. "We're redoing the wills," Janice reported cheerfully over the din, while in the background Miriam could hear plainly the words "Give me that Rainbow Brite right now, dumb face."

12   "Just give it some thought," Janice had said calmly, but Miriam hadn't needed to think. "Will you help out with my memoirs if I'm someday the President?" her sister might as well have asked, or "What are your plans in the event of a nuclear war?" The question seemed to Miriam more mythical than practical. Janice was a careful person, not given to adventure, and in any case tended to stick to those kids like some kind of maternal adhesive. Any act of God that could pick off Janice without taking the lot would be a work of outstanding marksmanship.

13   Late on Sunday night, while Miriam was hemming a dress of Rennie's that had fallen into favor, she'd had a phone call from her ex-husband Lute. His first cousin and her boyfriend had just been killed on a San Diego freeway by a Purolator van. Over the phone, Lute seemed obsessed with getting the logistics of the accident right, as though the way the cars all obeyed the laws of physics could make this thing reasonable. The car that had the blowout was a Chrysler; the cousin and boyfriend were in her Saab; the van slammed into them from behind. "They never had a chance," Lute said, and the words chilled Miriam. Long after she went to bed she kept hearing him

say "never had a chance," and imagining the pair as children. As if even in in-
fancy their lives were already earmarked: these two will perish together in
their thirties, in a Saab, wearing evening clothes, on their way to hear a friend
play in the symphony orchestra. All that careful mothering and liberal-arts
education gone to waste.

14   Lute's cousin had been a freelance cellist, often going on the road with the
likes of Barry Manilow and Tony Bennett and, once, Madonna. It was probably all much tamer than it sounded. Miriam is surprised to find she has opinions about this woman, and a clear memory of her face. She only met her once,
at her own wedding, when all of Lute's family had come crowding around like
fog. But now this particular cousin has gained special prominence, her vague
features crystallized in death, like a face on a postage stamp. Important. Someone you just can't picture doing the humdrum, silly things that life is made
of—clipping her toenails or lying on the bed with her boyfriend watching
Dallas—if you hold it clearly in your mind that she is gone.

15   Lute is probably crushed; he idolized her. His goal in life is to be his own
boss. Freelance husbanding is just one of the things that hasn't worked out
for Lute. Freelance fathering he can manage.

16   Miriam is thinking of Rennie while she waits through a yellow light she
normally might have run. Rennie last week insisting on wearing only dresses
to nursery school, and her pale, straight hair just so, with a ribbon; they'd
seen *Snow White*. Rennie as a toddler standing in her crib, holding the rails,
her mouth open wide and the simplest expectation you could imagine: a
cookie, a game, or nothing at all, just that they would both go on being there
together. Lute was already out of the picture by that time; he wouldn't have
been part of Rennie's hopes. It is only lately, since she's learned to count, that
Lute's absence matters to Rennie. On the Disney Channel parents come in
even numbers.

17   The light changes and there is a honking of horns; someone has done
something wrong, or too slowly, or in the wrong lane. Miriam missed it altogether, whatever it was. She remembers suddenly a conversation she had
with her sister years ago when she was unexpectedly pregnant with Rennie,
and Janice was already a wise old mother of two. Miriam was frantic—she'd
wanted a baby but didn't feel ready yet. "I haven't really worked out what it
is I want to pass on to a child," she'd said to Janice, who laughed. According
to Janice, parenting was three percent conscious effort and ninety-seven percent automatic pilot. "It doesn't matter what you think you're going to tell
them. What matters is they're right there watching you every minute, while
you let the lady with just two items go ahead of you in line, or when you lay
on the horn and swear at the guy that cuts you off in traffic. There's no sense
kidding yourself, what you see is what you get."

18   Miriam had argued that people could consciously change themselves if
they tried, though in truth she'd been thinking more of Lute than herself.
She remembers saying a great many things about choices and value systems
and so forth, a lot of first-pregnancy high-mindedness it seems to her now.
Now she understands. Parenting is something that happens mostly while
you're thinking of something else.

*   *   *

19   Miriam's job claims her time for very irregular hours at the downtown branch of the public library. She is grateful that the people at Rennie's day care don't seem to have opinions about what kind of mother would work mornings one day, evenings the next. When she was first promoted to this position Miriam had a spate of irrational fears: she imagined Miss Joyce at TenderCare giving her a lecture on homemade soup and the importance of routine in the formative years. But Miss Joyce, it seems, understands modern arrangements. "The important thing is quality time," she said once to Miriam, in a way that suggested bedtime stories read with a yogic purity of concentration, a mind temporarily wiped clean of things like brake shoes and MasterCharge bills.

20   Miriam does try especially hard to schedule time for the two of them around Rennie's bedtime, but it often seems pointless. Rennie is likely to be absorbed in her own games, organizing animated campaigns on her bed with her stuffed animals, and finally dropping off in the middle of them, limbs askew, as though felled by a sniper.

21   Today is one of Miriam's afternoon-shift days. After leaving Rennie she has forty minutes in which she must do several errands before going to work. One of them is eat lunch. This is an item Miriam would actually put on a list: water African violets; dry cleaner's; eat lunch. She turns in at the Burger Boy and looks at her watch, surprised to see that she has just enough time to go in and sit down. Sometimes she takes the drive-through option and wolfs down a fish sandwich in the parking lot, taking large bites, rattling the ice in her Coke, unmindful of appearances. It's efficient, although it puts Miriam in mind of eating disorders.

22   Once she is settled inside with her lunch, her ears stray for company to other tables, picking up scraps of other people's private talk. "More than four hundred years old," she hears, and "It was a little bit tight over the instep," and "They had to call the police to get him out of there." She thinks of her friend Bob, who is a relentless eavesdropper, though because he's a playwright he calls it having an ear for dialogue.

23   Gradually she realizes that at the table behind her a woman is explaining to her daughter that she and Daddy are getting a divorce. It comes to Miriam like a slow shock, building up in her nerve endings until her skin hurts. This conversation will only happen once in that little girl's life, and I have to overhear it, Miriam is thinking. It has to be *here*. The surroundings seem banal, so cheery and hygienic, so many wiped-clean plastic surfaces. But then Miriam doesn't know what setting would be better. Certainly not some unclean place, and not an expensive restaurant either—that would be worse. To be expecting a treat, only to be socked with this news.

24   Miriam wants badly to turn around and look at the little girl. In her mind's eye she sees Rennie in her place: small and pale, sunk back into the puffy pink of her goosedown jacket like a loaf of risen dough that's been punched down.

25   The little girl keeps saying, "Okay," no matter what her mother tells her.

26   "Daddy will live in an apartment, and you can visit him. There's a swimming pool."

27   "Okay."

28   "Everything else will stay the same. We'll still keep Peppy with us. And you'll still go to your same school."

29   "Okay."

30   "Daddy does still love you, you know."

31   "Okay."

32   Miriam is thinking that ordinarily this word would work; it has finality. When you say it, it closes the subject.

33   It's already dark by the time Miriam picks up Rennie at TenderCare after work. The headlights blaze accusingly against the glass doors as if it were very late, midnight even. But it's only six-thirty, and Miriam tries to cheer herself by thinking that if this were summer it would still be light. It's a trick of the seasons, not entirely her fault, that Rennie has been abandoned for the daylight hours.

34   She always feels more surely on course when her daughter comes back to her. Rennie bounces into the car with a sheaf of papers clutched in one fist. The paper they use at TenderCare is fibrous and slightly brown, and seems wholesome to Miriam. Like turbinado sugar, rather than refined.

35   "Hi, sweetie. I missed you today." Miriam leans over to kiss Rennie and buckle her in before pulling out of the parking lot. All day she has been shaky about driving, and now she dreads the trip home. All that steel and momentum. It doesn't seem possible that soft human flesh could travel through it and come out intact. Throughout the day Miriam's mind has filled spontaneously with images of vulnerable things—baby mice, sunburned eyelids, sea creatures without their shells.

36   "What did you draw?" she asks Rennie, trying to anchor herself.

37   "This one is you and me and Lute," Rennie explains. Miriam is frowning into the river of moving headlights, waiting for a break in traffic, and feels overcome by sadness. There are so many things to pay attention to at once, and all of them so important.

38   "You and me and Lute," Miriam repeats.

39   "Uh-huh. And a dog, Pickles, and Leslie Copley and his mom. We're all going out for a walk."

40   A sports car slows down, letting Miriam into the street. She waves her thanks. "Would you like to go for a walk with Leslie Copley and his mom sometime?"

41   · "No. It's just a picture."

42   "What would you like for supper?"

43   "Pot pies!" Rennie shouts. Frozen dinners are her favorite thing. Miriam rather likes them too, although this isn't something she'd admit to many people. Certainly not her mother, for instance, or to Bob, who associates processed foods with intellectual decline. She wonders, though, if her privacy is an illusion. Rennie may well be revealing all the details of their home

life to her nursery-school class, opening new chapters daily. What I had for dinner last night. What Mom does when we run out of socks. They probably play games along these lines at TenderCare, with entirely innocent intentions. And others, too, games with a social-worker bent: What things make you happy, or sad? What things make you feel scared?

44   Miriam smiles. Rennie is fearless. She does not know how it feels to be hurt, physically or otherwise, by someone she loves. The people at Tender-Care probably hear a lot worse than pot pies.

45   "Mom," Rennie asks, "does God put things on the TV?"

46   "What do you mean?"

47   Rennie considers. "The cartoons, and the movies and things. Does God put them there?"

48   "No. People do that. You know how Grandpa takes movies of you with his movie camera, and then we show them on the screen? Well, it's like that. People at the TV station make the programs, and then they send them out onto your TV screen."

49   "I thought so," Rennie says. "Do you make them sometimes, at the library?"

50   Miriam hears a siren, but can't tell where it's coming from. "Well, I organize programs for the library, you're right, but not TV programs. Things like storybook programs. You remember, you've come to some of those." Miriam hopes she doesn't sound irritated. She is trying to slow down and move into the right lane, because of the ambulance, but people keep passing her on both sides, paying no attention. It makes Miriam angry. Sure enough, the ambulance is coming their way. It has to jerk to a full stop in the intersection ahead of them because of all the people who refuse to yield to greater urgency.

51   "Mom, what happens when you die?"

52   Miriam is startled because she was thinking of Lute's poor cousin. Thinking of the condition of the body, to be exact. But Rennie doesn't even know about this relative, won't hear her sad story for years to come.

53   "I'm not sure, Rennie. I think maybe what happens is that you think back over your life, about all the nice things you've done and the people who've been your friends, and then you close your eyes and . . . it's quiet." She was going to say, ". . . and go to sleep," but she's read that sleep and death shouldn't be equated, that it can cause children to fear bedtime. "What do you think?"

54   "I think you put on your nicest dress, and then you get in this glass box and everybody cries and then the prince comes and kisses you. On the lips."

55   "That's what happened to Snow White, isn't it?"

56   "Uh-huh. I didn't like when he kissed her on the lips. Why didn't he kiss her on the cheek?"

57   "Well, grownups kiss on the lips. When they like each other."

58   "But Snow White wasn't a grownup. She was a little girl."

59   This is a new one on Miriam. This whole conversation is like a toboggan ride, threatening at every moment to fly out of control in any direction. She's enjoying it, though, and regrets that they will have to stop soon for some

errands. They are low on produce, canned goods, aluminum foil, and paper towels, completely out of vacuum-cleaner bags and milk.

60   "What I think," says Miriam, after giving it some consideration, "is that Snow White was a little girl at first, but then she grew up. Taking care of the seven dwarfs helped her learn responsibility." Responsibility is something she and Rennie have talks about from time to time. She hears another siren, but this one is definitely behind them, probably going to the same scene as the first. She imagines her sister Janice's three children bundling into her life in a whirlwind of wants and possessions. Miriam doesn't even have time for another house plant. But she realizes that having time is somehow beside the point.

61   "So when the prince kissed her, did she grow up?" Rennie asks.

62   "No, before that. She was already grown up when the prince came. And they liked each other, and they kissed, and afterward they went out for a date."

63   "Like you and Mr. Bob?"

64   "Like Bob and I do sometimes, right. You don't have to call him Mr. Bob, honey. He's your friend, you can call him just Bob, if you want to."

65   Instead of making the tricky left turn into the shopping center, Miriam's car has gone right, flowing with the tide of traffic. It happened almost before she knew it, but it wasn't an accident. She just isn't ready to get to the grocery store, where this conversation will be lost among the bright distractions of bubble gum and soda. Looping back around the block will give them another four or five minutes. They could sit and talk in the parking lot, out of the traffic, but Miriam is starting to get her driving nerves back. And besides, Rennie would think that peculiar. Her questions would run onto another track.

66   "And then what happened to the seven dwarfs?" Rennie wants to know.

67   "I think Snow White still took care of them, until they were all grown up and could do everything by themselves."

68   "And did the prince help too?"

69   "I think he did."

70   "But what if Snow White died. If she stayed dead, I mean, after the prince kissed her."

71   Miriam now understands that this is the angle on death that has concerned Rennie all along. She is relieved. For Miriam, practical questions are always the more easily answered.

72   "I'm sure the dwarfs would still be taken care of," she says. "The point is that Snow White really loved them, so she'd make sure somebody was going to look after them, no matter what, don't you think?"

73   "Uh-huh. Maybe the prince."

74   "Maybe." A motorcyclist dodges in front of them, too close, weaving from lane to lane just to get a few yards ahead. At the next red light they will all be stopped together, the fast drivers and the slow, shooting looks at one another as if someone had planned it all this way.

75   "Rennie, if something happened to me, you'd still have somebody to take care of you. You know that, don't you?"

76   "Uh-huh. Lute."

77   "Is that what you'd like? To go and live with Lute?"

78   "Would I have to?"

79   "No, you wouldn't have to. You could live with Aunt Janice if you wanted to."

80   Rennie brightens. "Aunt Janice and Uncle Paul and Michael-and-Donna-and-Perry?" The way she says it makes Miriam think of their Christmas card.

81   "Right. Is that what you'd want?"

82   Rennie stares at the windshield wipers. The light through the windshield is spotty, falling with an underwater strangeness on Rennie's serious face. "I'm not sure," she says. "I'll have to think it over."

83   Miriam feels betrayed. It depresses her that Rennie is even willing to take the question seriously. She wants her to deny the possibility, to give her a tearful hug and say she couldn't live with anyone but Mommy.

84   "It's not like I'm sending you away, Rennie. I'm not going to die while you're a little girl. We're just talking about what-if. You understand that, right?"

85   "Right," Rennie says. "It's a game. We play what-if at school." After another minute she says, "I think Aunt Janice."

86   They are repeating their route now, passing again by the Burger Boy where Miriam had lunch. The tables and chairs inside look neater than it's possible to keep things in real life, and miniature somehow, like doll furniture. It looks bright and safe, not the sort of place that could hold ghosts.

87   On an impulse Miriam decides to put off the errands until tomorrow. She feels reckless, knowing that tomorrow will already be busy enough without a backlog. But they can easily live another day without vacuum-cleaner bags, and she'll work out something about the milk.

88   "We could stop here and have a hamburger for dinner," Miriam says. "Or a fish sandwich. And afterward we could stop for a minute at Ice Cream Heaven. Would you like that?"

89   "No. Pot pies!"

90   "And no Ice Cream Heaven?"

91   "I don't need any more angel stickers. Leslie Copley gave me twelve."

92   "Well, that was nice of him."

93   "Yep. He hates bananas."

94   "Okay, we'll go straight home. But do you remember that pot pies take half an hour to cook in the oven? Will you be too hungry to wait, once we get home?"

95   "No, I'll be able to wait," Rennie says, sounding as if she really will. In the overtones of her voice and the way she pushes her blond hair over her shoulder there is a startling maturity, and Miriam is frozen for a moment with a vision of a much older Rennie. All the different Rennies—the teenager, the adult—are already contained in her hands and her voice, her confidence. From moments like these, parents can find the courage to believe in the resilience of their children's lives. They will barrel forward like engines, armored by their own momentum, more indestructible than love.

96   "Okay then, pot pies it is," Miriam says. "Okay."

QUESTIONS

1. Interpret the meaning of the short story's title: "Quality Time."

2. Kingsolver writes: "When people remark to Miriam about how well-organized she is, she laughs and declares that organization is the religion of the single parent." Explain the meaning of this statement as seen by Miriam.

3. Although the story revolves around the relationship of a mother and daughter, other family members play a role in the story. Describe their function.

4. Discuss the challenges Miriam faces in trying to balance parenting with work.

 THE TECHNOLOGY CONNECTION

Electronic technologies are affecting family life and changing the way family members work, play, and interact with one another. If you read Linda Ellerbee's excerpt in Unit Three, you've already had a taste of how television changed the author's family life. Parents and children often confront technology differently. In the next reading, Erma Bombeck relates how one device, the VCR, affected her family.

Technology's Coming . . . Technology's Coming

ERMA BOMBECK

Author and humorist, Erma Bombeck was a widely read syndicated columnist, a twice-a-week commentator on the television show Good Morning America *from 1975 to 1986, and a contributing editor of* Good Housekeeping *magazine. Her column "At Wit's End" was syndicated in over 900 newspapers. Erma Bombeck's many books focused on the universal truths of family living. Among her titles are* The Grass Is Always Greener over the Septic Tank *(1976),* If Life Is a Bowl of Cherries, What Am I Doing in the Pits? *(1978),* Motherhood: The Second Oldest Profession *(1983), and* Family: The Ties That Bind and Gag *(1987), from which the following excerpt is taken.*

GEARING UP

1. How do you view modern applications of technology like the VCR and the microwave? Do you have older family members (e.g., parents or grandparents) who refuse to use such technology? What is their thinking?

2. Have you ever programmed a VCR? Did you find it easy or difficult? Explain.

The Reading

Technology's Coming . . . Technology's Coming

by Erma Bombeck

Friday: 8 P.M.

1   The younger son made his move first. He jumped up from the table and said, "I've gotta get my laundry started or I can't go out. What time is it?"

2   I looked at my watch. "It's 6 A.M. in Hamburg, Germany, if that helps."

3   "Why do you know the time in Hamburg, Mom?"

4   "Because that is where the watch was made and set and the directions for resetting it are written in German."

5   "The clock on the oven says it's 11."

6   "That's wrong," said my husband. "Your mother can't see what she's twirling half the time without her glasses and sometimes when she sets the timer, she resets the clock."

7   "And the one on the VCR?" he asked.

8   ". . . is always 12 and blinking," I said, "because your father screwed up between steps two and five when the power went out."

9   "God, Mom, you and Dad are out of it. It's like the *Twilight Zone*. How do you two function around here? I'd be lost without technology. This little beeper," he said, patting his shirt pocket, "keeps me in touch with the world."

10   "He's right, Mom," said our daughter, "you oughta have one of those signals attached to your car keys and your glasses. Think of the time you could save."

11   It was a subject I hated.

12   "Maybe we should have tranquilized you with a dart and fitted you with a beeper to track your migratory habits when you were seventeen and we'd have all slept better," I snapped.

13   "Mom, why do you resist the twenty-first century? You don't even have a home computer."

14   "I don't need a home computer. What would I do with it?"

15   "A lot of things. You could store all your personal documents in one

place . . . your marriage license, your insurance policies, your warranties. Just think, you and Dad could punch up your insurance policies in seconds."

16   "We could die from the excitement," I said.

17   "You could even use a copier around here," piped in her brother, "to duplicate all of our medical records and your dental bills, not to mention a Christmas newsletter."

18   "We need a copier like the Osmonds need a cavity fighter," I said.

19   "She's hopeless," they shrugged.

20   I sat there alone, toying with my coffee. They had told me what I didn't want to hear. Their father and I were casualties in the war of automation. Why did we resist it? Maybe because there was a time when there weren't enough hours in the day to fulfill all the skills of my job description. I was chauffeur, cook, nurse, decorator, financier, psychologist, and social director. I was important. All the slick magazines said so.

21   Slowly but steadily I was replaced by beeps, switches, flashing lights, electronic devices, and monotone voices.

22   In the beginning, I taught my children how to tie their shoes and button and zip their clothing. Then along came Velcro tabs on their shoes and on their clothes where buttons and zippers used to be.

23   I used to tell them how to place an emergency call to Grandma if they needed her. Now it was a matter of pushing a button on a memory phone and it was done for them.

24   I used to enlighten them about the stove. I showed them how to turn it on and off so they wouldn't get burned. They don't have stoves anymore. They have microwave ovens that have little buttons to push and are cool to the touch.

25   At one time I pulled them on my lap and together we traced our fingers across the printed page as I read to them. I don't read anymore. All they have to do is insert book cassettes into their stereos and hear them read by professionals.

26   I have been replaced by ouchless adhesive bandages, typewriters that correct their spelling, color-coded wardrobes, and computers that praise them when they get the right answers. The future is here.

27   The kids are wrong. It isn't that we don't give technology a chance. We use the VCR. True, it was in our home for a full six months before we turned it on.

28   From time to time my husband would leaf through the manual with an intensity usually reserved for a nervous flier reading about the evacuation procedures on an aircraft. Then one day he said, "Since we are going out to dinner, I am going to tape 'Dallas' so we can watch it later."

29   I put my hand over his. "I want you to know that whatever happens, I think you're the bravest man I have ever met."

30   Looking back, that was the beginning of our march against time.

31   There are 24 hours in every day. I used to watch television 6 hours and 44 minutes a day, leaving me with 17 hours and 16 minutes.

32   After I scheduled 7 hours and 5 minutes to sleep and 2 hours and 15 minutes to eat, it only left me with 7 hours and 56 minutes to do my job.

33   Then we got cable television and what with the news channel, first-run movies, MTV, country western, spiritual, entertainment, and sports, my viewing cut into my workday. The VCR was supposed to solve our problem.

34   But when do you watch the shows you've taped?

35   I took time away from my 2 hours and 15 minutes eating time by eating in front of the TV set. Naturally, we began to buy cassettes to fit the VCR. I bought Jane Fonda so I could get my body into shape. However, I had to take time away from my 7 hours and 5 minutes of sleeping to do it.

36   On my birthday, a son rented two movies as a present. I panicked. They had to be viewed by 10 A.M. the next morning. Already I had a stack of shows that had been taped that I hadn't had time to view. I put the movies ahead of the tapes, rescheduled Jane Fonda for 4 A.M., and watched *Terms of Endearment* and *Easy Money* at 5 and 7 A.M. It was close but I made it.

37   Other scheduling problems were not so easily solved. Before dinner one night, I approached the VCR with my Julia Child cassette. My husband was watching Dan Rather. When I asked him to watch Dan in the bedroom, he said it wouldn't do any good as he was taping a *M*A*S*H* rerun on the other channel. I went into the kitchen, turned on another set, and watched *Wheel of Fortune*, and we didn't eat until 9:30 in front of *Magnum P.I.*

38   As the weeks go on, I feel the pressure more and more. With the VCR taping shows day and night, with my husband running from room to room, channel-searching to see what we're missing, the new cassettes on everything from how to repair your plumbing to how to be more assertive, the new films and video music, we're falling behind.

39   Already we're beginning to cut corners. We've got *60 Minutes* down to 30, *20/20* to 10/10, and anything on World War II we fast-forward because we know the ending.

40   But the cassettes are winning. We both know that. It's only a matter of time.

41   Our son returned to the kitchen with his father's running watch in his hand. "I don't believe you, Dad. You've been telling time by your memory/recall lap 4, total time. Here, let me show you how it works. You've got a multimode chronograph and multimode countdown timer with one-tenth second accuracy."

42   I watched the two of them hunched over the watch as my son patiently explained the mechanism.

43   Had it been twenty-some years since they had huddled over the kitchen table together and my husband brought forth the brand-new watch for his son and taught him how to tell time? They had "walked through" all the parts when they got down to the basics. When the big hand pointed toward the refrigerator and the small hand was toward the stove, it was 6 o'clock and time to eat. When the big hand was toward the mixer and the little hand was pointed toward the portable television set, it was time to go to bed.

44   If the kid went into a home or building where the furniture was not positioned in the same spot as our kitchen, he was to go to the nearest person and ask, "What time is it?"

45   With deft fingers, our son twisted dials and adjusted minute screws on the watch. My husband watched with admiration and awe. He had come a long way since that day twenty years ago at the kitchen table.

46   Minutes later, "Mr. Technology" yelled from the utility room, "Mom, how do you turn the washer on?"

47   Maybe not.

QUESTIONS

1. Describe the author's feelings toward technology. Why does she feel the way she does?

2. The author's children see technology in a different way from their mother. Explain why.

3. The author describes her husband's efforts to program a VCR. She is using humor but is also making a serious point. What is the underlying message of her humor?

4. Describe what happens to the author's daily schedule once she starts using the VCR. Do her experiences sound realistic, or do you feel she is exaggerating to be humorous? Explain.

MAKING CONNECTIONS

The Family

1. Analyze Spock's prescription for ensuring healthy families. Do Kingsolver's, Mitchard's, and Angelou's families fit this prescription? Explain.

2. Hochschild and Robertson list some of the changes the modern family has undergone. Study the Angelou article and interpret her observations regarding some of these changes.

3. Coontz suggests that the stereotypical nuclear family of the 1950s was more fanciful than fact. Interpret her observations with reference to Robertson's and Mitchard's comments on the evolving family.

4. Mitchard argues that preserving certain traditions and rituals is essential for healthy families. Select one other article that addresses family traditions and compare and contrast the views of the author with the observations of Mitchard.

5. Of the various issues and ideas raised in this unit, which do you believe will be most significant for the family of the future? Explain.

6. Every author writes from experience. The articles in this unit present different views of the family. Which article do you think best captures the spirit of the family? Explain on the basis of your experience.

7. Some of the articles in this unit present problems that modern families face, such as divorce, work-related pressure, technology, and day care needs. Select one problem and, using two articles in the unit, suggest some possible solutions. After you respond, state whether you agree or disagree with the proposed solutions and why.

8. "Raising a family can be both rewarding and stressful." Select any two readings in this unit and explain how the author would respond to this statement.

LIBRARY ASSIGNMENT

The Family, Past and Present

The library assignment in Unit One asked you to investigate what the world was like during the week you were born and contrast it with the world today. For this library assignment, you are to compare the world as it is today to the world the eldest living member of your family experienced when he or she was your present age. This assignment will give you a perspective on how things have changed or remained the same over a longer period of time than that in the first library assignment.

You will be required to gather information from various sources. You will need to use the library and study reference material such as newspapers, books, and magazines. In addition, you will need to interview your eldest relative to gain his or her personal view of history. Finally, you will need to relate events of the past to today's events. You will be asked to investigate seven topics and prepare answers to specific questions. Afterward, you will answer some general questions regarding your findings and conclusions.

Questions for Library Research and Interviewing

To answer the following questions, use the library first. After you have completed your library work, interview your relative to gain a personal account of how things were when he or she was your age. Many of the questions have several parts. Try to answer as many parts as possible and make your answers comprehensive and specific. Further suggestions for the assignment follow the questions.

1. Examine magazines, newspapers, and family photographs if available. Note clothing styles and compare them with today's styles.

2. List the most significant events that took place. Divide your answer into events that took place in the United States and throughout the world. Who were some of the newsmakers? Who were some of the notable government leaders? What was the mood of the nation? What were some of the major concerns and issues? Repeat the process for the present time.

Then compare the newsmakers, leaders, and concerns of the past to those of today.

3. Manufacturers constantly advertise their latest products. Cordless telephones, personal computers, portable videocassette recorders, and other examples of modern technology promise to make life better, easier, and more enjoyable. What were some examples of technology in the past, and how do they compare to today's? What features do today's products offer that were unavailable in the past?

4. Study the sports page of newspapers and magazines from your relative's time. Then do the same for the present. What were the major sports stories in both years? List similarities and differences between sports-related issues for both years (e.g., types of games played, salaries, rules, team composition, location of teams, presence of minority group members and women).

5. Examine the employment section of a newspaper from your relative's time and compare it with that of a current newspaper. What are some similarities and differences? Is the job you plan to pursue listed in both papers? If your relative worked, is his or her job mentioned in both papers? Find a job described in both papers. Compare working conditions, salaries offered, and qualifications. What conclusions can you draw? What jobs that formerly were restricted to men are now open to both sexes?

6. What persuasive techniques (for example, pictures, graphics, messages) did advertisers in both time periods use to promote their products?

7. Compare the entertainment pages of magazines and newspapers from both time periods.
   a. What motion pictures were featured in the past? Who were the popular stars? How do the types of movies produced in the past differ from those of today?
   b. Examine the radio and television listings (if these media were available by your relative). What kinds of programs were presented, and how do they compare to today's programs? What other differences and/or similarities in radio and television do you note?
   c. Compare other kinds of popular entertainment (e.g., theater, concerts) for both periods. What similarities and differences do you observe? How can they be accounted for?

Using the Library

To complete this assignment, you will have to spend time in the library reading and studying various reference materials. Your librarian can help you locate history texts, almanacs, newspaper indexes, back issues of magazines, and other references. Two texts that will give you a general picture of life in your relative's time are *The Timetable of History* by Bernard Grun (Simon and Schuster, 1975) and *The Timetable of American History*, edited by Lawrence Urdang (Simon and Schuster, 1981). Take notes and, if possible, photocopy relevant material (advertisements, photographs, etc.).

Interviewing Your Relative

After you have completed your library research, you are to interview your relative to learn what conditions were like when he or she was your present age.

For the interview, use the set of questions you completed for library research. You may need to adapt these questions to the interviewing situation. Your subject may wander off the topic at hand or focus on one event. It is important to keep the interview moving so that you can cover all the questions. If your subject does not object, you can tape-record the interview. This will free you from note taking and allow you to concentrate on the interview. The information you gather is to be added to that obtained in your library research and incorporated in your final report.

Find a place where you and your subject will be at ease and undisturbed. Recalling past memories may arouse strong emotions. Respect such responses, and don't pressure the person for answers.

Think of the interview as an extended conversation. Interview subjects need to be reassured that they have something worthwhile to say. Listen carefully, encourage your subject, and ask for additional information when necessary. Be patient; don't cut your subject off in the middle of an answer. Help him or her recall a particular answer. You can use the information gathered from your library research here—for example, photocopies of relevant material or lists of important events. Also, your relative may have photographs, scrapbooks, or other material from the time period you are studying. You may need more than one session.

Concluding Questions

The following questions are more general and will allow you to compare both time periods, summarize your findings, and present your conclusions. Answer these questions after you have completed your library work, finished interviewing your relative, and answered the preceding questions.

1. How different or similar is life today compared to the time when your relative was your age?

2. Name three things that have changed and three things that have remained the same.

3. Is the world a better place today? Explain.

4. Is life today easier or more difficult than in the past? Explain.

5. What is and is not missing from the "good old days"?

An Example

The following example should give you a better understanding of the assignment. Imagine that it is 1993 and you are twenty years old. Your eldest living relative is Aunt Helen, who was born in 1925 and reached age twenty in 1945. You are to find out what Aunt Helen's world was like when she was twenty and compare it to the present. To answer the assigned questions, you will need to go to the library and consult various sources to learn about the world in 1945.

After completing the library research and answering the questions on page 512, you are ready to interview Aunt Helen. During the interview, pay particular attention to what has changed and what appears to be the same for both time periods.

To see how you can combine the information obtained from your research with what you will learn from Aunt Helen, let's focus on a specific topic: question 2 on page 510, which asks for a description of major events, newsmakers, and issues. Because 1945 was the year in which World War II ended, there was no shortage of important news stories. A library search of various materials would reveal the following information.

In 1945, the United States was actively involved in World War II, both in Europe and Asia. President Roosevelt (United States), Winston Churchill (England), and Joseph Stalin (USSR) met in Yalta to plan the final defeat of Germany. During that year, President Roosevelt died and Vice President Harry Truman became president. In Europe, Germany surrendered, Hitler reportedly committed suicide, and Mussolini was captured and shot. In Asia, the United States dropped the A-bomb on Hiroshima and Nagasaki and Japan surrendered, which ended the war. The war dead were estimated at 35 million, plus 10 million who died in Nazi concentration camps.

Although World War II was not fought on U.S. soil, it had a profound impact on our country. A coal shortage developed, and brownouts were ordered to conserve fuel and energy. An examination of advertisements from 1945 reveal that as the war ended, many products that were previously rationed, such as shoes, butter, and tires, became available to the public once again. Advertisements proclaimed "Rationing is off" and "Available again!" The arrival of the Allied troops and the victory celebrations were important events.

Non-war-related events also made news. In sports, Jackie Robinson became the first black player in major league baseball. Detroit defeated Chicago in the World Series. The film *The Lost Weekend* won the Academy Award for best picture. Rogers and Hammerstein produced the long-running Broadway musical *Carousel*. Richard Wright published his autobiography, *Black Boy*. Popular radio shows of 1945 included "The Red Skelton Show," "The Green Hornet," "Superman," "Inner Sanctum," and "The Fred Allen Show." Other popular radio performers were Frank Sinatra, Eddie Cantor, and the Andrews Sisters. There were few FM radio programs. Although television had been invented some years back, there were only two stations and they broadcasted a very limited number of programs. In 1945, weather-detecting radar was developed, radiophones for automobiles became available, and thirteen people were killed when a B-25 bomber flew into the seventy-eighth and seventy-ninth floors of the Empire State Building.

This brief summary gives you a general description of 1945 as described in various reference sources. By interviewing Aunt Helen, you may learn how the war personally affected her as well as her family and friends. Most likely, she will recall specific stories and cite examples. A family scrapbook or photo album might stir up additional memories and emotions, as might photocopies of news stories or photographs from history books.

Finally, you would combine your library research information with the knowledge you gained from interviewing Aunt Helen to develop a picture of 1945. Then you would use this information to compare the world of 1945 with that of today. It will be important that you keep up with current events.

This assignment requires you to gather and organize much information. You may find it useful to keep notes of your work on index cards and organize the cards according to the following broad categories:

Family Member at My Age		Myself Today	
Library info	Response of person being interviewed	Library info	My reactions

ACKNOWLEDGMENTS

From *Everything But Money* by Sam Levenson. Reprinted by permission of Sterling Lord Literistic, Inc. Copyright © 1966 by Samuel Levenson. Pages 42–44.

From *The Autobiography of Malcolm X* by Malcolm X, with the assistance of Alex Haley. Copyright © 1964 by Alex Haley and Malcolm X. Copyright © 1965 by Alex Haley and Betty Shabazz. Reprinted by permission of Random House, Inc. Pages 53–56.

"To Young People Who Want to Know Why We Should Read," by Vincent Nowell. Reprinted with permission of the publisher, Teaching K-8, Norwalk, CT 06854. From the November/December 1996 issue of *Teaching K-8.* Pages 70–72.

Quotation on pages 87–88 of "The Proficient Reader" by Ira D. Epstein and Ernest B. Nieratka from an advertisement by *Good Housekeeping,* a division of The Hearst Corporation. This ad appeared in *The New York Times,* January 10, 1980. Reprinted by permission.

"History of Printing" by Geoffrey Rubinstein. Copyright © 1996 Jones Digital Century. All rights reserved. Used with permission. CD-ROM (Jones Telecommunications and Multimedia Encyclopedia) is available via the Product Ordering Line at 1-800-750-JONES. Pages 99–104.

"A Summer's Reading," from *The Magic Barrel* by Bernard Malamud. Copyright © 1950, 1958, and copyright renewed © 1977, 1986 by Bernard Malamud. Reprinted by permission of Farrar, Straus, & Giroux, Inc. Pages 115–120.

"In His Book, The Printed Word Will Live On." Interview with Geoffrey Nunberg by Mary Pupura and Paolo Pontoniere, April 21, 1997. Copyright © 1997 Los Angeles Times. Reprinted by permission. Pages 122–123.

"McDonald's—We Do It All for You," by Barbara Garson. Reprinted with permission of Simon & Schuster from *The Electronic Sweatshop: How Computers Are Transforming the Office of the Future into the Factory of the Past* by Barbara Garson. Copyright © 1988 by Barbara Garson. Pages 138–151.

"So You Want to Be a Physician/Opthamologist," from Insider Information. Article originally published on StudentCenter.com. ©1997, iVillage, Inc. Used by permission of iVillage, Inc. All rights reserved. Pages 157–163.

"Evaluating Information Found on the Internet" by Elizabeth E. Kirk, Electronic and Distance Education Librarian, The Johns Hopkins University. Reprinted by permission. Pages 206–211.

Lewis, Robert, "Looking for Work in All the Right Places." Reprinted by permission of the AARP. Pages 212–216.

Screen dumps on pages 218–223: page 218, reprinted by permission; page 219, reprinted courtesy of the Online Career Center; page 222, reprinted by permission; page 223, *The Riley Guide,* www.dbm.com/jobguide. Used with permission.

"How to Critically Analyze Information Sources." Reference Services Division, Olin*Kroch*Uris Libraries, Cornell University Library. Pages 224–226.

"Work to Make the World Work Better," by James Michener. Copyright © 1976 by James Michener. Reprinted by permission of William Morris Agency, Inc. on behalf of the author. Pages 228–231.

"How It Feels to Be Out of Work," by Jan Halvorsen, from the "My Turn" column of *Newsweek,* September 22, 1980. Pages 237–238.

"The Day the Mommies Went Home" by Anita Shreve. Reprinted by permission. Copyright © 1990 *Special Report,* Whittle Communications, 333 Main Avenue, Knoxville, TN, 37902. Pages 244–247.

"Managing Workforce Diversity in Organizations," from Griffin, Ricky W., *Management,* Fifth Edition. Copyright © 1996 by Houghton Mifflin Company. Used with permission. Pages 275–297.

"The Day's Work," copyright © 1996 by Barbara Holland. Reprinted by permission of McIntosh and Otic, Inc. Pages 310–318.

"Change and the Transformation of Work" from William Bridges, *Jobshift* (pages 10–17). Copyright © 1994 by William Bridges and Associates, Inc. Reprinted by permission of Addison Wesley Longman, Inc. Pages 320–324.

"Television Changed My Family Forever" by Linda Ellerbee. Reprinted by permission of G.P. Putnam & Sons, a division of Penguin Putnam, Inc., from *Move On* by Linda Ellerbee. Copyright © 1991 by Linda Ellerbee. Pages 341–343.

"Only Good If You Can Trust It," by Tom Brokaw. Reprinted by permission. Pages 345–346.

"Introduction to Mass Media, by Shirley Biagi, from *Media Impact: An Introduction to Mass Media,* 3/e. Copyright © 1996 Wadsworth Publishers. Reprinted by permission of the publisher. Pages 352–368.

"Television," from *The Read-Aloud Handbook* by Jim Trelease. Copyright © 1979, 1982, 1985, 1995 by Jim Trelease. Used by permission of Viking Penguin, a division of Penguin Putnam, Inc. Pages 377–389.

"Don't Blame TV," by Jeff Greenfield. Reprinted courtesy of Jeff Greenfield, CNN Senior Analyst. Pages 398–400.

"Can Your Students Read TV?" by Kathleen Tyner. Copyright © 1991, Cable in the Classroom. Reprinted by permission of the author. Pages 408–410.

Schrank, Jeffrey, "The Language of Advertising Claims," *Media and Methods,* March 1974, pp. 44–48. Copyright © 1974. All rights reserved. Reprinted by permission of the publisher. Pages 418–423.

Christine Lapham, author of "The Evolution of the Newspaper of the Future," is a technology writer, editor of *CMC Magazine,* and an instructor at The Sage Colleges in Troy and Albany, New York. Pages 432–438.

From *Bullet Park* by John Cheever. Copyright © 1967, 1968, 1969 by John Cheever. Reprinted by permission of Alfred A. Knopf, Inc. Pages 440–444.

"Too Much Information, Too Little Time," by Joe Saltzman. Copyright © 1997 USA Today. Reprinted by permission. Pages 445–447.

"The New Traditional Family," by Jacquelyn Mitchard. Reprinted by permission. Pages 455–457.

From Ian Robertson, *Society: A Brief Introduction.* Worth Publishers, New York, 1989. Reprinted with permission. Pages 458–474.

"The Way We Weren't—The Myth and Reality of the 'Traditional' Family," by Stephanie Coontz, reprinted from *National Forum: The Phi Kappa Phi Journal,* Volume 75, Number 3 (Summer 1995). Copyright © by Stephanie Coontz. Reprinted by permission of the publisher. Pages 476–481.

"Joey's Problem," from *The Second Shift* by Arlie Hochschild and Ann Machung. Copyright © 1989 by Arlie Hochschild. Used by permission of Viking Penguin, a division of Penguin Books USA, Inc. Pages 482–490.

"Put Family First," by Benjamin Spock, M.D. Copyright © by Benjamin Spock. Originally appeared in *Parenting.* This usage granted by permission. Pages 491–492.

From Maya Angelou, *Keeping Families Together: The Case for Family Preservation.* Reprinted by permission of Edna McConnell Foundation. Pages 493–496.

"Quality Time," by Barbara Kingsolver. Copyright © by Barbara Kingsolver. *Homeland and Other Stories 1989.* Published by HarperCollins. Reprinted by permission. Pages 497–504.

"Technology's Coming . . . Technology's Coming" from *Family: The Ties that Bind and Gag* by Erma Bombeck. Reprinted by permission. Pages 506–509.

INDEX

Adler, Mortimer, 243
Advertising, as persuasive writing, 68
Agree, as cue word, 7
Alice's Adventures in Wonderland (Carroll), 417
Allusions, 405–407, 416–417
Although, as signal word, 95–96
Analysis, in exposition, 77–78
Analyze, as cue word, 5, 7
Anecdote, definition of, 62
Angelou, Maya, 492
    Keeping Families Together: The Case for Family Preservation, 493–496
Annotation. *See* Marking text
Answer, framing, 40–41
Argument and persuasion, 68–69
    advertising using, 68
    as author's purpose, 68, 235
    editorials using, 68
    questions for, 68–69, 232
    reading strategies for, 273
    summary for, 70
Aristophanes, 242
Arrow, for marking text, 50
Assessment, periodic, 262–263, 431
Associated Press, 248
Asterisk, for marking text, 49, 377
Author, evaluating credibility of, 227
Author's purpose, determining, 166, 234–235, 345
Author's writing pattern, determining, 261–262
Autobiography of Malcolm X, The (Malcolm X and Haley), 53–56

Bar graphs, 180–181
Because, as signal word, 95
Biagi, Shirley, 348
    "Introduction to the Mass Media," 352–370
Bias, detecting and evaluating, 376
Boldface type, to present key ideas, 73
Bombeck, Erma, 505
    "Technology's Coming . . . Technology's Coming," 506–509

Boorstin, Daniel, 2
Bridges, William, 319–320
    "Change and the Transformation of Work," 320–325
Brokaw, Tom, 344
    "Only Good If You Can Trust It," 345–346
Bullet Park (Cheever), 440–444
Byline, newspaper, 248

"Can Your Students Read TV?" (Tyner), 408–410
Careers. *See* Work and careers unit
Carroll, Lewis, 417
Cartoons, satire in, 243
Cause-and-effect pattern
    examples of, 61
    in exposition, 77, 78, 97, 261–262
    noting in graphs, 179
CD-ROM databases, 450
"Change and the Transformation of Work" (Bridges), 320–325
Chapter projects, 256
Chapters. *See* Textbooks
Charts
    for collecting ideas, 30–31, 155–157
    for comparing and contrasting, 397
    for connecting ideas, 168–169, 334
    for organizing lists, 392–393
    principles for understanding, 179–180
    in textbooks, 255
Cheever, John, 440
    Bullet Park, 440–444
Circle, for marking text, 49, 244, 260
Circle graphs, 181–183
Cite, as cue word, 6
Clinton, Bill, 205
Clymer, Anne W., 165
    "Solving the Job Puzzle," 170–178
Collecting ideas, 29–31, 42, 155–157
    charts and, 155
    importance of, 29

reading and literacy unit and, 30–31
    work and careers unit and, 155–157
Comparative reading,
    chart for, 393, 397
    on television, 394–397
Compare and contrast
    as cue words, 7, 41, 52–53
    in exposition, 77, 166
    outlining and, 202
    using graphs to, 179–182
    see also Comparative reading
Competency, work and careers and, 133
Comprehension questions, 256
Computer-Mediated Communication magazine, 428
Connecting ideas, 51–53
    among units, 332, 430–431, 453–454
    collecting ideas and, 29
    family unit and, 453–454, 509–510
    focusing on areas for, 51–53
    mass media unit and, 332–335, 447–448
    reading and literacy unit and, 124–125
    work and careers unit and, 132–134, 168–170, 325–326
Connotation, 413–416
Consequently, as signal word, 98
Context, in predicting vocabulary, 21
Contrast. *See* Compare and contrast
Coontz, Stephanie, 475
    "The Way We Weren't : The Myth and Reality of the 'Traditional' Family," 476–481
Cramming for exam, 272
Critique, as cue word, 8
Cue words, 5–9
    examples of, 6–8, 135, 407
    exercise for, 8–9
    strategies for using, 11, 268
    see also Signal words

"Day's Work, The" (Holland), 310–319

"Day the Mommies Went Home, The" (Shreve), 244–247
Define, as cue word, 7
Definition
　in exposition, 78
　in predicting vocabulary, 21–22
Denotation, 413
Describe, as cue word, 5, 6
Despite, as signal word, 98
Diagrams
　principles for understanding, 179–180
　in textbooks, 255
Disagree, as cue word, 7
Discuss, as cue word, 135
Discussion, class, 264
"Don't Blame TV" (Greenfield), 398–401
Douglass, Frederick, 9
　The Life of an American Slave, 12–13, 25–28
Drucker, Peter, 131

EBSCOhost, 450
Editing
　an exam response, 269
　questions for, 136–137
Effort, work and careers and, 133
Ellerbee, Linda, 339
　"Television Changed My Family Forever," 341–344
Entertainment, as author's purpose, 235
Epstein, Ira D., 75
　"The Proficient Reader," 79–89
Essay exams
　sample, 301, 302–306
　strategies for writing, 267–269
　summarizing and, 63
"Evaluating Information Found on the Internet" (Kirk), 206–211
Evaluation
　of exam type, 266
　of grading schemes, 265
　of information on the Internet, 205–211
　of qualifications and sources, 224–228, 236
Everything But Money (Levenson), 42–44
"Evolution of the Newspaper of the Future, The" (Lapham), 432–438
Example, in exposition, 78

Exam preparation, 263–273
　checklist for, 272–273
　for essay questions, 267–269
　exam importance and, 265–266
　exam type and, 266
　for fill-in-the-blank questions, 271
　listing key concepts and, 265
　for matching questions, 271
　for multiple-choice questions, 269–271
　pre-exam strategies for, 263–264
　sample exam questions for, 300–309
　support discussion and, 264
　time planning and, 266–267, 266–270
　for true/false questions, 271–272
Experience, previous
　and framing an answer, 135
　and textbook studying, 252
Explain, as cue word, 5, 7
Exposition, 94–98
　analysis in, 77–78
　cause and effect in, 77, 78, 97
　comparison and contrast in, 77
　definition in, 78
　definition of, 75–76
　example in, 78
　example of, 76
　listing in, 77
　reading, 78–79, 261–262, 273
　sequence or process in, 77
　signal words in, 94–98
　summarizing of, 165–168

"Family" (Robertson), 458–474
Family unit
　connecting and, 332–333, 453–454, 509–510
　introduction to, 452
Feinberg, Leonard, 243
Fill-in-the-blank exams, 256, 266, 271
　sample of, 301, 308
Framing an answer, 40–41
　for essay questions, 267–269
　for "Looking for Work in All the Right Places," 211–212
　for "McDonald's—We Do It All for You," 135–137
　for *The Story of My Life*, 41
　steps for, 40–41, 134–135, 211
　for subjective tests, 266

Garson, Barbara, 134
　"McDonald's—We Do It All for You," 138–152
Gates, Bill, 3
Gearing up
　for "A Summer's Reading," 115
　for *The Autobiography of Malcolm X*, 51
　for *Bullet Park*, 440
　for "Can Your Students Read TV?," 405
　for "Change and the Transformation of Work," 320
　for "The Day's Work," 309
　for "The Day the Mommies Went Home," 242
　for *Everything But Money*, 42
　for "The Evolution of the Newspaper of the Future," 427
　for "Family," 458
　for "History of Printing," 93–94
　for "How It Feels to Be Out of Work," 234
　for "In His Book, The Printed Word Will Live On," 121–122
　for "Introduction to the Mass Media," 348
　for "The Language of Advertising Claims," 413
　for *The Life of an American Slave*, 9–10
　for "Looking for Work in All the Right Places," 205
　for "McDonald's—We Do It All for You," 134
　for "Managing Workforce Diversity in Organizations," 250
　for "The New Traditional Family," 455
　for "Only Good If You Can Trust It," 344–345
　for "The Proficient Reader," 75
　for "Quality Time," 497
　for "The Second Shift: Working Parents and the Revolution at Home," 482
　for "Solving the Job Puzzle," 165
　for "So You Want to Be a Physician/Ophthalmologist," 153
　for *The Story of My Life*, 29
　for studying, 258

for "Television," 375
for "Television Changed My Family Forever," 339
for "Tomorrow's Jobs," 178
for "Too Much Information, Too Little Time," 445–447
for "The Way We Weren't: The Myth and Reality of the 'Traditional' Family," 476
for "Why We Should Read," 68
for "Work to Make the World Work Better," 224
Graphs, reading and interpreting, 178–186
    bar, 180–181
    circle (pie), 181–183
    importance of, 178–179
    line, 183–185
    principles for, 179–180
    questions for, 185–186
    in textbooks, 255
Greenfield, Jeff, 394
    "Don't Blame TV," 398–401
Griffin, Ricky, 250
    "Managing Workforce Diversity in Organizations," 275–297
Grun, Bernard, 511
Gutenberg, Johannes, 330

Haley, Alex
    The Autobiography of Malcolm X, 53–56
Halvorsen, Jan, 234
    "How It Feels to Be Out of Work," 237–239
Headings
    chapter, 254
    and idea development, 429, 430
Hidden Persuaders, The (Packard), 416
Highlighting, for marking text, 48
"History of Printing" (Rubinstein), 99–105
Hochschild, Arlie, 482
    "The Second Shift: Working Parents and the Revolution at Home," 482–490
Holland, Barbara, 309
    "The Day's Work," 310–319
However, as signal word, 108
"How It Feels to Be Out of Work" (Halvorsen), 237–239

Idea map, 73
Ideas. See Collecting ideas; Connecting ideas

Identify, as cue word, 6
Idiosyncratic questions, 256
Illustrate, as cue word, 6
Indexes, magazine, 449–450
Inference questions, 256
Information mapping. See Mapping information
Information sharing, as author's purpose, 234–235
"In His Book, The Printed Word Will Live On" (Purpura and Pontoniere), 122–124
Inserts, textbook, 255
Internet
    career resource sites, 327–328
    evaluating information on, 205
    impact of, 330–331
    on-line journals on, 428
    research resources on, 450
Interpret, as cue word, 8
Interviews, reading, 153–155
    applications of, 154–155
    explanation of, 153
    questions for, 154
"Introduction to the Mass Media" (Biagi), 352–370

Jackson, Holbrook, 3
Journal, reading, 67, 114, 164–165, 204, 241, 249–250, 309, 374–375, 404, 426–427
Journal articles, strategies for reading, 428–429

Keeping Families Together: The Case for Family Preservation (Angelou), 493–496
Keller, Helen, 29
    The Story of My Life, 32–34
Kingsolver, Barbara, 496
    "Quality Time," 497–505
Kirk, Elizabeth E., 205
    "Evaluating Information Found on the Internet," 206–211
Knowledge worker, 131
Koop, Everett, 376

"Language of Advertising Claims, The" (Schrank), 418–424
Lapham, Christine, 427
    "The Evolution of the Newspaper of the Future," 432–438
Levenson, Sam, 41
    Everything But Money, 42–44

Lewis, Robert, 205
    "Looking for Work in All the Right Places," 212–217
Lexus/Nexus, 450
Libraries
    anthologies in, 394
    career resources in, 327
    index resources in, 450
    questions for research using, 510–511
    reference resources in, 227, 511
    research assignments in, 125–128, 326–328, 448–450, 510–514
    reserve textbooks in, 263
Life of an American Slave, The (Douglass), 12–13, 25–28
Line graphs, 183–185
List, as cue word, 6
Listing
    in analyzing text, 392
    in exposition, 77
Literacy
    definition of, 2
    in the workplace, 3–4
"Looking for Work in All the Right Places" (Lewis), 212–217

"McDonald's—We Do It All for You" (Garson), 138–152
McGregor, Elizabeth, 165
    "Solving the Job Puzzle," 170–178
Machung, Anne, 482
    "The Second Shift: Working Parents and the Revolution at Home," 482–490
Magazine Index, 450
Magazine indexes, 449–450
Main idea, in summary, 64
Malamud, Bernard, 114–115
    "A Summer's Reading," 115–120
Malcolm X, 51
    The Autobiography of Malcolm X, 53–56
"Managing Workforce Diversity in Organizations" (Griffin), 275–297
Mapping information, 348–351, 431
Marginal notation
    for marking text, 49, 260, 377
    in textbooks, 255

Marking text, 48–51, 53
  advantages of, 260, 431
  arrow for, 50
  asterisk for, 49, 377
  for *The Autobiography of Malcolm X,* 57–59
  building up to, 53
  circle for, 49, 244
  definition of, 48
  double underline for, 49
  highlighting for, 48
  for *The Life of an American Slave,* 14
  for longer selections, 377
  for "Managing Workforce Diversity in Organizations," 298–300
  marginal notes for, 49, 260, 377
  for "The Proficient Reader," 89–91
  purpose of, 243–244
  question mark for, 50, 244, 377
  for *The Story of My Life,* 35–37
  for summary, 64
  underlining for, 48, 49, 135
Mass media unit, 329
  assessment of media for, 331–332
  connecting and, 332–335, 447–448, 454
  graph use and, 178–179
  introduction to, 330–331
  satire and, 242–243
Matching questions exams, 256, 266, 271
  sample of, 301, 306
Michener, James A., 223–224
  evaluating credibility of, 227–228
  "Work to Make the World Work Better," 229–232
Mill, John Stuart, 69
Mitchard, Jacquelyn, 455
  "The New Traditional Family," 455–457
Modest Proposal, A (Swift), 242
Multiple–choice exams, 63, 256, 266, 267
  sample questions, 301, 306–308
  strategies for taking, 269–271

Name, as cue word, 6
Narrative
  reading strategies for, 10–11, 273, 340

sequence of events in, 76
  summarizing for, 165–166
Nast, Thomas, 243
News magazines, library research using, 126
Newspapers
  bylines in, 248
  editorials in, 235
  graphs used by, 178–179
  library research using, 125–126
  wire services and, 248
"New Traditional Family, The" (Mitchard), 455–457
Nieratka, Ernest B., 75
  "The Proficient Reader," 79–89
Notes, organizing for summary, 64
Nowell, Vince, 67
  "Why We Should Read," 70–72
Nunberg, Geoffrey, 121–122
  interview with ("In His Book, The Printed Word Will Live On"), 122–124

Objective exams, 266
  sample questions for, 301, 306–308
On Liberty (Mill), 69
"Only Good If You Can Trust It" (Brokaw), 345–346
Outline, chapter, 254
Outlining, 202

Packard, Vance, 416
Paraphrase, as cue word, 7
Paraphrasing
  to cite reference, 212
  to frame an answer, 136
  of key statements, 73, 107, 167
  of magazine articles, 449
  for summaries, 397
  to understand questions, 268
Persuasion. *See* Argument and persuasion
Pie graphs, 181–183
Plagiarism, 64
Pontoniere, Paolo, 121
  "In His Book, The Printed Word Will Live On," 122–124
Predicting vocabulary, 18–24
  before summarizing, 166
  in careful reading stage, 260–261
  for *The Life of an American Slave,* 23–24
  prediction in, 22, 31–32

steps in, 19–23
  synonym/definition in, 21–22
  target words in, 19, 21
  writing sentences for, 22–23
Prediction, in predicting vocabulary, 22, 31–32
Previewing
  of exam, 272
  of graphs/visual aids, 179
  of "McDonald's—We Do It All for You," 137–138
  of "The Proficient Reader," 79
  as reading overview, 274, 430
  and studying process, 258–259
  for summarizing, 63, 166
Prichett, Price, 131
Process, in exposition, 77
Process guides
  for *The Autobiography of Malcolm X,* 59–62
  for "Can Your Students Read TV?", 411–413
  for "The Day the Mommies Went Home," 248–249
  for "Don't Blame TV," 402–403
  for *Everything But Money,* 45–47
  for "History of Printing," 107–113
  for "How It Feels to Be Out of Work," 239–241
  for "Introduction to the Mass Media," 370–374
  for "The Language of Advertising Claims," 425–426
  for *The Life of an American Slave,* 15–18
  for "Looking for Work in All the Right Places," 217–223
  for "Only Good If You Can Trust It," 347
  for "The Proficient Reader," 92–93
  for *The Story of My Life,* 37–39
  for "Television," 392–393
  for "Tomorrow's Jobs," 201–204
  for "Why We Should Read," 73–75
"Proficient Reader, The" (Epstein and Nieratka), 79–89
Proofreading, questions for, 136–137
Purpura, Mary, 121
  "In His Book, The Printed Word Will Live On," 122–124

"Put Family First" (Spock), 491–492

Qualifications, evaluating. *See* Evaluating qualifications and sources
"Quality Time" (Kingsolver), 497–505
Question mark, for marking text, 50, 244, 260, 377
Questions
  for argument and persuasion, 68–69, 232
  based on section headings, 108–109
  for detecting bias, 376
  for editing an answer, 136–137
  framing an answer to, 40–41, 134–137, 302
  for graphs, 179, 185–186
  to guide reading, 274
  for interviews, 154
  for library research, 126–128, 510–511
  on mass media's impact, 331–332
  for narrative, 340
  for readings. *See* title of reading
  for satire, 243
  for summarizing, 64
  in textbooks, categories of, 256
Quotations, using, 64, 212, 449

Reader's Guide to Periodical Literature, The, 450
Reading
reasons for, 2–3
  for summarizing, 63–64
  in workplace, 3–4
Reading and literacy unit
  collecting ideas and, 29–31
  connecting ideas and, 124–125, 332, 453
Reading strategies. *See* Strategies
Reading/study process, for textbooks
  application of, 263
  exposition and, 260–261
  gearing up for, 258
  marking text and, 260
  periodic assessment and, 262
  predicting vocabulary and, 260–261
  previewing and, 258–260
  reading through and, 259
  signal words and, 262

References, citing specific, 212
Refute, as cue word, 8
Rereading, 135, 268, 302, 431
Research questions, 256
Research reports, summaries in, 63
Reuters wire service, 248
Reviewing, for exam preparation, 272
Robertson, Ian, 458
  "Family," 458–474
Roosevelt, Franklin D., 2
Rubinstein, Geoffrey
  "History of Printing," 99–105

Saltzman, Joe, 445
  "Too Much Information, Too Little Time," 445–447
Satire, 235
  as author's purpose, 235
  characteristics and history of, 242–243
  process guide for "The Day the Mommies Went Home," 248–249
  questions for reading, 243, 249–250
Schrank, Jeffrey, 413
  "The Language of Advertising Claims," 418–424
Search Bank, 450
"Second Shift: Working Parents and the Revolution at Home, The" (Hochschild and Machung), 482
Sequence of events, in exposition, 77
Short–answer exams, 266, 267
Shreve, Anita, 241
  "The Day the Mommies Went Home," 244–247
Signal words, 94–98, 166, 262
  see also Cue words
Simile, 46
SIRS Researcher, 450
"Solving the Job Puzzle" (Clymer and McGregor), 170–178
Sources, evaluating. *See* Evaluating qualifications and sources
"So You Want to Be a Physician/Ophthalmologist" (interview with Dr. Stephanie B.), 153, 157–164
Spock, Benjamin, 490
  "Put Family First," 491–492
State, as cue word, 6

Story of My Life, The (Keller), 32–34
Strategies
  definition of, 4–5
  important points for using, 98–99, 273–274
  see also Collecting ideas; Connecting ideas; Evaluation; Exposition; Framing an answer; Graphs, reading and interpreting; Interviews, reading; Mapping information; Predicting vocabulary; Previewing; Summarizing
Study groups, 264
Studying. *See* Reading/study process
Subheadings, chapter, 254
Subjective exams, 266
Summarize, as cue word, 8
Summarizing, 62–66, 165–168
  of argument and persuasion, 70
  of *The Autobiography of Malcolm X,* 65–66
  checklist for, 167
  to check understanding, 431
  components and importance of, 63–65, 397
  definition of, 62
  for exposition, 165–167
  in framing an answer, 136
  of magazine articles, 449
  of "Solving the Job Puzzle," 167–168
  of "Tomorrow's Jobs," 186
Summary, chapter, 255–256
"Summer's Reading, A" (Malamud), 115–120
Support, as cue word, 8
Surveying. *See* Previewing
Swift, Jonathan, 242
Syllabus, instructor's, 265
Synonyms, 21–22

Tables
  principles for understanding, 179–180
  strategies for reading, 336–339
  in textbooks, 255
Target words, in predicting vocabulary, 13–14, 19, 21
Technology
  and family life, 505
  and information overload, 444
  and mass media, 330, 454
  and work, 121, 319

"Technology's Coming . . .
Technology's Coming"
(Bombeck), 506–509
Television
research assignments in, 448–
450
satire featured by, 242–243
see also Mass media unit
"Television Changed My Family
Forever" (Ellerbee), 341–344
"Television" (Trelease), 377–389
Textbooks, 251–263
as alternatives sources, 264
chapters in, 251–253, 351–352
chapter outline for, 254
headings and subheadings in,
254
inserts used in, 255
instructor/time parameters for,
252
previewing, 137
previous experience with, 252,
252–260
questions/projects in, 256–257
study time expectations for,
257–258
visuals/graphics in, 179, 255
see also Exam preparation;
Reading/study process
Thesis statement, 107, 166, 232,
429

Time management
daily preparation and, 264
for exam preparation, 264, 272
for multiple–choice tests, 269
in sizing up exam, 266–267
*Timetable of American History,
The* (Urdang), 512
Timetable of History, The (Grun),
511
Title, predictions regarding, 429
Toffler, Alvin, 131
"Tomorrow's Jobs," 178, 186–201
"Too Much Information, Too Lit-
tle Time" (Saltzman),
445–447
Topic selection, 448–449
Transitional words, 64
Trelease, Jim, 375
"Television," 377–389
True/false exams, 256, 266,
271–272
sample of, 301, 308–309
Tutoring, 264
Tyner, Kathleen, 404
"Can Your Students Read
TV?," 408–410

Underlining, for marking text, 48,
49, 135, 260
Understanding, cue words helping
in, 6–8, 135

Urdang, Lawrence, 512
U.S. Statistical Abstracts, 330, 335,
336

Visual aids. *See* Graphs, reading
and interpreting
Vocabulary. *See* Predicting vocabulary

"Way We Weren't: The Myth and
Reality of the 'Traditional'
Family, The" (Coontz),
476–481
"Why We Should Read" (Now-
ell), 70–72
Wilson Web, 450
Wire services, 248
Work and careers
career planning and, 131–132
current trends and, 131
history of, 130
Work and careers unit
collecting ideas and, 155–157
connecting ideas and, 132–134,
168–170, 325–326, 332, 453
Workplace, literacy in the, 3–4
"Work to Make the World Work
Better" (Michener), 228–
231
Writing pattern, determining,
261–262